NAPOLEON
A BIOGRAPHY

Frank McLynn

JONATHAN CAPE
LONDON

First published in 1997

1 3 5 7 9 10 8 6 4 2

© Frank McLynn 1997

Frank McLynn has asserted his right
under the Copyright, Designs and Patents Act 1988
to be identified as the author of this work

First published in the United Kingdom in 1997 by Jonathan Cape,
Random House, 20 Vauxhall Bridge Road, London SW1V 2SA

Random House Australia (Pty) Limited
20 Alfred Street, Milsons Point, Sydney,
New South Wales 2061, Australia

Random House New Zealand Limited
18 Poland Road, Glenfield,
Auckland 10, New Zealand

Random House South Africa (Pty) Limited
Endulini, 5A Jubilee Road, Parktown 2193, South Africa

Random House UK Limited Reg. No. 954009

A CIP catalogue record for this book is available from the British Library

Papers used by Random House UK Limited are natural,
recyclable products made from wood grown in sustainable forests.
The manufacturing processes conform to the environmental
regulations of the country of origin.

ISBN 0-224-04072-3

Typeset by Deltatype Ltd, Birkenhead, Merseyside

Printed and bound in Great Britain
by Mackays of Chatham PLC

For Julie

CONTENTS

ILLUSTRATIONS

PREFACE

This book does not purport to be a definitive biography of Napoleon. Indeed I wonder if such a thing is possible, short of a multi-volume life along the lines of Martin Gilbert's lifetime work on Churchill, and even then there must be doubts whether any one individual could fully master all the sources dealing with the multitudinous aspects of such a complex life. As the great French scholar Frédéric Masson found, after spending a lifetime studying the Emperor, Napoleon becomes more elusive and more enigmatic the more one knows about him. I have therefore set myself the modest task of attempting a clear synthesis of our existing knowledge of this extraordinary colossus who convulsed the world for two decades.

Regrettably, I have decided that I cannot afford the luxury (self-indulgence?) of detailed footnotes and citations. In the case of Napoleon, in order to sustain a single proposition one would have to cite the conflicting evidence available sometimes from more than a dozen sources. Apart from the fact that this volume, which is already long enough, would have to double in size to accommodate the critical apparatus, I am not sure the reader is really interested in the agonizing that goes on before a historian makes his or her Thucydidean judgement on what is likely to have been the truth about a particular incident. I have therefore contented myself with a summary of 'indicative reading'.

My debt to the work of the great French scholars, especially Masson and Jean Tulard, will be evident. Among English students of the Emperor I would single out for special mention the seminal work by David Chandler on Napoleon as military commander. My thanks are due to a number of individuals who played a part in this book. Will Sulkin, Euan Cameron and Tony Whittome at Cape gave particular support, while to the generosity of Patrick Garland and Alexandra Bastedo I am indebted for hospitality in Corsica, enabling me to visit all the Napoleonic places on the island. Others who gave me encouragement at vital moments when my spirits were flagging were Melvyn Bragg, Nigella

Lawson, Colette Bowe and Professor Murray Pittock of Strathclyde University. But my greatest debt is to the three significant women in my life: Pauline, Lucy and Julie.

CHAPTER ONE

Napoleon Bonaparte was born at Ajaccio, Corsica, on 15 August 1769. Such a bald, even banal statement is necessary when we consider that every aspect of the man's life has been turned into the stuff of legend. In 1919 Archbishop Whateley tried to push beyond legend into myth by suggesting, tongue-in-cheek, in his *Historic Doubts Relative to Napoleon Buonoparte*, that Napoleon had never existed, that his was a proper name falsely attributed to the French people collectively. The psychologist Carl Gustav Jung, while accepting the reality of Napoleon's existence, argued that his significance was wholly collective and not individual: that he represented the resurgence from the depths of the French unconscious of the savage and irrational forces the Revolution had tried to suppress through the cult of Reason (*Déesse Raison*).

Even those who accepted the importance of Napoleon the individual argued about his origins and his date of birth. There has in some quarters been a curious reluctance to accept that he was a Corsican at all, even though born on the island. Some have asserted that he was descended from the Greeks, the Carthaginians or the Bretons. Others, remarking his 'Oriental complex' (of which more later), and noting that in the ninth century the Arab invaders of Europe reached Corsica, claim an Arab, Berber or Moorish strain in his provenance; hence (on this view) his excessive superstition, his belief in ghosts, Destiny and his own star, and his preference for Islam over Christianity. The historian and critic Taine traced his descent to an Italian *condottiere*, while Disraeli, on the grounds that Corsica had once been peopled by African Semites, claimed Napoleon as a Jew (presumably, given Napoleon's later antipathy to the Jews, an anti-semitic one). Kings of England, the Comneni, the Paleologues, and even the Julian tribe have been pressed into service as Napoleon's forebears. The prize for the most absurd candidate as Napoleonic ancestor must go to the Man in the Iron Mask and for the most unlikely parents to the footman and goat girl, proposed by his most scurrilous enemies.

At another level of mythmaking, Napoleon's champions claimed that he emerged from his mother's womb a born warrior because she gave birth to him immediately after a hazardous 'flight in the heather' – retreating through the *maquis* with Corsican forces after being defeated by the French. And the French writer Chateaubriand, who knew Napoleon well and worked for him as a diplomat, argued that the true date of his birth was 5 February 1768; according to this theory, it was Napoleon's brother Joseph who was born on 15 August 1769 and Napoleon was the eldest son.

The sober facts are less sensational. On 2 June 1764 Carlo Buonaparte of Ajaccio, an eighteen-year-old law student, married the fourteen-year-old Marie-Letizia Ramolino, also of Ajaccio. Both families were descended from Italian mercenaries in Genoese pay who settled in Corsica at the beginning of the sixteenth century. The Buonapartes came originally from Tuscany and could trace their lineage to the soldier of fortune Ugo Buonaparte, documented as a henchman of the Duke of Swabia in 1122. Ugo was a veteran of the struggle between Guelphs and Ghibellines and a devoted supporter of the Holy Roman Emperor in his conflict with the Pope. The loser in a Florentine power struggle, Ugo spent his last days in the seaport of Sarzana, and it was from there in the early sixteenth century that his descendant Francesco Buonaparte emigrated to Corsica.

Such at any rate was the Buonaparte family tradition; their surname was said to denote Ugo's Imperialist affiliations. The earliest unimpeachable record shows a member of the Buonaparte family, a lawyer, as a member of the Council of Ancients in Ajaccio in 1616; several more Buonaparte lawyers served on this council in the eighteenth century. The Buonapartes like the Ramolinos were part of the Corsican nobility, but it must be remembered that Corsican 'nobles' were as common as 'princes' in Czarist Russia. Carlo Buonaparte, born on 27 March 1746, had been studying law at Pisa University but left to marry Letizia without taking his degree. The romancers have seized on this fact to build up a *coup de foudre* love affair between Carlo and Letizia, but the match was certainly dynastic, even though some sections of the Ramolino clan objected to the marriage.

The Ramolinos were a cadet branch of the distinguished Collalto family, well entrenched in Lombardy since the fourteenth century; the Ramolinos themselves had been established in Corsica for 250 years. Where the Buonapartes were a family of lawyers, with the Ramolinos the tradition was military: Letizia's father was an army officer with expertise in civil engineering, who commanded the Ajaccio garrison and held the sinecure office of Inspector-General of Roads and Bridges. Both the

Buonapartes and the Ramolinos specialized in intermarriage with ancient families of Italian origin, so a dynastic match made sense. There was just one peculiarity: both the newly-weds' fathers had died young. Carlo's father, a lawyer, died in 1760 when his son was fourteen, which meant that Carlo could bring into the marriage the family house in the Via Malerba, two of the best vineyards in Ajaccio, some pasture and arable land, and also his claims to another estate.

Marie-Letizia Ramolino (born either in late 1749 or early 1750) was in a more complicated situation. Her father died when she was five, after which her mother Angela Maria turned for consolation to François (or Franz) Fesch, a Swiss captain in the French garrison forces at Ajaccio. Angela Maria married Fesch in 1757 and persuaded him to convert to Catholicism, but his father, a banker in Basle, responded by disinheriting him. From the union of Fesch and Letizia's mother came Joseph (born 1763), the future cardinal and Napoleon's uncle, though only six years his senior. The unfortunate Fesch, who died in 1770, gave Letizia away; her dowry comprised thirty-one acres of land, a mill, and an oven for baking bread.

The marriage of Carlo and Letizia was a solid, down-to-earth marriage of convenience. There is even reason to believe that Carlo hedged his bets by not marrying in the Church in 1764, or ever. It was well known that Corsicans took an idiosyncratic, eclectic attitude to the Catholic Church, which was why legal marriage on the island consisted in the agreement of the two male heads of families, the signature of a dotal contract, and the act of consummation. The likelihood is that Carlo simply refused to go through with a religious ceremony, and for reasons of pride and saving face the two clans kept quiet about it.

Again, contrary to the mythmaking, it is untrue that some of the Ramolinos opposed the match for political reasons, allegedly on the grounds that they supported the Genoese masters of the island while the Buonapartes backed the independence movement under Pasquale Paoli. Almost certainly, they simply had doubts that this was the very best dynastic bargain they could strike while, as for political ideology, both the Buonapartes and Ramolinos were notorious trimmers who made obeisance to whichever party in Corsica had the most power.

Carlo, a tall young man with a prominent nose, sensual lips and almond-shaped eyes, was a hedonist and sensualist. Cunning, self-regarding, unrefined, unscrupulous, he made it clear that his marriage was no love match by declaring a preference for a girl of the Forcioli family. The romancers claim that he was bowled over by Letizia's beauty, but portraits reveal a woman whose mouth was too small, whose nose was too long and whose face was too austere for a claim to real beauty to be advanced. It was true that she was petite (5'1"), with rich dark-brown hair and slender white hands; and what she had, incontestably and by common consent, were large, lustrous, deep-set eyes. As was normal at the time, Letizia was wholly uneducated and trained in nothing but domestic skills.

Letizia fulfilled the essential requirement of women of the time, which was to be an efficient childbearer. She gave birth to thirteen children in all, of whom eight survived. A son, named Napoleon, was born and died in 1765. Pregnant again almost immediately, Letizia next brought forth a girl who also died. Then came a mysterious interlude of about two years. Allegedly Paoli sent the twenty-year-old Carlo as his envoy to Rome, to appease the Pope when he launched his planned attack on the Genoese island of Capraia (Capraia and Genoa had originally been deeded to Genoa by papal gift), but the best evidence shows Carlo becoming a Paolista while he was in Italy. Carlo's time in Rome seems to have been spent in cohabitation with a married woman. His own story was that he returned from Rome after running out of funds, but a stronger tradition has it that he seduced a virgin and was run out of town. On his return to Corsica he again impregnated Letizia, who this time bore him a lusty son in the shape of Joseph (originally named Giuseppe), who was born on 7 July 1768.

Another prevalent myth about Napoleon's background was that he was born into indigence. The property brought into the marriage by Carlo and Letizia seems to have been nicely calculated, since Letizia's dowry was valued at 6,750 livres and Carlo's assets at about 7,000 livres. The joint capital generated an annual income of about 670 livres or about £9,000 a year in today's money. In addition, there was the money earned by Carlo. Pasquale Paoli employed the young man as his secretary on account of his unusually neat and clear handwriting. Carlo also worked as a *procureur* – approximately equivalent to a British solicitor. Letizia employed two servants and a wet-nurse – hardly badges of poverty.

What Carlo and Letizia suffered from was not poverty but relative deprivation. The Buonapartes and their great rivals, the Pozzo di Borgos, were among the richest families in Ajaccio, but they were aware that they were big fish in a very small pond. Across the water, in mainland France, their wealth would have counted for nothing and their pretensions to nobility would have been laughed at. The Buonapartes wanted to be as rich as the richest nobles in France and, since they could not be, they created a compensatory myth of dire poverty. Economic conditions in Corsica and their own pretensions worked against them. A sharecropping economy based on vineyards and a primitive barter system meant there were few opportunities for generating a surplus, hence no possibility for profits and making money. Even if there had been, Carlo Buonaparte's aspirations to noble status stood in the way, for to a noble the Church, the Law and the Army were the only acceptable professions, and even the lower reaches of the Law, such as Carlo's position as *procureur*, were essentially beyond the aristocratic pale.

Napoleon was often, to his fury, called 'the Corsican'. He always denied that his birthplace had any significance, but no human being can slough off early environmental and geographical influences just by say-so. The restlessness in Napoleon's later character must owe something to the confused and chaotic politics of the island, which he imbibed with his mother's milk, or rather that of his wet-nurse. As Dorothy Carrington has written: 'defeat, resistance, betrayal, heroism, torture, execution and conspiracy were the topics of the first conversations he overheard. Conversations that left a permanent imprint on his mind.'

After 1729 a Corsican independence movement gathered momentum against the Genoese overlords. In 1755 this took a more serious turn when the twenty-nine-year-old Pasquale Paoli put himself at the head of the Corsican guerrillas. Taking advantage of Corsica's mountainous terrain (a chain of high granite sierras runs down Corsica from the north-west to the south-east and the highest peaks are always snowcapped), the Paolistas drove the Genoese out of central Corsica, confining them to the coastal towns of Ajaccio, Bastia and Calvi. Regarding himself as the true ruler of Corsica, Paoli brought in a series of much-needed land reforms, which confirmed the ancient customs of the land in defiance of Genoese exploitation. In an early form of mixed economy, Paoli divided land into two categories: in the lowlands there was the *piage* or public land used for pasture and growing crops; but in the highlands, the vineyards, olive groves, sweet chestnut and other trees were in private hands. Paoli's power base was always the widespread support he enjoyed among the peasantry.

Paoli attracted admirers throughout Europe. Jean-Jacques Rousseau thought Corsica, with its tiny population, was the ideal laboratory for the political experiment he outlined in his *Social Contract*. An early exponent of 'small is beautiful', Rousseau thought that the 'General Will' could emerge in Corsica as the city state. The island was ideal, with a total population of no more than 130,000 and its cities were glorified villages; in the census of 1770 Bastia had 5,286 inhabitants and Ajaccio 3,907. Rousseau actually sketched a constitution for Corsica and announced: 'I have a presentiment that one day this small island will astonish Europe.'

Another admirer who actually visited Corsica and met Paoli was James Boswell, Dr Johnson's faithful companion and biographer. Boswell in his *Account of Corsica* (1768) famously compared the Corsicans, with their clans and martial traditions, with the Scottish Highlanders before the 1745 Jacobite Rising. The thought had occurred to others: at one time Bonnie Prince Charlie himself was proposed as a possible King of Corsica. So enthusiastic for Paoli was Boswell that Dr Johnson accused him of being a bore on the subject.

But Paoli had scarcely completed the conquest of the interior and introduced his reforms when Corsica once again became a pawn on the international diplomatic chessboard. Just before the outbreak of the Seven Years War in 1756, by treaty arrangement the French poured their troops into Calvi, Ajaccio and St-Florent. They pulled them out again when war broke out, but reintroduced them in 1764. French encroachment reached its apogee the year before Napoleon's birth, in 1768, when Genoa formally ceded the island to France; Paoli and his men learned that they had fought the Genoese only to be delivered to the suzerainty of Louis XV. In fury the Paolistas rose in revolt against the French. They scored a string of minor military successes but were decisively crushed on 8 May 1769 at the battle of Ponte Novo. Among those who fled with Paoli from this disaster were Carlo Buonaparte and his nineteen-year-old wife, now six months pregnant with the future Napoleon.

Napoleonic legend credited the embryonic conqueror with having been present in foetal form at Ponte Novo. What happened was dramatic enough, for Carlo and Letizia fled with the other rebels into the mountains towards Corte; it is therefore true to say that the embryonic Napoleon was literally on the march. When Paoli recognized the inevitable and accepted French surrender terms, Carlo and Letizia returned to Ajaccio by the mountain route; to the end of her life Letizia always remembered carrying Joseph in her arms while staggering and slipping along precipitous paths.

Back in Ajaccio Letizia came to full term. On the feast of the Assumption she was at mass in the cathedral when the labour pains started. Fortunately she was only a minute's walk away from the three-storey Buonaparte family home, and her sister-in-law Geltruda Paravicini helped her to walk the few yards. A curmudgeonly maidservant named Caterina acted as the midwife and laid the newborn infant on a carpet, on which were woven scenes from the *Iliad* and the *Odyssey*. The child was weak, with spindly legs and a large head, but sea air and the abundant milk from wet-nurse Camilla Ilari, a sailor's wife, saw him through the perilous early days. Tradition says that a priest came from the cathedral

6

on the day of birth to carry out a perfunctory baptism, but sober history must be content to record that the formal baptism did not take place until 21 July 1771, when it was performed in Ajaccio cathedral by Napoleon's great-uncle Lucien; the records show Lorenzo Giubeca of Calvi, *procureur du roi*, as the child's godfather. The little boy was christened Napoleone. It was an odd name, and its origin, predictably, is shrouded in controversy. Some claimed it was a name deriving from the Greek and meaning 'lion of the desert'. More plausibly, a Greek saint who suffered martyrdom in Alexandria under Diocletian is cited, but the most likely explanation is the simple and banal one that one of Letizia's uncles, a Paolista who had recently died, bore that name.

There is little hard evidence for the events of Napoleon's early boyhood. There is a strong tradition that he was sent in 1773 to a school for girls run by nuns and that he was the terror of the playground. The story goes that, when the children were taken for their afternoon walk, Napoleon liked to hold hands with a girl called Giacominetta. Noting also that Napoleon was sloppy with his appearance and often had his socks around his ankles, some juvenile wag composed the couplet:

> *Napoleone di mezza calzetta*
> *Fa l'amore a Giacominetta.*

If this provocative line was uttered, the sequel would have been predictable, which was doubtless where the boy Napoleon got his early reputation for fisticuffs.

It is certain that at about the age of seven he was sent to a Jesuit school, where he learned to read and write, to do sums and take in the rudiments of Latin and ancient history. But stories of tantrums and of a systematically destructive boy who pulled the stuffing out of chairs, wrecked plants and deliberately cut grooves in tables were later accretions bruited about by his enemies and are fairly obvious attempts to read back into his childhood authenticated adult traits.

Three items of anecdotal evidence relating to these early years seem to be genuinely grounded in fact, not least because Letizia and Joseph vouched for them in old age. Letizia recalled that when she gave her children paints to use on the wall of their playroom, all the other children painted puppets but Napoleon alone painted soldiers. Joseph recalled that at school, when they played Romans and Carthaginians, Napoleon was chosen by the teacher to be a Carthaginian while Joseph was a Roman. Wanting to be on the winning side, Napoleon nagged and wheedled at the teacher until the rôles were reversed and he could play the Roman. This would square with the tradition, which seems solidly grounded, that Napoleon picked on Joseph, fought with him at every opportunity and generally tried to browbeat and bully him. Joseph was quiet and mild, but Napoleon was rumbustious and belligerent.

Finally, there is Letizia's testimony that she was a stickler for the truth while Napoleon showed early signs of being a pathological liar. This was part of a general clash of wills between mother and son which saw Letizia frequently having recourse to the whip. Carlo spoiled his children, but Letizia was a fearsome martinet with a rather masculine nature and a natural love of power. A stern taskmistress who always punished for the slightest fault, Letizia laid about her with gusto when her second son misbehaved. She drove him to Mass with slaps and blows, whipped him when he stole fruit, misbehaved in church or – on one notorious occasion – laughed at a crippled grandmother. Letizia was also cunning and devious. When her son was eight and an altar boy, she vowed to mete out punishment for his less than reverent behaviour on the altar, but faced the problem that she would find it hard to lay hands on the agile and fully-clothed Napoleon. To lull his suspicions, she told him she would not beat him for his offence. But when he took his clothes off she pounced on him with the whip.

Napoleon never cried out under the lash, but fear and respect for his mother replaced genuine love. Napoleon resented her doctrinaire principles and her sacrifice of reality for appearances. A true Latin, Letizia believed that outward show was the most important thing and that it was better to go without food so as to be able to wear a smart suit. Naturally austere and penny-pinching, she had no qualms about sending her children to bed hungry, both because she thought such hardship was good for them and because she genuinely preferred to spend the money on furnishing the house and keeping up appearances. Superficially, at least, the challenge and response between mother and son worked out well, since Napoleon did learn the value of discipline; his siblings, by contrast, were notorious for the lack of it. Napoleon's testimony to his mother on St Helena is the truth, but it is not the whole truth: 'I owe her a great deal. She instilled into me pride and taught me good sense.'

But it was on Carlo that Napoleon's future prospects depended. Despite his later claims to have been at the heart of Paolista councils, Carlo was always held at arm's length by Paoli, who never admitted him to the inner circles. Perhaps Paoli sensed that his young secretary was a political opportunist pure and simple. After the retreat to Corte in May 1769, following the rout at Ponte Nuovo, Paoli and 340 of his most devoted followers continued on to Bastia and took ship for England rather than remain under the French heel. Significantly, not only did Carlo not go with them but he immediately threw in his lot with the new French overlords. In February 1771 he was appointed assessor of the Royal Jurisdiction of Ajaccio, one of eleven on the island. Certainly not coincidentally, in the same year, on 13 September 1771, Carlo obtained patents from the authorities declaring the Buonaparte family noble. Corsican nobility did not confer many advantages: there were no feudal privileges, no exemption from taxes, not even any particular deference from other classes; but the advantages of the declaration of nobility for the Buonapartes were significant in the long term.

Two aspects of Carlo's career in the 1770s are particularly noteworthy: his litigiousness and his truckling to the French Commissioners who ruled the island. In the eighteenth century modern notions of privacy were still largely unknown, and Carlo was quite content to have his cousins living on the top floor of Casa Buonaparte. He drew the line, however, at their emptying the slop-bucket over Letizia's washing and brought suit against them. He then petitioned for the ownership of the Mitelli estate. This had belonged to Paolo Odone, the brother of Carlo's great-great-grandmother, who had died childless and in a fit of piety bequeathed the property to the Jesuits. When the Jesuits were suppressed in 1767–69 throughout the Bourbon kingdoms and colonies, Carlo saw his chance. The incoming French tried to expropriate the Mitelli estate as a state asset, but Carlo brought an action to have it returned to his family. The protracted legal wrangling occupied the rest of Carlo's life, with the lack of clear documentary title and unimpeachable genealogical lines telling against him.

Carlo also turned his legal guns against the Ramolinos. A clause in the act of dowry that formed part of Letizia's marriage settlement expressly stipulated that if the value of Letizia's property ever slipped below 7,000 livres, the Ramolinos had to make up the difference. Pressing the letter of the law, Carlo in 1775 began proceedings against Letizia's grandfather, the eighty-four-year-old Giovanni Ramolino. His suit was successful, but then it turned out that Giovanni could not pay the amount owed. The old man's meagre belongings – two good barrels, two crates, two wooden jars, a washing bowl, a tub, five casks, six low-quality barrels, etc – were sold at auction in Ajaccio marketplace. It is probable that Letizia, already less than enamoured by Carlo and his conduct, was deeply angered by the public humiliation of her impoverished grandfather; she was, after all, a woman who believed deeply in 'face' and appearances.

Ironically, Carlo's litigiousness, which alienated Letizia, made her more vulnerable to the charms of Carlo's protector and patron, the

Comte de Marbeuf. French rule in Corsica essentially came down to the military governor and a civil intendant supported by a docile *conseil supérieur* (a president, six French councillors, four Corsican) sitting at Bastia. From 1772–86 the military governor was Charles Réné, Comte de Marbeuf, a favourite of Louis XV's, while the Intendant from 1775–85 was M. de Boucheporn. Marbeuf, from an old Breton family, was sixty when he took up his appointment as the virtual ruler of Corsica and soon showed himself an enlightened reformer and improver, interested in crop rotation and presiding in Cartesian benevolence over a strict administrative hierarchy of *paese* (village), *pieve* (canton), province and central government.

Marbeuf surrounded himself with male protégés and sycophants on the one hand and pretty women on the other. Having contracted a marriage of convenience in France, he also conveniently left his wife behind when he went out to Corsica as governor. A man whose virility belied his years, he at first kept Madame de Varesnes, the 'Cleopatra of Corsica', as his mistress. To his male protégés he distributed largesse, and one of the principal beneficiaries was Carlo. In 1777 Marbeuf secured his election as a deputy for the nobility, to represent Corsica at Versailles. Carlo was away for two years.

Marbeuf meanwhile turned his attention to Letizia. It was well known that he was besotted with her, but only in 1776, when he dropped Madame de Varesnes, did he begin the pursuit. There is very strong circumstantial evidence that Marbeuf and Letizia were lovers while Carlo was in Versailles; unfortunately, zealots for the theory that Letizia was habitually unfaithful to Carlo have tried to backdate the liaison to 1768 in order to sustain the thesis that Marbeuf was Napoleon's father. It can be stated categorically that he was not: at the probable date of Napoleon's conception, around November 1768, Marbeuf was with French troops in winter quarters and had no connection whatever with Letizia. Yet those who have refuted the 'straw man' theory that Marbeuf was Napoleon's father have made the unwarranted further assumption that he could not have fathered any of her other children. He certainly did not beget the third son, Lucien, who was born in 1775, nor the first daughter, Maria Anna Élisa (born 1777), but it is highly likely that the fourth Buonaparte son, Louis, was really the son of Marbeuf. The calendar favours Marbeuf as father far more than Carlo; additionally Louis was quite unlike his siblings in looks, character and temperament, and shared Marbeuf's brusque irascibility. Many biographers have asserted on no grounds whatever that Marbeuf's relationship with Letizia was platonic and that 'she had eyes only for Carlo'. Such writers fly in the face of probability and reveal themselves as poor judges of human nature.

Marbeuf repaid Letizia in an eminently practical and concrete way. Knowing of Carlo's parlous finances, he alerted him to a little-known procedure whereby the children of distressed French nobility could receive a free education. In theory, Joseph could be trained for the priesthood at the seminary at Aix, Napoleon could be sent to military school, while the eldest girl might secure a place at Madame de Maintenon's school at St-Cyr. There was just one snag: parental applicants had to submit both a certificate of nobility and of indigence, and competition for the free places was ferocious, only 600 being available in the whole of France. Nevertheless, with his contacts and patronage Marbeuf was confident of success. In 1778, while Carlo was still out of Corsica, Marbeuf solicited the Minister of War, Prince de Montbarrey for free places for Joseph and Napoleon, enclosing the certificates of poverty and of four generations of nobility. Montbarrey replied provisionally on 19 July 1778, granting Napoleon a place at the military academy at Brienne and Joseph his indentures at the Aix seminary. However, there were conditions: the two Buonaparte sons had to be clear that they could not both be trained for the same profession; they had to pass the entrance examinations; and final confirmation had to await a new certificate of nobility from the royal heraldist in Versailles. Final confirmation of Napoleon's place at a military school was not received from the Minister of War until 31 December 1778.

Marbeuf again pulled strings. The preliminary education, so necessary after the fragmentary instruction in Corsica, would be given at the school at Autun, run by his nephew the Bishop; Marbeuf guaranteed payment of Napoleon and Joseph's fees. Carlo gushed with gratitude and wrote a sonnet in praise of his benefactor, who does not seem to have reciprocated by ending the affair with Letizia. Such was the complex family situation as Napoleon, at the age of nine, prepared to depart for Autun. What was the impact of those first nine years, in which all the essential 'formation' of his personality was done?

The Corsican legacy may partly account for the ruthless pragmatism in Napoleon's personality, the impatience with abstract theory and the conviction that, ultimately, human problems are solved by main force. There is also the 'primitive' aspect of the adult Napoleon, frequently noticed by memorialists and biographers. The psychoanalyst A.A. Brill wrote: 'There is no doubt that Napoleon represents the very acme of primitivity,' and went on to argue that his universal fascination lies in his embodiment of those primitive qualities we can scarcely acknowledge consciously in 'civilized' society. This is not so very strange when we consider the backward and primitive nature of eighteenth-century Corsican life, where even the everyday sights, smells and sounds were primordial. Contemporary accounts speak of the streets of Ajaccio as suffused with the stench of animals slaughtered outside butchers' shops and the animal hides stretched out to tan in the sun. The noisome foetor in the streets was exacerbated by the clouds of flies, the stifling summer climate, and the acute shortage of water. There are grounds for believing that Napoleon's later addiction to lying in hot baths was compensation for a childhood marked by water shortage.

The other quintessentially primitive aspect of Corsica, noted by all travellers and visitors to the island, was the vendetta. The tradition of blood vengeance was handed down to the seventh generation, and a girl had the number of her cousins reckoned as part of her dowry so that wrongs done to the clan would never be forgotten; the males in the clan refused to shave and went about bearded until the affront to the family honour was avenged. It was this aspect of the Corsicans that *ancien régime* statesmen like the duc de Choiseul particularly hated. Rousseau, Boswell and other admirers might praise the Corsicans as shrewd, verbose, voluble, highly intelligent and as interested in politics as the inhabitants of an ancient Greek city-state. But against this, said the critics, was the fact that the Corsicans were also proud, prickly, arrogant, vindictive, unforgiving, implacable, vengeful and alarmingly quick to take offence or construe words and actions as insults.

The institution of vendetta knew no boundaries of class or status, only of family and clan. Napoleon himself clearly surmounted the tradition of vendetta, as he always killed his enemies for reasons of state not out of personal grievance; indeed he can be faulted for being absurdly tolerant of inveterate personal enemies. His enemies in Corsica, however, did not have his forbearance: the rival family of Pozzo di Borgo pursued the Buonapartes with vendetta to Napoleon's grave and beyond. They intrigued with his enemies, manipulated Czar Alexander and were among the first to suggest St Helena as a place of exile. Only after the fall of Louis-Napoleon in 1870 and the death of the Prince Imperial in the Zulu War of 1879 did the Pozzo di Borgos relax and build the castle of LaPunta as a monument to their final victory.

Far more important than the influence of Corsica on Napoleon was the impact of his family. It is quite clear from his later career, as indeed from the tenuous record of his first nine years, that Napoleon was obsessed by rivalry with Joseph and yearned to supplant him. The later political history of Napoleon the emperor is sometimes inexplicable without taking into account his 'Joseph complex'. In later years Napoleon indulged his elder brother shamelessly, leading one to conclude that the childhood hatred must have been compensated and the original aggression visited on others. It was this consideration that led Freud to write: 'To push Joseph aside, to take his place, to become Joseph himself, must have been the little Napoleon's strongest emotion. . . . Hundreds of thousands of strangers had to pay the penalty of this little fiend's having spared his first enemy.' The early feelings of hostility towards his brother may well have been compounded, in Napoleon's unconscious, by the idea that he was a 'replacement child' for the first Napoleon, who died in 1765; Joseph, therefore, had a clear identity and a clear focus in his parents' affections which he, as a 'substitute', did not have.

Towards his father Napoleon always evinced an ambivalence characterized by contempt for the real man coupled with idolization of Carlo or a Platonic form of Carlo; this maybe found expression ultimately in Napoleon's desire to be a second great French Emperor, the first being Charlemagne who, bearing the same Christian name as his father, was the ideal-type. Consciously, Napoleon disliked his father's extravagance and addiction to pleasure, but was proud of him as a patriot and Paolista. Yet it is universally conceded that during Napoleon's early life Carlo was a shadowy figure. The really important early parental influence came from his mother.

Some of the mistakes attributed to Letizia probably did not have the consequences ascribed to them. Wilhelm Reich speculated, from the mixture of great energy and passive tendencies, that Napoleon might have been a 'phallic-narcissistic' character, as a result of an 'overfeminized' early socialization, with the nuns at school and the overbearing Letizia at home. It is, however, unlikely that his brief attendance at the nuns' school had any significant role in his formation, and it is surely far-fetched to imagine Letizia's beatings as the genesis of sado-masochistic tendencies. However, the general thesis of an unconscious desire for revenge against the opposite sex seems well grounded in the evidence of his later life. In particular, he always thought of women as being totally without honour, duplicitous, deceivers, liars.

In later life Napoleon always showered lavish praise on his mother in public or when talking to inferiors. To intimates and confidantes it was a different story, for then he allowed himself to express his darker feelings about Letizia. In theory her meanness with money should have balanced Carlo's extravagance but the adult Napoleon felt, though he would obviously not have used the term, that both his parents were neurotic in countervailing and fissiparous ways. He hated the way his mother got him to spy on Carlo when he was drinking and gambling in the Ajaccio saloons. There were also more sinister suspicions about Letizia and Marbeuf that he dared not express consciously. But it is important to be clear that Napoleon's ambivalence about his mother was part of a general obsession with Letizia, and we would therefore be justified in adding 'mother fixation' to the other 'complexes' already noted.

All human beings struggle in vain against the determinism of the parental legacy, both biological and psychological. The curious paradox of being a charismatic workaholic, which was the character of the adult Napoleon, surely results from the very different and centrifugal qualities of his two ill-matched parents. From Carlo he would appear to have derived the histrionic and magnetic qualities, the self-dramatization and the ability to win men; from Letizia came the self-discipline and the fanatical devotion to work. It was the Letizia-derived qualities that would be most valuable to him during his virtual orphancy at Brienne.

CHAPTER TWO

On 15 December 1779 a veritable cohort of Buonapartes left Corsica, all ultimately headed in different directions. Carlo, once again named deputy for the nobility of the Estates-General of Corsica, was on his way to Versailles. In his charge were the young Fesch, who was beginning his studies at the seminary at Aix-en-Provence, Napoleon, who was to spend four months learning French before being assigned to a military school, and Joseph, likewise going to the school at Autun to learn French before beginning to study for the priesthood. The other adult in the party was Letizia's cousin, the Abbé Varèse, who had been appointed subdeacon at Autun Cathedral.

In his memoirs Joseph states categorically that the party crossed to La Spezia and visited Florence before proceeding to France, but the calendar tells against him, for he and Napoleon were definitely enrolled at the school at Autun in Burgundy on New Year's Day 1779. Carlo dropped off Fesch at the Aix seminary and then proceeded north with Varèse to Autun. Three weeks after his sons had started school, Carlo was notified by the War Ministry that Napoleon had, in principle, been assigned to the military school at Tiron, but that some final formalities concerning the title to nobility had still to be cleared up. However on 28 March 1779 Montbarrey informed Carlo that Napoleon was actually being sent to the military school at Brienne in Champagne. Since Carlo was by now in Versailles and detained on business, he asked Mgr Marbeuf, the Bishop of Autun, to take Napoleon up to Brienne to begin his education proper.

Serendipity intervened, so that Napoleon did not actually commence his schooling at Brienne on 23 April, official school records notwithstanding. A certain captain Champeaux, on leave from his regiment in Nice, arrived in Autun to convey his son from the school to Brienne. Learning that the Champeaux boy was going to the same place as the young Buonaparte, Mgr Marbeuf decided to save himself a journey and prevailed on Champeaux to take Napoleon with him. Joseph described the parting from his brother: he (Joseph) was red-eyed from weeping but Napoleon shed just a single tear. On 22 April the Champeaux family took

Napoleon with them for a three-week holiday at the family château in Thoisy-le-Desert. But Mgr Marbeuf, who had squared this arrangement with the school at Brienne, had not quite calculated all the odds, for at the end of the holiday the young Jean-Baptiste Champeaux was found to be too ill to continue to Brienne; Marbeuf thus had to send his vicar, the Abbé Hamey, to take Napoleon over to Brienne – something he could have done three weeks earlier.

Napoleon arrived in Brienne on 15 May 1779. The military 'college' there, originally a monastery, stood at the foot of a hill dominated by the château. A religious academy from 1730, it had become a military school in 1776, one of ten (later twelve) such schools set up to replace the École Royale Militaire in Paris, which had been wound up that year on grounds of cost. It was still run by monks and the religious ethos was dominant, but the Minimes of the Order of St Benedict were poor and ignorant, the Brienne school was underfunded so could not afford to engage top-class teachers, was the lowest-ranked of all ten military colleges and had the lowest student enrolment (around 150) as against a top military school like La Flèche (with nearly 500). Its aim was to prepare the sons of the nobility for eventual cadetships in the armed services but, apart from a course in fortification in the final year, the education was not remotely military, but rather a variant of the standard training of the eighteenth-century gentleman. The theory was that the best pupils would be selected for the artillery, the engineers and the navy, and the mediocre ones for the infantry; only those too stupid even for the cavalry would be sent back in disgrace to their families.

In this sleepy town on the vast open plains of Champagne Napoleon spent five years. He often professed an admiration for Sparta, but here he had to live like a Spartan of old. There were two corridors, both of which contained seventy cells, each six feet square, furnished with a strap bed, a water jug and a basin. Students were locked into their cells at 10 p.m., in a vain attempt to stamp out homosexual practices which were rampant at the Brienne school. In an emergency a pupil could press a bell which communicated with the corridor where a servant slept. At 6 a.m. reveille sounded. After a breakfast of bread and water and some fruit in a common dining-hall which seated 180 persons, lessons began. The morning was given over to Latin, history, mathematics, geography, drawing and some German. A two-hour lunch break followed, where the standard of food improved. A typical menu contained soup, *bouilli*, roast meat, salad and dessert. Teaching in the afternoon concentrated on fencing, dancing, music and handwriting. There was a brief break for 'tea' which was a repeat of breakfast, and later there was a dinner which repeated the lunch menu. Only on feast days did the monotonous fare vary: one Epiphany Napoleon noted down that the boys had been served chicken, cauliflower, beetroot salad, cake, chestnuts and hot dessert.

There was a strict dress code. Pupils wore a blue coat with red facings and white metal buttons; the waistcoat was blue faced with white; the breeches were blue or black and an overcoat was allowed in winter. No servants were permitted. Linen was changed twice a week, but only one rug was permitted on the bed, except in cases of illness. Up to the age of twelve the boys had to have their hair cut short but after that a pigtail was to be worn; powder could be worn only on Sundays and saints' days. The régime was austere in other ways. Boys were not allowed to visit home except in the case of death or severe illness of a parent, parental visits were discouraged, and there were no real holidays. During the short annual break between 21 August and 8 September classes were cancelled and the boys taken on long walks, though the Champagne countryside hardly inspired Romantic feelings: Brienne was situated in flat, agricultural and often flooded or waterlogged terrain, where the monotony was broken only by wretched, poverty-stricken villages, dilapidated cottages, smoking bothies and thatched hovels.

The teachers at the school were of poor calibre and sometimes downright incompetent. The Berton brothers, who had started life in the Army and now acted as Principal and Vice-Principal, did not run a tight ship and were even cavalier about religion: the younger Berton brother, Jean-Baptiste, used to race through Mass in nine or ten minutes. Vulgar yet pretentious, tough yet incompetent, cynical, worldly and *fainéant*, the Berton brothers, as their name suggests, would have been better running a circus than a military school. Official inspections of the school in 1785 and 1787 found laziness and carelessness in both staff and students, and the 1787 report recorded outright indiscipline. The Bertons' career was hardly a glittering success. Napoleon, in one of those flashes of genuine generosity his critics never acknowledge, rescued Louis Berton, the Principal, from poverty in later years and gave him a sinecure in educational administration, but the man died insane. The brother proved that his record-breaking time for saying Mass was no fluke by getting himself released from his vows after the Revolution.

The approach to teaching was as pragmatic as the brothers' general attitude. Latin was studied for moral example, not so as to provide models for rhetoric; the elements of logic were instilled by detaching them from their metaphysical and Aristotelian roots; German was taught because it might be useful in a future war; history, geography and mathematics for their use in topography and fortification, and so on.

Plenty of Latin authors were picked over – Virgil, Caesar, Sallust, Livy, Cicero, Horace, Cornelius Nepos – but Napoleon could never master Latin inflections (strangely for one with such mathematical talents). In any case, his favourite classical author was Plutarch, who wrote in Greek. What Napoleon liked most about the ancient world was the study of its military leaders such as Caesar. From the story of his assassination boys were meant to draw the moral that Caesar was a tyrant and Brutus the champion of liberty; but Napoleon concluded that Caesar was a great man and Brutus a traitor.

There were twenty teachers instructing six classes, but the only ones remembered by Napoleon with any affection were Father Patrault, the head of mathematics, and Father Dupuy, the head of French. He was unmusical, sang out of tune, hated dancing, fencing and deportment and was hopeless at all of them but evinced a flair for ancient history and was brilliant at mathematics. He liked geography but his actual knowledge was always shaky: in later life he confused the river Elbe with the Ebro and Smolensk with Salamanca. He never mastered the rules of spelling and always spoke French with an Italian accent, pronouncing certain words as if they obeyed Italian rules of phonetics.

No Greek was taught at Brienne and only the most elementary Latin; Napoleon read the classical authors in translation. He read omnivorously if erratically and was soon recognized as one of the more able pupils. In August and September each year the school opened its doors to the public for *exercices publics*, in which the cleverest boys answered questions put to them by the masters in the presence of Church and State dignitaries. After 1780 Napoleon was a prize exhibit each year at these sessions. In 1781 he was awarded a prize for mathematics by the duc d'Orléans; in 1782 he answered on mathematics and ancient history; and in 1783 he answered mathematical problems that were as difficult as his teachers could make them. Despite his brilliance, he never got his teeth into higher mathematics, simply because there was no one at Brienne with the talent to teach him.

If Napoleon's academic progress at Brienne was fair, his social and personal formation was disastrous. Three things combined to turn him into a misanthropic recluse when not yet in his teens: brutality, social snobbery and racial prejudice. Brutality was visited on him by both boys and masters. Corporal punishment was officially outlawed at Brienne as damaging to body and soul, but this proscription was honoured more in the breach than the observance. On one occasion Napoleon was punished by having to eat his dinner kneeling down in the refectory, wearing coarse brown homespun and a dunce's cap. This brought on hysteria and an attack of vomiting. Father Patrault, the head of mathematics, a tall, red-faced man who was the only one at Brienne to discern Napoleon's true intellectual potential, intervened and reproved the master who had inflicted the punishment.

Napoleon's initial problem with the other boys was that he would not consent to be a 'nymph', as the catamites in the school, well known to be honeycombed with homosexuality, were called. This inevitably led to beatings-up and fights. His sallow skin, his nationality and even his name set him apart. His schoolmates converted 'Napoleone' into *paille au nez* ('straw nose') – an insult he still remembered at the end of his life. Great mirth was occasioned by Napoleon's first encounter with ice, in his water jug. 'Who's put glass in my water jug?' he cried, to hoots of laughter. Napoleon's response to such humiliations was to insult his fellow-pupils in turn, which led to further fisticuffs. But he won grudging respect from his peers by not 'peaching' to the masters.

Yet the major source of tension was Napoleon's virulent Corsican nationalism and his worship of Paoli. His schoolmates scoffed at Paoli; he expressed his hatred for Choiseul; they jeered that the Corsicans were a defeated people and were natural cowards; he replied that they were the bravest of the brave and could easily have handled odds of four to one but not the ten to one they actually faced; moreover, he would one day make good his words by leading Corsica to independence. There is also this highly significant outburst to one of his teachers: 'Paoli was a great man: he loved his fatherland, and I shall never forgive my father, who was his adjutant, for helping to unite Corsica to France. He should have followed his fortunes and succumbed with him.'

The spiral of taunt, counter-taunt, playground fight and return match between Napoleon and schoolmates continued. The arrival in 1782 of another student from Corsica, Élie-Charles de Bragelonne, might conceivably have been a source of relief, but Bragelonne was the son of the French military commander in Bastia, and the strong anti-Napoleon schoolboy faction twisted this to its own advantage. Knowing that Corsicans hated Genoese even more than the French, they put Bragelonne up to pretending he was Genoese. The sequel was predictable: Napoleon flew at the boy and pulled out his hair in tufts, leading to another fight. But there is a tradition that Bragelonne later joined in Napoleon's anti-schoolmaster baiting and troublemaking and even aspired to inherit his mantle in this regard, for he was expelled in 1786. There must have been some kind of rapport, for Napoleon later made him one of his generals.

There are many accounts of Napoleon at Brienne by alleged

contemporaries but only four of them seem authentic, and even these have often been doctored or suffused with the 'wisdom' of retrospection. Hence the surfeit of apocrypha from these years – the plaintive pleas from Napoleon to his parents for pocket-money, the alleged visit to Brittany, etc. Napoleon himself, in his St Helena memoirs, doubtless exaggerated the misery at school, the violence and the loneliness. Yet all the evidence dovetails to underline the inescapable conclusion that he did not fit in, did not make friends easily, was unpopular and a lone wolf. Two of the best authenticated stories show him in the two moods he habitually demonstrated at Brienne: either a reserved, meditative loner who would turn to violence if provoked; or an aggressive gang-leader.

As part of the ethos of 'robust bodies, enlightened minds, honest hearts' so falteringly applied by the Berton brothers, all students were encouraged to take up outdoor recreations. Napoleon and three of his schoolmates opted for gardening, but Napoleon quickly bribed the others to give up their rights in the patch of garden and then enclosed his plot with a 'palisade'. He liked to retire inside this redoubt to be alone, private and *au dessus de la mêlée*, to work on an algebraic problem or read his favourite books – Plutarch, Macpherson's *Ossian* and Marshal Saxe on military campaigning. On the feast of St Louis the other boys let off fireworks, but Napoleon, as a pointed demonstration of his Corsican patriotism, held aloof. One of the fireworks exploded a fresh box of firecrackers, at which the boys panicked and stampeded through the gardens, trampling down Napoleon's stockade. In a fury he emerged with a spade and laid about him, as a retaliation for which he was later ambushed and beaten up. His peers took the line that Napoleon should have been able to see that the whole affair was a genuine accident and been rational about it. But to Napoleon, obsessed as he was with notions of defending Corsica against the French invader, the incident was a microcosm of all the events that caused him greatest grief.

The most famous event featuring Napoleon at Brienne comes from late in his years at the school, in the winter of 1783-84. There had been heavy snowfall and Napoleon, now fourteen, suggested to his bored fellow pupils that they build a snow fortress in the courtyard, and then divide into two groups, besiegers and besieged, for a massive snowfight. The idea was at first a huge success, with Napoleon commanding both sides, but things took an ugly turn when the boys began to cover large stones in an outer casing of snow; serious wounds were sustained as a result. Needless to say, this incident was always cited later as prefiguring Napoleon's military genius. A better index of his Promethean ambitions is his well-authenticated remark to the Inspector-General M. de Keralio in 1782, when Napoleon announced he wanted to devote his life to science – either producing a general theory of electricity or inventing a model of the cosmos to replace the Newtonian system.

By 1782 Napoleon had decided that he wanted to join the Navy. It was conceivable that, the following year, he could have been sent either to the naval training school in Paris or to the École Militaire in Paris, but the royal Inspector-General decided he had not yet spent enough time at Brienne to be transferred. In 1783 the Inspector-General, M. de Keralio, kept the boy's options open. 'M. de Bonaparte (Napoleon), born 15 August 1769. Height 5'3". Constitution: excellent health, docile expression, mild, straightforward, thoughtful. Conduct most satisfactory; has always been distinguished for his application in mathematics. He is fairly well acquainted with history and geography. He is weak in all accomplishments – drawing, dancing, music and the like. This boy would make an excellent sailor; deserves to be admitted to the school in Paris.'

What decided Napoleon's fate was a downturn in his family's fortunes. Since Napoleon last saw his father, Carlo had not fared well. Once in Paris in 1779, he tried to press to have the Odone estate returned to him or at least to be compensated for it, but in vain. With a letter of introduction from Marbeuf he was granted audience with Louis XVI who, impressed by the Governor of Corsica's patronage of the supplicant, granted him his secondary request: a subsidy for the planting of mulberry trees which, it was hoped, would eventually make Corsica a silk-producing centre. But Carlo claimed all this money was absorbed by his expenses in Paris and the costs of lobbying. In his accounts book he noted: 'In Paris I received 4,000 francs from the King and a fee of 1,000 crowns from the government, but I came back without a penny.'

Meanwhile his family continued to grow. When Napoleon went to Brienne he was already the second child in a family of five but by the time he next saw his father there had been two additions to the brood (Marie Pauline, born in 1780 and Maria Annunciata Caroline in 1782). At the same time Carlo had declined in health and lost weight – clearly the first signs of the stomach cancer that would carry him off in 1785. This reduced his earning power at the very time his financial resources were declining, for in 1784 Marbeuf ceased to be the generous patron of old. A man of exceptional sexual vigour, he married an eighteen-year-old and began keeping Letizia at arm's length. Carlo had hoped Napoleon would be promoted either to Toulon or Paris in 1783 and, with this in mind, had had Lucien brought over from Corsica to slot into Napoleon's vacant cadetship. Keralio's report ended his hopes, but he decided to visit

Brienne anyway, in hopes of getting the Bertons to take on the eight-year-old Lucien.

The farewell act of patronage Marbeuf had performed for Carlo was getting Elisa placed with the nuns at St-Cyr in Paris. Hoping to kill two birds with one stone, Carlo arrived at Brienne on 21 June 1784 en route to Paris with Elisa. Also in tow was Lucien, who had been with Joseph at Autun since the year before. Apart from generally gloomy news about the family's finances, Carlo had three further items of bad news to impart to Napoleon: Letizia was not in the best of health, having contracted puerperal fever after the birth of Caroline; Lucien was coming to stay at Brienne for some months; and Joseph had decided he had no vocation, so wanted to quit his studies as a seminarist.

Sullenly Napoleon accepted the custodianship of the now nine-year-old Lucien. The notoriously bad later relationship between the two brothers seems to have had its origin here, for Lucien reported that Napoleon was broody and withdrawn, greeted him without affection and showed him no tenderness or kindness. Lucien deeply resented this and always said it was because of Napoleon's attitude that he (Lucien) felt the greatest repugnance in bowing to him when Emperor.

Carlo's visit is described in some detail in the first authentic letter written by Napoleon, on 25 June 1784, to his uncle Nicolo Paravicini. Napoleon was outraged by Joseph's ambition to join the artillery after leaving the seminary, for the notorious inter-service rivalry meant that was probably the end of his own ambitions to enter the Navy. Although, therefore, we must realize that Napoleon had his own reasons for the unflattering portrait he painted of Joseph, the analysis still shows very shrewd insight into his elder brother's failings. The lucid, cold, pragmatic adult Napoleon is essentially on display here. He pointed out that Joseph had poor health and lacked physical courage, that he had not faced the reality of Army life but thought only of the social side of garrison existence. What a pity that Joseph was abandoning a career where, with Bishop Marbeuf's patronage, he too could soon have a bishopric. And how was Joseph going to make the grade, he who had shown no aptitude for mathematics? Even if he were not congenitally lazy, had he fully realized that he would have to spend five years learning his putative profession as an engineer?

At some stage Letizia also visited Napoleon at Brienne and was appalled at how thin and cadaverous he was. This must have been on a visit distinct from Carlo's, though careless historians have run the two together. But one visit Napoleon looked forward to with more trepidation was the arrival in September of M. Reynaud des Monts, the sub-inspector of military schools. On 22 September Des Monts examined Napoleon and found him qualified to enter the military school in Paris. The only question now remaining was whether a place would be found. Napoleon did not rate his chances highly, as he thought his lack of the classical languages would stand between him and the École Royale Militaire in Paris. Fortunately, at this very juncture the Ministry of War authorized a special intake of candidates outstanding in mathematics. Early in October word came through that Napoleon and three schoolfellows had been selected for the school in Paris; Lucien could have the Brienne berth after all.

This was the end of Napoleon's naval ambitions, once so intense that he actually thought of applying to the Royal Navy in England for a cadetship. To this unlikely historical might-have-been can be added a more sombre possibility. In expressing his continuing enthusiasm for the Navy in 1784, Napoleon mentioned his ambition of sailing with the great French navigator La Pérouse, then preparing for a Pacific expedition to rival those of Captain Cook. La Pérouse sailed in 1785 but three years later was shipwrecked with the loss of all hands at Vanikoro Island in the south-west Pacific, between the Solomons and the New Hebrides. But for an administrative decision in Paris, the great European conqueror could easily have died in obscurity in an oceanic grave.

Napoleon and his three schoolfellows, whose names have been preserved for history (Montarby de Dampierre, Castries de Vaux, Laugier de Bellecour) accompanied by a monk (possibly Berton himself), left Brienne on 17 October by water coach and, after joining the Seine at Pont Marie, began to enter the suburbs at 4 p.m. on the 19th. The cadets were allowed to linger until nightfall before entering the military school, so Napoleon bought a novel from one of the quayside bookstalls, allowing his comrade Castries de Vaux to pay. The choice of book was surely significant: *Gil Blas* was the story of an impoverished Spanish boy who rose to high political office. Then their religious chaperon insisted they say a prayer in the church of St-Germain-des-Prés before entering the École Royale Militaire.

Built by the architect Gabriel thirteen years before, the École Royale was a marvel of Corinthian columns and Doric colonnades looking out on to the Champ de Mars and already hailed as one of the sights of Paris. Inside the building, carved, sculpted, painted and gilded walls, ceilings, doors and chimney-pieces were picked out with a plethora of statues and portraits of military heroes. The classrooms were papered in blue with gold ornamentation; there were curtains at the windows and doors. Students slept in a large dormitory warmed by earthenware stoves, and each boy had a separate cubicle, with an iron bedstead, linen drapery to go over the bed, a chair and shelves, a pewter jug and wash basin. Everything was on a lavish scale. There were 215 cadets in Napoleon's time but staff outnumbered students for, apart from the thirty professors and a librarian, there were priests, sacristans, riding instructors, grooms, stable hands, armourers, a medical staff, concierges, guardians of the prison, doorkeepers, lamplighters, shoemakers, wigmakers, gardeners, kitchen staff and no less than 150 servants. When Napoleon's name was formally entered on the rolls as a gentleman cadet on 22 October, he was given a splendid blue uniform, with red collar, splashes of yellow and scarlet on the cuffs, silver braid and white gloves. Linen was changed three times a week and the entire uniform replaced every April and October.

The luxury at the military school rather shocked Napoleon, and when he came to power he insisted on Spartan austerity at military academies. On St Helena Napoleon told Las Cases of three delicious meals every day, with choice of desserts at dinner and said: 'We were magnificently fed and served, treated in every way like officers possessed of great wealth, certainly greater than that of most of our families and far above what many of us would enjoy later on.'

His memory was selective, for the daily routine was gruelling enough. Cadets began their studies at 7 a.m. and finished at 7 p.m. – an eight-hour day with breaks. Each lesson lasted two hours, each class contained twenty to twenty-five students, and each branch of study was taught by a single teacher and his deputy. Accordingly, there were sixteen instructors for the eight subjects on the curriculum: mathematics, geography, history, French grammar, fortification, drawing, fencing and dancing. Three days a week were spent on the first four subjects and three days on the second four, so there were six hours' instruction in each discipline. On Sundays and feastdays the cadets spent four hours in the classroom, writing letters or reading improving books. In addition, there was drill every day as well as, on Thursdays and Sundays, shooting practice and military exercises. Punishment for infraction of the rules was severe: arrest and imprisonment with or without water. The most common misdemeanours committed were leaving the building without official permission (almost never granted) and receiving unauthorized pocket-money from parents.

Napoleon's academic progress closely mirrored his years at Brienne. He was outstanding in mathematics, was an enthusiastic fencer, but poor at drawing and dancing, and hopeless at German; as became clear later, he had absolutely no linguistic talent. Once again he read omnivorously and by now had a distinct taste for Rousseau and Montesquieu. But also, once again, the student of Napoleon is confronted by a number of anecdotes of doubtful credibility. He is alleged to have gone to the Champ de Mars in March 1785 to see the balloonist Blanchard ascend in the type of hot-air balloon made famous by the Montgolfier brothers. The story goes that Blanchard kept postponing the moment of take-off, so that Napoleon became impatient, cut the ropes keeping the balloon earthbound, and thus caused a scandal for which he was punished. But the sober historical record finds nothing more to say than that on 15 May 1785 he was confirmed by the Archbishop of Paris, and on the 26th of that month he took part in a review presided over by the Minister of War, Marshal Ségur.

For the first time in his life Napoleon made a true friend. Alexandre Des Mazis, was an ardent royalist from a military family in Strasbourg, who was in the year ahead of him and a senior cadet in charge of musketry training. He needed to draw on the resources of this friendship when news came that Carlo Buonaparte had died and the family was in straitened circumstances. Sustained pain and vomiting had led the ailing Carlo to consult physicians in Paris, Montpellier and Aix-en-Provence, but they were powerless against cancer. Carlo died on 24 February 1785, leaving Napoleon in financial limbo. He wrote to his uncle Lucien, the archdeacon, asking him to sustain the family until he qualified as an officer, and set to work to cram two or three years' work into as many months.

Carlo's death caused Napoleon considerable financial anxiety but no great sorrow or grief. He despised his father and could not see that he had any achievements to his credit. The emotions he felt seem to have been indifference and relief. In 1802 he rejected a proposal by Montpellier Municipal Council to erect a monument to his father in these words: 'Forget it: let us not trouble the peace of the dead. Leave their ashes in peace. I also lost my grandfather, my great-grandfather, why is nothing done for them? This leads too far.' Much later he said Carlo's death was a happy accident, for he was an unsubtle political trimmer and in the post-1789 quicksands would certainly have made the kinds of blunders that would have finished off Napoleon's career before it got started. Yet Napoleon, especially as a Corsican, could not simply slough off his need for a father; at this stage he 'solved' the problem by elevating Paoli to the position of father-figure.

Napoleon immersed himself in his studies, now desperate to make the grade as an artillery officer. Entry to the élite corps of the artillery was normally a two-stage process. First came an examination on the first volume of Étienne Bézout's *Cours de Mathématiques*, the artilleryman's bible. There then followed a year in artillery school, after which cadets were examined on the next three volumes of Bézout; if successful, candidates were then commissioned as second lieutenants. Oustandingly gifted boys could take a single examination on all four volumes of Bézout and go straight into a regiment with a commission. Only a very few attempted this feat every year, but among them in 1785 was Napoleon Buonaparte.

Every summer an examiner came to the military school to test artillery candidates. Until 1783 it had been the renowned Bézout himself, but then his place was taken by Pierre Simon, marquis de Laplace. One of the great authentic scientific geniuses of the eighteenth century, Laplace was a brilliant mathematician who specialized in astronomy. His theories explained the motions of Saturn and Jupiter and its moons, the workings of the tides, the nebulae in deep space, electromagnetism and molecular physics. In September 1785 Laplace subjected Napoleon to a rigorous examination in differential equations and algebra as well as the practical applications of mathematics.

Only fifty-eight candidates were taken into the artillery from all schools and colleges in France. The École Royale Militaire in Paris should have had the edge but, of the seventeen boys put in for the examination, only four featured among the successful fifty-eight. Among them was Napoleon, placed forty-second, Des Mazis, placed fifty-sixth and Napoleon's bitter student rival Le Picard de Phélipeaux, who was forty-first. To be forty-second out of fifty-eight does not sound distinguished, and this fact has contributed to the persistent idea that Napoleon was not a particularly brilliant student, but it must be remembered that he was up against students who in some cases had had two years' more study than he. In September, just sixteen, he was commissioned as a second lieutenant. He and Des Mazis had expressed a wish to join the same regiment, and the request was granted; the two friends were gazetted to join the La Fère regiment at Valence in the Rhône valley. Some have speculated that Napoleon's request had an ulterior motive, since the La Fère regiment was known to have served in Corsica ever since 1769. But if there was Machiavellianism in his method, Napoleon was disappointed: by 1785 only twenty men from the regiment remained in Corsica and the rest were in Provence.

Napoleon's education was now complete and his personality formed in all essentials; there would be no decisive change in attitudes until 1792 and probably no fundamental shift in world-view until 1795, when he first tasted real power. He entered the Army shockingly ill-prepared for military life, at least by modern standards. Knowing nothing of the real conditions he might encounter on a battlefield, and still less of Army regulations, he was rather like the nineteenth-century English gentleman with a classical education sent out to administer India; he was to learn the craft of soldiering on the job. Cynics have claimed that the École Royale Militaire was little more than a finishing school, but that even so it left Napoleon as much of a primitive savage as when he entered it.

If the military schools at Brienne and Paris had been designed to promote social inequality, as was claimed, they failed miserably with Napoleon. The experience of being a poor boy among rich cadets embittered him and left him cynical. If the idea of racial and cultural equality had been taken seriously at Brienne, he would not have been bullied for his Corsican origins. At the École Royale in Paris the official lip service paid to equality between the eighty-three paying students and the 132 scholarship boys simply resulted in a kind of crude 'levelling up' where the poor were trapped by peer pressure into living beyond their means. Napoleon grew to hate aristocrats whose only 'virtue' was that they had been born in the right bedroom. He referred to them as 'the curse of the nation . . . imbeciles . . . hereditary asses', and his hatred was compounded by the aristocratic contempt for those of lesser breeding, even if they were a hundred times more talented. Actually, in the context of the *ancien régime*, Napoleon was luckier than he knew for the artillery, to be entered only by those of great mathematical talent, was the only branch of the Army where a career genuinely was open to talent.

It may be that contempt for an organized religion that could condone blatant injustices contrary to its own official teachings was what finished Catholicism for Napoleon. Certainly by the time he left Brienne he had lost his faith, though still obliged to make public obeisance to its forms. Napoleon's later explanation for his alienation from the Church was threefold. First there was the hypocritical force-feeding of rote-learned religious doctrine at Brienne, often inculcated by monks, like the Bertons, whose own credentials as believers were open to doubt. Then there was his reading of Rousseau, who believed in a civil religion that was the ideology of the State, and loathed Catholicism for forming a middle layer between the citizen and society. Additionally, Rousseau, like Machiavelli, believed in the old civic virtue of Ancient Rome and Sparta, and in line with this theory believed Christianity turned out effete, emasculated soldiers and citizens. Finally, Napoleon's love of the ancient world was affronted by the bigotry of the monks at Brienne who taught that the classical authors, for all the brilliance and elegance of their writings, were

roasting in Hell because they were pagans. This idea seemed spectacularly absurd to the young Napoleon. We might add that although
Napoleon believed, along with the Catholic Church, in original sin, he
was a thoroughgoing pessimist about human nature and did not believe in
redemption in any form.

At this stage Rousseau was still the lodestone Napoleon steered by. It is
easy to see the appeal: Napoleon in his teens was also a fanatical Corsican
nationalist and Rousseau had praised Corsica as the one society in Europe
where true freedom and equality might emerge. The visionary view of
Corsica as a society where Spartan simplicity, civic virtue, equality and
austerity contrasted with the corruption of mainland France, almost as
though Rousseau's Social Contract had been given physical form, was
reinforced by his worship of Paoli, who by the later years in Brienne had
already displaced Carlo as father-figure. Napoleon's critics then and since
have argued that his Francophobia was deeply illogical, given that he was
drawing on French funds to obtain an education and had obtained the
place at Brienne solely because he was accepted as belonging to the *French*
nobility. One senior officer at the military school in Paris finally got a
bellyful of Paoli and Corsica and rounded on Napoleon sternly: 'Sir, you
are a King's cadet; you must remember this and moderate your love for
Corsica, which is after all part of France.'

Slighted for his low-grade Corsican nobility, regarded as a bore for his
island nationalism, Napoleon had further reason to believe, on the
evidence of his school years, that he was an Ishmael, with every man's
hand turned against him. He experienced severe difficulty in making
friends, was let down by most of those he did make, but on the other
hand seemed to make bitter enemies by the mere fact of his existence. At
Brienne he was taken up by Fauvelet de Bourrienne, who later painted an
idyllic picture of the two supposed friends bathing in the ice-cold waters
of the Aube. Bourrienne's Army career was a failure but in 1797
Napoleon appointed him as his secretary. His reward was to find that
Bourrienne cheated him at every opportunity. Bourrienne was a
fraudster, embezzler, defalcator and money launderer on a grand scale.
Napoleon treated him with great indulgence, but again received scant
recompense. Bourrienne's ghosted memoirs – a cynical moneymaking
exercise – were a work of blatant propaganda, still uncritically used by
Napoleon's critics as an authentic picture of the man.

Another Brienne schoolfriend was one of those who accompanied
Napoleon to the military school in Paris: Laugier de Bellecour, the son of
a baron. Laugier had flirted with the homosexual set at Brienne, but
Napoleon warned him that if he succumbed to their blandishments, that

would be the end of his friendship. Laugier either did resist, or was able to persuade Napoleon that he had. But once in Paris the temptation was simply too great. Laugier 'came out', to Napoleon's disgust, and when the Corsican coldly told him their friendship was over, Laugier, angry and distraught, assaulted him. Laugier came off the worse from the encounter, and a contemplated charge of assault against Napoleon was dropped, since the school authorities knew all about Laugier's proclivities.

At the military school in Paris Napoleon had the first of the 'hate at first sight' experiences that were to dog him through life. His enemy was Le Picard de Phélipeaux, who just pipped him into forty-first place in the artillery examination, became an émigré after the Revolution, and fought with the British against Napoleon at Acre in 1798. But Napoleon had the gift for rubbing up the wrong way against young females as well as male rivals. In 1785 he sometimes visited Madame Permon, a Corsican and an old friend of Carlo; she had married a rich French commissary officer and had two daughters, Cécile and Laure. There seems to have been an instant antagonism between Napoleon and Laure who, seeing his long legs in officers' boots, laughed at him and called him 'Puss in Boots'. Although Napoleon tried to turn the whole thing into a joke, it was clear he was deeply affronted. He would not have liked Laure anyway: she had been dressed as a boy until the age of eight and was as assertive as only men were supposed to be in that era. Later she married Napoleon's friend Junot and was a persistent thorn in the Bonaparte side. A kind of female Bourrienne, like him she would do anything for money and in that capacity later brought out eighteen volumes of memoirs which rival Bourrienne's for their unreliability.

Napoleon could never abide any gender uncertainty or 'unnatural' behaviour by assertive or strident women. His ambivalent feelings about his mother are at the root of this, but if tradition is any guide, as a cadet he had further experiences that made him wary of women. He was said to have met up with two young women, then been shocked and incredulous to find they were lesbians. The other story from his cadet years concerns the attempt to seduce him by a much older woman. But the sixteen-year-old Second Lieutenant Bonaparte was still sexually timid and repressed. He was allegedly the only successful artilleryman in Paris posted to the La Fère regiment who did not visit a brothel in Lyons on the way south.

With a chip on his shoulder about his social origins and his nationality, an uncertain touch with his male peers and a fear and suspicion of women, Napoleon needed little else to make him feel as though he were one of nature's loners. But, to cap all, he was short of stature, only 5'6" when fully grown. Alfred Adler has made us aware that this is a key feature in the overcompensation of despots; most dictators have been small men – Caesar, Hitler, Mussolini, Stalin and Franco as well as Napoleon. It is no exaggeration to say that the sixteen-year-old Napoleon's experience of life denoted the authoritarian personality in the making.

CHAPTER THREE

Napoleon left the École Royale Militaire, Paris, on 28 October 1785. Before heading south to join the La Fère regiment at Valence he went to see his patron, Bishop Marbeuf, whose luxurious quarters were at the Abbey Palace in St-Germain-des-Prés. Marbeuf gave him letters of introduction to a cleric of equivalent standing in Valence, Monsignor Tardivon. Although Napoleon was finished with Catholicism, he was still prepared to milk it for worldly advantage.

Two days later he departed southward on the Lyons stage. His route took him through Fontainebleau, Sens, Autun and Chalon-sur-Saône where, on 1 November he took the water coach down the Saône to Lyons. He completed his journey by post-boat and arrived in Valence on 3 November. Splendidly arrayed in the uniform of the La Fère regiment – blue breeches, blue waistcoat, royal blue coat with red facings, pockets braided in red and epaulettes with gold and silver fringes – he was assigned to the bombardier company of Captain Masson d'Autevrive. The garrison at La Fère had seven artillery regiments (in turn divided into gunners, bombardiers and sappers) plus fifteen companies of workmen and miners. The La Fère regiment had the reputation of being a crack unit; it rose early, worked hard, and drilled as perfectly as an élite infantry regiment.

Second Lieutenant Bonaparte was the Number Four man in one of four bombardier companies. Each regiment contained twenty companies, fourteen of gunners, four of bombardiers and two sappers. Each company of about seventy men was commanded by a captain with three lieutenants under him. In the French system, five companies made up a brigade (commanded by a major), two brigades a battalion and two battalions a regiment. Napoleon underwent ten weeks of basic training, drilling first as a private, then as a corporal and finally as a sergeant. He afterwards paid tribute to this method of learning from the grass-roots up and attributed to it his famous 'common touch'.

On 10 January 1786 he completed his probation as an officer. His duties were scarcely onerous: mounting guard, looking after the men, attending classes on mathematics, fortification, chemistry and physics. There was plenty of free time. From the copious notes Napoleon kept we know a great deal about how he spent his time: climbing Mont Roche Colombe, skating, visiting the towns of Romans and Tournon. He records that Valence, a town of 5,000 inhabitants, then chiefly notable for its citadel and a plethora of abbeys and priories, had more than its fair share of pretty women. Girls begin to be mentioned: on 4 December 1785, at a fiesta, he danced with a certain Mlle Mion-Desplaces. He was friendly with a Madame Grégoire de Colobier and her daughter Caroline, though the episode of eating cherries in the countryside with Caroline sounds suspiciously like a Rousseauesque fantasy (Rousseau did likewise with Mlle Galley).

Napoleon's principal problem was money. He had an income of 1,120 livres a year, made up of a basic salary of 800 livres, plus 200 livres royal bounty and 120 livres lodging allowance. But because Carlo had died virtually penniless and Letizia had lost the protection of Marbeuf, Napoleon had to remit most of his earnings to Corsica to help his impoverished family; Letizia had a total of 1,200 livres a year on which to keep herself and the younger children. Somehow or other she inveigled money for extras out of the notorious skinflint Archdeacon Luciano, who was the family miser. Napoleon therefore had to make do with very basic lodgings. He found a noisy room on the first floor of the Café Cercle, at the corner of the Grand-Rue and the rue du Croissant, where the landlady was a fifty-year-old spinster, Mlle Bou, who washed and looked after his clothes; the room and services cost just over eight livres. He took his meals in a cheap café named the Three Pigeons in rue Perollerie.

At Valence Napoleon launched himself on a career as a would-be writer. He penned a refutation of a book attacking his hero Rousseau. He wrote a story called *The Prophetic Mask* about an Arab prophet who is defeated after a string of victories and commits suicide along with all his followers. Apart from underlining Napoleon's continuing fascination with the world of the Middle East, the tale and the sixteen-year-old lieutenant's notebooks testify eloquently at this time to a morbid preoccupation with suicide. How seriously should we take this? Partly it seems a fashionable Romantic pose, for Goethe's Werther, with his tired-of-life melancholia, was a role model for educated young men of the time. But part of Napoleon's reflections on suicide do suggest a genuine pessimism about the world and the beginnings of a depressive illness. He wrote:

Always alone in the midst of men, I return to dream with myself and give myself up to all the force of my melancholy. What madness makes me desire my own destruction? Without doubt, the problem of what to do in this world . . . Life is a burden to me because I feel no pleasure and because everything is affliction to me. It is a burden to me because the men with whom I have to live, and will probably always live, have ways as different from mine as the light of the moon from that of the sun. I cannot then pursue the only manner of living which could enable me to put up with existence, whence follows a disgust for everything.

The uneventful external tenor of life at Valence ended in August 1786 when the regiment was ordered up to Lyons to suppress a strike by silk workers; three 'ringleaders' were hanged and the strikers effectively cowed. Napoleon, who had often expressed his homesickness for Corsica, applied for leave and was granted it, to run from 1 October. Since officers in far-flung corners of France were allowed a month's travelling time in addition to leave, Napoleon set out for Corsica as soon as the military intervention in Lyons was complete. At Aix-en-Provence he visited his uncle Fesch, who had not yet completed his theological studies, and also Lucien, who had abandoned Brienne and come down to Aix to be trained as a priest. He finally reached Ajaccio on 15 September 1786, having been absent from the island for nearly eight years.

The reunion with Letizia and great-uncle Lucien was a particularly joyous one, though clouded by the financial shadows that hung over the family. Napoleon was shocked to find his mother doing all the household chores when he arrived home. He enquired about Joseph and learned that, in obedience to his father's wishes, he had given up all hope of a military career and turned to the paternal study, law. Hearing that he was now studying law at Pisa University, Napoleon wrote to him to say that the family honour required that Letizia be relieved of the worst drudgery; would Joseph therefore bring back a reliable servant? When Joseph came home a few months later, he brought with him the Italian domestic maid Saveria, who remained in Letizia's service for forty years.

To Joseph we owe a meticulous analysis of Napoleon's reading at the time: the classical authors in translation, especially Plutarch, Cicero, Livy, Cornelius Nepos and Tacitus; Macpherson's *Ossian*, Racine, Corneille, Voltaire, Montaigne, Montesquieu and, above all Rousseau and the Abbé Raynal. However, all the evidence suggests that Napoleon's reading was wide rather than deep. His knowledge of Rousseau was superficial and he was ignorant of much of Voltaire; he knew little of Montesquieu and less of Diderot; most surprising of all, he had not heard of Pierre Laclos's *Les Liaisons Dangereuses*, published four years earlier and significant both because it was heavily influenced by Rousseau and because Laclos, like Napoleon, was an artilleryman.

The entente between Napoleon and Joseph was particularly close during this leave. The two brothers held long, animated discussions on all the subjects that fascinated Napoleon. Joseph was said to have remarked later: 'Ah, the glorious Emperor will never compensate me for Napoleon, whom I loved so well, and whom I should like to meet again as I knew him in 1786, if indeed there is a meeting in the Elysian fields.' But over both young men a financial shadow continued to hang, and in particular there was the problem of Carlo's mulberry groves. His investment was predicated on a subsidy from the French government which had been suspended because of financial retrenchment. Joseph had to return to his studies in Pisa, so it fell to Napoleon to try to sort out the implicit breach of contract.

On 21 April 1787 Napoleon wrote to Colonel de Lance, his commanding officer in the La Fère regiment, enclosing a medical certificate stating that he was suffering from 'quartan ague', and requesting an extension of leave on grounds of illness. This was granted readily: Napoleon was informed he need not report back for duty until December 1787. To obtain leave after only nine months' service and then to be away from the regiment for what eventually turned out to be nearly two years suggests an extremely complaisant attitude to the professional officer by the *ancien régime* military authorities. Nor does there appear to have been any liaison between government departments, for nobody seemed to have questioned how Napoleon was too ill to be on military duty yet fit enough to make a long journey to Paris to lobby the financial bureaucracy about Carlo's mulberry groves. Such laxity was common in the pre-1789 years: a colonel, for example, was required to be present with his regiment for only five months a year.

Napoleon's financial mission began when he left Corsica on 12 September 1787. By the beginning of November he was installed at the Hôtel de Cherbourg in the rue du Faubourg-St-Honoré in Paris. For the first time he really got to know the French capital, having been a virtual prisoner at the École Royale; he made the most of his time, visiting as many theatres as possible, with the Italian Opéra a particular favourite. His audience with the Comptroller-General of Finance was abortive: nothing for the groves was offered. As if in compensation, Napoleon received the six-month extension of leave he had requested before leaving Corsica. This time he asked for prolongation on the ground that he wished to attend a meeting of the Corsican Estates; since he did not ask for pay, the request was granted.

The most significant event in the eighteen-year-old Napoleon's sojourn in Paris was that he lost his virginity. On the freezing night of 22 November 1787 he went to the Palais-Royal, then the red-light district, and picked up a prostitute. The Palais-Royal, bordering the Louvre and the Tuileries, had once belonged to Cardinal Richelieu and the duc d'Orléans. In 1776 the gardens became the property of the duc de Chartres, a libertine, who engaged the architect Victor Louis to build a theatre. While this was being constructed, a wooden gallery was put up, running alongside the gardens. Known as the *camp des tartares*, by 1784 it was notorious for prostitution and petty theft; as the private property of the duc de Chartres, it was safe from police raids. Meanwhile the theatre itself gradually took shape in the inner area of the Palais, which then became a centre for culture in its widest sense, both élite and popular.

It was here that Napoleon made his first timid approaches to a *fille de joie*. He approached one who proved willing to talk about her experiences and what had driven her to this life. Encouraged by her ingenuousness, he took her back to his lodgings. They talked, then made love. Napoleon records that she was slight, slim and feminine and that she was a Breton, from Nantes, who had been seduced by an army officer.

On New Year's Day 1788 he arrived back in Ajaccio. The family's financial situation had worsened if anything and Letizia still had four children entirely dependent on her; in 1788 Louis had his tenth birthday, Pauline her eighth, Caroline her sixth and Jérôme his fourth, and in addition there were fees payable for Lucien at the Aix seminary and Joseph at the University of Pisa. It is remarkable how quickly Napoleon, as the only breadwinner, was accepted as the head of the family, and how Joseph was quite prepared to defer to him. But by the time Napoleon departed from Ajaccio on 1 June 1788 he had at least had the pleasure of seeing Joseph return from Pisa with the coveted title of Doctor of Laws.

The La Fère regiment was by now stationed in Auxonne. Once again Napoleon dedicated himself to a Spartan existence. He lodged near the barracks, at the Pavilion de la Ville, where his room had a single cell-like window and was austerely furnished with just a bed, table and armchair. There was even less to do here than at Valence, and appearance at parade was required just once a week. In this period Napoleon became a genuine workaholic, alternating his writing of apprentice pieces with omnivorous reading, with special emphasis on history, Corsica and the theory of artillery. He was already learning to get by with a minimum of sleep; he rose at 4 a.m., took just one meal a day at 3 p.m. so as to save money, and went to bed at 10 p.m. after eighteen hours at his books.

The ascetic way of life seriously affected his health. Poor diet, overwork and the cold and damp climate triggered physical exhaustion, which made his body prey to malaria. His only real friends in the barracks were the faithful Des Mazis and a Captain Gassendi, who appealed to Napoleon on three separate counts: as a man of letters, a distinguished geometer and an admirer of Corsica. But he fell out with an officer named Belly de Bussy; a duel was arranged, but intermediaries forced the two officers to compose their differences for the sake of the regiment. Evidently Napoleon did sometimes try the patience of the senior command, for he suffered a 24-hour arrest for reasons unknown; he was shut up in a cell with just a single law book for company – an experience he later claimed was useful when he came to draw up the Code Napoléon.

But on the credit side Napoleon attracted the attention of the mathematics instructor, Professor Lombard, who in turn mentioned him to the commanding officer of all troops in Auxonne, Baron Jean-Pierre du Teil, as 'one to note'. Napoleon acquired an unrivalled knowledge of projectiles and ballistics and also honed his talents as a draughtsman. Among the most important influences on Napoleon the theoretician of artillery were the general's brother, Jean de Beaumont du Teil, whose handbook, published ten years earlier, stressed the massing of big guns at decisive moments in battle. Napoleon was also influenced by Jacques de Guibert, whose books stressed that a successful army depended on speed and should be prepared to live off the land. Yet another influence was the recently published work by Pierre Bourcet, which prescribed the separation of army divisions for the purpose of rapid movement, followed by their rapid concentration just before a battle.

Such was Napoleon's dedication that in fifteen months at Auxonne he filled thirty-six manuscript notebooks with writings on artillery, history and philosophy. In August 1788 he was singled out for his special aptitude and appointed commander of a demonstration company trying to devise ways of firing mortar shells from ordinary cannon. The danger of the work was offset by the opportunity to put favourite theories to the test. Napoleon also became the only second lieutenant to sit on a select regimental artillery committee. On 28 August he wrote to Fesch complaining of fever and warning that his appointment to the committee, over the heads of many captains, had caused considerable irritation and jealousy.

Du Teil liked to send his junior officers into the countryside to test their talent at choosing ground and spotting any topographical draw-backs; often they would be asked to write a situation paper, explaining how a particular hill or village could be attacked or defended. The combination of assiduous fieldwork with voracious reading turned

Napoleon into an artilleryman nonpareil. The one obstacle to rapid promotion under du Teil's benevolent eye was the nineteen-year-old's uncertain health. There was another protracted attack of fever in the final months of 1788, after which Napoleon wrote to his mother that several fevers had laid him low; in common with most people in the eighteenth century, who knew nothing of the anopheles mosquito, he attributed his attacks of malaria to 'miasmata' arising from the nearby river. In similar vein he wrote to Archdeacon Lucien on 18 March 1789: 'I have no other resource but work. I dress but once in eight days; I sleep but little since my illness; it is incredible; I retire at ten (to save candles) and rise at four in the morning. I take but one meal a day, at three; that is good for my health.'

At the beginning of April in the fateful year 1789 du Teil received word of grain riots in the nearby town of Seurre. Napoleon was among one hundred officers and men immediately put on the twenty-mile march to Seurre to quell the disturbances. The rioters dispersed before the military came on the scene, but Napoleon and the troopers were kept on for two months, as a warning against any further uprising. After taking lodgings in the rue Dulac, Napoleon made his mark with the Intendant of Burgundy, who gave a supper for the officers and asked for the young Bonaparte as his personal escort on a horseback ride to Verdun-sur-les-Doubs. On 29 May he returned to Auxonne, where he shortly afterwards wrote a famous letter to Paoli, lamenting that he was born at the very moment independent Corsica expired:

As the nation was perishing I was born. Thirty thousand Frenchmen were vomited on to our shores, drowning the throne of liberty in waves of blood. Such was the odious sight which was the first to strike me. From my birth, my cradle was surrounded by the cries of the dying, the groans of the oppressed and tears of despair. You left our island and with you went all hope of happiness. Slavery was the price of our submission. Crushed by the triple yoke of the soldier, the law-maker and the tax inspector, our compatriots live despised.

Napoleon liked swimming, but in the summer of 1789 he was seized by cramp in the Saône and nearly drowned. Superstitiously, he linked his own near-tragedy with the alarming events taking place that summer in Paris. On 15 July he wrote to Archdeacon Lucien in high excitement about the 'astonishing and singular' news reaching them. Soon the revolutionary current sweeping France affected Auxonne and even the La Fère regiment. On 19 July the local people rose in revolt, burnt the register of taxes and destroyed the offices of a Farmer-General. The men of the La Fère regiment stood idly by and, a little later, caught the spirit of mutiny themselves. They marched to du Teil's house, demanded money with menaces, got drunk and compelled some officers to drink with them and dance the farandole. Order was eventually restored, but du Teil thought it best to break up the regiment and canton it in different locations along the banks of the Saône. Napoleon, who on 23 August took an oath of fidelity to Nation, King and the Law, apparently confessed that he would have obeyed du Teil and turned his guns on the mutineers, even though his ideological sympathies were with the Revolution.

For some time Napoleon had been requesting another period of furlough, and this was eventually granted on 21 August, but after the trouble with his regiment, du Teil thought that no leave at all should be granted. He was, however, overruled by the provincial governor who sensibly thought that such punitive action would simply increase the sum total of resentment. Napoleon's leave was granted from 15 October but, given the usual month's 'long-distance' travelling time, he left for Corsica on 9 September. He accompanied the Baron du Teil as far as Lyons, then continued alone to Valence, where he took the river coach to the mouths of the Rhône. In Marseilles he visited his hero the Abbé Raynal before crossing to Ajaccio, where he arrived at the end of September 1789.

On this leave, Napoleon began his career as Corsican politician – or troublemaker, as his critics would have it. Learning that the new military commander in Corsica, the Vicomte de Barrin, was a timid and irresolute man with just six battalions at his call, Napoleon trimmed and temporized with the Revolutionary faction, now dominant on the island. The politics of Corsica were of quite extraordinary complexity, with personal politics and class conflict overlying clan loyalties and ideological struggle. Early in 1789, the situation had been reasonably clear. To the famous meeting of the Estates-General in Versailles went the comte de Buttafuoco, who had asked Rousseau to write a constitution for Corsica, representing the nobility; Peretti della Rocca for the clergy; and for the Third Estate Colonna Cesari and X Saliceti.

However, the outbreak of the French Revolution in 1789 was, for Corsica, like applying a match to a powder-keg. On the royalist side the vicomte de Sarrin was soon outflanked by firebrands like his deputy General Gaffori. Corsica largely embraced the Revolutionary cause, and the first Constituent Assembly adopted a resolution that the island was no longer conquered territory but an integral part of France. In February

1790 Saliceti was instrumental in getting the Assembly to grant an amnesty to Paoli and invite him to return to the island.

This was the context in which Napoleon, together with Joseph, who was turning himself into a professional politician, started to acquire a reputation as a small-time 'fixer'. He was in Bastia in early November 1789, and the fact that a popular rising took place there five days after his arrival has always seemed more than coincidence. The first three months of 1790 saw him active with Joseph in the election campaigns for the new Corsican assembly, and on 12 April he and Joseph were present at a nine-hour meeting of the new Assembly at Orezza. It was no wonder that the commander of the Ajaccio garrison complained to the Minister of War in December 1789 as follows: 'This young officer was educated at the École Militaire. His sister is at St-Cyr and his mother has received countless kindnesses from the government. This officer had much better be with his regiment since he spends all his time stirring up trouble.'

On 16 April 1790 Napoleon wrote to du Teil to request a prolongation of his leave, on the grounds that he was suffering from anaemia and needed to take the waters of Orezza. The request was so clearly bogus that it is surprising that du Teil granted an extension of four-and-a-half months with pay until October, but we must remember that by this time he was something of a cynosure with his commanding officer. It was not the water at Orezza Napoleon was interested in, but the hot air of political disputation, for between 9 and 27 September he and Joseph were in daily attendance at the Paolistas 'party conference'. The sessions were dominated by Paoli, who, aged sixty-six and whitehaired, had made a triumphant return to Corsica, landing at Bastia on 17 July, where Napoleon met him.

The Assembly held at Orezza halted the growing move for the partition of the island (for in addition to every other complexity, there was a separatist movement *within* Corsica) and settled on Bastia as the capital. The stage was now set for head-to-head conflict in the Corsican Assembly between the partisans of Buttafuoco and Paoli. In this tactical battle Saliceti decisively outpointed Buttafuoco and the clerical representative Peretti; the Third Estate and the Paolistas now held the whip hand in Corsica.

For the whole of 1790 Napoleon was in effect a Corsican politician. He did try to rejoin his regiment in October, but his ship was driven back to Ajaccio several times by adverse winds. He used the time to get Joseph elected to the Ajaccio municipal council, even though the Bonapartes' enemies produced Joseph's birth certificate to show that he was too young to serve. With the Republican majority on the Council behind him,

Napoleon advocated stern measures against the island's reactionaries; hounding them from office Napoleon justified under the formula *salus populi suprema lex*. By the time of his departure in January 1791 he was both founder member and leading light of the Ajaccio Jacobin Club and was commissioned to write a philippic denouncing Paoli's enemy Buttafuoco.

At the end of the month Napoleon left Corsica, taking with him his twelve-year-old brother Louis, in order to ease the financial pressure on his mother. After spending a few days in Valence, he arrived in Auxonne on 11 February 1791. Technically he had overstayed his leave and was therefore liable to lose pay since the end of October, but he brought with him certificates from the municipal council at Ajaccio, stating that repeated and sustained storms in the Mediterranean had made a sailing impossible all that time. Colonel de Lance accepted this and put in a request, rubber-stamped by the Ministry of War, that the back salary be paid.

Napoleon's relations with Louis at Auxonne seem to have been largely a rerun of the disastrous overlap with Lucien at Brienne in 1784. The twelve-year-old slept on a mattress in a cabinet adjoining Napoleon's room and was taken aback at his brother's poverty: here was just a single room, poorly furnished, without curtains, a bed and two chairs and a table in the window covered with books and papers, at which Napoleon worked for fifteen to sixteen hours a day. Napoleon did his best to look after the lad, cooking him meals, including a cheap but nourishing broth, and teaching him a smattering of French, geography and mathematics. But the two were ill-matched in temperament, sensibility and intellect, and Louis was an ingrate. Napoleon wrote to Fesch that Louis had acquired some social graces and was a favourite with women, who wanted to mother him, but Louis himself hinted in a letter to Joseph that he hated it at Auxonne and wanted to go home.

If Napoleon still retained his favour with du Teil and his regimental colonel, he seems by his new-found Jacobin sympathies to have alienated the largely royalist officers in the mess. After one particularly acrimonious altercation a group of his brother officers tried to throw him in the Saône; this was reported to the commanding officer, who did his best to pour oil on troubled waters. Perhaps for this reason he was judiciously 'kicked upstairs' with a promotion to first lieutenant and a transfer at the beginning of June to the 4th Artillery Regiment at Valence.

Another factor in Napoleon's transfer was the general reorganization of artillery following a decree of the National Assembly in early 1791. To break down the old allegiances and substitute 'rational' solidarity with the new régime, the Assembly abolished the names of regiments, which were henceforth to be designated only by numbers. The La Fère became the First Regiment. Napoleon's new regiment, the Fourth, was formerly known as the Grenoble regiment. Napoleon once again showed himself scarcely to be a man of the 'new' rationalistic ideology of the Revolution, for he had a powerful sentimental attachment to the La Fère, and even petitioned to stay where he was. But the order was confirmed, so on 14 June he left Auxonne.

He arrived in Valence on 16 June and took his old room with Mlle Bou. Once again he tried to involve Louis in his ambitions as a polymath, introducing the boy to astronomy, law, statistics, English politics, Merovingian history and the writings of Racine, Corneille and Rousseau. Yet Napoleon could not quite be the recluse of old, for the pace of events at Paris was forcing all Army officers to decide where they stood politically. Four days after Napoleon joined his new regiment at Valence, Louis XVI was involved in the disastrous flight to Varennes, which was the beginning of the end for the monarchy. As a result of the Varennes imbroglio, all Army officers were compelled to take a new oath, to the new Constitution and the National Assembly: to maintain the Constitution against all enemies internal and external, to resist invasion and to obey no orders except those validated by the Assembly's decrees; the oath had to be written by each officer in his own hand and signed by him.

The oath caused schism in the Army, setting brother against brother, friend against friend. For example, Desaix, Napoleon's greatest general in later years, threw in his lot with the new régime, while his two brothers resigned. The net result was that royalist officers resigned in droves, opening up thousands of vacancies in the officer class and giving meaning to the Revolutionary ideal of social mobility. Many joined the émigrés abroad. Thirty-two officers in the 4th Regiment refused to take the oath, but Napoleon signed his on 6 July. He had the reputation of being an ultrapolitical, overserious officer and had to pay heavy fines for violating the mess code against talking shop; because of his outspoken political views some of his comrades refused to speak to him and others would not sit next to him at table.

Napoleon joined the Club of Friends of the Constitution, the Jacobin society of Valence. There was an all-day meeting of two hundred members on 3 July which Napoleon attended. As yet, however, he was still running with the hare and the hounds, for on 25 August he ostentatiously celebrated Louis XVI's birthday with his brother officers at the Three Pigeons.

Napoleon was by now bored and restless, and his workaholic reading programmes gave way to visits, to Grenoble, Tain, Tournu. One of his excursions had more point, for he visited General du Teil at his château of Pommiers and came away with yet another dispensation for leave, this time on the grounds that Archdeacon Lucien was dying. Behind this seemingly innocent visit was great Machiavellian calculation. On 4 August 1791, finding itself short of troops, the National Assembly authorized the raising of volunteer battalions in each *département*. It was also decreed that serving officers could hold posts in such battalions without forfeiting their regular army rank. Napoleon applied to his new colonel, Campagnol, for leave, speaking vaguely of family business, but Campagnol turned him down, almost certainly because Napoleon had already spent thirty-two months of his first six years' service on leave. The ambitious young lieutenant simply went above his head to du Teil, who was now Inspector-General of Artillery.

The likelihood is that the Bonaparte brothers set off for Corsica, and a certificate from the municipality of Ajaccio shows Napoleon to have landed there in September, but historians have raised the difficulty that his name also appears as being among those present at a review of his regiment on 30 October. The most likely explanation is that some friendly officers covered for him to avoid becoming ensnarled in Army bureaucracy, perhaps even calling out 'present' when his name was called. Certain it is that by 16 October he and Louis were back in Ajaccio, at the Archdeacon's bedside.

There is an apocryphal sound to the story in Joseph's memoirs that the dying Lucien said: 'Napoleon, you will be a great man,' and then bade Joseph defer to him. On the other hand, Napoleon did later refer to the deathbed scene as 'like Jacob and Esau'. But there was nothing mythical or apocryphal about the money Lucien left the Bonapartes. The old miser, who was said to keep a chest of gold coins under his bed which he claimed was not his but the Church's, left a significant amount of money. By the end of 1791 Napoleon and Joseph were co-owners of a house and a vineyard in the environs of Ajaccio; in addition, Napoleon estimated he spent 5,000 francs getting himself elected as Lieutenant-Colonel and second-in-command of a regiment of Corsican volunteers in 1792 – in an episode which merits further examination for the light it throws on Napoleon the Machiavellian.

Napoleon's release from abject poverty in late 1791 launched him into the final phase of his abortive career as a Corsican politician. What kind of political views did the ambitious first lieutenant hold at this juncture, itself a turning point in the wider French Revolution? To establish this we must examine the copious writings he churned out in the period

1786–91. What becomes clear is that Napoleon wrote under a dual stimulus: he was still a fanatical Corsican nationalist and partisan of Paoli whom he worshipped only just this side of idolatry; and he took his immediate inspiration from his undisciplined and eclectic reading.

The 1786 composition *Sur le Suicide* reveals a mixture of Napoleon as fervent Paolista and young Werther. It evinces a hatred of France and his immediate physical surroundings, a barely suppressed eroticism and a ruthless desire for pleasures either forbidden or unaffordable, a thirst for fame and, as ever with the young Napoleon, the gallery touch. Napoleon so far seemed to have derived from his reading of the classical authors only the tawdry tricks of fustian rhetoric, as in the following: 'Frenchmen! Not content with bereaving us of all we cherish, you have, besides, corrupted our morals.'

His next significant composition was *Sur l'Amour de la Patrie*, written in Paris in 1787. The basic notion of love of a fatherland is illustrated entirely from antiquity or the history of Corsica, and France features merely as the personification of *hubris* or overweening ambition. But the most significant thing about this essay is that it was composed just five days after he lost his virginity to the Breton prostitute in the Palais Royal. Napoleon's guilt about sexuality is evident, for he pitches into modern woman and suggests that the female sex should emulate the women of Sparta. 'You, who now chain men's hearts to your chariot wheels, that sex whose whole merit is contained in a glittering exterior, reflect here upon your triumph [i.e. in Sparta] and blush at what you no longer are.' This essay is a priceless clue to Napoleon's inner psychic development. In thrall to a 'mother complex', Napoleon clearly found the encounter with the prostitute traumatic, as it threatened his ties to Letizia. At the unconscious level, therefore, the Spartan matron content to see her dead son brought home on a shield is conflated with the idealized picture of the 'Spartan' Letizia carrying Napoleon in the womb while fleeing in the *maquis*.

Usually, however, the spur for Napoleon's writings lay nearer the surface, in the books he had just devoured. His taste in reading was catholic, embracing a historical novel about Alcibiades, the back-to-nature novel *La Chaumière Indienne* by Bernardin de Saint-Pierre, a popular psychology book *The Art of Judging Character from Men's Faces* by Jean Gaspard Lavater, Buffon's *Histoire Naturelle*, Marigny's *History of the Arabs*, Voltaire's *Essai sur les Mœurs*, Rollin's *Ancient History*, Lavaux's biography of Frederick the Great, Plato, Machiavelli and Coxe on Switzerland. The famous example of dramatic irony, which all biographers comment on, occurred when he was perusing the Abbé de la

Croix's *Géographie* and wrote in his notebook 'St Helena, small island'. He was at one time totally absorbed in John Barrow's *History of England* and made a hundred pages of manuscript notes on it. Some critics of Napoleon say that he read too many second-rate authors, who simply put the reader through a series of paradoxical hoops in the eighteenth-century manner and produced a warped view of the world and historical events. But we should remember that he was also reading Montesquieu, Corneille, Plutarch, Adam Smith and other classics at the same time, so this thesis cannot be pushed too far.

A more interesting study is the use to which Napoleon put his omnivorous reading in his own writings. His early short story, *Le Masque Prophète*, derives heavily from Marigny's history of the Arabs, and the ghost story, *Le Comte d'Essex*, set in England in 1683, relies wholly on Barrow's history. Another piece of fiction, inspired by his research for the projected history of Corsica, and containing a very strong subtext of support for the island's 'code of honour', was the romantic horror story he began to write in 1789 entitled *Nouvelle Corse*. Ostensibly a fantasy of utopia on a desert island, it is actually a *grand guignol* catalogue of murder and atrocity, where Frenchmen are slaughtered in droves because of an oath of vendetta. The story ends after eight pages, leaving critics to wonder how Napoleon could possibly have topped his opening which, in its absurdity, reminds one of the Goldwynism: Start with an earthquake and build up to a climax.

In many ways Napoleon's non-fictional output is even odder. The *Lettres à Buttafuoco*, written on 23 January 1791, reveal him as, at this stage of his life, a very unsubtle propagandist: he simply accuses the Corsican-born field marshal of treason and then produces a feeble version of Cicero or Demosthenes in full flight.

> O Lameth! O Robespierre! O Pétion! O Volney! O Mirabeau! O Barnave! O Bailly! O Lafayette! This is the man who dares to sit beside you! Drenched in the blood of his brothers, tainted with every sort of crime, he dares to call himself the representative of the nation – he who sold it.

Paoli, whether through annoyance at the 'over the top' style or because Napoleon had mentioned representatives who sat on the left wing of the assembly, wrote curtly to Joseph: 'I have received your brother's pamphlet. It would have been more impressive if it had said less and been less partisan.'

But 1791 saw a more important work, for the Academy of Lyons offered a prize of 1,200 livres (a year's salary) for an essay answering the question: 'What are the most important truths and feelings to instil into men for their happiness?' During the long periods of leisure at Auxonne and Valence in the spring and summer of 1791, the talented young lieutenant got down to work. Although Napoleon did not win the prize (the Academy decided that none of the essays submitted was of sufficient quality), Napoleon's forty-page dissertation is an invaluable source for his political views as he passed his twenty-second birthday.

Napoleon's basic tenet that morality is a function of freedom is simply a *rechauffée* of Rousseau and Raynal and it sets the tone for what is to follow, which is eclectic when it is not being directly derivative. Napoleon poses himself the problem of reconciling feelings and reason and, not surprisingly, fails – not surprisingly, when we consider that Rousseau himself had not solved the conundrum. As Bertrand Russell later impishly remarked, Byron's Corsair, with his limitless freedom, is the clearest manifestation of the Romantic movement inspired by Rousseau, but the actual corsair, in Rousseau's ideal society, would find himself behind bars.

Napoleon's essay is remarkable for four things: the paradoxical insistence that the much trumpeted 'apostles of freedom' were the true tyrants, while the so-called tyrants were the real patriots; a sense of sexual confusion 'solved' by draconian prescriptions; social nostrums which, if written in the twentieth century, would merit the epithet 'quasi-fascistic'; and a continuing Francophobia and dislike of Christianity as a religion not of this world and hence an irrelevance in social theory. For Napoleon magnanimity is weakness – as when in Voltaire's *Azire* the dying hero forgives his assassin instead of crying out for vengeance and vendetta – and the true hero is not the 'bleeding heart' but the statesman who recognizes the iron dictates of necessity; hence Caesar was a great man while Brutus is an 'ambitious madman'.

Napoleon's fulmination against adultery, as when he says that adulterous bachelors should be denounced to the whole community, strongly suggests that sexuality in general, and this aspect in particular, contained some hidden menace which Napoleon dared not admit; in this sense his essay was a continuation of the thoughts expressed in *Sur l'Amour de la Patrie*. The dislike of capitalism, and preference for traditional, medieval types of society, which is such a feature of modern fascism, is clearly on view in Napoleon's contempt for documentary title over customary right as the key to ownership of land: 'What! are those the title deeds of such gentry? Mine are more sacred, more irrefutable, more universal! They reveal themselves in my sweat, they circulate with my blood, they are written in my sinews, my heart; indispensable to my existence and, above all, to my happiness.'

Coursing through the essay, is the Rousseauesque conviction that Corsica was the acme of social and moral achievement. Scholars may dispute the fine points, but it is possible to discern for the first time a slight ebbing in the hitherto overt Paoli-mania. One factor may have been the snub Napoleon received from the great man while he was writing the Lyons essay. On 14 March 1791 Napoleon sent some chapters of his history of Corsica to Paoli and requested his help in getting access to certain documents that would make the projected history better grounded in unpublished sources. This was a fairly simple favour to ask, as Paoli's word on such a matter was tantamount to a command. But Paoli rebuffed the young man brutally, scouting the entire enterprise and writing curtly (on 2 April): 'Youth is not the age for writing history.'

The career of the young Napoleon and his early writings alert us to contradictory aspects of his personality that he never succeeded in integrating. The most obvious contradiction was that between the mathematician and the romantic dreamer. Napoleon was a devotee of science and believed in bringing logic and mathematical clarity to bear on problems. He also had a Gradgrind-like appetite for facts: in his early notebooks he lists the 40,000 *lettres de·cachet* issued by Cardinal Fleury between 1726–43, Mohammed's seventeen wives, Suleiman's consumption of meat, and so on. This passion for encyclopedic knowledge and exact science collided with a countervailing current of extreme irrationality. As a disciple of the gathering Romantic movement, Napoleon entertained wild and unrestrained fantasies about war, tragedy and high adventure. As Bertrand Russell pointed out, this convergence of extreme rationality and extreme unreason was perhaps the most striking thing about Rousseau himself, and Rousseau at this time continued to be Napoleon's supreme intellectual mentor.

It is probable that the romantic fantasist represented the true Napoleon more deeply than the mathematician and man of science: the latter was what he was, the former what he aspired to be. This is borne out by his subsequent behaviour. Napoleon liked to cultivate a surface of calm, no matter how grave the crisis. The calmness and unflappability were supposed to denote a 'mathematical' rationality, but they concealed a volcano beneath, which would often come spewing out in the form of violent rage. Certainty on this point is prevented only by another characteristic of Napoleon: his thespian persona, which meant that he often staged bogus rages to achieve certain ends or to observe their effects.

The tacking between contradictory polarities also explains Napoleon's ambiguous political persona. He was deeply committed to the anti-monarchism and the anticlericalism of the French Revolution, yet had a visceral attraction for the hierarchical order of the *ancien régime*. Harsh critics said Napoleon was so keen to get to Corsica on leave in 1791 because he had worked out that his career prospects were better there. Naturally there is a lot of truth in this, but it is also probable that Napoleon felt paralysed by the contradictory political impulses afflicting him in France in 1791 and wanted to escape to Corsica to 'solve' the dilemma.

Overlaying Corsican culture with the values and ideology of Rousseau and the Enlightenment was bound to create confusions and contradictions. Some point to the conflict between Napoleon's shameless indulgence of the Bonaparte family and his claim to represent modernity and reason, and conclude that the extreme irrationality noted above was the Corsican legacy, with France contributing the Revolutionary cult of reason. But the contradictions in Napoleon's thought and behaviour persisted long after he had jettisoned Corsica and all its works, so it may be that Napoleon's 'traditional' manifestations – the hatred of anarchy, the fear of the mob, the strong family feeling – simply meant that his heart was with the *ancien régime* even if his brain was with the Revolution. The deepest obstacle to Napoleon as a man of the Revolution always remained his profound pessimism about human perfectibility and his conviction that human beings were fundamentally worthless.

The final aspect of the young Napoleon worth dwelling on is a continuing uncertainty about sexual identity. This part of the early record is particularly murky. In 1789, at Auxonne, Napoleon is said to have asked for the hand in marriage of one Manesca Pillet, stepdaughter of a wealthy timber merchant. Since Napoleon had no worthwhile prospects at this time and his suit was unlikely to be entertained by a wealthy bourgeois family, it may be that if such an overture was made, it was made, unconsciously at least, so that it would be rejected and Napoleon could continue to regard himself as a perfect Ishmael.

Another puzzling liaison from these early years is the friendship he allegedly struck up with a Corsican sculptor nine years his senior, Joseph Ceracchi by name. Certain students of Napoleon, Belloc among them, have hinted that the relationship was homosexual, and that the young Bonaparte was therefore fundamentally bisexual in orientation. All we know for certain is that Ceracchi tried to renew the acquaintance when Napoleon was famous, that he was rebuffed, turned against his old friend and was eventually executed for conspiracy in 1802. However, it seems likely that Napoleon's sexual difficulties lay along quite other lines, which involved the island of his birth. The key psychological moment that saw the birth of the mature Napoleon was the traumatic dénouement of the Corsican saga in 1792–93.

CHAPTER FOUR

By the time Archdeacon Lucien died, leaving the Bonaparte family comfortably off, Napoleon's ambitions had moved on a notch. With Joseph already president of the Ajaccio Directory, the Bonapartes were making progress. Fortified by the gold of the late miser Lucien, Letizia, still a striking woman habitually dressed in black, was able to abandon her chores as housekeeper and start spending money on home and children. The family dynamic was beginning to grow complicated. At sixteen Lucien was a spoiled neurotic who resented the eminence of his two older brothers. Thirteen-year-old Louis, whom Napoleon was glad to be able to offload, was a good-looking mother's boy and favourite with women but something of a 'hop out of kin'. Seven-year-old Jérôme was apparently as tiresome as a child as he was to be ineffective and useless as an adult. With Élisa, aged fourteen, absent at St-Cyr and the pale-skinned nine-year-old Caroline a quiet child with some musical talent, Pauline, aged eleven, was already usurping the role of most striking female Bonaparte. Emotional, charming, humorous and showing signs of her later stunning beauty, Pauline seemed to have inherited Letizia's looks and Carlo's love of pleasure.

To advance in Corsican politics meant making a minute analysis of the power structure on the island – something Napoleon, with his love of detail, was good at. On the outbreak of the French Revolution in 1789, Corsica had at first been bedevilled by the extreme factionalism between the royalists led by Buttafuoco and Peretti, who relied for support on the Army, and the Paolists, whose power came from strong popular support. Throughout 1790 and 1791 the Paolists had won victory after victory, culminating in the royalist defeat when they tried to prevent the two Paolist representatives, Gentile and Pozzo di Borgo (delegates from the 1790 Orezza assembly) taking their seats at the National Assembly. But almost immediately after this decisive rout of the royalists, the Paolistas had themselves begun to splinter, basically between those loyal to France and revolutionary principles and those who distrusted the Revolution's anticlericalism and its attitude to property and hankered after an independent and separate Corsica. Paoli, at first the champion of the Revolution against the old régime, increasingly emerged as a conservative figure, moving back into reaction even as many of his followers swung left into Jacobinism. The fissiparous nature of the Paolist movement resulted in violent religious riots in Bastia in June 1791. There was bloodshed, Bastia lost the rank of capital city and, more ominously, Paoli's authority and prestige were compromised and a parliamentary opposition arose against him.

Napoleon in late 1791 still retained his faith in Paoli. His strategy now was to parlay his furlough into a quasi-permanent leave while becoming an Adjutant-Major in a volunteer company; this would make him a significant military force in the land. But in December 1791 the National Assembly came close to torpedoing this strategy with a law requiring all officers in the regular army to return to their regiments for a nationwide census, to be carried out between 25 December and 10 January 1792. Fortunately for Napoleon, the deputy military commander in Corsica, General Antonio Rossi, had already petitioned Minister of War Narbonne for Napoleon's commission in the Ajaccio volunteer regiment, and a favourable reply to the request arrived in January 1791. Rossi wrote to Colonel Campagnol of the 4th Regiment to inform him that First Lieutenant Bonaparte was now an Adjutant-Major in the Corsican Volunteers.

But Napoleon's problems were not yet over, for in February 1792 the National Assembly passed a further law, requiring all officers of volunteer battalions to rejoin their regular army regiments by the end of March; the only exception permitted was to the handful of colonels of important volunteer battalions. There were only two such lieutenant-colonelships in Corsica, and it was now Napoleon's task to obtain one of them or see his career as a Corsican political fixer in ruins.

The two colonelships were elective positions, in which the five hundred or so National Guardsmen cast two votes for their two chosen candidates, in order of preference. Napoleon began by getting Paoli's backing for himself and Quenza as the two Lieutenant-Colonels. They faced stiff opposition, particularly from Jean Peraldi and Pozzo di Borgo, scion of another of Ajaccio's great families. Napoleon began by laying out a good part of Archdeacon Lucien's legacy on bribery: more than two hundred voting volunteers were lodged free of charge in the grounds of the Casa Buonaparte and provided with lavish board for the two weeks before the elections. Then Napoleon thought of other ways to scupper the opposition. Tradition says that he actually tried to eliminate Pozzo di Borgo physically, by challenging him to a duel which Pozzo did not accept. What is certain is that Napoleon added intimidation to the bribery he had already employed.

Three commissioners had been appointed to supervise the election. One of them, Morati by name, made the mistake of choosing to lodge the night before the vote (31 March 1791) at the house of the Peraldis, well known as opponents of the Bonapartes and supporters of Pozzo. Napoleon's men simply arrived at the Peraldi house at dinner time and abducted Morati 'to ensure his impartiality'. Next day, the election took place in the church of San Francesco. 521 volunteers arrived to record their preferences, but Pozzo di Borgo harangued them on the infamy of the Bonapartes; for his pains he was pulled off the platform and narrowly escaped a knifing. It is said that Pozzo, who had hitherto not been Napoleon's rival, swore eternal vengeance by the code of vendetta; he certainly made good his threat in later years. Then the voting started. Quenza received the highest number of votes and was elected the first lieutenant-colonel. Napoleon, with 422 first and second preferences, was a comfortable second and so found himself, not yet twenty-three, a lieutenant-colonel of the Corsican volunteers. Since Quenza had no military experience, Napoleon was the effective commander and at once evinced his ability to remember every last detail about the personnel and organization of any body he commanded.

Although the royalists on Corsica had been decisively routed in a political sense, they still retained the support of the Army in key strongholds. Paoli and the Directory, the centrally directed administration of Corsica, decided that the final stage in taking power in Corsica was to replace these royalist troops with the volunteers, and an obvious first target was the citadel at Ajaccio. General Rossi protested, but was overruled by the Directory, supported by Paoli. In response the royalists played the clerical card, counting on the monarchist sympathies of most of Ajaccio. The National Assembly had already decreed that monasteries and religious orders were to be dissolved, but in March 1792 a town meeting in Ajaccio petitioned that the Capucin order be excepted. The Corsican Directory reiterated the decree and added that the town meeting had no authority, being merely an unlawful assembly.

This was the juncture at which Christophe Antoine Saliceti, already a delegate to the National Assembly in Paris and a rising star in the Corsican opposition to Paoli, first appeared in full Machiavellian skill. A tall, sinister-looking man with a pockmarked face, Saliceti spread the whisper that Paoli was a fence sitter who had secret sympathies with the royalist rump in Ajaccio, and urged Napoleon to settle scores once and for all with the diehards in that town. Accordingly Napoleon entered the town with four companies of republican volunteers, in full knowledge of the hatred that existed between the pious, royalist townspeople and his rural guardsmen.

On Easter Sunday 8 April 1792 a group of priests who had refused to swear an oath of primary loyalty to the French republic held a service in the officially dissolved convent of St Francis and announced a religious procession – actually a political demonstration under another name – for the following day. At 5 p.m. Napoleon, hearing of disturbances around the cathedral, took a platoon of his men to investigate. Outside the cathedral he found a hostile mob who, it transpired, had already disarmed another platoon of volunteers and taken their muskets. When Napoleon heard of this, he demanded the weapons back and an angry altercation ensued. Suddenly a shot rang out and Lieutenant Rocca della Serra of the volunteers fell dead. Napoleon and his men rushed for cover, then made their way back to their headquarters by back streets.

It did not take a man of any great military talent, let alone Napoleon's superlative gifts, to work out that the key to the control of Ajaccio lay in command of the citadel. The snag was that this stronghold was held by a Colonel Maillard, commanding 400 men of the 42nd Infantry Regiment, and both commander and troops were loyal to Louis XVI. Napoleon went to see Maillard, who predictably proved uncooperative. Napoleon's argument was that his men were in mortal danger from angry townspeople and needed to take refuge in the citadel or at the very least to have access to the ammunition there. Maillard not only refused to accept either of these points but ordered Quenza and Napoleon to withdraw their volunteers from the town centre to the Convent of St Francis.

Napoleon responded by getting from his friend, the *procureur-syndic* of the district, an order overruling any orders issued by Maillard or the municipality. The *procureur* did so, adding the rider that Maillard was duty bound to protect the volunteers. Maillard, however, was adamant that he would accept only the orders of the municipality. Despite the version of those who try to present Napoleon as a Machiavellian bully in this incident, it is quite clear that he had the law on his side.

Napoleon and Quenza refused to withdraw but offered a compromise. If Maillard withdrew his proviso about the volunteers' retreating to the convent of St Francis, they for their part would show good will by sending home the particular individuals in the National Guard most objected to by the townspeople. Maillard grudgingly accepted this, but Napoleon followed up the offer by surreptitiously extending his control in the town. The armed royalists in the town and the volunteers now began fortifying the houses they occupied, ready for a bout of grim streetfighting, while Napoleon unsuccessfully tried to suborn the troops in the citadel to rebel. To twist the knife still further, he instituted a food blockade by the republican peasantry. Napoleon's men killed cattle, ravaged orchards and cut off water supplies.

The conflict escalated when the municipality got Maillard to wheel out cannon from the citadel, preparatory to expelling the volunteers by force. Napoleon then produced a letter from the Directory authorizing him to stand fast and, if necessary, bring in more volunteers. It was quite clear that the municipality was putting itself in a position where it was defying the elected government of Corsica and thus making itself legally responsible for all damage sustained in the expected fighting. Evidently the hotheads in Ajaccio finally perceived they were getting into very deep water; they backed down and agreed a compromise peace with Napoleon. Maillard, however, refused to be party even to this, claiming to be upholding the law. Since both the Directory and the municipality were now in agreement, it is difficult to see what this 'law' could be. In his own mind it involved the supremacy of the claims of Louis XVI, as interpreted by him, against those of the French Republic, but in strictly legal terms his action was treason. Historical precedents were all against him, for the legitimacy of the House of Stuart in England had not prevented the execution of Charles I or, in the following century, dozens of Jacobites.

Eventually two Commissioners arrived from the Directory to sort out the fracas. They arrested some of the troublemaking members of the municipality but the defiant Maillard simply retired to the citadel and challenged Paoli and the Directory to blast him out. Napoleon, Quenza and the volunteers had won the moral victory and Napoleon had shown himself to be exceptionally intrepid, energetic and resourceful, but the affair left a nasty taste in Ajaccio. Henceforth his reputation there plummeted, and Pozzo di Borgo was able to make significant propaganda ground in his vendetta.

When peace was made, Napoleon went to Corte, where he had an interview with Paoli. But his mind was on France, where his position with his regiment was precarious. At the review held on 1 January 1792 the regimental record stated: 'Buonparte, First Lieutenant, whose permission of absence has expired, is in Corsica.' He was expressly left out of the list of those recommended to the National Assembly as having legitimate reasons for absence. It was evident that to clear his name Napoleon would have to go to Paris, for he was now virtually regarded as an émigré, as appears from the following note placed against his name in a list of lieutenants at the Ministry of War: 'Has given up his profession, and has been replaced on February 6th, 1792.'

Some time early in May 1792 Napoleon left Corsica on his urgent mission to Paris. He reached the French capital on 28 May, to find that war had broken out with Prussia and France had sustained its first defeats. He wrote to Joseph that the capital was in a tense state, with financial chaos and the *assignat* at half its old value. It seemed to be a season for meeting old acquaintances, not all of them pleasant, for when Napoleon booked in at the Hôtel des Patriotes Hollandais in the rue Royale, he found his old enemies Pozzo di Borgo and Peraldi staying there. Next day he bumped into a different sort of acquaintance, for he went to a session of the Assembly and met Bourrienne. For once Bourrienne's memoirs, noting the event, are probably trustworthy:

> Our friendship dating back to childhood and college was completely revived ... adversity weighed him down and he was often short of money. We spent our time like two young people of twenty-three who have nothing to do and not much money; he was even harder up than I was. Each day we thought up new plans. We were trying to make some profitable speculations. Once he wanted us to rent several houses which were being built in the rue Montholon in order to sub-let them immediately. We found the demands of the landlords exorbitant. Everything failed.

On 16 June he went to St-Cyr to visit his sister, who asked him to get her out of the convent as soon as legislation promised by the revolutionary government made this possible. On 20 June he had arranged to dine with Bourrienne in the rue St-Honoré, near the Palais Royal, but, seeing an angry crowd, some 5–6,000 strong, debouch from the direction of Les Halles and head towards the river, the two young men decided to follow. Two huge crowds organized by Antoine Santerre headed for the Tuileries. After browbeating the Legislature, the crowd, chanting the revolutionary song *Ça Ira* pressed on into the undefended palace grounds themselves. In the Salon de l'Oeil de Boeuf they came upon Louis XVI himself, with just a handful of attendants. For the whole of that afternoon the monarch was systematically humiliated, unable to escape, forced to listen to the taunts and abuse of the crowd. Finally, he put on a red hat – 'the crowning with thorns' – and was forced to drink the health of the people of Paris. It was well past six o'clock before Jérôme Pétion, the representative of the Assembly, persuaded the now placated multitude to leave. This was a much greater affront to the monarchy even than the return to Paris after the abortive flight to Varennes, and few observers doubted that it was the beginning of the end for Louis XVI. Napoleon, however, thought that if he had been king it would have been an easy matter to disperse the crowd.

All this time Napoleon had been submitting documents and affidavits to the Ministry of War, trying to prove his version of events against the hostile counter-testimony of Peraldi. On 21 June a departmental committee of the Artillery accepted that Napoleon's reasons for not returning from Corsica by 1 April were entirely satisfactory. The committee rejected the Peraldi submission – which has been endorsed by some modern critics of Napoleon – that to accept Napoleon's version was to reward crime: it was preposterous, on this view, that a man who had been leading a riot against the King's army in Corsica, should be commended for it, and even secure the promotion he would have got normally only by being with his regular army regiment. Whether Napoleon was a master manipulator, or just lucky, or whether he convinced the committee that he was a true son of the Revolution, the result was the same. On 10 July the Ministry of War informed him that he would be reinstated in the 4th Artillery Regiment, with the rank of captain.

This new commission was backdated to 6 February 1792 – which meant Napoleon would receive the equivalent of £40 in back pay. To warn him against further legerdemain, the Ministry announced that it expected him to return to his regiment as soon as his promotion was ratified; meanwhile, some minor complaints brought from Corsica by Peraldi and Pozzo di Borgo would be dealt with by the Ministry of Justice. Napoleon was delighted. He knew, as did his opponents, that the Ministry of Justice was a labyrinth where complaints disappeared. The only thing keeping Napoleon in Paris now was the formal ratification of this decision, in the name of the King, by Minister of War Joseph Servan. Despite his triumph, Napoleon was gloomy. On 7 August he wrote to Joseph that the interests of the family necessitated his return to Corsica, but he would probably have to rejoin his regiment.

Before that, on 23 July he had written to Lucien words that show the youthful idealism about Corsica giving way to generalized cynicism: 'Those at the top are poor creatures. It must be admitted, when you see things at first hand, that the people are not worth the trouble taken in winning their favour. You know the history of Ajaccio; that of Paris is exactly the same; perhaps men are here even a little smaller, nastier, more slanderous and censorious.'

On 10 August Jean-Paul Marat masterminded the decisive blow

against royal power. Of the revolutionaries, Danton, Robespierre, Rossignol and Santerre were all implicated in the day's gory events. Thousands of armed revolutionaries obeyed the tocsin call and converged from right and left banks of the Seine on the Tuileries, defended by 2,000 troops, half of them members of the Swiss Guard. The scenes that followed were among the most terrible in the French Revolution. Confused by contradictory orders, the Swiss Guards were overwhelmed by superior numbers and slaughtered mercilessly. Six hundred died in the palace courtyard in a hecatomb of stabbing, stoning, clubbing and gunshot. Women stripped the bodies of clothes, and the most savage members of the crowd gelded and mutilated the corpses. When all was over, the dishonoured dead were carted away to mass burial in lime pits.

Napoleon was an eyewitness of these terrible events, and he later told Joseph that no battlefield carnage ever made such an impression on him. His words to Las Cases on St Helena are worth quoting:

> I found myself lodging in Paris, at the Mail in the Place des Victoires. At the sound of the tocsin and on learning that the Tuileries were under attack, I ran to the Carousel to find Bourrienne's brother, Fauvelet, who kept a furniture shop there. It was from this house that I was able to witness at my ease all the activities of that day. Before reaching the Carousel I had been met in the rue de Petits Champs by a group of hideous men bearing a head at the end of a pike. Seeing that I was presentably dressed and had the appearance of a gentleman, they approached me and asked me to shout 'Long live the Republic!' which you can easily imagine I did without difficulty . . . With the palace broken into, and the King there, in the heart of the assembly, I ventured to go into the garden. The sight of the dead Swiss Guards gave me an idea of the meaning of death such as I have never had since, on any of my battlefields. Perhaps it was that the smallness of the area made the number of corpses appear larger, or perhaps it was because this was the first time I had undergone such an experience. I saw well-dressed women committing acts of the grossest indecency on the corpses of the Swiss Guards.

Some say his hatred and distrust of the mob dated from that day, and a conviction that only a bourgeois republic could hold in check the forces of anarchy and the dark impulses of the *canaille*.

Napoleon judged that a resolute defence by the King could have saved the Tuileries and that, if he had been in charge, he could have routed the mob. His disdain for the hydra-headed monster of the crowd was increasing daily.

If Louis XVI's luck had run out, it was beginning to turn Napoleon's way. A new government decree, on 17 August, ordered the dissolution of all religious houses and the confiscation and sale of their assets. Since St-Cyr was no more, Élisa had to leave for Corsica, but the college directors, by now terrified of their own shadows, refused to allow her to leave without two sets of orders, one from the municipality and another from the Versailles directorate. Napoleon therefore persuaded the local mayor, a M. Aubrun, to go to the college with him. Elisa then made a solemn declaration that she needed her brother to escort her back to Corsica. Aubrun copied this down, then endorsed the copy with his own affidavit that permission was necessary. Napoleon then took the document to Versailles and requested that the directorate pay travelling expenses. Amazingly, Versailles voted the sum of 352 livres (which represented one livre for every league of the distance between Versailles and Ajaccio) and authorized him to remove his sister, together with her clothes and linen.

Napoleon's trip to Paris therefore ended in total triumph. He had cleared his name, won promotion and back pay, had avoided the necessity to return to his regiment and was now returning to Corsica with all expenses paid. The details of his journey are unknown, but it is probable that he left Paris on 9 September, as soon as the War Minister had ratified his promotion, took the water coach at Lyons to Valence, then stayed at Marseilles for the best part of a month before embarking for Corsica from Toulon on about 10 October, arriving at Ajaccio on 15 October.

Once in Corsica Napoleon proceeded to Corte to rejoin his volunteer battalion. Shortly after his arrival he had an interview with Paoli, which left both men dissatisfied. Paoli again turned down a Bonaparte request, this time that Lucien be appointed his aide-de-camp. Coming so soon after Joseph's defeat by the partisans of Pozzo di Borgo in recent elections, this was a very clear confirmation of the rumour that Paoli had been won over by the Pozzo di Borgos. For his part, Paoli was animated by a number of considerations. He never cared for the Bonapartes, disliked Joseph and was merely irritated by the young Napoleon's excessive admiration; most of all, he thought the entire clan a set of political trimmers and had never forgiven Carlo for his too-rapid defection to the French after 1769. At the ideological level, Napoleon's Jacobinism, contrasting with Paoli's growing disenchantment with revolutionary France, made them unlikely bedfellows.

Napoleon came away from the interview injured in his pride and needing time to lick his wounds and take stock. He began to feel that all his scheming to get back to Corsica had been a mistake, that maybe the future did, after all, lie with the 4th Artillery Regiment. Or perhaps he should throw up his career and go to India or somewhere else in the East as a mercenary. Certainly it was a subdued and unwontedly quiet Napoleon who spent the last months of 1792 in Corte, at least until 15 December, when he brought down to Ajaccio two hundred men from his battalion for a proposed expedition against Sardinia. Apart from a brief trip back to Corte, he was in Ajaccio from Christmas 1792 to 18 February 1793, and it was during this limbo period that Lucien remembers his brother often talking to his mother about the opportunities for service in India with Tippoo Sahib, Britain's mortal enemy on the subcontinent.

By February 1793 the French Revolution had taken a dramatic turn. Staring military defeat in the face, by a massive effort (the *levée en masse*) the revolutionaries had turned the tables on the Prussians and Austrians. At the 'Thermopylae' of Valmy on 20 September 1792 Dumouriez decisively defeated the Prussians. By the end of the year the new armies of revolutionary France had invaded the Rhineland and the Austrian Netherlands, officially 'exporting' the ideology of the revolution but actually in search of loot to shore up the value of the tottering *assignat*. January 1793 was a key date in the Revolution, for Louis XVI was executed and Danton declared the doctrine of France's 'natural frontiers' (the sea, the Alps, the Pyrenees and the Rhine). In line with these national aspirations, the revolutionary executive or Convention declared war on England and Spain.

The French plan for an expedition against Sardinia was a sign of the new expansionist policies. Sardinia had an obvious strategic importance in the Mediterranean, and the invasion was meant to demonstrate France's new found power and to overawe Florence and Naples; there were additional objectives of seizing the island's corn and alleviating shortages in the south of France. Admiral Truguet arrived in Ajaccio with a large body of regulars and a flotilla of ships, intending to incorporate the Corsican volunteer battalions in his force. On the way over from France there had been tension between soldiers and sailors; to this was now added acrimony and bad feeling between the regulars and the Corsican volunteers. Paoli, who was now close to an overt breach with Revolutionary France, bitterly opposed the venture but was shrewd enough to see that Truguet's regulars might combine with Napoleon's volunteers to depose him if he came out openly against the expedition, especially since there were rumours that Truguet was already a fast friend of the Bonapartes and was besotted with the sixteen-year-old Élisa. He therefore schemed to denude the island of Napoleon's volunteers while secretly taking steps to ensure the ultimate failure of Truguet's project.

Because of the ill-feeling between regulars and volunteers, Paoli persuaded Truguet to mount two attacks: the main assault under Truguet would be at Cagliari, and a diversionary thrust would be made against La Maddalena, the largest of the eleven Buccinari islands that lie between Corsica and Sardinia. For the diversionary attack on La Maddalena, with its two forts, Paoli successfully intrigued to have his nephew Colonna Cesari named as colonel, with Napoleon as third-in-command (for Quenza was also participating). After carrying out half-hearted artillery manoeuvres at Bonifacio, Napoleon embarked with 450 volunteers on 18 February 1793. Altogether the assault force on Maddalena comprised six hundred men (150 regulars) and four guns, conveyed in sixteen transports escorted by a single corvette.

The omens for the expedition were inauspicious from the very beginning. Heavy gales forced the ships back to Ajaccio, so that it was the evening of 22 February before they anchored off the western end of the channel between La Maddalena and the neighbouring island of San Stefano. A surprise attack at nightfall was the obvious ploy, but Cesari ruled this out. Napoleon was already despondent: 'We had lost the favourable moment, which in war is everything,' he wrote. But he stuck to his task. On 23 February, after troops had landed, secured a beachhead on San Stefano and captured the island's fort, he set up a battery of two cannon and a single mortar within range of La Maddalena. 24 February saw the bombardment commence, and Colonna Cesari promised that the main assault would take place next day.

Dark deeds were afoot on the 25th and even today it is not easy to follow the exact sequence of events. First the sailors on the corvette appeared to have mutinied and forced Cesari to call off the entire venture, even obliging him to send a formal letter to this effect to Quenza. But Napoleon, and many later analysts, believe there was no genuine mutiny at all, that this was all part of a preconcerted stratagem between Paoli and Cesari. Certainly the corvette departed with Cesari, leaving behind the message that operations should be abandoned. Quenza's version of the subsequent events was that he consulted with Napoleon and together they laboriously broke off the shelling of La Maddalena. But on St Helena Napoleon accused Quenza of reembarking on the 25th without telling him, with the consequence that he and his fellow artillerymen were left dangerously exposed, vulnerable to a sortie from the Maddalena garrison. The one certainty is that the bombardment was abandoned, and that Napoleon and his platoon manhauled the one-ton guns through muddy fields to the embarkation point. Their labours were anyway in vain, for only a single ship's boat was sent in to San Stefano to take off the men. Unable to retrieve his cannon, Napoleon was forced to spike them.

The Maddalena enterprise was fiasco with a capital 'f' and made Napoleon almost apoplectic with rage. It left him with a keen sense of betrayal as a key factor in warfare and a distaste for amphibious operations which, some say, was the unconscious factor in his ill-considered later plans for the invasion of England. But the immediate effect of the fiasco was to finish Paoli with Napoleon for good. Restless, ambitious, aggressive and treacherous – all the adjectives Paoli applied to the Bonapartes – were exactly the epithets Napoleon now fastened on the 'saviour' of Corsica, the man he had worshipped for years.

On 28 February Napoleon landed at Bonifacio to find that his suspicions of Paoli were shared by the Convention in Paris, for on 5 February they appointed three Commissioners to investigate the worsening situation on the island; leading the deputation was Napoleon's ally Christopher Saliceti. But Napoleon had his own deteriorating position to consider, for at the beginning of March, in the Place Doria at Bonifacio, there was an attempt on his life in which Napoleon again claimed to see the hand of Paoli. Some sailors denounced him as an aristocrat and formed a lynching party, which was foiled by the arrival of a group of Napoleon's volunteers. Napoleon became convinced that the 'sailors' were disguised Paolistas, possibly the selfsame ones who had fomented the 'mutiny' on board the corvette off Maddalena.

He decided to beard the elderly lion in his den. He requested an interview with Paoli at the convent of Rostino, which turned into an acrimonious confrontation. To begin with Napoleon tried to softpedal, aware that if it came to civil war on the island, the Paolistas were likely to win, the Bonaparte properties then being confiscated and his family reduced to destitution. He urged Paoli not to turn his back on the Revolution which had brought him back from exile and to take the long view of the nation's interests. Paoli spoke angrily of the way the French Revolution had gone sour, how its leaders wanted a subservient, not independent, Corsica and of how Marat, Danton and the others had forced people in the west of France into open rebellion. Most of all, he said, he was disgusted by the execution of Louis XVI, which for him was the last straw. Napoleon protested that Louis had met his fate deservedly for conspiring with foreign powers and inviting their armies on to the sacred soil of France. At this point Paoli stormed from the room. The two men never saw each other again.

April 1793 found Corsica at crisis point. Saliceti saw his chance to topple Paoli and become the number one man in the island. He opened a formidable propaganda campaign against the 'father of Corsica' by playing on French suspicions of Paoli's Anglophilia, nurtured by the twenty years' exile after 1769. The Convention was irritated by Corsica's ambiguous status, supposedly loyal to France yet paying no taxes, sending no volunteers to fight in the wars and in a permanent state of anarchy. Saliceti kept the pot boiling by insinuating in his dispatches that this state of affairs would never end while Paoli was top dog in Corsica. His initial aim was to get the pro-Paolista volunteer regiments disbanded and replaced by regulars from the mainland but, although he and his two fellow Commissioners (Delcher and Lacombe St-Michel) had plenipotentiary powers from the Convention, the snag was that it was Paoli's writ, not the Convention which ran in Corsica. Accordingly Saliceti and the two Commissioners spent two fruitless months trying to make contact with their enemy, who hid away in a mountain fastness.

Unknown to Napoleon, his brother Lucien had been a major catalyst in the deepening crisis. In March, at the Jacobin club in Toulon, he denounced Paoli as a traitor who was preparing to sell out to the English. All the evidence suggests that Paoli knew of this denunciation when he met Napoleon at the convent of Rostino, but Napoleon did not. On 7 April 1793 the Marat faction in the Convention decided to summon Paoli to Paris to answer serious charges laid against him by Lucien and others – for soldiers returning from the Maddalena fiasco were now openly saying that the expedition had been sabotaged by Paoli – on pain of outlawry should he fail to appear. The declaration was an arrest warrant in all but name. On 18 April the Convention's formal decree to this effect was promulgated in Corsica, prompting Napoleon to write to Quenza that this made civil war on the island certain.

However, Paoli played the cleverest of clever hands. On 26 April he wrote a dignified letter of reply to the Convention, regretting that 'old age and broken health' made it impossible for him to come to Paris. This was calling the Convention's bluff with a vengeance. With so many calls on their manpower, they baulked at sending the numbers of troops to Corsica necessary to bring the Paolistas to heel. The Convention saved face by rescinding the arrest decree and appointing two more (this time pro-Paoli) Commissioners from the mainland. The initiative therefore shifted back to Paoli.

Irritated at this turn of events, Saliceti and the two other Commissioners already on the island colluded with Napoleon to force a military solution before their tame colleagues arrived to patch up a peace that would leave Paoli with the spoils of victory. Napoleon's first idea was to bribe the new military commander of Ajaccio, Colonna Leca, to open the gates of the citadel, but he refused. His next project was a plan to visit the Sanguinaires isles to set up a safe military haven. But before he could implement this, he was warned that Paolistas planned to assassinate him once he left Ajaccio. He therefore stayed on in the town until 2 May.

Paoli meanwhile summoned a convention at Corte to concert measures for the defence of Corsica against the French and their allies. One of the first decisions taken was to proceed against the Bonapartes, expropriate their property and arrest Napoleon. Ignorant of this, Napoleon set out for Corte, intent on another meeting with Paoli. On the road he was met by his cousins the Arrighi, who advised him that Paoli had intercepted a letter from Lucien to Joseph, making it clear that his denunciation had triggered the virtual decree of outlawry from the Convention. Amazingly, Napoleon seemed undeterred by this intelligence and pressed on to Arca de Vivaria, where he lodged with the parish priest, another Arrighi connection. Next day he continued his journey and made the overnight stop with another set of relations, the Tusoli, in the hamlet of Poggiolo.

On 5 May Napoleon was at Corsacci, trying to persuade some Corsican delegates not to attend Paoli's convention at Corte. But he was already in enemy territory, for the local magnates were his old enemies the Peraldis. Marius Peraldi secured the help of the Morelli brothers to place Napoleon under arrest. It was lucky for him that he still had many friends and that some of them were resourceful. Two of them, Santo Ricci and Vizzavona by name, cooked up an ingenious plan and persuaded the Morellis to bring their prisoner to Vizzavona's house for a meal. Once there, they spirited Napoleon away down a secret staircase to a waiting horse. He and Santo Ricci then made their way back to Ajaccio by backtracks and entered Ajaccio in secret on 6 May.

After hiding out with his friend Jean-Jérôme Lévie, three days later Napoleon was able to secure sea passage to Macinaggio, from where he travelled overland to Bastia. In Bastia he was reunited with Joseph, Saliceti, Lacombe St-Michel and the principals of the anti-Paolista party. After two weeks of plotting and preparing, the conspirators sailed from St Florent in two ships with 400 men and a few guns. Ironically, on the very day of departure the Bonaparte house in Ajaccio was being sacked by the Paolistas and their farms gutted. Letizia fled with her daughters and hid in bushes near the ruined tower of Capitello, across the bay from Ajaccio, while the Paolistas looked for them. Once again Letizia experienced the pendulum of fortune and was forced to become a fugitive.

A week later the ill-fated expedition anchored in the Gulf of Ajaccio but was fired upon by the fort. Since only thirty people rallied to their standard in Ajaccio, the coup was abandoned next day. Napoleon meanwhile had landed at Provenzale on 29 May and made rendezvous with his refugee family, getting them by longboat on to a three-masted xebec, which took them to Giralda. Letizia remembered making yet another of her perilous night journeys before being united with her family at Calvi. Napoleon himself arrived there disconsolately on 3 June. Calvi was in friendly hands, but was being blockaded by the English. Eight days later, after enjoying the hospitality of the Giubega family, the entire family embarked for Toulon, virtually penniless. They risked capture by the British by taking passage on a coaster navigated by a noted blockade-runner.

Paoli's triumph was complete. To cement it, on the very day of the Bonapartes' departure the Paolista National Assembly declared them to be 'traitors and enemies of the Fatherland, condemned to perpetual execration and infamy'. Paoli's success, in socioeconomic terms, meant the triumph of the mountain folk, the shepherds and the peasants over the great landowners, the nobility and the bourgeoisie of the ports and cities. Most of those who fled into exile with the Bonapartes were merchants or landowners; the paradox was that Napoleon the 'Rousseau-ist revolutionary' was from the viewpoint of social class more 'reactionary' than the 'counter-revolutionary' Paoli. The French still maintained a precarious toehold in Corsica, for they still held a few towns and villages, and Commissioner Lacombe St-Michel stayed on to encourage them.

Paoli's triumph was shortlived. Fearing the inevitable French invasion to restore their position on the island, he ended by inviting the British in. When Admiral Hood anchored at San Fiorenzo with 12,000 troops, Paoli added his 6,000 men and proceeded to besiege the French in Calvi and Bastia. In June 1794 the Council of Corsica, with Paoli at its head, proclaimed perpetual severance from France and offered the crown to the King of England. George III accepted and sent out Sir Gilbert Elliot as viceroy. Paoli, who was officially in retirement, still wanted to be the power on the island and, not surprisingly, soon quarrelled bitterly with Elliot. The British, tired of his prima-donnaish antics, hinted broadly that Paoli might like to retire to England. Paoli hesitated, saw France still in the grip of anarchy and then thought of the possible consequences of war with both France and England. He accepted the offer. His victory over the Bonapartes was therefore a hollow one. His loyal ally Pozzo di Borgo left Corsica for a diplomatic career that would eventually find him in the service of the Czar of Russia.

What is the explanation for Napoleon's violent split with Paoli? The cynical view is that he realized that there was no future in Corsica for an ambitious young man, that Paoli had already snatched anything that was valuable in the way of power and prestige, and that the 'glittering prizes' were to be found only in France. The conventional view is simply that both men backed different horses in the Corsican power struggle and thus ended up as enemies; an additional factor was Paoli's personal dislike of the young man. Another view is that when Napoleon became a Jacobin he lost his faith in Rousseau and came to despise him. But it was Rousseau's *Social Contract* that had inspired his original visionary view of Corsica as a society of Spartan simplicity, civic *virtu*, social equality, poverty and nobility of soul. Simultaneous with his loss of faith in Rousseau, and possibly a contributory factor, was the extreme factionalism and in-fighting in Corsica in the early 1790s, which Napoleon witnessed at close quarters. As Masson put it: 'Just as France had made him Corsican, so Corsica made him a Frenchman.'

Yet it seems unlikely that it was merely the contingent circumstances during February–March 1793 that turned the Paolista Napoleon into Paoli's enemy or that a negative attitude to the Bonapartes alone could have turned off such an oil-gusher of adulation as that from Napoleon to Paoli. The psychologist C.G. Jung has warned us that 'lightning conversions' are seldom that and even coined the word 'enantiodromia' to describe the process whereby Saul becomes Paul – not, on this view, through seeing the light on the road to Damascus but because the experience crystallized a process of gradually dawning illumination. If Napoleon's violent breach with Paoli had in fact been brewing for years, we may ask another question of more general import. Was Napoleon simply boundlessly ambitious, in the way Brutus hinted Caesar was, and was his ambition an irreducible and dominant psychological factor in his makeup? Or was his ambition a more complex manifestation reducible to other factors, which in turn might give us the clue to the deep dynamic of the quarrel with Paoli?

The key may lie in two apparently insignificant remarks. To one of his close friends Napoleon once confided that at some time in the Corsican period he had surprised Paoli having intercourse with his (Napoleon's) godmother. And in the anti-Paoli essay he wrote in July 1793 *Le Souper de Beaucaire* he said that Paoli's greatest fault was that he had attacked the fatherland with foreigners; by uniting Corsica to France in 1790 without thinking through all the implications he had in fact lost any chance of an independent Corsica. We may, then, reasonably infer that Napoleon was deeply worried about three things: illicit sexual relations, the attempt to fuse Corsica and France, and the idea of a fatherland invaded.

Since it is a commonplace of psychoanalysis, confirmed in hundreds of case studies of neurotics, that concern about the fatherland really indicates concern about the mother, and we know in any case of Napoleon's ambivalent feelings towards Letizia, it seems reasonable to assume that Napoleon's antagonism towards Paoli was, at the unconscious level, something to do with his mother. And since Paoli was consciously acknowledged by Napoleon as a father-figure, it is clear that what needs further investigation is what depth psychologists would call Napoleon's 'paternal image'. There seem to have been four paternal images significant in the mind of the young Napoleon: of Paoli, of his actual father Carlo, of Louis XVI and of the Comte de Marbeuf. At any given moment, the association of 'father' could have been to any one of the quartet.

The role of Marbeuf as protector of the Bonapartes needs no further elucidation. Moreover, on returning from France on his first leave, Napoleon bracketed Marbeuf with Carlo when he expressed sorrow that he had lost the two significant older men in his life. We have also noted Napoleon's uncertainty how to respond to Louis XVI, the father of the nation to whom he had taken oaths of loyalty. The flight to Varennes did not alienate Napoleon, and in Paris in 1792 his dominant emotion during the two savage mob irruptions into the Tuileries were sympathy with the King rather than fellow-feeling with the crowd. The ambivalence Napoleon felt for Carlo was mirrored in his uncertain attitude to Louis XVI; he was partly for the Revolution against all kings, but partly for this particular King against this particular mass of revolutionaries. What finished Louis for Napoleon was when he became convinced that the monarch had called on foreign powers to invade French soil.

The quartet of father-figures all represented men who, in Napoleon's mind, were betrayers. Whether or not Letizia and the Comte de Marbeuf were lovers – and circumstantial evidence overwhelmingly indicates they were – Napoleon certainly thought they had been. This trauma explains so much in his later life especially his sexuality, his misogynism. The horror he expressed at finding Paoli with his godmother may refer, not to an actual event, but to a transmogrified fantasy, hinting at Letizia's infidelity with Marbeuf. Napoleon's 'mother complex' owes something to the neurotic feeling that he could not be certain who his own father was – even though, as we have seen, Letizia's probable infidelity with Marbeuf had no actual connection with Napoleon, who was certainly Carlo's son. The important thing is that he *thought* it did, and we surely find an echo of the anxiety in that pithy clause in the later Code Napoléon: 'Investigation of paternity is forbidden'.

It is very probable that the excessive concern about the union of Corsica and France expressed in *Le Souper de Beaucaire* – 'he helped unite Corsica to France', 'he attacked the fatherland with foreigners' are an unconscious manifestation of anxiety about Letizia's infidelity with Marbeuf and of anger towards Carlo for letting such a state of affairs develop. The conscious anger Napoleon felt about his defeat by Paoli in Corsica tapped into an unconscious well of rage about quite other matters. Since Paoli was a father-figure, Napoleon could discharge his anger about Carlo and Marbeuf on to him.

The rage against France as a young man, the violent outburst against the schoolmates who invaded his 'fatherland' at Brienne in the garden incident, the violent Francophobia in general are all explained on this hypothesis. But, it may be asked, why did the outburst against Paoli take place at this very time? Almost certainly the answer lies with the execution of Louis XVI in 1793. With Carlo and Marbeuf out of the picture, Napoleon's conscious adoration of Paoli coupled with an unconscious antagonism towards him for the 'sins of the fathers' was dispersed for a while as Louis XVI took centre stage. In late 1792 the anger against a man who would deliver the fatherland to foreigners was obviously directed by the Jacobin Napoleon against the perfidious Bourbon king. It is a characteristic of ambivalence to divide the love/hate object so that all negative feelings can be decanted against the 'Hyde' aspect and all positive ones retained for the 'Jekyll'. Put simply, in late 1792 Louis XVI attracted the fire that would later fall on Paoli.

When Louis XVI's execution redeemed him in Napoleon's eyes, the undischarged hatred arising from Letizia's infidelity with Marbeuf had to find a new focus. And it was only at this precise time (January 1793) that Napoleon attached himself to France in a decisive and unambiguous way. It is sometimes overlooked by those who regard the breach with Paoli as purely contingent and political that Napoleon made common cause with Saliceti and the anti-Paolist faction *before* the breach was inevitable. In any case, once Louis XVI was dead, it made sense, at the unconscious level, that Napoleon should rid himself of the one remaining figure so that *he* could become the father. In symbolic terms, his infantile Oedipal phantasies were now partly assuaged. These had become exacerbated into a mother complex by the conviction that, though Carlo denied Letizia's body to his son, he had allowed it to other men.

It must be stressed that by falling out with Paoli Napoleon lunged into disaster, losing all his family's property without any good reason for thinking that he could retrieve the Bonaparte fortunes. From the point of view of rationality and self-interest, Napoleon's opposition to Paoli in early 1793 makes no sense at all. Yet one of the reasons historians have so violently debated 'Napoleon, for and against' is the conviction that Napoleon, with his great intellect, must always have had sound reasons for his actions. An examination of the dark recesses of the Napoleonic psyche shows that this is not necessarily so and that self-destructive psychological impulses usually played some part, and sometimes the major part. This was not the last time in his life that Napoleon, pleading ineluctable necessity, *raison d'état* and 'there is no alternative', plunged into reckless adventures that defy rational explanation.

European States 1792

NORTH SEA

ATLANTIC

OCEAN

GREAT

BRITAIN

London

Har

HANO

HOLLAND

Ems

CLEVE

AUSTRIAN

LIÉGE

Rhine

GER

NETHERLANDS

Coblenz

Mainz

Paris

Seine

Loire

FRANCE

SWITZERLAN

Lyons

SARDINIA

Rhône

Garonne

Toulouse

GEN

Nice

Marseilles

PORTUGAL

SPAIN

CORSICA

MEDITERRANEAN

CHAPTER FIVE

The refugee Bonaparte family reached Toulon to find the Terror at its height. As 'aristocrats' the Bonapartes might have been at risk, but Lucien was already a prominent member of the Toulon Jacobin club, and the family was penniless. Just to be on the safe side, however, Letizia and her three daughters were described on their passports as 'dressmakers'. But Toulon was not secure even for the Jacobins: in July the townspeople rose against the Terror and let in the British under Admiral Hood, forcing Lucien and his fellow politicos to flee.

Toulon's action was not an isolated case. In the summer of 1793 the spark of civil war lit up two-thirds of the Departments of France. The Girondin faction, expelled from the Convention by the Jacobins and 'Men of the Mountain', raised the provinces in revolt against Paris. There was a serious uprising in Lyons, and the defection of Toulon and Marseilles conjured visions of a counter-revolutionary link-up with the rebels at Lyons, taking Provence out of the Jacobin orbit.

Letizia initially took lodgings in the small town of La Vallette, near Toulon, but when the rising took place Joseph moved her to Marseilles and installed her in two rooms there: desperately hard up, she was forced to queue for soup at the municipal soup kitchen. She eked out an existence on money supplied by Napoleon who continued to evince a talent for manipulation by rejoining his regiment in Nice and getting 3,000 francs in back pay. He also received additional funds as unofficial secretary to Saliceti, who now stood forth as the Bonapartes' doughty champion. Saliceti wrote to the Convention in Paris, backing the Bonapartes' claim for compensation for their expropriated property in Corsica, alleging that Napoleon had sacrificed all for the Revolution. The Convention voted a grant of 600,000 francs compensation and notified Joseph, who had gone to Paris to lobby for recompense, but not a penny of the money was ever paid.

Napoleon was in favour when rejoining his regiment partly because the brother of his old friend General du Teil was in charge. After being employed on the supervision of artillery batteries on the coast, Napoleon was ordered up to Avignon to supervise a convoy bringing powder to the Mediterranean for use by the Army of Italy. Napoleon's exact movements in July and August are hard to follow, so it is not clear if he took part in the fighting when Jacobin General Carteaux stormed Avignon on 24 July; the probability is that he did not.

It was while proceeding south through Tarascon and Beaucaire on 28 July that he wrote his last major essay *Le Souper de Beaucaire*. The work is cast in the form of a Socratic dialogue, with 'an army officer' (clearly Napoleon) and a Marseilles businessman as principals; also participating are a manufacturer from Montpellier and a citizen of Nîmes. The businessman defends the right of Provence to fight Carteaux, while the officer castigates the men of the South for plunging France into civil war, arguing that this cannot be justified while France has external enemies to contend with. Napoleon's main point was that the conflict between Girondin and Montagnard was unnecessary and played the royalists' game for them: the real enemy of both sides were the rebels of the Vendée. Needless to say, the army officer wins the argument, and in 'gratitude' the businessman stays up late and buys him champagne. An unashamed work of propaganda designed to justify the Jacobin position, *Le Souper de Beaucaire* is notable for the vehemence of its attacks on Paoli:

> Paoli, too, hoisted the Tricolor in Corsica, in order to give himself time to deceive the people, to crush the true friends of liberty, and in order to drag his compatriots with him in his ambitious and criminal plots; he hoisted the Tricolor, and had the ships of the Republic fired at, he had our troops expelled from the fortresses and he disarmed those who remained ... he ravaged and confiscated the property of the richer families because they were allied to the unity of the Republic, and all those who remained in our armies he declared 'enemies of the nation'. He had already caused the failure of the Sardinian expedition, yet he had the impudence to call himself the friend of France and a good republican.

Le Souper de Beaucaire was published as a pamphlet at the urging of Saliceti, who saw that Napoleon had the makings of a propagandist of genius. He in turn brought it to the notice of Augustin Robespierre, brother of the leader of the new twelve-man executive in Paris, the Committee of Public Safety. Robespierre thought the work brilliant and was equally impressed by the author when he met him soon afterwards. A great advance in point of style, economy and lucidity over his earlier literary efforts, it shows Napoleon to be extremely well-informed on the political and military issues of the day, and is the first time we see the ideas of the mature Napoleon clearly on display. 'All of Napoleon is to be found in the *Souper de Beaucaire*,' Jean Tulard wrote, and perhaps too much is on show, for as First Consul Napoleon ordered the police to destroy every copy they could lay hands on.

The immediate result of this successful foray into political propaganda was to encourage Saliceti, now a political commissar (*député-en-mission*) of enormous power, to wrap the Bonaparte family even closer around him. He began by fixing Joseph's appointment as an assistant commissary of the Republic, attached to the Army of the South on a salary of 6,000 francs. He then kept a close eye on Napoleon, who led an itinerant life for the next weeks: he was at Arles at the beginning of August, then travelled up to Valence and at the beginning of September was back in Auxonne. It was mid-September before Saliceti got his chance to reward the most valuable of the Bonapartes. Back in Marseilles on 15 September, Napoleon was assigned to the escort of powder wagons from Marseilles to Nice, ready for use by the French Army of Italy. Learning of this, Saliceti set it up that Napoleon should stop at Beausset to 'pay his respects' to him and the other *député-en-mission*, Gasparin, also a Bonaparte supporter. He then introduced the young Bonaparte to General Carteaux, who was conducting the siege of Toulon, and suggested him as a replacement for the artillery commander Dommartin, who had been seriously wounded. Carteaux was reluctant, but as political commissar Saliceti had superior hire-and-fire powers even to a commander and chief; and so the appointment was made.

When the men of Toulon admitted the Anglo-Spanish fleet on the night of 27–28 August 1793, they brought about a potentially critical situation for the Jacobins. Toulon was the most important naval arsenal in France and the key to French control of the Mediterranean. Even more importantly, it posed a problem of credibility for the Montagnards. Not only did its loss damage the image and reputation of the Republic, but it was looked on as a test case; if not recovered it could fan the flames of the Vendée into wholesale civil war. It was fortunate for the revolutionaries that England had already committed most of its troops to the West Indies and that no more than 2,000 of them landed at Toulon. Six thousand Austrian soldiers were promised as reinforcements, but never arrived, thus leaving 7,000 poor quality Neapolitans and 6,000 lacklustre Spaniards to bear the brunt of defence.

General Carteaux had been given 12,000 men to retake Toulon, plus 5,000 detached from the Army of Italy under General Lapoype. Both commanders were basically nonentities, who commenced an unimaginative blockade of Toulon, with Lapoype approaching from Hyères and the east and Carteaux from the west. The two generals immediately fell foul of their energetic young artillery officer who, with Saliceti's endorsement, wrote to the Committee of Public Safety in Paris to denounce their incompetence. The response from Paris was a good sign of the favourable position Napoleon now occupied: he was promoted major with effect from 18 October. Napoleon complained that he could not get Carteaux to appreciate the importance of big guns and he himself lacked the clout to force through what needed to be done. As was the case with all Napoleon's memoranda at this time, it received the endorsement of both political commissars and of Augustin Robespierre. The result of Napoleon's complaint was therefore predictably favourable: Saliceti and Gasparin appointed Brigadier du Teil. Since he was ill and elderly and anyway a patron of Major Bonaparte, Napoleon virtually had a free hand on artillery matters during the siege.

During his time on the island, Napoleon had made a close study of Corsican ports and their fortifications, and had even sent a report to the Convention. Having gone over the topography of Ajaccio with a fine-tooth comb, he was immediately struck by the remarkable similarity in the geography of Toulon and Ajaccio. This enabled him to zero in on Toulon's weak spot: Fort Eguillette, commanding the western promontory between the inner and outer harbour, whose capture would make both harbours untenable by the enemy fleet. 'Take l'Éguillette,' he wrote to Carteaux, 'and within a week you are in Toulon.' Yet even with the backing of the two commissars, Napoleon found it difficult to persuade Carteaux, who believed in crude frontal attacks with the bayonet.

If given the green light, Napoleon could have taken l'Éguillette almost instantly but Carteaux's dithering gave the British time to identify the weak spot and fortify it. Napoleon had to settle in for a long haul. He started by making the artillery arm as strong as possible, drawing in cannon from as far away as Antibes and Monaco. With a battery of one 36-pounder, four 24-pounders and a 12-pound mortar he forced the Royal Navy to keep its distance. Seeing the looming threat, the British made several sorties and fought tenaciously. Meanwhile a political battle developed in tandem with the military one, as Napoleon kept plugging away to Saliceti and Gasparin on the theme of Carteaux's incompetence. The Chinese whispers against the official commander reached the point where Carteaux's wife is said to have advised him to give Napoleon his head: the best thing was to distance himself, just in case the young major failed; but if he succeeded, Carteaux himself could take the credit.

Fortunately on 23 October the commissars' negative reports finally had their effect, and Carteaux was posted away to take command of the Army of Italy. Another timid commander, General Doppet, a former dentist who allegedly could not stand the sight of blood, came and went within three weeks. Finally, on 17 November, Napoleon got a commander after his own heart in the shape of General Dugommier. Behind this appointment lay a complex story of politicking in Paris. Saliceti found a powerful new ally there in Lazare Carnot, who was the member of the Committee of Public Safety entrusted with the organization and deployment of France's fourteen armies. Carnot saw the merit of Napoleon's scheme and overruled the other, inferior, plans that had been put to him. There was no more dithering. 'There is only one possible plan – Bonaparte's,' Dugommier wrote to the Ministry of War.

For all that, Dugommier ordered one final attack across a broad front before bowing to the inevitable. But after a frenzied combat – when the English sortied and bloody hand-to-hand fighting took place, yielding hundreds of casualties on both sides and the expenditure of 500,000 cartridges – he signed the order endorsing Napoleon's scheme.

Éguillette point was dominated by the fort called Mulgrave, which the French nicknamed 'Little Gibraltar'. Having amassed a powerful artillery park and demonstrated the accuracy of his gunners by shelling British ships – 'artillery persistently served with red-hot cannonballs is terrible against a fleet,' he wrote later – Napoleon began on 11 December to bring up his guns to very close range. He made good use of the rolling, hilly terrain to construct new batteries and then commenced a 48-hour artillery duel with the twenty guns and four mortars inside the fort. On 16 December, during this 'softening up' process, he narrowly escaped death when he was knocked off his feet by the wind from a passing cannonball.

It was at Toulon that Napoleon met the first of his faithful followers. Androche Junot was then a young sergeant from Burgundy. When Napoleon asked for a volunteer soldier with good handwriting, Junot stepped forward. While Napoleon was dictating, already impressed with the man's calligraphy and spirit, a cannonball from a British warship fell nearby and sprayed Junot's writing paper with sand. 'Good,' said Junot. 'We won't need to blot this page.' This was exactly the sort of humour Napoleon appreciated, and he immediately appointed Junot to his personal staff.

By 17 December Napoleon judged that he had effectively silenced the fusillade from the fort and called on Dugommier to deliver the final attack. Heavy rainfall and low clouds that evening almost led the general to call it off, since the weather would affect the accuracy of musketry by troops whom he knew not to be top flight, but this raised suspicions in the political commissars that Dugommier's heart was not in the job. They toyed with asking Napoleon himself to lead, but he quickly talked Dugommier round into leading an attack by 5,000 men, arguing that artillery and the bayonet were all that was needed. Advancing in heavy rain and taking heavy casualties, Dugommier's troops hesitated in face of a desperate defence. Then Napoleon led a charge with 2,000 more troops. Despite having a horse shot from under him, he led his men to the walls. Still taking losses, the French swarmed over the timber-spiked parapets. Two hours of bitter hand-to-hand fighting ensued, with bayonet and sabre playing a greater role than musketry. By 3 a.m. it was all over, and the fort was in French hands.

Saliceti and Gasparin arrived after the fighting to confer their political 'imprimatur'. They found their favourite, Major Bonaparte, lying wounded on the ground, having taken an English sergeant's pike in his inner left thigh just above the knee. At first there was panic, and it was thought amputation would be necessary to prevent gangrene. But a military surgeon was brought in for a second opinion and pronounced the wound not serious. Ever after, however, Napoleon bore a deep scar.

More seriously wounded in the final assault was a man who would loom large in Napoleon's later life: Claude-Victor Perrin, the future Marshal Victor. At that time, the twenty-nine-year-old Victor outranked Napoleon, being a lieutenant-colonel, but after Toulon both men were promoted together to the same rank of brigadier-general. Other future marshals to make their mark at Toulon were Marmont, then a nineteen-year-old captain, and a twenty-three-year-old lieutenant, Louis-Gabriel Suchet. It was at Toulon also that Napoleon first met the greatest of all soldiers whom ever commanded his armies, twenty-five-year-old Louis Charles Desaix, and the man who would be his greatest friend, twenty-one-year-old Géraud Christophe Duroc.

But not all Napoleon's new acquaintances were of high calibre: one, who would soon marry into his family, was the stupid and pretentious blond-haired Victor Emmanuel Leclerc.

Napoleon's prediction about L'Éguillette was soon borne out: on the 18th the British took the decision to abandon Toulon. The twenty-nine-year-old English sailor Sidney Smith, already knighted for feats of gallantry, and Hood's right-hand man in Toulon, remarked that troops 'crowded to the water like the herd of swine that ran furiously into the sea possessed of the devil'. Hood and Smith set fire to the military arsenal and gutted all the ships they could not use, then put to sea under cover of darkness. The terrific explosion when the arsenal finally blew up at 9 p.m.

that evening made a great impression on Napoleon's romantic soul. The French began to enter Toulon next day.

Toulon was a great triumph for Napoleon's nascent military genius, but it was marred by wholesale massacre once the French armies got inside the city. The surrender of Toulon to the British had given the Committee of Public Safety a terrible fright, and they reacted with the vengeful reflex common on such occasions. The mass executions began on 20 December: two hundred officers and men of the naval artillery, then another two hundred 'collaborators' the next day. A Jacobin official named Fouché, later to be heard from, put forward a pilot version of General Franco's infamous twentieth-century credo of redemption through bloodshed: 'We are shedding much blood, but for humanity and duty.' Napoleon, anxious that his great moment should not be besmirched by hecatombs of blood, and anyway unable to do more than stumble about, largely shut his eyes to what was going on around him. It was anyway inexpedient to take notice. Dugommier did so, and was immediately suspected of being an enemy of the people. But black propaganda linking Napoleon with the Toulon massacres can be disregarded. Even if Napoleon's later claim that 'only the ringleaders' were shot is humbug, so too is Sidney Smith's assertion that Bonaparte personally mowed down the innocent in hundreds.

Toulon was a significant milestone in Napoleon's career and he always looked back on it with romantic nostalgia. Anyone who was with him at Toulon could, in later years, be certain of promotions and rewards, even the useless Carteaux. It is interesting to note that he had already met many of the people who would loom large in the consular and imperial periods: Desaix, Duroc, Junot, Marmont, Victor, Suchet. Napoleon had now made his reputation among élite circles, even if he was still a long way from being a household name. The political commissars hastened to promote him to brigadier-general on 22 December, and this was ratified by the Committee of Public Safety on 16 February 1794. Du Teil reported to the Ministry of War: 'I lack words to convey Bonaparte's merit to you; much knowledge, equal intelligence and too much bravery; that is but a feeble sketch of this rare officer's virtues.' Yet Toulon was no guarantee of a glittering future for Napoleon. The political situation was still too uncertain, and too many revolutionary generals had been sacked, shot or guillotined to make Toulon the inevitable prelude to his rise.

After recovering from his wounds, Napoleon was in Marseilles until the end of the year and was then given command of the artillery arm of the

Army of Italy, with headquarters at Nice. With his general's pay of 15,000 livres a year – a twelvefold increase in income since joining the La Fère regiment seven years earlier – he was able to instal Letizia at the Château Salle, a pretty country house near Antibes set in groves of palm, eucalyptus, mimosa and orange trees. Always down-to-earth and practical, Letizia impressed the locals by doing her own laundry in a stream that ran through the garden, even though funds were plentiful enough.

Napoleon now took stock of his family. Of the younger brothers, so far his favourite was Louis, a bookish fifteen-year-old. 'Louis has just the qualities I like,' Napoleon wrote, 'warmth, good health, talent, precision in his dealings, and kindness.' Lucien was mainly antagonistic. He was annoyed that Napoleon had secured Joseph a sinecure with Saliceti but had left him (Lucien) to rot as a commissariat storekeeper in the village of St-Maximin (where he was also president of the Revolutionary Committee) on a pittance of 1,200 francs a year. Partly out of pique, and to show his independence, Lucien married an illiterate and penniless inn-keeper's daughter without even consulting Letizia: so much, he seemed to say, for the Bonaparte pretensions to nobility. Another looming cloud on the family horizon was Napoleon's favourite sister, Pauline, rising fourteen. Already a stunning creature, who combined beauty with magnetic sex-appeal (not actually all that common a combination), she was already turning heads and inviting unwelcome attention. Androche Junot, promoted to lieutenant for his feats at Toulon, was one of those bowled over when he accompanied his general on a visit to Château Salle.

The one success in the family, Napoleon apart, seemed to be Joseph. In Marseilles lived a rich merchant in the silk, soap and textiles trade named François Clary, a man with royalist sympathies. In the troubles of 1793 Clary backed the wrong horse and, when Marseilles fell to government troops, had the Jacobin firebrand Stanislas Fréron on his neck. One of Clary's sons was thrown into jail and the other committed suicide to avoid a firing squad. Broken by grief and anxiety, François Clary pined away and died. His widow came to Saliceti to petition for her son Étienne's release and to lift the anathema of 'counter-revolutionary running dogs' that had fallen on the family. At Saliceti's she met Joseph, charmed him and invited him to dine. There he met the elder daughter Julie Clary, aged twenty-two, and, learning that she was to inherit 80,000 francs once her father's will was settled, promptly issued a certificate, exonerating the family of all royalist sympathies. Out of gratitude, Julie agreed to be his wife, and a wedding date was fixed for August 1794.

After a short spell as inspector of coastal fortifications between

Marseilles and Toulon, while he waited for the ratification of his new appointment to come through, Napoleon moved to Nice, with the faithful Junot in tow, to take up his post as senior gunner in the Army of Italy. Until mid-July 1794 he was to be found commuting from Nice westwards to Antibes and Fréjus and eastward to San Remo and Vintimiglia, tirelessly working on new military schemes and confirming the battle-readiness of his units. After two years of warfare against Austria, the Army of Italy was stalemated in a fruitless campaign against Piedmont, which was being constantly rearmed, reinforced, supplied and sustained by the British Navy operating through Genoa. Napoleon began by writing up a stratagem for capturing Oneglia. When this fell, on 9 April 1794, his reputation was skyhigh and he was asked to write a general memorandum on grand strategy.

Basing his strategy on the writings of Guibert de Bourcet, Napoleon devised a plan that enabled the Army of Italy to advance to the watershed of the Maritime Alps, having secured control of the passes of Col d'Argentière, Tende and St-Bernard. With the enthusiastic support of Augustin Robespierre, who took Bonaparte's memorandum to Paris with him, Napoleon argued that if the French attacked in Piedmont, Austria would be forced to come to the aid of her Austrian possessions and thus weaken her position on the Rhine, allowing the French to strike a knockout blow there. Napoleon's chances of getting the plan accepted looked good, for his new commander-in-chief, General Dumerbion, deferred in all things to the political commissars; Saliceti and Augustin Robespierre, in turn, nodded through anything military that came from the pen of Napoleon.

The one obstacle to the implementation of Napoleon's plans was Carnot in Paris. Carnot argued instead for an invasion of Spain, in the teeth of the explicit advice in the Bonaparte memorandum that Spain was too tough a nut to crack – ironically advice Napoleon himself was to ignore later in his career. But Carnot was adamant that the Piedmont venture would not proceed. There are even some historians who argue that the fervent advocacy of the Italian invasion by the Robespierre brothers was what turned Carnot against them and sealed their fate.

The famous 'Thermidorean reaction' of 27 July 1794 (9 Thermidor), which brought the Robespierre brothers and the Jacobin leaders to the guillotine, was the end of the French Revolution in all but name. After three years in which the Left had ruled the roost in Paris, it was now the turn of the Right. As a committed Jacobin and friend of Augustin Robespierre, Napoleon was in danger. It has sometimes been suggested that he was not really in deadly peril from the ideological point of view, for he was perceived in Paris as a military technician *par excellence* and in the very month of Thermidor had become a general-elect and sworn an oath to the Revolution itself. That may be true in a general sense, but unfortunately for him, at the very moment of Thermidor, Napoleon found himself in a compromising situation through having undertaken a secret mission to Genoa.

There was really no great mystery about this visit. Napoleon was authorized to go to Genoa by Ricord, one of the political commissars, as part of the general scheme for preparing a counter-stroke against Austria in Piedmont. But it was unfortunate that just before he went he fell out with Saliceti. The reasons are obscure, but there was a persistent rumour that they had been rivals for the favours of the same girl in Nice. Annoyed by Napoleon's refusal to leave the amatory field clear for him, after all he had done for the Bonapartes, Saliceti also had to save his own skin after Thermidor, so came forward to denounce the chief of artillery. Saliceti now claimed that Napoleon had gone to Genoa on secret instructions from the Robespierres, to hatch a contingency plan with the enemy, to be activated in case the brothers fell from power; in his letter to the Committee of Public Safety on 6 August, Saliceti spoke of dark deeds, including the deposit of French gold in a Genoese bank account.

The accusation was preposterous, but in the feverish, paranoid atmosphere after Thermidor anything was believed possible. On 10 August Napoleon was placed under house arrest at his residence in the rue de Villefranche in Nice and later lodged either in the prison of Fort Carre in Antibes or under house arrest with Comte Laurenti in Nice – incredibly the record is confused, with evidence pointing either way and partisans for one or other view claiming that the documentation supporting the rival view is 'forged'. His papers were seized and sent to Saliceti for examination, and Lucien Bonaparte was arrested as an accomplice. The different attitudes of the two brothers are instructive. Lucien grovelled, debased himself and asked for mercy. Napoleon wrote a dignified rebuttal, rehearsing his services to the Republic and his exploits at Toulon. In confinement he showed himself an optimist by reading and taking notes on Marshal Maillebois's account of his campaign in Piedmont in 1745. But in his heart he thought his number was up, and discussed with Junot plots to spring him from captivity.

Suddenly, on 20 August, Saliceti and his fellow commissars announced that Napoleon's papers and his meticulous accounts completely vindicated him. The explanation for Saliceti's *volte-face* was that he realized the men of Thermidor were not calling for extensive blood sacrifices, and that he himself was in the clear. Executing Napoleon was a pointless indulgence for, in Saliceti's view, there was still political mileage to be made out of exploiting his military talent. To his credit, Saliceti urged that Napoleon's continuing presence at the front was necessary if the Army of Italy was to succeed. Even before Saliceti had his change of mind, General Dumerbion had been telling the *députés-en-mission* and the War Ministry that he could not afford to lose an officer of Bonaparte's calibre.

Once restored to the Army, Napoleon continued to submit memoranda on his Piedmontese project, this time dealing with a threatened Anglo-Piedmontese assault on French-held Savona, but Carnot, firmly in the saddle after Thermidor, rejected his ideas even more forthrightly than before. Not even Dumerbion's victory against the Austrians at the first Battle of Dego (September 1794) could shake him. Nevertheless Dumerbion sent envoys to Paris to plead for a general offensive in Italy and wrote that the military achievements of 1794 were entirely due to Bonaparte: 'It is to the ability of the General of Artillery that I owe the clever combinations which have secured our success.' The most Carnot would do was to hold out hopes of an expedition against Corsica. From December 1794 to February 1795, therefore, Napoleon was in Nice, Marseilles and Toulon, preparing an expedition that he would never take part in.

1794 saw some significant developments in the Bonaparte family dynamic and in Napoleon's personal circumstances. In August Joseph married Julie Clary, but Napoleon was still in Genoa and could not attend the wedding. If his older brother had secured his position by marrying money, Louis seemed to be faring much better than the cross-grained Lucien. Napoleon appointed Louis to his staff, and the young man saw action against the Piedmontese in the Alps before being posted to a coastal battery at St Tropez. Napoleon himself, after a long period apparently in limbo, rediscovered his sexuality. Soon after the flight from Corsica there was another encounter with a prostitute, this time in the stews of Toulon, from which Napoleon emerged complaining of the 'itch'. The evidence is tenuous, but he seems to have scratched and torn at his skin, eventually bringing on eczema.

There was a heavy flirtation, at the very least, with Emilie, daughter of the Comte de Laurenti, in Nice, just before his arrest. It is also certain that on 21 September 1794 he made the acquaintance of a M. Turreau de Lignières, yet another political commissar, and his charming and vivacious wife, that he carried on a heavy flirtation with Madame, and may even have made her his mistress. Certainly he had intercourse with her either in 1794 or 1795, and there were even rumours that he fathered a child on her. He later numbered her among his conquests and confessed sheepishly that he had needlessly sacrificed the lives of some of his men in a futile attack on an enemy position on the Italian front simply to show off to her. There seems an element of fantasy about this ill-documented 'affair' which, however, Frédéric Masson accepts as a genuine liaison. Perhaps the true fantasy, as the psychoanalyst Ernest Jones suggested, was not the affair, which was real enough, but the sacrifice of the men. A psychoanalytical reading of the business with Mme de Lignières would suggest that the words Napoleon uses to describe the alleged incident – 'some men were left on the field of battle' – could refer to the husbands he had cuckolded. Napoleon's confession might therefore be the Sartrean ploy of pleading guilty to a 'lesser' misdemeanour: in Napoleon's confused mind the loss of soldiers might weigh less than the 'sin' of adultery about which he always had such strong feelings.

The year 1794 certainly ended Napoleon's flirtation with Jacobinism and other forms of political radicalism. The Thermidorean reaction meant that landowners and men of property were entrenched as the true beneficiaries of the Revolution, and that there would be no further pandering to the *sans-culottes* or other dispossessed groups. This hard line by Carnot and his colleagues, together with the famines, harvest failures, unemployment and price rises – for after Robespierre's fall there was a year of chaos with depreciating *assignats*, unpaid armies and therefore zero recruitment – brought the old revolutionaries out on the streets again. The crowd stormed the Convention on 12 Germinal Year III (1 April 1795) and were dispersed by the National Guard. They tried again on 1 Prairial (20 May 1795) and were again dispersed by the Guard. But the heart had gone out of the revolutionary crowd: these manifestations lacked the zeal and organization of previous post-1789 insurrections and were more like the old-fashioned *ancien régime* bread riots. Put down ruthlessly, these street revolts proved to be the last hurrah of the Revolutionary crowd, which was not seen in action again until after the Napoleonic era.

The Thermidorean defence of property meant most of all the defence of new property, for the men of Thermidor – the profiteers, hoarders, black marketeers, speculators in military supplies or the falling *assignats* – were the true beneficiaries of the Revolution. Most of all, the new class was made up of those who had cornered large public monopolies or who had purchased what was euphemistically called 'national property' – in other words, confiscated Church lands or real estate previously belonging to exiled aristocrats. The Thermidorean alliance of the bourgeoisie with the upper peasantry gave Napoleon a valuable lesson in political management. Quite apart from the fact that the executive was now chock-full of regicides, he saw clearly that their economic interests precluded a return to the *ancien régime* as surely as the Angel barring the return to Eden. This meant that a man could make himself a kind of king without fear of competition from the Bourbons.

Napoleon's ready abandonment of his old friends, the Robespierres, has seemed to some of his critics the most cynical form of *realpolitik*. He distanced himself from the executed leader in a letter to Tilly on 7 August 1794 (just before he was arrested) and this explanation has often been condemned as skin-saving doubletalk: 'I have been somewhat moved by the catastrophe of the Younger Robespierre whom I loved and whom I believed to be pure, but were he my brother, I would have stabbed him with my own hand had he aspired to tyranny.'

Yet there may be more to it than simple expediency. At the deepest level Napoleon and Maximilien Robespierre, the 'sea-green incorruptible', would always have made unlikely bedfellows. It is true that some superficial similarities can be pointed to: both had difficult childhoods, both were proud and aloof, both Romantic dreamers. But where Robespierre genuinely did dream of a utopia of perfect equality, the non-existence of poverty, the triumph of morality and Rousseau's General Will, Napoleon never paid more than lip-service to those ideals. At bottom, Napoleon's heart was with the *ancien régime*, with its patterns of hierarchy and order. He was a meritocrat, not an egalitarian: his quarrel with the pre-1789 world was that talent was not hailed as the supreme value, over birth and inherited wealth. Thermidor ushered in a kind of crude entrepreneurial meritocracy, where the craftiest, the most cunning, the most corrupt and the most manipulative were preferred to the old aristocracy or the new would-be levellers.

There was another deep psychological factor making it easy for Napoleon to switch horses from Robespierre and Jacobinism to Carnot and the Thermidoreans. The core of Robespierre's thought was Rousseau, but Napoleon was already turning his back on Rousseau long before 27 July 1794. The reason is obvious. Rousseau was associated in his mind with Corsica and with Paoli. Once he allowed his hatred for native island and father-figure to come gushing out of its subterranean caverns, it was obvious that Rousseau would be the next to go. Once again, as so often in Napoleon's life, a dramatic event, in this case the fall of Robespierre, crystallized a process that was already under way in his mind.

CHAPTER SIX

The exact date when Napoleon met the first significant woman in his life (Letizia apart) is not known, but by the time Joseph married Julie Clary, Napoleon was deeply interested in her sixteen-year-old sister Bernardine Eugénie Clary, also known as Désirée. Both girls were brunettes, and at this stage Désirée had not shed all her puppy fat so that, petite as she was, she had a somewhat dumpy appearance. But she was warm, affectionate and good-natured, with a smile like Mediterranean sunshine, and she had large, lustrous, slightly popping brown eyes; her portraits show her as sexy rather than beautiful.

The initial attraction for Napoleon is easy to explain, but before September 1794, Désirée probably rated no higher in his affections than Emilie de Laurenti, whose hand he once lukewarmly solicited from her father, in the certain knowledge that he would be turned down. As is quite clear from the events of 1795, Napoleon liked to 'test the water' by making frivolous marriage proposals, just to see how his social status was perceived by others. But we can certainly discount the wild story that Joseph really wanted to marry Désirée until Napoleon 'leaned on' him by pointing out that stable should marry flighty and flighty stable; this meant the pairings should be Joseph/Julie and Napoleon/Désirée. Joseph made a hardheaded marriage of convenience to solve his financial problems, and there was never any suggestion of an automatic second connection between the Bonaparte and Clary families.

There was certainly nothing special about Napoleon's feelings for Désirée in September 1794, as his first letter to her (he always called her Eugénie), from the Italian front, makes clear: 'Your unfailing sweetness and the gay openness which is yours alone inspire me with affection, dear Eugénie, but I am so occupied by work I don't think this affection ought to cut into my soul and leave a deeper scar.' Scarcely *coup de foudre*. The epithet best describing Napoleon's letters to Désirée at this juncture is 'patronizing'. He advised her on what books she should read, how she could improve her piano playing (though his technical advice on scales, tones and intervals is nonsensical), how to develop an acknowledged musical talent, and how she could brush up her deportment and manners. When Désirée, unsurprisingly, rebuked him for his unromantic tone, he replied with a list of her shortcomings.

Yet the visits to her house from December 1794 onwards, while he was preparing the Corsican expedition, obviously increased his ardour, for the tone of his letters changes. 'You are always in my thoughts. I have never doubted your love, my sweet Eugénie, how can you think I could ever cease to love you?' The romance caught fire, and on 21 April 1795 Napoleon became engaged to Désirée. Although it has often been said that Madame Clary opposed the match, there is no sign of this at this stage, nor of Joseph's supposed objection on the grounds that one Bonaparte in the family was enough. Since Désirée would bring in a healthy dowry – up to 100,000 francs on some estimates – the marriage made sense to the hardheaded Napoleon.

It is clear from subsequent events that at some time between 21 April and his departure for Paris on 7 May Napoleon made Désirée his mistress. When the guilt-ridden Napoleon admitted this on St Helena, his confession was disregarded as the fantasy of a 'dirty old man', but to construe his remarks in this way reveals an astoundingly superficial view of his psychology. To take the virginity of a girl and then not marry her was against his own old-fashioned code of honour – it was vastly different in the case of experienced women – and he always felt guilt about this. Why he did not marry her he scarcely knew at the conscious level and continued to hark back to her wistfully. But there are some important clues to the relationship and its eventual failure in the outline for a novel Napoleon wrote during the affair with Désirée, *Clissold et Eugénie*.

It is obvious that Eugénie is Désirée (Napoleon thought the name more refined and dignified than the erotically charged 'Désirée') and that Napoleon is Clissold. This is how he described hero and heroine:

> Clissold was born for war. While still a child he knew the lives of all the great captains. He meditated on military tactics at a time when other boys of his age were at school or chasing girls. As soon as he was old enough to shoulder arms, brilliant actions marked his every step. One victory succeeded another and his name was as renowned among the people as those of their dearest defenders . . . Eugénie was sixteen years old. She was gentle, good and vivacious, with pretty eyes and of medium size. Without being ugly, she was not a beauty, but goodness, sweetness and a lively tenderness were essential parts of her nature.

Clissold is the Romantic hero, a loner who has reached high rank in the army while still a young man, thus making him prey to insane jealousy and insane rumour. In the countryside near Lyons he meets two sisters, Amélie and Eugénie. After some inconsequential flirting with Amélie, Clissold falls in love with Eugénie and she with him. Thereafter Clissold renounces fame and lives only for the love of Eugénie. Years go by and they have children. In what is surely a reference to his affair with Désirée, Napoleon writes: 'Every night Eugénie slept with her head on her lover's shoulder or in his arms ... In his new life with Eugénie Clissold had certainly avenged men's injustice, which had vanished from his mind like a dream.'

The incomparable idyll comes to an end when Clissold is recalled to the Army. He is away for years but every day gets a letter from Eugénie. Wounded in battle, he sends his right-hand man, Berville, to comfort Eugénie. Berville and Eugénie fall in love and, hearing of this, Clissold decides to die in battle. At two in the morning, just before the battle, he writes a letter of farewell to Eugénie:

How many unhappy men regret being alive yet long to continue living! Only I wish to have done with life. It is Eugénie who gave me it ... Farewell, my life's arbiter, farewell, companion of my happy days! In your arms I have tasted supreme happiness. I have drained life dry and all its good things. What remains now but satiety and boredom? At twenty-six I have exhausted the ephemeral pleasures of fame but in your love I have known how sweet it is to be alive. That memory breaks my heart. May you live happily and think no more of the unhappy Clissold! Kiss my sons. May they grow up without their father's ardour, for then they would be like him, victims of other men, of glory and of love.

The theme of betrayal by a woman hints at what was in the Napoleonic unconscious. It squares with what we know of his deep ambivalence towards Letizia, and the conviction that she had betrayed Carlo. The seeds of disaster for the love affair with Désirée are already on show here. To marry Désirée, Napoleon seems to hint, is to expose himself to the full blast of romantic love with its almost inevitable heartache and, given his opinion of women, virtually certain betrayal. Désirée's very status as a virgin when Napoleon took her is, paradoxically, felt to be what is most threatening about her.

Any chance of a spontaneous development of the romance was destroyed when Napoleon suddenly received orders to join the Army of the West, engaged in fighting the royalist counter-revolutionaries of the Vendée. This posting to an infantry command was, in effect, a demotion and Napoleon decided to go to Paris to protest it. Accompanied by

Marmont and Junot, he set off north in a post-chaise, travelling via Avignon, Montelimar, Valence, Lyons and the Saône to the Marmont family home in Burgundy. As the coach drove off, Désirée wrote: 'You left half an hour ago . . . Only the thought of knowing you forever faithful . . .' at which point the letter tailed off on a tear-splotched page.

That Napoleon, though possibly sexually besotted, was not in love in any true sense became clear even before he reached Paris. At the Marmont house he met a bright young woman named Victorine de Chastenay, who fell under his spell at once, as she herself testifies. At dinner Victorine sang a ballad and asked Napoleon if her pronunciation was correct. He said 'No' rather boorishly and otherwise spoke to her only in blunt monosyllables. But she was much taken with this very pale and thin general with the long greasy hair, and set out to impress him. Evidently she succeeded for the following day after dinner she spent four hours alone with him, while he held forth as a literary critic: he told her he loved Ossian, hated happy endings in the theatre, and thought Shakespeare's plays were pathetic and unreadable. It is quite clear that Victorine threw herself at him; whether the encounter ended with sexual consummation is unclear.

Napoleon and his companions proceeded via Chalon, Châtillon-sur-Seine and Semur and arrived in Paris on 25 May. Once in the capital Napoleon went to the Ministry of War to protest his demotion from the rank of artillery general. A stormy interview followed, after which it looked likely that Napoleon would end up on a supernumerary list as an unemployed general. The Minister reiterated that the artillery quotas were full and that, as he was the last to be promoted, there was nothing for it but he must command a brigade in the Vendée. Napoleon, as usual in such an emergency, stalled by asking for three weeks' leave, intending in the meantime to lobby his influential friends to get him off the hook. He began collecting evidence of victimization and discovered that a number of politicians, including the Minister of War himself, held the rank and pay of a brigadier-general though not on active service.

When there was no resolution of the stand-off after the expiry of the leave period, Napoleon found himself on half pay and reduced to living in a cheap hotel, wearing a shabby uniform, muddy boots and no gloves, and getting by on a pittance sent by Joseph. He was said to have been so poor that when dining out he wrapped the money for his bill in a piece of paper, to conceal how little he was spending. No longer able to maintain Louis, he managed to find him a place in the artillery school at Châlons. Despondent and disillusioned, he cut a poor figure, as described by Laure Permon, the future duchess d'Abrantes:

At this time Napoleon was so ugly, he cared so little for his appearance, that his uncombed and unpowdered hair gave him a disagreeable look. I can still picture him, entering the courtyard of the Hôtel de la Tranquillité, and crossing it with an awkward, uncertain step. He wore a nasty round hat pulled down over his eyes, from which his hair, like a spaniel's ears, flopped over his frock-coat . . . an overall sickly effect was created by his thinness and his yellow complexion.

Other contemporary descriptions mention his short stature and his deep-set, grey eyes, which could look gloomy or fiery and could be changed in a trice to produce either a charming or a terrifying effect. Some observers noted his unusually delicate features or his 'spaniel's ears' haircut – cut square under the ears and falling to the shoulders – while others spoke of the peculiar charm of the lines of his mouth and his palpable physical presence – something no other Bonaparte possessed. But all were agreed about the predominant tone of depression.

Certainly in these dark days in Paris in the summer of 1795 Napoleon contemplated suicide. At other times he thought of going into service with the Sultan of Turkey, always provided his beloved Joseph would agree to serve as French consul at Chios. He actually submitted a formal application to the War Ministry to be allowed to serve in Turkey, but the application was not immediately processed because of incompetence by Ministry clerks. The mixture of depression and emotion for Joseph comes through in a letter written to Joseph in June:

Whatever may happen to you, remember that you cannot possibly have a warmer friend than I, one to whom you are more dear or who is more sincerely desirous for your happiness. Life is a mere dream that fades. Should you go away and suspect that it may be for some time, let me have a miniature of yourself. We have lived together for so long and been so close that our hearts have become as one – you know more than anyone how completely mine belongs to you.

Napoleon's letters from this period, both to Joseph and Désirée, are gloomy and depressive. The epistles to Joseph oscillate between the sentiment that life has little meaning and he would welcome death and a hyper-cynicism and money obsession, heightened by the presence all around him in Paris of quick-fix speculators, shady get-rich-quick characters, *parvenus, arrivistes* and the *nouveaux riches*: 'There is only one thing to do in this world and that is to keep acquiring money and more money, power and more power. All the rest is meaningless.' There is much about the Napoleon of 1795 to back Madame de Rémusat's assertion that Napoleon was bold and resourceful only when luck was running his way, but when at a low ebb he was timid, circumspect and uncertain. There was little encouraging news from Joseph: just that Lucien, still destitute in St-Maximin, had been arrested as a Jacobin a full year after Thermidor but then released after two weeks.

To Désirée he wrote that he had a 'romantic soul', an imagination of ice, a head of ice, a bizarre heart and melancholy inclinations. This was hardly what she wanted to hear, for she was busy writing that she was doing everything she could to make herself worthy of him, adding, however, that she feared he would forget all about the pleasures of Marseilles in the heady, hedonistic atmosphere of Paris. So uninterested was Napoleon in Désirée that he let nine days go by before going down to the *poste restante* to retrieve her tear-stained letters. But it was typical of him to blow hot and cold. On 24 June he decided to have his portrait painted for Désirée. In July, when she was with her family in Genoa, he complained to Joseph that he never heard from her, did not know whether she was alive or dead, and chided Joseph with never mentioning her.

Maybe Désirée, from the vantage point of the French capital, now looked small beer or, more likely, she was a card he cynically kept in play while he investigated his prospects of making a more financially lucrative or politically advantageous match. Certainly he did the rounds of eligible women, sounding out prospects. He probably did make overtures to Laure Permon's forty-year-old widowed mother, and it may well be, as l'Abrantes relates, that he was scornfully rejected. On the other hand, the story that he proposed marriage to the sixty-year-old Mlle de Montansier seems like obvious black propaganda spread by his enemies. Other women whom he may have reconnoitred with a view to a marriage of convenience include Mme de la Bouchardie and Mme de la Lespada.

Also in his sights for a while was thirty-year-old Grace Dalrymple, later Lady Elliott, a Scotswoman who was an adventuress in a double sense, having given birth to an illegitimate daughter by the Prince of Wales and been imprisoned in France during the Terror. A walk in the Tuileries convinced them there could never be a meeting of minds. Napoleon, a one-time admirer of the English, now associated them with Paoli's treachery and had all the fanatical Anglophobia of the newly converted. He told Grace he wished the earth would open and swallow up all Englishmen. She replied that the remark was scarcely tactful in her presence. Napoleon protested that he believed all Scots loved France more than they did England, but Grace hastened to assure him that her heart was in England even more than Scotland.

One woman who certainly was a salient consideration to Napoleon during the dreadful limbo of summer 1795 was Thérésia Tallien. How Napoleon came into her orbit is uncertain. Junot recalls that he and Marmont ran into Napoleon's schoolmate Bourrienne in Paris; the three of them then played a penurious version of the Three Musketeers to Bonaparte's d'Artagnan, roaming around Paris and knocking on the doors of the influential. For some reason, possibly his memory of Napoleon at Toulon, one of the doors opened to them was that of forty-year-old Paul Barras (who had been a commissar at Toulon), one of the five most powerful men in Paris. Barras was part of the famous salon which met at 'La Chaumière' – the elegant house made up to look like a cottage, where lived Jean-Lambert Tallien, architect of Robespierre's downfall and president of the Thermidorian Convention.

But the more significant inhabitant was his new wife Thérésia Cabarrus. At the influential 'Chaumière' salon could be found Barras, Stanislas Fréron, the young financial genius Gabriel Ouvrard, Joseph Chénier – said to have connived at the guillotining of his brother André, the poet, during the Terror – the American envoy James Monroe, together with Germaine de Staël and notorious women of the time, including Fortunée Hamelin, Juliette Récamier and Rose de Beauharnais. It was overwhelmingly a milieu of the powerful, the beautiful and, above all, the young: Ouvrard was twenty-eight, Tallien twenty-seven, and at forty Barras and Fréron counted as old men.

Still only twenty-two 'la Cabarrus', the reigning beauty of Thermidorian society, had already packed a lifetime's adventure into her glittering career. She had been married and divorced by twenty-one and had narrowly escaped the guillotine during the Terror. Both pleasure-loving and philoprogenitive, she had numerous lovers, including Barras and the banker Ouvrard and would end her career as the Princesse de Chimay. Napoleon was at once fascinated and repelled by her: fascinated by her bewitching beauty and power over men, yet repelled by her promiscuity and the airs and graces she gave herself. The story that Napoleon made overtures to her and was rebuffed is absurd: at this juncture Napoleon was a nobody and Thérésia could have her pick of any man in the Thermidorian élite – and did so.

Thérésia Tallien symbolized the new hedonistic Paris, given over to sensuality and gratification. Paris was a world away from the repressed revolutionary society Napoleon had last seen in 1792. The Thermidorian reaction released rivers of the pleasure principle, pent-up by Robespierrean austerity, and in this the new society resembled Restoration England after the puritanism of Cromwell, or the luxury and opulence of the

Second Empire after the 1848 Revolution. Theatres flourished as never before, conspicuous consumption was the order of the day as women spent fortunes on gowns and men on coaches, fine wines and their losses at the card table. Sensualists found new avenues to explore, and the Thermidorian period is even credited with the invention of lunch, as the old-style dinner hour was pushed back and back and a new 'forked' meal took its place. Needless to say, all this ostentatious luxury at the top contrasted with the most crippling poverty and destitution in the Parisian slums. For the common man, it seemed, five years of Revolution had been in vain.

Most of all, the new order was a 'permissive society' with sexuality and hence the role of women underlined. In July Napoleon wrote to Joseph: 'Everywhere in Paris you see beautiful women. Here alone of all places on earth they appear to hold the reins of government, and the men are crazy about them, think of nothing else and love only for and through them . . . A woman needs to come to Paris for six months to learn what is her due, and to understand her own power. Here only, they deserve to have such influence.'

Apparently Désirée read this letter, for she wrote an incoherent letter to Napoleon containing the following: 'A friend of Joseph's, a deputy, has arrived. He says that everyone enjoys themselves immensely in Paris. I hope that the noisy pleasures there will not allow you to forget the peaceful country ones of Marseilles, and that walks in the Bois de Boulogne with Madame Tallien will not allow you to forget the riverside ones with your *bonne petite* Eugénie.' Napoleon wrote a reassuring letter to say that when he last dined with Madame Tallien, her looks seemed to have faded. Whether Désirée was taken in by this transparent lie about a glowing twenty-two-year-old beauty is unlikely, but she can hardly fail to have noticed that one of Napoleon's subsequent letters was scarcely the effusion of a man madly in love: 'Tender Eugénie, you are young. Your feelings are going to weaken, then falter; later you will find yourself changed. Such is the dominion of time . . . I do not accept the promise of eternal love you give in your latest letter, but I substitute for it a promise of inviolable frankness. The day you love me no more, swear to tell me. I make the same promise.'

Napoleon's new patron, Paul comte de Barras, typified the post-Thermidor and Directory régime. A former career soldier and voluptuary from Provence, who had been bankrupted in 1789, Barras had a career as an ex-Jacobin – he was one of the regicides of 1793 – and turncoat. A deeply unpleasant man even by the not very elevated standards of the Thermidorian régime, he was corrupt, amoral, cynical, venal, sardonic and opportunistic. A cardsharp who was known to cheat when his instincts failed him, he ran a house that was little more than a glorified brothel, full of crooked stockjobbers and ladies of the night.

Napoleon was never so much an opportunist as during this period under Barras's wing at the Tallien salon. Here was the erstwhile firebrand Jacobin, friend of the Robespierres, dining at the house of the most reactionary man of Thermidor, the man who had compassed the downfall of the 'sea-green incorruptible'. Napoleon had already learned the lesson that ideology was for fools, that the ambitious man went where the power was. And whatever his private feelings about Tallien's wife, he kept them to himself, and tried to charm and cajole her. Although as an officer not on the active list he was not entitled to a new uniform and was reduced to wearing his old, threadbare one at her parties, Thérésia listened sympathetically to his tale of woe and used her immense influence to have a new one issued to him.

Gabriel Ouvrard, the banker, recalled that of all the visitors to the Chaumière, Napoleon was the least memorable. How it must have galled this young man, who wanted always to be first in everything, to have to take a back seat! He became more and more aware that in Paris, his exploits at Toulon notwithstanding, he was regarded as just an insignificant officer with a provincial accent. Received Parisian pronunci-ation was almost becoming a Thermidorian badge of honour, but Napoleon retained an unwitting Jacobin legacy in the coarseness of his demotic speech. Having become used to the knee-jerk foulmouthery appropriate to 'citizen Bonaparte', he found it hard to adjust to the refined elegance of La Chaumière, where the finely-turned epigrams of Germaine de Staël contrasted with the barefaced sexual promiscuity behind closed doors

Napoleon took a particular dislike to de Staël's close friend Juliette Récamier, possibly because she was virginal and had a known dislike of sex, whereas to Napoleon sexuality was woman's destiny. Fortunately, the nineteen-year-old Creole beauty Fortunée Hamelin, who was reputed to have paraded up the Champs-Elysées barebreasted for a dare, also disliked Récamier as a pretentious prude, and made common cause with Napoleon. She became an admirer and close friend, and the support Napoleon got from her and Thérésia led him to a tactless revelation in a letter to Désirée that he now admired royalist women; she, on the other hand, had first known him as a devout Jacobin. 'Beautiful as in old romances and as learned as scholars . . . all these frivolous women have one thing in common, an astonishing love of bravery and glory . . . Most of them are so violently royalist, and their labour and their pleasure is to win respectable people over to their cause.'

Suddenly, on 17 August 1795, the bombshell burst. Napoleon received an express order to join the Army of the West or see his military career at an end. Napoleon was desperate and at his wits' end. To comply meant accepting that he had been demoted from the rank of artillery general to a common-or-garden infantry brigadier in the endless Vendée campaign, from which could come no glory or advancement. It almost meant serving under the Republican hero Lazare Hoche, who had driven the Austrians out of Alsace in 1793. Napoleon shrewdly sensed that the ambitious Hoche, just one year older, was in competition for the same space and the same glittering prizes, and that to serve under him might mean ending up in front of a firing squad. Jealous of his prestige and aware that Hoche had a reputation as a martinet and would not tolerate the slightest insubordination, Bonaparte, the free-wheeling political intriguer and shameless adventurer, knew that the Vendée was the end of the line. Hoche would not permit a day's leave, never mind years of it, and took the same draconian attitude to furlough that Napoleon himself would take when Emperor.

Napoleon did his best to avoid the inevitable. First he tried the old dodge of sending in a sick note, but the War Office trumped that ace by declaring that the doctor who wrote the certificate was not competent to do so. In despair Napoleon appealed to Barras as his last hope. Influenced by Thérésia Tallien as well as his own partiality for the young supplicant, Barras got him a post in the Topographical Bureau of the Committee of Public Safety. It was an exalted position, guaranteeing his rank as brigadier-general, but not quite so elevated as Napoleon boasted when he told Joseph he had 'replaced' Carnot there: in fact the Bureau was run by a quadrumvirate of generals. Carnot had set up the Bureau in 1792 as a kind of general staff and it was supposed to be a preserve of the brightest and best military minds.

Barras's quick action to help his protégé was aided by the turn of events. On 29 June an Austrian counter-offensive routed General Kellermann and undid all the French victories of 1794. Kellermann claimed that Nice was in danger and asked for help. The government was already searching for men with Italian experience when Barras put forward Napoleon's name. His first memorandum, arguing for a significant transfer of troops from the armies of the Rhine and the Pyrenees to the Italian front, where Scherer now took over from Kellermann, simply mirrored his 1794 arguments.

Ironically, on the very day he was appointed, his old project for going to Turkey came to life again. The bureaucratic muddle at the Ministry of War had been sorted out and passed to the Commission of the Exterior, who now informed him that his proposal to go to Turkey as head of a military mission to the Sultan had been approved. But there was still a snag. He had not informed the Committee of Public Safety of his Turkish application. Having just stretched a point and given him a prestigious post, the Committee was offended at being approached with this fresh request and turned it down.

Perhaps this contretemps was still in the Committee's mind a few weeks later, or perhaps it was simply a change in the personnel on the Committee, but on 15 September Napoleon was informed that he had been struck off the list of generals. The reason given was his refusal to serve in the Vendée campaign, but this was grossly illogical for, if the argument was valid, he should never have been offered the post in the Topographical Bureau in the first place. His position was now the worst ever, and for three weeks he was in desperate straits, beset by pressing financial worries.

Foreseeing now that all his ambitions might come to naught, he decided to reactivate the relationship with Désirée. She must have been surprised, after all the previous cold missives (in one of which he told her, 'If you love someone else, you must yield to your feelings') to receive a warm and enthusiastic screed, talking excitedly of his plans for introducing her to Parisian society and adding: 'Let us hurry, beloved Eugénie, time flies, old age is almost upon us.' But after that, nothing. In the meantime Napoleon's career had taken another, successful twist, and he no longer needed Désirée. If we judge from his conscious actions alone, Napoleon's treatment of Désirée seems despicable. To apply for service in Turkey even while he spoke to a seventeen-year-old of introducing her to high society, denotes a secretive, unscrupulous, duplicitous and chillingly ambitious personality.

Yet if Napoleon in late September stared career disaster in the face, his protector Barras confronted an even more serious situation, one where his very life was in jeopardy. A new constitution on 21 June 1795 placed executive power in the hands of a five-man 'Directory' and vested legislative authority in a lower Chamber of 500 and an upper house of 'Ancients'. But the Decrees of 22 and 30 August 1795 – the so-called 'Decree of Two-Thirds' – stipulated that two-thirds of the new assembly had to be chosen from members of the old Convention; the intention was to protect the new men of property and prevent royalists returning to power.

On 11 Vendémiaire (3 October 1795), led by the royalist Le Peletier, seven Parisian sections declared themselves to be in rebellion. General Menou, commander of the Paris garrison, made it plain that he sympathised with the rebels. There were 20,000 National Guardsmen in the capital who could conceivably be swayed to the royalist side. Having experienced Red terror and the revolt of the *sans-culottes*, Paris now faced White terror and that ultimate paradox: counter-revolution from the Right against an extreme right-wing government. The distinction was that the threat was directed against the men of 'new' property by a motley alliance between ultramontane royalists and dissatisfied sections of the National Guard.

There is considerable controversy over Napoleon's exact movements and motives in the forty-eight hours following the Paris rising. Both Barras and Napoleon in their very different memoirs grossly distort the record. Some have claimed it is black propaganda to suggest that Napoleon flirted with the royalists. Napoleon allegedly said to Junot: 'If only the Parisians [the rebels] would name me their chief, I would see to it that the Tuileries would be invaded within two hours, and we would chase those miserable deputies out of there.' Since this story comes from Laure, duchess of Abrantes, it is safest to disregard it. Yet on St Helena Napoleon told General Bertrand he was undecided which way to jump, and was inclining to the royalists' side when Barras sent for him. Barras stoked up the rumours in his memoirs by claiming that when the trouble broke out he at once thought of Napoleon and sought him out, but that he could not be found at his lodgings, his café or any of his usual haunts; the obvious inference was that he had been bargaining with the other side. Yet another story was that Napoleon was in bed with a blonde called Suzanne when he was 'missing'. According to Barras, he discerned Napoleon's duplicity but outfoxed him by offering him command of the artillery, *provided* he accepted within three minutes. Napoleon did so, whereupon Barras took him to the session of the Committee of Public Safety in the Tuileries and got an order signed on the spot, readmitting Napoleon to his full army rank.

The historian can only cut through the thickets of rumour and innuendo, sidestep Napoleon's inflated claim that he was officially designated second-in-command under Barras, and concentrate on what actually happened. Throughout 12 Vendémiaire (4 October), the tocsin call to arms never ceased to sound. The men of Thermidor were in a panic and looked to Barras to save them. He began by releasing hundreds of Jacobins from prison and hiring a number of unemployed officers. He then sent word to Napoleon who heeded the call, whether immediately or after a judicious interval is uncertain. Napoleon did a quick head count.

Disregarding the paper figures, which showed the Convention with 60–70,000 men under their command, he soon established that Barras disposed of no more than 5–6,000 effectives; moreover, ammunition was low and Barras had no artillery. Facing them were 20,000 well-armed royalists, moving in towards the Tuileries in an ever-contracting ring of steel. It was time for inspired measures.

Realising from his observations on 10 August 1792 that the key to the coming engagement was artillery, Napoleon ordered the squadron commander of the 21st Chasseurs to seize the National Guard's artillery in the Place des Sablons. The time was midnight, 4 October, and the man to whom he gave the order was destined to loom large in his life: Joachim Murat, a twenty-eight-year-old Gascon from Lot with a chequered background. Murat, a huge man with a large nose, strong southern brogue and a Gascon's arrogance to match, was an inspired cavalry leader whose courage always outran his intelligence, but on this occasion he bore himself superbly. He arrived at the Place des Sablons with 260 men at the same time as a company of National Guardsmen, intent on the same errand. Murat curtly told the opposition they would be cut to pieces if they interfered, and under this threat they backed off. Murat then requistioned horses and carts and dragged the forty big guns back to the Tuileries.

Napoleon and Barras placed four thousand men in a protective cordon around the Tuileries. Napoleon's strategy depended on using artillery fire to prevent the insurgents from concentrating their forces under the Palace windows and then overwhelming the defenders. He set up his main battery ready to rake the rue St-Honoré. Then he waited. He was lucky, for the National Guardsmen proved pusillanimous and the royalists' military commander, Danican, incompetent. Despite the fact that rain had been pelting down all the day before, the royalists decided to wait until it stopped before launching their onslaught. If they had attacked at first light, Napoleon would not have had time to set up and sight his batteries correctly.

Finally, at about 4.45 on the afternoon of 5 October, the attack on the Tuileries began. The onrushing rebels ran into murderous artillery fire of a kind never yet experienced in the revolutionary street battles. Taking heavy losses, the attackers pulled back into the rue St-Roch and regrouped at the church of that name. The boldest of them climbed the church roof and took up sniper positions behind the chimneys and on the steeple. Their movements could not have suited Napoleon better, as he personally commanded the battery of two 8-pounders loaded with case-shot, facing the church. He called up more cannon and then unleashed a deadly fusillade, mowing down the insurgents in droves. This was the action he later euphemistically called 'the whiff of grapeshot'. Meanwhile the guns he had positioned to command the Seine prevented the rebels on the Left bank from crossing over to aid their comrades. By 6 p.m. these too fell back discomfited, and both 'horns' of the intended attack withdrew. That night the rain pelted down again, washing away the gore of an urban battlefield. There were four hundred corpses inside St-Roch church and another thousand bodies lay dead on the streets.

Next day Barras and his henchmen left the gates of Paris open so that the surviving rebels could escape. Barras informed the government that Napoleon was the hero of the hour and must be promoted to major-general, but his colleagues in the Directory claimed to be incredulous that this General Bonaparte, still an unknown, had played any part in the victory. A week later Barras resigned his post as Commander-in-Chief of the Army of the Interior and recommended Napoleon as his successor. The story was that Barras told his colleagues: 'Promote this man or he will promote himself without you.' Over great opposition, particularly from Carnot, Napoleon was named as the new commander. He was to receive an annual salary of 48,000 francs and would have the *de facto* position of Governor of Paris, as well as controlling the police and secret service.

At twenty-six, Napoleon was rich and famous. In euphoria he wrote to Joseph that he would now be able to enrich the Bonaparte clan with places and perquisites. The process began at once. Letizia received 60,000 francs and, with her daughters, relocated from the wretched garret in Marseilles to the best apartment in the plushest house in the city's most sought-after quarter. Joseph was made consul in Italy and given money to invest in Genoese privateers, while Lucien was appointed commissary with the Army of the North in the Netherlands. Louis was promoted lieutenant in the 4th Artillery Regiment and joined Napoleon's staff as military secretary and aide-de-camp. The eleven-year-old Jérôme was sent to an expensive Irish school near Paris, where Napoleon, mindful of his own schooldays at Brienne, spoiled him outrageously and loaded him with pocket money. Fesch, the financial brains of the Bonaparte clan, temporarily left the priesthood for the lucrative post of commissary to the Army of Italy.

To Madame Clary Napoleon sent a *de haut en bas* note informing her of his new status, ostensibly for the purpose of introducing his henchman Stanislas Fréron, but to Désirée he wrote not a word. To Joseph he wrote on 15 November, clearly revelling in his new status as a man of wealth:

I have just received 400,000 francs for you. I have given it to Fesch who will pay it into your account. I may instal the family here [Paris]. Let me have much more news of you and your wife and of Désirée. Goodbye, my good friend, I am all yours. My only worry is the knowledge that you are so far away and to be deprived of your company. Were not your wife pregnant, I would try to persuade you to come and spend some time in Paris.

For the first time since Toulon Napoleon was unquestionably on the winning side, and he revelled in his new status. His letters now bespeak a confidence that he was born under a lucky star. He moved at once from his dingy quarters in the Marais to a splendid new house. The man who just a few days before was destitute now drove around Paris in a fine carriage, invited guests to a private box at the Opéra, and gave lush parties at his headquarters in the Place Vendôme. If Napoleon had been unknown to the wider public before Vendémiaire, now he was a household name. Fréron's extravagant praise, during a session of the Convention on 11 October, saw to that, even if the frightful Fréron had an ulterior motive, since he was slavering with lust at the thought of the stunning fifteen-year-old Pauline Bonaparte, and had plans to marry her.

As Commander-in-Chief of the Army of the Interior, Napoleon was responsible for internal order and for tranquillity in Paris, that notorious powder-keg. Since the economic crisis showed no signs of abating, he began by striking at the most likely focus of discontent: he closed the Panthéon Club, the nerve centre of the Jacobin party. With 40,000 men at his disposal, he divided them into cohorts and heavily policed potential trouble spots, with an ostentatious display of 'showing the flag'. The pressing problem, as always, was the Parisian bread supply; throughout these years the search for real bread, made from white flour, sold at reasonable prices was the abiding concern of the proletariat. Napoleon liked to tell a story, probably apocryphal, of a menacing situation that developed when would-be bread rioters surrounded a platoon he was commanding. A monstrously fat women jeered at the soldiers and tried to work up the crowd by calling out that the military grew fat while the poor starved. Napoleon was at this time extremely thin, and called out: 'My good woman, look carefully at me. Which of us is the fatter?' The contrast in profiles was too much. All tension dissolved in gales of laughter.

October 1795 was the great turning point in Napoleon's life for, immediately after the Vendémiaire triumph, he became heavily involved in an affair with Rose de Beauharnais which led to marriage. The two events should be seen as cause and effect, not coincidence, as in the versions of some credulous biographers. The usual story is that after 13 Vendémiaire Napoleon issued a decree that Parisians should hand in all weapons. In the light of this decree, Rose de Beauharnais's fourteen-year-old son, Eugène, went to see Napoleon to ask him if he could keep his father's ceremonial sword, which had been bequeathed him. Napoleon agreed, Rose called to thank him, and the affair took off from there.

This is obvious legend. Rose de Beauharnais was Thérésia Tallien's best friend, and Napoleon would have seen her many times at the gatherings at La Chaumière. But then he was nothing, and would not have excited her interest. After Vendémiaire he was a rising star. The fable about Eugène was invented later to save face on both sides. Rose wanted to conceal the fact that she had set her cap at the young general, while Bonaparte wanted to rewrite the historical fact that he had been Barras's creature and that it was Barras who suggested the liaison. If we discount the transparent story about the sword, what is left is the historical fact that on 15 October Napoleon made his first visit to her house in the rue de Chantereine.

Who was this Rose de Beauharnais, who would be known to history and legend as Josephine? She was born on 23 June 1763 in the French colony of Martinique in the West Indies and christened Marie-Josèphe-Rose. Her father was the struggling plantation owner Joseph Tascher de la Pagerie. At sixteen, despite being in love with the son of a Scots Jacobite émigré, she had been sent to France to wed Alexandre de Beauharnais in a marriage arranged by her aunt, who was the mistress of the bridegroom's father. Rose's marriage was turbulent, and in the first four years Alexandre spent just ten months with her, long enough to beget a son, Eugène, born in 1781. When she was pregnant with a second child (her daughter Hortense), Alexandre decided to visit Martinique and departed with a former mistress, Laure de Longpré. The jealous Laure poisoned his mind against Rose and, once in Martinique, bribed and threatened the la Pagerie slaves to say that Rose had led a promiscuous life before she left for France. In letters to Rose full of bitterness, Alexandre repudiated the paternity of Hortense. When he returned to France, he abducted Eugène, but was forced to give him up.

During the separation that followed, Rose seems to have undergone a change of personality, for it is in these years that the sensual, pleasure-loving, promiscuous woman first emerges. In 1788 Rose took Hortense with her to Martinique on a transatlantic voyage that no one has explained satisfactorily. Some say she was pregnant when she boarded ship and certainly not by her husband. A possible abortion on board ship could explain her later childlessness. At all events, Rose stayed in Martinique for two years. In 1790 she returned to Paris where, though still separated, she was on reasonable terms with Alexandre de Beauharnais.

During the Revolution the ex-oligarch de Beauharnais moved ever leftwards until he was one of the Mountain faction. However, he was caught up in the collective madness of the Terror, where one species of Jacobin shark ate another. Falling foul of Robespierre and St-Just, he was imprisoned in the notorious Les Carmes prison in April 1794. For petitioning for his release, Rose suffered the same fate. In Les Carmes, which had the reputation of being a gigantic brothel, where the soon-to-die coupled frenziedly to thumb their noses at the guillotine, Alexandre de Beauharnais was having an affair with Delphine de Custine. Rose, who had turned to casual liaisons after her return to Paris in 1790, took General Hoche as her lover. In prison there was an amazing cameraderie of the damned. Once they had locked their charges securely inside the prison, the warders were indifferent what they got up to. The result was a kind of combination of perpetual orgy with social club for the doomed. Among women friends Rose made in jail were Grace Dalrymple and Thérésia Tallien.

Alexandre de Beauharnais was taken out for execution on 22 July, just five days before Robespierre's downfall in the Thermidorian coup. Ten days after the coup Rose herself was at liberty. Attaching herself to Thérésia Tallien and the Chaumière set, she became Barras's mistress and lived a life of luxury totally at odds with her private financial situation, which was desperate; this trait seems to have been a cultural legacy of Martinique where insolvent plantation families indulged in conspicuous consumption to overawe their slaves.

Apart from her relentless frivolity – she never read a book but spent a fortune on clothes – Rose most impressed her contemporaries by her sexual appetite. When she came out of prison and found that Hoche had not, after all, been guillotined, she tried to resume her affair with him. Hoche admitted that she was wonderful in bed but, alongside his desire for her, was disgusted by her voracious appetite. He snubbed her with the words: 'Such an amour can be pardoned in a prison but hardly outside . . . One may take a prostitute for a mistress but hardly for a wife.' According to Barras's later testimony – but it must be remembered that by this time he hated both Napoleon and Josephine and spewed out malicious rumour – Hoche was disposed to resume the affair until he found the lecherous Rose in the arms of his giant Alsatian groom named Van Acker. The cynical libertine Barras, however, cared nothing about the background of the women in his informal harem and was happy to add Rose to his collection.

The friendship between Rose and Thérésia Tallien, ten years her junior, was celebrated; they often wore identical clothes to establish the rapport. Both were generous and compassionate women, both had been married young to unsuitable men and both had been imprisoned during the Terror and come close to the guillotine. From the sexual point of view, the most intriguing similarity was that they were both mistresses of Barras, who in his memoirs left a devastating comparison of the lubricious charms of each. Barras claimed that Thérésia was a genuinely passionate woman, but that behind Rose's pretended ecstasies in the bedchamber was a calculating machine, mentally clocking up francs and livres. But other memoirs contradict this: the consensus is that Rose/Josephine was a woman of genuinely high sex drive, only this side of nymphomania, and that Barras's testimony is unreliable for obvious reasons (it has even been suggested that his executor wrote the passage in question).

Such was the thirty-two-year-old woman with whom Napoleon became involved in October 1795. Not really pretty, past the bloom of youth, with no outstandingly good features and with teeth so bad and blackened (they were described as being 'like cloves') that she had trained herself to smile without showing them, Rose de Beauharnais was at best a *jolie laide*. Some descriptions make her sound like a southern belle of the pre-American Civil War type: she had fine, silky, chestnut hair, magnetic dark-blue eyes and long lashes. She had trained herself to be sexy: hence the sweet smile, the graceful walk and the husky, drawling voice which she tried to render mellifluous. She made the best of a good skin tone by dressing elegantly, surrounding herself with jewels and flowers.

At first the affair with Napoleon was little more than flirtation. On 28 October she wrote to him: 'you no longer come to see a girlfriend who loves you. You are wrong, for she is tenderly attached to you. Come tomorrow to dine with me. I need to see you and talk about your interests.' Napoleon replied at once: 'I cannot imagine the reason for the tone of your letter. I beg you to believe that no one desires your friendship as much as I do, no one could be more eager to prove it. Had my duties permitted, I would have come in person to deliver this message.'

From 29 October Napoleon spent every night for five months with Josephine. For the first few days contact was restricted to dining but early in November the affair was consummated. The morning after they first made love, Napoleon wrote to her, fixing her for all time as 'Josephine':

'Seven in the morning. I awaken full of you ... The memory of yesterday's intoxicating evening has left no rest to my senses ... Sweet and incomparable Josephine, I draw from your lips, from your heart, a flame which consumes me ... A thousand kisses, but do not give me any for they burn my blood.'

Josephine had set out quite cynically and calculatedly to snare Napoleon. She needed a powerful protector and she needed money, and General Bonaparte seemed to fit the bill under both heads. There are hints that Barras was becoming tired of her and thought that an ingenious solution would be to get rid of her on to Napoleon, so that his two protégés would be bound to each other by sex and to him by gratitude. Yet it was Josephine who took the decision, and the deciding factor seems to have been her old lover Lazare Hoche.

Having defeated the Vendée rebels, Hoche returned to Paris to take over command of the projected invasion of Ireland – the one which came within an ace of success in 1796. Reluctant to return to his wife in Lorraine, Hoche stayed on in Paris, apparently having regrets about his intemperate outburst to Josephine the year before. He did not mind sharing her with the powerful Barras but he was angry to find the very general who had refused to serve under him not only his superior in rank but installed in the rue Chantereine as her lover. Josephine, it seems, would have been willing to take Hoche back, but two things worked against this. First, she made a false move by telling him she would use all her arts and influence to get him a top command. Hoche, however, was a proud man who was determined to achieve his ambitions on his own merits, and not through the machinations of a woman. Second, word came through that his wife had given birth to a daughter. On 3 January 1796 Hoche reluctantly left Paris. He later rationalized with bitterness his failure to get Josephine back and wrote to a friend: 'I have asked Mme Bonaparte to return my letters. I did not wish her husband to read my love letters to that woman ... who I despise.'

Once it became clear that she could never become Madame Barras, Josephine decided her interests were best served by marriage to Napoleon, but there were a few early hiccups in the relationship. Apparently each of the lovers thought the other had money. Josephine begged Barras not to tell Bonaparte the true situation. There was one contretemps before the marriage when Napoleon visited her lawyer to enquire about her allegedly extensive property in Martinique. The mixture of panic and anger drew from her a stern reproof which brought him to heel, for he hastened to reassure her that he was no fortune hunter: 'You thought I did not love you for yourself alone.'

Many of Josephine's friends thought that Napoleon was a strange choice for her. Their personalities clashed, as she was indolent while he was violent and passionate. He was not really a man of sufficient means, as he had no 'old money', had a numerous family to support and could end up penniless if the wheel of fortune turned once more. Her lawyer, Ragudeau, warned her that she was on shifting sands: 'Can you be so foolish as to marry a young man who has nothing but his cloak and his sword?' Others of her friends pointed out that Bonaparte was physically unappealing and – the most obvious objection of all – that she neither loved him nor was in love with him.

Josephine weighed all this, but against the minuses were some powerful pluses. Her own charms were fading fast, and the supply of influential admirers would sooner or later dry up. She felt she had a hold over Napoleon, which she never had over Barras, and only fleetingly with Hoche. Also, Bonaparte had the makings of an excellent stepfather, and Eugène, in particular, needed a male guardian he could look up to. During the Terror, when it was mandatory for all children to learn a trade, he had been apprenticed to a carpenter. Then he had spent a year as Hoche's orderly in the Vendée and had witnessed terrible atrocities. Josephine felt that her son had seen too much of the seamy side of life too soon, and hoped that he would be wrapped thereafter in Napoleon's mantle. It was true that her daughter Hortense did not appear to care for her prospective stepfather, but time could cure that. Whether Josephine's estimate of Hortense's feelings was accurate is a moot point. In her memoirs Hortense speaks of being overwhelmed by Napoleon's intellect and exhausted by his energy; she recalled a dinner with Barras at the Luxembourg on 21 January 1796, when she sat between her mother and Bonaparte, and he seemed besotted with Josephine, as an emotionally draining experience.

On 7 February 1796 the marriage banns between Napoleon and Josephine were announced and on 9 March the wedding took place – but not before Napoleon had kept the bride waiting three hours. Barras, Tallien and her lawyer acted as the witnesses on Josephine's side, and an eighteen-year-old Army captain, Le Marois, played the rôle for Napoleon. Although Napoleon was twenty-six and Josephine rising thirty-three, they both declared themselves to be twenty-eight: according to the marriage certificate Josephine had been born in 1767 and Napoleon in 1768.

This was not the only false aspect of a somewhat sordid marriage ceremony. Josephine had cynically opted for a civil ceremony to make divorce easier, but in fact there is doubt that the couple had been legally married at all. The mayor was not present, possibly because of the wedding's extreme lateness, and the ceremony was conducted by his assistant, who had no legal authority to do so. Moreover, as a minor Le Marois could not legally be a witness. To cap all, Josephine had continued her affair with Barras right up to the eve of her wedding, showing the shape of things to come. The honeymoon itself was scarcely auspicious. First, Josephine's dog Fortuné, whom she insisted on having in bed with her, bit Napoleon – whether or not *in flagrante* is not recorded. Napoleon turned in his usual perfunctory love-making performance – said to be so rapid it came close to being *ejaculatio praecox*. Josephine, frustrated by this 'expeditious' approach to intercourse, took to telling her close friends that Bonaparte was *bon à rien*.

A week earlier, Barras's 'wedding present' had been made official: Napoleon's nomination as Commander-in-Chief of the Army of Italy. The background to this was Napoleon's abiding obsession that the key to victory over Austria lay in Italy. While Commander of the Army of the Interior, he continued to bombard the Directory with criticisms of the conduct of the war on the Italian front. Increasingly, an undeclared struggle for power took place between Napoleon in Paris and General Scherer in Nice. Scherer, more and more irritated at Napoleon's sniping, complained to the Directory that its boy wonder's plans were chimerical and quixotic. After getting his way a couple of times by threatening to resign unless the Directory backed him, Scherer finally overplayed his hand, and the Directory accepted his resignation, effective 2 March 1796. But when Napoleon was appointed in his stead, the Parisian press reacted hostilely, alleging that Barras had rewarded one of his favourites because he feared generals of real talent: Hoche, Moreau, Marceau and Pichegru were mentioned in this category.

Once he had decided to marry Josephine, Napoleon's first task was to get out of his engagement with Désirée. As soon as the thought of marriage entered his mind, he started distancing himself from Désirée. The ending of a letter to Joseph in November is eloquent: he merely sent his regards to Désirée, no longer referring to her as 'Eugénie'. Once his mind was definitely made up, in January 1796, he informed Désirée that unless she got the consent of her family immediately, they must end their engagement. This was Machiavellian, for he knew perfectly well that Madame Clary opposed the match on grounds of her daughter's youth and would withhold her consent while she was still a minor. The next Désirée knew was the announcement that her beloved was married. There is no need to doubt the sincerity of the heartbroken letter she sent Napoleon:

You have made me so unhappy, and I am weak enough to forgive you!
You married! Poor Désirée must no longer love you or think of you?
... My one consolation is that you will know how steadfast I am ... I
have nothing more to hope for but death. Life is a torment to me, since
I may no longer dedicate it to you ... You married! I cannot grasp the
thought – it kills me. Never shall I belong to another ... And I had so
hoped soon to be the happiest of women, your wife! Your marriage has
shattered my happiness ... All the same I wish you the greatest joy and
blessing in your marriage. May the woman you have chosen make you
as happy as I had intended to make you and as happy as you deserve to
be. In the midst of your present happiness do not quite forget poor
Eugénie, and be sorry for her fate.

What possessed Napoleon to marry a penniless Creole, six years his
elder and with fading looks? There can be many answers, ranging from
the banal to the pathological. At the simplest level, it can be argued that
Napoleon anchored himself to the ruling élite by this marriage to one of
its leading female icons. Some have gone so far as to say that Barras *forced*
him to marry Josephine as a *quid pro quo* for the supreme command in
Italy. But this view hinges on the mistaken idea that Napoleon had no
relationship with Barras before Josephine; in fact he was a firm favourite
long before Rose de Beauharnais ever featured in his life.

An alternative view is that Napoleon was naïve, thought Josephine was
of higher rank than she was, and imagined that he had married into the
aristocracy. It is true that in a letter to Joseph he described the
Chaumière circle as 'the most distinguished society in Paris', and if we
incline to this view Napoleon would emerge as a victim of snobbery,
imagining that he now had entrée into royalist and aristocratic circles.
Marmont thought this was the explanation and wrote in his memoirs:
'Napoleon almost certainly believed at the time that he had taken a
greater step upwards than ever he felt when he married the daughter of
the Caesars.'

But all this makes the match a marriage of convenience and it was
never that. Napoleon himself, aware that he had lost his head over
Josephine, tried to rewrite this episode on St Helena, as he rewrote all the
others in his life, and insinuated that reason of state was involved.
Perhaps he hated himself for the one spontaneous, unmeditated action of
his life. What decisively refutes the idea of marriage of convenience is
Napoleon's sexual besottedness with Josephine, for which the evidence is
overwhelming. 'She had the prettiest little cunt in the world, the Trois
Islets of Martinique were there,' is one of many expressions of his
appreciation of her physical charms. Besides, Josephine was exactly the

kind of woman who was likely to appeal to a man who was sexually insecure and misogynistic. She was unchallenging, featherbrained, feminine in all the traditional ways. She was luxury-loving, obsessed with clothes and make-up, hopeless with money; she spoke in a little girl voice, lied transparently and could burst into tears apparently at will. Napoleon's own judgement is interesting: 'She was a woman to her finger-tips. I really did love her but I had no respect for her.'

But what is often overlooked or forgotten by students of this ill-matched pair and analysts of this improbable marriage is that after Vendémiaire Napoleon could have had almost any woman in Paris. So why this one? Why a woman of mediocre looks and fading beauty? Some have speculated that Napoleon was sexually inexperienced and needed the reassurance of an older woman well versed in the arts of love. His own words are often quoted: 'I was not insensible to women's charms but I had hardly been spoiled by them. I was shy with them. Madame Bonaparte was the first to give me confidence.' That could be construed as referring to lack of sexual confidence, but it suggests more strongly a man in need of maternal feelings and training in *social* graces and savoir-faire. It is by no means so clear that Napoleon was the sexual novice this theory requires him to be.

The Bonaparte clan were united in their dislike of Josephine. Lucien referred to her contemptuously as an 'ageing Creole', and Letizia in particular, who had wanted her son to marry Désirée, always hated Josephine. The conventional view is that Letizia was enraged that Josephine was of higher rank than she, that she had a chip on her shoulder accordingly, and that her charming letter of friendship to her daughter-in-law (dictated, some say, by Napoleon himself) masked a vengeful fury. The shrewdest critics have seen that Letizia is important to this story in a quite different sense. Dorothy Carrington wrote: 'Was his marriage to Josephine, who combined all the traits of character Letizia deplored, his masterpiece against the adored mother who had deceived him?'

There are two aspects of Josephine that strike observers who have only the most cursory knowledge of her: she was an older woman, and she was habitually unfaithful. If we accept that Napoleon had a 'complex' about Letizia, then it is interesting to note what C. G. Jung has to say about the 'mother complex' in general. 'If a young man loves a woman who could almost be his mother, then it always has to do with a mother complex. Such a union is sometimes quite fruitful for many years, particularly in the case of artistic persons who have not fully matured. The woman in such a case is helped by an almost biological instinct. She is hatching eggs. The man as the son-lover benefits by the partially sexual, partially mother interest of the woman. Thus such a relationship can be satisfactory in every respect for an indefinite period, but the advancing years would certainly put a definite limit to it as it is not quite natural. It may even be that an artistic nature becomes so adult that the need of becoming a father and a grown-up man in general begins to prevail against the original son-attitude. When that is the case the relationship is overdue.'

Jung's formulation by no means covers all aspects of the Napoleon-Josephine relationship. Josephine was only six years older than her husband, he himself, though a genius, was scarcely an 'artistic person', and it was not really the 'maturing' of Napoleon that brought the relationship to an end. But Jung does convey the important insight that a relationship with a significantly older woman may show that the mother is lurking in the male unconscious. Freud suggested that Napoleon's 'complex' about Joseph was why he insisted on renaming Rose de Beauharnais Josephine. But it seems more plausible to assume that the deep dynamic in this case focused on Napoleon's unconscious feelings about Letizia rather than Joseph.

It has sometimes been suggested that Napoleon was so naïve about Josephine that he knew nothing of her chequered past and was thus astonished when he was first cuckolded. Theories about Napoleon's alleged 'naïveté' seldom convince; he was always exceptionally well informed and as soon as he had a whiff of power employed a host of spies and secret agents. Of course Napoleon reacted with anger to slights to his pride and honour caused by his wife's infidelity, but at the unconscious level it was what he expected. His ambivalent emotions about Letizia, and his love for his mother alongside the certainty that she had been unfaithful to his father, could coexist without conflict in the unconscious, but at the conscious level had to be displaced on to other women. Hence his contemptuous and discourteous behaviour later when he had a court of his own. But most of all, he needed to find a woman who was at once entirely dissimilar to Letizia yet at root the same kind of female.

In taking an older and promiscuous woman as his wife, Napoleon showed himself to be in thrall to a peculiar mother-complex. His mother, the object of his unintegrated emotion, was also someone he loved but did not respect, and the principal reason was her infidelity. This is undoubtedly the most profound reason why he opted for Josephine rather than Désirée. As a young girl who was almost religiously faithful to him during his long absence in Paris, Désirée did not have the attributes required. Josephine, the unfaithful 'mother', on the other hand, satisfied all the deep drives in the Napoleonic unconscious.

CHAPTER SEVEN

The grand strategy for the 1796 campaign against Austria was the brainchild of Lazare Carnot, though he drew heavily on the thinking of others, Napoleon not least. Including Kellermann's 20,000-strong Army of the Alps and a reserve of 15,000 stationed in Provence and the Var, France could put 240,000 men into the field. The French offensive was three-pronged: 70,000 troops, then in the Lower Rhine under Jourdan's command, would strike along the Main valley, invest the fortress of Mainz and then advance into Franconia; another 70,000 under Moreau would advance into Swabia and the Danube valley; and the third, under Napoleon, would engage the Austrians in the Po valley. The Italian campaign was designed as a sideshow, but if it proved unexpectedly successful, there was provision in Carnot's plan for an advance up the Adige valley to Trent and the Tyrol, there to link with Moreau for the *coup de grâce*.

Two days after his wedding Napoleon left Paris with Junot and arrived in Marseilles on the night of 20–21 March. Along the road they had discussed Carnot's threefold intention in the great campaign against Austria: to divert growing unrest at home with a foreign adventure; to consolidate the Revolution and export its principles; and, most importantly, to stop the drain on the French treasury by getting the nation's armies to live off the soil or by plunder and thus in effect exporting France's military expenses. Napoleon has often been censured for turning the Italian campaign into a gigantic quest for booty, but this possibility was already implicit in the Directory's grand strategy.

At Marseilles he visited his mother. She told him that the sixteen-year-old beauty, Pauline Bonaparte, was now beyond parental control and had a magnetic effect on men. Napoleon's idea of using Stanislas Fréron as his agent to tidy up loose ends in the south, principally the Désirée business, had backfired disastrously. Fréron, a notorious rake with syphilis, had been smitten with the luscious Pauline, and she with him. If Napoleon had not already known of the forty-year-old's unsavoury past, Josephine would have enlightened him. It was bad enough that the man was unreliable: he was a former Robespierre acolyte who had trimmed successfully to emerge from Thermidor as a Barras protégé. But it was intolerable that he might infect Pauline with venereal disease, and that she could end up married to the most promiscuous man in Paris. Just at the moment Napoleon lacked the power to cross Barras over Fréron, so he advised Letizia to stall and await further instructions.

On 24 March he was at Toulon, where he met and greatly impressed Denis Décrès, later to be his Minister of Marine. Next day he was at Antibes, where he conferred with Louis Berthier, his forty-three-year-old chief of staff. Berthier, a veteran of the American War of Independence and the Vendée, was a man of great energy and lucid mind; he was a brilliant organizer and a master of the terse dispatch. Napoleon sensed his quality straight away. Never one to judge men, at least, by external appearances, he ignored Berthier's physical ugliness, his gaucherie, his stammering and his compulsive nail biting, and concentrated on his great administrative talents – enhanced, in Napoleon's eyes, by Berthier's lack of ambition for a field command.

Yet the supreme test of Napoleon's ability to overawe rivals and bend them to his will came in Nice on 27 March, when he met his three principal generals: Sérurier, Augereau and Masséna. Sérurier was a tall man with a scar on his lip, a fifty-three-year-old martinet who had fought in the Seven Years War and in Corsica in 1770. Although he was the son of a molecatcher at the royal stud at Laön, he had the demeanour of an aristocrat and it was said that, after the Revolution he went in danger of his life every time he entered a new army camp, such was his foppish, oligarchic air. He had less energy than Berthier or Augereau, but was a man of greater integrity.

The thirty-eight-year-old Augereau, who had begun life in the Parisian gutters, was the son of a stonemason and had had a chequered career. A devotee of the first real communist, Gracchus Babeuf, who was in this very year executed by the Directory, Augereau was a genuine man of mystery. He had deserted from the French Army at seventeen, and then led an intinerant life as an adventurer. According to his own (either unreliable or unverifiable) account he had at various times sold watches in Constantinople, given dancing lessons, served in the Russian army and eloped with a Greek girl to Lisbon. The French Revolution was the making of him. He commanded the 'German Legion' in the Vendée and then won a spectacular victory against the Spanish with the Army of the Pyrenees in 1795. A man of little education and indifferent intellect, Augereau was a great fighting general, with a tendency to melancholia, as he would brood depressively the evening after a battle, regardless of whether he had won or lost. Popular with his troops, tall, talkative, foul-mouthed, with a great hooked nose, Augereau was memorably described by Desaix as follows: 'Fine, big man; handsome face, big nose, has served in many countries, a soldier with few equals, always bragging.'

André Masséna, aged thirty-eight, was the greatest general of the three and would prove to have military talents of a high order. Dark, thin and taciturn, a dedicated hedonist and womaniser, Masséna started life as a cabin boy and had been a non-commissioned officer and smuggler. He looked like an eagle and was said to have an eagle's eye for terrain, but the quality Napoleon most prized in him was his indefatigable energy. Dauntless, stubborn, imperturbable, he seemed to spend all his days and nights on horseback. Nothing ever made him feel discouraged: if he was defeated heavily, he went jauntily to work next day as if he was the victor.

Sérurier, Augereau and Masséna were tough characters in anyone's book, and most twenty-six-year-olds would have quailed at the prospect of asserting superiority over them. Additionally, they were disposed to be contemptuous of the newcomer, thinking him merely one of Barras's favourites and a boy general. Masséna and Augereau both thought they should have had the command themselves and poured scorn on Napoleon's ideas for the Italian campaign: Masséna said that only a professional intriguer could have come up with such a plan, while the blunt-speaking Augereau used the epithet 'imbecile'.

By the end of the meeting Napoleon had won all three men round. Legend has perverted the reality of what took place and credited Bonaparte with Svengali-like powers, but it is certain that the trio of generals thenceforth looked on him with new respect. Masséna remarked that when Napoleon put on his general's hat he seemed to have grown two feet, while Augereau allegedly remarked: 'that little bugger really frightened me!' What is certain is that Napoleon tried to calm their minds over the drawbacks in Carnot's strategy. It did not take outstanding insight to see that the three main French armies were operating too far away from each other and that, if any of the offensives flagged, the Austrians would simply transfer troops from one front to another. The Directory had not appointed a supreme commander to coordinate the movements of all three armies, assuming, absurdly, that Jourdan, Moreau and Bonaparte would all cooperate willingly and without rivalry, and had compounded their error by seeming to assume that the Alps, which lay between the Army of Italy and the other two, was simply a paper obstacle.

At his headquarters Napoleon found 37,000 ill-fed, unpaid and demoralized troops, with which he was supposed to clear 52,000 Austrians out of half a dozen mountain passes between Nice and Genoa. He was fortunate to have at his side his old Corsican friend Saliceti, who raised a loan in Genoa to see to the Army's most pressing supply problems. Even so, Napoleon reported to the Directory on 28 March: 'One battalion has mutinied on the ground that it had neither boots nor pay,' and a week later wrote again: 'The army is in frightening penury . . . Misery has led to indiscipline, and without discipline there can be no victory.' The famous proclamation Napoleon is said to have made to his troops at this time is apocryphal. It was written in St Helena and represents the Aristotelian spirit of what might have been said and even what ought to have been said. It also shows Napoleon as a master of propaganda and already sedulously at work on his own legend:

> Soldiers, you are naked, ill-fed; though the Government owes you much, it can give you nothing. Your patience, the courage you have shown amidst these rocks, are admirable; but they procure you no glory, no fame shines upon you. I want to lead you into the most fertile plains in the world. Rich provinces, great cities will lie in your power; you will find there honour, glory and riches. Soldiers of the Army of Italy, will you lack courage or steadfastness?

Napoleon saw at once that his best chance of breaking into Italy was by separating the Austrians from their allies the Piedmontese. His intelligence sources told him there was bad blood between the two commanders, the allies were scattered in three different locations, and the Austrian commander, Beaulieu, thought the main French blow would fall on the Riviera coast. Napoleon therefore decided to engage the Austrian right in the mountains and take out the war-weary Piedmontese, ensuring himself local superiority in numbers at all times. On 12 April he won his first victory, at Montenotte, employing Masséna adroitly and using a combination of clouds of skirmishers with charges from battalion columns, which inflicted 3,000 casualties on the enemy. Further successful actions followed at Millesimo (13 April) against the Sards and Dego against the Austrians (14 April). Having split the allies, Napoleon then turned to deal with the Piedmontese and broke them in the three battles of San Michele, Ceva and Mondovi (19–23 April). On 23 April Colli, the Piedmontese commander, requested an armistice. Within ten days Napoleon was in control of the key mountain passes and had destroyed a superior enemy force piecemeal by rapidity of movement.

Although 'Hannibal merely crossed the Alps, we turned their flanks' is probably another St Helena accretion, there can be no doubting Napoleon's genuine euphoria at the time. To the Directory he sent back glowing letters with Joseph, who had been acting as his unofficial aide. After the armistice of Cherasco on 28 April gave him control of the mountain fortresses and the lines of communication into Lombardy, he wrote: 'Tomorrow I shall march against Beaulieu, force him to cross the Po, cross myself immediately after and seize the whole of Lombardy: within a month I hope to be on the mountains of the Tyrol, in touch with the Army of the Rhine, and to carry the war in concert into Bavaria.' To his soldiers, ever mindful of propaganda advantages, he made a proclamation (genuine, this time), which exaggerated his achievements in typical manner: 'Soldiers! In fifteen days you have gained six victories, taken twenty-one colours and 55 pieces of artillery, seized several fortresses and conquered the richest parts of Piedmont. You have taken 15,000 prisoners and killed and wounded more than 10,000.'

At this stage realism and propaganda still vied for supremacy. On 24 April he wrote to the Directory: 'The hungry soldiers are committing excesses that make one blush to be human. The capture of Ceva and Mondovi may give us the means to put this right, and I am going to make some terrible examples. I will restore order or I will give up the command of these brigands.' Yet to Barras personally he wrote on the previous day a sycophantic letter boasting about the six battles he had already won and the twenty-one captured enemy standards Joseph was bringing back to Paris.

Napoleon's next task was to prevent the Austrians withdrawing to the comparative safety of the far bank of the Po. The French armies debouched from the mountains and entered the plains of Lombardy. The Austrians dug in and waited for them on the left bank of the Po near Pavia. Again employing the war of rapid movement, he took Serurier and Masséna on a sixty-mile route march which ended with their divisions making a classic river crossing at Piacenza in sight of the enemy. The hero of the hour, who crossed with 900 men and established a bridgehead on the far bank, was Jean Lannes, a dashing twenty-six-year-old colonel whom Napoleon had first noticed at Dego.

Napoleon now advanced on Milan, outflanking Beaulieu's main army. Barring the route to Milan was a 12,000-strong Austrian army at Lodi, on the river Adda. Trying to ford the swiftly-flowing river would be costly, so Napoleon opted for an assault on the bridge at Lodi, heavily defended by the Austrians. The bridge, 200 yards long and twelve feet wide, forced attacking troops into a bottlenecked killing ground, and Napoleon's generals advised him that to attack artillery along such a narrow front was suicide. But Napoleon was determined to take the bridge by storm. First, he worked on the feelings of his 4,000 assault troops, alternately cajoling them and telling them that they lacked the courage for the planned enterprise. Then he sent his cavalry on a wide sweep in search of a ford; they were to cross and fall on the Austrians from the rear.

At 6 p.m. on 10 May Napoleon released his assault force of Frenchmen and Savoyards on to the bridge. Predictably they took terrible casualties from the massed Austrian guns. Seeing their men falter, Lannes and Masséna led an élite squad of grenadiers on another attack across the bridge. Fifty yards from the other side, they dived into the river to avoid point-blank fire. In response the Austrians unleashed their cavalry, which drove the élite squad back into the water. Just when all appeared lost, the devious circling French cavalry, which had taken an unconscionable time to find a suitable ford, swept in on the Austrian flank. Once it had silenced the big guns, Napoleon's troops streamed across the long line of planks. As dusk fell, the Austrians broke and ran, leaving behind all sixteen guns, 335 casualties and 1,700 prisoners. But the French had paid dearly for the victory and left two hundred dead on the bridge and in the river.

Even though he had not been able to vanquish Beaulieu decisively – a fact disguised and obfuscated by Bonapartist mystique and triumphalism – Lodi was a psychological breakthrough for Napoleon. To have pulled off such a feat of arms gave him confidence in his star. He wrote later: 'It was only on the evening of Lodi that I believed myself a superior man, and that the ambition came to me of executing the great things which had so far been occupying my thoughts only as a fantastic dream . . . After Lodi I no longer saw myself as a mere general, but as a man called upon to influence the destiny of a people. The idea occurred to me that I could well become a decisive actor on our political scene.' His troops too believed, after seven clear victories, that they were led by an ever-victorious general. It was now that the nickname of the 'little corporal' was first bestowed. Apparently one of his units decided to see how long he would take to become a 'real' general, starting from the ranks and getting a promotion after each victory. But the later image of Napoleon leading the first wave of attackers over the bridge is the stuff of legend: Napoleon did not lack personal courage, but on this occasion he was supervising his artillery.

Napoleon entered Milan in triumph on 15 May. Marmont remembered him saying: 'Well, Marmont, what do you think they'll say in Paris? Will this be enough for them? They've seen nothing yet. In our time nobody has had a grander conception than mine, and it's my example that must point the way.' But what the Directory said in Paris, albeit in private, was that Napoleon, after seven victories, had grown too powerful. They informed him that the Italian command would be split: Kellermann would command in Lombardy while he (Bonaparte) was to march south to secure Genoa, Leghorn, Rome and Naples. Napoleon replied with a thinly veiled threat of resignation, employing some masterly irony: 'Kellermann will command the army as well as I, for no one is more convinced than I am that the victories are due to the courage and audacity of the men; but I believe that to unite Kellermann and myself in Italy is to lose all. I cannot serve willingly with a man who believes himself to be the first general in Europe; and, besides, I believe that one bad general is better than two good ones. War, like government, is a matter of tact.' The Directory backed down and informed him there was no longer any question of dividing the command. But, they added, he should not think of moving north into the Tyrol in the foreseeable future; first he had to put the Pope in his place – he had to 'cause the tiara of the self-styled head of the Universal Church to totter'.

The week Napoleon spent in Milan was notable for the Janus face he displayed. On the one hand, he held himself out as an apostle of Italian unification; on the other, he presided over the most barefaced and systematic looting seen in Lombardy since the sixteenth century. He began by replacing the old aristocratic government with a new régime of bourgeois liberals. The Dukes of Parma and Modena immediately sued for peace, which Napoleon granted on payment of a hefty tax. On 17 May, influenced by the enthusiastic reception he had received in Milan, he wrote to the Directory to urge the creation of a northern Italian republic, and followed this with a declaration to the people of Milan that he would give them liberty. In later utterances Napoleon argued that Italy had to go through the crucible of war before becoming a united nation. 'As those skilful founders, who have to transform several guns of small calibre into one 48-pounder, first throw them into the furnace, in order to decompose them, and to reduce them to a state of fusion; so the small states had been united to Austria or France in order to reduce them to an elementary state, to get rid of their recollections and pretensions, that they might be prepared for the moment of casting.'

Yet this apparent idealism was belied by Napoleon's ruthless financial exactions and expropriations. The terrible shape of things to come was evident even before the French army debouched from the mountains on to the Lombardy plain. At Mondovi Bonaparte commandeered 8,000 rations of fresh meat and 4,000 bottles of wine, and in Acqui he requisitioned all the boots in town at a knockdown price. But it was in Milan that his army really cut loose. An orgy of looting took place, with French generals sending houseloads of art treasures back to Paris in wagons. Napoleon's apologists claim that he was merely carrying out the wishes of a corrupt and venal Directory, but this is not the picture that emerges from his correspondence. On 9 May, *before Lodi*, Napoleon wrote to the Directory as follows: 'I repeat my request for a few reputable artists to take charge of choosing and transporting all the beautiful things we shall see fit to send to Paris.'

In Milan Napoleon soon lost his initial popularity when he levied two million livres in hard cash to pay off the accumulated back pay of the Army. His prestige with the rank and file shot up, since this was the first time since 1793 that the army had been paid in cash: usually, the perennial arrears of pay were made good in useless *assignats*. All this might have been justified as 'living off the land' but Napoleon went further by extracting a surplus for the Directory's coffers from Milan, Parma, Modena and the other cities of the Lombardy plain. On 22 May he informed the Directorate that 8 million francs in gold and silver awaited their disposal in Genoa, and by July the tally of funds mulcted for the Directory amounted to sixty million francs. One obvious result was a change in the balance of power. Napoleon now had the whip hand and, if the Directory wanted to survive, its five members had to keep on the right side of their most successful general. The political commissars, even in their new diluted manifestation as *commissaires aux armées* were a busted flush and would be suppressed altogether by the end of 1796.

If Napoleon the public figure was now almost in the position of a victorious legionary commander whose exploits terrified the emperor at Rome, the private man was suffering grievously. For 127 days, from 8 March until his reunion with her on 13 July, he wrote to Josephine at least once a day. The letters were fervent, poignant, despairing, tender, melancholy, sometimes even prolix and incoherent, full of sexual longing and frustration. On 30 March, before any of his great military successes, he wrote: 'In the middle of all my business and at the head of my troops, I think of nothing but my adorable Josephine who is alone in my heart.' On 23 April, after his ten-day lightning campaign, he wrote: 'Come quickly! . . . You are going to come, aren't you? You're going to be here, beside me, in my heart, in my arms, kissing my heart.' Another letter from the same period shows clearly the source of his anxiety: Josephine did not write to him, and it was clear that she had no intention of joining him. 'Ah! this evening if I do not get a letter from you, I shall be desperate. Think of me, or tell me with contempt that you do not love me, and then perhaps I shall find some peace of mind.'

To get Josephine to come down to Italy, and find out what was detaining her, Napoleon sent back three important envoys. First was Joseph, despatched on 24 April with letters for the Directory and with a letter of introduction for Josephine. Joseph and his female namesake met but did not get on; the elder Bonaparte was no more impressed by the 'fading Creole' than Lucien had been. Then on 25 April Napoleon sent the faithful Junot to Paris with captured standards, instructing him to take the longer route to Paris via the Riviera; he bore an explicit command to Josephine to join her husband. Finally, on 26 April he sent Murat via Piedmont and the Mont-Cenis with letters for Carnot and Barras and a detailed itinerary for Josephine to follow on her travel south.

Both men reached Paris on 6 May, but Murat was first at the rue Chantereine. Napoleon's letter proved to be one of his wilder screeds: '. . . A kiss on your lips and on your heart . . . There's no one else, no one but me, is there? . . . And another on your breast. Lucky Murat! . . . little hand!' A few hours later Junot arrived, with another besotted message: 'You must return with Junot, do you hear, my adorable one, he will see you, he will breathe the air of your shrine. Perhaps you will even allow him the unique favour of a kiss on your cheek . . . A kiss on your heart, and then another a little lower, much *much lower*.' The last two words had been so emphatically underlined that the pen sliced through the paper.

Josephine had no intention of going to Italy. Soon after Napoleon left, she took a new lover, named Hippolyte Charles. A lieutenant of Hussars but only 5'2" tall, Charles was a noted gambler, rake and man-about-town, part of a hard-drinking, loose-living Army set. From Josephine's point of view he had two valuable assets: he could make her laugh, as Napoleon never could, and he was an accomplished lover who took his time and was able to bring her to climax.

Josephine bluntly told Junot she could not leave Paris, so he remained in Paris awaiting further orders. Her way with Murat was more subtle. Sensing that he was attracted to her, she invited him to a champagne breakfast, then spent the day with him on the Champs-Élysées, lunching and dining. Murat later boasted he had bedded her and provided many circumstantial details in the officers' mess. Josephine's biographers usually affect to doubt this on the grounds of her romance with

Hippolyte Charles, but since she was to all intents and purposes a nymphomaniac, Murat's version is not inherently implausible. At all events she prevailed on Murat sufficiently that he sent a letter to Napoleon, saying she could not travel as she was pregnant! Murat was never wholly trusted by Napoleon once he learned the truth of this unsavoury episode.

Meanwhile the ardent letters from Napoleon flooded in. Most of the time Josephine did not even bother to open them. As far as she was concerned, she enjoyed the social advantages of being General Bonaparte's wife but, in her own mind at least, the liaison was a pure marriage of convenience. Lovers of dramatic irony may relish the following letter which arrived while the affair with Charles was at its height. 'You know very well I could never bear your taking a lover – much less seriously suggest one to you . . . A thousand kisses upon your eyes, your lips, your tongue, your cunt.' Josephine took the correspondence as an elaborate charade. The playwright Antoine Arnault remembered her reading from one of Napoleon's letters which was full of jealous suspicion and ended: 'If it were true, fear Othello's dagger!' Josephine simply laughed and said in her inimitable Creole accent: *'Qu'il est drôle, Bonaparte!'* ('He's so amusing.')

Napoleon stayed in Milan until 21 May, waiting for the peace with Piedmont to be confirmed. But no sooner did he move east once more against Beaulieu than Milan and Pavia rose in revolt. This was the worst possible news, as it seemed to mean that every time Napoleon conquered a territory in Italy, he would have to detach part of his army to hold it in subjection. A stern lesson was called for. He invested Pavia and bloodily retook the town, giving it over to sanguinary plunder by his troops as punishment. His first draconian instinct – to put to death the entire 300-strong garrison – was overcome only in favour of savage looting *in terrorem*. After dealing with Pavia Napoleon won another victory – at Borghetto – on 30 May, which involved his setting foot on the territories of the Venetian Republic. But the message of Pavia had got though to the burghers of Milan. When Napoleon turned back to besiege the city, the Milanese sent envoys at once to tender their submission.

Napoleon next proceeded to the siege of Mantua, which opened on 4 June. Just before returning to Milan, Napoleon was at the village of Vallejo and was nearly taken prisoner by an Austrian scouting party (1 June); he had to bolt over several garden walls wearing only one boot. This taught Napoleon the lesson that he needed a bodyguard, and from this incident date 'the Guides' – an élite corps or praetorian guard later to be greatly expanded in numbers to form the Imperial Guard. But at least by the beginning of June he could tell himself that he controlled the entire Lombardy plain except the fortress of Mantua.

Returning to Milan on 7 June, he was bitterly disappointed not to find Josephine waiting for him. Instead, there was a 'scrap of a letter' in which she claimed she was ill, with three doctors in attendance. In despair he wrote to her that a thousand daggers were tearing at his heart. 'My emotions are never moderate and since the moment I read that letter I have been in an indescribable state . . . the ardent love which fills me has perhaps unbalanced my mind.' To Joseph he wrote: 'You know that Josephine is the first woman I have ever adored . . . I love her to distraction and I cannot remain any longer without her.' By now he had heard from Murat and did not like what he heard. Always a superstitious man, Napoleon was deeply troubled by the apparent coincidence that on the very day Murat arrived in Paris, the glass broke on the miniature of Josephine he carried on his person. According to Marmont, he went pale when the glass broke and said: 'Marmont, either my wife is very ill or she is unfaithful.'

Receiving no further word from Josephine and unable to work out what was detaining her in Paris, Napoleon decided to put his private woes before the Directory. On 11 June he wrote to Barras: 'I hate all women. I am in despair. My wife has not arrived, she must be detained by some lover in Paris.' Four days later he wrote to Josephine: 'Without appetite or sleep, without interest or friendship, no thought for glory or Fatherland, just you. The rest of the world has no more meaning for me than if it had been annihilated.' The hatred for women he acknowledged to Barras found expression in one of his few peevish letters to Josephine, in which he accused her of loving everyone more than her husband, including the dog Fortuné; in the latter assessment of the featherheaded Josephine's cynophilia he was certainly correct.

Napoleon followed his broadside to Barras by an explicit statement to Josephine that, since she was ill, he would return to Paris within five days. Becoming more and more fearful that the distraught Napoleon might really return to Paris to fetch his wife himself, bringing the ever-victorious army with him, possibly for a final settling of political accounts, the five men of the Directory exerted maximum pressure on Josephine to join her husband. Carnot concocted a ludicrous letter, claiming that the Directory had kept Josephine in Paris, lest her presence distract Bonaparte from his victories but that, now he held Milan, there could be no further objection. There is an element of farce in the way the Directory colluded with Josephine to conceal her infidelity. The dalliances of women have often threatened to shake régimes and dynasties but surely seldom in such an indirect, convoluted and comical way as this.

According to contemporary witnesses, the Directors virtually had to bundle a sobbing Josephine on to the Milan-bound carriage. Her friend Antoine Arnault noted: 'She wept as though she were going to a torture chamber instead of Italy to reign as a sovereign.' A bizarre six-carriage convoy wound its way south. In the first of them sat Josephine with the dreaded pug Fortuné, together with Junot, Joseph and Hippolyte Charles. Joseph had spent his time in Paris in the corridors of power, making new friends among the powerful, lobbying for an ambassadorship and extending his impressive portfolio of real estate investments in the environs of Paris. Charles was returning to his post as aide-de-camp to Colonel Victor Emmanuel Leclerc, another of Bonaparte's Toulon 'finds', who repaid Napoleon's patronage by seducing the beautiful Pauline.

Josephine went out of her way to make the journey south as protracted as possible. At night she and Charles would contrive to end up in the same bedroom. Joseph, egomaniacal as ever, and reportedly suffering from gonorrhea after an encounter in Paris, worked on a new novel. Only the faithful Junot properly consulted Napoleon's interests but Josephine solved that problem by flirting outrageously with him, often in front of Charles, to the cynical amusement of that most depraved Hussar. After an eighteen-day journey, during which she and Charles had made love several times each day, Josephine and entourage arrived in Milan early in July, to Napoleon's great relief. His letters to and about his wife had previously been full of suicidal despair.

In Milan Napoleon was installed in the glittering and gorgeous Palazzo Serbelloni. For forty-eight hours he slaked the pent-up passions of the past four months. Junot told him about the liaison with Charles and was surprised to find that his chief, instead of having Charles shot on the spot, allowed him to depart for Brescia on his official duties. Only later did he cashier him and send him packing back to Paris. Here is yet one more piece of circumstantial evidence that, consciously or unconsciously, Napoleon actually liked the fact that Josephine was habitually unfaithful; what he hated was overt evidence of the fact, which would bring him into ridicule and contempt as a cuckolded husband.

Having set his mind at rest about Josephine, Napoleon could now turn to urgent military matters. On paper his position was good, since only the fortress of Mantua held out against him, but his situation was fraught with potential peril. Already the Austrians were switching reinforcements to the Austrian front to start a counter offensive, and meanwhile French lines of communication were too long, with hostile and disgruntled cities on their flanks. Napoleon saw clearly enough that his chief problem was going to be that of taking Mantua while the Austrians were trying to relieve it, even while diverting significant parts of his own army to keep control of conquered territory. He became impatient when no word was received from Moreau and Jourdan on the other fronts. Unless they took the offensive soon, Austria could pour troops into Italy. On 8 June he had written testily to General Henri Clarke in the Topographical Bureau in Paris: 'I see only one way of avoiding being beaten in the autumn: that is to arrange matters so that we are not obliged to march into the south of Italy. According to all the information reaching us, the Emperor is sending many troops to his Italian army. We wait impatiently for news from the Rhine.'

Under pressure from the Directory to lay hands on the wealth of Florence, Rome and Naples, Napoleon decided to risk a quick southern expedition before bringing the siege of Mantua to a conclusion. He sent two divisions south to occupy Bologna, Ferrara and Tuscany. Augereau defeated the forces of the Papacy near Bologna, and negotiations opened with Pius VI. Napoleon played a double game, writing fiery philippics about the 'infamy of priestcraft' to the Directory, while writing secretly to Cardinal Mattei about his great reverence for the Holy Father. The Pope soon signed an armistice, conceding the occupation of Ancona and agreeing to pay a huge indemnity, including art treasures to be taken from the Vatican galleries. Faced with this defection, Tuscany surrendered, Florence and Ferrara opened their gates, and the French occupied Leghorn (29 June), thus denying the Royal Navy a valuable base.

Napoleon's life after Josephine's arrival was schizoid, divided as it was between quickly snatched meetings with his wife in Milan and urgent rushing to a political or military flashpoint. Just before she arrived he had visited Tortono, Piacenza, Parma, Reggio and Modena. Later he was in Bologna and was lionized by the Grand Duke in Florence. As far as possible he left the day-to-day siege of Mantua to Sérurier. In Milan he moved his military headquarters from the Palazzo Serbelloni to the Villa Crivelli at Mombello outside the city, where it was said that a vast throng of army officers, administrators, contractors and lobbyists could always be found in a huge marquee he had set up in the gardens. He never really cared for the Serbelloni Palace but spent his time with Josephine there. Under her influence he began to cut a quasi-imperial dash, dining in public or parading with an escort of three hundred red-uniformed lancers.

Josephine relished the imperial style, but at first the Milanese burghers found her hard to take and the manners of her entourage outrageous; particular offence was given by the marchesa Visconti, who doubled as Josephine's lady-in-waiting and Berthier's mistress. But soon it became chic to ape the easy-going hedonism of the Josephine circle. Even as the new Milanese élite followed her into sensualism, they deluged her with presents on the understanding that she would get her husband to stop the looting.

When he was away from Milan, Napoleon chafed at the separations. The love letters recommenced and were just as impassioned as before. From Lake Garda, where he was conferring with Sérurier, he wrote on 18 July: 'I have been in Virgil's village, by the lake side, in the silver light of the moon and not a single second without thinking of Josephine.' That he was suspicious of her is clear from the many exhortations to marital fidelity and his (probably deliberately exaggerated) disgust for the illicit pleasures of the flesh. When his officers consorted with prostitutes and caught venereal disease, he wrote: 'Good God, what women! What morals. Tell my brother Joseph to be faithful to his Julie.'

At the end of July there was a reunion in Brescia. Napoleon wrote that 'the tenderest of lovers awaits you.' Since this was where Hippolyte Charles was based, the presumption must be that Josephine agreed to meet Napoleon there rather than elsewhere because of the presence of the rake-Hussar. But Napoleon's planned idyll was cut short by the sudden advance of a new Austrian army down the Brenner pass. He sent Josephine back to Milan with Junot and the dragoons by a circuitous route. When Josephine heard of Napoleon's success against this new army, which made it safe to return to Brescia, she sped back to the city. Napoleon's headquarters was just twenty-five miles away and she found an urgent appeal from him to join him there. Pleading exhaustion, she spent the night with Hippolyte Charles instead. Her biographers have predictably had fun with the dramatic irony about the 'tenderest of lovers' who awaited Josephine in Brescia.

It was 29 July when Napoleon got definite news that an Austrian counter-offensive was under way. From then until February 1797 a titanic struggle took place for the besieged Mantua and the other three fortresses – Peschiera, Verona and Legnago – which formed the famous quadrilateral on the southern tip of Lake Garda, guarding the entrances to the Lombardy plain from the Brenner pass and the Alps. Since Mantua was so bitterly fought over, it has acquired a symbolic importance in the Napoleonic story, but it was not Mantua itself

Napoleon was interested in, but control of the routes to and from the Tyrol.

The new Austrian army was commanded by Count Dagobert Wurmser, who had been detached from the Rhine with 25,000 to reinforce Beaulieu. The combined army of 50,000 men made rendezvous at Trent and marched on Mantua in three columns, the right via Chiesa, the centre converging on Montebaldo between the Adige valley and Lake Garda, and the left through the Adige valley itself. The Austrians scored some early successes, leaving Napoleon temporarily despondent, and took Lonato on 31 July. But Wurmser made the cardinal error of concentrating on the relief of Mantua (whose fall he mistakenly thought imminent) instead of uniting the three wings of his army. This allowed Napoleon to indulge his favourite strategy of the 'centre position', where a numerically inferior army got between two sections of a superior army to defeat them piecemeal. Napoleon threw the enemy out of Lonato with heavy losses on 3 August: three divisions of the Austrian right and part of the centre were forced to surrender. Wurmser then belatedly moved to support his right but was caught at Castiglione (5 August) before his left could come up. In a tough, brutal action, which Napoleon always considered Augereau's finest hour, he punctured the Austrian centre at Castiglione (5 August), while Napoleon routed the left wing. Because of Wurmser's blunders, Napoleon had been able to achieve local superiority of 27,000 against 21,000.

The Lake Garda region had seen a week of hard fighting. Including the 'mopping up' operations until 12 August, the French inflicted 25,000 casualties, and took 15,000 prisoners, nine standards and seventy pieces of cannon. On their own side they lost 5,000 wounded, 600 dead and 1,400 prisoners. On the other hand, Wurmser's advance had forced Napoleon to break off the investment of Mantua, losing 179 guns in the process, including all his heavy artillery. Wurmser could now do little for Mantua. After leaving two fresh brigades in the city, he returned to Trent to lick his wounds. Napoleon resumed the siege but, without the big guns, the blockade was less effective than before. Hearing of the victories, and mistakenly thinking Moreau was achieving similar results on the Rhine, the Directory ordered Napoleon to pursue Wurmser and attempt the link with Moreau which they had previously vetoed.

Napoleon ignored the Directory's orders. Even if he had wanted to collaborate with Moreau, the idea was chimerical as there was no secret code allowing the two commanders to communicate. Besides, his men were exhausted and in need of rest and recreation, and he could scarcely advance to the Brenner pass with Mantua still in his rear. Even more seriously, he could not leave behind an unpacified Italy. The clashes with Wurmser had been politically valuable to him, since at first there were rumours of French defeats, which encouraged Napoleon's enemies within Italy to come out from the woodwork. The pattern of loyalties was now reasonably clear. Milan, Lombardy, Parma, Bologna, Ferrara and Reggio had kept faith with him, but Modena, Cremona, Pavia and the Papal states had thrown off the mask and revealed their pro-Austrian sentiments.

Bearing all this in mind, Napoleon proceeded cautiously. A game of wits developed between him and Wurmser. Napoleon began by leading 33,000 French troops against Wurmser. After a victory at Rovereto, he took Trent on 4 September, but Wurmser outwitted him by heading south for Mantua via the Brenta valley. The object was to force Napoleon back down the Adige valley to meet this new threat to Mantua, but Napoleon proceeded to trump Wurmser's ace. He did not retrace his steps but simply blocked the gorges north of Trent and set off south after the Austrians, taking the same pass Wurmser was using. This was a calculated risk: Napoleon was hoping to live off the land without actually knowing that Wurmser's army had left enough to subsist on. On the other hand, Wurmser could not relieve Mantua, since he would be forced either to turn and give battle or to retreat to the Adriatic.

Napoleon caught up with the Austrians at Bassano on 8 September and inflicted another defeat, ably supported by Augereau on the left and Masséna on the right. To his annoyance, however, Wurmser did not, as expected, veer off towards Trieste and the Adriatic but kept on for Mantua. Beating off his pursuers, he crashed through the besieging perimeter around Mantua on 12 September and entered the city, raising the total strength of the defence to 23,000 men. When the pursuers joined forces with the besiegers heavy fighting took place in the suburbs, following which the Austrians were penned inside the old city. The accession of Wurmser seemed to make the fortress impregnable, but in fact the arrival of so many more mouths to feed placed a terrible burden on Mantua's food supply. By Christmas 1796 the defenders were eating horseflesh and dying at the rate of 150 men a day from malnutrition and disease.

Scarcely had he blocked up Wurmser inside Mantua than bad news came in from the German front. On 24 August Archduke Charles defeated Jourdan. Moreau fell back before the Austrians and by the beginning of October was back on the west bank of the Rhine. Napoleon always thought that Moreau's 1796 campaign in Germany was a textbook illustration of all the errors he himself had avoided in Italy. Moreau had divided his army and left the flanks unprotected, so that with three different corps it was vulnerable to six different flank attacks; moreover, he had left the two great fortresses of Phillippsburg and Mannheim in his rear without blockading them. Bonaparte did not intend to make the same mistake with Mantua. But his position was potentially troublesome. He had to keep the pressure on Mantua while guarding the northern passes against a surprise Austrian attack, and at the same time had to have one eye open for possible internal revolts in Italy – very likely as the Directory's demand for official exactions was compounded by the private looting and pillaging by the troops. And all this at a time when Moreau's retreat meant the Austrians were certain to make a massive effort on the Italian front.

Mid-September saw Napoleon back in Milan and again enjoying Josephine's embraces. Antoine Hamelin, the financier who had accompanied Josephine to Italy, reported that Napoleon could scarcely keep his hands off his wife. He would often caress her passionately and coarsely in the presence of others, embarrassing Hamelin to the point where he would pretend to look out of the window. In her letters to friends in Paris Josephine rarely mentioned her husband except to disparage him or claim that she was bored. In her letters to Barras she used the name of Bonaparte as power play. She missed her children, she hankered for the pleasures of Paris and the power-broking with Barras, and found the limelight in Italy poor consolation.

Napoleon meanwhile played the role of imperial proconsul impressively. His family came to visit him in Mombello – all but Lucien, who still remained aloof. Caroline and Jérôme came to Milan for their school holidays, while the most prominent man from the clan was Fesch, wheeling and dealing in army supplies. Napoleon was mightily displeased with Lucien and actually complained about him to Carnot in August, suggesting he be sent to the front with the Army of the North to end his 'troublemaking'. But the favoured Louis he recommended to Carnot, and the Minister of War was so impressed that he promoted him to captain.

On the political front Napoleon compelled Genoa to accept a French garrison, occupied pro-Austrian Modena and tried to browbeat Venice. A treaty signed with Naples on 10 October nipped in the bud a papal intrigue to put 30,000 Neapolitans into the field against the French. Meanwhile, in the teeth of determined vested interests, he tried to advance his project for a northern Italian republic. He set up three interim 'republics': the Cisalpine, incorporating Milan; the Cispadane linking Modena and Reggio; and the Transpadane, uniting Bologna and

Ferrara. But always his eye was on the Brenner pass, waiting for the Austrian offensive that was bound to come now that Moreau had failed so dismally in Germany.

In November the Austrians began their campaign. Two armies descended on Italy: one, 28,000 strong, was commanded by Joseph Alvinzi and advanced over the Venetian plain through Vicenza towards Verona; the other, under Davidovitch, contained 18,000 troops and debouched in the Adige valley. The strategy was for Alvinzi's army to feint towards Mantua while Davidovitch took Trent. Napoleon's response was to attack Alvinzi while General Vaubois dealt with Davidovitch. Unfortunately Vaubois was badly beaten outside Trent, and was forced to retreat in confusion. Napoleon himself was forced out of Verona and was now in great peril. His forces were dispersed, 14,000 men were on the sick list and he had only 10,000 effectives to meet Alvinzi. If the Alvinzi and Davidovitch armies now combined, and Wurmser sortied from Mantua to link with them, the French position would be hopeless.

This was Napoleon's darkest hour in the entire Italian campaign. His pleas to the Directory for reinforcements had produced just twelve battalions. The War Ministry preferred to waste its resources on the incompetent Moreau in Germany, whose failure had unleashed Alvinzi in the first place. Morale was low in the Army of Italy, with a prevailing feeling that, whatever efforts the men made and however many victories they won, they would still be let down by the Army of the North, so that more and more Austrian reinforcements poured in. It was in this condition, outnumbered and demoralised, that Napoleon and his army sustained a definite defeat at Alvinzi's hands on 12 November, at Caldiero, outside Verona. Next day he wrote despondently to the Directory:

> Perhaps we are on the verge of losing Italy. None of the expected help has arrived. I despair of being able to avoid raising the siege of Mantua, which would have been ours within a week ... In a few days we will make a last effort. If fortune smiles, Mantua will be taken and with it Italy.

Napoleon decided to concentrate on Alvinzi, before the Austrian finally realized the obvious and coordinated effectively with Wurmser and Davidovitch. He opted for a daring flank march to cross the Adige south of Verona and strike Alvinzi in the rear. Unfortunately, he ran into a strong Croat detachment defending the village and bridge of Arcole. The

Croats called up reinforcements, as did the French, and a three-day slugging battle commenced in the marshes, ditches and dykes around the bridge.

Arcola (15–17 November) was Lodi all over again, with the same terrible loss of life from frontal attacks by the French on prepared positions. But this time Napoleon did try to lead his men across the bridge in a do-or-die effort. He describes his efforts as follows:

> I determined to try a last effort in person; I seized a flag, rushed on the bridge, and there planted it; the column I commanded had reached the middle of the bridge, when the flashing fire and the arrival of a division of the enemy frustrated the attack. The grenadiers at the head of the column, finding themselves abandoned by the rear, hesitated, but being hurried away in the flight, they persisted in keeping possession of their general; they seized me by the arm and by my clothes and dragged me along with them amidst the dead, dying and the smoke; I was precipitated in a morass, in which I sank up to the middle, surrounded by the enemy. The grenadiers perceived that their general was in danger; a cry was heard of 'Forward, soldiers, to save the general!' the brave men immediately turned back, ran upon the enemy, drove him beyond the bridge, and I was saved.

Such, at any rate, is the account of Napoleon the mythmaker. Louis claimed that his brother seized the tricolour to lead the charge but fell into a dyke as he ran along the causeway through the marshes towards the bridge and would have drowned had not he (Louis) pulled him out. The version of his aide, the Polish officer Sulkowski, has a more authentic ring of truth; he described Napoleon raising the standard on the bridge and then berating his men for cowardice. This is borne out by Napoleon's report to the Directory on 19 November where he admits, almost in throwaway fashion: 'We had to give up the idea of taking the village by frontal assault.' What happened was that he threw a pontoon bridge across the Adige farther downstream at Albaredo and was then able to attack the Austrian rear over firm ground. Alvinzi then retreated, even though his position in point of supplies and reinforcements was superior to Bonaparte's. Napoleon had been lucky: his nerve held better than Alvinzi's. A good general could have defeated the French decisively while they were bogged down in the marshes. But the upshot was certainly favourable to Napoleon: Alvinzi took 7,000 casualties as against 4,500 for the French, and could no longer link up with Davidovitch.

Napoleon next turned his attention to Davidovitch, who had beaten Vaubois in every encounter. But it was not until 17 November that he began his campaign in earnest. Had he done so two days earlier, Napoleon would again have been severely defeated. As it was, Davidovitch himself came within an ace of being encircled by Napoleon's victorious army. Another three days of French successes followed around Ronco, in which Davidovitch took heavy casualties. Both he and Alvinzi retreated northward; once again the Austrians had failed to relieve Mantua. The French army, which had quit Verona by the Milan gate when Alvinzi approached, re-entered it three days later in triumph by the Venice gate.

Napoleon won the Arcole campaign by the narrowest of margins. He made a grave mistake in getting bogged down around Arcole and should have found the Albaredo crossing much earlier. Alvinzi should have destroyed him in the swamps and Davidovitch should have struck earlier. Louis Bonaparte reported that French morale was near cracking point: 'the troops are no longer the same, and shout loudly for peace.' Even Bonaparte's admirers concede that Arcole was a near-run thing. The great German military theorist Karl von Clausewitz thought that Napoleon won because of superior tactics, greater boldness, mastery of the strategic defensive and, ultimately, because of his superior mind. Yet the crucial factor was his nerve: in an eyeball-to-eyeball confrontation Alvinzi blinked first. Even though Napoleon did not achieve encirclement and decisive victory, his protean abilities depressed the Austrian government, who began to sue for peace at the end of November. But talks broke down over Austrian insistence that they be allowed to reprovision Mantua.

Napoleon wrote to Josephine in euphoria about his latest victory. But two days later his thoughts had turned to erotica. 'How happy I would be if I could be present at your undressing, the little firm white breast, the adorable face, the hair tied up in a scarf *à la Créole*. You know that I never forget the little visits, you know, the little black forest . . . I kiss it a thousand times and wait impatiently for the moment I will be in it.'

Six days later, on 27 November, he arrived at the Serbelloni Palace, eager for another encounter with the 'black forest'. But Josephine had used the pretext of her husband's preoccupation with the military campaign to go to Genoa, where she found solace in the arms of Hippolyte Charles. So devastated was Napoleon to find Josephine absent that he almost fainted with shock on the spot. Later that day, as he got out of his hot bath, he suffered something akin to an epileptic fit. In the nine days he waited for her to return, he sent her three letters that oscillated between rage and lust. 'I left everything to see you, to hold you in my arms . . . The pain I feel is incalculable. I don't want you to change any plans for parties, or to be interested in the happiness of a man who lives only for you . . . I am not worth it . . . When I beg you to equal a love like mine, I am wrong . . . Why should I expect lace to weigh as much as gold? . . . O Josephine, Josephine!'

Josephine finally returned from Genoa on 7 December and three days later gave a grand ball in the Palazzo Serbelloni. But by now Napoleon had political problems to handle. The parting of the ways had finally come with his old friend Saliceti, the Directory's political representative. He and his colleague Garrau looted one church too many and went too far in selling the proceeds openly on the street. When Napoleon clamped down, Saliceti wrote a poisonous letter to Paris, stressing Bonaparte's overweening ambition, his high-handed unilateral conclusion of peace terms with Piedmont in May, the refusal to accept a joint command with Kellermann, and much else. The Directory in some alarm sent General Henri Clarke to Italy as its special representative, charged with making a detailed report on the situation there.

The initial contacts between Napoleon and Clarke were scarcely propitious. Clarke arrived in Milan on 29 November, the day after the bombshell discovery that Josephine was in Genoa. Napoleon was in a foul temper and Clarke reported that he looked emaciated and cadaverous, having picked up fever, probably in the ditches of Arcole. Napoleon remarked snappishly that he was opposed to an armistice with Austria. Clarke snapped back: 'That is the intention of the Directory and there's an end of it.' But three days later, after minute investigation, Clarke changed tack and admitted that Napoleon was right. On 7 December, when Josephine arrived, he was ready to pen the following highly favourable report to Barras and Carnot:

Everyone here regards him as a man of genius. . . . He is feared, loved and respected in Italy. I believe he is attached to the Republic and without any ambition save to retain the reputation he has won . . . General Bonaparte is not without defects . . . Sometimes he is hard, impatient, abrupt or imperious. Often he demands difficult things in too hasty a manner. He has not been respectful enough towards the Government commissioners. When I reproved him for this, he replied that he could not possibly treat otherwise men who were universally scorned for their immorality and incapacity . . . Saliceti has the reputation of being the most shameless rogue in the army and Garrau is inefficient: neither is suitable for the Army of Italy.

Whatever their misgivings, the Directors had to admit that their suspicions of Bonaparte could not be sustained. They promised him full support and gave him virtual *carte blanche* in Italy – psychologically of the greatest importance, for in January 1797 the Austrians exerted themselves for one final effort to wrest the peninsula from the French grasp. As a result of a nationwide recruiting campaign in Austria, Alvinzi was able to put 70,000 troops in the field. It was fortunate for Napoleon that the Directory finally made good their promise to send reinforcements to the Army of Italy. Napoleon reorganized his forces so as to put them in five different divisions (the germ of the later corps system), led by Generals Masséna, Augereau, Rey, Sérurier and Joubert.

The success story of this part of the campaign was Barthélemy Joubert, who had replaced the disgraced Vaubois in November 1796. Tall and thin, with a weak constitution which he strengthened by deliberate hardship, Joubert was intrepid, vigilant and active, the perfect complement to Masséna. It was on these two most of all that Napoleon relied when Alvinzi launched his offensive in January 1797, this time aiming at Rivoli between the river Adige and Lake Garda, with diversionary attacks from Bassano and Padua.

Napoleon waited at Verona to make sure he knew where the weight of the attack would fall. Joubert's division came under heavy pressure at Rivoli, so on 13 January Napoleon decided to ignore the supplementary offensives and concentrate his forces there. He arrived on the plateau of Rivoli at 1 a.m. on 14 January and attacked at dawn, at first running into stiff resistance and once almost being outflanked. But he timed the playing of his trump card perfectly. Masséna completed another of the gruelling night marches that were becoming legendary on this campaign and covered the fifteen miles to the plateau of Rivoli by dawn, marching on a fine moonlit night but sloshing through snow and ice. Alvinzi had nearly succeeded in outflanking Joubert, even though he had thereby separated his infantry from his cavalry. The arrival of Masséna transformed the situation. The Austrians were blasted off the outflanking positions on two hills, then Masséna ruptured the Austrian centre. Next Joubert's men counter-attacked to recover ground already lost. But the Austrians bitterly contested every inch of ground, and Napoleon had several horses shot under him during the day.

At dusk on 14 January Napoleon and Masséna left the scene to intercept another Austrian army trying to relieve Mantua. At Rivoli Joubert won another victory next day. Total Austrian losses on the two days were 14,000 as against 2,180 French casualties. Masséna's division, meanwhile, performing prodigies, marched another thirty miles to catch up with General Provera, who was bearing down on Sérurier and the besiegers of Mantua after giving Augereau the slip. On 16 January the French completely defeated Provera at La Favorita; 7,000 Austrians and 22 guns were captured. Mantua, with its garrison at starvation point, now sued for terms. Bonaparte acclaimed Masséna in front of his troops as 'the child of victory'. In five days 48,000 Austrians on the offensive had been reduced to a rabble of 13,000 fugitives.

Wurmser sent an aide to negotiate with Napoleon and tried to secure decent terms by claiming that there was still a twelve-months supply of food in Mantua. Napoleon, in a typical jape, hovered round the negotiations in disguise. Only when he finally sat down and wrote his terms on the margins of Wurmser's draft proposals did the Austrian envoy realize who he was. Overcome by the generosity of the terms, the envoy then blurted out that they had just three days' food left. However magnanimous Napoleon was in victory, he could not accept that Wurmser was in any sense his equal, and made a point of being absent when the Austrian commander came to sign the surrender terms with Sérurier. Mantua opened its gates to the French on 2 February.

No military obstacle now remained to the invasion of Austria via the Brenner Pass and the Tyrol. Yet the Directory insisted that before Napoleon gave the Austrians the *coup de grâce*, he had to settle accounts with the Pope, who had refused to sign a treaty with France in the belief that Austrian military power would prevail. Early in February Napoleon led his army on a sweep through the papal states, subduing successively Bologna, Faenza, Forli, Rimini, Macerata and Ancona. At Ancona he already evinced clear signs of the 'oriental complex' that was to be so striking a feature of the irrational side of his political projects. On 10 February he wrote to the Directory: 'The port of Ancona is the only Adriatic port of importance, after Venice. From any point of view it is essential for our links with Constantinople. In twenty-four hours one can be in Macedonia.' It does not require brilliant insight to see that it was Macedonia's greatest hero, Alexander the Great, who was on his mind as he wrote.

By the time Napoleon reached Ancona on 10 February, Pius VI was ready to come to terms. By the treaty of Tolentino (19 February 1797), the Pope ceded Bologna, Ferrara and the Romagna and paid an indemnity of thirty millions. Napoleon accepted this, even though atheistic firebrands in the Directory, like Louis La Révellière-Lépeaux, wanted Pius deposed. Napoleon reasoned, and argued thus to the Directory, that the deposition of the Pope would not serve French interests; the Papacy was a stabilizing factor in central Italy and, if it was removed, the power vacuum would be filled by Naples, then an even more embittered enemy of France than Rome was. He was also mindful of the likely consequence that he would ignite a second Vendée or religious war in Italy if he pressed the Pope too hard; the invasion of Austria would then be delayed indefinitely.

Making the obvious contrast between French failures on the Rhine and the spectacular successes achieved by Bonaparte in Italy, the Directory decided to concentrate on the Italian 'soft underbelly' approach to Austria. They reinforced Napoleon to a strength of 80,000 by sending him the divisions of Generals Bernadotte and Delmas, who had previously been operating in Germany.

The arrival of Jean-Baptiste Bernadotte signalled the advent in Napoleon's life of one of the three most bitter and devious enemies he would ever encounter in his career. Bernadotte's fundamental problem was that his proper mark was as a second-rate regimental colonel, yet he considered himself a genius. Tall, immaculately dressed, a vainglorious genius of the mouth who put new meaning into the term 'gasconnade', Bernadotte was born in Pau, joined the army at seventeen and worked his way up through the ranks, rising rapidly on the great surge of revolutionary promotions. An opportunist and adventurer who masked his egomania beneath a profession of extreme Jacobin principles, Bernadotte was promoted to general in 1794 at the age of thirty-one, in the very year that his close associate St-Just perished on the guillotine. Nothing better illustrated the vulpine nature of the man who outdid his fellow Gascon, La Fontaine's fox, in humbug.

During the Rhine campaign of 1796 Bernadotte threatened to burn the German university town of Altdorf to the ground when the academics objected to his troops' rape and pillaging. A notable hothead, Bernadotte once fought a duel with his own chief of staff and, when the Altdorf incident was reported in the Paris press, asked the Directors to imprison the offending editor. When they demurred, Bernadotte fumed that his honour had been impugned and was prevented from throwing up his command only by the shrewd advice of his friend and fellow Jacobin General Kléber. Bernadotte had barely set foot on Italian soil than he was at odds with Napoleon's indispensable chief of staff, Berthier. Bernadotte's ability to start a row in an empty room can perhaps be inferred from the trivial pretext he used to challenge Berthier to a duel. Berthier addressed all generals as 'Monsieur' but the Jacobin firebrand Bernadotte insisted that the only proper form of greeting was 'citoyen'; Napoleon had to intervene to compose this storm in a teacup.

Predictably, the first meeting between Napoleon himself and Bernadotte was scarcely propitious. Bernadotte thought, on no grounds whatever, that he was a superior military talent to Bonaparte and should be commanding the Army of Italy. When Napoleon overawed him as he had overawed Augereau and Masséna, the sulky Bernadotte grumbled to his cronies: 'Over there I saw a man of twenty-six or twenty-seven who wants to appear fifty. It bodes no good for the Republic.' Napoleon ordered Bernadotte to commence the offensive on 10 March with the vanguard off the right. The Gascon general crossed the Tagliamento and Isonzo rivers but complained when he was sent to besiege the Austrian fortress of Gradisca. His paranoia was well to the fore in this open lament to his senior officers: 'I see it all. Bonaparte is jealous of me and wants to disgrace me. I have no resource left but to blow my brains out. If I blockade Gradisca I shall be blamed for not having stormed it. If I storm it I shall be told I ought to have blockaded it.'

Napoleon's offensive was a great success. After taking meticulous precautions against a possible Austrian attack, he sent Joubert through the Brenner pass, and himself swept Archduke Charles aside at the Tagliamento and took Klagenfurth on 29 March. Moreau was supposed to be coordinating movements on the Rhine but did not stir. Napoleon suspected that the Directory, fearful of the suspect loyalty of the Army of Italy and its commander, had given secret instructions to Moreau not to move a muscle. Realizing that he could not hope to take Vienna unaided, Napoleon decided on a bluff. He advanced as far as Leoben, just seventy-five miles from Vienna, and then offered a truce. The Austrians agreed a five-day cessation of hostilities while Napoleon, who was stalling, tried to learn Moreau's intentions.

Confused and suspicious about the actions and motives of the Directory, Napoleon then decided to take a further gamble. He actually proposed a full set of peace terms and gave the Austrians until 18 April to accept. This was high-risk poker playing, for if the Austrians turned him down and Moreau did not open his offensive, his bluff would be called spectacularly. The peace terms were, however, very generous: Austria was to cede Belgium to France, allow her to occupy the left bank of the Rhine and the Ionian islands, and also recognize Bonaparte's new Cisalpine Republic of Milan, Bologna and Modena; Austria would be allowed to keep a foothold in Italy by retaining the territories of Istria, Dalmatia and Frioul.

A day before the peace offer was due to expire, the Austrians conceded defeat, heavily influenced by the urgings of their best general, Archduke Charles. Preliminaries of peace were signed at Leoben on 18 April. To his fury, Napoleon then learned that two days earlier Moreau had finally crossed the Rhine. In composed mood he later wrote: 'I was playing *vingt-et-un* and I stopped at twenty.' But at the time he was angry with the Directory for what he considered a calculated double-cross.

As a sweetener to get Austria to accept the Leoben terms, Napoleon had included a secret clause promising that the Habsburg empire could swallow up the republic of Venice. Since Napoleon was master of Italy, it now remained for him to make the gift-wrapped presentation of the Most Serene Republic. Napoleon was never more Machiavellian than in his treatment of Venice in 1797. He had long been angered by a so-called Venetian neutrality that actually benefited Austria and was well aware that the oligarchs of Venice detested the French Revolution and its principles. He also realized that it was pointless to consult the Directory: at best they would equivocate and at worst actively intrigue against him. On the other hand, a direct attack on Venice might suck the Army of Italy into a prolonged siege, since the republic could easily be reinforced and provisioned by sea and any sort of sustained defence would give the rest of conquered Italy dangerous ideas about resisting the French invader.

Fortunately for Napoleon, the Venetians played into his hands. When Napoleon paused at Klagenfurth, false rumours reached Italy that the French had received a military check. In Verona the people rose and massacred a French garrison; in this action they were warmly encouraged by the Doge and his ministers. But when the Veronese heard that the Austrians had accepted French peace terms, their nerve cracked and they threw in the towel. Napoleon sent the faithful Junot to Venice to read a grave and thunderous letter to the Senate. Too late the Venetian oligarchy realized it had jumped the gun by supporting Verona.

Panic-stricken, the Doge exerted all his power to lobby, bribe and cajole the Directors in Paris into ordering Napoleon to leave Venice well alone. But Bonaparte had foreseen this reaction and was able to find excuses, based on technicalities, for ignoring the Directory's instructions about Venice. On 3 May Napoleon sent his troops into the waterbound republic. Deprived of any possibility of succour from Austria, the demoralized oligarchy resigned and handed power to the 'democratic' faction that had allowed the French into the city. The French looting of Italy reached new heights even by the rapacious standards of the Army of Italy. Among the myriad treasures to be removed from the city and sent back to Paris were the treasures of the Arsenal, the Lion of Venice and the four bronze horses of St Mark's.

The final stage of Napoleon's settling accounts with Venice came on 26 May when he sent his troops to occupy the Ionian islands of Cephalonia, Corfu and Zante. There was no opposition. Napoleon told his commander to show outward deference to Venetian authority but keep real control in his own hands. Once again he showed himself to be a master of cynical propaganda: 'If the inhabitants should prove to be inclined towards independence [i.e. freedom from Venetian rule], you are to encourage that inclination, and in proclamations you will be issuing you must not omit to speak of Greece, Sparta and Athens.' It was typical of his independence and highhandedness that he did not bother to notify the Directory of the occupation of the islands until the beginning of August.

By June 1797 Napoleon was back in Milan. This time he moved his court and family from the Palazzo Serbelloni to the baroque palace of Mombello outside the city. Josephine, who had not been able to effect a meeting with Hippolyte Charles since December, told Napoleon she needed to return to Paris for her health. But the mysterious malady cleared up miraculously once she heard that among the guard of honour at Mombello that summer would be the bold chevalier Charles; there was no longer any talk of returning to Paris.

Charles was aide-de-camp to General Victor Emmanuel Leclerc, son of a rich Pontoise miller and one of the Toulon set whose mere presence at the siege meant they were automatic favourites with Bonaparte. When Napoleon returned to Milan, one of his first actions was to uncover a potential family scandal. Roaming the Mombello palace one day, he came upon Leclerc making love to his sexually overcharged sister Pauline, already a stunning beauty of fabled lubricious charms. Napoleon insisted that the pair get married at once, and by chance was able to arrange a double family wedding. The shrewish, sourfaced and mannish Maria Anna Bonaparte, who had taken the name Elisa, was marrying the extremely stupid Corsican aristocrat Pasquale Bacciochi, with all her family present. Napoleon presided over a double ceremony on 14 June in the Oratory of St Francis. He had, as he thought, solved the problem of Pauline's voracious sexual appetite. With hindsight we can appreciate the irony whereby Leclerc serviced one Bonaparte nymphomaniac while his aide attended to another.

The double family wedding in Milan on 14 June saw the entire Bonaparte clan face to face with Josephine for the first time. Predictably, perhaps, there was no love lost. The Bonapartes could not understand why Napoleon was so complaisant about his wife's love affairs and her spendthrift ways – which meant spending 'their' money. There was particular animus between Josephine and Pauline, who tried to mete out a family revenge by setting her cap at Hippolyte Charles. The cynical hussar made history by being the only man known to have resisted

Pauline's charms. Letizia also detested Josephine, but her ill-feelings were assuaged with the prospect of a triumph she enjoyed the following month. The French had finally cleared the English out of Corsica and winnowed out all the fervent Paolistas. Armed with 100,000 francs compensation from the Directory, Letizia returned to Ajaccio and set about restoring and redecorating the Casa Buonaparte. Now at last she was a woman of substance and her second son was, potentially if not actually, the most powerful man in France.

CHAPTER EIGHT

Napoleon's Italian campaign of 1796–97 has always provoked military historians to superlatives. His contemporaries were equally enthusiastic. In October 1797 the Directory presented the Army of Italy with an inscribed flag. This recorded that the Army had taken 150,000 prisoners, 170 enemy standards, 540 cannon and howitzers, five pontoon trains, nine 64-gun ships of the line, twelve frigates, eighteen galleys, in addition to sending to Paris masterpieces by Michelangelo, Guercino, Titian, Paolo Veronese, Corregio Albano, Raphael and the Caracci. More saliently, the army had fought sixty-seven actions and triumphed in eighteen pitched battles enumerated as follows: Montenotte, Millesimo, Mondovi, Lodi, Borghetto, Lonato, Castiglione, Rovereto, Bassano, St George, Fontana Viva, Caldiero, Arcola, Rivoli, La Favorita, Tagliamento, Tarnis and Neumarcht.

What enabled Napoleon to win so many battles and with such apparent ease? Did luck or military genius play the greater part? Were the revolutionary armies different in kind from the Austrian forces? Was Napoleon a tactical or strategic innovator? Was he a political visionary who used his victories to promote a pilot form of Italian federation? Or was he just a glorified pillager? And what precisely was it that made him an object of fear, envy and hatred by the Directory, who by their actions tacitly acknowledged that he was already the single most powerful man in France?

There were four main factors that contributed to Napoleon's remarkable military success: technology, the effects of the French Revolution, the superior morale of his men, and his own genius as tactician and strategist. Overwhelming defeat in the Seven Years War had the result that the French thereafter bent their energies to be abreast of all the latest military technology. The most encouraging results were in the field of artillery, which Jean-Baptiste de Gribeauval had first begun modernizing in 1763. Lighter gun-barrels and carriages made it possible to produce 12- or 24-pounder calibres for field-guns, which was the ordnance hitherto thought possible only for siege-guns.

Gribeauval's new artillery was at the technological forefront until 1825, but the Revolution provided a new fillip after Valmy in 1792, which was far in advance of any battle yet fought in terms of big guns and artillery rounds fired. The war fever of 1793 saw massive production of artillery weapons – seven thousand cannon in that year alone – and the efforts of scientists like Gaspard Monge made sure that France remained at the technological cutting edge. The know-how was therefore in place, ready to be exploited by an artilleryman of high talent. No more perfect individual for this particular historical moment could be imagined than the young Bonaparte, schooled as he was in the doctrines of du Teil and Guibert.

Yet if France had the edge in big guns, its superiority in infantry firepower was marginal. Battlefield firearms were still mainly muzzle-loading, smooth-bore flintlocks, and the standard issue was the 1777 Charleville musket (in use until 1840) – a .70 calibre weapon, fifty inches long (without bayonet). This was virtually useless against compact bodies of troops at ranges greater than 250 yards, and even a sharpshooter needed one hundred yards range or less to pick out an individual. The crudity of this weapon was the reason battlefields were often blacked out with dense clouds of smoke. Every soldier carried into battle fifty cartridges, powder charges and three spare flints, but the coarse black powder used by the French resulted in excessive fouling of the barrels, so that they had to be cleaned after every fifty rounds; the flint also needed to be changed after a dozen shots. Muskets misfired on average once in six shots, which in the heat of battle often led to soldiers double-loading their weapons.

The crudity of gunfire in this period needs emphasis. Reloading was a clumsy, complicated, time-consuming business. Typically an infantryman would take a paper cartridge from his pouch and bite off the end containing the ball, which he retained in his mouth; then he opened the 'pan' of his musket, poured in a priming charge and closed it; next he tipped the remainder of the powder down the barrel, spat the musket ball after it, folded the paper into a wad and then forced both ball and wad down the barrel on to the powder charge with his ramrod; finally he took aim and fired. The mere recital shows how many things could go wrong: a soldier could double-load after an unnoticed misfire, or forget to withdraw his ramrod before pulling the trigger; most commonly, clumsy or malingering soldiers would spill most of the powder charge on the ground to avoid the mule-kick of the weapons at their shoulder.

When to the crudity of the musket is added generally poor marksmanship by the French, it can be readily understood why Napoleon thought artillery was the key to winning battles. Although an expert marksman could get off five shots a minute, the average was only one or two. Slowness was compounded by inaccuracy. At a range of 225 yards only 25% of shots could be expected to hit their target, 40% at 150 yards and only 60% even as close as 75 yards. French infantrymen were generally poor shots because musketry practice was neglected, partly to save ammunition, partly to avoid casualties from burst barrels but most of all out of a doctrinaire conviction that killing by shot was the job of the artillery; the infantry went in to 'mop up' with cold steel. Even so, deaths from the bayonet were few: its impact tended to be psychological rather than actual, causing fear but not death. On the other hand, at ranges less than fifty yards ('whites of eyes' range) even the 1777 musket was deadly and could produce horrific casualties.

When it came to individual weaponry, Napoleon laid most emphasis on the rifled carbines – lighter, smaller-calibred weapons – issued to snipers, sharpshooters, skirmishers, *voltigeurs* and non-commissioned officers. Dense clouds of these skirmishers, in numbers sometimes amounting to regimental strength, would engage and harass the enemy while the main column approached with drawn bayonets. If the morale of the main body of attackers was low, an élite grenadier company would be placed in the rear to urge others forward; if morale was good, the élite corps would lead the right wing into battle.

Napoleon planned his battles to maximize the advantages of technology and minimize the disadvantages of infantry and muskets. First he would unleash a devastating bombardment from his big guns to inflict heavy losses and lower resistance. While this barrage was going on, snipers and *voltigeurs* used the cover to advance within musketry range in hopes of picking off officers and spreading confusion. The next stage was a series of carefully coordinated cavalry and infantry assaults. The cavalry would attempt to brush aside the enemy's horse and then force his infantry to form square; French infantry then moved up to close quarters to prevent the enemy in square from reforming in line. The square was usually proof against cavalry charges but it left those forming it highly vulnerable to an infantry attack, since men drawn up in a square or rectangular formation could fire only in a limited number of directions, enabling the advancing French columns to come to close quarters without sustaining the withering fire and unacceptable casualties normal when engaging an enemy drawn up in line. The final stage came when the infantry forced a gap in the enemy lines: horse artillery would widen the breach; and then French cavalry would sweep forward for the breakthrough. Time and again the Austrian method of relying on infantry unprotected by cover or cavalry screens played into Napoleon's hands and proved useless against the combination of massed artillery and highly-trained sharpshooters.

Objectively, then, the French Army of Italy, though outnumbered, disposed of superior technology which a commander of high talents could use to open up a decisive gap. Yet Napoleon was unimaginative when it came to the exploration of new technologies. He showed no interest in the use of military observation balloons, even though he had been formed in a revolutionary culture where Danton's balloon flight was a central image. Nor did he show any interest in inventions which had the potential for producing a military 'quantum leap', such as Fulton's submarine and steamboat. This is puzzling, since Napoleon prided himself on his interest in science and was closely associated with scientists like Monge, Laplace and Chaptal. Some historians have argued that Napoleon sensed the contemporary limitations of technology, and it is true that the technical breakthrough in metallurgy which would usher in railways, the steamship and the breech-loading rifle, was a post-1815 phenomenon.

The second great advantage Napoleon had in the Italian campaign was that he had a relatively homogeneous army infused with the spirit of the Revolution, whereas the Austrian army was polyglot (composed of Serbs, Croats and Hungarians as well as Austrians), stymied by paperwork and excessive bureaucracy, and still in thrall to the frozen hierachies of the *ancien régime*. The Revolution made possible new tactics and organization, provided fresh pools of manpower and talent and provided a citizen army with positive ideals, images and ideologies. It is not necessary to go all the way with the theorists Clausewitz and Georges Sorel and claim that a citizen army was a *sufficient* explanation for Napoleon's success in Italy, but it was a necessary one. Military service by citizens who genuinely felt they were participating in a state enterprise of which they approved produced a highly motivated force of what Sorel called 'intelligent bayonets'.

The Revolution, with its 'career open to talents', produced for a while a meritocratic gap, especially in the Army, through which proceeded highly talented men who would have been born to blush unseen under the *ancien régime*. Without the Revolution Napoleon himself could not have had his meteoric rise, nor would he have had Lannes, Murat, Davout, Masséna, Augereau and his other favourite generals at his side. While a hundred flowers bloomed in France, their enemies remained petrified in the social immobility of the old régime. Napoleon's dictum, that every soldier carried a marshal's baton in his knapsack, was anachronistic by the time he uttered it, when most of the avenues for advancement had already been choked off, but it still had meaning during the Directory.

However, there was considerable irony in that Napoleon himself discounted this factor, except for propaganda purposes, and quickly moved to replace a revolutionary ethos with a purely military one. *Esprit de corps* replaced civic virtue and patriotic virtue as the ideological cement in Napoleon's army. By the imperial period the process was complete, but Napoleon's army of 1796–97 was already very far from the citizen army raised by *levée en masse* in 1793–94: one obvious pointer is that the lust for booty replaced zeal to export the Revolution.

This involves the question of morale and how Napoleon was able to bind the troops to him, so that they were prepared to endure amazing hardships on his behalf. The discipline of his army needs stressing, since to switch from column to line, as in the *ordre mixte* which Napoleon used in Italy, required precise coordination if the result was not to be a shambles. In theory it was all straightforward: the line provided superior firepower and the column superior mobility, weight and shock. Napoleon's instructions sounded simple, but they were always based on the ability of highly trained units to implement them.

Napoleon's military maxims presuppose an army keyed to the highest pitch of élan and commitment. What sounds like armchair theorizing turns out on closer inspection to require every single army corps to be an élite unit. Take the following: 'When you are driven from a first position, you should rally your columns at a sufficient distance in the rear, to prevent the enemy from anticipating them; for the greatest misfortune you can meet with is to have your columns separately attacked before their junction.' What is merely implicit in that prescription becomes explicit with this: 'An army should be ready every day and at all hours to fight . . . an army ought always to be ready by day, by night, and at all hours, to make all the resistance it is capable of making.'

To get entire army corps committed to his principles Napoleon had to win hearts and minds. This he was able to do for a number of reasons. For a start, he had a track record of almost continual onwards and upwards triumph over his enemies. Nothing succeeds like success, and morale increased almost geometrically at the thought of being part of an ever-victorious army. Napoleon headed off the possible sources of his troops' discontent: he clothed and equipped them well, paid them in specie, and turned a blind eye to their pillaging expeditions. Victory in battle was not just the largely meaningless prelude to diplomacy it had been under the *ancien régime*; to win a battle now meant there was a serious chance of riches.

Yet the brilliance of Napoleon lay in his understanding of human psychology. He realized that at root human beings are driven by money but that they hate to admit this is what actually motivates them and are therefore grateful to leaders who can mystify and obfuscate the quest for filthy lucre. The best possible scenario is that of the conquistadores where the quest for riches could be rationalized as the desire to serve God. Napoleon could not use religion in this way, but he spoke of glory, immortality, the judgement of posterity. Hence the swords of honour and, eventually, the institution of the Legion of Honour. 'A man does not have himself killed for a few halfpence a day or for a petty distinction. You must speak to the soul in order to electrify the soul.'

On the Italian campaign Napoleon really learned human psychology. He realized that men liked to be rewarded in their pockets while being appealed to in their minds and hearts. This was why, many years later, when he came to establish the marshalate, he took great care to combine the most elaborate titles, duchies, princedoms and even thrones with the most elaborate emoluments of 'benefices'. And that was why, while conniving at the looting of his old sweats, he liked to flatter and cajole them. With his amazing memory for detail, he could remember the names of obscure rankers and make them feel ten feet tall by an appreciative word. The men actually liked his habit of tweaking their ears in parades, for this was a general who could deliver on his promises.

For such a man, who rewarded them, understood them and even remembered their names, the troops could not do too much. Some of his victories were possible only because of a highly committed army, at the peak of morale. During the Rivoli campaign, Masséna's division fought at Verona on 13 January, marched all night to reach Rivoli early on the 14th, fought all day against the Austrians, marched all night and all day on the 15th towards Mantua and completed their epic of endurance with a battle at La Favorita on the 16th. In 120 hours they had fought three battles and marched 54 miles.

Yet above all credit for the triumph in the Italian campaign must go to Napoleon's own superb talents as strategist, tactician and military thinker. Napoleon liked to avoid frontal attacks, which were costly in lives and rarely yielded a clear-cut result, in favour of enveloping attack on the flanks. 'It is by turning the enemy, by attacking his flanks, that battles are won' was a favourite saying. The enveloping type of battle partly broke down the age-old distinction between strategy and tactics, for it was planned well in advance yet adapted to circumstance. The key to Napoleon's success in his favourite battle-plan (the so-called *mouvement sur les derrières*) was his reorganization of the army into a corps system.

Each corps became in effect a miniature army, each with its own cavalry and artillery arm, and each capable of operating independently for forty-eight hours or more; at the limit, it had to be capable of taking on an enemy force three times its size.

When contact was made with hostile forces, Napoleon ordered the corps nearest the enemy to pin him down, often encouraging an all-out assault from the opposition by the very paucity of its own numbers. Meanwhile the rest of the army would be engaged in forced marches to fall on the enemy flanks and rear at a predetermined moment. Perfect timing and coordination were necessary to achieve outright victory by this method, and tremendous courage and stamina on the part of the 'pinning' corps, which was sure to take heavy losses. Even if the enemy managed to punch through the 'pin', it could find itself cut off from its base or in hostile territory.

Usually, however, the pinning corps would not have to stand and fight for twenty-four hours, since Napoleon arranged for his various corps to arrive at the battle at different times. The enemy would find to his consternation that he was fighting more and more Frenchmen, and would then commit his reserves to achieve victory before further French reinforcements arrived on the scene. Meanwhile, hidden by a cavalry screen, the main enveloping force would move towards the weak spot on the flanks or rear. Napoleon always tried to envelop the enemy flank nearest his natural line of retreat, but was aware that this required meticulous timing. 'The favourable opportunity must be seized, for fortune is female – if you baulk her today, you must not expect to meet with her again tomorrow.' This was why the command of the final enveloping force was always given to his most trusted general, for everything depended on arriving at exactly the right place and time.

What this meant in practical terms was that Napoleon had to work out through the smoke of battle exactly when the enemy commander committed his final reserves. The commander of the enveloping force had to keep his troops like greyhounds on the leash, lest a premature attack betray their presence. The signal to the envelopers to make their presence felt would either be a pre-arranged barrage from certain guns or, if geography permitted it, a message from an aide. The *coup de grâce* was meant to be a combined offensive from front and rear. When the enveloping force appeared, the enemy commander would either have to weaken his front to meet the new challenge at the very moment Napoleon was launching a frontal attack, or he could opt for retreat – supremely perilous in the teeth of attacking forces. Napoleon liked to launch his final frontal attack at the 'hinge' of the enemy's weakened front so as to cut his army in two.

This aspect of military tactics appealed to Napoleon the mathematician. He liked to time his battles with a watch and showed uncharacteristic patience while he waited for events to unfold. As he put it: 'There is a moment in engagements when the least manoeuvre is decisive and gives victory; it is the one drop of water which makes the vessel run over.' He also liked the chessplaying aspects of varying cavalry and infantry attacks. In the final assault a cavalry charge would make the enemy form square, thus making the advancing infantry columns less vulnerable. When once a hole was made in the enemy line, his forces would quickly fall into disarray. In the final stage of exploitation of a victory the cavalry came into its own, aiming to turn defeat into rout by relentless pursuit.

However, it was not always possible, for geographical and logistical reasons, or because the enemy anticipated the move, for Napoleon to employ his favourite enveloping strategy. In such a case, he liked to take up the 'central position', interposing his forces between two parts of the enemy army so as to destroy it piecemeal. Overwhelming the enemy in detail was particularly suited to a situation where the battlefield itself was divided, by a hill, river or some other natural feature. Time and again Napoleon defeated overall superior numbers by gaining local numerical superiority. He had a genius for finding the 'hinge' or joint between two or sometimes even three different enemy armies. He would then concentrate his forces, crash through the hinge and interpose himself between two armies. Forced apart and thus, in technical language, operating on exterior lines, the enemy would be at a natural disadvantage.

Having selected which enemy force he would deal with first, Napoleon deployed two-thirds of his forces against the chosen victim while the other third pinned the other enemy army, usually launching assaults that looked like the prelude to a full-scale attack. After defeating the first army, Napoleon would detach half his victorious host to deal with the second enemy army, while the rest of his victorious troops pursued the remnants of the vanquished force. There were two snags to this strategy. The obvious one was that, since Napoleon himself could not be in two places at once, it was likely that a less skilled general would botch the operation Bonaparte was not supervising personally. The other, more serious, problem was intrinsic to the strategy itself: because he needed to divert half his victorious force to deal with the second enemy army, he did not have the resources to follow up the vanquished foe and score a truly decisive victory. For this reason the 'central position' as a strategy was always a second best to the golden dream of Cannae-style envelopment.

From the Italian campaign evolved certain military principles that Napoleon never altered. These may be summed up as follows: the army's lines of communication must always be kept open; the army must have a clear primary objective with no secondary distractions; the enemy army, not his capital or fortified towns, must always be the objective; always attack, never remain on the defensive; always remember the importance of artillery so that ideally you go into battle with four big guns for every thousand men; the moral factor is to the material as three is to one. Above all, Napoleon emphasized the importance of concentration of force, speed and the factor of time, and the cardinal principle of outflanking.

Each of these ideas fed into each other. Speed of response would demoralize the enemy even as it allowed for concentration of force. A favourite Napoleonic ploy was to disperse in order to tempt the enemy into counter-dispersal, followed immediately by a rapid concertina-like concentration that caught the enemy still strung out. Speed was the single key to successful strategy and called for careful research and preselection of the shortest practicable routes. As Napoleon wrote: 'Strategy is the art of making use of time and space . . . space we can recover, time never.' Once contact was made with the enemy, concentration on the flanks was crucial; the army should always strive to turn the enemy's most exposed flank. This meant either total envelopment with a large force or an outflanking movement by corps operating apart from the main army.

Napoleon's military genius is hard to pin down, but certain categories help to elucidate it. He was a painstaking, mathematical planner; a master of deception; a supremely talented improviser; he had an amazing spatial and geographical imagination; and he had a phenomenal memory for facts and minute detail. He believed in meticulous planning and war-gaming, aiming to incorporate the element of chance as far as possible. By logic and probability he could eliminate most of the enemy's options and work out exactly where he was likely to offer battle. By carefully calculating the odds he knew the likely outcome of his own moves and his opponent's. His superb natural intelligence and encyclopedic memory allowed him to anticipate most possible outcomes and conceivable military permutations days, months, even years in advance. Madame de Rémusat quotes what is surely an authentic observation: 'Military science consists in calculating all the chances accurately in the first place, and then in giving accident exactly, almost mathematically, its place in one's calculations. It is upon this point that one must not deceive oneself, and yet a decimal more or less may change all. Now this apportioning of accident and science cannot get into any head except that of a genius. Accident, hazard, chance, call it what you may, a mystery to ordinary minds, becomes a reality to superior men.'

Napoleon was also a prince among deceivers, who placed fundamental reliance on his network of spies, agents and informers. It was a central part of his methods that when he made contact with the enemy, he would immediately seek to mislead their spies as to his real numbers, adding a division here, a brigade there at the very last moment and using a thick cavalry screen to hide the concentration of infantry. His highly fluid corps system gave him flexibility in drawing up his battle lines, which was always designed to bamboozle the enemy. He liked to deploy along very wide fronts, sometimes more than one hundred kilometres, so that his opponents could never know exactly where he was going to mass for the vital blow. In order to cover all of his presumed options, the opposing general was likely to disperse his forces, with fatal results. The front tended to narrow as his prey was spotted but, to prevent anticipation, Napoleon would often narrow the front and then widen it again to keep the enemy guessing. A favourite ploy was to station his forces two days' march away from the enemy on, say, a Sunday, leaving the enemy to conclude that battle would be joined on a Tuesday; the French army would then stage a night march and catch their opponents unawares on Monday.

But if things went wrong, Napoleon was usually equal to the occasion as he was a superb improviser. One of his maxims was that you should always be able to answer the question: if the enemy appears unexpectedly on my right or on my left, what should I do? Naturally, improvisation was made easier by the previous mathematical calculation of all chances, no matter how far-fetched. It was, for example, essential for a commander always to have at his disposal at any given moment both an infantry and a cavalry arm; and the worst perils could be anticipated by never having more than one line of operations and never linking columns in sight of or close to the enemy. 'No detachment should be made on the eve of the day of attack, because the state of affairs may alter during the night, either by means of the enemy's movements in retreat, or the arrival of great reinforcements, which may place him in a situation to assume an offensive attitude, and to turn the premature dispositions you have made to your own destruction.'

Napoleon additionally possessed an almost preternatural eye for ground and battlefield terrain, including a minute awareness of the strengths and weaknesses of every possible vantage point. From looking at a relief map he could visualize all the details of a potential battlefield and work out how an enemy was likely to deploy on the ground. He particularly liked manoeuvring an opponent on to ground where geographical features like mountains and rivers told against an overall enemy numerical superiority. His frequent use of the 'centre position' was possible only because of his eye for landscape. He also liked to conceal part of his forces behind natural topographical features, such as woods or hills, and then unleash them to the surprise and consternation of the enemy.

However, for all his military genius, Napoleon was never a commander in the same league as Alexander, Hannibal or Tamerlane. His chessplaying qualities were never absolute, for an imp of the perverse manifested itself in a deliberate decision to leave certain things to chance, almost as if he were testing his own abilities at the limit or superstitiously pushing his luck to see how far it would run. Side by side with his mathematical propensity went a certain empirical pragmatism, summed up in the following statement: 'Tactics, evolution and the sciences of the engineer and the artillery officer may be learned from treatises, much as in the same way as geometry, but the knowledge of the higher branches of the art of war is only to be gained by experience and by studying the history of man and battles of great leaders. Can one learn in a grammar to compose a book of the Iliad, or one of Corneille's tragedies?'

Napoleon's military talents were essentially practical rather than theoretical. It has been suggested that he never put his ideas on strategy and tactics on paper so as to keep his generals (and later his marshals) in the dark but the truth is that he was not much of an innovator anyway. Initially he got most of his ideas from books and did not change his approach very much. Napoleon himself made no great claims as a military theoretician. 'I have fought sixty battles and I have learned nothing which I did not know at the beginning' is a statement that has sometimes raised eyebrows but, self-mocking cynicism aside, he was being starkly realistic. The obvious snag was that his enemies would learn his methods and devise counter measures.

From a military point of view, two propositions about the Italian campaign seem warranted. His great skill notwithstanding, Napoleon was lucky. He did not have to build a military machine from scratch, inherited a potentially excellent army, and then fought indifferent generals. He took many gambles at long odds, notably at Arcola, where the French army could and should have been trapped in the swamps. The men he faced – Beaulieu, Wurmser and Alvinzi – did not have his burning will to win; they were eighteenth-century generals, essentially amateurs ranged against a professional. But the element of luck can be stretched too far to explain the Bonapartist triumph. Napoleon's willpower should not be discounted as a factor in his success: he never abandoned the tactical offensive for a single day and devoted fiendish energy to bringing the greatest possible number of men on to the battlefield by unremitting mobility and surprise; time and again he contrived to defeat the Austrians in detail.

There were other factors in Italy that produced the result where Napoleon, mistakenly, thought it was his destiny always to be Fortune's darling. The plethora of talent unleashed by the Revolutionary meritocracy and the short-lived period of social mobility played to Napoleon's strength. So too did his idea that the army should live off the land. His army never carried more than three days' supplies, while the Austrians always carried nine. The sheer size of the armies of 1793–96, making it impossible for any conventional commissariat to supply them, forced them to live off the land, even if the Directory had been able to pay for the campaign in Italy instead of being bankrupt. Long-term, the seizures, requisitioning and plundering by Napoleon's armies would provoke a terrible civilian backlash, where hideous atrocities became the norm. Again Napoleon was lucky in 1796–97 in that he did not elicit this reaction from the Italians.

The second caveat one must enter about the Italian campaign is that Napoleon did not manage to carry out his own prescriptions. He neither destroyed the enemy's armies nor sapped his will to resist further. Partly this was because of the obsession with Mantua – again in defiance of his own principles. In 1796–97 he wavered between making the siege of Mantua his supreme objective and searching out and destroying the enemy armies. Nor did he break the Austrians' will, for they resumed the military struggle in Italy in 1800.

There are many who hold, with Stendhal, that the Italian campaign was Napoleon's finest achievement and that with the occupation of Venice the greatest chapter of his life came to an end. Yet no account of Napoleon in Italy is complete without a discussion of the massive sums in cash and kind he expropriated from the conquered territories. Napoleon, it is true, was under orders from the Directory to make the war pay for itself and to remit any surplus obtained to Paris. One of the reasons the Directors connived at his frequent defiance of them was the multi-million-franc sweeteners he sent them. But he went far beyond this and extracted the kind of surplus from Italy for which the only proper word is exploitation. He turned a blind eye to the peculations and embezzlements of notorious money-grubbers like Augereau and Masséna, provided he got his cut from them. An authentic story from Hamelin about some confiscated mines shows how the Bonapartist system worked. Napoleon himself received a million francs and his henchmen in the affair proportionate sums: Berthier got 100,000 francs, Murat 50,000, Bernadotte 50,000. Napoleon's hagiographers point to his stern treatment of Saliceti and Garrau for their defalcations, but this misses the point: his intention was to discredit the political commissioners, so that he was no longer subject to effective control.

The looting of Italy's art treasures was a particularly nefarious aspect of Napoleon's triumph. All conquered peoples or those who signed treaties with Bonaparte had to pay an indemnity in the form of precious paintings, sculptures and other works of art. The Duke of Parma was forced to disgorge Coreggio's *Dawn*; the Pope was mulcted of a hundred paintings, statues and vases; Venice yielded up some of its most priceless Old Masters: and everywhere the pattern was the same. Works by Giorgione, Mantegna, Raphael, Leonardo, Fra Filippo Lippi, Andrea del Sarto and many others were removed to France, either as official prizes of war or as objects of private rapine by Augereau, Masséna and others.

Napoleon's defenders claim that he was under orders from the Directory to repatriate these works of arts, that it was standard Revolutionary practice to confiscate the artefacts of a 'corrupt aristocracy'. Carnot's instructions to this effect on 7 May 1796 are often cited, ordering Napoleon to send back works of art 'in order to strengthen and embellish the reign of liberty'. But Napoleon and his generals did not just send back money and art treasures: they kept the majority of the loot for themselves. One estimate is that only a fifth of the surplus in money and art extracted from Italy found its way to the Directory. Of the fifty million francs uplifted, the most conservative estimate is that Napoleon kept back three millions for himself. Tens of millions remain unaccounted for, and the obvious inference is that Napoleon, his family, his favourites and his generals lined their pockets to an astonishing degree. Napoleon always considered that the best way to bind the talented but ambitious generals to his cause was to associate himself with the idea of unlimited wealth; any commander following the Bonaparte star would end up with the wealth of Croesus.

Napoleon claimed, absurdly, that he himself brought nothing back from Italy but his soldier's pay, and has even found biographers and historians prepared to swallow this transparent lie. Circumstantial evidence alone is overwhelmingly against him. Napoleon connived with his brother Joseph to have a vast quantity of treasure extracted from Rome with which Joseph built a palatial house in Paris not too far from the rue de la Victoire; Joseph pretended he had bought the property with his wife's money, though everyone knew the Clarys did not have money on that scale. The rest of the Bonapartes received substantial handouts: Letizia received enough to rebuild and refurbish the family home in Ajaccio, Caroline and Jérôme were sent to expensive schools, and Pauline and Élisa received lavish dowries. On his own account Napoleon purchased the house in the rue de la Victoire which he had previously rented, acquired a large estate in Belgium and, when he was in Egypt in 1798, had Joseph buy a vast country house with three hundred acres of parkland for Josephine at Malmaison on the banks of the Seine, just six miles west of Paris, at a price of 335,000 francs. Napoleon used Joseph as the family banker: only his elder brother knew all the secret accounts where the treasure looted from Italy was stored. Napoleon's apologists also like to divert attention to his experiments with Italian republicanism but here the record is less clear than it needs to be to sustain the case for Bonaparte as Revolutionary liberator. Officially Napoleon was supposed to be exporting the values and ideals of the Revolution to Italy as well as looting it, but the Directory was always ambivalent about the political side of the programme. Their only true ideological aim was a desire to humble the Pope but thereafter the project to republicanize Italy scarcely interested them, if only because it would make it more difficult to exchange the conquered territories with Austria. Napoleon was under strict instructions to make no binding promises to the Italians that could in any way impede a cut-and-run peace with the Austrians if the military campaign went wrong.

However, Napoleon had ideas of his own. His Army needed to be supplied, its communications required safeguarding and its situation was potentially perilous, between hostile armies and sullen and superficially subdued Italian city-states. Napoleon had to carry out the difficult balancing act of encouraging the pro-French party without provoking a backlash from the conservative, aristocratic and pro-Austrian factions. To his mind, the best way to find equilibrium was to co-opt the conquered Italians in a new scheme for Italian federation; it would be time enough to dwell on the ultimate reality of the plan when military victory in Italy was secure.

He began in May 1796 by abolishing the Austrian machinery of government in Lombardy and enacting a new constitution, with a Congress of State and municipal councils under the direction of French military governors. 'Milan is very eager for liberty,' he wrote to the Directory. 'There is a club of eight hundred members, all business men or lawyers.' After the Lombardy experiment, in October 1796 he presided over the creation of a Cispadane republic, incorporating Modena, Ferrara, Reggio and Bologna, to be confirmed by an elected Assembly in December. This became a reality in February 1797 after final Austrian defeat, the capitulation of the Pope, and his cession of Bologna, Ferrara and the Romagna in the Treaty of Tolentino on 19 February 1797.

At the end of 1796 Napoleon explained his thinking on the Transpadane republic to the Directory and again revealed himself a master of political Machiavellianism. 'The Cispadana republic is divided into three parties:1) the friends of their former government, 2) the partisans of an independent but rather aristocratic constitution, 3) the partisans of the French constitution and of pure democracy. I repress the first, I support the second, and moderate the third. I do so because the second is the party of the rich landowners and priests, who in the long run will end by winning the support of the mass of the people which it is essential to rally around the French party.' There is much evidence that Napoleon trod very carefully in Italy when the Roman Catholic Church was involved. In answer to the taunts of the anticlericals in February 1797 for failing to enter Rome and depose the Pope, he explained that the combination of the thirty-million-franc indemnity and the loss of Bologna, Ferrara and the Romagna amounted to the euthanasia of the Papacy. Yet at the very same time he wrote warmly to the Pope in terms that made it clear he had no such expectation of the imminent demise of the Vatican as temporal power.

There were even times when he wondered whether he had been too soft on the Catholic Church, for the elections in the Cispadane republic showed how strong was the influence of the Church. On 1 May 1797 Napoleon wrote to the Directory about the disappointing results in the ballot. 'Priests have influenced all the electors. In the villages they dictate the lists and control all the elections . . . I shall take steps in harmony with their customs to enlighten opinion and lessen the influence of the priests.'

By this time signs of strain were evident between Napoleon and the Directory over Italian policy. The Directors thought Italy too backward to republicanize and such a policy likely to antagonize Austria permanently. But Napoleon seemed impressed by the Republican spirit and the commitment to his cause and was contemptuous of Austria. Napoleon won the struggle and began the move to fuse the Lombardy government and the Cispadane republic into a greater Cisalpine republic. By July 1797 most of the territory Napoleon had conquered in Italy was united in the new Cisalpine state, with an elaborate constitution patterned on the

French one, complete with five Directors and a bicameral legislature of Ancients and Juniors. The murder of pro-French democrats in Genoa in May 1797 gave Napoleon the excuse he needed to intervene there too: he set up a Ligurian republic, with twelve Senators, a Doge and two elective chambers.

Napoleon's desire to promote an incorporating union of Italian states was, however, always predicated on his power struggle with the Directors. About the thing in itself he was cynical. In October 1797 he wrote to Talleyrand: 'You do not know the Italian people. They are not worth the lives of forty thousand Frenchmen. Since I came to Italy I have received no help from this nation's love of liberty and equality, or at least such help has been negligible. Here are the facts: whatever is good to say in proclamations and printed speeches is romantic fiction.'

In August, too, having carried his point with the Directors, he changed his line in communication with them and argued that the islands of Corfu, Zante and Cephalonia were much more important to the French national interest than the whole of Italy put together. Presumably his reasoning was that the islands were important centres on Mediterranean and eastern trade routes and could generate continuing wealth, whereas Italy had already been bled dry. His cynicism was borne out in 1798 when the Republican experiment in Italy collapsed virtually overnight.

His changing attitude to Italy during 1797, moving from sanguine euphoria to cynical defeatism, was almost certainly the result of the tortuous six-month negotiation with Austria, when he and the Directory seemed to be more concerned with winning the power struggle in France than forcing the Austrians to sign a final treaty. Each of the five Directors had good reason to be suspicious of their victorious general, but in addition the Directory was divided against itself in a political imbroglio of frightening complexity. Of the five directors Barras wanted peace at any price while Reubell, the only true ex-Jacobin among them, wanted to continue the revolutionary policy of exporting the ideas of '89. Neither saw eye to eye with Bonaparte, for Barras thought Napoleon too hardline in his dealings with the Austrians, while Reubell wanted to sacrifice the gains in Italy to secure France her 'natural' frontiers on the Rhine.

Yet overlying these conflicts was an even more menacing development. In May 1797 France lurched rightwards, as signalled by the elections to the legislative councils. This was hard on the heels of the execution of 'Gracchus' Babeuf, who had plotted to destroy the Directory and replace it with an extreme democratic-communistic system. Of the two standard bearers of the 'new Right' François Barthélemy entered the Directory while General Charles Pichegru, as president of the Five Hundred, openly intrigued for a royalist restoration. In Paris signs of rightist reaction were palpable: churches were reopening, the tricolour was seldom seen, and the title of 'Citizen' used only ironically. Disabled or wounded veterans of the Army of Italy found on their return that they were insulted or worse if they did not cry, 'Long live the King.'

Napoleon followed internal events in France closely. As he saw it, there were three main power groupings in Paris: the determined republicans who sided with the majority in the Directory (Barras, Reubell and La Révellière); the out-and-out royalists led by Pichegru and Barthélemy; and a cabal of 'don't knows' clustered round the Clichy club and led by Lazare Carnot. It was this latter group that particularly incensed Napoleon. Royalists he could understand but he despised fence sitters. 'The Clichy party represented themselves as wise, moderate, good Frenchmen. Were they Republicans? No. Were they Royalists? No. They were for the Constitution of 1791, then? No. For that of 1793? Still less. That of 1795 perhaps? Yes and No. What were they then? They themselves did not know. They would have consented to such a thing, *but*; to another, *if*.' However, he suspected Carnot and Barthelémy of being the most dangerous of the five Directors: Carnot because he hated the Thermidorians and resented their assiduous propaganda that all the bloodshed in the Revolution was due to the men of '93; Barthélemy because he was the front man for Pichegru, whom Napoleon suspected of wanting to play General Monk in a Bourbon restoration.

For their part, the Directors had various grievances against Bonaparte. The so-called 'rape of Venice' still rankled. Representative Dumolard in the tribune of the Five Hundred denounced the commander-in-chief of the Army of Italy for intervening in Venice and Genoa without the authority of the Directory and the Assemblies and without even consulting them. The new incumbents in political office denounced his looting in Italy, doubtless because they came too late to share in the spoils. The 'unconstitutional' offer of terms to the Austrians at Leoben was raked over and the prospect of an imminent peace laughed to scorn. Most of the Parisian journals were anti-Bonaparte and plugged away at the 'shame' of his Venetian policy; some went so far as to deny that any Frenchmen had ever been massacred in Verona.

Another motif was that a restoration of the monarchy would bring a lasting European peace. There was some warrant for this assertion, for war-weariness in England was palpable. Even the Francophobe firebrand Pitt was prepared to discuss terms and sent Lord Malmesbury to Paris to negotiate with the new French Foreign Minister, Talleyrand. The war was not going England's way: the French invasion of Ireland in 1796 had come within an ace of success, and was thwarted only by storms; Spain went over to the French side in the same year, causing the Royal Navy to withdraw from the Mediterranean; and at home there was financial crisis and a possible harbinger of general social unrest in the shape of the Nore and Spithead naval mutinies, which struck at the heart of Britain's traditional first line of defence. Pitt made it clear that Napoleon's actions in Italy were a sticking point, and this was played up in royalist propaganda.

Napoleon had three principal weapons of counter offensive. In the first place he had his own press and his own tame organs of propaganda. His two newspapers, distributed free to soldiers in the Army of Italy and even smuggled into France itself and distributed widely and gratis there too, were *Le Courrier de l'Armée d'Italie ou le patriote* and *La France vue de l'Armée d'Italie*, of which the former was edited by an ex-Jacobin who had been involved in the Babeuf conspiracy. *Le Courrier* was aimed at the crypto-Jacobites in the Army of Italy and stressed the way the revolution was being betrayed by the rightward swing in France; *La France*, on the other hand, was aimed at moderate opinion and stressed the qualities of Napoleon himself as leader and thaumaturge. The very real achievement in the Italian campaign was exaggerated tenfold, to the point where all Napoleon's errors were 'deliberate mistakes' designed to lure the enemy to his doom; it has been well said that the Napoleonic legend was born, not on St Helena, but in Italy.

The Bonapartist press liked to portray known opponents of Napoleon, like Dumolard and Mallet du Pan, as English agents in the pay of Pitt. By the time the Right appeared as the ascendant power in France in May 1797 Napoleon had founded a third newspaper, this time in Paris, using the vast booty he had accumulated in Italy. This one was called *Journal de Bonaparte et des hommes vertueux*. He kept in reserve the secret that his spies had intercepted correspondence from the most important royalist agent, the comte d'Antraigues, implicating Pichegru and other rightist figures in France. For the moment he contented himself with a formal letter of protest to the Directory, complaining that he was being persecuted by jealous souls purely because of his great services for the Republic. Accusing Dumolard of being a stalking horse for the émigrés, he enclosed with his letter a dagger, symbolizing the dagger aimed at his heart by the Five Hundred.

The second major weapon of retaliation against the Right was the alliance Napoleon built up with Barras, using as middleman the newly returned French ambassador to the U.S.A. Charles Maurice de Talleyrand. The wily and Machiavellian Talleyrand, whose name would later be a byword for double-dealing, quickly sized up the political situation on his return and saw that Napoleon was the key. Another newly returned exile, Madame Germaine de Staël (ostracised for marital infidelity), was part of this circle and worked earnestly for a Barras-Bonaparte alliance, even sending to Italy gushing letters of admiration for the Commander of the Army there, which succeeded only in alienating Napoleon by their 'impertinence'.

Officially Napoleon encouraged the alliance with his onetime benefactor. He acquiesced when Josephine wrote to her ex-lover to stress that her husband was of one mind with him. Barras responded by appointing Joseph Bonaparte, engaged in Paris in some lucrative real-estate speculations, as the Directory's envoy in Madrid. Yet, despite these emollient superficial contacts, Napoleon was in no hurry to do Barras's dirty work for him. If he acted too quickly to extirpate Barras's enemies, he might find the moderate Directors too well entrenched on his return to Paris, and that did not square with his own already vaulting political ambitions. The truth was that he despised Barras, Reubell and Larevelliere only slightly less than Carnot and Barthelemy and referred to the Five as 'five little city courts, placed side by side and disturbed by the passions of the women, the children and the servants'. Napoleon's table talk often focused on the alleged mindlessness of the Directors, and a favourite example was their attempt to reform weights and measures and introduce decimalization. Napoleon liked to tell his bemused comrades that, as a mathematician, he knew better: complex numbers were better attuned to the deep structure of the human imagination, as witness the fact that the number ten had only two factors, five and two, whereas the 'complex' number twelve had four – two, three, four and six.

In conversations with Miot de Melito at Mombello that summer Napoleon made his contempt for all five Directors explicit: 'Do you believe that I triumph in Italy for the Carnots, Barras, etc . . . I wish to undermine the Republican party, but only for my own profit and not that of the ancient dynasty . . . As for me, my dear Miot, I have tasted authority and I will not give it up. I have decided that if I cannot be the master I will leave France. But it's too early now, the fruit is not yet ripe . . . Peace would not be in *my* interest right now . . . I would have to give up this power. If I leave the signing of peace treaties to another man, he would be placed higher in public opinion than I am by my victories.'

Napoleon's third, and most obvious weapon against the rightists was his victorious Army of Italy. He now had his soldiers' intense loyalty, partly because he had paid them half their wages in cash and allowed them to loot, partly because he was head of an 'ever-victorious army' and partly because they had been brainwashed by Napoleonic propaganda. Bonaparte could not only appeal over the heads of the Directory to the people of France but, like a Roman legionary commander of old, launch his cohorts against his country's capital, if that became necessary. Over and over again he referred to the 80,000 heroes who were just waiting for the chance to defend the constitution against 'royalist conspirators, cowardly lawyers and miserable chatterboxes'. On 14 July there appeared this ominous proclamation to the Army of Italy: 'Mountains separate us from France: but if it were necessary to uphold the constitution, to defend liberty, to protect the government and the Republicans, then you would cross them with the speed of an eagle.'

The resolution of the struggle for power on the Directory between Right and Left took an unconscionable time, partly because Barras and Talleyrand dithered about whether they really wanted to use Napoleon as their 'sword' to settle accounts with Carnot and Barthélemy. There were only two other possible candidates in mid-1797: Bernadotte and Hoche. Bernadotte was soon out of the running because of his putative ultra-Jacobin views, but for a long time Barras favoured Lazare Hoche as his hatchetman. Barras's plan was to make Hoche Minister of War as a prelude to a military coup, but this plan was leaked to the Councils, and Hoche became temporarily the prime target for the pro-royalist journals. Something happened to him at this stage, which is most charitably described as 'going to pieces'. A man who lived for honour and prestige, Hoche could not take the virulent assault on his reputation and buckled under the strain. Not yet thirty, he seemed suddenly to have the vigour of a man of seventy and capped all by dying in mysterious circumstances: some said it was melancholia, depression and despair that broke his heart, others claimed he was swept away by tuberculosis, while still others subscribed to the persistent canard that he had been poisoned by persons or factions unknown.

Barras now had no choice, if he wanted to survive, than to turn to Bonaparte. Delighted by the turn of fortune which had wiped out a dangerous rival, Napoleon sent Augereau to Paris with an unambiguous message: 'If you fear the royalists, call for the Army of Italy who will swiftly wipe out the Chouans, the royalists and the English.' The brilliance of this move was that Napoleon accepted his role as Barras's 'sword' and thus preempted an alliance between the Directors and any other general, while holding himself aloof from the direct fray, so that it could never be said that he had once again put down a rising of the people of Paris.

Augereau proved an efficient arm of Bonaparte's wrath. During the night of 17–18 Fructidor (3–4 September), in concert with Barras, Reubell and La Révellière, he surrounded the Tuileries with troops, forced the Councils to decree the arrest of Barthélemy and Carnot and annulled the results of the recent elections. Carnot escaped in his nightshirt through the garden to exile, but Barthélemy and Pichegru were arrested. Sixty-three marked men of the Right were proscribed and deported in iron cages to the penal colony in Guyana, that bourn from which few travellers returned. Draconian new laws against émigrés and royalists (and incidentally against ultra-Jacobins) threatened a return of the Terror. As justification for all this, Augereau posted up on the walls of the city the incriminating correspondence between d'Antraigues and Pichegru which Napoleon had been holding in reserve as his trump card.

The legend of the egregious corruption of the Directory dates from Napoleon's masterly use of press propaganda. Naturally, the five Directors *were* corrupt, venal and ineffectual, but in terms of rapacity they were nowhere alongside the French generals in Italy, the Bonapartes and, it must be said, Napoleon himself. Their worst fault was to give Napoleon *carte blanche* in Italy and to make no attempt to stop him when he used his almost absolute power to intervene in internal French politics. However, even Napoleon's enemies must accept that the opposition in the Five Hundred to his Italian policy *was* either overtly royalist or was being manipulated by monarchists whose aim was the overthrow of the constitution. In such a context, bluster about Bonaparte's proxy despotism at Fructidor is out of place.

Fructidor destroyed the monarchist faction and brought to a head the latent tension between Napoleon and Barras's party. Fortunately, perhaps, the Austrians seemed unaware of the latter nuance, and had pinned all their hopes on the triumph of the rightists in Paris. This is the context in which the protracted negotiations and sustained Austrian stalling that summer should be seen. Some of the prevarications of the foppish Austrian plenipotentiary the Marquis of Gallo at the talks that summer in Milan reached *opéra bouffe* proportions. Napoleon played along, for until he had crushed the monarchists in France he did not want a treaty signed. The result was a lazy, sensuous summer at Mombello which many of the Bonaparte entourage remembered as the happiest time of their lives. Josephine was in her element, for her husband indulged her love of animals by constructing a menagerie for her in the vast grounds. However, Napoleon did not extend this indulgence to all animals. Josephine's friend, the poet and playwright Antoine Arnault, remembered the general's joy when the beloved cur Fortuné was killed by a cook's dog. Josephine ordered the culprit banned from Mombello park, but Napoleon restored both cook and animal. 'Bring him back,' he said, 'perhaps he will rid me of the new dog too.'

In August the stalled peace talks moved to Passeriano near Venice. After a tour of Lake Maggiore, Napoleon removed there on 22 August. Josephine found an excuse to remain in Milan, where she spent nine days in dalliance with Hippolyte Charles before he departed on leave; she then condescended to rejoin her husband. After Fructidor Napoleon moved quickly to settle matters both with the Austrians and the Directory. In secret correspondence Talleyrand warned him he would have to move fast, as Barras and Reubell opposed his ideas on the treaty and in particular would never agree to ceding Venice. Augereau, meanwhile, forgetting who had made him, began imagining himself the true author of Fructidor and started criticizing his leader. Napoleon cut the Gordian knot by sending an impassioned letter to the Directory, stressing that there could be no peace unless his proposals about Venice were accepted; if the Directors did not like this, they should replace him:

> I beg you to replace me and accept my resignation. No power on earth could make me continue to serve after this dreadful sign of ingratitude from the government, which I was far from expecting. My health . . . needs rest and quiet. My soul also needs to be nourished by contact with the great mass of ordinary citizens. For some time great power has been entrusted to me and I have always used it for the good of the country, whatever those who do not believe in honour and impugn mine might say. A clear conscience and the plaudits of posterity are my reward.

This letter was written on 23 September. The Directory received it seven days later. Barras and Reubell were placed in an impossible situation. Their position was not yet secure enough to be able to dispense with a 'sword' and all other possible candidates had to be ruled out: Jourdan and Moreau for suspected sympathy with the ousted faction of monarchists, Augereau because he daily manifested himself as a vainglorious loud-mouth and Bernadotte because he seemed to be ultra-Jacobin in sympathies. Barras and Reubell had no choice but to accede to Napoleon's demands. The day after receiving his ultimatum, they in effect gave him *carte blanche* to conclude the treaty.

It was time to deal firmly with the Austrians, already demoralized as the implications of Fructidor sank in. The new Austrian plenipotentiary Ludwig Cobenzl was an even more consummate artist of diplomatic procrastination than his predecessor, frequently nitpicking over points of protocol and seeking by every means to drag out the talks in hopes that something – perhaps a new English initiative – might turn up. In the end Napoleon lost his temper with the delaying tactics. When Cobenzl disingenuously claimed that the Austrian emperor had no power to dispose of the destinies of the Rhine states, Napoleon exploded. 'Your emperor is nothing but an old maidservant accustomed to being raped by everyone!' He picked up a precious tea service – a gift to Cobenzl from the Russian Empress Catherine – and smashed it on the ground. 'This is what will happen to your monarchy!'

Shaken by this outburst and advised by his government that there was no power in France that could oppose Bonaparte, Cobenzl signed terms. On 17 October the peace of Campo Formio was signed. Austria ceded Belgium and recognized the Cisalpine Republic, which included Bologna, Modena, Ferrara and the Romagna. As a sop Austria was given Venice, Istria and Dalmatia but France retained the Ionian islands. In a secret article Austria agreed to support the French claim to the left bank of the Rhine at a Congress to be held at Rastadt.

Wiser heads in France saw that this treaty was scarcely the glittering triumph portrayed by the Bonapartist press. The original war aims of 'natural frontiers' had been transmogrified into Napoleon's quixotic dream for a new Italy, and the destruction of Venice was widely seen as a blot on French honour. Worst of all, Austria had been left with a foothold in Italy, which was bound to cause conflict in future and, in general, the empire that had sustained so many reverses in Italy had got away astonishingly lightly. There were many who agreed with another rising political star, the Abbé Emmanuel Sieyès: 'I believed that the Directory was to dictate the conditions of peace to Austria but I see now that it is rather Austria which has imposed them on France. This peace is not a peace, it is a call for a new war.'

It took four hours of impassioned discussion before the Directors agreed to ratify Campo-Formio. They wanted to oppose Napoleon, but he had the military power and their resources were uncertain. Besides, a great wave of relief swept over war-weary France and the tide of public opinion was running so strongly in favour of peace and Bonaparte that the executive did not dare to oppose it. Their foremost fear now was that the Corsican ogre would soon be back in Paris. To forestall this, they announced that the Commander in Italy was to be given two new honours: he was simultaneously appointed plenipotentiary to the Rastadt conference and nominated Commander of the Army of England, the would-be invasion force collecting in the Channel ports.

Though proud of the honour conferred on him, Napoleon was under no illusions about the Directors. In Turin on 19 November he confessed to Miot de Melito: 'The Parisian lawyers who have been put in the Directory understand nothing of government. They are mean-minded men . . . I doubt that we can stay friends much longer. They are jealous of me. I can no longer obey. I have tasted command and I would not know how to give it up.' The appetite for power shows Napoleon already not letting the right hand know what the left hand was doing, for a month earlier he had written to Talleyrand from Milan that he was so exhausted he could barely get into the saddle and needed two years' rest and recuperation.

On 16 November 1797 Napoleon left Milan to head northwards through Switzerland to the conference at Rastadt. After travelling via Chambéry, Geneva and Berne he arrived at Rastadt only to be advised that the Directory wished to confer with him urgently in Paris about the proposed invasion of England. Napoleon tarried four days, then sent word on 30 November that he would be leaving within forty-eight hours. He was travelling without his wife, for Josephine had seen another opportunity to be alone with Hippolyte Charles. She pretended she wanted to visit Rome, and Napoleon had arranged for a quasi-regal reception there by the peripatetic Joseph, who had meanwhile been appointed by the Directory as their envoy to the Holy See. But as soon as Napoleon left for Turin on 16 November, Josephine 'changed her mind' about Rome. She got Marmont to accompany her instead to Venice, where she was fêted like royalty by more than 100,000 onlookers. To the surprise of no one who knew Madame Bonaparte well, by pure coincidence also in Venice was Hippolyte Charles.

However, Josephine was now skating on dangerously thin ice. At Rastadt, Napoleon's spies informed him of what was afoot. There were rumours that Charles was to be executed by firing squad. In fact Napoleon curtly ordered Charles to report to Paris at once and await further orders. But the ingenious Josephine was not so easily baulked. She contrived to intercept the courier bearing these orders – none other than her old friend General Berthier – at an Alpine wayside inn and got the orders rewritten so that Charles was granted a three-month leave in Paris to attend to family business. Josephine then proceeded at a snail's pace through southern France while Charles, alerted, rode several post horses into the ground from Milan to Lyons in pursuit of her. He finally caught up with her at Nevers on 28 December. For five days and nights, proceeding as slowly as possible towards Paris, they made love, so that it was 2 January 1798 before Josephine finally arrived in Paris.

She was a month overdue, for Napoleon, who had arrived in Paris at 5 p.m. on 5 December after travelling through eastern France incognito, had been expecting her daily in the rue Chantereine. On arrival in the French capital, he made a point of meeting Talleyrand as his very first item of business. In the early days the entente between Bonaparte and Talleyrand was a true meeting of minds, and their first encounter, in the Grand Salon of the Ministry of Foreign Affairs, was marred only by the presence of the pushy Germaine de Staël. Napoleon cut her and concentrated instead on Talleyrand's other guest, the celebrated Pacific navigator Admiral de Bougainville, the man whose reports from Tahiti in 1767 had done most to boost the cult of the 'noble savage'. Only after a long consultation did Napoleon and Talleyrand go on to the Directory to meet his five nominal overlords. There he was received warmly by Barras and La Révellière, more coolly but still amicably by Reubell but in frozen silence by the two new men, Merlin and François de Neufchâteau.

Napoleon was now the focus for hysterical hero-worship as the ideal citizen-soldier, a kind of mélange of George Washington and Cincinna tus. While he pondered his next move, Napoleon cultivated the image of a demi-god, above the small change of quotidian politics, linked to no faction or party. At a dinner party on 11 December he was in sparkling polymath form, discussing metaphysics with Sieyès, poetry with Marie-Joseph Chénier and mathematics with his old teacher Laplace. But the more he remained above the mêlée, the more intense was the desire of Parisians to catch a glimpse of him. The entrances to his house in the rue Chantereine were sealed off with judiciously placed porters' lodges. Inside his fortress Napoleon seethed at Josephine's absence and at the bills presented by the decorator and cabinetmaker George Jacob for refurbishments done at Josephine's request. Even on St Helena he bridled at the bill from Jacob of 130,000 francs for custom-built salon furniture alone.

After enjoying a quasi-Roman triumph in the Luxembourg, where he was introduced by Talleyrand to cheering crowds and made a short non-committal speech in response to Barras's exhortation to him to lead his legions across the Channel, Napoleon got down to the serious business of planning the invasion of England. Much had happened on this front since his departure for Italy. In December 1796 an invasion force under Hoche, 15,000 strong in forty-five ships, and carrying Wolfe Tone the Irish revolutionary leader, set out for Bantry Bay. The fleet evaded the Royal Navy and reached landfall, all bar the frigate carrying Hoche himself. The army commander General Grouchy (later to be Napoleon's nemesis) took the fateful decision not to disembark his forces until Hoche arrived. After lying indolently at anchor for three days, the invasion fleet was hit by a severe storm which sent them scuttling back to France. Two months later, in Wales, Hoche tried again, this time sending an army of convicts to disembark on the Pembroke coast, but when Tate's 'Black Legion' surrendered after three days, Hoche's reputation took another knock; there were those who claimed that these two fiascos precipitated him into terminal depression.

On 21 December 1797 Napoleon got down to serious planning at the Ministry of Marine. In close conference with him was the head of the United Irishmen, Wolfe Tone, who had had such a close call in the great storm at Bantry Bay twelve months earlier. Tone was not impressed by Bonaparte's grasp of the politics and geography of the British Isles and reported with derision that the Corsican seemed to imagine that the population of Ireland was less than two million. Two days later Tone continued uncertain whether the appointment of this new invasion commander boded ill or well for the United Irishmen. He reported that Napoleon was cold and distant, said little, seemed bored and appeared to mask his indifference to Irish affairs under a mask of courteousness and hyper-affability.

Yet on paper Napoleon's invasion plans were elaborate and spectacular. Sixty specially designed gunboats, with capacity to carry 10,000 men, were ordered constructed and another 14,750 troops were to be conveyed across the Channel in 250 fishing boats. Both gunboats and fishing vessels were deployed over a very wide range: Honfleur, Dieppe, Caen, Fécamp, St-Valéry, Rouen, Le Havre, Calais, Boulogne, Ambleteuse, Étaples and Dunkirk were all to be embarkation points. And because the French now had the Dutch as allies, Antwerp and Ostend were to be used as well. Particularly high hopes were pinned on the gunboats designed by the Swedish engineer Muskeyn, who had long argued that the flank of the Royal Navy could be turned by the use of such vessels. Armed with a 24-pounder in the bows and a field-piece in the stern, these boats were the cynosure of Napoleon's invasion project. In January 1798 the Minister of Marine wrote to him: 'I remark with pleasure that by means of large and small gunboats, Muskeyn's craft, the new constructions, and the fishing boats of the district, the Havre flotilla can carry 25,800 troops for landing.'

While his military preparations proceeded satisfactorily, Napoleon continued to cultivate his image as saviour. He knew he could seize power in a moment, especially as he had incriminating evidence from d'Antraigues intercepted correspondence to blacken and discredit most of the leaders of the Directory but, using that genius for timing that was such a feature of his battles, he judged that the fruit was not yet ripe. Meanwhile his immense popularity played into his hands. Songs, poems, even paintings reinforced the propaganda message he had initiated in

Italy. A play based on his Italian exploits, *Le Pont de Lodi*, was a smash hit at the theatre, and the street where he lived, rue Chantereine, was renamed rue de la Victoire. Yet Napoleon proceeded cautiously: he knew that the bubble of a reputation could burst overnight, as it had with Hoche, and that a single unguarded aside could be the trigger for a change in fickle public opinion.

He therefore burnished his performance as the Republican hero whose active life is over and who wishes to devote himself to the disinterested pursuit of science and knowledge. He sat through official receptions and banquets taciturn and poker-faced, attended the theatre without cere-mony in a private box, refusing all offers by theatre managers of gala performances, and held dignified and quiet dinner parties. He assumed the vacant seat at the Institute left by Carnot's departure, and milked the action for symbolism by taking up the seat on Christmas Day 1797. His entry into the First Class (Sciences) of the Institute was a clever piece of Machiavellianism, winning the support of the 'ideologues' and the intellegentsia. Thereafter he was frequently seen in the company of the Institute crowd and assiduously attended its meetings, seated between Laplace and the other great mathematician Joseph Lagrange.

Next he concentrated on behind-the-scenes domination of the five Directors and the elimination of troublesome rivals. Irritated with Augereau's independence, he had him removed from command of the important Army of the Rhine and shunted into the backwater of the Pyrenees command. Hearing that the Directors were about to appoint Bernadotte to command of the Army of Italy, he intervened with the objection that Bernadotte was 'too able a diplomat' to be used as a mere commander and had him sent out to Vienna as the Directory's envoy to Austria.

Meanwhile he attended the daily meetings of the Directory at the Luxembourg, ostensibly working on the continuing negotiations at Rastadt on the future of the Rhine and on the proposed descent on England, but in reality bending the Directors to his iron will. Only Barras held aloof, but the other four were soon reduced to the most craven currying of favour. They showed him secret police reports on the popular perception of Bonaparte, which were a mélange of sycophantic nonsense specially brewed for the occasion. When the Directors had their agents assassinate two young aristocratic hotheads at the Garchi coffee house, Napoleon dissociated himself from the act and called it murder. In alarm the Directors sent him a deputation to justify their conduct as an act of exemplary terror.

In January 1798 a fête had been arranged to commemorate the fifth anniversary of Louis XVI's execution. Both for personal and political reasons Napoleon did not want to be involved in such a controversial project, but the Directors pressed him, alleging that his absence would be construed as a snub to them. Napoleon solved the problem by agreeing to appear at the ceremony on 20 January as a private person, part of a delegation from the Institute. The incident anyway caused the Directors embarrassment, for Napoleon was recognized as he entered the church of St Sulpice, and the cry went up: 'Long live the General of the Army of Italy.'

By 27 January 1798 Napoleon had had enough of the stifling boredom of the daily sessions at the Luxembourg that inevitably went on until dinner time. Joking but serious, he said to Barras that the way forward would be his own appointment as Director followed by a fresh coup by the two of them. Angered by Barras's frosty response to this overture, he pointedly absented himself from further meetings at the Luxembourg. Mindful of the potentially murderous inclinations of the Directors, as of royalists and ultra-Jacobins, none of them with cause to love him, he took careful precautions against an assassination attempt. Reubell recalled that Bonaparte took his own plates and cutlery to public functions, had his own private wine taster and for a time tried to live on boiled eggs alone. Napoleon himself admitted to a daily fear of arrest, always had a horse waiting already saddled in his stable and never removed his spurs during the day.

In this tense atmosphere he scarcely needed anxiety from Josephine also but, apart from keeping Barras ticking over calmly with her effusive letters, she merely added to his burdens in this period. The fact that she did not arrive in Paris until the New Year of 1798 considerably embarrassed her husband. A fabulous display of sumptuous luxury and patriotic triumphalism was planned in the shape of a grand ball on Christmas Day, nominally to welcome home the hero's wife. When Josephine did not appear, the ball was cancelled and a new date set for 28 December. When Josephine still did not appear, a final date of 3 January was set. Fresh from the embraces of Hippolyte Charles the fading creole beauty arrived in time for a quasi-royal evening, with Talleyrand as master of ceremonies.

Napoleon's misogyny had already surfaced during his 10 December speech when the svelte Juliette Récamier had tried to upstage him. The glacial anger he displayed on that occasion was surely in part 'transference' of his feelings towards Josephine. The anger Napoleon felt towards Josephine for embarrassing him was also projected on to Germaine de Staël, whom he already cordially disliked as an interfering feminist busybody who did not know her place – a woman, in his eyes, whose alleged beauty and brains were absurdly overrated. The ball was held in the great Hôtel Gallifet in the rue Grenelle, and the contumacious Madame de Staël took it into her head to ambush the conqueror at the foot of the great staircase. There she plied him with a series of quick-fire questions on his attitudes to women, hoping for some gallant persiflage. At first Napoleon tried to freeze her out but when Germaine refused to take the hint and pressed on, he decided sterner measures were called for. 'Which woman do you love and esteem most?' she asked. 'My wife, of course,' he replied coldly. 'And which woman in history, alive or dead, do you most admire?' 'Whoever has borne the most children,' said the conqueror, pushing past her and leaving her agape with stupefaction.

For a while Josephine played the dutiful wife at small dinner parties in the rue de la Victoire, always playing the useful role of transmission belt to Barras. But once again her turbulent private life threatened to catch up with her. First there was a crisis over the unreturned love letters from Josephine to Hoche, which were highly incriminating. She implored Hippolyte Charles to help her and he in turn enlisted the aid of Rousselin de St-Albin, guardian to Hoche's nineteen-year-old niece and heiress. Rousselin successfully retrieved the damning correspondence, but Josephine proved herself an ingrate and won Rousselin's undying enmity.

The next and more serious crisis, involved Charles himself. Napoleon learned from his spies, and a variety of other contacts including his brother Joseph, that Josephine was seeing Charles again, at a house in the Faubourg St-Honoré belonging to a M. Bodin. By this time Charles had resigned from the Army but was putting his military experience to good personal use as a middleman, working on commission for the shady merchant house of Louis Bodin of Lyons, who specialized in supplies and provisions for the Army, invariably of a shoddy or sub-standard kind. Charles knew the right contacts in the Ministry of War to set up lucrative contracts, involving multiple sweeteners and kickbacks for the principals involved. Because Josephine was a vital link in the chain, she too was on a retainer from Bodin, and had additionally used the Bodin-Charles network to smuggle diamonds looted in Italy into France, as part of a transaction utterly distinct from the 'official' loot she had received from her husband. The latest wheeze cooked up by Josephine and Charles was a lucrative contract for supplying the entire Army of Italy through Bodin.

Apprised of what was afoot by his contacts, Napoleon confronted Josephine with his findings. Was she seeing her lover again after she had promised Napoleon faithfully not to do so after he had spared Charles's life in Italy? And did she have her hand in the till in the manner described? Josephine begged, pleaded, cajoled, wept, waxed piteously and finally fainted. When she came to, she once more denied everything hysterically, threatened suicide and offered him a divorce if he did not believe her. Napoleon affected to be impressed. It is absurd to imagine, as some naïve biographers do, that he actually believed her. What he wanted from Josephine was external submission, deference and respect and what he feared most of all was a public scandal that would dent his reputation. He knew very well that she was continuing her affair with Charles, but for the reasons already adduced he enjoyed participating in his own secret humiliation – a masochistic urge made even more piquant by the quasi-sadistic way he would toy with Josephine and break her down. Napoleon actually cared more about the potential scandal from the Army provisioning by the corrupt Bodin company, but here Josephine successfully enlisted Barras to cover her tracks and obfuscate the record. A letter from Josephine to Charles on 19 March, the day after the dramatic showdown with Napoleon, is eloquent: 'Please tell Bodin to say that he does not know me, that it was not through me that he obtained the Army of Italy contract.'

Disillusioned with both Directory and Josephine, Napoleon departed on 8 February 1798 for a two-week tour of inspection of the Channel ports, travelling incognito from port to port through Normandy, Picardy, the Pas-de-Calais and Belgium, but concentrating on Boulogne, Calais and Dunkirk. In Belgium his itinerary took him to Nieuport, Ostend, Antwerp, Ghent, and Brussels. In Antwerp he conceived a great plan for rebuilding the port installations, which he actually put in hand many years later. But his idea for taking his gunboats from Flushing to Dunkirk and Ostend by canal, thus avoiding the risk of British attack on the open sea, was foiled a little later by a British commando raid, when 1,200 crack troops destroyed the sluices of the Bruges canal and many of the gunboats. The one positive achievement was that Napoleon followed in the footsteps of previous commanders of the French 'Army of England' by concluding that Boulogne was a better launching point for an invasion than Calais.

Although invasion preparations were reasonably well along in all the ports, Napoleon did not like what he saw. He had no confidence in the ability of his unwieldy flotilla to run the gauntlet of the Royal Navy. In his heart he still believed in the traditional French military thinking that an invasion of England was possible only after a victory at sea. Even if it were possible, he reasoned, for small vessels to cross the Channel under cover of darkness, this could be done only in the winter when the nights were long, since the estimated time for a crossing was eight hours minimum. By spring such an operation was no longer feasible and, as everything would not be ready before April 1798 that seemed to rule out the possibility of a descent on England.

On 23 February, three days after returning to Paris via St-Quentin, Douai and La Fère, Napoleon indited a long letter to the Directors, setting out his reasons why he considered an invasion of England chimerical: 'However hard we try, we will not achieve naval supremacy in a few years. To undertake an invasion of England without being masters of the sea would be the boldest and most difficult operation ever carried out and would require the long nights of winter. After the month of April it would be impossible to attempt anything.' He suggested instead either throwing in the towel and concluding peace terms with England or launching an attack on Hanover which, though it might ignite a premature war in Europe, would at least chime with the analysis he made elsewhere of Barras and his colleagues: 'The Directory was dominated by its own weakness; in order to exist it needed a permanent state of war just as other governments need peace.'

Next day there was a stormy meeting in the Directory. The Five Directors seemed unable to grasp that Bonaparte was actually refusing to proceed with the descent on England. They asked him what his terms were. When he replied with what he thought were impossibly steep demands, they agreed to meet them. In frustration he suggested deputising his protégé General Caffarelli Dufalga as *de facto* commander of the invasion attempt, but Reubell countered by putting up his own candidate, who would not be under Bonaparte's thumb. At this point Napoleon lost his temper and exclaimed: 'Do what you will, but I am commanding any descent on England.' His threat to resign if the Directors were dissatisfied was met by the now equally agitated Reubell with a histrionic flourish: 'Here is a pen. The Directory awaits your letter.' At this point Barras, realizing that there might soon be blood on the streets of Paris, before he had considered his own position carefully enough, intervened to pour oil on troubled waters. Napoleon promised to let the Five have a memorandum on his further thinking.

What Napoleon did not say in his letter of 23 February was that his own future prospects precluded a descent on England. This was a venture fit for a political gambler betting on a rank outsider, and Bonaparte was too well ensconced to need to take such risks. He had never yet been associated with failure and did not intend to start in the Channel. But how to prevent his star from slipping over the horizon? After three months on a precarious political tightrope in France, his lustre was beginning to dim. He had either to engineer a coup and make himself the absolute ruler of France or he had to win fresh laurels in the field. With this in mind, he included yet another possible scenario in his letter to the Directors. If he could not emulate his hero Julius Caesar by setting foot in England as a conqueror, he would rival his other hero Alexander the Great by winning glory in the East. His thoughts now increasingly turned to Egypt.

CHAPTER NINE

Napoleon's interest in a specific adventure in Egypt, as opposed to his general mania for the Orient, can be traced back to 1797. In July of that year Talleyrand, newly arrived from the U.S.A. and soon to be the Directory's Foreign Minister, lectured to the Institute of Sciences and Arts in Paris on 'The Advantages of Acquiring New Colonies'. Talleyrand argued that Egypt was an ideal colony, as it was closer to France than her possessions in Haiti and the West Indies and not so vulnerable, either to the Royal Navy or the rising power of the U.S.A. He pointed out that the great eighteenth-century French statesman the duc de Choiseul had wanted to buy Egypt from Turkey. The idea had been in the air from other sources too: from Magallon, the onetime French consul in Cairo who stressed that this was the obvious gateway to India; and from Volney's *Considérations sur la guerre actuelle des Turcs* (1788). It was perhaps no coincidence that Talleyrand was appointed Foreign Minister fifteen days after making this speech.

Whether prompted by Talleyrand or not, on 16 August 1797 Napoleon wrote from Mombello to the Directors as follows: 'The time is not far distant when we shall feel that, in order to destroy England once and for all we must occupy Egypt. The approaching death of the vast Ottoman Empire forces us to think ahead about our trade in the Levant. ' Soon he and Talleyrand were deeply involved in the project, at least at a theoretical level. On 13 September Napoleon wrote to the Foreign Minister to suggest that as a prelude to the conquest of Egypt France should invade Malta: the island had a population of 100,000 who were disgusted with their hereditary rulers, the Knights of St John, while the Knights were a shadow of their former military selves and could easily be suborned from the Grand Master. Through his secret agents on the island Napoleon had already learned that the Order was in a terminal state of decline. When the French Revolution swept away feudal dues and benefices and confiscated Church property it unwittingly signed a death sentence on the Knights. Besides most of them were French, and would they really oppose an army from the French mainland when the only possible beneficiaries were the English?

After the débâcle in the Directory on 24 February, Napoleon went away to compose a memorandum, stressing the advantages of an Egyptian expedition and setting out the minimum requirements in men and matériel. The Directors baulked at the size of expedition Napoleon proposed, especially as it would divert military resources from the European front, but they desperately wanted to be rid of Bonaparte so agreed to the enterprise on 5 March. The much-touted idea that the Directors opposed the adventure vehemently is false. Secret preparations were at once put in hand. Napoleon meanwhile ostentatiously attended the Institute daily, as if he were intending to withdraw into private life; as a further blind he was renamed commander of the descent on England with much public trumpeting.

Napoleon's motives for going to Egypt were a curious mixture of the rational and the irrational, in which expediency and cold calculation went hand in hand with his 'Oriental complex'. Some of the ideas in his memorandum were highly attractive to the Directory, though it is not clear how practicable they were. The most tantalizing notion was that of establishing a French colony without slaves to take the place of Santo Domingo and the sugar islands of the West Indies, which would provide France with the primary products of Africa, Syria and Arabia while also providing a huge market for French manufactures.

In the short term, there were cogent military arguments, even if based on rather too many imponderables. *If* the conquest of Egypt was wholly successful, it could be used as a springboard for reinforcing Tippoo Sahib, sultan of Mysore, and the Mahrattas and ultimately expelling the British from India; links with Tippoo had been all but severed when the British captured the Cape of Good Hope. *If* a Suez canal could be dug, this would destroy the efficacy of the route round the Cape and neutralize British seapower. An immediate consequence of the conquest of Egypt might be that France could use the country as a bargaining counter against Turkey. Certainly the threat to India would pressurise Pitt towards peace. Above all, the invasion of Egypt would be easier to achieve and less expensive than a descent on England.

These points could be argued for and against and were well within the realm of the feasible. But some of Napoleon's utterances suggest an unassimilated obsession with the Orient, where the motives cannot be integrated into a rational framework. His reading of Plutarch, Marigny and Abbé Raynal had augmented his desire to emulate Alexander the Great and Tamerlane. He was always interested in the Turkish empire and, even if we did not know of his early hankering to serve the Porte, we would be alerted to the romantic side of his perception of the Orient by his many asides to Bourrienne. 'We must go to the Orient; all great glory has been acquired there.' On 29 January 1798, two days after protracted talks with Talleyrand about all the implications of an Egyptian adventure, he remarked to Bourrienne: 'I don't want to stay here, there's nothing to do ... Everything's finished here but I haven't had enough glory. This tiny Europe doesn't provide enough, so I must go east.'

In the early months of 1798 Napoleon's 'Oriental complex' chimed perfectly with his own objective self-interest. After three months in Paris, he was ceasing to be an object of universal fascination. Convinced of the need for ceaseless momentum, he knew he had either to attempt a coup in Paris or to find an adventure elsewhere. He felt he would probably lose if he attempted an invasion of England, but would probably win if he went to Egypt. True, there was great risk from the Royal Navy but, after the loss of Leghorn and Hoche's invasion attempts in 1796, the British had pulled their fleets out of the Mediterranean. If cross-Channel invasion fever could be kept up, it was likely they would stay out.

For two months from 5 March Napoleon moved heaven and earth to put together a viable expedition. He had to raise the money, troops and ships needed while maintaining secrecy about the destination of his forces. He had to find a means of 'selling' the idea of Egypt to the French population at large when the secret became known. And he had to be absolutely sure in his own mind that he was doing the right thing, that his absence would not, after all, play into the hands of his enemies and political rivals. France was not yet psychologically ready for the fall of the Directory, and the Five must be given enough rope to hang themselves with; on the other hand, if things went wrong in Egypt or he was away too long, Napoleon could come back to find that he was yesterday's man and that Bernadotte, a new Hoche or maybe even Barras still was the man of the hour. Napoleon's actions throughout March–May 1798 were those of a gambler playing for very high stakes, and it is this that accounts for the many 'blips' in the preparation of the expedition.

The first problem was that of men, money and matériel. Napoleon had originally projected a total army of 60,000 for his ultimate advance into India: these were to comprise 30,000 Frenchmen and 30,000 recruits he hoped to find in Egypt, conveyed on 10,000 horses and 50,000 camels, together with provisions for sixty days and water for six. With these, a train of artillery, 150 field-pieces and a double issue of ammunition, he estimated he could reach the Indus in four months. The very mention of the Indus, with its association with Alexander the Great, is suggestive.

However, Napoleon was prevailed on by Talleyrand to do separate estimates for Egypt alone, so as not to alarm the Directors. He therefore asked for 25,000 men and the use of the Toulon fleet already in being, making the costings far less than for the descent on England, and the Directors granted him this without demur.

Next he assembled a galaxy of military talent. The thirty-year-old Louis Charles Desaix was a military hero Napoleon had met in Rastadt the previous November. Desaix was an ex-aristocrat who as a young man had refused to become an émigré; ugly, with a sabre scar across his face, he was still an avid womanizer. He had won his laurels in Moreau's Black Forest campaign in 1796 and the following year held the fortress of Kehly for two months against the Austrians where a lesser man would have capitulated after a week. He and Napoleon had a rare rapport and perhaps not coincidentally he was the greatest military talent ever to fight at Bonaparte's side. The forty-five-year-old Jean-Baptiste Kléber, on the other hand, never liked Napoleon but was invaluable in the field. His pedigree included the Vendée War and victories at Fleurus and Altenkirchen in 1794–96.

Additionally Napoleon had as his chief of cavalry General Dumas, future father of the novelist, and the one-legged General Louis Caffarelli as chief of engineers; the reliable Louis Berthier acted as chief of staff and Androche Junot as principal aide-de-camp. Most of the other generals were 'new men': d'Hilliers, Menou, Bon, Reynier. Napoleon was lucky in being able to take so much military talent with him at a time when warfare threatened France on other fronts, but the Directory played into his hands by turning down his offer to give up Desaix and Kléber so that they could concentrate on descents on the British Isles.

Money was a particular problem, for Talleyrand and Napoleon had sold the idea of Egypt to the Directors on the ground that it would pay for itself. This meant that Napoleon would have to raise nine million francs before the expedition could sail. He demanded from the Directors permission for handpicked men to go abroad to extract this sum and accordingly sent Joubert, Berthier and Brune to, respectively, Holland, Rome and Switzerland to obtain the funds. These plundering expeditions were the most barefaced Napoleon had yet authorized. Brune's ruthless campaign in Switzerland, where he uplifted fourteen million francs, achieved notoriety and Brune himself became a byword for plundering. When the Directory appointed him to Italy, he had the audacity to levy a further 200,000 francs for the 'expenses' of his previous looting. On the journey south the bottom of his carriage collapsed under the weight of stolen gold he had stashed in its boot. In Italy Brune continued his career as a kind of licensed pirate and went from strength to strength until his disgrace in 1807.

Having by the most brutal methods raised the funds for his expedition, Napoleon faced the next problem, that of persuading the French people that their hero had embarked on a worthwhile, prestigious and glorious venture. His ploy was to surround the expedition with the aura of scientific discovery. Without telling his chosen candidates exactly where they were going, Napoleon invited scores of eminent scientists to accompany him on a tropical voyage of adventure. Given that they were taking a leap into the unknown, it is surprising how few of the savants turned him down; it was doubtless his rôle and status at the Institute that persuaded them. If the British had intercepted and sunk Napoleon's Egyptian flotilla, much of France's intellectual talent would have gone to the bottom.

Among the celebrities who accepted his invitation were Gaspard Monge, the highly talented mathematician, physicist and inventor of descriptive geometry; Jean-Baptiste Fourier, the equally brilliant mathematician; Claude-Louis Berthollet, the great pioneering chemist; Geoffroy St-Hilaire, the naturalist, Nicholas Conté, the inventor and ballooning expert; Gratet de Dolomieu, the mineralogist for whom the Dolomite mountains are named; Matthieu de Lesseps, father of Ferdinand, whose journey to Egypt sowed the idea of a Suez canal which he passed on to his son; Vivant Denon the engraver, and a host of others, including astronomers, civil engineers, geographers, draughtsmen, printers, gunpowder experts, poets, painters, musicians, archaeologists, orientalists and linguists. In all, over 150 distinguished members of the Institute answered Bonaparte's call.

It was a brilliant stroke of propaganda genius to include these 'ideologues' as it enabled Napoleon to obfuscate the true motives for the Egyptian expedition. His claim to be engaged on a civilizing mission has fooled many people and the myth persists even today. To seek out new worlds in order to enhance pure knowledge and to bring the light of Western civilization to benighted regions of the globe provided superb ideological rationalization for an enterprise that was always part hardheaded Machiavellian calculation and part romantic fantasy. The two sides of Napoleon, ruthless, cynical, down-to-earth pragmatist on the one hand, and dreamer and fantasist on the other, were rarely so perfectly dovetailed. The ideological camouflage provided in addition by the scientists and intellectuals who accompanied him makes the Egyptian venture something of a motivational masterpiece.

Finally, Napoleon had to keep his destination secret. This he did with remarkable success, aided by the undoubted fact that troops continued to collect in Channel ports; they would eventually be used in the ill-fated Hardy-Humbert expedition to Ireland in August. Only the English agent at Leghorn correctly guessed the true destination of Napoleon's men but his view was dismissed sceptically at the Admiralty. Another factor helping Napoleon was that at the very time he set out for Egypt, a great rebellion broke out in Ireland, which occupied a good deal of English attention. The one serious miscalculation – it was nearly fatal – that Napoleon made was to assume that the Royal Navy would not re-enter the Mediterranean. Some instinct – or was it merely the Jeremiah laments of his right-hand man Henry Dundas? – led the warmongering and ferocious Francophobe William Pitt to send a strong naval squadron under Nelson into the Mediterranean, when the obvious course would have been simply to bottle up the exit from the Straits of Gibraltar.

Ironically, it was land-based events in Europe rather than the Royal Navy which nearly torpedoed the Egyptian expedition. Napoleon's Machiavellian suggestion that Bernadotte be appointed envoy to Vienna had succeeded in discrediting the vainglorious Gascon, just as Bonaparte had hoped, but the boomerang effects threatened to unhorse him as well. On 22 April Napoleon wrote to Admiral Brueys, commanding the Toulon fleet that was to cover the expedition on its perilous track to Egypt, that he would be leaving for Toulon tomorrow. Suddenly urgent word came from the Directory that Napoleon was required to return to Rastadt, there to demand satisfaction from the Austrian emperor for the 'Bernadotte affair'. Once ensconced in Vienna as ambassador, the ultra-Jacobin Bernadotte ran up the tricolour on the masthead of his 'hôtel'. This was construed as an insult by the Viennese, who flouted diplomatic immunity, invaded the house, tore down the flag and plied Bernadotte with insults.

The Directors' instinctive reaction was to declare war, but Napoleon advised them strongly that they should not reopen hostilities because of the folly of Bernadotte. He declared himself satisfied that the Austrians would give satisfaction for the incident and, besides, French forces were now too dispersed – in Rome, Switzerland, Holland, the Channel ports – to make a campaign against Austria feasible. The response of the Directors was that Napoleon should go to Rastadt with all speed. Napoleon told them forthrightly that his involvement with Campo Formio and Rastadt had ended the year before and he would not be going.

Here was yet another stand-off, and for the first time since his return to Paris Napoleon began seriously to consider seizing power as the only way to rid himself of the troublesome Directors. On the very day he wrote to Brueys, and just before the courier from the Directory arrived, he had told Bourienne, who asked him how long he would be in Egypt: 'A few months or a few years, depending. They don't want me here. To make things right I suppose I should overthrow them and make myself King but it's not time to think of that yet.' Doubtless Barras intuited something of what was on Bonaparte's mind, for on 27 April, four days after the lengthy and acrimonious session in the Directory, he informed the general that the Directory had decided not to send him to Rastadt and he was therefore free to leave for Toulon. Even so, friends like Arnault urged Napoleon right up to the last moment to stay and seize power. Napoleon declined. The day before he left Paris he told Arnault: 'The Parisians complain but they would not take action. If I mounted my horse, nobody would follow me. We'll leave tomorrow.'

Leaving Paris on 4 May, Napoleon sped southwards to Lyons via Chalon, then took a boat down the Rhône and arrived in Aix-en-Provence on the 8th. The next day he was in Toulon, conferring with Brueys, proudly overseeing the armada that had been collected there. The formal orders from the Directors, originally issued on 12 April, had been reconfirmed. These instructed Bonaparte to seize Malta and Egypt, dislodge the British from the Middle East, construct a Suez Canal and build good relations with Turkey by remitting the annual tribute from Egypt to Constantinople. At this date Egypt was a Turkish possession in name only, having for centuries been in the grip of a ruling military élite, the Mamelukes, who did not recognize the sovereignty of the Porte. The Directors had agreed on a twin-track strategy towards Turkey whereby, while Napoleon was conquering Egypt, Talleyrand would head a mission to Constantinople to explain that the expedition, far from being aimed at Turkey, actually served their interests.

After ten weeks of frenzied preparations, twenty-one brigades had been detached from armies in Italy, Rome, Corsica, Switzerland and northern France, although most of the units were veterans of the Army of Italy. By legerdemain Napoleon had greatly exceeded the numbers agreed with the Directory. Instead of 25,000 there were actually 38,000 troops, ready to embark in four hundred transports from five ports: Toulon, Marseilles, Genoa, Ajaccio, Civitavecchia. There were sixty field-guns, forty siege-guns, hard rations for one hundred days and water for forty; only 1,200 horses were taken along as Napoleon expected mainly to use camels as transport. The convoy was escorted by Brueys and thirteen ships of the line, including the flagship *L'Orient*. To maintain secrecy it was agreed with Brueys that all shipping of whatever kind should be forbidden to leave Marseilles and Toulon for five days after the Armada left.

Josephine accompanied her husband as far as Toulon and, to all appearances, was determined to travel with him all the way to Egypt. That she did not has sometimes been attributed to her cunning and machiavellianism, but the sequence of events strongly suggests that she ended up staying behind by pure accident. Napoleon was fearful that he might encounter Nelson and the Royal Navy, so arranged with Josephine that, once he passed the coast of Sicily safely, he would send back a courier to have her embark on a fast ship. Only four days out, he missed her so badly that he sent back the frigate *Pomone* to pick her up at Naples as agreed.

The fact that Josephine had meanwhile departed north for a spa at Plombières in Lorraine has made some biographers suspicious that she never intended to go to Egypt. But the more likely explanation is simply that Josephine was birdbrained when it came to business appointments, punctuality or logistics and had not allowed herself enough time to get down to Naples. Whatever the explanation, on 20 June she and two female companions were seriously injured when a wooden balcony collapsed under them while they stood gazing out at the street from the first floor. Josephine was at first thought to be partially paralysed and to have sustained severe internal injuries. She recovered only after a long convalescence in Lorraine.

Meanwhile, after being delayed for two weeks by contrary winds, the Egyptian armada finally stood away from Toulon on 19 May. All unawares, the French fleet was actually in the gravest danger from the Royal Navy, whose intelligence was first-rate despite all the French disinformation. While Pitt ordered Nelson to re-enter the Mediterranean, Admiral St Vincent detached three frigates from the Cadiz fleet to help Nelson watch Toulon. Nelson was actually off Toulon on 17 May while the French fleet was becalmed, but its departure two days later took him by surprise. The French were able to run before the wind past the east coast of Corsica, but when Nelson set off in pursuit on a more westerly track he ran straight into the teeth of the gale, took severe damage and had to put into Sardinia for repairs.

The amazingly fortunate French fleet in the meantime made rendez-vous with the Genoa squadron on 21 May and the flotilla from Ajaccio two days later; the Civitavecchia ships were not encountered until 9 June at Malta. For the first part of the voyage feelings ran high between the scientists and intellectuals on the one hand and the soldiers and sailors on the other, who treated them with amused contempt. The fault was

Napoleon's for, with a foot in both camps, he could not see any reasons for disharmony and was impatient with complaints from either side. Intending as he did to found an Egyptian Institute, he turned the deck of his ship into a kind of floating university, where daily seminars were held on a wide variety of topics.

It was now that Androche Junot, Napoleon's chief aide, first revealed the qualities that would eventually lead to his fall from his master's favour. Two years younger than Napoleon, the twenty-seven-year-old Junot was already showing signs of a world-weary cynicism, verging on nihilism, that was more appropriate to a much younger man. He had not always been thus: when his father asked sceptically after the siege of Toulon in 1793, 'Who is this unknown General Bonaparte?' Junot had replied: 'He is the sort of man of whom Nature is sparing and who only appears on earth at intervals of centuries.'

Junot never entirely lost his hero-worship of Napoleon but, almost as compensation, he was devastatingly sardonic and philistine about virtually everyone and everything else. During one of the first shipboard 'seminars', which Napoleon expected his officers to attend, he was discovered asleep and snoring loudly. When aroused he was unrepentant: 'General, it is all the fault of your confounded Institute: it sends everyone to sleep, yourself included.' Always ready to poke fun at the academicians on *L'Orient* and with a pronounced taste for levity, he once made a pun on Lannes's name, pronouncing it as *l'âne* (ass). 'General,' he said, 'why hasn't Lannes been made a member of the Institute. Surely he ought to be included on his name alone.' Junot was now beginning to irritate Napoleon. After all, the scene with Josephine in March was really his fault, for Josephine dismissed her personal maid Louise Compoint for sleeping with the philandering Junot. It was in revenge for this that Compoint came to Napoleon and spilled the beans about Hipployte Charles, the Bodin Company and Josephine's infidelities.

On 9 June the French fleet reached Malta. On paper this should have been a formidable obstacle, as the city of Valletta had walls ten feet thick and was defended by fifteen hundred guns and three hundred Knights of the Order of St John of Jerusalem. But a combination of demoralization and the corrupting gold of Napoleon's secret agents had done its job well. The two hundred Knights of French origin resented the fact that the French Grand Master de Rohan had been succeeded by the Prussian Hompesch and let it be known they would not oppose their compatriots. Hompesch, a defeatist, seeing the scale of external and internal opposition ranged against him, surrendered after token resistance of a day. This was the same order of St John that had held Malta against the cream of the Ottoman army for a whole year in the sixteenth century.

For just three attackers dead the French secured a great naval base and a vast treasure. In five days Napoleon swept through the island like a whirlwind. He abolished the Order of St John, deported the Master and his Knights, abolished slavery and feudal privileges, reformed education and the monasteries, and ordained equal rights with Christians for Jews and Moslems. Most significantly, he seized the assets of the Order and those of many of the monasteries. When he sailed on, leaving behind General Vaubois and a garrison of 3,000, he took with him seven million francs of official exactions and countless millions more as loot.

Meanwhile Nelson's search for his elusive prey continued. Reinforced on 7 June so that he had thirteen ships of the line, he wrote to the Admiralty on the 15th to say that the French destination must be Alexandria if they went beyond Sicily. Three days later he heard that the enemy was heading for Malta. Even as he prepared to catch them unawares at Valletta, he learned on 21 June that Napoleon had sailed on on the 16th. Figuring that since the French had a six-day lead, he should be able to catch them at anchor off Alexandria, he made for that port with all speed. But the French had taken a different tack, to Crete and then south to Alexandria. On the night of 22–23 June the two fleets actually passed each other in the dark. Five days later Nelson arrived at Alexandria but, finding no sign of the French, went north to search for them along the Turkish coast, leaving behind the Captain Hardy who would feature in his dying words at Trafalgar seven years later. Hardy, chafing impatiently off Alexandria, finally quit station just two days before the arrival of Napoleon's vanguard.

The latter stages of the French fleet's voyage to Alexandria were marked by high seas and food shortages, with some units reduced to eating biscuit and drinking brackish water; additionally there was a continuing atmosphere of tension from fear of encountering Nelson and the Royal Navy, so at night all lamps were dowsed. It is to this voyage that we owe Bonaparte's adage about novels: that they were fit only for chambermaids – an observation provoked when he found Bourrienne, Duroc and Berthier all reading romances. The fact that Berthier's choice was *Werther* did not assuage his leader's derision.

On 30 June the coastline of Egypt was spotted and next day Napoleon selected the beach at Marabout, eight miles from Alexandria, for his landfall. Disembarking troops in high surf on this sandy beach was hazardous, but far less so than a frontal attack on Alexandria. After getting 5,000 men ashore, Napoleon did not wait until he had achieved full disembarkation (this was completed only on 3 July) but pressed on to the outskirts of Alexandria. On 2 July Menou seized the Triangular Fort outside the city while Kléber and Bon took the Pompey and Rosetta gates. From 8 a.m. to noon a fierce battle raged as the French, spurred on by thirst, gradually broke down the Arab defences at a cost of three hundred casualties. Napoleon spent the morning sitting on a pile of ancient potsherds as he watched the unfolding battle, occasionally flicking at the shards with his whip.

Alexandria was not sacked, for Napoleon gave strict instructions that Islam was to be respected and there was to be no looting. This had the effect of making his men's morale plummet still farther. Matters reached crisis point on the subsequent march. Leaving Kléber in Alexandria with a garrison, Napoleon marched south with the main army on 7 July, with Desaix well ahead as a probing vanguard. Desaix's men experienced a 72-hour nightmare when confronted by the desert, the filth and squalor of the villages, and the hostility of the Bedouin. Encountering wells deliberately fouled by the Arabs, mirages and suffering from ophthalmia, the army was on the point of disintegration and many men went mad. On 10 July Desaix's vanguard reached the Nile, where his men, desperate with thirst, threw themselves into the river; many died here through overindulgence in slaking their thirst. It became very clear that Napoleon had timed his invasion for the very worst part of the year. The refusal to take account of seasons or the weather was always to be his Achilles' heel as a military commander.

Napoleon's main army of 25,000 also went through the slough of despond during almost a fortnight of desert marches, when water shortages and hostile Bedouin were daily features, exacerbated by dysentery, scorpions, snakes and swarms of black flies. The French commissariat had been incompetent, water flasks had been left behind, and terrible scenes were the result. When one division halted in the desert beside two wells, thirty soldiers were trampled to death in the rush for water, while others, finding the well drunk dry, turned their guns on themselves. One eye-witness wrote: 'Our soldiers were dying in the sand from lack of water and food; the intense heat forced them to abandon their booty; and many others, tired of suffering, simply blew their brains out.' François Bernoyer, chief of supplies to the Army, wrote to his wife: 'I have tried to find out what our government expected when it sent an army to invade the Sultan's territory without declaring war and without any valid reason for a declaration. Use your intelligence, I was told. Bonaparte, by reason of his genius and victories won with an invincible army, was too powerful in France. He was both an embarrassment and an obstacle to those who manipulate the levers of power. I could find no other reason for this expedition.'

Faced with outright mutiny, Napoleon had to concentrate the four most unreliable divisions at Damanhour, where he rebuked their commanders vociferously and unfairly. What was needed was a quick victory, followed by some looting. On 10 July the French were the victors at a skirmish at Damanhour. On 13 July there was a brisk river battle at Shubrakhit between the rival Nile flotillas, which the French won. On land the army formed into squares to receive a charge from the Mameluke cavalry, but the Mamelukes sheered off. With his army still teetering on the brink of outright mutiny, the hard-driving Napoleon forced it on to Wardan (reached on 18 July).

By 21 July the French were very near Cairo. At Embabeh they could see the Pyramids shimmering in the heat-mists fifteen miles away. It was now clear that the Mameluke commanders Murad and Ibrahim Bey were preparing to stand and fight. Napoleon drew up his 25,000 men in a line of rectangular squares, then exhorted them in a pre-battle speech containing the famous lines which may yet be almost genuine. Pointing to the Pyramids he said: 'Soldiers, remember that from those monuments yonder forty centuries look down upon you.'

The stage was set for the inaptly named Battle of the Pyramids (the Pyramids were some way distant), more properly the Battle of Gizeh. Facing the enemy with roughly equal numbers but with a huge technological superiority, Napoleon felt supremely confident. He drew up his men in a huge field of watermelons, allowing the soldiers to slake hunger and thirst on the fruit. As soon as he felt their shattered morale had recovered sufficiently, he ordered a general shift to the right so that his army would be out of range of the guns in the Mamelukes' entrenched encampment. Murad Bey, the Mameluke commander, spotted the manoeuvre and ordered all his cavalry out to arrest it. This was just what Napoleon had hoped for, for Desaix and Reynier on the right had orders in such a case to get between the enemy cavalry and its infantry.

At 3.30 that afternoon the French squares took the full force of a Mameluke cavalry charge, but the enemy horse was unsupported. In the six-deep squares, the French did not open fire until the Mamelukes were just fifty yards away. The volley, when it came, was devastating; the charge faltered, then turned into a massacre. All that valour could do was done, but the Mamelukes charged the bristling porcupines that were the French squares for a full hour, all in vain. The fire from the French infantry was so intense that the bullets set fire to the Mamelukes' flowing robes, so that wounded horsemen writhed on the ground in agony or burnt to death just yards away from the intact squares. The repulsed cavalrymen fled back to the entrenched camp, causing confusion and chaos just when the Mameluke infantry were already being hard pressed by Desaix and Reynier.

Taking advantage of the confusion, the two divisions on the French left under Bon and Menou also advanced on the camp. To make matters worse, many of the terrified and disoriented Mamelukes fled the wrong way, thus finding themselves cut off between the victorious squares of the French centre and the left and right who were attacking the camp. Total panic ensued, with thousands of Egyptian infantrymen rushing into the Nile, where they were drowned. French victory was complete but then and since triumphalists have exaggerated the achievement. It is true that in two hours the Mamelukes had lost 10,000 dead as against just twenty-nine Frenchmen killed and 260 wounded, but Murad Bey escaped from the field with 2,500 horse intact and a majority of the infantry did manage to find boats and reach the other side of the Nile. The Battle of the Pyramids then, though a great triumph, was scarcely what one historian has called it, 'a massacre as complete as Kitchener's victory at Omdurman a century later'.

The great significance of the battle was the way it transformed the morale of the French army. It was not just the victory itself that sent spirits soaring but the realization that in Egypt there were treasures to be looted as great if not greater than those the army had plundered in Italy. The Mamelukes had gone into battle in traditional style, bedizened with jewellery and precious stones and thousands of bloated corpses bearing these valuable trinkets were rotting in the Nile. In addition, in despair at their unexpected defeat the Mamelukes had tried to burn sixty treasure ships in the Nile, but most of the hoard was intact. The victorious troops spent a week fishing out the dead Mamelukes and extracting their prizes. There were to be grumblings and murmurings in the army again during the harsh year in Egypt, but never again did the problem of morale reach such crisis proportions as it had during the first three weeks of July 1798.

Napoleon acted quickly to occupy Cairo before the dazed Egyptians could recover from the shock of defeat. On 24 July he entered the city, declared that the Mameluke era had come to an end and put the administration of Cairo in the hands of a committee of nine sheikhs or pashas, with a French commissioner as adviser. He reiterated and repromulgated all the manifestoes he had had published in Alexandria, in which he declared he came to Egypt as the friend of Islam, advancing as proof his campaigns against the Pope and his destruction of the Knights of St John on Malta. Against the day when Egypt would be completely conquered he announced that the country would be run in the same way as its capital, with each of its fourteen provinces ruled by a committee of nine Egyptians and a French adviser. He himself would be overall ruler, assisted by a senate of 189 Egyptian notables.

In Cairo Napoleon had two disasters to mull over, one public, the other private. The public disaster was the loss of the French fleet at Aboukir. Nelson finally got definite news of the movements of the French fleet while he was off Greece and put about for Alexandria on 31 July. Next day he came on Brueys's thirteen ships of the line in Aboukir Bay and came close to annihilating them; the flagship *L'Orient*, containing the boy who stood on the burning deck, exploded around midnight and only two French ships survived the naval holocaust. This was Nelson's greatest victory to date, made possible because Brueys stupidly left his flank between the bay and the shallows unguarded. Nelson sent his ships into the narrow gap, thus catching the French between two fires.

Napoleon has sometimes been held personally to blame for this disaster through the imprecision of his orders to Brueys. The French admiral claimed he had remained at anchor because he was obeying Bonaparte's orders. Napoleon was adamant that he had instructed Brueys to enter the port of Alexandria or, if he was unable to do so, to proceed to Corfu. The best evidence suggests that Napoleon did issue unclear or imprecise orders, for on his own admission it suddenly came to him at Cairo that Brueys was in great danger. He therefore sent his aide Julien north with explicit orders, but Julien was murdered by Arabs before he reached Alexandria.

Yet even if Napoleon's orders appeared to constrain Brueys, this does not explain why he did not make his left impregnable by placing a battery on (or a floating battery near) the isle of Aboukir. Brueys was, after all, an admiral in the French Navy and should have been able to work out for himself that he had either to plug that gap, to anchor inside the port of Alexandria, or at least stand away for Greece. A good admiral exercises initiative and disregards orders that make no sense, just as Nelson habitually did. Only an incompetent seaman would at once have permitted himself to be out of range of his covering shore batteries *and* provided a gap between the shore and his ships which Nelson's captains could enter.

This may be the point to raise a general issue. Napoleon's critics make a point of leaping on any of his instructions that contains an ambiguity and saying that it was therefore he, not his subordinates, who was at fault. Yet it is surprising how often his subordinates interpreted these orders to their own advantage or disobeyed them when it suited their book; far less often do we hear of a subordinate disregarding Napoleon's orders to the leader's eventual disadvantage. Brueys was just one of many in a long list of unimaginative or self-serving commanders that would include such names as Villeneuve, Bernadotte, Ney and Grouchy.

Whatever the rights and wrongs of the Battle of the Nile, it was a major disaster for the French and perceived as such by Napoleon, who tried to put a brave face on circumstances and make a virtue of necessity. The French army was now marooned in Egypt it was true, but did not all great conquerors, from Alexander to Cortés, dispense with their fleets in order thereby to win even greater glory? Yet in his heart he knew the Battle of the Nile was a grave setback and would have dire political consequences. He was right: Turkey immediately broke off talks with France and prepared for a full alliance with France's enemies; the Second Coalition, formed in February 1799, would contain Turkey, Naples and Portugal as well as Britain, Austria and Russia.

Napoleon could slough off responsibility for naval defeat, but there was no hiding from the humiliation when his cuckolding by Hippolyte Charles passed into the public domain. Two days before the Battle of the Nile Junot took it into his head to divulge to his chief all that he knew – and he knew *everything* – about Josephine's affair with Hippolyte Charles. He produced letters detailing Josephine's return from convalescence in Plombières, full of circumstantial evidence making it clear that she and Charles were lovers. This he did in the presence of Bourrienne and Berthier. Napoleon turned pale and reproached the other two for not having told him what they must have known.

This scene has been consistently misrepresented, and it is alleged that Junot thereafter fell from favour, a victim of 'shoot the messenger'. It is true that Junot did fall from favour as a result of this incident, but not because he told Napoleon something hitherto unknown to him. Napoleon had his spies everywhere, he had expressly been given the same information by Joseph in March, and Josephine had already confessed. What was unpardonable about Junot's action was that he made the knowledge *public*, that he told the story in the presence of others. This meant Napoleon could not feed his masochistic fantasies but had to act. Hence the histrionics as reported by Bourrienne. 'Divorce, yes, divorce – I want a public and sensational divorce! I don't want to be the laughing-stock of Paris. I shall write to Joseph and have the divorce pronounced . . . I love that woman so much I would give anything if only what Junot told was not true.'

Misrepresentation of Junot's famous gaffe extends to character interpretation of Napoleon himself, so that we are supposed to see the incident as a turning point in his life. According to this view, from being idealistic he became cynical and ambitious, and it was in Egypt that the first strains of tyranny appeared. But Napoleon was always both idealistic *and* cynically ambitious, so the alleged antinomy does not hold. As for tyranny, Napoleon's most resolute critics always claim this was in evidence already in Corsica in the events of Easter 1792.

None the less, Napoleon's response to Junot's indiscretion is puzzling. In Cairo, before the Battle of the Nile was fought and he still expected to be back in France in a couple of months, he wrote to Joseph:

> The veil is torn ... It is sad when one and the same heart is torn by such conflicting feelings for one person ... Make arrangements for a country place to be ready for my return, either near Paris or in Burgundy. I expect to shut myself away there for the winter. I need to be alone. I am tired of grandeur; all my feelings have dried up. I no longer care about glory. At twenty-nine I have exhausted everything. There is nothing now left for me but to become completely selfish.

Joseph, who had put all the relevant facts before Napoleon in March, must have wondered why his brother should have waited until reaching Egypt before writing in this vein. He retaliated by drawing the purse-strings tighter and making Josephine sweat for her prodigious advances; Josephine hit back by alleging that Joseph was siphoning off her allowance to fund his own property speculations.

The day before Napoleon wrote this letter (24 July) the seventeen-year-old Eugène Beauharnais, torn between love of his mother and devotion to Napoleon, wrote to Josephine to warn her that her husband now knew everything about Charles: he added, with more filial piety than conviction, that he was sure all the stories were just idle rumours. Just after the Battle of the Nile both letters were intercepted in the Mediterranean by British cruisers. Here was a golden opportunity to turn the propaganda tables on the master of propaganda. Both letters appeared in the London *Morning Chronicle* of 24 November. By the end of the month they were printed in the French press as well and Napoleon was the laughing-stock of Paris.

In Cairo he turned to the problem of extinguishing the military menace from the Mamelukes. His forces caught up with Ibrahim Bey and defeated him heavily at Salalieh on 11 August, but the French hold on Egypt was still tenuous. After a number of massacres of outlying French garrisons he was forced to send out more search-and-destroy missions.

The main task, that of hunting down Murad Bey, was given to the brilliant Desaix, who had already settled in well in Egypt and gathered around him a polyglot harem. On 25 August 1798 Desaix set out on an expedition which, in terms of sheer military brilliance sustained month month after month, equalled if not surpassed Napoleon's own great achievements. Time and again, often hugely outnumbered and usually with only 3,000 men at his disposal, Desaix defeated the Mamelukes: principally at El Lakun (7 October 1798), Samhud (22 January 1799) and Abnud (8 March 1799).

Meanwhile in Cairo Napoleon achieved his ambition of founding an Egyptian Institute, with four sections: mathematics; physics; political economy; literature and the arts. At last the scientists and savants were coming into their own, for so far they had had a hard time of it, constantly the butt of derision from generals and privates alike. A roar of laughter invariably went up from the ranks just before an engagement when the cry was heard: 'Donkeys and scientists to the centre of the square.' Now, though, they proved their worth and achieved things of permanent importance which echoed down the years long after the purely military exploits of Napoleon's army were forgotten. Together with the nine local administrators the scientists supervised the building of hospitals (both civilian and military), sewage systems, street lighting, irrigation schemes, windmills for grinding corn, a postal system, a stagecoach service, quarantine stations to combat bubonic plague, and many other projects.

Since most of the scholars' books and instruments had been lost in the débâcle at the Battle of the Nile, Conté, head of the balloon corps, built workshops to manufacture what was needed. Napoleon and Monge, president of the Egyptian Institute, supervised the construction of libraries and laboratories, the installation of a printing press (which later published two newspapers), the beginnings of a geographical survey of Egypt, and complex mathematical studies of the Pyramids. A red-letter day for the Institute came in July 1799 when they discussed the Rosetta Stone, brought back from Upper Egypt by the academicians who had accompanied Desaix's expedition. The paper read that day by Napoleon's principal Egyptologist later inspired the brilliant French linguist Jean-François Champollion to decipher the seemingly impenetrable hieroglyphics. Napoleon in person took a party of savants to survey the ancient Suez Canal and draw up plans for a new one. The amazing energy of the Egyptian Institute membership covered so much ground that their work needed several magisterial volumes to do it justice; these were published over twenty years and the final volume did not appear until 1828.

On the political front Napoleon tried to tighten his hold on Egypt by having his régime recognized as legitimate by the keepers of the Islamic flame. He approached the muftis at the Mosque of El Azhar – a kind of theological university – for a *fatwa* declaring that the Moslem faithful should consent to his régime without infringing religious scruple. The muftis at first suggested that Napoleon and his army convert to Islam or at least be circumcised and avoid alcohol. These terms were predictably perceived as too steep, and some hard bargaining ensued. Finally, a compromise was reached whereby, in return for complete non-interference with religious worship, the muftis issued a statement, confirmed from Mecca, that the French were allies of Islam and were exempt from the usual prescriptions concerning circumcision and teetotalism.

This was a great and underrated propaganda victory by Napoleon, and without it he could scarcely have held down a country entirely hostile to him. But its effect was severely vitiated by lack of support from France. Although Napoleon in his letters to the Directory continued to harp on about the necessity that Talleyrand should depart urgently for Constantinople on his peace mission, it soon became obvious that Talleyrand was playing a double game of his own and had no intention of doing anything of the sort. Given the febrile state of Turkish emotions after the Battle of the Nile, only a top-level French diplomatic mission, prepared to make significant concessions, could have averted Turkey's drift into the British camp. When no attempt at all was made to extend an olive branch to the Porte, Turkey predictably declared war on France on 9 September, and the Sultan issued a *firman*, declaring holy war on France.

The long-term effects of the Battle of the Nile continued to eat away at Napoleon's position in Egypt. Not only was Turkey now hostile, trying to fan the flames of holy war against the infidel but, because most of the bullion Brune and others had looted in Europe had gone to the bottom of the sea with *L'Orient*, Napoleon had to raise taxes and exact forced loans to pay for the day-to-day administration, thus mathematically cutting down on the amount he and his army could hope to extract by looting. The resentment of taxation in turn fed into the religious crusade being preached from Constantinople.

The resentment found expression in a great uprising in Cairo on 21 October, which demonstrated dramatically how shaky the French grip on the country was. Fanatical Moslems from the university of El Azhar, sustained by dreams of immortality, took the French by surprise and slaughtered 250 Frenchmen before Napoleon was able to bring overwhelming force to bear. After two days of vicious and desperate fighting he gained the upper hand, at a total cost of 300 Frenchmen dead and some 2,000 Arabs. Among the French casualties were General Dupuy and Napoleon's favourite aide-de-camp Captain Sulkowski. Despite the propaganda picture later painted by Guérin, Napoleon did not pardon the rebel ringleaders but executed them out of hand. What he did do, out of purely prudential motives, was to refrain from burning down the Mosque of El Azhar, lest the entire country rise against him. But even this act of political judgement evoked complaints from the Army, who had wanted to put Cairo to the torch in reprisal.

Napoleon's position in Egypt was precarious and, cut off as he was in Egypt with no news of the outside world, worse than he knew. Having intended to be absent from France for just a few months, he was now in limbo, not knowing how soon or if ever he could be reinforced. The recent revolt in Cairo showed how uncertain was the temper of the people, and he intuited that Nelson's naval victory would already have tempted the Turks to a declaration of war. He was not to know that the Directory had already effectively written him off and were concentrating on grave crises in Europe. The new confederations in Italy collapsed like a house of cards under a fresh Austrian assault. The indigenous rebellion in Ireland failed to coordinate with the French and ended ingloriously; Humbert eventually landed and won a string of small victories but he was forced to capitulate. On 4 November Talleyrand wrote to Napoleon to tell him he was on his own and that if he could maintain himself there he had *carte blanche*; but this letter was not received until 25 March the following year.

The last two months of 1798 were an ordeal for Bonaparte even without the depressing news from Europe. The British blockade was tight and morale in the ranks was crumbling. Battle, suicide and disease had already drastically reduced manpower and in addition by the end of October 15% of the Army was on the sick list. In December bubonic plague broke out in Cairo, Alexandria and Damietta, claiming seventeen victims a day on average and leaving behind a further 2,000 dead. It was not surprising that spirits were low even among the officers: Menou, Kléber, Dumas and even Berthier put in their resignations only to have them rejected.

Reversing Sir Walter Scott's polarity, Napoleon's dreams of honour and of arms gave place to dreams of love and lady's charms. Since he said farewell to Josephine in Toulon in May, he had been largely sexually inactive. An eleven-year-old daughter of a sheikh, named Zenab el Bekri, had been presented to him as a virgin prize but he did not find the experience satisfactory, and this is in line with the sexual profile we have adumbrated above. Napoleon liked his women experienced and in addition, deflowering a virgin would have brought him uncomfortable reminders of Désirée at a time when he had already admitted, in his letter to Joseph, that he might have made a mistake in his treatment of her.

There has always been a persistent rumour that in Egypt Napoleon allowed himself his one and only homosexual encounter, on the Voltairean prescription of 'once a philosopher, twice a pervert'. Allegedly he agreed to experiment because it was put to him that all great conquerors, such as Caesar and Alexander, made a point of tasting 'forbidden fruit'. But it is interesting that this tradition also holds that the encounter was unsuccessful. This surely indicates that the idea of Napoleon's bisexuality, much trumpeted since Sir Richard Burton popularized it in his notes to his translation of the *Arabian Nights*, is not really convincing. It is true that Napoleon had distinct traces of bisexuality in his psychic makeup, but this is very different from saying that he was bisexual in an active sense. Whatever the unconscious impulses, the conscious Napoleon disliked any suggestion of sexual deviancy and punished the Marquis de Sade accordingly. On the other hand he cannot have been unaware that homosexual practices were rampant in any army deprived of women.

This was a germane consideration on the Egyptian expedition, for officers and men had been expressly forbidden to take wives, mistresses or girlfriends with them. Many blatantly defied the proscription and dressed their women as men to embark at Toulon; once safely at sea an epicene army appeared, with large numbers of the soldiers proving to be females in disguise. Among those who came to Egypt in this way was the twenty-year-old blue-eyed blonde Pauline Fourès from Carcassone. She and her husband were considered by undiscriminating judges to be an ideal couple, but when Napoleon met her on 30 November, she soon made it clear she had no objections to becoming his mistress.

Yet first there was a serious contretemps which once again showed Junot to be a master of the gaffe. After the initial meeting in a public garden in Cairo, when smouldering eyes and other obvious body language made it clear to Pauline that the generalissimo wanted her, Napoleon dispatched Lieutenant Fourès away on a trumped-up errand and then sent Junot to Pauline as his ambassador of love. Junot, an earthy sensualist, botched the mission by making the proposition in terms of extreme crudity; Pauline replied with affronted dignity that she would always remain faithful to her husband.

Napoleon's anger with Junot when he heard the outcome was overdetermined. By an obvious association of ideas he linked Junot's lack of discretion over Josephine and Hippolyte Charles with this further instance of gross insensitivity on sexual matters. It seems quite clear that Napoleon never forgot the two linked incidents, for when marshal's batons were handed out to old friends six years later, Junot's name was conspicuously absent. For the repeat overture Napoleon put his trust in the faithful Michel Duroc, with whom he sent not just his apology for Junot's behaviour but the gift of an Egyptian bracelet studded with precious stones and diamonds.

Duroc performed his task well, though we may take leave to doubt the story that he called every day for two weeks with a different present. In a comic opera subterfuge that can scarcely have fooled Pauline, she was invited to dine on 19 December with General Dupuy, the military commandant of Cairo. As the coffee was being served, Napoleon burst into the room and 'accidentally' tipped a cup of the liquid over her dress. He departed with her into Dupuy's private suite to 'remove the stains'; it was two hours before the couple emerged. At least this is the story. Napoleon's strategy for getting the lady into the bedroom sounds like the kind of ploy used by a cad from the 1940s rather than the action of a great conqueror, but the circumstantial detail about the coffee cup rings true. The latent hostility a misogynist like Bonaparte would have felt because Pauline kept him waiting before succumbing to his overtures may well have found expression in just this way; it is well known that a favourite form of aggression by men who do not really like women is to try to impair their beauty or that of their clothes.

By all accounts Pauline was extremely pretty and very accomplished at lovemaking. Napoleon's next task was to get rid of the inconvenient husband. He sent him to France with dispatches, but the troublesome Fourès wanted to take his wife with him and was only prevented from doing so by an express order. Laure Abrantès, who had the story from Junot, reported that she said goodbye to her husband 'with one eye streaming with tears and the other wet with laughter' and that, after going to bed with her husband for a farewell marital embrace, she 'buttered the bun' by going straight to Napoleon's quarters and spending the night with him.

It is clear that Pauline's charms had affected the great leader, for he sent orders to Admiral Villeneuve at Malta to provide a warship to convey Fourès to Paris; dalliance with la Fourès was evidently worth the sacrifice of a man-o'-war. But now came a case of history repeating itself, the first time as comedy, the second as farce. Just as Junot had been mixed up in both the case of Josephine's infidelity and the tryst with Pauline, so the British lent a hand in both cases to make life difficult for Bonaparte. Scarcely had the dispatch-boat *Le Chasseur* cleared from

Alexandria, than it was captured by the Royal Navy vessel *Lion* (29 December). The British, who had an excellent spy network in Cairo, had already heard the gossip about Napoleon and his new mistress and saw a chance to make mischief. The captain of the *Lion* put Fourès ashore near Alexandria, after securing his parole not to serve against England for the duration of the war.

Fourès arrived in Alexandria and insisted on pressing on for Cairo, despite the exhortations of Marmont, the commandant on the coast, that he should remain there pending further orders. Marmont foresaw a damaging scandal but was uncertain on his ground and weakly let the lieutenant proceed. When he reached Cairo a week later he was at once informed by his messmates that Pauline was openly living with Bonaparte. He burst into the palace, found her in the bath and whipped her severely, drawing blood. Hearing the outcry, her servants rushed in and threw the husband out. Napoleon then ordered a military court to dismiss Fourès the service for conduct unbecoming, and urged Pauline to divorce him and she agreed; her husband had destroyed the last vestiges of her affection for him by his brutality.

Thereafter Pauline was seen everywhere on Napoleon's arm. The troops called her 'Cleopatra', which accurately suggested that her hold on the leader was wholly sexual. As usual in such cases, the affair began to peter out once the first flames of passion were dowsed. In the end Napoleon grew tired of her and did not take her back to France with him in August 1799. She became General Kléber's mistress, which irrationally annoyed the dog-in-the-manger Bonaparte, but was soon discontented and yearned to return to France. Grudgingly Kléber allowed her to depart for Rosetta and the north coast where, while waiting to take ship to France, she succumbed to the predatory Junot, always a man with an eye to the main chance where women were concerned. In Marseilles she was detained for some time in a quarantine hospital and when she eventually reached Paris Napoleon had her pensioned off and married to Comte Henri de Rauchoup. Napoleon always had a sentimental streak when it came to his former mistresses.

Josephine meanwhile was matching infidelity with infidelity. According to Barras, when she received a false report that her husband had been killed in Egypt, she burst out laughing, jumped for joy and told Barras how glad she was that 'that cruel egoist' was dead. She even contemplated divorcing her absent husband and marrying Hippolyte Charles. It was said that Louis Gohier, the new president of the Directory, encouraged her in this ambition, hoping that he in turn could become her lover, but both Charles and Barras cautioned against the idea. In yet another melancholy twist of the *ronde de l'amour*, Désirée in 1798 took as her husband none other than Napoleon's bitterest enemy Jean Bernadotte.

The idyll with Pauline Fourès came to an abrupt end on 10 February 1799 when Napoleon left Cairo for Syria. He had received intelligence that the Turks planned a two-pronged attack, with their so-called Army of Rhodes being ferried across the Aegean by Napoleon's old opponent Commodore Sir William Sidney Smith while a separate Army of Damascus advanced on eastern Egypt via Palestine and Sinai. Napoleon's strategy was to avoid being caught between two fires: leaving a token force to control Egypt, he intended to march to Palestine, seize the fortress of Acre, defeat the Damascus army and then double back to meet the Army of Rhodes.

For the invasion of Syria he relied on 13,000 infantry, 900 cavalry and some fifty big guns; a garrison of barely 5,000 was left in Cairo. The march across the arid Sinai desert was gruelling, even in winter, and the army had to slaughter many of its mules and camels to survive. Entry into the lemon and olive groves of the Gaza plain promised better things, but there was a disappointment in the unexpectedly strong resistance of the fortress of El Arish. The defenders repelled several frontal attacks before Napoleon forced a surrender on 19 February by opening a formal siege. Together with the unintended consequences of the siege, Napoleon calculated that the delay at El Arish had cost him eleven days – days, it turned out, which he could ill afford and which affected the outcome of the entire campaign.

Perhaps the frustration at El Arish was one factor in the obscene butchery Napoleon ordered at Jaffa two weeks later. Gaza fell on 25 February, yielding 2,000 prisoners, and by 3 March the French army was at the gates of Jaffa. The 3,000 defenders here accepted the word of a French officer that their lives would be spared if they surrendered. But once in possession of the city, Napoleon ordered them all executed, plus about 1,400 of the prisoners taken at Gaza. This mass slaughter was by any standards a war crime, but it reached a fresh dimension of horror in the way it was carried out. Anxious to save bullets and gunpowder, Napoleon ordered his men to bayonet or drown the condemned thousands. The resulting holocaust revolted hardened veterans who thought they already knew about atrocities: there are well authenticated reports of soldiers wading out to sea to finish off terrified women and children who preferred to take their chances with the sharks.

This dreadful massacre was one of several incidents that haunted Napoleon ever afterwards, not in the sense that he felt guilty – he did not – but because he realized posterity would judge him harshly unless he could plead compelling necessity. He and his supporters have mounted several lines of defence, some specious, some with a certain *ad hoc* force, but none convincing. The argument that his aides were not authorized to accept a Turkish surrender is casuistry. Not much better is the *tu quoque* proposition: that the defenders of Jaffa had killed a French herald who approached under a flag of truce, and that in Acre the ferocious Turkish commander Djezzar Pasha had announced he would behead any French prisoners. If Napoleon had come to Egypt to civilize, as he claimed, this rejoinder was not really open to him. More compelling is the defence that he had barely enough food to feed his own army, would therefore have to release the prisoners to fend for themselves and would thus risk having Acre reinforced by men to whom a word of honour meant nothing. It is known that he was particularly enraged to find that most of the Gaza prisoners who had been released on parole had simply gone on to fight at Jaffa.

Perhaps Napoleon genuinely thought that military ends justified any means. Perhaps he was supremely ruthless and wanted to give his enemies convincing proof of his awesome qualities; the issue, in a word, was credibility. Or perhaps he considered that Arabs and Turks were lesser breeds without the law and that atrocities visited on them did not thereby legitimate war crimes when two European nations were locked in combat. The issue of atrocities in the Napoleonic wars is a complex one, but it must be conceded that Napoleon was the first one to set foot down that gruesome road. On the other hand, it is true that the Turks habitually used massacre to cow their enemies, that they recognized no rules of war and that, as in Spain later, the British made no attempt whatever to dissuade their hosts and allies from frightful atrocities against French prisoners.

As if the massacre was a sin crying to heaven for vengeance and heaven had answered, the French army was immediately struck by plague and had to stay a week at Jaffa. Morale plummeted, and Napoleon decided he had to assert his role as thaumaturge and inspired leader. He followed one of the darkest episodes in his life by one of the most courageous by visiting the hospital where his plague-stricken men lay dying (11 March). Fearlessly he touched the expiring men and helped to carry out a corpse. Always Shavian in his attitude to illness and doctors, he assured his petrified officers that willpower was everything and that the right mental attitude could overcome plague. This is one of the great moments in Napoleonic iconography, Gros's painting *Napoleon visiting the plague victims of Jaffa* portrays the leader as a Christ-like figure. But the effect on morale of his courage was real enough at the time. By the end of March he was able to resume the march on Acre, even though he left 300 plague cases behind.

The Fates were not smiling on the Syrian campaign, for the delays at El Arish and Jaffa effectively precluded a successful conclusion. If Napoleon had arrived at Acre any time before 15 March, he could simply have walked into the city. But meanwhile two things happened. On 15 March Sir Sidney Smith appeared off Acre in the Royal Navy ships *Tigre* and *Theseus*, just in time to prevent Djezzar Pasha evacuating the town. Smith had faced Napoleon at Toulon but, in an even more bizarre turn of events, he brought with him the very same Phélipeaux, now an émigré officer of engineers, who had once been Napoleon's classmate at the Paris Military Academy. Smith at once landed some companies of British troops, while Phélipeaux put Acre in a sound state of defence.

Even so Napoleon might still have prevailed had not British naval power once more tilted the odds. His flotilla bearing most of his siege-guns was intercepted by the Royal Navy off Mount Carmel, with the consequence that when the French assaulted Acre they came under fire from their own artillery. With proper siege-guns Napoleon could have blown Acre apart, but without them he was reduced to slow sapping and mining or costly frontal assaults on prepared positions. Smith concentrated his fire on the French trenches, making good use of the lighthouse mole and being supported by broadsides from *Theseus* and *Tigre*. All the time fresh supplies reached Acre, while in the French lines the sick list continued to grow. Morale was not aided by the news that Djezzar Pasha was paying a large bounty for every infidel head brought to him.

Operations went into temporary abeyance in the first week of April at word of the approach of the Army of Damascus. Once contact was made with the enemy, the French won all the early rounds. On 8 April an outnumbered Junot was the victor in a cavalry skirmish near Nazareth, while on 11 April Kléber with 1,500 men routed 6,000 Turks in a more substantial battle at Canaan. In yet another engagement the dashing cavalry leader Joachim Murat crossed the Jordan to the north of Lake Tiberia and defeated 5,000 Turks.

Emboldened by these easy successes, on 16 April Kléber with just 2,000 men attempted a surprise dawn attack on the entire 25,000-strong Army of Damascus as it lay unsuspecting in its tents. Not surprisingly, the attack failed and soon the French had their backs to the wall, in a desperate position under Mount Tabor, with stocks of ammunition running low. They formed square and prepared to sell their lives dearly. Suddenly, at about 4 p.m. Napoleon appeared, having made a forced march from Acre. A devastating barrage from his cannon and some well-aimed volleys from his advancing squares panicked the Turks, who had seen what just 2,000 Frenchmen could do and were terrified at the thought of being caught between the two armies. The retreat became a rout, and soon the threat from the Army of Damascus was no more. Amazingly, Kléber's army, which had fought all day, had lost just two killed and sixty wounded in a ten-hour battle with 25,000 horsemen.

If everything had gone right against the Army of Damascus, at Acre everything was still going wrong. When, on 1 April, the French sappers exploded a large mine under the 'Tower of the Damned' guarding the city, against all predictions it failed to crack the masonry and provide the breach needed. In a frontal assault Napoleon narrowly escaped death from an exploding shell through the quick action of his personal bodyguard, the Guides. There was a shortage of food and essential matériel, also of ammunition and cannonballs. Even when the rest of the siege artillery arrived safely at Jaffa and Napoleon was able to bring big guns to bear on Acre, he still could not take the city. Then plague broke out again, with 270 new cases by the end of April.

On his return from Mount Tabor Napoleon ordered a series of desperate frontal assaults. For the first ten days of May the tide of battle ebbed and flowed with fury. On 8 May Lannes actually breached the defences and got inside the fort, sustaining serious wounds in the process, only to find himself confronted with a second line of defence, even more formidable. One of his generals – it may have been the irrepressible Junot – remarked that Turks were inside and Europeans outside yet they were attacking Turkish-style a fortress defended European-style. Reluctantly Napoleon concluded that the citadel, continually reinforced by sea and with fresh forces pouring in daily from Rhodes, could never be taken. He had no option but to raise the siege; sixty-three days of investment and eight costly all-out attacks had all been for nothing.

This was the first serious setback in Bonaparte's military career. In the three months' fighting so far the French had lost 4,500 casualties (including 2,000 dead) from an army of 13,000. Four generals had perished outside Acre: Bon, Caffarelli, Dommartin and Rambaud. Napoleon failed at Acre partly through bad luck and partly through miscalculation. First he lost half his 24-pounders to the Royal Navy, then he failed to equip his other guns adequately: he had allowed only 200 rounds per 24-pounder and 300 shells per mortar, when he needed twice the quantity of shells and five times the rounds. Most of all, he had calculated that Acre would surrender without a fight, which of course it would have done had he not been delayed at El Arish and Jaffa. Moreover, if the usually reliable François Bernoyer is to be believed, some of Bonaparte's generals, notably Dommartin, worried that victory at Acre would lead Napoleon to march on Persia and India, actively conspired to prevent its fall. Furious at the blow to his prestige, Napoleon set his propaganda machine to work to mask the defeat by dwelling on the glorious victory at Mount Tabor. But his fury found expression in the public humiliation and foul-mouthed abuse of the 69th Regiment which had failed in the final assault; he announced that until such time as the regiment retrieved its laurels he refused to acknowledge its existence.

Napoleon now prepared for a hazardous retreat, anxious lest the emboldened enemy dog his footsteps across the desert – exactly what happened in fact. A particular problem was the 2,300 men wounded or on the sick list. If he tried to take them with him, his already seriously depleted army would not be able to march fast enough to elude pursuers and the result might well be a form of death by a thousand cuts, with daily attacks on the rearguard gradually nibbling away at the strength of his effectives. On the other hand, if the sick and wounded were left behind, they would be beheaded and otherwise mutilated by the Turks.

To his chief of medical staff Dr Desgenettes Napoleon suggested a simple solution: euthanasia of the worst cases by opium. Desgenettes refused but, to sugar the pill, experimented by giving thirty plague-stricken victims laudanum, in some cases with beneficial effects. Reluctantly, the troops man-hauled the rest of them back to Jaffa, while Napoleon covered the operation by continuing to bombard Acre until 20 May, using up all the siege-gun ammunition thereby. He then spiked the big guns, leaving himself with just forty pieces of field artillery.

In Jaffa, where the French paused four days, a final decision about the fate of the sick and wounded could no longer be postponed, especially since the occupants of the hospital where Napoleon had visited the plague victims on 11 March simply swelled the throng of non-combatants. After desperate attempts to evacuate all military hospitals had proved unavailing, a three-fold strategy was adopted: on all the hopeless cases mercy killing was used; those who were on the mend but could not yet be moved were left to the mercy of the Turks; walking wounded and convalescent were mounted on horses and mules. For the euthanasia Napoleon has of course been much criticized, but this was a different case from the massacre of the Turks, and it is difficult to see what realistic option he had, especially since the incoming Turks did behave to the abandoned Frenchmen in line with the worst possible predictions.

It was a gloomy and demoralized French army that trekked back to Gaza (reached on 30 May). But the real nightmare came next, in the shape of a four-day crossing of the Sinai desert. This had been an ordeal even during winter on the outward march, but now, sweltering in temperatures that rose as high as 54° C, with food and water low, a long train of wounded and a mounting casualty list, and Turkish horsemen harassing their rear, the French experienced exquisite torment and came close to outright mutiny. Finally, on 3 June, the exhausted survivors traipsed into Katia, with its ample supplies of food and water. The Syrian campaign, in some ways a miniature forerunner of 1812, had achieved nothing, except possibly to delay the Turkish landing at Alexandria while reinforcements were sent to Acre. Casualties had been terrific, and even Bonaparte's formidable propaganda machine was hard put to it to talk up the doomed campaign as a glittering success.

Defiantly Napoleon staged a triumph in Cairo on 14 June as he re-entered the city. The one thing he did have to celebrate was the quite extraordinary military achievement of Desaix in Upper Egypt. Although seemingly engaged in a Sisyphean task of pacification – in that each conquered area rose in revolt as soon as Desaix moved on and Murad Bey continued to receive reinforcements from Arabia – Desaix never relaxed his grip in a remorseless war of attrition. He won three great battles: at El Lahkun on 7 October 1798, Samhud on 22 January 1799 and at Abnud on 8 March. In the end Murad and the Mamelukes cracked under the strain of continuous campaigning. Desaix's campaign concluded trium-phantly just when Napoleon was emerging from Syria: the French General Belliard captured the Red Sea port of Kosjeir on 29 May, thus driving a wedge between the two hostile armies and preventing Murad from linking up with his allies in Syria.

Yet the impossibility of holding Egypt in subjection, marooned as he was and without hope of reinforcement from France, must have struck Napoleon forcibly when he heard that in addition to Desaix's ceaseless endeavours there had been two large-scale revolts in the Nile delta during his absence, one led by the emir El-Hadj-Mustafa and the other, a more serious outbreak headed by a fanatic claiming to be the angel El Modi of the Koran or, in some versions, the Mahdi or promised one. General Desaix proceeded to Lanusse, defeated El Modi and his army, then executed 1,500 'ringleaders' including the Mahdi himself. Yet all these successful French campaigns entailed losses in manpower Napoleon could ill afford, and there continued to be isolated massacres and ambushes of his troops.

It was therefore immediately on his return to Cairo that Napoleon began to think seriously about how to return to France. The usual version is that it was only after Sidney Smith, in an obvious bout of psychological warfare, allowed French ships to deliver newspapers with news of the Directory's disastrous setbacks in 1798–99, that Napoleon decided to leave Egypt. In fact some individual French spies managed to get to Egypt with news, and it would indeed be surprising if Napoleon had genuinely been without all intelligence for almost an entire year; after all, the interests of too many people, from Joseph to Barras, depended on keeping Bonaparte fully informed.

First, though, he had to pacify Egypt. To cow internal opposition, he organized the show trials of thirty-two members of the Cairo élite whom he suspected of treachery and, after having them convicted on trumped-up charges, executed them during 19–22 June. His propaganda machine got to work, exaggerating his successes everywhere, and threatening dire retribution if the Army of Rhodes dared land at Alexandria. To boost the morale of his men, he claimed that bubonic plague was only contracted by men who already had a death wish and that there was nothing to fear from the disease. But when Napoleon tried to force Dr Desgenettes to make a public declaration that the plague was not contagious, Desgenettes protested he could not be party to such a blatant lie. At this Napoleon exploded with rage, and a violent altercation took place between him and Desgenettes. Angrily Napoleon accused the doctor: 'You're all the same with your principles, you teachers, doctors, surgeons, chemists, the whole pack of you. Rather than sacrifice one of your precious principles, you'd let an entire army perish, yes, even an entire society!'

The blow Napoleon had long been expecting fell on 11 July, when Sidney Smith's fleet escorted Turkish landing craft into Aboukir Bay and disembarked 15,000 troops. The French garrison at Aboukir under Marmont valiantly held out until 18 July, giving Napoleon his chance to strike at the ageing commander Mustapha Pasha. But Napoleon was supremely ungrateful for their sacrifice. He claimed to have given orders for razing the town of Aboukir and fortifying the citadel, which Marmont had not carried out. When 1,300 defenders (including Marmont) and one hundred élite fighters in the citadel finally surrendered, having bought valuable time, Napoleon simply raged about their perfidy and cowardice.

Napoleon headed north from Cairo on forced marches, together with Lannes, Bon and their corps; Desaix was urgently recalled from Upper Egypt. The worst anxiety for Bonaparte was that, while he was engaged in the north, a new Turkish army might advance on Cairo from Syria. But a planned Turkish pincer movement foundered on the incompetence of Murad Bey. Murad was supposed to advance to Alexandria, bringing thousands of horses to mount the Turkish host and draw the big guns.

Murad, however, got no farther than the Pyramids before he was chased ignominiously back into the desert by Murat.

Napoleon arrived at Alexandria with 6,000 men, fully aware that it would take another fortnight for the other French corps, 10,000 strong under Kléber, to arrive. Learning that the Turks had not yet disembarked any cavalry or big guns, he decided to make a lightning strike with his own thousand-strong cavalry. The manoeuvre was perilous but plausible, since the enemy, by stationing its wings on high ground, had left a weak spot in the centre. There were three successive lines of Turkish entrenchments to be carried, and at first it was Napoleon's intention simply to force the enemy back to their second line of defence, where he could pin them with howitzers and shells from artillery swiftly brought up to the abandoned first line.

Outnumbered two to one, the French performed miracles. Murat's dashing cavalry attack through the centre, supported by Lannes on the left and Destaing on the right, cut the Turkish army in two; the ill-disciplined Janissaries played into French hands by leaving their defences in search of French heads. The Turks abandoned the first line of defence and rushed back to the second, but Murat's cavalry got between the two lines, forcing the Turkish right into the sea and the left into Lake Maadieh. Meanwhile, Lannes and Destaing on the wings had taken the high ground and came on at the double; it was estimated that thousands of panic-stricken Turks drowned at this point.

Encouraged by this easy success, Napoleon increased the stakes and gambled that he could take the third line of defence as well. Observing that Lannes was likely to turn his left, the enemy commander Mustapha Pasha sortied from the entrenchment with 5,000 men. There was a short and ferocious struggle, during which Murat and Mustapha actually fought each other from horseback and Murat took a wound in the cheek. Now Napoleon showed his genius for timing by throwing in the reserve at exactly the right moment to reinforce the struggling Lannes. The outflanking movement was completed and Lannes was in the rear of the redoubt. When Destaing came charging in, the despondency and terror of the Turkish defenders was total. Most of them fled in disarray and a further 3,000 were driven into the sea; Mustapha himself and his reserve of 1,500 Janissaries were surrounded and taken prisoner. By 4 p.m. only 4,000 Turkish effectives remained on the field and they barricaded themselves in the town and citadel of Aboukir which they had taken with such difficulty just a week before. Not wishing to suffer further losses in house-to-house fighting, Napoleon brought up his heavy artillery for a final period of slaughter.

It was a notable French victory, one of the few occasions when Napoleon actually carried out his textbook destruction of an enemy. For a loss of 220 killed and 750 wounded, he had defeated an army between twice and three times as large; Turkish losses amounted to at least 5,000 dead. The 69th Regiment, publicly humiliated at Acre for its allegedly poor showing and condemned to the task of escorting the sick on the retreat across the Sinai desert, fought with a desperate tenacity and fully retrieved their laurels. Sidney Smith, who had confidently selected Mustapha's defensive positions and advised him on the choice of ground, was lucky to escape back to his sloop.

Back in Cairo Napoleon could now make leisurely plans for the departure which he had strongly hinted at as early as 21 June, when he asked Admiral Ganteaume to be ready to sail for Europe in the frigates *La Muiron* and *La Carrière*. To put pressure on the Directory to recall him, he sent a dispatch to Paris on 29 June, acknowledging the loss of 5,344 men and asking for 6,000 reinforcements – knowing very well that they would not be forthcoming. Whether the political situation in France meant that the fruit was finally ready for the picking he knew not, and there was grave risk of interception by the Royal Navy as he travelled virtually the entire breadth of the Mediterranean. But his own future demanded that he get out of Egypt as soon as possible.

On 11 August a fresh sheaf of newspapers arrived in Cairo, leaving no doubt of the scale of disaster in Europe. At last the worst was widely known: that France faced a coalition of England, Austria, Russia, Turkey and Naples; that the Russians seemed ubiquitous in Europe; that an Anglo-Russian army had invaded Holland and an Austro-Russian army had gained control of Switzerland; that a Turco-Russian fleet had captured Corfu; and that another Austro-Russian army had swept into northern Italy and undone all Bonaparte's work there in a matter of weeks. France was reported to be on the verge of economic collapse and royalist sentiment was running high.

Napoleon knew all this already, but in a carefully stage-managed histrionic outburst put on for the benefit of his generals, he rehearsed the scale of the disaster in Europe: France facing Austria on the Rhine, Austrians and Russians in northern Italy and Neapolitans and Sicilians in the south; Austrian victories at Stockach on the Rhine and at Magnano and Cassano in Italy; 18,000 British troops and 18,000 Russian dominating Holland; Neapolitans entering Rome, the Russians in Turin, the Austrians in Milan, and withal the Royal Navy still the master of the Mediterranen. He inveighed against the Directors: 'Can it be true? . . . Poor France! . . . What have they done, the idiots?' He put it to the assembled company that he wanted to stay with them but now had no choice. It was fortunate for him that on 26 May the Directors had sent him a dispatch authorizing him to evacuate if he thought it necessary; this precious document would later give him a tenuous *ex post facto* justification for his decision to cut and run.

What Napoleon did not tell his generals was that he was deeply disturbed by a strong rumour that in Paris Sieyès was trying to engineer a coup and had called in General Joubert as his 'sword'. On 17 August Admiral Ganteaume informed his leader that the Anglo-Turkish fleet had left Egyptian waters. This was the chance Napoleon was waiting for. On 17 August he left Cairo for the coast and six days later put to sea in the *Muiron*. He took just a handful of his favourites and most trusted personnel with him. Of the savants, only Monge and Berthollet were allowed to accompany him; of the generals only Berthier, Lannes and Murat made the journey. Marmont, Bessières, Duroc, Eugène de Beauharnais, Bourrienne, the newly acquired Mameluke servant Roustam and two hundred Guides were among the favoured few; notable for her absence was Pauline Fourès.

Command devolved on Kléber, who later claimed he had been presented with a *fait accompli* and knew of Bonaparte's departure only after he had gone. Choking back the fury he felt, Kléber read to his troops the brief communiqué Napoleon had left: 'Extraordinary circumstances alone have persuaded me, in the interests of my country and its glory and of obedience to pass through the enemy lines and return to Europe.' In his instructions to Kléber, which included the order to send Desaix back to France in November, Napoleon claimed that he would move heaven and earth to reinforce the army in Egypt: 'The arrival of our Brest squadron at Toulon and of the Spanish squadron at Cartagena leaves no doubt as to the possibility of transporting to Egypt the muskets, sabres, pistols and ammunition of which you and I have an exact list, together with enough recruits to make good the losses of two campaigns . . . You can appreciate how important the possession of Egypt is for France.' He also authorized Kléber, in the event that no reinforcements arrived by May 1800 or if plague cut a swathe through the army, to conclude a peace with Turkey, even if this meant evacuating Egypt, but he thought the most likely outcome was that the future of Egypt would be subsumed in a general European peace treaty.

Did Napoleon simply abandon the French army in Egypt to its fate, in the full and cynical knowledge that Egypt was a lost cause? Kléber certainly thought so. After he had read the instructions he told his brother officers: 'He's left us with his breeches full of shit. We'll go back to Europe and rub it in his face.' Technically, Napoleon was within his rights, since the letter from the Directory authorized him to return with or without his army. And it must be pointed out that he sent Ganteaume back several times with a force of 5,000 reinforcements but on each occasion the admiral was unable to make landfall. The fact that Napoleon was unlikely to achieve much in Egypt and was needed more urgently in Europe is irrelevant to the argument, since this was already the case when he left France in May 1798. An honourable general would have stayed with his men and taken his chances, even if it meant capitulating with them. But Napoleon did not work from moral principles and despised notions like honour if they could not be yoked to his self-interest. A man who would remain with his army in Egypt in the context of August 1799 was not the stuff of which a future emperor was made.

The sequel in Egypt is easily told. As soon as Napoleon left, Kléber disregarded his instructions and contacted Sidney Smith to act as mediator between France and Turkey. By the treaty of El Arish of 13 January 1800, Kléber agreed to leave Cairo within forty days for Alexandria, where he and the French army would be given safe conduct back to France. But the hardline Pitt in London refused to countenance any terms but unconditional surrender. Two more years had to elapse and many more battles were fought before there was an end of bloodshed in the desert; it was not just Napoleon who was careless of human life in this epoch. Kléber, with just 10,000 men, won a spectacular victory against yet another invading Turkish army at Heliopolis on 20 March 1800. In December that year he was assassinated by a Moslem fanatic and succeeded by the lacklustre General Menou, the only Frenchman in Egypt who actually converted to Islam.

Faced by what seemed to be a permanent French colony astride British trade routes to the Orient, the government in London decided in October 1800 by a bare majority to send General Abercromby to reconquer Egypt. The landing in Aboukir Bay in March 1801 was bitterly contested but ultimately successful. Two weeks later a night battle was fought at Aboukir, which the British won (though Abercromby was killed). The French General Belliard cravenly surrendered the 10,000-strong French garrison in Cairo in June, and after a protracted campaign Menou capitulated at Alexandria in September with his remaining 7,300 effectives. Ganteaume, heading yet another French relieving expedition, reached Derna in Libya, 400 miles west of Alexandria but was forced to turn back. In October the men who surrendered and their dependants arrived back in France. Among them was Pauline Fourès, who was met off the ship by Duroc, who forbade her access to Napoleon but pensioned her off with the gift of a country mansion.

What did Napoleon achieve in his fourteen months in Egypt? From the viewpoint of immediate French interests, almost nothing. Nearly 40,000 troops, many of them élite units, who would have been better employed on the battlefields of Europe, were gradually diminished in numbers by endless and ultimately pointless battles against Mamelukes and Turks. By aiming at Malta he brought the Russians into the Mediterranean ambit and by striking at Egypt he brought the Royal Navy back into the Levantine seas. It is not too much to say that the Egyptian adventure uniquely allowed the Turks and Russians, those traditional enemies, for once to make common cause.

Even if Napoleon had not failed beneath the walls of Acre, it is difficult to see what the end result could have been. The idea of a link-up with Tippoo Sahib and the Mysores was dealt a death blow by the great victory at Seringapatam by General Harris and the Wellesley brothers in the spring of 1799. French losses in battle and from disease were high, and were not compensated by hoards of loot, as in Italy, since there was no way to transport looted artefacts back to France. A few privileged members of the officer class doubtless enjoyed a degree of sexual freedom they could not have had in France. Only long-term and indirectly, in the shape of a burgeoning European intellectual interest in Egyptian history and culture, can one see benefits from the three-year sojourn of the French.

For Napoleon himself it was a different matter. By the time his propaganda machine had winnowed the details of the military campaigns, his very real martial achievements in Egypt had been apotheosized. He himself throve in Egypt and, even if we accept that his diet was immeasurably superior to that of his men, it is surely significant that he remained untouched by plague. His health in fact was never better than during 1798-99; he rid himself of all ailments for a time, only to find them returning when he got back to Europe. He loved the sights, sounds and smells of the Arab world and felt an instinctive sympathy for the culture of the Arabs and the folkways of the sheikhs and *fellahin*. He told Madame Rémusat that he loved aping Alexander the Great by putting on eastern garb and that the East appealed uniquely to his sensibility:

In Egypt I found myself freed from the obstacles of an irksome civilization. I was full of dreams. I saw myself founding a religion, marching into Asia, riding an elephant, a turban on my head and in my hand a new Koran that I would have composed to suit my needs. In my undertaking I would have combined the experience of two worlds, exploiting for my own benefit the theatre of all history, attacking the power of England in India . . . the time I spent in Egypt was the most delightful of my life because it was the most ideal.

Napoleon's ease with Islamic culture is worth stressing. He understood the mind-set of the Arabs extremely well. When the Bedouin raided a village friendly to the French and killed a fellah, he sent 300 horsemen and 200 dromedaries to apprehend and punish the culprits. The Sheikh El Modi, who witnessed Napoleon's anger and heard his orders, said with a laugh: 'Was this fellah thy cousin, that his death excites so much anger in thee?' 'Yes,' replied Bonaparte. 'All whom I command are my children.' '*Taib* [it is well],' said the sheikh. 'That is spoken like the Prophet himself.'

We may discount Freud's fanciful notion that Napoleon, with a brother complex, revelled in Egypt because it was, in a Biblical sense, the land of Joseph. But that he had a genuine 'Oriental complex' is hard to deny. However, it must be understood that this was a purely romantic fantasy. Some incautious biographers have speculated that on this campaign he imbibed the spirit of Oriental despotism from the soil, so to speak, and that this explains a 'new' Napoleon, as evinced by the massacre at Jaffa, the judicial murders in Cairo, the plan to poison the sick with opiates and the dubious Machiavellian justification of his return to France. But it is a misreading of Bonaparte to speculate that the man who returned from Egypt was not the man who set out. Probably as early as the initial victories in Italy, Napoleon harboured a yearning for supreme power. Nothing experienced in Egypt affected the lust for power, but Napoleon returned from the East even more clearheaded about how to achieve it.

CHAPTER TEN

La Muiron set sail on a moonless night on 23 August 1799 with one other frigate as escort. At first they hugged the North African coast and twice saw British sails in the distance. On one of these occasions Napoleon was sufficiently alarmed to make preparations for landfall, intending to proceed across the desert to some other port of embarkation; but the ships of the Royal Navy stood away at the last minute. Sailing for much of the time in bad weather, *La Muiron* was forced into the gulf of Ajaccio on 30 September by contrary winds. This was to be Napoleon's last visit to his native island, and he spent a few nights in the family home which Letizia had so expensively refurbished. But all the time he was plagued with anxiety. When learning the latest news from Paris he was heard to say despairingly: 'I will be there too late.'

On 6 October *La Muiron* put to sea again, only to fall foul of the weather once more. And no sooner had the full storm on the 7th blown itself out than English ships under Lord Keith were again spotted. Napoleon ordered the captain to make for Fréjus, where landfall was achieved in the bay of St Raphael on 9 October. Without doubt Napoleon had been lucky to escape naval interception. When the British realized that Napoleon had passed through their fleets on the return run as well, after a perilous 47-day voyage in the Mediterranean, popular fury was unbounded. A London caricature showed Nelson dallying with Emma Hamilton while *La Muiron* passed through his legs.

Napoleon was lucky in a second sense, in that he arrived in France just four days after the news of his great victory at Aboukir reached Paris. The Directory, fearful that the huge and growing army of malcontented ex-servicemen might flock to his banner, dared not impose on Napoleon the strict quarantine regulations governing all arrivals from the Orient at France's Mediterranean ports; still less could they object that Bonaparte had deserted his army in Egypt. At 6 o'clock on the evening of the 9th, Napoleon set out on a seven-day journey to Paris, hoping vainly to arrive in the capital before the Directory even knew he was in France. Using rapid relays of post horses, he passed through Aix-en-Provence, Avignon,

Valence, Lyons, Chalon and Nevers, arriving in Paris on the morning of 16 October. He was delighted with the tumultuous reception he got, especially in Avignon, where the people seemed to regard him as a deliverer.

At first sight Napoleon's gamble in going to Egypt and returning only when the Directory was discredited seemed to have paid off. Until the news of Aboukir reached France, he appeared to be losing the propaganda battle: the Battle of the Nile, the revolt of the 'angel' El Modi and British disinformation about atrocities had been cleverly played up by his enemies. Most of all, it became obvious that, no matter how many victories Napoleon won in Egypt, in the context of a general European war these made little impact. The sensational news about Aboukir cut through all that, but Napoleon's position was by no means as good as he would have liked. The principal problem was that France's military position had stabilized by the time he returned.

In Cairo Napoleon had read a litany of French disasters. In 1799 the Allies finally put their differences behind them and launched a new coalition against France. The Russians under General Suvorov joined the Austrians in a campaign in northern Italy which rapidly undid all Bonaparte's work. The Allies overran the Cisalpine Republic, occupied Turin and forced the French to quit Rome (which they had occupied in February 1798). Suvorov then defeated in succession the French generals Scherer, Moreau and MacDonald, while the British reoccupied Naples. By the end of June 1799 the French had lost all their Italian conquests except Genoa and a narrow strip of the Ligurian coast. Meanwhile in Germany the Archduke Charles repeatedly defeated Jourdan and opened the passes between Germany and Italy. In Holland the military initiative was held by an Anglo-Russian army under the Duke of York.

Such was the situation when Napoleon left Egypt. By the time he arrived in Paris, there had been a rapid turnaround in military fortunes. Facing disaster, the Directors made a string of mistakes, but these were capped by the Allies. First, in June 1799, the Directory enacted a conscription law which led to wholesale evasion by draftees. The Directors then compounded their error by detaching large sections from Jourdan's hard-pressed army on the Rhine to round up the draft dodgers, and then ensured that Scherer lost Italy by insisting on sending every available soldier against Naples.

However, the Allies made the egregious mistake of insisting on clearing the Danube and Po valleys of opposition before moving against Switzerland, the strategic key to Europe. Then the Austrian minister Thugut inexplicably decided to switch commanders, with Archduke

Charles being transferred from Switzerland to Holland and Suvorov moving from Italy to Switzerland. This caused a delay in campaigning which the French exploited. In September Masséna won the second battle of Zurich (in the first, in May, he had been defeated by Archduke Charles), routing the Russians while Suvorov was being transferred. Even more significant than the military check to the Allies was the suspicion and mutual recrimination the setback engendered. Austria and Russia blamed each other bitterly, and the final upshot was that Russia left the coalition in dudgeon in January 1800.

Taking advantage of the confusion and bickering, General Ney defeated the Austrians on the Rhine. In Holland General Guillaume Brune brought the Anglo-Russian adventure to an inglorious end and earned the Duke of York eternal obloquy by a stunning victory in October which had the English scurrying for their embarkation vessels. The consequence was that when Napoleon arrived in Paris on 16 October the immediate military crisis was over, removing the justification for a *coup d'état*. In particular, the victories by Brune and Masséna made it very difficult for the Bonapartist propaganda machine to present its man as the 'sword' badly needed by the Republic. Since Ney, Brune and Masséna were the new military heroes and fickle public opinion was likely to turn away from him, Napoleon needed to act fast. On the other hand, because there was no obvious necessity now for a coup, he had also to move with extreme caution.

While he pondered his next move, he had one immediate decision to take: what to do about Josephine? When they were reunited with their brother, Joseph and Lucien confirmed the stories about Josephine's habitual adultery with Hippolyte Charles. The affair had recommenced in earnest at the end of 1798; Charles would often stay weeks at a time at Malmaison, decamping when visitors arrived. Charles and Josephine were also a byword for corruption. In addition to the retainers from Louis Bodin for putting army contracts his way, Josephine was also on a huge sweetener of 500,000 francs from another military contractor, Compagnie Flachat. Almost predictably, when Napoleon arrived at his house on the rue de la Victoire at 6 a.m. on 16 October, Josephine was not there. He flew into a rage and decided to divorce her without more ado. Barras urged Napoleon to be stoical, but made no impression. Only when the banker Jean-Pierre Collot put the affair in the context of *raison d'état* did Bonaparte cool down. Collot argued that Napoleon would lose prestige if it became widely known that he had been cuckolded; the best course was to wait until he had supreme power and then settle accounts with his errant wife.

Had he known the full extent of her treachery, Napoleon would have been even more angry. She told Barras that she found his letters from Egypt either odd or droll and, while sending him tepid notes, would be composing passionate and lubricious ones to Charles. According to Barras, her verbal indiscretion was notorious. In a masterpiece of projection she described her husband thus: 'He is a man who has never loved anyone but himself; he is the most ingrained and ferocious egotist the Earth has ever seen. He has never known anything but his own interest and ambition.'

Unaware of these dark currents, Napoleon contented himself with a policy of humiliation. Though urged by his family to move to the rue du Rocher, Napoleon stayed put and decided to lock Josephine out. He cleared the house of her enormous wardrobe of clothes and sent them down to the porter's lodge, with instructions to the porter that he was on no account to admit her. Napoleon assumed she was with her lover, but the truth was more singular. Alerted by letters from her son Eugène and by confidential advice from Fouché, with whom she was developing a kind of business relationship, she hastened south to meet her husband, hoping to get her version of events in before Joseph and Lucien arrived with the truth. But when she arrived in Lyons, expecting to meet him on the Burgundy road at any time, she learned that Napoleon had already gone north by a different route, via Bourbonnais. She turned round and headed for Paris. Forty-eight hours after Napoleon got to the rue de la Victoire, a despairing Josephine arrived with her daughter Hortense after a long and tiring journey, the latter stages through thick fog.

It was 11 p.m. The porter told her he had orders not to let her in, but Josephine softened him with tears or browbeat her way to her husband's door (the account varies). When Napoleon refused to admit her, she camped outside the door on the last spiral of a narrow staircase, from where she directed sustained and piteous pleas through the wooden threshold. Eugène and Hortense arrived to add their lachrymose pleas to those of their mother. At last Napoleon relented sufficiently to allow Eugène and Hortense to enter. Tearfully they pleaded her case, adding that her heart was broken. Finally Napoleon admitted Josephine herself. An initial angry explosion and bitter reproaches were followed by a cooling-off period, then by sexual overtures. When Lucien called next morning he found Napoleon and Josephine in bed, beaming with seraphic expressions. The entire Bonaparte family was scandalized and furious at this unexpected outcome, but even Letizia dared say nothing. None the less, the balance of power in the marriage had decisively shifted and from this point on Napoleon had the psychological advantage.

During this honeymoon period Josephine put him in the picture about his old love Désirée Clary. Napoleon had earmarked her as the wife of General Duphot, but he was assassinated in Rome late in 1797, thus triggering French occupation of the eternal city. On 17 August 1798 she married Bernadotte, apparently more for a desire to be married than because of any overpowering *coup de foudre* for the Gascon. The marriage was a scheme by the Bonapartist clan to neutralize or co-opt a dangerous political rival. Joseph, Lucien and their wives had attended the wedding ceremony and Désirée now regularly passed on to her sister Julie (Joseph's wife) full intelligence on the Bernadotte household: who visited, what was discussed, what was the attitude to Napoleon. Josephine had apparently done her best to conciliate Désirée, but Désirée strongly disliked her and used to mimic her mercilessly to Julie, the only member of the Bonaparte clan to have a soft spot for Napoleon's wife.

The dynamics of the extended Bonaparte family were becoming increasingly complex. The constant was the hatred felt for Josephine by all female members of Napoleon's family – Letizia, Pauline and, especially, Elisa. Désirée's distaste is more easily explained as simple jealousy. There is even evidence that Désirée was still besotted with Napoleon and dreamed of displacing Josephine and getting him back. When she became a mother in 1799 she asked Napoleon to be godfather. The subtext was clear: she could bear children while Josephine could not. Napoleon asked that the boy be called Oscar after Ossian, the hero of his beloved Macpherson epic, and Désirée duly obliged. Désirée was an important transmission belt between the ultra-Jacobin circle of Bernadotte and friends and the Bonapartes. She supported Napoleon's ambitions even to the point of spying on her own husband; Bernadotte, besotted with her, turned a blind eye. But she was the focus of sexual jealousy, with Napoleon resentful that an enemy like Bernadotte was married to 'his' Eugénie, and Bernadotte fuming that Napoleon had had his wife's virginity.

Napoleon had a talent for making mortal enemies, and no enemy was more inveterate than Jean Bernadotte. Tall, slight, with thick black hair, a colourless face and a huge hook nose, Bernadotte was reputed to have Moorish blood but, like many of Napoleon's followers, was in fact a Gascon. Energetic, ruthless, mendacious and treacherous, Bernadotte professed Jacobinism and had received his political 'education' in the sergeant's mess. Unlike his fellow Gascon Murat, who continued to speak with a thick country brogue, Bernadotte had polished up his accent and gone to some pains to conceal his rude origins. Bernadotte was actually an egomaniac of the first order, whose political beliefs were always a mask for the promotion of Jean Bernadotte. He has attracted widespread odium, and rightly so. Frédéric Masson described him as 'the most unbearable of Jacobins and schoolmasters, a Béarnais with nothing of the Gascon smartness and happy repartee about him, but whose calculating subtlety always concealed a double game and who regarded Madame de Staël as first among women because she was the first of pedants and who spent his honeymoon dictating documents to his young wife.'

A hot-tempered, paranoid Gascon boaster, Bernadotte had ambitions which always outran his abilities. The fiasco of his two-month incumbency as French ambassador to Austria in 1798 was matched by the farce of his two months as Minister of War in July 1799. The rising star in the Directory, the Abbé de Sieyès, grew tired of his intrigues and prima donna antics at the Ministry. The last straw came after Brune's victory when Bernadotte delivered a gasconnade to the effect that he would rather be in the field as a soldier than behind the Ministry desk. Sieyès sacked him abruptly, but Bernadotte managed to have the last word by leaking a 'resignation letter' to the press in which he thanked Sieyès ironically 'for accepting a resignation I had not offered'.

Of his legendary hatred for Napoleon there can be no doubt. When Napoleon arrived so unexpectedly in France, Bernadotte proposed to the Directory that Napoleon be arrested and court-martialled, both for deserting the army in Egypt and for evading the quarantine regulations. He was the only one of Napoleon's former generals not to call on him at the rue de la Victoire to offer congratulations for a safe return from Egypt. He then refused to subscribe to an official dinner being arranged by the generals for Napoleon until he explained his reasons for leaving the army in Egypt. He added that since Napoleon had not been through quarantine and might therefore have brought back the plague, he, Bernadotte, had no intention of dining with a plague-ridden general.

Yet Bernadotte was only one of a host of dangerous political rivals Napoleon had to fend off or neutralize when he arrived in Paris to take stock of the Directory's brittle position. Fortunately for him, few of the rest of them possessed Bernadotte's overweening ambition. Sieyès was already engaged on a scheme of his own to topple the Directory but needed a 'sword'. His first choice was Joubert, but he was killed in Italy. His second choice was MacDonald but he refused to take part, as did Moreau, the victor of Hohenlinden. A reluctant Moreau was explaining his hesitation to Sieyès on 14 October when news of Napoleon's landing in France came in. 'There's your man,' said Moreau. 'He will make a better job of your *coup d'état* than I could.'

Nevertheless, in his bid for supreme power in October 1799 Napoleon faced a situation of frightening complexity. The only certainty was that the Directory was discredited for economic reasons. It was the Army that sustained the Directory, and a system of symbiotic corruption resulted. Army officers and war commissioners demanded the right to loot and requisition in order to line their pockets, while the Directory had to bow to the demands of the Army, as the government in turn needed the spoils of war to pay bankers, army contractors and other creditors and to raise revenue. But inflation gnawed away at the Directors' position. In 1794 the gold franc was worth 75 paper francs, but by 1798 the rate had soared to 80,000 paper for one gold franc.

The Directory had inherited an impossible financial situation. The State was virtually bankrupt, credit was non-existent and the worthless *assignats* had been withdrawn. Left with nothing but taxation to finance the war, the Directors struggled manfully and even introduced worthwhile administrative reforms and improved the tax system. But there was no way to avoid inflation, and the pressing need for money explained the collaboration of Army and government in exacting revenue from the conquered territories. Meanwhile the government steadily added to its tally of enemies. Having already alienated the Catholic Church by its anticlericalism and the Jacobins by its conservatism, by its forced levy of one hundred million francs on the rich the Directors also lost caste among the privileged. Nor was there any hope of support from the urban proletariat or the *sans-culottes*. Butter and cheese were already luxury items, sugar was heavily rationed, and the price of basics was astronomical: 250 grammes of coffee cost 210 francs, a packet of candles 625 francs, two cubic metres of wood 7,300 francs. Many families were reduced to hanging a lump of sugar from the ceiling, and this would be dipped into a cup of coffee for a few seconds.

The corruption of the Directory was legendary and the hatred entertained for the government proportional. On the opening night of the play *La Caverne*, a melodrama featuring four thieves as principal characters, a wag in the audience called out: 'Only four? Where's the fifth?' The entire theatre dissolved into laughter, with the actors actually applauding the audience. Many other contemporary stories testified to the intense unpopularity of the Directors. A perfume vendor in the rue de la Loi was said to have made a fortune out of selling a fan with five lighted candles painted on one side, with the middle candle much taller than the others. On the other side of the fan were the words: 'Get rid of four of them. We must economize.' Another story, relating to the swelling throng of Directory clients and hangers-on, concerned a Gascon, said to have sent a letter to the Council of 500,000; when reproved for adding three more noughts than necessary, the Gascon replied that he could not put in more than there actually were. And when news of Napoleon's victory at Aboukir reached Paris, the enemies of the Directory went about wearing a pendant, showing a lancet (*lancette*), a lettuce (*laitue*) and a rat (*rat*). Spoken quickly, the rebus signified '*L'An Sept les tuera*' ('Year Seven will kill them').

Yet if the Directory seemed doomed by its inability to satisfy any significant social sector, what was to replace it? Apart from supporters of the *status quo*, there were three main groups contending for power should the Directors lose their footing. Perhaps the most powerful were the monarchists, who had only just failed to seize power at Vendémiaire and Fructidor. Particularly strong in the south and west of France, the royalists spoiled their chances by in-fighting, split between the ultramontane supporters of the comte d'Artois, who wanted a return to the *ancien régime*, and champions of constitutional monarchy. Although some saw a Bourbon restoration as inevitable, there remained the obstacle that too many people stood to lose from such an eventuality: bourgeoisie, peasants, merchants, businessmen, war contractors and all other profiteers. The only members of the middle class who had been unable to buy up confiscated property (or 'national' property as it was termed in the euphemism) were those without capital, such as pensioners and members of the liberal professions.

On the left were the neo-Jacobins, a powerful force in provincial electoral assemblies and supported by the petit-bourgeoisie, artisans and shopkeepers. They were influential in the Council of Five Hundred where the tempestuous Lucien Bonaparte, still theoretically a Jacobin, had been elected as president, but were ill represented in the Council of Ancients. Having learned from the failure of Gracchus Babeuf that there was no constituency for extremism, they espoused a moderate programme of greater democracy, accountability by the Directors, and greater provincial autonomy. It was the Jacobins who in 1799 had pushed through the Hostage Law, making the relations of émigrés responsible for any crimes committed within France; and it was at the Jacobins' insistence that the Directors had levied the compulsory loan on the rich. The weakness of the Jacobins was that they were a mere coalition of special interests. Their power was on the wane in 1799, as the attraction of emergency powers and committees of public safety had dimmed after the victories at Bergen and Zurich in September 1799. A sign of the times was the ease with which Minister of Police Fouché closed down the

'Constitutional Society' – a Jacobin club which had hitherto been a bugbear for the Directory.

The third party in the ring was the Thermidoreans who wanted to end the Revolution on an 'as is' basis, leaving them as the beneficiaries of the sale of national property. They wanted neither the true social revolution of the Jacobins nor the restoration of the monarchy. These were in essence the people who had held power since the fall of Robespierre in 1794, the veterans of the revolutionary assemblies who now wanted a cosmetic change of régime that would allow them to emerge untarnished by the image of the Directory yet in possession of all their economic gains. These were the men who held power as a result of a whole series of illegal actions, principally the Decree of Two-Thirds against the royalists and the Floréal coup against the Jacobins; their hallmark was the ruthless sacrifice of their weakest members so as to cling to power. At root the Thermidoreans wanted a Republic dedicated to the interests of the rich – rather like the U.S.A. at that time under Washington and Jefferson.

Since the great personalities of the royalist movement were in exile and those of the Jacobin club were generals like Bernadotte, Jourdan and Augereau, it was on the Thermidoreans and the five Directors that Napoleon directed most of his attention during the critical period from 16 October to 9 November 1799. General Moulin and Roger Ducos were the two minor Directors, basically nonentities. The three key figures were Barras, Sieyès and Gohier. Barras was still ostensibly the key man, still linked to Bonaparte through Josephine, but increasingly perceived as erratic and harbouring secret royalist sympathies. Gohier and his stooge Moulin supported the *status quo*, but because Gohier was physically attracted to Josephine, there were obvious possibilities for Napoleon to neutralize him in any power struggle.

The most dangerous man in the Directory, was the fifty-one-year-old Emmanuel Joseph Sieyès, who had gradually usurped Barras's premier position on the executive while Napoleon was in Egypt. Sieyès had betrayed Danton, and later Robespierre, and when asked what he had done during the Terror, replied: 'I survived.' This grim cynic now had Barras firmly in his sights, and to this end had constructed a loose coalition of intriguers, including Talleyrand, Fouché and Lucien Bonaparte. The hotheaded Lucien, who had brought the Bonaparte family close to disaster by his denunciation of Paoli, nearly ruined things again by shooting from the hip. He started a whispering campaign that Barras had deliberately sent Napoleon and the cream of the army into the 'deserts of Araby' to perish. To cover his tracks he bracketed Talleyrand with Barras as the two men jointly responsible. Barras knew how to deal with the insolent young cub. He brought up the subject of Lucien's illegal under-age recruitment to the Council of 500. To save face yet not be expelled Lucien had to continue his bluster while backtracking on the accusations against Barras. The absurd result was that he ended up accusing his co-conspirator Talleyrand alone of sending his brother and his army to their deaths.

By August Sieyès felt reasonably confident that events were moving his way. Veteran of the 1789 National Assembly, the Fructidor coup of 1797, in which he had had a hand, and a diplomatic mission to Berlin in 1798, Sieyès was a long-time opponent of the 1795 Constitution of the Year Three. Supported by his minion Roger Ducos he nursed his hatred of the Constitution and had long wanted to subvert it; since there was a waiting period of nine years before the Constitution could be amended, Sieyès's only chance to achieve his aims was through a coup.

The arrival of Napoleon in Paris on 16 October added a fresh ingredient of uncertainty to this turbid stew of ideologies, policies and personalities. Perhaps as a result of Josephine, Gohier greeted him cordially on the 16th and scouted Bernadotte's suggestion of a court-martial. However, at a meeting next day with the full Directory the atmosphere was decidedly frosty. Dressed in a round hat, an olive cloth frock-coat, with a Turkish scimitar at his waist, Napoleon affected not to notice and assured the Directory he was on its side. But immediately afterwards, at his house in the rue de la Victoire, he was importuned by rival groups of plotters and conspirators, each trying to make him over. During 19–20 October he was positively besieged by visitors: Talleyrand, Roederer, Reynaud, Maret, Bruix, Boulay de la Meurthe and Brueys were some of the élite names who called during a twenty-four-hour period. Napoleon affected to be interested only in the newly reconciled Josephine, and when the trio of Talleyrand, Brueys and Roederer made an after-dinner call at the rue de la Victoire, they found Bonaparte playing tric-trac with Josephine.

Napoleon's camouflage in the last fortnight of October 1799 was clever. He returned to his old ploy of appearing interested only in the affairs of the Institute, meanwhile taking soundings from the principal Directors. At first he made overtures to Gohier, intending to become one of the Directors. Gohier, who was all affability and reported a conversation in which Sieyès had recommended that Napoleon be shot, expressed his regret that there was no way round the rules stipulating a minimum age of forty for a Director. Influenced by Josephine, Napoleon then inclined towards Barras. Barras wanted to get rid of this dangerous interloper and suggested that he take the field again. Napoleon replied blandly that he had to stay in Paris for reasons of his health. The sparring continued, until at a dinner on 30 October Barras publicly insulted Napoleon by suggesting that he should return forthwith to command the Army of Italy. Napoleon decided to stop beating about the bush. On 4 November he asked Barras bluntly how he would react to a coup to replace the Directory; Barras said he had no tolerance at all for such an idea. This meant that Napoleon had no choice but to throw in his lot with Sieyès, whom he heartily disliked.

Meanwhile Napoleon tried to marginalize the dangerous maverick Bernadotte. The Gascon went to the rue de la Victoire and told Napoleon in his typical charmless manner that he was exaggerating the corruption of the Directory for his own purposes. 'I don't despair of the Republic and am convinced it will see off both internal and external enemies,' Bernadotte continued. When he spoke the word 'internal' he glared at Napoleon; an embarrassed Josephine quickly changed the subject. A few days later Napoleon tried again when he and Josephine visited Bernadotte in the rue Cisalpine. After dinner the two families drove to Joseph's country house at Montefontaine, where there was another violent altercation in the park between Napoleon and Bernadotte.

Detailed planning for the coup now went on. There were innumerable meetings with Sieyès and Roger Ducos in the rue de la Victoire. Fouché, also a party to the plot, made sure the police did not disturb them. Only Napoleon, Sieyès, Talleyrand, Fouché and Ducos knew the full details of the plot; others were informed on a 'need to know' basis. Sieyès, Fouché and Talleyrand, all ex-clerics, agreed with Napoleon that Bernadotte should be excluded as unreliable, a Jacobin and an opportunistic egomaniac, but made strenuous eleventh-hour efforts to bring Barras into their camp. A key day in the preparation of the coup was 6 November. Sieyès and Napoleon finally composed their severe differences and agreed that after the coup a commission would draw up a new constitution. There would be a parliamentary strike against the Directory backed by a show of force. Meanwhile, Joseph, Talleyrand and Fouché spent the sixth vainly trying to win over Barras. That evening a disappointing day ended in virtual farce with the subscription dinner held at the Temple of Victory (formerly the Church of St Sulpice). Napoleon and Moreau were the guests of honour, but Bonaparte attended with great reluctance and brought his own food – some bread, a pear and a bottle of wine – making it clear he trusted nobody; the Jacobin generals, Bernadotte, Jourdan and Augereau completed the farce by refusing to attend.

The coup was originally planned for 7 November, but at the last moment some of the key conspirators lost their nerve. Napoleon gave them twenty-four hours to make a definite and final commitment, and postponed the attempt until Saturday 9 November, since he was superstitious about Fridays. On the seventh he lulled Jacobin suspicions by dining at Bernadotte's with the other Jacobin lions, Jourdan and Moreau, taking Talleyrand, Volney and Roederer as his entourage.

By the evening of 17 Brumaire (8 November 1799) all was finally ready. In return for forcing a change of constitution, Bonaparte had been promised by Sieyès that he would be provisional consul. He and Josephine dined early at the Ministry of Justice with Jean-Jacques Cambacérès, one of Sieyès's henchmen. Cambacérès was an eminent jurist, a Grand Master of the Freemasons and also the central figure in the Parisian gay network. Cambacérès expressed anxiety about Bernadotte, but Napoleon assured him he had found a way to marginalize him. Back at home Napoleon made careful preparations for next day. His aim was to force the Directors to resign; the two chambers of the Assembly would then have to decree a new constitution; and meanwhile all potential enemies had to be neutralized. But it is important to be clear that the objectives of Napoleon and Sieyès were already divergent. Sieyès envisaged an almost peaceful transfer of power backed by a show of force, but Napoleon had in mind a more significant rôle for the Army.

Busy with the meticulous planning for next day, Napoleon could not afford the time for the nightly meeting he had held with Barras for the previous week, partly to gull him, partly to convince waverers that Barras was with them. At 11 p.m. he sent Bourrienne to inform Barras he would not be coming because of a 'headache'. According to Bourrienne, this was the moment when the truth of what was afoot first hit Barras and he allegedly replied: 'I see that Bonaparte has tricked me. He will not come back. It is finished. And yet he owes me everything.' Barras was at least more perceptive than Gohier, who suspected nothing until the very morning of 18 Brumaire. So contemptuous were Napoleon and Fouché of him that they played an elaborate charade. Fouché one afternoon arrived while the Bonapartes and Gohier were taking tea. Fouché, who had come straight from a meeting of the conspirators, launched into a tirade to the effect that he was tired of hearing rumours of a conspiracy. Gohier reassured Josephine that there could not be any truth in the rumours, for otherwise the Minister of Police would not have repeated such frightening intelligence in the presence of a lady!

On 9 November (18 Brumaire) Napoleon rose at 5 a.m. and began to implement the coup proper. It was still dark, so first, ever superstitious, he located his 'lucky star' in the sky. Reassured, he dressed hurriedly while whistling (out of tune) a popular ditty of the time: '*Vous m'avez jeté un regard, Marinette'.* Then he sent round letters to all members of the Ancients (where Sieyès had a majority of supporters), summoning them to an urgent meeting at the Tuileries at 7 a.m. on a matter of national emergency. At 6 a.m., as planned, four hundred dragoons under Colonel Sebastiani received their final orders and began making their way to the Tuileries; the clattering of the horses' hooves brought bleary-eyed citizens in nightgowns and cotton nightcaps to their windows and shutters were flung open. One of Fouché's spies claims to have jotted down a verbatim exchange at the time.

'So today's the day for clearing out the rubbish dump?'

'It could be!'

'Perhaps we'll have a king tonight!'

'For God's sake shut up!'

'I'm only repeating what I've been told. It's said that Barras invited the comte de Provence to ascend the throne.'

'Shut up! We haven't had a revolution merely to see the King back. What we need is a good republican – someone really decent and with clean hands . . . I hope General Bonaparte has made up his mind to clear the five swine out.'

By 6.30 p.m. a stream of generals had begun arriving at Napoleon's door in answer to urgent summonses: Murat, Lannes, Berthier, Moreau, MacDonald. A little later Joseph arrived in company with Bernadotte who, alone of the generals, was not wearing uniform. When Napoleon coldly asked Bernadotte why he was wearing mufti, the Gascon replied that that was how he always dressed when off duty. 'You'll be on duty soon,' said Napoleon. But Bernadotte swore up and down that he would do nothing to harm the Republic and could not be swayed. The most Napoleon could get from him was a promise to remain neutral during the day's proceedings. To Joseph was allotted the task of shadowing Bernadotte during the day to make sure he kept his word.

Among those summoned to the rue de la Victoire was the military governor of Paris, General François Lefebvre. Napoleon asked for his help in saving the Republic. Lefebvre simply asked whether Barras was with them and, on being told (falsely) that he was, pledged his support. Napoleon's next ploy was to summon Gohier and then detain him so that he could not interfere with the day's events. He had Josephine send round one of her would-be *billets doux*, inviting Gohier for breakfast at 8 a.m. Since all previous breakfast invitations at the Bonapartes had been for 10 a.m., even the obtuse Gohier smelt a rat and sent his wife instead. When she arrived, Napoleon angrily demanded her husband's presence, so Madame Gohier, doubly alerted, scribbled her husband a note warning him on no account to accept the invitation.

Meanwhile the Council of Elders had been meeting since 7 a.m. at the Tuileries. Sieyès used his majority to panic the Elders into voting a decree to move their session to the Palace of St-Cloud outside Paris to avoid becoming victims of a Jacobin plot; constitutionally it was the Elders who decided where the two-chamber Legislative Body should sit. A four-article decree transferred the Legislative Body to St-Cloud and the session was prorogued until noon on 19 Brumaire; all continuation of the two councils' functions was forbidden until that place and time. In the final two articles 'General Bonaparte' was charged with the application of the decree and was formally summoned before the Ancients to swear an oath of loyalty.

At 8.30 Napoleon mounted his horse and, accompanied by a retinue of all the military talents (except Bernadotte) rode to the Tuileries. He strode into the Council of Ancients and solemnly swore to uphold the Republic he was even then in the process of subverting; the chorus of echoing cries of 'We swear it' from Berthier, Marmont, Lefebvre and the others introduced an ominous military dimension that did not go unnoticed by some deputies. Having received the decree making him commander-in-chief of all troops in the Paris area, Napoleon straightaway altered it so as to include the bodyguard of the Directory. Next he addressed his troops, whipping up their indignation over the real and alleged way the Directory had betrayed the heroism of the Army. Already Napoleon was thinking in terms of a genuinely military coup and anticipating the time he would have to deal with Sieyès.

By 11 a.m. the news of the Ancients' decree reached the Council of the Five Hundred. There were some protests but no real resistance to the idea of removal to St-Cloud. Meanwhile Gohier and Jean Moulin, learning that Sieyès and Roger Ducos were no longer in the Luxembourg, made their way to the Tuileries. Napoleon informed them that Sieyès and Ducos had resigned as Directors (which was true), as had Barras (which was not) and therefore the Directory no longer existed. But when he asked for their resignations, they refused; Gohier, moreover, questioned the legality of the Elders' decree giving Napoleon command of all armed forces in Paris. Since the two Directors were still a potential rallying point for his enemies, Napoleon had them escorted back to the Luxembourg and placed under house arrest. General Moreau posted sentries with orders to let no one in or out, and the surveillance was so effective that Gohier claimed he could not even sleep with his wife that night.

Talleyrand meanwhile had dealt with Barras. Talleyrand and Admiral Bruix arrived at Barras's house shortly after eleven o'clock and informed Barras (also falsely) that the other four Directors had resigned. It was surely understood that Bonaparte had appeared on horseback only because the Republic was in supreme danger and in the circumstances Barras would surely not demur at offering his resignation. Barras signed without comment and appended a note saying that it was 'with joy that he rejoined the ranks of the ordinary citizens'. Barras then set out for his country seat at Grosbois. The morning's events were a spectacular triumph for the venal Talleyrand. Napoleon had given him two million francs to bribe Barras if necessary. When Barras caved in without a struggle, a delighted Talleyrand pocketed the funds. Barras's inertia is surprising, and there may be merit in the idea that he was temporarily 'dissociated', semi-catatonic with shock at the treachery of Bonaparte and Josephine.

All this time the usually volatile Parisian population had not stirred a muscle. Night fell on a scene of apparently total triumph for the conspirators. Bonaparte's military stranglehold on the city was complete. Yet neither he nor Sieyès were confident that they had won the struggle yet, and indeed it was an egregious error on their part to plan a coup extending over two days, allowing their opponents time to recover their nerve and regroup. Napoleon told Bourrienne: 'Today has not been too bad. Tomorrow we shall see.' All the same he placed two loaded pistols under his pillow. Bourrienne himself next morning drove past the Place de la Revolution where the guillotine had stood and told a friend: 'Tomorrow we will either sleep at the Luxembourg or we will end here.' Sieyès, too, was concerned that the events of tomorrow would be no walk-over. There were three principal dangers. First, Gohier and Moulin might escape or contrive to get word out that they had not resigned. Secondly, the ultra-republican army might not react favourably to the coup. Thirdly, and most importantly, none of the conspirators had thought through exactly how the Legislature could be persuaded to endorse a legal transfer of power.

The drama of 19 Brumaire quickly unfolded at the Château of St-Cloud. Napoleon surrounded the palace with 6,000 men under General Murat and stiffened the military presence with Sebastiani's dragoons. In part the show of force was meant to overawe the Guardsmen in the inner château, whose job it was to protect the assemblymen. The legislators arrived early for the scheduled noon meeting and found a scene of confusion, as contractors and workmen tried to get the palace, uninhabited since 1790 when Louis XVI and his family had spent their last carefree days there, into shape for the bicameral session. The arrangement was that the Elders were to sit in the Gallery of Apollo – a vast hall with a ceiling painted for Louis XIV by Mignard – while the Five Hundred occupied the Orangerie. But because of the delay members of the Elders and the Five Hundred freely hobnobbed together – the exact situation Sieyès had hoped to avoid by keeping them in separate quarters between which communication was difficult. As feelings ran high among the angry Councillors, now sceptical that there was any compelling danger to the Republic, it was counterpointed by an equal and opposite anger among the six thousand men under Murat who surrounded the Château. Clearly visible to the Councillors, the soldiers kept up an angry bray of grievances which they imputed to the 'lawyers and speechifiers' of the Council.

The meeting of the Ancients began an hour late, at 1 p.m. Immediately there was an altercation between Sieyès's creatures and those members who had purposefully not been summoned the day before. Napoleon waited anxiously in another room while points of order and acrimonious debate protracted proceedings interminably. When it was proposed as a reaction to the resignation of the Directory that a new one be appointed, Napoleon could stand it no longer. He burst into the chamber, interrupting the debate – in itself an illegal action – and began haranguing the red-coated senators. The Elders yelled at him to name the conspirators. 'Names! Names!' the cry went up. Others yelled out: 'Caesar, Cromwell, tyrant!' Napoleon became confused and blustered about his military prowess, adding that his soldiers would obey him not the Ancients. 'Remember that I walk accompanied by the god of war and the god of luck!' was one of his effusions. As the unimpressed Bourrienne reported: 'He repeated several times "That is all I have to say to you," and he was saying nothing . . . I noticed the bad effect this gabbling was having on the assembly, and Bonaparte's increasing dismay. I pulled at his coat-tails and said to him in a low voice: "Leave the room, General, you no longer know what you are saying."'

Napoleon emerged from the gallery to find further bad news. From Paris Talleyrand and Fouché warned him that the two councils' hostile reaction to him was already generally known in Paris, that the Jacobin generals Jourdan and Augereau were outside the Château, urging Murat's men to have nothing to do with the coup. Napoleon had been bruised by the encounter with the Ancients and it was ill-advised to meddle further, but it seemed to him he had no choice. He strode determinedly towards the Orangerie.

It was now 4 p.m. Flanked by two giant grenadiers Napoleon entered the chamber where the Five Hundred were engaged in impassioned debate. The conspirators were in a clear minority here, and awkward questions had already been asked about the legality of Barras's resignation. Napoleon's appearance created a sensation. Once again he was present illegally, in full uniform and troops could be seen through the open door. A red mist of rage seemed to descend on the deputies. They began climbing over benches, overturning chairs, desperate to lay hands on the trio. The immediate cries of 'Get out!', 'Kill, kill' were finally replaced by the ominous call for Bonaparte's outlawry: *'Hors la loi!'* Deputies laid hands on the grenadiers and began beating them up; Napoleon himself was seized and shaken like a rat.

Murat and Lefebvre and a body of troops rushed in to the rescue. Walking backwards, with great difficulty they extricated a dazed and bleeding General Bonaparte from the chamber. The cry continued: *'Hors la loi!'* There is controversy about the blood on Napoleon's face. Some say he was wont to scratch at facial pimples when under stress and it was this that had drawn blood. Whatever the case, when he dazedly joined Sieyès and the ringleaders, he made the most of it and claimed he had narrowly escaped assassination. Sieyès, who knew the deputies were unarmed, was sceptical.

Matters had now reached a crisis. There was no longer any possibility of a purely parliamentary coup. Force was required, and the question was whether the Guardsmen, who guarded the Château and officially owed their loyalty to the Assembly, would heed the calls for outlawry. It was Lucien Bonaparte who cut the Gordian knot. Laying down his seals of office as President of the Five Hundred, he rushed outside, jumped on to a horse and exhorted the Guard to do its duty. Inside the Orangerie were knifemen, assassins in the pay of England, who had just tried to assassinate General Bonaparte. He urged the guardsmen to go in and flush out the traitors.

There was a moment of hesitation. Some deputies were still hanging out of the window and calling for Bonaparte's outlawry. Then the drum beat the advance. All afternoon the Guardsmen had been considering their position. The deciding factor had been their conviction that if they did not obey Napoleon and his allies, he would unleash on them Murat's irate troopers slavering outside the Château and they would thus suffer the same fate as the unfortunate Swiss Guardsmen in the Tuileries on 10 August 1792. The guard commander ordered the deputies out of the chamber on the double. When they refused, he told his men to clear them out, lock, stock and barrel. The Guardsmen swarmed forward. Seeing that this was no drill, the panic-stricken deputies scrambled out of the windows into the Orangerie gardens. Next day hundreds of red togas were found caught up in the branches of trees or strewn on the ground.

It was now 5.00 p.m., dusk was descending, and a thick bank of fog swirled around the palace. Demonstrating admirable presence of mind for the second time that day, Lucien had a quorum of stragglers from the Five Hundred rounded up – some from local wineshops, others still cowering in the bushes. At 2 a.m. that morning fifty deputies from the lower chamber, together with the remaining Elders, formally wound up the Directory and swore an oath of loyalty to a triumvirate of provisional consuls: Napoleon, Sieyès and Ducos. The Legislature was adjourned and two commissions were charged with drawing up a new constitution within six weeks. At 11 p.m. Napoleon issued a proclamation putting his own slant on the events of the day and emphasizing the alleged assassination attempt by English agents.

Why did Napoleon succeed in the coup of 18 Brumaire? In the first place he was an immensely skilful politician, able to play off one rival against another, aware that the best way of telling a lie is to tell the truth but not the whole truth. He had learned from his bitter early experiences in Corsica that the way to emerge from the ruck was to appear to be above party considerations, to be beholden to no faction, to be *au-dessus de la mêlée*, and to appear to assume power reluctantly. He understood the importance of propaganda, image and myth-making in a way none of his rivals did. He had not won at Fleurus, Geisberg or Zurich and yet he was more popular than Jourdan, Hoche, Masséna or Moreau. This was because he had known how to convert the Italian campaign into the stuff of heroic and epic legend and to present the Egyptian adventure – actually a military failure – as a dazzling triumph.

Most of all, he was lucky. Disregarding the bad omen on 30 October, when he was thrown from his horse and concussed while out riding, he believed in his star and was confirmed in his belief. In the dangerous context of a coup, self-confidence is half the battle. Objectively, he appeared at just the right moment, when the French people had had enough of the Revolution and wanted peace and retrenchment. The Jacobin experiment of decentralizing on a democratic basis seemed merely to have weakened France against the threat from abroad. All the other would-be *putschists* – Lafayette, Dumouriez, Pichegru – had appeared too soon and were too compromised by party political allegiances. Above all, Napoleon made his bid at the precise moment the all-important bourgeoisie was willing to contemplate one-man rule. He had shown himself willing to deal harshly with the urban proletariat and with bread rioters and this endeared him to the bourgeoisie, now the key class given that the Revolution had devoured its own communalist children.

His mastery as politician was particularly evident in the analysis he made of the roots of power. He realized that the key to stability lay in entrenching the power of those who had benefited from the sale of national property. And he saw clearly the consequences of support for either of the two rival groups: to throw in his lot with the Jacobins entailed endless external war, while to endorse the royalists meant sparking a bloody civil war. His reading of the popular mood was shrewd. The Paris crowd, that much-feared Behemoth of the Revolution, did not stir a muscle, and though the Jacobins in the provinces tried to foment trouble, the people were too weary to face civil war.

The coup of 18 Brumaire was really a dual affair. At one level it seemed simply the recognition of necessity: the confirmation in power of a wing of the Directory, a more sophisticated cabal of neo-Thermidorians representing the interests of the bourgeoisie and those who had benefited from the sale of national property. By excluding Jacobins and royalists from national representation, Napoleon seemed merely to be consolidating the bourgeois revolution and to represent continuity rather than change. Indeed 18 Brumaire was the first coup since 1789 that unequivocally embraced the notion of private property as the supreme value. Thus far it can almost be bracketed under the rubric of historical inevitability.

Yet at another level 18 Brumaire was the conduit that led Napoleon ultimately to imperial power. It is at this level that the coup seems a botched affair, a plot that succeeded only because of public apathy and the Army's determination. The coup was twofold: there was Sieyès's 'structural' putsch and Napoleon's personal bid for power. This explains why what was planned initially as a transfer of parliamentary power by political legerdemain was finally attained only at the point of a bayonet. Consciously, Napoleon involved the Army in a way that had never been agreed with Sieyès. Unconsciously, particularly on 19 Brumaire, Napoleon operated on the margin and took the risks he always liked to take, on the battlefield and elsewhere, so that a successful outcome multiplied his power and prestige. What seem on the surface blundering and inept interventions in the Ancients and the Council of Five Hundred actually answered deep drives in Napoleon's psyche. There was unconscious method in his conscious madness.

A few specific consequences of 18 Brumaire seem worth remarking. Bernadotte was a loser while Fouché, Talleyrand, Murat and Lucien

were spectacular winners. Joseph had successfully marginalized Bernadotte on 9 November, taking him for lunch outside Paris while the
Directory was being dissolved. Next day Bernadotte did manage to get
some half-hearted messages through to the Jacobin Société du Manège,
urging opposition to Bonaparte, but it was Jourdan and Augereau who
did the (unavailing) spadework outside the Château of St-Cloud. Later an
apocryphal story was bruited about to the effect that Bernadotte panicked
on the evening of 19 Brumaire, fled in disguise with Désirée (dressed as a
boy), and hid for three days in the forest of Seuart. Though blatantly
false, the story did express symbolically the depth of Bernadotte's
humiliation. According to Lucien's memoirs, Bernadotte later reproached
himself bitterly for not having taken more vigorous action. He explained
his ineptitude partly as weakness of will and partly because Désirée and
Julie bound him ineluctably to the Bonapartes. Napoleon, as always,
forgave him his disloyalty for Désirée's sake and because, through
Joseph's marriage to Julie Clary, he was 'family'. Early in 1800 Napoleon
made him a member of the Council of State with lavish emoluments and
gave him command of the Army of the West.

As Bernadotte's fortunes dipped (albeit only momentarily), those of his
fellow Gascon Murat rose, to the point where he aspired to the hand of
Napoleon's sister Caroline. Now thirty-two, Murat cut a dashing figure.
With thick, jet-black curls, dark-blue eyes and good features marred only
by a coarse, sensual mouth, Murat was the idol of the cavalry; he usually
charged with his men in the front rank and was both adored and
respected by them. A vulgar man with a Jacobin past and a strong Gascon
accent, Murat was among the least intelligent of those in Napoleon's
inner circle. Napoleon despised him for being an innkeeper's son and
having been a draper's assistant and strongly opposed his bid for
Caroline's hand. But he allowed himself to be persuaded by Joseph, with
the result that the marriage took place at the Luxembourg on 18 January
1800. All the Bonaparte clan (including Bernadotte) was present except
Louis, and Joseph gave Murat an appropriate wedding present by
inducting him into the secrets of property speculation.

Talleyrand, who would sacrifice any person and any principle for
money, had pocketed two million francs from Brumaire. Some scholars
have protested that Barras's inactivity on 19 November is inexplicable,
and that Talleyrand must have given him at least some of the bribe – a
figure of half a million francs is sometimes mentioned. But the plain fact
seems to be that Talleyrand got clean away with all the loot. Duplicity of
a different kind was practised by Joseph Fouché who waited until dusk
on 19 Brumaire to see how events would fall out. He closed the gates of

Paris and kept them shut until he knew the certain victor, fully intending to arrest Napoleon and Sieyès for treason if the coup miscarried. Lucien Bonaparte, however, usually a thorn in his brother's side, acquitted himself splendidly on 19 Brumaire, assured the success of the plot, and wrapped a cloak of legality around a barefaced use of military power. Without question, if nonentities like Boulay de la Meurthe or Danon, had been presiding over the Five Hundred that day, Napoleon would have been outlawed.

The financing of 18 Brumaire remains a murky issue. Prosperous tradespeople, alienated by draconian Directory laws on tax returns, undoubtedly subsidized the operation, and it is known that the banker Collot advanced 500,000 francs. Some idea of who the other big contributors were can be gauged from the preferential contracts granted to certain individuals once Napoleon was First Consul. But although bankers in general were sympathetic, they waited to see how events would turn out before committing themselves; in any case, the granting of large scale loans required some convincing demonstration that the new régime was legitimate and enjoyed widespread support.

Napoleon can be faulted for many things, but the idea that he destroyed liberty by his coup of 18 Brumaire is simply absurd. As the great French historian Vandal said: 'Bonaparte can be blamed for not having founded liberty, he cannot be accused of having overthrown it, for the excellent reason that he nowhere found it in being on his return to France.' It is a supreme historical irony that the master of propaganda has been out-propagandized on 18 Brumaire by Madame de Staël, who claimed that Napoleon had a unique opportunity for introducing into France perfect freedom of the 'let a hundred flowers bloom' variety. Contemporary criticisms of Napoleon as 'undemocratic' have to be treated with extreme caution. Madame de Staël and her circle did not want democracy as it is understood in the twentieth century – theirs was a demand for hegemony by an intellectual élite at best and by a cultivated section of the bourgeoisie at worst – and even the Jacobins wanted a 'democratic dictatorship'. It is an unjustified slur on Madame de Staël to say that she bitterly criticized Napoleon just because he rejected her as a woman. But of her general criticism one can only say that Napoleon was excoriated for not granting a freedom Rousseau had not had under the *ancien régime*.

After Brumaire Napoleon resorted to scheming and broken promises to get rid of the limitations on his power which still remained. On 20 Brumaire he and Josephine left the house on the rue de la Victoire forever; henceforth Josephine was always to be found in her dream house at Malmaison. Napoleon spent most of his time in his office at the Luxembourg, manoeuvring to get rid of Sieyès and Ducos, who had been named as provisional consuls alongside him. He was, however, happy to reward his friends, and the new appointments after Brumaire had a strong Napoleonist tinge. Fouché was confirmed as Minister of Police, Talleyrand was entrusted with Foreign Affairs, while Cambacérès received the Justice portfolio. Berthier was made Minister of War, Lefebvre Lieutenant-General and Murat was given command of the consular guard. The army commands too were all Bonapartist appointments: Masséna as commander of the Army of Italy, Moreau as supremo of the Army of the Rhine and MacDonald in charge of the Army of Reserve.

For the next five weeks a constitutional commission met in the Luxembourg. Sieyès had the reputation of being the great expert on constitutions but he believed in government by assemblies, which did not suit Bonaparte's purposes. At first Napoleon listened gloomily to the legalistic wranglings, cutting the arm of his chair to pieces with a pen-knife as he listened, in a characteristic gesture of stress. Tensions rose when Napoleon objected to Sieyès's proposed Constitution. On 1 December there was a particularly stormy meeting, in a private three-man session chaired by Talleyrand. Exasperatedly Sieyès said to Napoleon: 'Do you want to be King, then?' Sieyès left the meeting in a black mood and Napoleon, equally irritated, told Roederer that he could get a new Constitution ratified in a week if only Sieyès would retire to the country. Next day he got his wish. In the presence of Talleyrand, Roederer and Boulay there was a calm, polite discussion between Napoleon and Sieyès, which Roederer described as being like an academic symposium on political science. At the end of the meeting Sieyès tendered his resignation as provisional consul.

Sieyès then tried to get Napoleon to show his hand by proposing that he be given the position of 'Grand Elector'. Napoleon turned this down and made sure his propaganda machine got the people of Paris to know of his 'magnanimity'. Confident that he had the people behind him, he commenced a war of attrition against Sieyès. In eleven successive evening meetings with the constitutional commissioners at the Luxembourg palace he wore down the opposition of Sieyès and his faction, prolonging meetings deep into the night and seeking to destroy his enemies through sheer physical exhaustion. In this contest the thirty-year-old Napoleon held all the cards: he had physical magnetism and presence, he could concentrate on detail for hours on end without tiring, and he impressed everyone with his pithy commonsense and exceptional intelligence.

The internal coup which consolidated Napoleon's power came on 12 December. Working on his famous principle that constitutions should be short and obscure, Napoleon presented a constitutional document which was a masterpiece of ambiguity. Ostensibly following Sieyès's principles, but really tailoring the draft to favour his own ambitions, Napoleon proposed that there should be a First Consul with executive powers, flanked by two other consuls with advisory powers and 'checked' by four assemblies: a Council of State with 30–40 members, a Tribunate with 100 members, a 60-strong Senate and a Legislature of 300 souls. The object was to paralyse the legislative arm with a maze of checks and balances, leaving the First Consul with virtually untrammelled power. Ministers were to be responsible to the Consuls and theoretically powerful figures in their own right, but Napoleon had already calculated that he could divide and rule by, for example, countering the ambition of Talleyrand with that of Fouché, or setting Lucien as Minister of the Interior against Fouché as Minister of Police. A further weakening of Ministers' powers came in the 'flanking' proposal whereby two director-generals drawn from the Councils of State would 'shadow' each Minister. The entire Constitution was to be ratified by plebiscite.

On 12 December Napoleon brought his draft Constitution into the legislative chamber and got it adopted by fifty commissioners. The three consuls were supposed to be elected by secret ballot but Napoleon, in a clever show of 'magnanimity' suggested that Sieyès should nominate them. He rubber-stamped Napoleon as First Consul for ten years and chose as his advisory Second and Third Consuls Cambacérès and Charles Lebrun; this was supposed to be an act of balancing, with Cambacérès, a one-time member of the Committee of Public Safety as a sop to the Jacobins and Lebrun a concession to the monarchists. The vote in the chamber then took place by acclamation.

There remained now only the hurdle of the plebiscite, which Napoleon insisted on turning into a personal vote of confidence for him. The referendum was an odd affair, where the only possible answer was yes or no to the proposed constitution. The ballot was not secret, the vote was given on property qualifications which favoured those who were beneficiaries of Brumaire and the scope for intimidation was immense, given that the vote did not take place simultaneously nationwide. The result seemed to be an overwhelming victory for Napoleon: 3,011,007 'yes' votes and only 1,562 'noes'; in Paris the figures were 12,440 'yes' and 10 'noes'. Interestingly, there was a high 'no' vote in Corsica. However, in an electorate of over nine million, there was a huge abstention rate. Lucien at the Ministry of the Interior doctored the result by 'rounding up' the individual figures for the departments, and then proceeded to add 500,000 notional votes from the Army, which had not in fact been polled, on the ground that they 'must be' in favour of Napoleon. In fact only one-sixth of the electorate (about one and a half million) voted for the constitution.

Napoleon now had dictatorial power in all but name. The people of France had agreed to one-man rule as they desperately wanted peace, stability, consolidation and an end to uncertainty. The royalist resistance, backed by the British, was degenerating into chronic banditry. The Catholic Church was in schism, with anti-revolutionary priests regarded as enemies of the people and pro-revolutionary clerics regarded as traitors by the faithful. The army was badly equipped even while shady military suppliers made fortunes. The Directory had scotched the snake of Jacobinism but not killed it, and seemed violently opposed to liberty, equality and fraternity despite all the blood that had been spilled since 1789. General relief was palpable when a man on horseback appeared with clear-cut goals, a man wedded to authority, hierarchy and order, a realist and a reconciler. The people of France – or enough of them to make the difference – were impressed by Napoleon's sureness of touch and cared little if he flouted constitutional niceties. Historical necessity, it seemed, had produced Napoleon. No one yet realized that his genius was of the kind that needed constant warfare to fuel it and that all the hopes vested in him were illusory.

CHAPTER ELEVEN

By New Year's Day 1800 France and Napoleon desperately needed peace. Throughout the nation there was a general war-weariness, and meanwhile the flames of the Vendée still burned strongly in western France. The sticking point was the fanatical hostility of the Austrian Baron Thugut to Napoleon, and Pitt's equally intransigent refusal to make peace with France while Belgium and Holland remained in French hands. The theory was that the south coast of England which faced France was steep and difficult to attack, but the flat east coast, together with an unfavourable wind pattern, made it difficult for the defenders. The abiding British fear was that an enemy could assemble large fleets of transports in the estuaries of the Rhine, Scheldt and Maas, ready to cross the North Sea in a trice; there was a particular British phobia about the Scheldt estuary, because the port of Antwerp is inland and cannot be observed by seaborne blockaders.

How legitimate were these fears? Austria, it is true, having reconquered most of Italy, could scarcely be expected to return to the Napoleonic terms of Campo Formio. But the British obsession with the Low Countries bordered on the irrational, since throughout the eighteenth century France had proved over and over again incapable of mounting an invasion of England, with or without the Belgian and Dutch ports. Moreover, the French revolutionary ideology of 'natural frontiers' – which on the eastward side meant the Rhine – was as much an item of faith, and entrenched in all post-1789 French constitutions, as a united Ireland is in the constitution of Ireland today. It was the irresistible force against the immovable object: either France would have to abandon 'natural frontiers' or the British would have to give up their traditional concern with Belgium. Given that France was led by Napoleon and England by Pitt, the prospects did not look bright.

The intransigence of Thugut and Pitt was a gift to Bonapartist propaganda. French newspapers played up their implacable hostility, while Napoleon made all the right moves, using Talleyrand as his agent. On Christmas Day 1799 Talleyrand put out peace feelers to England, which Lord Grenville promptly rejected. In response, on 16 February 1800 Napoleon discussed with Talleyrand the possibility of a French landing in Ireland; this seemed like a return to the Directory's strategy of 1798 but was merely a halfhearted riposte, a desire to seem to be doing something about the British. But the ploy of whipping up French public opinion against contumacious Austria and perfidious Albion worked brilliantly. By April 1800 even the war-weary French were clamouring for decisive action against their ancient foes.

Napoleon used the time between 18 Brumaire and May 1800 to reorganize the Army, making sure it was paid up to date, well supplied, and provided with new recruits. It was clear to everyone that Austria, not England, was the target of his preparations. In April he appointed Berthier to the Army of the Reserve, while coaxing Carnot back from voluntary exile in Germany to take over at the Ministry of War. He got the money he needed for the campaign by the simple expedient of imprisoning the banker Gabriel Ouvrard 'on suspicion of treason' until he provided a 'loan'. Napoleon planned a strategic offensive, aiming to defeat General Kray and his army of 100,000 men in the Black Forest and Danube area at the same time as he took out Melas and the second Austrian army of 90,000 in Italy. The overall objective was the destruction of both armies and the occupation of Vienna.

At first Napoleon intended to fight the main campaign in Germany, but this idea foundered on the intransigence of Moreau, who refused to accept the First Consul's orders; apparently he considered that he was still constitutionally on a par with Bonaparte, whom he anyway despised as a Corsican upstart. Napoleon was angry at Moreau's insubordination, but as yet his power base was not secure enough to proceed against a highly popular general, who could act as a rallying point for the disaffected. Stifling his rage, on 15 March he wrote a flattering letter to Moreau to keep him sweet, contrasting the cares of consular office with the joys of command in the field: 'I am today a kind of mannequin who has lost his freedom and his happiness . . . I envy your happy lot.'

Napoleon was now obliged to alter his plans so as to make Italy the main theatre of operations, thereby reducing Moreau to a secondary rôle. He aimed to use the Army of Reserve as a feint, moving it into Switzerland as if guarding Moreau's lines of communication, then swinging south to Italy through the Alpine passes. He therefore ordered Moreau to launch an offensive against Kray in mid-April and push him back to Ulm. Once Moreau had driven Kray back to a point where he could not intervene, half of the Army of the Reserve would head for Italy, leaving the other half to secure its communications back through

Switzerland. Also, Moreau was instructed to release a division from the Rhine Army which, reinforced by French units in Switzerland, would then make a final 12-day forced march of 192 miles from Zurich to Bergamo to take the Austrians in the rear on the Po just when they were facing the main French army.

The most successful military strategies are the simplest and most economical ones. On the Austrian campaign of 1800 Napoleon was creating problems for himself by the extreme and needless complexity of his ideas. Military historians have identified at least six major errors in the strategy for the second Italian campaign. First, the new Italian plan needed two separate lines of operation while the original German scheme needed just one. Secondly, a victory on the Po would not meet France's war aims; it would be 1796 all over again, with an endless series of battles. Thirdly, it was unlikely that Moreau could defeat Kray decisively in the first place. Fourthly, the Austrian army selected for destruction was not the enemy's main one. Fifthly, success depended on Moreau's full cooperation in releasing Lecourbe and his men at precisely the right moment. Sixthly, and most importantly, the plan assumed the Austrians would be purely reactive and have no strategies of their own. But the Austrians surprised Napoleon in two ways. They launched an unexpected offensive against Masséna and the weak French force at Genoa. And, amazingly, they decided to make Italy *their* main theatre of operations.

The Austrians achieved signal early success. They penned Masséna up in Genoa, and cut him off from his right (under Suchet) and his left (under Soult). With the help of the Royal Navy, by the third week of April they had Genoa tightly blockaded, leaving Napoleon's strategy in tatters unless Masséna, by some miracle, could hold out until the First Consul arrived. At this stage, however, Napoleon had not even decided which of the Alpine passes he should use: should it be the Great St Bernard, the Simplon or the St Gotthard?

Things were not going well for the French in any sector. Berthier proved to have been a mistaken appointment, so that Napoleon virtually had to take over the direction of the Army of the Reserve. He was reduced to going against his own principle of concentration of force by sending small French detachments through other passes so as not to clog up the Great St Bernard. Nor was congestion the only problem, for the Alpine passes were not clear until the end of May, so that the men still had to contend with ice, snow and avalanches. Moreau, too, delayed unconscionably before opening the spring campaign in Germany. And even when he drove the Austrians back to Ulm, he still proved reluctant to release Lecourbe. An increasingly anxious Napoleon got a message to Masséna that he must hold out until 4 June.

Two things helped Napoleon to recover from the disastrous start to his campaign. In Genoa the valiant Masséna held out until 4 June, with the French garrison on half rations. And the Austrian General Melas, confident that he held all the cards, had no thought of a French attack through the Alps. Logically, once Genoa had fallen, Provence lay open to an Austrian offensive and it was there that he expected the French to concentrate. But Napoleon confounded expectations. Leaving Paris on 6 May, he proceeded south via Avallon, Auxonne (where he spent two hours at his old school), Champagnole, Rousses, St Cergue and Nyon to Geneva, where he arrived on 9 May.

He spent five days in Geneva assembling his 50,000 troops before moving on to Lausanne and then Martigny-Ville at the foot of the Alps. Cheering news came in that his great commander Desaix had returned from Egypt, so Napoleon ordered him to join the army with all speed. Then the epic crossing of the St Bernard began on 15 May. There was fierce fighting between Lannes and the French vanguard and the Austrians, but Melas failed to evaluate the intelligence adequately and did not realize a full French army was on the move. On 18 May Napoleon took up his quarters in a Bernardin convent at the foot of the pass.

Once again the campaign lurched close to disaster. The French vanguard, it turned out, were in danger of being trapped from the exit to the pass at Fort Bard, strongly held by the Austrians. The spectre of another El Arish loomed. Instead of cursing his own lack of contingency planning, Napoleon moaned to Bourrienne about the inadequacy of Lannes and his other field commanders. On 19 May he told his secretary: 'I'm bored with this convent and anyway those imbeciles will never take Fort Bard. I must go there myself.' Next day he made a perilous passage through the pass on muleback, slipping and sliding uncontrollably on the downhill stretches. He solved the problem of getting his artillery past Fort Bard by spreading straw and dung along the streets near the fort and having the two 4-pounders, two 8-pounders and two howitzers dragged along noiselessly under cover of night (24–26 May). But his achievement, which was later distorted by propaganda, was bought at great cost. Napoleonic iconography portrayed the leader as a second Hannibal crossing the Alpine passes in snow and ice and the famous painting by David showed him astride a rearing horse rather than a lowly mule; but the sober fact was that so much equipment had been lost in the St Bernard that he entered Italy almost as ill-equipped as in 1796.

By 24 May 40,000 French troops were in the Po valley. Another 26,000 were expected which, combined with Masséna's 18,000 in Genoa, would give France virtual military parity with Austria in Italy. From Aosta, where he had Duroc and Bourrienne in attendance he wrote to Joseph: 'We have fallen like a thunderbolt, the enemy did not expect us and still seems scarcely able to believe it.' Overconfidence was nearly his undoing next day for he was surprised by an Austrian patrol, which called upon him to surrender. Fortunately his escort came up in the nick of time and it was the Austrians who had to surrender.

On the 26th Napoleon moved on to Ivrea, where the artillery had been taken on its nocturnal journey past Fort Bard, then proceeded by quick stages through Vercelli, Novara and Turbico to the occupation of Milan, which he entered in triumph on 2 June. After receiving a spontaneous and touching welcome by the Milanese, he spent a week building up his strength for the coming encounter with Melas. 5 June brought the welcome news that Fort Bard had fallen and therefore that needed reinforcements of artillery would soon be arriving. Meanwhile his forces spread out to take Pavia and Piacenza before concentrating at Stradella, which Napoleon had earmarked as his fallback position if defeated. While taking Piacenza Murat intercepted dispatches from Melas which revealed that Genoa had surrendered on 5 June.

When Napoleon arrived in Milan, Melas did as expected and marched back to meet him, in order to keep his lines of communication open. But if Napoleon hoped he had thereby saved Masséna in Genoa, Murat's news soon disabused him. Napoleon has been criticized for tarrying in Milan instead of marching to Masséna's aid. This shows a misunderstanding of his strategy, but the First Consul *can* be criticized for his peevish remarks when he heard that Genoa had fallen. In fact, Masséna by holding out a day longer than Napoleon had ordered him to, had far exceeded expectations. Melas moved back towards Milan when he was confident that the fall of Genoa was imminent; the valiant Masséna, obedient to his chief, had opened negotiations on 2 June and dragged them out for three priceless days.

The Austrian capture of Genoa was worrying to Napoleon on two grounds. In the first place, with the spectre of Acre always in the unconscious, he feared that the Austrians might turn the city into an impregnable fortress; this was not an unreasonable presumption, for the Royal Navy began supplying the city as soon as it fell into Austrian hands. Secondly, the very fact of British supply and reinforcement meant that Napoleon could no longer wait at Stradella in the certain knowledge that Melas would have to come to him to reopen his communications with Mantua; he had to go to the Austrian.

Napoleon set off in search of Melas, but the Austrians proved elusive. Lannes and Victor engaged and defeated the Austrian vanguard at Montebello on 9 June, but immediately afterwards Melas vanished once more. Napoleon was desperate to intercept Melas before he returned to the fortified safety of Genoa, but in order to find him he took the nearly fatal decision to split up his force and send out separate detachments. The only favourable development was the arrival of his strong right arm Desaix on 11 June.

It was now that Napoleon made the final mistake in a blunder-strewn campaign. Convinced that Melas would never stand and fight but would retreat all the way back to Genoa, he sent out two strong divisions under Desaix and Lapoype to find the elusive Austrians. But Melas meanwhile, convinced that there was no future if he allowed himself to be bottled up in Genoa, decided to turn and attack his pursuer. On 14 June, after concentrating his army on the Bormida he found Napoleon's main force, now heavily outnumbered, and launched an attack notable for its aggression. Around the farmhouse at Marengo – one of the many farms at which Napoleon was destined to fight – Napoleon with 24,000 men faced an Austrian army greatly superior in numbers and overwhelmingly superior in cannon. At first Napoleon suspected a feint, but when the truth of the situation dawned, and he saw himself in imminent danger of defeat, he sent out frantic messages to recall Desaix and Lapoype. It was fortunate indeed that Desaix had been held up by a swollen river, for the courier found him at 1 p.m.; Lapoype, however, had already ranged farther afield, was not contacted until 6 p.m. and therefore took no part in the battle.

Despite heroic efforts as the battle swirled around Marengo, especially by the eight hundred Consular Guardsmen, by early afternoon the French were in full retreat. By 3 p.m. Napoleon's was a parlous position: he had committed every single man to the struggle but had still been forced back to the village of San Guiliano. The fighting withdrawal, carried out while the Austrians reformed for pursuit, was a classic of the trading-space-for-time variety. At 3 p.m. Desaix galloped up to announce that his division was close at hand. Napoleon counterattacked an hour later. He sent in a cavalry charge scheduled to coincide with an exploding ammunition wagon, which was a masterpiece of timing and succeeded perfectly. The Austrian right was routed, and the French surged forward to victory. At the very moment of victory, at 9 p.m. after twelve hours continuous fighting, Desaix, the hero of the hour, was mortally wounded in the chest. The usually cynical Napoleon mourned his friend deeply. He wrote to his fellow consuls: 'I cannot tell you more about it: I am plunged into the deepest anguish from the death of the man whom I loved and esteemed more than anyone.'

By 10 p.m. the defeated Austrians were streaming back across the Bormida. They had lost 6,000 dead together with 8,000 prisoners and forty guns at Marengo. It was a great victory for Napoleon, but hardly the stunning success depicted in his official propaganda. In reality Napoleon rewrote history after a series of botches. He had been duped by Melas, he had detached Desaix and Lapoype against his own military principles, he had wrongly divined Melas's intentions as regards Genoa, and in general had risked destruction of his numerically inferior troops at the very climax of the campaign. The real victory, as he knew, was Desaix's. In the bulletins issued immediately after the battle Napoleon was too shrewd to deny Desaix's role but disingenuously claimed that his return had been preplanned. Much later, on St Helena, he tried to write Desaix out of the scenario altogether. With Lannes he followed an opposite course. Initially he denied him credit for Montebello, but later tacitly conceded the point by making him Duke of Montebello.

However, in evaluating the second Italian campaign we should not omit to mention the areas in which Napoleon evinced a singular talent: the eye for detail, for instance, and the talent for administration which made the crossing of the Alps a success. The refusal to aid Masséna in Genoa may seem callous, but Napoleon justified his action as a desire to avoid Wurmser's mistake over Mantua in 1796; for a man like Napoleon the destruction of the enemy was always going to loom larger than the relief of a friend. Moreover, critics of Napoleon consistently discount the fact that he fought at Marengo with 40,000 fewer men than he planned, simply because of Moreau's delays, his refusal to cooperate or to send Lacourbe with the requested force. Masséna, too, could be faulted for splitting his army into three and pointlessly dispersing the wings under Soult and Suchet.

Victory at Marengo was no Cannae-style annihilation, and there seemed no good reason why the Austrians should not have continued the struggle. But Melas lost heart and immediately asked for an armistice. By the convention of Alessandria the Austrians undertook to withdraw all their armies to the east of the Ticino and to surrender all remaining forces in Piedmont, Lombardy, Liguria and the territory of Milan. Defeat for Napoleon at Marengo would not have been a military disaster, but politically it would have been a catastrophe. Without Marengo Napoleon could not have become consul for life and, ultimately, Emperor.

He knew very well the political risks he was taking. He had left Paris secretly at the beginning of May to mitigate the inevitable period of plotting that would result from his absence. Sure enough, for two months Paris was once again in the grip of coup-fever, with Jacobins, royalists, Thermidorians and Sieyès's partisans all prominent. Alternative consuls proposed by one faction or another included Bernadotte, Carnot and Lafayette. Fouché, who would have found a way to intrigue if he was alone on a desert island, was well to the fore, sometimes as a simultaneous participant in rival plots. All the conspiracies and bids for power were swept away in a torrent of euphoria once the news of Marengo reached Paris. The peace-thirsty population of Paris seemed to take collective leave of its senses, with illuminated windows, fireworks, gunfire and huge popular demonstrations in favour of the First Consul. Cambacérès remembered it as 'the first spontaneous public rejoicing in nine years'.

The second Italian campaign was over in weeks, in contrast to the protracted campaigns of the first in 1796–97. There was another difference. Napoleon still corresponded regularly with Josephine, even though she, as usual, did not bother to reply, but there was no longer the yearning and the sexual longing of four years before. One even suspects irony in his order to army women and camp followers to leave the army and return to France: 'Here is an example to be followed: Citoyenne Bonaparte has remained in Paris.'

He reached Milan on 17 June and stayed there a week. Although he wrote that he hoped in ten days to be in the arms of his Josephine, by now such sentiments were purely formulaic. The reality was that in Milan he found himself another mistress, in the shape of opera singer Madame Grazzini. So taken with her was he that he insisted on bringing her back to Paris, dallying with her on his return journey through Turin, Mont-Cenis, Lyons, Dijon and Nemours. Arriving in Paris on 2 July, he installed her in a house at 762, rue Caumartin, where he visited her every night, shrouded in a huge greatcoat. La Grazzini received an allowance of 20,000 francs and was admitted to all the best circles. The affair came to an end when Grazzini met a young violinist named Pierre Rode and began running him and Napoleon in tandem. Tipped off by Fouché, Napoleon expelled her and Rode from Paris, giving them just one week to leave the city.

Protracted peace negotiations with Austria occupied much of Napoleon's attention for the rest of 1800. Although beaten on both fronts, the Austrians stalled and dragged out the peace talks, as they had in 1797. In order to keep Austria in the war Pitt signed a new subsidy treaty, which allowed the Austrian plenipotentiaries to plead that its treaty commitments to England precluded a separate peace before February 1801. Exasperated, Napoleon reopened hostilities and presided over a string of victories: Dupont was successful at Pezzolo and MacDonald in the Alps while in Italy Murat drove the Neapolitans out of the Papal states and other French armies occupied Tuscany. To Napoleon's fury, the greatest success was achieved by Moreau. On 3 December he scored a dazzling victory over Archduke John at Hohenlinden, opening the way to Vienna. In February 1801 Austria agreed to the treaty of Lunéville – in effect a reaffirmation of Campo Formio. In Italy Austria was left with only Venice; the King of Naples was to be restored; and the Duke of Parma took over Tuscany in return for his small principality which was incorporated in the Cisalpine Republic. Austria was forced to agree to the Rhine as the boundary between France and the Austrian empire and to accept the existence of the French satellite states: not just the Cisalpine Republic but the Batavian (Dutch) and Swiss as well.

This left England to fight alone, for a disillusioned Paul I had pulled Russia out of the war. Even alone, the British were a formidable enemy: in September 1800 they recaptured Malta and the following year regained Egypt; in 1800 they brought the wars in India to a triumphant conclusion, conquered French and Dutch colonies in the East, began prising open Spain's Latin American empire through large-scale smuggling. Napoleon's initial response was to propose an alliance with Russia. The Czar bitterly opposed the Royal Navy's self-assigned right of search and had by now concluded that the real danger to European peace came from the British. Whereas Napoleon had imposed order and stability on the chaos of the French empire, Paul saw England determined to stir the diplomatic pot so as to pin France down while she (England) acquired a global empire.

Accordingly, Paul took two drastic steps. In December 1800 he formed a League of Neutral Nations – Russia, Sweden, Denmark and Prussia – and closed the Baltic to British trade. The British responded with the bombardment of Copenhagen on 2 April 1801 – the action in which Nelson famously distinguished himself – and effectively destroyed the League. Paul's second endeavour was more intriguing. He proposed an alliance with Napoleon that would aim at the dismemberment of the Turkish empire and eventually the overthrow of the British position in India. This was exactly the sort of thing to appeal to Napoleon, with his 'Oriental complex'. Indeed, Paul was so impressed by Masséna's victory over Suvorov that he wanted him to command the expedition. The plan was for 35,000 French troops to link with 35,000 Russians on the Volga, ready for a march on India; just before his demise the Czar ordered an advance guard of 20,000 Cossacks to Khiva and Bokhara.

But this was an era when the British thought nothing of using assassins to compass their ends. To facilitate their conquest of Egypt, they first used an Islamic fanatic to murder the able General Kléber in Egypt. Next they turned their attention to the dangerous Paul of Russia. In March 1801 Paul was strangled in his bedroom by officers who had taken bribes from British agents. Deprived of this powerful ally, Napoleon tried vainly to make inroads on British seapower by treaties with other littoral nations. A treaty with Spain yielded not just six warships but the more important prize of the vast Louisiana territory in North America; the King of Naples ceded Elba to France and closed his ports to the British; and important naval agreements were signed between France and the U.S.A, Algiers, Tunis and Tripoli.

By 1801 Britain and France both desperately needed peace. The government in London had the violent aftermath of the '98 in Ireland, domestic riots, inflation and the bad harvests of 1799–1800 to deal with, to say nothing of a mad king. The principal personal obstacle to peace was removed when the warmongering Pitt stood down (in March 1801) and was replaced by Addington, who immediately put out peace feelers. A draft peace was negotiated on the basis that Britain would pull out of Malta and France out of Naples. The Egyptian campaign of reconquest being waged by the English complicated matters, but it was provisionally agreed that Egypt should be returned to France. When Napoleon heard of Menou's defeat in Egypt and realized that word of this had not yet filtered through to England, he ordered his negotiators to rush through a treaty before Egypt could become a factor in the negotiations. The peace of Amiens was accordingly signed on 1 October 1801 and in March 1802.

Napoleon's official negotiators at Amiens were his brother Joseph and Talleyrand, between whom an odd entente had sprung up. In 1800 Joseph speculated on a rise in government stocks but lost spectacularly when the reverse happened. The sums involved were so vast that not even Napoleon could bail him out, but the crafty Talleyrand came to Joseph's rescue by suggesting an ingenious 'scam' involving the state sinking fund. But as a negotiator Joseph was naïve, being convinced that the British sincerely wanted a lasting peace.

In fact both sides were simply playing for time and needed a breathing space before recommencing hostilities. For the time being, exhausted as she was and discouraged by the collapse of the Continental coalition and the defection of Austria and Russia, Britain was ready to allow France to retain the Rhineland and Belgium. British public opinion demanded peace, and the élite was worried about a rising tide of domestic disaffection in a country where 15% of the population was classified as indigent. None the less, giving up all colonial conquests except Trinidad and Ceylon was a bitter pill for the English leadership to swallow. Pitt consoled himself with the thought that British finances would soon make a speedy recovery, putting the country on a sound footing for further wars and that disappointments arising from the peace would soon make a renewal of hostilities acceptable to public opinion. But it is utterly mistaken to assume, as some have, that by the peace of Amiens Britain genuinely gave up the Continent as a lost cause and concentrated on the extra-European position.

For Napoleon, too, the peace was always only a truce, enabling him to strengthen his internal position, to consolidate his mastery of Germany and Italy and in general to gain time. Public opinion in France was the most important consideration. The peace of Amiens was particularly welcomed in Atlantic coast towns like Bordeaux, which had been ruined by the British naval blockade. Economic and social forces meant that Napoleon was never entirely master in his own house. This is an aspect of the important general truth that Napoleon made history but never in circumstances of his own choosing. As he said on St Helena: 'I may have conceived a good many plans, but I was never free to execute one of them. For all that I held the rudder, and with so strong a hand, the waves were a good deal stronger. I never was in truth my own master; I was always governed by circumstances.'

The debate about whether Napoleon was the master or the puppet of circumstances goes to the heart of the much-discussed issue of his foreign policy and his aims. Could Napoleon at any time have abandoned the global struggle with England or the continental one with Austria, or was he in thrall to forces over which he had limited control? One view is that the peace of Lunéville was a wasted opportunity, that Napoleon should have headed off any future four-power coalition by concluding a lasting peace with Austria. The argument is that Britain could never be reconciled since her economic imperative of worldwide empire dictated a meddling 'divide and rule' policy in Europe; anything less than economic surrender by France would be unacceptable to Britain.

To make a lasting peace with Austria would have meant that France let her have a free hand in Italy and accepted that Germany east of the Rhine was an Austrian sphere of influence. Such a policy was not inherently implausible, even though 'natural frontiers' meant that renouncing the Rhineland seemed not really to be on the agenda. It is often said that 'natural frontiers' was a revolutionary legacy that Napoleon could not jettison. But he jettisoned many other parts of the legacy in 1800 and was to rid himself of even more as the years went by. The real barrier to a lasting accord with Austria was fourfold. Napoleon had won fame and glory in Italy and regarded it as his own personal province; his 'Oriental complex' meant that he was bound to intrigue in areas which sooner or later would entail conflict with Austria; he was arrogant enough to think that he could defeat both Britain and Austria provided he made Russia and Prussia his allies; and, most importantly, making war was Napoleon's *raison d'être*.

It can thus be seen that it was Napoleon himself who was the real barrier to a *European* peace. Sorel goes much too far in his famous defence of Napoleon – that, situated as he was, with England as it was, Austria as it was, the French revolution as it was, and even French history as it was, that Napoleon could not be otherwise than *he* was. 'The lovers of speculation,' Sorel wrote, 'who dispose of his genius so light-heartedly, require a manifestation of that genius more prodigious than all he ever vouchsafed to the world; not only that he should transform himself, but that he should modify the nature of things, that he should become another man in another Europe.'

The idea of Napoleon as the creature of circumstances and the product of historical inevitability works well in the context of the global struggle with Britain for world supremacy. This was a conflict that had raged, with brief intermissions, ever since 1688. During Napoleon's fifteen years of supremacy savage wars were fought between Britain and France in Ireland, India, South America, West Africa, Mauritius, Malaysia, Ceylon, Malacca, Haiti, the Cape of Good Hope, Indonesia and the Philippines. Sea battles were fought in the Indian Ocean; armies of black slaves were confronted in Haiti; a difficult see-saw relationship was maintained with the United States throughout the period. This was a struggle that would probably have gone on even if there had been no Napoleon. Thus far historical inevitability. But the argument does not work in Europe, where Napoleon's wars were of three main kinds: campaigns that had a high degree of rationality, *once granted Napoleon's initial premises*, such as the conflicts with Austria, Prussia and Russia from 1805–1809; conflicts he blundered into, as in Spain after 1808; and irrational wars fought because of the 'oriental complex' or vague dreams of Oriental empire, such as Egypt in 1798–99 and possibly the 1812 campaign. Napoleon was neither perfectly free nor perfectly constrained. In many areas he was the victim of circumstance, but in many others he himself created the circumstances.

Further evidence for the 'oriental complex' arises if we accept the notion of compensation. It is very significant that during the years of peace from 1801–03, when the dreams of a march on India with the Russians had been so brutally stifled, Napoleon toyed momentarily with the idea of an empire in the western hemisphere. The purchase of the

Louisiana territory from Spain in 1801 was one sign of this new bearing; another was the disastrous decision to send an expedition to Haiti.

The island of Haiti was the scene of nearly twenty years uninterrupted warfare since the early 1790s. Three years' warfare by the black ex-slaves against the British in 1793–96 led to total victory by the islanders, though the principal general fighting on the Haitian side was yellow fever. According to some estimates, in five years on the island the British lost 50,000 dead and another 50,000 permanently incapacitated to the dreaded 'yellowjack'. These years saw the rise of the 'black Napoleon', Toussaint l'Ouverture, a man whom the white original in France at first treated like a favourite son. After Brumaire Napoleon issued a proclamation, 'From the First of the Whites to the First of the Blacks,' lauding Toussaint to the skies: 'Remember, brave negroes that France alone recognizes your liberty and your equal rights.'

In 1799 there was a power struggle on the island between Toussaint in the north and Rigaud in the south. When civil war loomed, Napoleon came down on Toussaint's side, appointed him commander-in-chief and recalled Rigaud to France. Throughout 1800 and 1801 Haiti answered Napoleon's purposes. But Toussaint became increasingly independent and began to disregard orders from France. It became clear that Napoleon would either have to use force to remove him or acquiesce in a move towards total independence. Napoleon dithered over the options. On the one hand, to concede independence to Haiti meant the ruin of French planters there. On the other, French commercial interests in the West Indies in general would not be affected, sending an expedition would be costly, and there was also the prospect of an army of 30,000 blacks in the hemisphere distracting the U.S.A. and making them less inclined to interfere in his plans for Louisiana and Canada; this of course assumed that Toussaint would obligingly use his army in this way.

All such considerations became academic when Toussaint foolishly made the matter one of credibility by making a unilateral declaration of independence and sending a copy of Haiti's new constitution to France as a *fait accompli*. Even worse, Toussaint claimed the right to nominate his successors, who were likely to be the Francophobe firebrands Dessalines and Christophe. This was an overt affront to the honour of France, which Napoleon could not condone. He therefore placed his brother-in-law Leclerc in command of an army of 25,000 troops and with the expedition sent the Rochefort squadron under the command of his most talented admiral, Louis de la Touche-Tréville. With the expedition Napoleon sent a decree, proclaiming that the blacks would be free in Santo Domingo, Guadalupe and Cayenne but would remain slaves at Martinique and the isles of France and Bourbon. He explained that the differential decree of 28 Floréal 1801 was necessary because Martinique, just obtained by the Treaty of Amiens from the British, was as yet in too volatile a state for abolition.

It has sometimes been said that the dispatch of such a powerful expedition to Haiti alarmed the British and hardened their resolve to renew hostilities. In fact, far from opposing the endeavour, the British secretly approved, as they feared the example of the black Jacobins could spread to their own plantations in Jamaica. English historians of the Victorian period liked to portray the struggle between Pitt and Napoleon as one between liberty and tyranny, but both sides were cynically concerned with economic interests, and even England's 'saviour' Horatio Nelson was in favour of slavery.

Leclerc was as inadequate a military commander as he was a husband. He threw both his best cards away. Hating his most able general Humbert, who had achieved wonders in Ireland in 1798, he gave him a minor post in Haiti where his talents could find no expression. Then he disregarded Napoleon's express instructions to work with and through the mulattoes of the island against Toussaint and the blacks. Influenced by the creoles, who loathed the mulattoes even more than the blacks, Leclerc disregarded his instructions.

The result was a two-year nightmare campaign. Toussaint was captured by a trick, transported, and imprisoned in an icy dungeon in France where he died within a few months. As Napoleon had foreseen, Christophe and Dessalines took up the struggle, and after 16 May 1803, with the resumption of general hostilities, they could count on powerful British naval assistance. Meanwhile the French army was progressively reduced by the ravages of yellow fever. 25,000 men landed in Haiti in 1801 but by 1803, when they surrendered to the British, only 3,000 were left; Leclerc was among the casualties.

Napoleon's brief dream of empire in the West crumbled in the swamps and bayous of Haiti. When general war broke out again in 1803, he concluded that his position in America was hopeless and the Louisiana territory untenable. He opened negotiations with President Thomas Jefferson, whose authority to purchase new chunks of land was constitutionally unclear. But Jefferson pressed ahead and Napoleon was glad of the money from the sale. Over the strenuous protests of Lucien and Joseph, Napoleon sold Louisiana to the United States for eighty million francs. His heart had never really been in the western hemisphere and it is significant that he abandoned the area as soon as war broke out again in Europe. Yet in his failure to think through the consequences of the military adventure in Haiti, Napoleon gave the first signs of an impatience with very long-term calculation that was to prove his fatal flaw in the future.

CHAPTER TWELVE

From the very first day Napoleon addressed the Senate as First Consul, he made it clear that he had a new era in mind. A shrewd observer could have deduced a lot from significant little touches. A double row of troops lined the streets from the Tuileries to the Luxembourg Palace. An eight-horse coach carried the First Consul. Behind him came six more carriages, containing the Second and Third Consuls, the Ministers of State and a military retinue designed to be representative of the whole army: generals, aides, inspector-generals. At the foot of the steps of the Senate ten of the elders greeted him deferentially.

Napoleon was already aiming at a quasi-imperial style, and Josephine too was caught up in it. Now that she was the spouse of the First Consul, Napoleon insisted on correct sexual behaviour and refused to let her see any women of less than spotless behaviour, which meant that all her old friends were excluded. The staff at Malmaison were under strict orders to admit nobody who did not have the oval ticket or *laissez-passer* signed by Bourrienne.

But if he could curb her sexual promiscuity to some extent, Napoleon could do little about her profligate spending. Even with her various retainers from shady military suppliers and her lavish allowance from her husband, Josephine spent money like a woman possessed. She bought nine hundred dresses a year – at her most extravagant Marie-Antoinette bought no more than 170 – and a thousand pairs of gloves. When ordered by Napoleon to investigate her finances, Bourrienne discovered a bill for thirty-eight hats in one month alone, another bill of 180 francs for feathers and another of 800 francs for perfume. The incorrigible Josephine would regularly buy new jewellery and, when Napoleon commented on it, would claim she had had it for years. As in all such cases of husbands with wives, he believed her.

Bourrienne discovered that Josephine's total debt was 1,200,000 francs of which she admitted half. She told Bourrienne she could not face her husband's anger if he knew the truth and asked for his help. As predicted, Napoleon flew into a rage even when informed of the reduced figure of 600,000 francs. For the sake of his prestige he ordered the sum paid. Bourrienne then persuaded the various tradesmen to accept half; he pointed out that if they sued and the affair became public, Napoleon might be forced from office and they would receive nothing. Reluctantly the duped milliners and haberdashers settled.

Almost at his wits' end with his wife's extravagance, Napoleon tried to persuade her to live a quiet life at Malmaison, where he encouraged her to entertain lavishly. Josephine was always a talented hostess, charming, kind, tactful, with a remarkable memory for names and faces. Malmaison symbolized part of Napoleon's new bearing. He had moved there from the rue de la Victoire on 21 November 1799, just after Brumaire. Three months later, on 19 February 1800 he made the transition from the quasi-republican to the quasi-imperial even more obvious by moving his official residence from the Luxembourg to the Tuileries, and spent his first night there occupying the bed last slept in by Louis XVI.

By one of those curious twists for which the psychologist Carl Jung invented the term 'synchronicity', the very next day a letter arrived from Louis XVI's younger brother, Louis Stanislas Xavier, the future Louis XVIII. Louis assumed, as did so many Frenchmen at the time, that Napoleon's consulate was a brief interregnum before the inevitable restoration of the Bourbons; Napoleon, in short, was thought to be a kind of General Monk making straight the ways for a return of the monarchy. Louis wrote *de haut en bas*: 'You are taking a long time to give me back my throne; there is a danger that you may miss the opportunity. Without me you cannot make France happy, while without you I can do nothing for France. So be quick and let me know what positions and dignities will satisfy you and your friends.'

Napoleon's prompt reply was devastatingly brief: 'I have received your letter. I thank you for your kind remarks about myself. You must give up any hope of returning to France: you would have to pass over 100,000 dead bodies. Sacrifice your private interests to the peace and happiness of France. History will not forget. I am not untouched by the misfortunes of your family. I will gladly do what I can to make your retirement pleasant and undisturbed.' Three years later he suggested that Louis face facts and give up his claims to the French throne. Trusting to his star, the stubborn Bourbon refused.

The perception that Napoleon intended to restore the Bourbons in 1800 was odd, for by his vigorous suppression of the Vendée revolt he surely served notice of his intentions. The Vendée rebels were the military arm of Bourbon royalism and, as soon as he was confirmed as First Consul, Napoleon dealt harshly with them. Rejecting all overtures from the Vendeans, he announced there would be peace only when the rebels had submitted. He sent some of his best generals, including Brune, against them and won a string of military victories. One of the most important Vendée leaders, the comte de Frotte, surrendered with six other rebel luminaries, under the impression they had been offered safe conduct. They were executed at once, possibly because Frotte had personally insulted the First Consul in a manifesto. But Napoleon himself was not directly responsible: 'I did not give the order,' he said later, 'but I cannot claim to be angered by its implementation.' Disheartened by this act of treachery, dismayed by their run of military failures, and bitter towards the English, whom they accused of not providing the resources to make the rebellion in western France a serious threat, the Vendeans signed a truce.

For the rest of 1800 royalist opposition to Napoleon took the form of conspiracies and assassination plots. There was a plan by one of General Hanriot's aides to assassinate Napoleon on the road to Malmaison; this aborted. There was the 'dagger plot' of 10 October 1800, when Napoleon was to be stabbed to death with a stiletto in his box at the Opéra; but the ringleaders – the painter Topio-Lebrun, the sculptor Ceracchi and the adjutant-general Aréna – were rounded up and executed before the plot could be implemented. And there was the most serious assassination attempt of all: the *machine infernale* of December 1800.

On Christmas Eve 1800 Napoleon, Joséphine and her family, together with Caroline Murat, were due to attend the opening of Haydn's *Creation* at the Opéra. Napoleon was in front in one coach with three of his generals, while Josephine, her daughter Hortense and Caroline Murat followed in the second. The royalists had rigged up an 'infernal machine' – actually a bomb attached to a barrel of gunpowder concealed in a cart – and timed it to explode at the precise moment Napoleon and his entourage drove down the rue St Nicaise. Two things thwarted a cunningly laid plot. The two carriages were supposed to keep close together, but the women's coach had been delayed when Josephine at the last moment decided to change a cashmere shawl; meanwhile a drunken coachman on Napoleon's carriage was driving at speed. A gap opened up between the two conveyances and it was at that point that the device exploded, missing both carriages but killing or maiming fifty-two bystanders and some of the Consul's escort. Napoleon continued to the Opéra as though nothing had happened.

It was not only from royalists that the Consul had to fear plots. The Jacobins were active too, especially in the Army, where they could count on the support of generals like Bernadotte, Moreau, Augereau, Lecourbe,

Delmas and Simon. Yet Napoleon was always kept well informed of Jacobin plots by his spies and made a point of sending dissident generals to remote foreign troublespots, excepting only Bernadotte, who as Joseph's brother-in-law and Désirée's husband, consistently got away with blatant disloyalty and even treason. The Jacobins' position was difficult, for press censorship made any propaganda offensive chimerical, and Napoleon, who detested the Jacobins far more than the royalists, did not hesitate to mete out execution and deportation, or to open mails and plant *agents provocateurs*. If ever Napoleon faced opposition from the legislature, he would cow them with his favourite threat: 'Do you, then, want me to hand over to the Jacobins?'

The one card the Jacobins held was that the loathsome Fouché, chief of police, was secretly on their side. Systematically duplicitous – to the point where, when asked by Napoleon to keep Joséphine under surveillance, Fouché secretly recruited her as an agent to report the goings-on in the First Consul's household – Fouché covered up for his political comrades and directed Napoleon's attention towards the royalists.

Yet the sequel to the 'infernal machine' showed Napoleon for once outfoxing the fox. He was determined to use the occasion to purge the Left opposition and, despite reluctance from his colleagues, he forced through an extraordinary measure: 130 known republicans were dubbed 'terrorist' and proscribed without legal process. They were then either interned or sent to a slow death in Guyana and Devil's Island. An enraged Fouché took no more than a few days to bring Napoleon incontrovertible proof that the perpetrators of the 'infernal machine' were royalist, not republicans. Napoleon authorized the guillotining of the new batch of prisoners but did not free the deported Jacobins. His cunning emerges in the wording of the emergency decree, which condemned the 130 Jacobins in phrases which referred to the safety of the state in general, not to the Christmas Eve outrage.

Throughout the year 1800 Napoleon proved himself a master at navigating the political shoals, playing off one party against another, now appearing to incline to the Right, now to the Left. He leaked his correspondence with Louis XVIII to the Jacobins to show that he had no royalist sympathies, then purged the Jacobins to reassure the Right. The situation after Marengo even allowed him to jettison his Thermidorian rump of former supporters. Because Marengo was at first reported in Paris as a defeat, the partisans of Sieyès and Barras showed their hand openly, which allowed Napoleon to marginalize them when he returned to Paris. More importantly, it revealed to people at large that Napoleon

The legend in the making: Bonaparte at the Bridge of Arcole, 1796

Devious, manipulative, pessimistic: Madame Mère (Maria Letizia Bonaparte)

The acme of lubricious beauty: Pauline Bonaparte

Joseph,
Napoleon's 'complex' elder brother

Louis,
the reluctant accomplice

Lucien,
the enemy within

Jerome,
Napoleon's 'Benjamin'

The Christ-like Bonaparte heals the sick at Jaffa
in this hagiographic study by Gros

(*Opposite page*) Marengo, 1800: the first of many close-run affairs

Josephine Beauharnais,
Creole beauty and Empress

A second Hannibal but without the elephant:
Napoleon crosses the Alps by mule

Austerlitz: Napoleon's finest hour

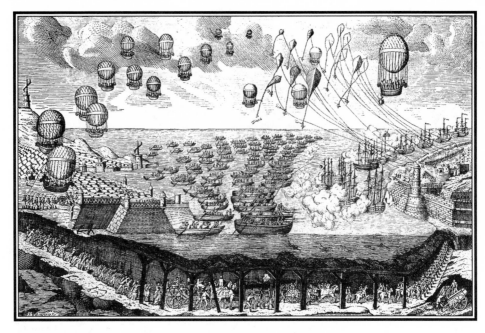

The invasion scare, 1803-04:
an early vision of the Channel Tunnel

The First Consul becomes Emperor:
Napoleon's coronation, December 1804

and the other Brumairians were things apart. Napoleon thus not only avoided all the unpopularity currently felt towards the men of Brumaire but was able to appear above faction and thus as national reconciler.

It was always the threat from the Right that most exercised the First Consul, even before the 'infernal machine', and he decided to cut the ground from under their feet by co-opting their traditional supporter, the Catholic Church. This was yet another opportunity provided by Marengo, which in political if not military terms has claims to be considered one of Bonaparte's most decisive battles. When Napoleon seized power in November 1799, French Catholicism was in a parlous state. The Church had been under sustained attack for ten years, first from the revolutionaries who equated it with the *ancien régime* and latterly from the blundering reformers of the Directory. The episcopate was for the most part in exile and systematically counter-revolutionary. The expropriation of church property and the institution of civil marriage left most of the priesthood irrevocably alienated, and even those priests who collaborated with the post-1789 régime had to heed the instructions of their émigré bishops. Under the Directory was no civil society, no middle range of institutions between the individual and the state; the Church therefore had a legal existence only as a collection of individual priests, which naturally weakened its position. Pius VI, a virtual prisoner of the Directory in Rome, was dying. The Church seemed to have reached the point of terminal crisis.

But Napoleon knew that Catholicism was still a potent force among the peasantry, from whom he derived much of his support. He saw an important potential source of authority in the 40,000 priests who would support his régime if he came to an agreement with the Church. He also saw the short-term advantages of getting rid of a counter-revolutionary element which would also bind closely to him the émigré aristocracy and the middle classes. He needed to ensure that the Vendée did not break out again and to cut the ground from under Louis XVIII. Above all, Napoleon seriously considered that society could not exist without inequality of property. Only the Church could legitimate social inequality, for secular attempts to justify it would trigger revolution.

There were two ways of going about the religious problem. Napoleon could allow the separation of Church and State to work itself out spontaneously, which would probably entail a *de facto* restoration of Catholicism; or he could actively seek a formal agreement with the Pope. On temperamental and political grounds, it was always likely that he would opt for the latter solution. He liked to stamp his authority on every aspect of national life and, if the Church was to be restored, he personally wanted the credit for it. Hence the paradox of the vigour with which this man, with no love for Christianity *per se*, forced through an agreement with the Papacy.

After Marengo, Napoleon made immediate overtures to the new Pope Pius VII, who was elected after a protracted conclave on 14 March 1800. The Consul celebrated a *Te Deum* in Milan Cathedral on 18 June and a week later, at Versilia, informed Cardinal Martiniana of his wish to come to an agreement with the Pope. The news was conveyed to Rome, where Pius VII at once accepted the principle of talks. Detailed negotiations opened in Paris in November, with Archbishop Spina of Corinth and the reformed Vendéan Bernier as the principals on either side; Bernier, an accomplished diplomat, was under the direction of Talleyrand who, as an unfrocked priest, could not negotiate directly.

At this time there were three groups in the French Catholic Church: the constitutionals, who had made their peace with the Revolution early on; the reformist *refractaires* who had come to terms with Napoleon after Brumaire; and the ultramontane faction of diehards. These three groups were mirrored within Napoleon's own circle by those who thought like him, those sympathetic to the Church (men like Fontanes and Portalis) who wanted to enshrine it as the State religion, and the crypto-Jacobins led by Fouché, who were violently anticlerical and detested the entire project of rapprochement with Catholicism. This confused situation produced some remarkable *ad hoc* convergences. Both the devout and the anticlerical party would have preferred no treaty with Rome but merely *de facto* separation of Church and State: the former thought religion would revive best this way, while the latter thought it would wither on the vine. The 'constitutionals' meanwhile thought Napoleon was on their side, but in his heart he preferred the authoritarian mentality of the ultramontanes. He was suspicious of the insidious 'democracy' of the constitutional church and the elections which the *constitution civile* had introduced.

Bernier proved an inspired choice for the negotiations. There were three main obstacles to a general agreement. The first concerned the appointment of bishops. Who should have the power to nominate to sees, and what about those who had fled or been forced to resign by previous Popes? The second was the desire of Pius VII that Catholicism should be the state religion in France. The third, naturally, concerned the revolutionary confiscation of Church property. Eight months of often acrimonious negotiations followed. Napoleon pretended sympathy for the idea of Catholicism as state religion but told the Pope that public opinion would not tolerate a return to the *ancien régime* in any form. Since those

who had benefited from the sale of national property were the mainstay of
Napoleon's régime, he could hardly grant the Pope's economic demands,
but as a *quid pro quo* Napoleon offered to put all the clergy on a salary and
treat them as state officials. A very decent compromise on the episcopate
had almost been worked out when the venal Talleyrand spotted that
married ex-clergy like himself would be at a disadvantage; he managed to
intrigue to get the 'offending' clauses scrapped.

As the negotiations stretched out into 1801, attitudes on both sides
hardened. After the 'infernal machine' incident, Napoleon's desire for an
agreement with the Catholic Church became more intense and he grew
impatient with the stalling tactics of the papacy. At one point he
threatened a military occupation of Rome if Pius VII did not come to
heel. The Pope, meanwhile, considered that Spina had already conceded
too much and sent his Secretary of State, Consalvi, to Paris, to conduct
the talks. Two eleventh-hour crises threatened to turn the proposed
treaty into débâcle. Consalvi tried to get a recantation from the bishops
who were then in schism through having accepted the revolutionary
constitution civile. Napoleon was outraged and angrily charged the papal
delegate with not realizing the extent of Republican, Jacobin and Army
opposition he had had to overcome even to reach this point in the talks.
Finally, a draft agreement was reached, but Bernier warned Consalvi that
he was being asked to put his signature to a text which was not the one
agreed.

There were outraged protests from Consalvi. Napoleon, angry at
having been caught in such an obvious deception, threw the draft treaty
on the fire and dictated a ninth at speed, which he insisted had to be
signed then and there without cavil. Consalvi refused and called
Bonaparte's bluff. Napoleon appeared to back down and signed the treaty
of Concordat at midnight on 15 July 1801. In a conciliatory preamble,
Napoleon recognized the Roman Catholic faith as the religion of most
French people. In the detailed articles that followed it was stipulated that
French government and Holy See together would work out a new
division of dioceses; that the First Consul would nominate bishops, to be
ratified and invested by the Pope; and that in return for an oath of loyalty
to the government the clergy would receive state salaries, without
prejudice to the benefits churches could enjoy from endowments.

The Pope considered the Concordat a great triumph. He ratified the
treaty on 15 August 1801, and in the bull *Tam Multa* he ordered the
ultramontane bishops to resign, pending the new reorganization of sees.
Most did so, but in the west of France a handful of rebels set up an anti-
Concordat church, royalist and schismatic. The new dioceses were

speedily agreed and bishops appointed in a spirit of compromise: twelve were former constitutionals, sixteen former non-jurors and thirty-two new ones, including Bernier. The naïve pontiff took it as a positive sign that Napoleon appointed his uncle Fesch, now a cardinal, as his ambassador to the Vatican.

Pius VII took the view that with the Concordat schism had been avoided, the unity of the Church restored and its finances put on a sound footing. The attempt by the Revolution to exclude the French Church from papal influence had manifestly failed and, having been invited to dismiss all existing bishops, the Pope now had a precedent for further interventions. Catholics in general gained from a State church in all but name, financial advantages, the end of schism and a privileged rôle in education. Above all, though, Pius VII felt that the impact of the Enlightenment and the Revolution had brought Catholicism close to collapse; in the context of a ten-year battering from revolutionary anticlericalism, Napoleon seemed like a godsend.

Napoleon was satisfied that he had achieved most of his objectives, appeased the peasantry and torn the heart out of royalist resistance. Piqued at Consalvi's valiant rearguard action, he tacked on to the main protocol of the Concordat the so-called 'organic articles', which forbade the publication of any bull, pastoral letter or other communication from senior clergy without the permission of the French government. Further articles forbade unauthorized synods or unwanted Papal legates, prescribed French dress for the clergy and ordained that the same Catechism should be used in every work. In order to rebut the canard that the Concordat made Catholicism the state religion in all but name, Napoleon ordered Chaptal, his Minister of the Interior, to draw up further 'organic articles' providing state salaries for Protestant pastors. The organic articles showed clearly that Napoleon was never really interested in genuine compromise and that in effect he had duped Pius. Such a mentality did not bode well for future relations with the Papacy.

The Concordat was the purely political act of a man indifferent to religion but conscious of its role as social pacifier. It successfully neutralized royalist opposition for the next eight years, to the point where the royalist Joseph de Maistre wrote: 'With all my heart I wish death to the Pope in the same way and for the same reason I would wish it to my father were he to dishonour me tomorrow.' Royalist wrath fell on Pius VII not Napoleon, but the First Consul had to face determined resistance from the opposite direction. The Concordat was construed as a gross offence to Republican sentiment. The Council of State greeted its promulgation in silence; in the Tribunate the treaty was mocked; the

Legislature pointedly elected an atheist as its president; and the Senate coopted a leading 'constitutional' who had opposed the accord. Resentment in the Army was even more vociferous. Napoleon was able to ride out these waves of dissent because the Concordat was hugely popular with ordinary people, and especially the peasantry, who had now got its old church back but shorn of its feudal privileges.

Radicals of all stripe thought the Concordat a mistake. Charles James Fox, talking to Napoleon after the Treaty of Amiens, blamed him for not insisting on a married clergy. Napoleon replied: 'I wanted, and still want, to pacify; theological volcanoes are to be quenched with water, not with oil; I should have found it less easy to introduce the confession of Augsburg into my empire.' Jacobins, and later historians sympathetic to them, saw the Concordat as the final betrayal of the Revolution. On this view, what had made France unable to throw off the claims of absolutism, despite the events of 1789–94, was the dead hand of Catholicism, and here was Napoleon making common cause with it, in a treaty signed by two separate despotisms. Some historians have even speculated that the Concordat was fundamentally 'unFrench' and that by concluding it Napoleon showed himself clearly a man of Italian sensibility, a true Constantine in his attitude to religion.

Certainly the reopening of churches for general worship inflamed Jacobins wedded to Voltaire's aim of 'wipe out the infamy!' (religion). The solemn *Te Deum* in Notre Dame cathedral on Easter Day, 18 April 1802, held to celebrate the Concordat, degenerated into farce. Napoleon ordered all his generals to be present to display unity, but the idea backfired. The only ones in Napoleon's entourage who knew when to genuflect were the two defrocked clergymen: ex-bishop Talleyrand and ex-Oratorian priest Fouché. The others went up and down at will. At the elevation of the host during the Consecration, senior officers responded by presenting arms, and throughout the Mass the booming voices of Lannes and Augereau could be heard chatting and laughing. After the service Napoleon asked one general (reputedly Delmas) how he thought it had gone. 'Pretty monkish mummery,' said the general. 'The only thing missing were the million men who died to overthrow what you are now setting up again.'

The Concordat allowed Napoleon to take a more relaxed view of the royalist threat, and the first sign of his increased confidence was the law to permit émigrés to return. In 1802 amnesty was declared, allowing the return of all refugees from the Revolution except those who had actually borne arms against France; it was to be a point of understanding that there would be no return of real estate already sold as 'national property'.

Some 40,000 émigrés or 40% of the total availed themselves of the opportunity, making Napoleon's rightward drift ever more evident. Josephine was a crypto-royalist and even corresponded with people who were officially enemies of the state. Napoleon, amused, indulged her but told Fouché to keep a close eye on her activities; a vicious circle was thus set up, wherein Fouché reported to Napoleon on Josephine and she reported to the chief of police on her husband.

By this time Bonaparte was increasingly confident that events were moving his way, even in areas where a year or two before there had been little reason to be sanguine. He had inherited a disastrous financial legacy from the Directory and economics is less obedient to the dictates of consuls and premiers than are political factions. When he became First Consul, the economy was a shambles: it was widely reported that only 167,000 francs remained in the state coffers. Highway robbery and brigandage were rampant, especially in the south and west, industry, trade and finance were in ruins, there were beggars and soup kitchens in Paris, the navy was non-existent, the desertion rate in the army at epidemic level, and yet Napoleon had to find the means of waging war for another full year.

Until he pushed his luck to the point where it could not possibly hold, Napoleon was always fortune's darling. There had been an early instance of this when an intemperate letter of complaint arrived from Kléber in Egypt, containing a blistering attack on 'General Bonaparte' and all his works. Addressed to the Directory, it arrived in Paris when that body was no more and was delivered into the hands of the cynically amused First Consul, who published it together with a tendentious rebuttal. At Marengo too he was lucky, and even more in its after-effects. First, there were the negotiations for the Concordat. Then came a dramatic fall in the price of bread, which convinced many that it was in some sense caused by Napoleon's military victory. At the same time bankers, persuaded both by the plebiscite and by Marengo that Napoleon was there to stay, began opening their purse strings. The First Consul told his Finance Minister Gaudin: 'The good days are coming.'

With his new popularity Napoleon felt confident enough to impose an additional 25-centime tax, which under the Directory would have brought the people on to the streets. Instead they applauded him. By 1801 economic recovery was in full swing. It is true that Napoleon was lucky, whereas the Directory's rule had coincided with a long period of economic depression. But he had worked hard for his success, which was possible only because he had won the complete confidence of the bourgeoisie. Among his most successful economic measures during

1800–02 were the system of direct taxation by central government, which balanced the budget by 1802; a sinking fund to diminish the National Debt by buying back government stocks; a Bank of France which aimed to mitigate the worst effects of the trade cycle by loans, discounts, promissory notes, etc; and a new coinage and payment in cash of government rents.

Napoleon's economic policy was a classic of state intervention. The Bank of France, which controlled the National Debt, also had the monopoly on the issue of paper currency. It was therefore possible to reform the currency and abolish the worthless *assignats*. Heavier taxation was avoided by the further sale of national property and the loot from the second Italian campaign. Bonaparte's policy of state intervention led to an upsurge in both agriculture and industry. Wool production increased by 400%. As far as possible tight control was kept on grain prices, which were kept low and not allowed to find their market level. There were even halting experiments with elementary health insurance schemes and workhouses were modernized. Trade unions, however, were suppressed as 'Jacobin' institutions: all workers had to carry a labour permit on pain of imprisonment.

Yet under this veneer of welfarism Napoleon always feared the common people. Mindful of his early experiences with food rioters, Napoleon had something of a perennial obsession with the price of bread. Suddenly, at the time of the peace of Amiens, the price started shooting up, and rising unemployment served warning that the initial prosperity might be a flash in the pan. For a while Napoleon confronted a grave economic situation, with serious food shortages. After ordering a newspaper blackout on the subject of famine and dearth, Napoleon blatantly used the power of the state to prime the economy. He gave concessions to a financial holding company, which was charged to buy up all the bread in European ports and flood Paris with it. The price soon came tumbling down beneath the danger level of eighteen sous a loaf; famine and popular uprising were averted. Next he tried reflating the economy by giving interest-free loans to manufacturers provided they took on more hands. Further banks were set up to provide loans in the different industries. The policy worked, and by his brilliant success in handling the economy Napoleon secured a third triumph to set alongside Marengo and the peace of Amiens.

The centralizing trends in economic policy were even more pronounced in public administration, where Napoleon was at the apex of a pyramid. Ninety-eight prefects in each Department answered to him and in turn transmitted orders to 420 under-prefects in the *arrondissements*, who in their turn controlled 30,000 mayors and municipal councils. The prefects ran the country rather in the manner of the Intendants under the *ancien régime*. According to a decree of 1802 every *département* had to have a secondary school and every commune a primary school; in large cities grammar schools or *lycées* were opened. The curriculum was rigidly controlled, and showed the bias against humanities typical of all dictatorships. Mathematics and science were emphasized but the liberal arts were banned or restricted. No modern history was taught, and the muse of Clio was placated instead with an intensive study of the reign of Charlemagne. In its exact reversal of 'democracy from the grass-roots up' the Napoleonic system could scarcely have been more authoritarian, though it was a good forerunner of Lenin's 'democratic centralism'.

The area where Napoleon experienced most difficulty in his path to supreme power was in his relations with the legislature. The sixty-strong Senate was loyal, but the 300 Deputies of the Legislative Corps were a thorn in his side, and especially troublesome was the 100-strong Tribunate, which opposed both the Concordat and the later Code Napoléon. But Napoleon had many powerful weapons of counter-offensive. He hit back by increasing the size of the Senate to one hundred in 1803 and halving the Tribunate and Legislative Corps. He used three other main devices for bypassing legislative obstruction: the use of *senatus consultum* or decrees which bypassed the Tribunate and Legislative Corps; *arrêts* or orders in council, promulgated by the Council of State; and, as the ultimate deterrent, the plebiscite.

Other measures for neutralizing opposition included playing Ministers off against each other or against the Council of State, or diminishing their powers by subdividing and duplicating the Ministries; another obvious ploy was to appoint second-raters to the Ministries. Later, he liked to appoint younger men bound to him by loyalty rather than the older generation. And, since one-fifth of Tribunes and Legislators were renewed annually, Napoleon used Cambacérès, the Second Consul, to get rid of opponents. Instead of drawing lots, which was the normal procedure, the Senate named the three hundred who were to keep their seats, and simply nominated twenty-four new members, even though the Constitution did not permit this. In the Legislative Body those who were removed were the friends of Sieyès and Madame Staël the so-called ideologues who had made the egregious mistake of thinking that their intellectual preeminence alone exempted them from the task of building a proper political power base.

Napoleon was ruthless towards individual opponents or potential enemies. He kept Sieyès under surveillance at his country estate. When

Barras, in exile at Grosbois, appealed to Napoleon but foolishly tempered his appeal by reproaching him with ingratitude, Napoleon sent his police to make sure Barras moved his place of exile beyond French borders. When Lafayette opposed the amendment of his consular powers in 1802, Napoleon at once removed the name of Lafayette's son and all his in-laws from the Army promotion list. The enemy he loathed most was Madame de Staël, whose salon, much visited by Moreau and Bernadotte, became the focus for the political opposition. When Germaine de Staël incautiously published *Delphine*, which contained many obvious coded criticisms of the First Consul, Napoleon exiled her from Paris and forbade her to come within 120 miles of the capital. Not even members of his own family escaped his ruthlessness if they did not act as he wished. In November 1800 he dismissed Lucien as Minister of the Interior, replaced him with Chaptal, and sent him as ambassador to Madrid. Lucien's crime was his tactlessness. On 8 April that year he had become engaged in an unseemly shouting match with Fouché at the Tuileries. Faced with Fouché's obvious sympathy for the Left, Napoleon's inclination was to conceal for the moment his animosity towards the Jacobins. But Lucien, by arguing for a hardline before his brother had consolidated his power, came close to ruining Napoleon's chessplaying strategy.

By 1802 Napoleon had made peace with France's external enemies, suppressed the Vendée, come to an agreement with the Catholic Church and cunningly conciliated the émigrés while yielding not a jot over confiscated property. His supporters felt that his great achievements merited overt recognition, and a motion calling for the First Consul to be given lifetime tenure was engineered in the Tribunate on 6 May 1802. However, the Senate, usually docile, was on this occasion whipped up by Fouché and the Jacobins and offered only the premature election of the First Consul for ten years. Cambacérès, placing an each-way bet, suggested a plebiscite to solve the problem. Napoleon insisted that the wording of the referendum should refer to a consulate for life rather than premature re-election for ten years. The question to be put was: 'Should Napoleon Bonaparte be consul for life?' This new nomenclature – hitherto he had always been 'General Bonaparte' or 'citizen Bonaparte' – was significant, and it has been pointed out that thereafter he was generally known as Napoleon rather than Bonaparte.

The plebiscite on the issue of a consulate for life returned 3,600,000 'yes' votes and 8,374 'noes'. The Senate ratified the result on 2 August 1802. Naturally, there was some iregularity in the voting, but the result was probably a reasonable reflection of the First Consul's popularity:

after all, here was a man who had delivered economic prosperity, the peace of Amiens, a religious settlement and a new deal for the émigrés. Royalists, moderates and the bourgeoisie flocked to him, but there was an ominous undertow in that most of the 'noes' came from the Army. In military circles, where Jacobinism was rife, intimidation was the order of the day. One soldier wrote in his memoirs: 'One of our generals summoned the soldiers in his command and said to them: "Comrades, it is a matter of nominating General Bonaparte consul for life. You are free to hold your own opinion; nevertheless, I must warn you that the first man not to vote for the Consulate for life will be shot in front of the regiment." '

The ratification by the Senate in August 1802 increased Napoleon's powers. He could now decide on peace treaties and alliances, designate the other consuls, nominate his own successor and had the right of reprieve (*droit de grâce*). As an apparent *quid pro quo* the Senate was given the power to dissolve the Legislature or the Tribunate. But Napoleon could now bring the Senate to heel whenever he wished as he also had unlimited powers to swamp it with new members. He had other powers to constrain the Senate. He allowed senators to hold other public offices simultaneously – previously forbidden – and had the right to distribute *senatoreries* – endowments of land for life together with a house and an income of 20–25,000 francs. As Napoleon confided to Joseph, his vision of the Senate was that 'it was destined to be a body of old and tired men, incapable of struggling against an energetic consul.'

The most enduring monument from the years of the First Consulate was the Code Napoléon. It appealed to Napoleon to think that he could be not just a great general like Caesar, Alexander and Hannibal but also a great law-giver like those other famous names of the Ancient World: Lycurgus, Hammurabi, Solon. Starting in 1800, for four years he summoned councils to oversee a drastic revision of the Civil Code. He began by appointing two separate law reform commissions, then combined them and put them under Cambacérès's direction. The joint commission's proposals would then be considered by the Judicial Committee of the Council of State before going to the First Consul for final approval. Altogether Napoleon attended fifty-seven out of 109 meetings to discuss the Code; these were exhaustive and exhausting affairs that would often go on until 4 a.m. The First Consul surprised everyone with his lucidity, knowledge and depth of insight. He had done his homework well and devoured a number of mammoth tomes given him by Cambacérès. Napoleon was beginning to impress even the sceptics as a man who could do anything; first there was his military talent, then his diplomatic skill, next his administrative ability and finally his prowess as a legislator.

The provisions of the new Civil Code began to be promulgated in 1802 and the final clauses were published in 1804. Later there would follow a Commercial (1807), Criminal (1808) and Penal (1810) Code. Napoleon's intentions in framing the Civil Code have been much disputed, but he declared that he genuinely wanted to create a civil society, with a middle range of institutions between the individual and the State; this was needed, he claimed, because the Revolution had introduced a spirit of excessive individualism. His famous declaration in the Council of State was that the Revolution had turned the French into so many grains of sand, so that it was now his task 'to throw upon the soil of France a few blocks of granite, in order to give a direction to the public spirit.'

The essence of the Code was its eclecticism and its clear intention to benefit the new bourgeoisie, the bulwark of Napoleon's power. Essentially a compromise between old and new law, between the modalities of pre-1789 and the new circumstances and conceptions of the Revolution, it mixed customary and statute law, intertwined legal and philosophical concepts and at times emerged with the worst of both worlds. The Tribunate, in particular, found the various drafts hurriedly prepared and ill-digested and thought that too many Revolutionary principles had been sacrificed to those of the *ancien régime*. The Code was meant to benefit wealthy men of property and had nothing to say to the propertyless. Philosophically, it was designed to extirpate feudalism and to enthrone bourgeois privilege, seeing property as an absolute and transcendental right, logically prior to society.

It is sometimes said that the Code was progressive, but such a view does not survive a scrutiny of the various clauses. The propertyless emerged with very few rights at all. The Code proclaimed freedom of labour but did nothing whatever to safeguard workers' rights; in any labour dispute the word of the employer was to be taken as gospel. Napoleon's anti-worker stance was in any case overt. By decrees of 1803 and 1804 he placed all proletarians under police supervision, obliged them to carry identity cards, prohibited unions and strikes on pain of imprisonment and charged the Prefect of Police with the arbitrary settlement of wage disputes. Amazingly, in the years of his success Napoleon was not perceived as being anti-labour. The workers supported him because of his policy of low food prices – to ensure which he placed bakers and butchers under state control – and the rising wages caused by a revival of industry. His victories in the field attracted their working-class chauvinism, so that the proletariat always listened to Bonapartist propaganda rather than the criticisms of the liberal opposition.

The most reactionary aspect of the Code, however, was its treatment of women. Until 1794 feminism and women's rights enjoyed halcyon days: in September 1792 the revolutionaries enacted a law allowing divorce by mutual consent, with the unsurprising result that for the rest of the 1790s one in three French marriages ended in divorce. The Directory had attempted to reverse the progressive legislation of 1791–94, but the death blow to feminist aspirations was dealt by the Code Napoléon. The First Consul's misogyny lay at the root of this. Always hostile to female emancipation, he declared: 'Women these days require restraint. They go where they like, do what they like. It is not French to give women the upper hand. They have too much of it already.' It is interesting to observe that the fiercest critic of Macpherson's *Ossian*, Napoleon's most beloved book, was Samuel Johnson but that he held exactly similar sentiments to Napoleon on the 'woman question': 'Nature has given women so much power that the Law has wisely given her little.'

The extent of anti-female sentiment in the Code Napoléon is worth stressing. The Code retained divorce by consent only if both sets of parents agreed also. Under Articles 133–34 the procedure was made more difficult. Marital offences were differentially defined under Articles 229–230: a man could sue for divorce on grounds of simple adultery; a woman only if the concubine was brought into the home. Articles 308–09 stipulated that an adulterous wife could be imprisoned for a period of up to two years, being released only if her husband agreed to take her back; an adulterous husband was merely fined. Patriarchy was reinforced in a quite literal sense by Articles 376–77 which gave back to the father his right, on simple request, to have rebellious children imprisoned. And the notorious articles 213–17 restored the legal duty of wifely obedience; these clauses, compounded by articles 268 and 776, severely restricted a wife's right to handle money, unless she was a registered trader. Finally, a woman who murdered her husband could offer no legal defence, but a husband who murdered his wife could enter several pleas.

The Code Napoléon has been much admired, but it is difficult to see it as anything other than a cynical rationalization of Napoleon's personal aims, in some cases cunningly projected into the future. The criticism that the Code quickly became out of date because it tried to fix the transitional society of the Napoleonic era in aspic is otiose. Much the same thing could be said of the US Constitution of 1787, but both documents proved supremely flexible. The more telling criticism is that the Code's talk of liberty and equality was largely humbug. The Code insinuated the oldest dodge in the book of right-wing theorists: the notion that equality before the law is in some sense real equality. It is noteworthy that whenever the Code speaks of abolishing privilege, it is *feudal* privilege that is meant. Napoleon wished to strike off all the fetters that chained the high bourgeoisie but he was most emphatically on the side of privilege. He tried to obfuscate the Revolutionary demand for an end to privilege by, in effect, pretending that the only forms of privilege were feudal rights and benefices, not glaring inequalities of wealth.

As has been well said, the 'dust' of individualism easily survived the Code. Napoleon's treasured legal system totally failed to create a civil society and indeed there is good reason to think that he never had any intention of creating such a society, but merely to create a chain of *ad hoc* interest groups bound to him personally by expediency. Faced with a conflict between the interests of the rich and the principle of *la carrière ouverte aux talents*, he decisively set his face against meritocracy; his basic position was that he believed in talent provided it was also wealthy. Later, with the creation of an imperial nobility and the cynical claim that one cannot govern nations without baubles, further nails were driven into the coffin of equality.

Some historians have even claimed that Napoleon devised his eponymous code as a kind of infrastructure for the future conquests he envisaged. Centralization and uniformity, after all, would be useful tools for crushing local and national customs. The cardinal purpose of the Code for Napoleon personally was the replacement of *ancien régime* inefficiency with a streamlined centralized bureaucracy whose main purpose would be raising troops and money. In the rest of Europe the Code could be used for putting Napoleon's power and that of his vassals beyond dispute. The purpose of destroying feudal privileges was to place all property not entailed at the disposition of his vassal rulers. The hollowness of the Code would be seen later but even in 1802–04 Napoleon showed how little it meant, in his governance of Italy. There the estates of deposed princes, émigrés and the clergy provided a steady stream of money, but often the income was in the form of tithes and feudal benefits, officially outlawed by the Code. Where money collided with the Code, Napoleon ignored his own 'masterpiece' and took the money.

By 1804 Napoleon's grip on France was complete. His power rested on a social basis of support from the peasantry and the upper bourgeoisie or 'notables'. Normally a single socio-economic class forms the basis of a régime's power, but the Napoleonic period was an era of transition, with the declining class (the aristocracy) too weak to dominate and the ascending class (the bourgeoisie) not yet quite strong enough. Napoleon held the ring, so to speak, by a trans-class coalition of peasantry and bourgeoisie based ultimately on the sale of national property. Napoleon was not a man of the Revolution, but it was the economic upheaval of the Revolution that made his autocracy possible.

By 1794 the feudal yoke had been thrown off and more than a third of all peasants in the north and east of France had acquired enough confiscated real estate to assuage the worst land-hunger. Overwhelmingly the 'national' property seized from émigrés, aristocrats and the clergy had been bought up by peasants. One survey shows over 70% of such lands being transferred to the peasantry between 1789–1799, with another 10% acquired by dealers and merchants, 10% by lawyers and 7-8% by former noblemen and returning émigrés. Upper peasants (those who owned their own land and employed others to work it) were major beneficiaries from the Napoleonic era: in time of famine, particularly in 1801, they grew rich thanks to capital investment and the productivity of their lands; and in time of war they benefited from increased trade outlets following Bonaparte's victories.

The lower peasants or rural proletariat – those who owned no land and worked as journeyman labourers for others – profited from the shortage of farm hands following conscription. There was a 20% rise in their wages between 1798–1815, enabling some of them to buy small amounts of national property, such as individual fields, and thus become middle peasants, working their own land. By becoming conscious of their scarcity value, and hence power, as a result of conscription, these journeymen workers annoyed the upper peasants, especially when the hitherto pliable rural proletariat acquired their own servants – a kind of 'sub-proletariat' of cowherds, shepherds, carters, etc. Under pressure from the upper peasants, Napoleon was forced to head off excessive pay rises by forbidding servants and seasonal labourers and harvesters to form unions or associations.

Yet unquestionably the greatest beneficiaries of the Napoleonic period were the moneyed élite, or upper bourgeoisie, who enjoyed continuous good fortunes from before 1789 to 1815. The big business people and bankers of the *ancien régime* were also the plutocrats of the Napoleonic empire. Behind them in economic fortunes, but still doing well, were the middle bourgeoisie from politics and administration and the new breed of post-Thermidor entrepreneurs, speculators in national property, colonial produce, *assignats* and military supplies; men from this stratum often ascended to the upper bourgeoisie through conspicuous success or intermarriage. In Napoleon's time the foundations for a true bourgeois society, in which money rather than rank was the salient consideration, were laid, although in some ways, as will become clear, the Napoleonic system also acted as a bar on the development of a society dedicated to Mammon alone.

The key to Napoleon's social and administrative system was the rule of the so-called 'notables'. These, in a word, were the people in each Department who paid the highest taxes. Typically, the notables were landowners, rentiers and lawyers with an annual income of more than 5,000 francs from real estate. Financiers, merchants and manufacturers joined the ranks of the notables by investing in land their profits from colonial produce or those generated by the boom given industry by new continental outlets. A man who was one of the six hundred most highly taxed people in his Department had a chance of entering the electoral college in the principal towns or being appointed a Senator or Deputy to the Legislature. The amount of land-tax paid was *the* determinant of a notable, who was often in any case a highly paid official. It did not take much to reach the magic figure of 5,000 francs from real estate when lavish salaries were being paid to officialdom: a Councillor of State was on 25,000 francs a year plus perks, a Parisian prefect received an annual salary of 30,000 francs, a provincial prefect anywhere between 8–24,000, an inspector-general of civil engineering 12,000 and a departmental head 6,000. Even the lower officials were in with a chance of ultimate distinction: a departmental deputy received an annual salary of 4,500, an ordinary solicitor or drafter of deeds 3,500 and a clerk 3,000.

It was undoubtedly the solidity of his régime in the years 1800–04 that encouraged Napoleon in his imperial ambitions, but there were straws in the wind from the very beginning of his consulate. He loved to hold military reviews and stirring marches in the Champs de Mars or the Place du Carousel, where he would preside in brilliant red uniform. The informal sumptuary laws extended to the consular guard, where the horsemen were dressed all in yellow. There were dinner parties in the Tuileries and balls at the Opéra, just as in the *ancien régime*. In 1801 he reintroduced court dress for men, with silk knee-breeches and cocked hats, and encouraged Josephine and Hortense to pioneer a female fashion of dressing in white; Josephine additionally received a bevy of ladies-in-waiting drawn from France's most noble families. After he had been appointed Consul for life, Napoleon's imperial proclivities became more marked. In 1802 he was declared President of the Cisalpine Republic and Protector of the Helvetic Republic. In 1803 coins bearing his effigy were struck, his birthday (15 August) became a public holiday, and his swordhilt was adorned with Louis XVI's diamonds.

Yet Napoleon was a clever politician who liked to camouflage and obfuscate what he was doing. The most consummate act of mystification was the introduction of the Legion of Honour, instituted on 19 May 1802. To offset his own imperial demeanour and the obvious dominance of the notables and upper bourgeoisie, Napoleon tried to pretend that he was still wedded to the Revolutionary ideal of meritocracy by seeming to introduce a parallel élite based on talent and achievement. There were to be four classes in the Legion: simple members, officers, commanders and grand officers; the highest award was the Grand Eagle. Originally divided into sixteen cohorts with 408 award holders each, the Legion by 1808 contained 20,275 members.

Napoleon's honours system was a great success, and there was keen competition for the familiar white enamel crosses on strips of red ribbon. Seeing in the Legion the germ of a new nobility, the returned émigrés hated and despised it, but they were not alone. The Legislature, packed with notables, absurdly opposed the Legion because it offended the principle of inequality; they saw no such offence in the glaring inequality of wealth and property of which they were the beneficiaries. It is a perennial peculiarity of societies to object to inequalities of race, sex, title, distinction and even intellect while remaining blithely untroubled about the most important form of inequality: the economic. A more telling criticism, which few made at the time, was that the honours system was overwhelmingly used to reward military achievement, usually to honour generals and others who had already done very well for themselves by looting and pillaging. An honours system, if it is to work well, should reward people who have not already received society's accolades and glittering prizes. Napoleon himself came to see the force of this argument and later regretted that he had not awarded the Legion of Honour to people like actors, who had no other form of official prestige.

The institution of the Legion shows Napoleon at his most cynical. He viewed human beings as despicable creatures, fuelled by banality and led by clichés, which he himself endorsed enthusiastically: 'It is by baubles alone that men are led'; 'bread and circuses'; 'divide and rule'; 'stick and carrot' – all these tags express an essential truth about Napoleon's approach to social control. He played off every class and social grouping against every other, and manipulated divisions within and between the strata: the urban proletariat, the petit-bourgeoisie, and the clergy were particular victims of his Machiavellianism but he dealt with recalcitrant lawyers, generals and financiers in essentially the same way.

It will be clear enough from the foregoing that in no sense can Napoleon be considered an heir of the French Revolution and its principles. It is possible to see him as a man of the Revolution only if one ignores the social and political tendencies of the early years 1789–93, to say nothing of the radical phase in 1793–94. Those who claim that Napoleon was in tune with Revolutionary principles are forced back on the absurd argument that the Revolution was really about returning to the *status quo ante*, before the legacy of the American war of 1775–83, which almost bankrupted France, forced Louis XVI to tamper with a fragile social fabric. On this view the Revolution was purely an economic and administrative transformation, and Jacobinism was simply the Revolution taking a wrong turning; equality and fraternity and all the rest of it was just so much hot air. Another influential view is that French history is a perennial quest for social order, which is why it is punctuated by bouts of absolutism and Caesarism; the obvious implication is that Napoleon was an organic growth but the Revolution was an aberration.

But this view of the Revolution, and hence of Napoleon, is nonsensical, and is really only a modern gloss on the way the men of Thermidor rationalized their recantation of the principles of 1789: they denied there ever were such principles. The other main way some historians try to present Napoleon as a man of the Revolution is to say that he was so unintentionally, that his armies spread the doctrines and ideologies of the Revolution by their victories. Some even claim that by his later assaults on the Inquisition in Spain and his overthrow of feudalism in Italy, he was at once the precursor of Italian unity and a kind of proto-apostle of European unity. But it must be stressed once again that Napoleon merely abolished feudalism and in no sense ushered in true equality. What happened was that Napoleonic victories gave the French a sense of superiority and that they therefore proselytized for certain Revolutionary ideals such as 'civil liberty' in conquered territories, much as though they were late-Victorian missionaries bringing the gospel to the heathen in benighted Africa.

Napoleon himself always made his position crystal-clear to his intimates. He told them he became disenchanted with the Jacobins very early because they prized equality over liberty. He always favoured the old nobility over the Jacobins and, beyond France, his attempts to introduce even the most basic rights of the Revolution were spasmodic. Outside France, administrative positions in the conquered territories were invariably filled by nobles, which made it impossible to carry out radical agrarian reforms and in turn meant that the peasantry outside France was always lukewarm about him. His apologists say that he favoured the foreign nobility because of the poor level of education outside France, but the truth is that for Napoleon *la carrière ouverte aux talents* was largely a meaningless slogan. As he once told Molé explicitly, the ideas of 1789 were 'nothing but weapons in the hands of malcontents, ambitious men and ideologues'.

CHAPTER THIRTEEN

During the years of peace (1801–03), sightseers and tourists thronged Paris, which became the same kind of Mecca to the curious it would be after 1945. The pent-up demand for things French was a particular feature of English travellers, who had been effectively barred from the country since 1792. In these years Paris was regarded as the arbiter of elegance and fashion; the permissive sexuality and the provocative clothes of the women, with dresses décolleté, tight and clinging were especially remarked on. Among the innovations in manners and morals from these years was the idea of the 'late' (7 p.m.) dinner, the 'barbarous' fashion for place cards at formal meals, and the introduction of menus in restaurants. Napoleon may have signed the Concordat to regularize religion, but the true god during the two-year breathing space between wars was conspicuous consumption, which in turn engendered more work than the capital's goldsmiths, jewellers and milliners could handle.

The two years of peace saw Napoleon almost entirely Paris-based and preoccupied with affairs of state. In January 1802 there was a quick visit to Lyons to review the troops who had returned from Egypt, and on 29 October the same year he made a fortnight's lightning tour of Normandy, taking in Évreux, Rouen, Honfleur, Le Havre, Dieppe and Beauvais. He told Cambacérès that he was everywhere received with ecstasy and, two months after his overwhelming triumph in the plebiscite on the Consulate for life, there is no reason to doubt this. Another significant development in 1802 was the move to the palace at St-Cloud. The commute between his official headquarters at the Tuileries and Joséphine's 'petit Trianon' at Malmaison – both, incidentally, on the 'must see' list of all British visitors to Paris in these years – came to irritate him and, once he was Consul for Life, he felt the need of an official residence more in keeping with the grandeur of his new status. The palace at Versailles was too redolent of the *ancien régime* and St-Cloud fitted the bill better, being a short drive from the Tuileries.

The move to St-Cloud was of course yet another imperial manifestation, much regretted by those who thought a First Consul should aspire to the Roman republican qualities of thrift, austerity and asceticism. Instead Napoleon spent millions on the fountains, waterfalls and frescoes at the palace. The soldiers of the Consular Guard made a resplendent show in the courtyard, but this initial impression of imperial splendour was dwarfed by the great marble staircase within, where hung the great propaganda masterpiece by David, *Napoleon Crossing the Alps*.

Napoleon's move to St-Cloud coincided with a downward spiral in relations with Britain, which brought the two nations back to open warfare by mid-1803. By December 1802 Napoleon had evacuated Taranto, as required by the Treaty of Amiens, but the British were still ensconced on Malta in blatant defiance of the same treaty. Moreover, they had not evacuated Alexandria, also as required by the treaty. As their ambassador to France, the British government had sent Lord Whitworth, an arrogant, supercilious oligarch who made it plain that he thought Napoleon was a low-born Corsican upstart. Meanwhile the British press carried on a scurrilous campaign of defamation against the First Consul. Something had to be done urgently.

Responsibility for the resumption of hostilities in 1803 is usually laid at Bonaparte's door, but the facts do not bear out this judgement. The fact that the war party in England, led by Pitt but also including the other two of the 'three Williams', Pitt's cousin Grenville and Windham, was out of office, did not significantly alter the basically bellicose thrust of British foreign policy. So powerful was the war party that the new prime minister Addington had to appease it by appointing Whitworth, a known opponent of the peace of Amiens, as ambassador to Paris. Whitworth entertained a particular animus towards Napoleon, which Bonaparte reciprocated. The mutual ideological and class-based antagonism was reinforced at the personal and visceral level: there is a lot of circumstantial evidence indicating that Napoleon resented the physical presence of the six-foot tall Whitworth.

On 21 February 1803 Napoleon summoned Whitworth for a dressing-down. He told him he was very disappointed that the Treaty of Amiens had not led to friendship between the two countries but had produced 'only continual and increasing jealousy and mistrust'. When he asked why Malta and Alexandria had not been evacuated, Whitworth alluded to the situation in Piedmont and Switzerland; in the former case France had annexed the territory and in the latter they had imposed a new constitution. Since it is often alleged that Napoleon's actions in these two cases justified the eventual British declaration of war, it is worth establishing what had happened.

In Piedmont Napoleon asked the exiled and ultra-Catholic king

Charles Emanuel to return to his throne so as to ensure stability in northern Italy. Charles Emanuel refused, so Napoleon, not wishing to leave a dangerous gap between France and the Cisalpine Republic, annexed Piedmont – a move that was welcomed by the majority republican party of the Piedmontese. In 1802 he also revised the Swiss constitution along federal lines and regulated relations between France and Switzerland by an 'Act of Mediation'. Again this angered the British who, as in Piedmont, were in league with the reactionary and aristocratic factions; Windham had even been sent with money to foment trouble among the aristocracy in Switzerland.

To the oft-repeated assertion that these two actions constituted unbearable 'provocation', three counter-arguments seem appropriate. In the first place, Switzerland and Italy were within the Austrian sphere of influence, not the British; if Napoleon's actions there gave cause for concern, it was for the signatories of the Treaty of Lunéville to react, not those of the Treaty of Amiens. Secondly, for precisely this reason the Treaty of Amiens contained no accords about Switzerland or Italy and said nothing whatever about affairs there. As Napoleon correctly stated: 'All this is not mentioned in the treaty. I see in it only two names, Taranto, which I have evacuated, and Malta, which you are not evacuating.' Thirdly, it was hardly in order for the English to speak of imposing constitutions, allegedly against the will of the majority, when they had just (1801) incorporated Ireland into the United Kingdom, *incontestably* against the will of the Irish.

Napoleon also raised the question of the vile propaganda cartoons about him being printed in the English newspapers, portraying him as a tyrant and ogre. The *Morning Post* had just described him as 'an unclassifiable being, half African, half European, a Mediterranean mulatto'. In cartoons he was usually portrayed as a pygmy with an enormous nose. Other organs portrayed Josephine as a harlot and claimed that Bonaparte was sleeping with her daughter Hortense. When taxed with this, Whitworth disingenuously claimed that press liberty was part of the traditional English freedoms and the government could not interfere; this from a creature of Pitt whose repressive 'Two Acts' of 1795 had silenced all pro-French newspaper opinion. Nor did Whitworth admit that he had been sending to London dispatches that were the purest fantasy, alleging that nine-tenths of the population in France opposed the First Consul.

Finding Whitworth intractable, Napoleon published in *Le Moniteur* a long article by Colonel Sebastiani, who had recently been on a mission to Turkey and the Near East, which warned that if Britain did not honour her treaty obligations, France might be forced to reconquer Egypt. This, an attempt by Napoleon to apply pressure on the recalcitrant English, was a bad mistake, for it allowed London to portray the First Consul as a sabre-rattler. By early 1803 it was abundantly clear to any dispassionate observer that Britain intended to go to war again. In the speech from the throne in March 1803 George III declared the nation to be on a war footing and falsely claimed that French invasion forces were fitting out in French and Dutch ports; even Whitworth was forced to concede that this was nonsense.

On 13 March, at a diplomatic reception at the Tuileries, Napoleon finally lost patience. He began to rant and rave at Whitworth about George III's speech from the throne and said it was now quite clear that England wanted another decade of war. He then turned to the ambassadors of Russia and Spain and said at the top of his voice: 'England wants war, but if they're the first to draw the sword, I'll be the last to sheathe it. They don't respect treaties.' He then stormed angrily from the room. He was playing the British game for them. In March Grenville told his henchman the Marquess of Buckingham (the same who had dubbed Bonaparte 'His Most Corsican Majesty') that Napoleon would have to go to war to avoid an unacceptable loss of face. The cynical Grenville then instructed Whitworth that when the next round of negotiations with Talleyrand and Joseph opened on 3 April, he should try to bribe them to see that London's wishes were fulfilled.

Two days after his explosion with Whitworth Napoleon addressed the Council of State and explained that Britain was determined to humiliate France: if they backed down over the continued occupation of Malta, the next thing would be a demand from the British for the port of Dunkirk, and after that always some fresh demand. The Council gave him their support. As a sop to England Napoleon proposed that once they evacuated Malta, they be allowed a Mediterranean base on Crete or Corfu. Under instructions from London, Whitworth then raised the stakes and replied that Malta must be handed over to England for ten years, and France must pull out of Switzerland and Holland. He freely conceded to Talleyrand that this was an ultimatum but cynically refused to put his outrageous demands on paper. Even Talleyrand, who thought that a renewed war with England was a bad mistake, described the proposal as the first verbal ultimatum in the history of modern diplomacy.

When Napoleon predictably rejected this demand, Whitworth asked for his passport. Still trying to head off a conflict he did not want at this time, Napoleon made a final offer: England could stay in Malta for three years, after which the island would be occupied by Russia. Naturally Whitworth turned this down, for London was set on war, and added fresh conditions to his original demand for a ten-year tenure of Malta.

On 11 May Napoleon wearily addressed another meeting of the Council of State in St-Cloud. The latest terms, he told them, were that Britain should occupy Malta for ten years, and in addition possess the island of Lampedusa in perpetuity; France meanwhile was to withdraw from Holland within a month. Even the most purblind pacifist could now see that Napoleon was right: there would never be any end of new British terms and conditions. As he rightly said: 'If the First Consul was cowardly enough to make such a patched-up peace with England, he would be disowned by the nation.' The Council enthusiastically voted to insist on the original terms of the Treaty of Amiens.

Even so, Napoleon made an eleventh-hour bid for peace. He told Whitworth that England could occupy Malta for ten years if France could reoccupy Taranto. This would be a face-saver to cancel out the most difficult clauses in the Treaty of Amiens. Whitworth forwarded the proposal to Addington, who disingenuously turned it down on the grounds of Britain's obligations to the King of Naples; that monarch in fact was in no position to do any other than what England ordered him to do.

So it was war. On 16 May 1803 George III authorized letters of marque for the seizure of French shipping and a state of war followed two days later. All fairminded statesmen in Europe agreed that the war was England's responsibility. Fox condemned Addington for playing Pitt's warmongering game, while the great anti-slavery crusader William Wilberforce declared that Malta was being retained only at the cost of a violation of public faith – something no nation could afford to lose. Napoleon, for whom the renewal of war came at least two years too early, tried to put a brave face on it. He told his sister Élisa's chamberlain Jérôme Lucchesini: 'I am going to try for the most difficult of all enterprises but the one which will be most fruitful of results of any I have conceived. In three days misty weather and a bit of luck could make me the master of London, Parliament and the Bank of England.'

The war thus begun would finally end only in 1815. It is therefore crucial to establish the responsibility for its outbreak and to see how the revival of hostilities in 1803 fitted Napoleon's ulterior designs. From Talleyrand to Pieter Geyl, so many people have alleged that going to war in 1803 was the beginning of the end for Napoleon that scrupulous examination is called for. Above all, why did Britain want war so badly in

1803 and why, despite this, has the responsibility so often been pinned on Bonaparte?

Some of the explanations for war in 1803 can be dismissed at the outset. The French historian Coquelle, for instance, argued that Napoleon consciously set his course for war as he hoped to achieve his imperial crown thereby. This falls down on all fronts: the dynamic towards empire was internal events in France, not the international scene and, as has been demonstrated, Napoleon made repeated efforts to avoid war. Pieter Geyl alleged that France had got a good deal at Amiens and that Britain had already gone as far as she intended to go with Bonaparte. According to this argument, the British had already granted him a position of great power on the Continent, and his 'gratitude' was to intervene in Switzerland, annex Piedmont, interfere in Italy and keep troops in Holland. By so doing he made enemies of people who thought that Britain had been foolish and generous in the first place, and the peace of Amiens dangerous and humiliating. Napoleon, it is said, observed the letter of Amiens but not its spirit. Other apologists for the British return in effect to Addington's own 'sabre-rattling' thesis and allege that Sebastiani's ideas, outlined in *Le Moniteur* were an attempt to blackmail England, by claiming that if the First Consul was forced to go to war with Britain, he would retaliate by conquering the whole of Europe.

Still others claim that Napoleon's apparent ambitions for empires in the East and West seriously alarmed London. It was not so much the expedition to Haiti, of which the British, for their own cynical reasons, secretly approved but the prospect of a Caribbean triangle of influence stretching from New Orleans to Cayenne via Santo Domingo. Then there were the Oriental ambitions at which Sebastiani hinted. Finally, it is claimed that Napoleon should not have closed Continental markets to British goods, as this was the one thing a trading nation could not tolerate. The one area where the 'provocation' argument rings true is in Napoleon's refusal of a commercial treaty and the introduction of economic and financial measures discriminating against the English.

The problem with all these attempts to fasten the responsibility for war on Napoleon in 1803 is that they make the error of imagining that the national self-interest of England was 'natural' and that of France unnatural. Why are 'national frontiers' unacceptable but a Belgium in hands friendly to Britain part of the natural order of things? Why was it legitimate for Britain to insist on a balance of power in Europe but not for France to insist on a balance of power and colonial trade in the rest of the world? If Napoleon's actions in Piedmont and Switzerland are construed as provocative, how much more provocative was England's refusal to evacuate Malta and Alexandria and to return Pondicherry and other enclaves in India to French rule? As Napoleon and others many times pointed out, the former were matters for Austria and were not mentioned in the treaty, while the latter were expressly mentioned in the text of Amiens and concerned no one but France and Britain.

The sober conclusion must be that on paper Britain went to war in 1803 out of a mixture of economic motives and national neurosis – an irrational anxiety about Napoleon's motives and intentions. The sale of Louisiana and the withdrawal from Haiti exposed the hollowness of the threat in the western hemisphere, while if Addington took the advice of his secret agents rather than the nonsense of Whitworth, he would have known that Admiral Denis Décrès, the French Navy Minister, did his best to sabotage any expedition Bonaparte proposed fitting out against India, and was particularly negative about the Consul's favourite project – a two-pronged assault on India and Egypt.

On the other hand, if we judge by the long-term rather than the short-term circumstances of 1803, the British decision for war contains more rationality. Napoleon was certainly no pacifist and his long-term plans clearly envisaged both further European expansion and a decisive settling of accounts with England. But for Napoleon in 1803, as for Hitler in 1939, the war came too soon. He had not yet built up his navy to the point where it had any prospect of challenging Britain's: he had just thirty-nine ships of the line and thirty-five frigates to throw against the massive power of the Royal Navy, whose numbers were 202 and 277 respectively. Nor had he finished the task of domestic consolidation. From the point of view of ultimate British self-interest, as opposed to the pharisaical reasons actually advanced, Britain made the right choice, catching Napoleon before he was ready to fight in time and circumstances of his own choosing. The problem for London was that it was going to be a very long haul and she faced the prospect of going it alone in the foreseeable future. Napoleon's rightward drift in France meant there was no enthusiasm or indeed occasion, as in 1792 for an ideological anti-Revolutionary crusade. None of the other powers wanted war or saw it as conducive to their interests. And there was little sympathy for the transparent 'justifications' of perfidious Albion.

Even as he wrestled with foreign and domestic policy, Napoleon had constantly to indulge or satisfy the aspirations of a large family of prima donna-ish siblings and an unscrupulous tail of in-laws and other hangers-on in the family circle. In many ways the least troublesome was Joseph, happy in his alliance with Talleyrand and content to grow fat on his real-estate investments. Joseph was full of a sense of his own importance, which Napoleon encouraged. His warm feelings for Joseph are surprising in light of his youthful desire to push Joseph aside, to take his place and in effect to become Joseph. Freud is probably correct in assuming that the childhood hatred had become transmogrified in love, thus requiring compensation in other-directed aggression: 'Hundreds of thousands of strangers had to pay the penalty of this little fiend having spared his first enemy.'

Napoleon may have revered Joseph but he never liked Lucien, doubtless because of the younger brother's insane jealousy. A third-rate politician with a taste for intrigue, Lucien had been a dismal failure as the short-lived Minister of the Interior and particularly angered Napoleon in 1800 by publishing a pamphlet entitled *Parallèle entre César, Cromwell et Bonaparte*, arguing for the establishment of the Bonapartes as an imperial dynasty – in effect letting the cat out of the bag. Nevertheless, when Napoleon sacked him at the end of 1800, Letizia intervened to see that he got the lucrative post of French ambassador to Spain. In Madrid Lucien became notorious for the massive bribes he took from the Spanish and Portuguese to further their interests. Growing bored, he returned to Paris at the end of 1801, simply throwing up his embassy on a whim, without permission from Napoleon or anyone else.

Returning with an immense fortune and with a German mistress (the so-called Marquesa de Santa Cruz) on his arm, Lucien set about buying up real estate in Paris and investing his ill-gotten gains in England and the U.S.A. A familiar figure at his 'town house', the Hôtel de Brienne on the rue St-Dominique, the short-sighted and small-headed Lucien was tall and swarthy, always a favourite among the Bonaparte women. He told all who would listen that Napoleon was an ingrate and that the coup on 18 Brumaire had been entirely his work. He especially loathed Josephine, but was outpointed in this particular contest, since Josephine's ally Fouché, who also despised Lucien, leaked the details of his sordid business details and his anti-Napoleon outbursts to the First Consul.

Napoleon responded by keeping Lucien at arm's length and showering his largesse on Louis. Although he revered Joseph, he liked Louis most of all his brothers, his habitual vacuous and quasi-moronic expression notwithstanding, possibly because he was most comfortable with one who did not challenge him in any way. Louis was a neurotic fantasist, an idler and wastrel, forever on leave on grounds of 'ill health', forever dreaming of a literary career or some other absurd fantasy. Misanthropic and mentally precarious, Louis suffered from jealous fits and paranoid delusions; the evidence does not permit us to correlate it exactly with a mysterious physical malady, from which he suffered, possibly gonorrhea, which engendered disabling attacks of rheumatism. But it is certain that Louis had difficulty with physical movements, had a speech impediment and curvature of the spine.

One of the most bizarre events in the Napoleon family saga was the marriage on 4 January 1802 of Louis and Josephine's daughter Hortense. Cardinal Caprara, Archbishop of Milan and papal legate, officiated at the ceremony and also bestowed on Murat and Caroline the nuptial benediction they had forgotten two years before. It was with great difficulty that Napoleon had got Louis, a repressed homosexual, to the altar. When the First Consul first suggested the match, Louis panicked and tried to bolt, but Napoleon insisted. Matters were not helped by Hortense's reluctance to wed this lacklustre Bonaparte scion; she wanted to marry Napoleon's faithful aide Christophe Duroc. Napoleon dealt with this in his usual ruthless way. He told Duroc he could marry Hortense provided he accepted an obscure command in Toulon and never came to court again. Duroc indignantly turned down this affront to his 'honour' and so was forced to reject Hortense. Josephine, meanwhile, anxious that her hold on her husband was slipping, nagged Hortense to contract the dynastic marriage for her sake.

The result was the farcical marriage in the rue de la Victoire, where the contracting parties were a sullen Louis and a tear-stained Hortense who had spent the night weeping. Joseph and Lucien, abetted by their sister Elisa, fumed at this further victory for Josephine, but they would have been delighted by events on the honeymoon. Louis callously went through the entire list of Josephine's known lovers and warned his bride that if she emulated her mother in this regard just once, he would cast her off immediately. Barred by her husband from spending the night under the same roof as her mother, Hortense then became the butt of scandal when Lucien started a rumour, eagerly taken up by the British, that she had been Napoleon's lover; when she became pregnant, it was further whispered that the child was the First Consul's.

The canard may just possibly have contained some truth. One theory is that Napoleon, convinced that he and Josephine could never have children yet determined to unite the blood of the Beauharnais and the Bonapartes, fathered a child on Hortense, then married her off to Louis when she became pregnant. The calendar seems against this, for Napoleon-Charles Bonaparte, Hortense's son was born on 10 October 1802 and Napoleon last saw Hortense in January. Undaunted, the incest theorists allege that the child was born earlier and the official birth date set much later. Two pieces of circumstantial evidence seem to support this idea. One was Louis's honeymoon tirade, when he threatened to divorce Hortense if she gave birth to a child even one day before the prescribed term; was he simply afraid that Hortense had already emulated her mother, or was there a darker suspicion? The other was that when the five-year old child died in 1807, Napoleon seemed for a time inconsolable and told his confidantes there was no longer any impediment to his divorcing Josephine. Working against the theory, on the other hand, is the known fact that it was Josephine's cousin, Stéphanie, whom Napoleon lusted after, though of course the one liaison by no means precludes the other.

The fourth of Napoleon's brothers, his 'Benjamin', was the supremely useless Jérôme. Seventeen in 1802, the fresh-faced Jérôme was a classic spoiled brat, an unprepossessing character with curly-black hair, a bull neck and a cruel little mouth; also a spendthrift, whose lavish bills were picked up by the First Consul. Napoleon sent him to sea with Admiral Ganteaume, hoping to make a sailor out of him, but in the Caribbean the swaggering Jérôme merely antagonized his brother officers by the gap between his high position and his non-existent abilities. Like Lucien, Jérôme ignored all the orders from Napoleon he found inconvenient. Despite repeated advice that he was being reserved for a dynastic marriage and should seek permission from his brother for any permanent liaison, Jérôme took up with the daughter of a wealthy shipowner in the U.S.A. and on Christmas Eve 1803 was married to Betsy Patterson. An enraged Napoleon gave orders that if 'Mrs Jerome Bonaparte' tried to set foot on French soil, she should be put back on a ship for the United States.

It was with reason that Napoleon used to remark bitterly that his brothers were all useless and to lament that, unlike Genghiz Khan, he did not have four able sons whose only object was to serve him. But Napoleon in his attitude to his family was a true product of Corsica. Even if he was disinclined to advance his siblings, the gadfly Letizia was always on his back, protesting that every advancement made on pure merit had to be balanced, for the sake of family 'honour', with an equal promotion for one of her brood. Now in her fifties, Letizia still retained her good looks, though she had lost her teeth. She refused to adapt, spoke Italian and could manage French only with the thickest of brogues. Her sole interest in life was her family and investing money. If Letizia's meddling had ended there, Napoleon could doubtless have borne it, but she kept up an incessant vendetta against Josephine and proved herself just as grasping as the children she had brought into the world. Napoleon flattered her by suggesting she go to Rome to see Cardinal Fesch and be presented to the Pope, but his real motive was to get rid of her.

Napoleon scarcely fared any better with his three sisters. Caroline, whom Talleyrand described as having 'the head of Cromwell on the body of a pretty woman', acted treacherously towards Napoleon, to whom she owed everything, and schemed and intrigued constantly to further her own ambitions and those of her husband Murat. As a reward for his sterling performance in the Marengo campaign Napoleon at the end of 1800 appointed Murat head of the élite Army of Observation – a kind of Praetorian guard – deliberately snubbing Bernadotte, Joseph's protégé and candidate for the post.

Bernadotte, incidentally, came close to forfeiting Napoleon's favour at this time. His farewell address to the Army of the West in 1802 contained coded criticisms of the First Consul, and he continued plotting with other discontented Jacobins. Exasperated, Napoleon threatened to have him shot if he did not mend his ways, but once again the tears of Julie and Désirée Clary saved the treacherous Gascon's skin. Appointed ambassador to the United States in 1803 he followed in the Lucien tradition of envoys by returning, unauthorized, to Paris when the Louisiana purchase was agreed. This led to another year in disgrace until, in 1804, he was made Governor and Commander-in-Chief of Hanover. In Germany he settled in to carve himself a share of the peculations of the corrupt intendant Michaux.

Meanwhile Murat's lust for money soon saw him Commander-in-Chief in Italy, looting in the grand tradition. He and Caroline were united by vaulting political ambitions and jealousy of Napoleon but in Milan, where they lived like royalty, they were habitually unfaithful to each other, Caroline discreetly, Murat less so. The driving force with Caroline was always power, not sex. The same was true of the cynical Elisa, the ugly sister of the family, who had been forced to marry an obscure Corsican officer, Félix Bacchiocchi, for lack of more impressive suitors. Madame de Remusat scathingly wrote of her: 'Those things we call arms and legs looked as though they had been haphazardly stuck on to her body . . . a most disagreeable ensemble.' Elisa always sided with Lucien in the family feuds, and she and Bacchiocchi went with him on his money-making exile to the embassy in Madrid in 1800–01. The family bluestocking, she thereafter ran a salon at her house in the rue Maurepas, where the painters David and Gros were frequent visitors. She intervened with Napoleon on behalf of her friend Chateaubriand, staged theatricals, and ran a circle for literary women. The henpecked Bacciocchi was given a job as commander of a garrison town and effectively expelled from her life. Elisa and Caroline Bonaparte were classic examples of what C.G. Jung called 'power devils'.

But sexuality had its triumphant showpiece in the third sister, Pauline, a byword for nymphomania and lubriciousness. Incorrigibly frivolous, with a strong Italian accent, Pauline behaved in a vague and absent-minded way as if not in full possession of her faculties. She spent vast sums on clothes and fortune tellers and was an embarrassment to Napoleon if she ever appeared at the Tuileries; she was not above sticking her tongue out defiantly at Josephine if the mood took her. In private she had a string of lovers and an unassuageable sexual appetite. As one of her studs remarked: 'She was the greatest tramp imaginable and the most desirable.' One of her early escapades was a 72-hour sexual marathon with the future Marshal MacDonald, for which she laid in a carefully prepared stock of food and drink.

When her husband Leclerc was given command of the army sent to defeat Toussaint l'Ouverture in Haiti, Pauline was brokenhearted, for it meant saying farewell to her latest lover, Pierre Lafon, an actor at the Comédie-Française. To celebrate her unwilling exile, before she left she had an orgy, in which five different lovers shared her bed. On the voyage out to Haiti she made sure she was accompanied by three more, her first paramour Stanislas Fréron, General Humbert the hero of the '98 in Ireland, and General Boyer, but these were not the only ones to share her bed in Santo Domingo. She sailed in December 1801, showed courage in Haiti, and dabbled in voodoo. When Leclerc died of yellow fever she returned to France (arriving New Year's Day, 1803). For 400,000 francs she bought the Hôtel de Charost in the Faubourg St-Honoré and was soon back to her promiscuous ways, embarrassing Napoleon at all points.

Her career came to a brief halt when she had to seek a cure (successful) for gonorrhea. Then in 1803 Napoleon made one of those bizarre decisions that so baffle historians. Despite the fact that Leclerc was a nonentity, Napoleon ordered a ten-day period of mourning for his brother-in-law; he later conceded that this had been a great public relations error and blamed it on Josephine's poor advice. The period of mourning was turned to farce by Pauline who, despite her brother's urging that appearances should be kept up, remarried in August 1803, with the papal legate Caprara officiating. This time her husband was Prince Camillo Borghese, the richest man in Italy. Aged twenty-eight, diminutive, dapper and elegant, Borghese had embraced Republican principles to save the family fortune, but showed where his heart lay by becoming the first man to appear in court dress at the Tuileries since the days of Louis XVI.

Pauline, who always hated Josephine, rubbed her nose in her new-found wealth by visiting her at St-Cloud wearing the entire Borghese collection of diamonds – the most beautiful in Europe – on a green velvet dress. But her madcap career did not end there. Discovering that Camilo Borghese was hopeless in bed – she told Cardinal Fesch she would rather have stayed Leclerc's widow on 20,000 francs than marry Borghese – and was in fact yet another repressed homosexual, Pauline again cut loose on a life of sexual adventure. Her most notorious exploit was the visit to Florence in 1804. Pleading ill-health, she commissioned the artist Canova to paint her as a naked Venus. When someone later asked whether she had posed nude in Canova's studio, she replied: 'Why not? There was a perfectly good fire in the studio.' Scandalized by her behaviour, Borghese put her under house arrest in his palace, but Pauline responded by smuggling in a further raft of lovers. The distraught Borghese was forced to appeal to Napoleon, who warned Pauline that she could never be received at the Tuileries without her husband.

Almost as though by a process of osmosis through contact with his hedonistic family, Napoleon in the latter years of his consulate seemed to take more interest in sex; indeed the evidence of the years 1802–4 points to a morbid craving or satyriasis of the John F. Kennedy kind. Perhaps as his appetite for Josephine waned, his attentions increasingly wandered; it is certain that at this time the Consul and his wife ceased to sleep in the same room and occupied separate apartments. In June 1802 he had an affair with the young actress Louise Rolandeau. This was no more than a 'fling' but in November the same year he began a more sustained liaison with another actress, the statuesque tragedienne Marguerite George, whose previous lovers had included Lucien and the polish Prince Sapiepha. With her the Consul was able to indulge his taste for buffoonery, schoolboy japes, practical jokes and general horseplay. Napoleon's affair with George soon became common knowledge. When she was playing *Cinna* at the Théâtre Français, she reached the line: 'If I have seduced Cinna, I shall seduce many more.' The audience roared, rose in a body, turned to the Consul's box and applauded. Josephine, who was in the box with her husband, was distinctly unamused.

By this time she was used to his infidelities. She vacillated between jealousy and indifference. One night she decided to catch the lovers red-handed in Napoleon's apartment and began mounting the narrow staircase that led there, before taking fright at the idea that the faithful bodyguard Roustam might suddenly emerge from the shadows and behead her, mistaking her for an assassin. Yet on another night she found herself in the love nest willy-nilly. Piercing screams from Mlle George echoed round St-Cloud. Josephine and the consular valets rushed upstairs to find Napoleon in the grip of an epileptic-like seizure, and 'Georgina' (as Josephine dubbed her) in a state of undress, terrified that her lover was dead and she would be accused of murdering him. When Napoleon came to and realized the situation he fell into such a rage that onlookers thought he was going to have a second fit.

Marguerite George's attraction dipped after this scandalous incident and for a while Napoleon kept her at arm's length. But he was always generous with his women and when he departed for Boulogne in 1803 to oversee the preparations for a descent on England, he shoved 40,000 francs down the front of her dress. By this time he was interested in a third actress, Catherine Josephine Raffin, known as Mlle Duchesnois. This was another brief affair, which ended when Napoleon insulted her as a woman. Busy with affairs of state, he asked his valet Constant to tell her to wait in a room adjoining his study. After an hour she knocked on his door and Napoleon asked Constant to tell her to get undressed. Duchesnois did so and shivered for another hour before knocking a second time. This time a disgruntled Napoleon barked that she should go home, thus making yet another unnecessary enemy.

The final woman in the bevy of actresses 'entertained' by the Consul was Mlle Bourgoin, the mistress of Chaptal, Minister of the Interior. Indulging his taste for the humiliation of others, Napoleon arranged to have la Bourgoin brought to him while he was in conclave with Chaptal; he thus gratuitously made another mortal enemy. But this affair did not last long either, for Bourgoin had a taste for coarse jokes which Napoleon did not like in women. By the end of 1804 this liaison too had fizzled out. Bourgoin went on to a notable career as *grande horizontale*, specializing in sleeping with men in some way close to her greatest conquest: she was the mistress of Czar Alexander and also of Jérôme, when he was King of Westphalia, in 1812.

Yet, despite his philandering, Napoleon's attitude to women was basically contemptuous and even boorish. He took the conqueror's line that women were there for him to avail himself of when the fancy took him, and became irritated if he encountered opposition. Laure Permon, who first observed Napoleon when she was eleven, married Androche Junot, the general who had been an early Bonaparte favourite but who never really came back into favour after his indiscretions in Egypt. In 1803 the Junots came to stay at Malmaison, and the First Consul decided that he did after all find Laure physically appealing. He sent Junot away on an errand.

The sequel was bizarre. At 5 a.m. one morning Napoleon entered her bedroom unannounced and sat on the bedside. After reading his morning's correspondence, he gave her a pinch and, getting no response, departed. When the same thing happened the next morning, Laure locked her door and gave strict instructions to her maid that no one was to be admitted. Next morning there was a rattling sound at her door, followed by animated conversation outside between Napoleon and her maid, who repeated her mistress's orders. Thinking she had seen off the persistent First Consul, Laure went back to bed but within minutes Napoleon was again at her bedside; he had opened another door into the room with a private key.

Since Laure Junot was a notorious liar, we might be inclined to suspect that this story, where she emerged one up, was really a smokescreen to conceal an actual infidelity with the Consul. But the next day Junot himself returned to Malmaison and was able to testify to his master's eccentric behaviour. His orders forbade him to be absent from Paris overnight, but Laure persuaded him to stay with her. Next morning Napoleon appeared as usual and was both surprised and irritated to find Junot in bed with his wife. Junot, summoning what dignity he could, asked Napoleon what he meant by bursting into his wife's bedroom; Napoleon at first blustered and became angry, reminding Junot that he could be punished for disobeying orders; finally he subsided and insinuated that the temptress Laure was really to blame. It is not recorded that he ever again tried to seduce her, though he did get his revenge by revealing to Laure the details of the informal harem Junot kept in Egypt.

A deep current of misogyny, almost certainly deriving from his early experiences with Letizia and doubtless exacerbated by Josephine's infidelities, underlay all Napoleon's dealings with women. Although he liked to bed them, he had nothing but contempt for their values and aspirations, and his behaviour suggests strongly the profile of a sexual neurotic. With the normal male, heterosexual lust is usually tempered by genuine admiration for the physical beauty of women, an appreciation of their role as nurturers and comforters and some kind of sentimental feelings of chivalry or protectiveness. With Napoleon there was only the lust, and instead of the other qualities there was aggression and resentment. Such men like to 'do the dirt' on women by cutting their hair, throwing ink on their beautiful clothes, and so on. It is worth noting that Napoleon often repeated his Pauline Fourès trick of 'accidentally' spilling coffee on a woman's dress; his later mistress Éléonore Denuelle was one of the sufferers.

There were other examples of this neurotic aggression. When he first met Marguerite George he tore off her veil and trampled it on the floor. He seldom said anything agreeable to women but was habitually rude, indiscreet, malicious or unflattering. Among his quoted slights are: 'What an ugly hat!' 'Your dress is none of the cleanest.' 'Do you never change your gown? I have seen you wearing that at least twenty times!' He specialized in asking young women impertinent questions about their private lives. He once ordered that camp followers who did not leave the Army when ordered to should be smeared with soot and exposed for two hours in the marketplace. Bourrienne reported that he had a particular aversion to fat women or to bluestockings like Germaine de Staël. Other oft-quoted remarks are in the same vein: 'Madame, they told me you were ugly; they certainly did not exaggerate.' 'If you appear again in that despicable dress, you will be refused entry.'

It was often remarked that Napoleon praised the backside as the most beautiful part of a woman, which has led some commentators to speculate that he was a repressed homosexual. There is no good evidence to support this though, in an age when we are less inclined to make hard and fast distinctions about sexuality, we may perhaps allow that there were some bisexual undercurrents in Napoleon. He was a man's man who preferred the company of men – a not unnatural trait in a soldier – and was impatient with any form of deviance. He ordered the commencement of formal dances as though he were on the parade ground and was puritanical in his public persona, maintaining a straitlaced court, though reserving for himself the right of sexual licence. When he heard that orgies were going on in a noted trysting place in the park of Fontainebleau – the *mare aux loups* – he was incandescent with rage. If he discovered through his spy network that the wife of an important soldier or courtier was unfaithful, he always informed the husband and threatened to exile the couple unless the husband took his wife in check.

Many farfetched theories have been advanced for Napoleon's misogyny. It is suggested that he suffered from a 'castration complex' or that his 'organ inferiority' (in his case phallic) led to military overcompensation. It is asserted, on no grounds whatever, that he had abnormally small genitals, and that this explained both his resentment of women and his lofty ambition ('masculine protest'). It is significant that Josephine never made such an accusation. Her complaint was that her husband made love too fast and suffered from *ejaculatio praecox*. Nor are there grounds for saying that Napoleon was anything other than heterosexual. Rather than bisexuality in the full sense, what we can detect in Napoleon's psyche is some form of sadism or sexuality transmogrified as aggression.

He liked to strike people of both sexes, to slap them, pull their hair, pinch their ears and tweak their noses. Slapping servants across the face and shoulders with a riding crop was not unusual. He once seized Marshal Berthier by the throat and hammered his head against a stone wall; he also kicked minister Molé in the genitals for presenting an unpalatable set of statistics. Court observers often reported fine ladies reduced to tears by his physical antics, generals suffering indignities and soldiers suffering nosebleeds. His sadistic impulses would if necessary be directed against children and animals, especially those dear to Josephine: at Malmaison he caused her great grief by shooting her pet swans and other wild fowl and rooting up plants. When she protested on one occasion that he ought not to shoot animals during the breeding season, he said scathingly and publicly: 'It seems that everything is prolific at Malmaison – except Madame.' That his aggression had a sexual basis is clear from one of Bourrienne's stories. It appears that during the siege of Toulon in 1793 a young wife approached General Bonaparte and asked him to excuse her husband from duty, as she had a clear premonition of his death. Napoleon refused but later told Madame Bourrienne laughingly that the young wife's intuition was right: the husband was killed when a bomb took off his genitals.

The cruel streak in Napoleon meant that although he had wit, and could therefore laugh *at* people, he was totally without a real sense of humour or the absurd – which enables one to laugh *with* people. Cambacérès, the Second Consul and later Grand Chancellor, was well known to be homosexual. One morning he excused himself for being late at Council by saying he had been detained by a lady. To general laughter Napoleon said: 'Next time you are detained by a lady, you must say, "Get your hat and stick and leave, monsieur. The Council is waiting for me."' An Italian woman once upstaged him in the wit department when she avenged one of his verbal slights. She was among the company at a court ball shortly afterwards when Napoleon decided to have a crack at the land of his ancestors. '*Tutti gli Italiani danzano si male,*' he announced ('All Italians dance so badly'). The quickwitted woman replied: '*Non tutti, ma buona parte*' (a clever play on words, meaning either 'Not all but a good part,' or 'Not all but Bonaparte does').

The magnetic charm Napoleon is said to have exercised on men appears to have left women cold. Clearly for them power rather than personal charisma was the aphrodisiac. And whereas Napoleon never used cajolery on women for any purpose other than seduction, with men he could be wheedling and insinuating. He possessed that most valuable attribute of the true charmer: the ability to make the person being spoken to feel that he alone counted. He had an amazing ability to sway other men to his purposes. The musicality of his voice as he addressed the troops at Marengo was said to have been worth an extra corps. Fond of the theatre and the company of actors, he had a highly developed sense of the histrionic and of stage management. Most of all, he was a skilled manipulator. As he himself said: 'If I want a man, I am prepared to kiss his arse.'

But the male beneficiaries of his charm had to be prepared for an equal and opposite rage if crossed, when he would swear profanely, belabour the offender with a riding crop on head and shoulders and even kick him in the stomach. The fixed, motionless and unblinking eyes produced an unsettling basilisk effect on victims. As with Hitler – with whom he is often compared – and the *Wehrmacht*, so with Napoleon and his generals and marshals. When the volcano erupted and he was in full flight, nobody dared gainsay him. Observers reported that the typhoon was fearsome: the large grey eyes would spit with rage as if he were a leopard, but his anger would subside very quickly. It is sometimes claimed that Napoleon's tantrums were all part of the gallery touch, and it is true that he could stage-manage them for effect when he chose. More usually, however, the rages were genuine manifestations, as evidenced by the volleys of obscene vituperation.

Napoleon could be supremely ruthless. He mowed down the royalists in the square at Toulon in 1793, he tore the heart out of the Parisian royalists at Vendémiaire in 1795, he butchered 5,000 Turkish prisoners on the beach in Syria in 1799, he poisoned his own troops at Jaffa when he might have got reasonable terms from Sir Sidney Smith had not his own prestige stood in the way. There is no reason to doubt the authenticity of the remark to Gourgaud on St Helena: 'I care only for people who are useful to me – and only so long as they are useful.' But he was ruthless only intermittently, harboured few grudges, and was sentimental. His sensibility was light years away from that of a Hitler or a Stalin, and indeed he can be faulted for not being ruthless enough at times. His indulgence of his worthless family and his repeated pardoning of the treacherous Bernadotte, the duplicitous Talleyrand and the treasonable Fouché are only the most obvious examples. Napoleon had the temperament of an old-style autocrat but not that of a modern totalitarian dictator.

Napoleon had not the grim peasant patience of a Stalin, the cold remorseless ability to win a long campaign of attrition. His personality was closer to Trotsky's in the romantic voluntarism, the grand gesture and the impatience. The famous Napoleonic tantrums were often a function of pure impatience, frustration and intolerance. Woe betide any servant who placed something on the right-hand side that belonged on the left or misplaced his toiletries. He would always tear off any clothes that constricted him, throw them on the fire and then hit whoever had laid them out for him or dressed him. At night he would often throw his clothes all over the floor, then slap the person nearest to him as 'punishment' for the chore of having to divest himself. Sometimes he played a game, shouting 'lands' as he took off one item of clothing, 'castles' when he took off another, and so on through 'provinces, kingdoms, republics, etc.

The same impatience explained why he always bolted his food, sometimes with the consequence of stomach cramps or vomiting. Napoleon's eating habits have always compelled astonishment. No meal with him ever lasted more than twenty minutes, for he would immediately rise from the table when he had finished dessert. He liked to eat little, fast and often, and expected his favourite food to be ready at any hour of day or night. Duroc made sure that his favourite repast – a roast chicken – was always to hand and kept a careful inventory of the beloved fowl. Another favourite Bonaparte dish was potatoes fried with onions. He drank little wine and always unmixed, his favourite tipple being a glass of Chambertin. Napoleon would demolish his food in silence and at express speed, sometimes eating the courses in reverse order and even eating with his fingers if he had pressing matters on his mind. At home he would dine with Josephine or with favourites such as Duroc, Berthier and Caulaincourt. In the field he would take a frugal lunch in the saddle or eat with the officer commanding the unit he was visiting. Although dinner was supposed to be at 6 p.m., often he would not eat until nine or ten or even midnight.

Another Bonaparte peculiarity was his insistence on always having a fire lit, winter or summer. Forever complaining of the cold, he would kick the blazing logs while he talked. Hot baths were another prerequisite – so hot that his staff wondered any man could get into the water. He hated cats – to the point of genuine ailourophobia – and had the most acute sense of smell that caused him agony on the battlefield, when the stench of burned and rotting bodies assailed his nostrils. A further mania was a horror of open doors. Anyone entering his room had to open the door just wide enough to squeeze through, then hold the door tight shut by the handle, sometimes doing so with hands behind the back, until dismissed.

These quasi-neurotic symptoms seem to have been the response of an over-stressed organism. Nobody reviewing Napoleon's daily routine can doubt that he taxed physical and mental strength to the limit. His enemies speak of pride, contempt for human beings, neurasthenia, nervous anxiety and indecision, and it is true that he had all these qualities. But to offset them he had a prodigious memory, a lucid mind and an intellect of awesome range. Most of all, he was one of history's great workaholics and regularly put in an eighteen-hour day.

The normal starting point would be a 6 a.m. breakfast, a rapid perusal of the newspapers and police reports brought to him by Duroc, an examination of household bills and any other domestic administration, a quick review of the day's business, then interviews with important officials or foreign visitors. Next he would enter his office to begin the day's work proper. As he sat at his desk and sifted through documents, he would scrawl brief minutes in the margin, dictate answers to a secretary or fling the papers to the floor if he thought them unworthy of his attention. More dictation and interviews followed, and by 10.a.m. the new letters and dispatches were ready for his signature – the famous 'N' scrawled at the bottom; a few very ticklish documents he would put aside to sleep on. The peacetime routine found him attending sessions of the Council of State, the Council of Ministers or some administrative body. Dinner was officially at 6 p.m. but often would not begin until 7 p.m. or be switched back to 5 p.m.

The wartime routine would follow the same pattern until midday. Usually he would then set off on horseback and visit a unit or corps headquarters. He never neglected the army and realized the vital importance of the common touch in building up and sustaining the Napoleonic legend. The famous 'common touch' he used with the rankers was spurious, theatrical but very effective. He knew how to inspire and also how to give the sort of dressing down that would not produce undying hatred but merely a determination to do better next time. Even greater ingenuity was exercised in the manipulation of his officers: he believed in keeping them guessing, maintaining them in suspense, uncertain whether they would be the recipients of smiles and jokes or the dreaded rages – which, as a great actor, he could summon at will. He liked to keep his officers on tenterhooks by issuing sudden orders which required instant execution; he would brook no delays, prevarication or excuses.

After his military tour he would return to his headquarters to read the latest bulletins, sign more orders, give more interviews, dictate more correspondence. He liked to go to bed at around 9 p.m. for four or five hours, with the faithful Roustam outside the door. But he was liable to wake at any hour and call out for an aide or a secretary; if they were not on hand, the consequences were steep. Many were the stories of nervous breakdowns among staff, particularly in the later imperial period. Yet there was never any rigid timetable. Sometimes he would linger after dinner and glance through the most recent books recommended by his librarian. Never retiring later than midnight, he would also never rise later than 3 a.m.; if he retired early, at 8–9 p.m. he would get up at midnight. After mulling over the most urgent affairs of state, he would take one of his famous boiling hot baths, then go back to bed at 5 a.m. for an hour.

With such a punishing régime, it was hardly surprising that Napoleon rarely looked well. His sallow complexion was often remarked on. The muleteer who guided him over the St Bernard pass in May 1800 said that the whites of his eyes were as yellow as a lemon and his face the same colour. An English traveller who saw him review troops at the Tuileries in 1802 reported that his complexion was dark yellow. At Brussels in August 1803 he coughed up blood, and a plaster was applied to his chest to draw out 'a deep-seated humour'. Later medical observers have attempted diagnoses as various as nervous ischuria, schistosomiasis, stones in the bladder or venereal disease, but sheer overwork must have had a lot to do with it.

Because we feel a moral repugnance for dictators we sometimes underrate their intellectual powers. It must be stressed that only a man superabundantly endowed with intellect could have achieved what Napoleon did. The historian Gabriel Hanotaux spoke of 'the richest natural gifts ever received by mortal man'. To maintain an iron grip on domestic, foreign and military affairs year after year while subjecting himself to such a régime denotes a mind of great stature. He combined the great gifts of a clear, mathematical, concise, economical and lucid mind with a fantastic memory for exact figures, the exact location of each regiment, the names of its officers and the details of its equipment. He also had perfect recall for faces and combinations. Yet since the clichéd picture of Napoleon as a man carrying within the seeds of his own destruction contains much truth, we must also point to the deficiencies in this formidable brain.

Napoleon's critics have alleged that his memory for detail and faces was not that impressive, and that this too is part of the stage-managed Bonaparte legend. It is true that he did not know the names and background of every soldier in his army – no one could. On the other hand he pretended that he had this degree of knowledge and before reviewing a parade would get his staff to point out various individuals, so that he could memorize their names and careers. That seems merely a venial sin of misrepresentation, and in any case speaks volumes for his intelligence and insight into human psychology.

The more serious flaw in Napoleon's intellectual makeup was his impatience, his low boredom threshold, his sacrifice of reason in favour of the imagination, and his (unconscious?) desire to make policy on the wing, to improvise and to sacrifice the simple solution for the more complicated. The impatience had many manifestations. He could never remain still, would feel in his waistcoat for snuff, take out his watch, file his nails or get up to throw pebbles at the invariably roaring fire or kick at the embers. When in a rage he would smash furniture and even when not angry would often fiddle with rare porcelain figures until he broke off the arms and legs; then he would scoff at those, like Josephine, saddened by the damage. When dictating, he would twitch his right shoulder and keep on twisting his right arm so as to pull down the cuff of his coat with his hand. Bourrienne reported that there would often be an involuntary shrug of Napoleon's right shoulder, accompanied by a movement of the mouth from left to right, especially when absorbed.

Students of Napoleon have often speculated on the possible medical or psychological causes of his many quirks and oddities. An investigation in this area is not helped by the tense relationship that existed between Napoleon and his medical advisers. Although the Bonaparte family in general had a tendency to hypochondria, Napoleon himself took a Shavian attitude to medicine and regarded all doctors as quacks or impostors. He had long-running relationships with many physicians, but never cared for any of them. The surgeon Larrey was the one he respected most (although Dr Yvan, in attendance from 1796–1814, was the longest-serving) but he never liked him, for Larrey combined three qualities Napoleon despised: he was introverted, sycophantic and money-grubbing. Larrey, like a later doctor, Antommarchi, always took the view that Napoleon's health problems stemmed from the liver.

The most obvious aspect of Napoleon's medical profile is that he suffered from fits. The seizure he had while in bed with Mlle George was the most dramatic example, and he never really forgave her for making this widely known through her panic and thus bringing him into ridicule and contempt. Medical opinion is divided on whether Napoleon suffered from *petit mal*, a minor form of epilepsy, or whether, like Julius Caesar, he was a victim of the full-blown variety; still others have claimed that the fits were the result of a disorder of the pituitary gland or (bearing in mind also that he suffered from urinary disorders) were a symptom of venereal disease. Yet another theory is that the temporary loss of consciousness was the consequence of a heart blockage, which might explain his abnormally low pulse rate of forty a minute.

Another constant physical symptom which assailed Napoleon was a skin disease, variously described as neurodermatitis or psoriasis. Napoleon himself believed that this skin ailment was the result of handling an infected ramrod at Toulon in 1793, but modern opinion inclines either to venereal disease or psychosomatic causation. The blood on his face at Brumaire, which so inflamed the troops, was not the consequence of an attempted assassination but resulted from his own scratching at the pimples on his face. His valet Constant reported that his master often drew blood in this way. He also had a scar on his thigh from a wound sustained at Toulon, at which he would pick and draw blood.

Put together with the nervous cough, which Napoleon tried to combat with frequent hot baths, and the difficulty in passing water, Yvan concluded (though he did not use modern phraseology) that his patient's problems were largely psychosomatic. Modern psychoanalysts have seen Napoleon as a man ill-suited for stress by reason of his sexual personality. Adler made much of the fact that Napoleon masturbated before battle to relieve stress. Fromm saw his nervous excitability as a sign of an unconscious thirst for destruction. Reich associated the ritual 'bleedings' of scars, scabs and pimples as the tension that resulted from the failure to achieve proper orgasm, and linked it with the known problem of *ejaculatio praecox*.

The almost pathological impatience manifested itself in a tendency to calculate the immediate odds without taking into account the more distant possible consequences, and in the demand he made for immediate results without giving his lieutenants adequate resources to carry out his will. The boredom was apparent at meetings of the Council of State when the First Consul would often be lost in thought, often seeming to be thinking aloud when he spoke. Secretive, trusting no one, disingenuous in his correspondence and unable to admit the truth about certain incidents even to himself, Napoleon's profound silences often scared those around him, who feared to interrupt his reveries. Only Talleyrand seemed similarly abstracted and when the two of them were together in Council those of a historical turn of mind recalled the partnership of the glacial Louis XI and the impassive Richelieu.

The intellectual in Napoleon was always at war with the artist *manqué*. He was once walking with Roederer through the state apartments of the Tuileries. Roederer remarked that the palace was a gloomy place, for it always reminded him of the sad fate of the Bourbons. Napoleon replied: 'Sad, yes – but so is glory.' This poetic insight – the kind of thing that made Chateaubriand call him 'a poet in action' – is not so far in sensibility from his account of his own relationship to Fate: 'I had risen from the masses so suddenly. I felt my isolation. So I kept throwing anchors for my salvation into the depths of the sea.' Then there is of course the famous utterance from the St Helena period: 'What a novel, anyhow, my life has been!'

Napoleon was always conscious of his place in history even as he made it, and it is this, as much as his many theatrical and histrionic touches, that have led people to speak of him as 'nothing but' an actor. The remark he made when he and Josephine first occupied the Tuileries is typical: 'Come along, my little Creole, go and lie down in the bed of your masters.' But a truer assessment would be to say that Napoleon's reason was always the servant of his imagination. His great memory for facts was transmuted by the imagination just as a great orchestral conductor 'magics' a dry score. He spoke of the 'after-midnight presence of mind' to denote the same kind of unconscious process an artist like R. L. Stevenson referred to as his 'Brownies'; Napoleon would often wake up in the middle of the night with an intuition comparable to that of a Coleridge or an Einstein.

Because Napoleon was an artist *manqué* and saw his life as a novel, nothing in it surprised him. People have often wondered how it was that an obscure Corsican could ascend an imperial throne like a duck taking to water. But wearing the purple to such a man would simply be another chapter in the book of his life. This is surely the hidden subtext to his own apology: 'It is said that I am ambitious, but this is an error; or at least my ambition is so intimately allied to my whole being that it cannot be separated from it.' Some have even speculated that Napoleon was a 'dual man' in a unique sense, that he was a man who lived in space and time and who observed the 'other self' doing so many remarkable things, that, to put it another way, he lived on an equal footing with his own destiny. This is why some writers, on the analogy of the historical Jesus and the numinous Christ, have elected to separate the historical Bonaparte from the legendary Napoleon and to consider them as things apart. Graphologists' study of Napoleon's penmanship, revealing hyperimpatience, identity problems and a discord between brain and hand, also demonstrate that the handwritings of the young General Bonaparte and the middle-aged Emperor Napoleon, are virtually those of two different people.

The penchant for making policy on the wing meant that politically, as well as militarily, Napoleon was a pragmatist who reacted to events: he had no blueprint, no overarching aim and therefore claimed that he was entirely the victim of circumstances. He failed to see that the brilliance and originality of his mind was such that it could never be happy in peacetime administration; there was a sense in which Napoleon's great intellect required war for its satisfaction, just as the Church Fathers used to speculate that God needed to create Man to be complete. The short-termism did not denote, as might be expected, the art of the possible but a quasi-existentialist mode of living dangerously.

Yet the propensity to improvise and to opt for short-term solutions, combined with the impatience and boredom, explains many things otherwise inexplicable. For a man so gifted, it is surprising how many failures, impracticable schemes and false starts there were in his career. A great decision-maker, who however seemed to forget so many of his own decisions, Napoleon took up and dropped a bewildering variety of plans which at the time he declared to be indispensable for the future of France. First he dreamed of an empire in the western hemisphere, then abruptly abandoned the idea and sold Louisiana to the U.S.A. He signed the Concordat to ensure permanent peace with the Catholic Church then engaged in a running battle with the Papacy. From 1803–05 he was busy on a dozen different schemes for the invasion of England, which he promptly dropped after Trafalgar as if any such idea had never entered his head. This tendency never to concentrate on any one objective but also to go for the *ad hoc* explains his proneness to motifs unintegrated into a general world-picture – the 'Oriental complex', for example. It would also increase the general mental and psychic overload that would finally exhaust Napoleon.

The answer to those, like Sorel, who see Bonaparte purely as a creature of historical inevitability is that they have concentrated solely on the rational side of the man. His unitary state is the product of a classical sensibility: in this sense Napoleon is the heir of the *philosophes*; he is the *cérébrale* who wishes to possess all knowledge. But the Promethean energy, the voluntarism, the fatalism and superstition, the gloom and melancholia, the risks he took, his love of Ossian, his hankering after the glittering and mysterious East, all this comes from the Romantic imagination which the Sorels have neglected. In Napoleon a cynicism about human nature and a pessimistic assessment of human motivations coexists with a countervailing desire to change human nature and to master the woodenheaded world; this after all was what the heroes of Plutarch and Corneille appeared to have done.

Historians have always divided as between those like Thiers, who saw Napoleon as the epitome of France, and those who consider that the key to his personality and career is that he was an outsider. It is certainly true that he was both rootless and classless. Neither a nobleman nor a plebeian, in his early days he faced both ways, being willing to serve either King or Revolution. He was ideology-free, being constrained neither by Richelieu's dynastic loyalty nor by the civic *virtu* of the republicans. But if he was *déclassé*, he was also *déraciné*. He became a Frenchman in his late youth and never really identified with the traditions and interests of the country, as opposed to his own Romantic and Platonic idea of France. On this view he understands France but is not French. He is at once sufficiently imbued with the French spirit to get people to identify their interests with his yet sufficiently 'other' to stand apart. Of patriotism there is not a scintilla: as one cynic remarked, Napoleon loved France as a horseman loves his horse, for only a simpleton would imagine that the tender grooming given the horse is for the animal's benefit. This has led historians like Taine and Quinet to see him as the quintessential Corsican, which in turn they interpret to mean an Italian from the Renaissance period, like Cesare Borgia; Bonaparte is therefore a *condottiere* who seized France and falsely identified the Revolutionary tradition with himself.

By this stage in his career we are perhaps better able to assess what Napoleon drew from Corsica and what was the long-term impact on him of the island. Romantic egoism – with oneself at the centre of things and no other motive obtaining than one's personal greatness – can be seen as a cast of mind fostered and enhanced by a lawless society, where no notions of civil society or the common interest moderated the violent struggles of chiefs and clan. The chaos of France after the Revolution produced a unique conjuncture, replicating Corsica on a large scale: this was what gave this particular individual his unique historical opportunity.

Certainly those who stress that Napoleon was a pure creature of the Enlightenment and the *philosophes* have a lot of explaining to do when it comes to Bonaparte's irrationality. This goes beyond the Romantic rôle of the imagination, or even the unintegrated 'complexes', to a deep and irreducible Corsican superstition. Napoleon was a deist who yet believed that demons lurked in the shadow of the heedless Almighty. He made use of all the superstitious rites practised in Corsica: at the critical moment of a battle or at times of strong emotion he would make the sign of the cross with wide sweeps of the arm, as did the Corsican peasants of the *maquis* when they heard bad news. A believer in omens, portents and numerology, he disliked Fridays and the number 13 but thought certain dates were lucky for him, notably 20 March and 14 June. If forced to begin any enterprise on a Friday, he was gloomy at the thought that the venture was ill-starred. He thought comets worked in pre-established harmony with terrestrial events.

Brought up on the Corsican notion of the 'evil eye', Napoleon thought that certain people were irremediably doomed to bad luck and communicated this lack of fortune to those around them. Hence the famous question he always asked of his generals: is he lucky? One of the reasons he stayed married to Josephine long after she had outlived her usefulness and attraction was that he thought she brought him good luck. There are numerous stories linking Josephine with her husband's superstitions. During the Italian campaign of 1796–97 he always wore a miniature of her; when it fell and broke, he was devastated and told Marmont (incidentally, later to be the classic 'unlucky' general) this meant his wife was either ill or unfaithful. On another occasion during a row with Lucien he accidentally knocked Josephine's portrait off the table, smashing the glass; he at once turned pale with superstitious dread.

Yet perhaps the most bizarre aspect of Napoleon's abiding belief in the paranormal or supernatural is the attachment he had to two 'familiars', one ghostly, the other sidereal. Many people claim to believe in a lucky star but Napoleon did so literally and often searched for his favourite dot of light in the night sky. When the Concordat began to unravel and he treated Pius VII badly, his uncle, Cardinal Fesch, came to protest. Napoleon asked him to step outside and look up at the sky. 'Do you see anything?' he asked. 'No,' said Fesch. 'In that case, learn when to shut up. I myself see my star; it is that which guides me. Don't pit your feeble and incomplete faculties against my superior organism.'

But even the lucky star pales alongside the familiar spirit or phantom he called the 'Little Red Man'. According to legend, Napoleon made a ten-year pact with a genie just before the Battle of the Pyramids, and the agreement was renewed in 1809. The spirit promised to advise and protect Napoleon provided he ushered in the Brotherhood of Man and the Universal Republic; if Napoleon reneged, the Red Man was to give him three formal warnings before abandoning him to his enemies. The legend says that the Red Man appeared at the time of his coronation in 1804, in Moscow in 1812 and at Fontainebleau in April 1814; in other versions of the legend the spectre advised him against invading Russia and appeared on the eve of Waterloo. It is not unknown for individuals under great stress to, as it were, exteriorize aspects of their own unconscious, as Carl Jung did with his familiar Philemon, and it is not beyond the bounds of the possible that Napoleon conversed with his Red Man just as Jung did with Philemon. The predisposition to believe in such apparitions was quintessentially Corsican; psychologically, of course, the tale of the Red Man points to a huge weight of guilt bearing down on Napoleon.

The supersitition may possibly be connected with the salient 'Oriental complex', for which so much evidence exists. He always hankered after Egypt as a 'lost domain' and told Madame de Rémusat that the years 1798–99 were the best of his life: 'I saw myself marching into Asia . . . riding an elephant, a turban on my head, attacking the power of England in India.' On St Helena he recalled his entry into Cairo: 'I felt the earth flee from beneath me, as if I were being carried to the sky.'

Other writers on Napoleon like to stress that his ancestors were Italian and that it is to Italy rather than Corsica or the Orient that we should look for the key to his personality. Those who speak of Napoleon as a Cesare Borgia like to add that in his mature political thought he most resembles Borgia's admirer, Machiavelli. All are agreed that he abandoned his early idol Rousseau and some allege that his later switch of favour from the notables to the old nobility shows, in terms of political theory, the passage from Rousseau through Montesquieu to Machiavelli. The historian Edgar Quinet considered that Napoleon was a uniquely Italian figure, that he had inherited the Ghibelline tradition from his ancestors, and that his true idols were not Charlemagne but Constantine and Theodosius. Quinet writes: 'When he dreams of the future, it is always of the submissive world of a Justinian or a Theodosius, as imagined by the medieval imperialist thinkers. In the midst of such concepts, modern freedom seemed an anachronism; worse, to him it could appear only as a people's whim, as a snare for his power.'

What is certain is that, as he himself moved closer to imperial power, his fascination with the Roman Empire increased. In his early career it was the Republic, its heroes and its writers that he was most interested in – Brutus, the Catos, the Gracchi, Livy, Plutarch – but he came to believe that history repeated itself. Just as the Bolsheviks after 1917 looked back to the French Revolution and saw parallels everywhere with their own experience, so Napoleon looked back to the chaos of the last days of the Roman Republic and saw history taking a cyclical course. The Pompey/Caesar struggles ended with the rule of a strong man: Augustus. In the same way historical inevitability seemed to suggest that the Robespierre/Danton struggle must logically end with the rule of a dictator; so now it was Caesar, Tacitus and the Julio-Claudian emperors who obsessed him.

Napoleon never visited Rome, perhaps because he felt that the Rome of reality could never match the Eternal City of his reading and imagination. In psychoanalysis, not to visit a place that obsesses one is the classic sign of a 'complex'. It is fascinating that by 1804 we can see the

'Rome complex' feeding other streams of the Napoleonic conscious and unconscious. Britain is now the new Carthage that must be destroyed and Russia is the Parthia – the powerful military neighbour on the borders of putative empire that must be conquered or conciliated. Moreover, the Pope, with whom he concluded the Concordat, is the true prince (or emperor) of Rome and so stands as an obstacle and reproach to Napoleon's imperial ambitions. As these ambitions came to fruition, they inexorably widened the gap between the rational and the irrational in Napoleon, between the classical and the Romantic, and between the art of the possible and the realm of fantasy.

CHAPTER FOURTEEN

The second half of 1803 saw Napoleon once again on his travels, after three Paris-bound years. On 25 June he began an extensive northern tour lasting two months. First he toured the towns of northern France that would be important in the coming campaign against England: Amiens, Abbeville, Boulogne, Calais, Dunkirk, Lille. Then he crossed the border into Belgium and proceeded through Nieuport, Ostend, Bruges, Ghent and Anvers to Brussels, where he arrived on 21 July. After a ten-day sojourn there, he made his way back to St-Cloud in a leisurely itinerary that took in Maastricht, Liège, Namur, Mézières, Sedan and Rheims. He arrived back in the palace on 11 August. Throughout the late summer and autumn he seemed obsessed with the idea of a descent on England and spoke excitedly to his family about planting the French flag on the Tower of London. Very optimistic by now about his chances of bringing off a Channel crossing, he made an extended visit to Boulogne from 3–17 November.

Absurdly overconfident of his ability to vault over the Channel and the Royal Navy, Napoleon was brought down to earth in November 1803 by the first whispers of the most serious conspiracy yet against his autocracy. In the autumn of 1803 several Chouans were arrested in Paris, taken before a military commission and sentenced to death. One of the condemned asked to make a statement before his death and revealed a wide-ranging plot against Napoleon. Other condemned conspirators then broke silence. It turned out that the ringleaders in the latest conspiracy were General Moreau, the hero of Hohenlinden and General Pichegru (once Napoleon's tutor at Brienne), who had been deported after the Fructidor coup in 1797 but had since returned secretly; the plot called for the assassination of the First Consul and the return of the Bourbons.

A further twist came on 29 January 1804 when one Courson, a British secret agent, was arrested. To save his life he revealed further details of the plot: there was to be a triumvirate consisting of Pichegru, Moreau and Cadoudal, the Chouan leader, which would pave the way for a Bourbon restoration; Pichegru and Cadoudal were known to be already in Paris.

Fouché's deputy, Pierre François Réal, solemnly but gloatingly told Napoleon: 'You've only uncovered about a quarter of this affair.' Acting on Courson's information, Real and the secret police were able to arrest several minor conspirators who, under torture, divulged the further intelligence that a Bourbon prince was privy to the plot. They did not reveal the name of the prince, but both Fouché and Talleyrand told Napoleon their sources pointed strongly to Louis de Bourbon Condé, the young duc d'Enghien, who was then at Ettenheim, across the Rhine from the French border. D'Enghien had given hostages to fortune by writing a note to another British secret agent, affirming his willingness to serve under the British flag and referring to the French people as his 'most cruel enemy'. Fouché had a copy of a letter in which d'Enghien claimed to have spent two years on the Rhine suborning French troops.

Napoleon dearly wanted to arrest Moreau, who had been a thorn in his side for so long, but he feared the effect on public opinion, as the victor of Hohenlinden was still a popular hero. When the police brought in Pichegru and the seriousness of the plot could not be gainsaid, Napoleon pondered his next step. It was the cynical Talleyrand who suggested that d'Enghien, being so close to the French border, should simply be kidnapped. On the night of 20 March 1804 a French snatch squad seized the Bourbon prince and brought him back to France. It needs to be emphasized that this was against every canon even of the rudimentary international law that existed at the time. D'Enghien was not a prisoner of war, nor a civil prisoner, nor was he wanted for any crime and neither had France formally made a demand for his extradition; the abduction was piracy pure and simple.

In the Château of Vincennes on the night of 20 March police captain Dautancourt interrogated the prisoner, under the general supervision of Fouché's deputy, Pierre François Réal. The chain of command was supposed to run from the First Consul to Murat, as military governor of Paris, and then to Real, but this clarity was later obfuscated as all parties to the affair denied they were the effective decision-makers. The interrogation, and the later summary trial before a military commission, scarcely provided the proof required for a retrospective justification of the kidnapping. D'Enghien was indicted on six counts before a military tribunal, consisting of General Hulin, five colonels and a captain, but in reality nothing more than a kangaroo court. The six counts were: bearing arms against the French people; offering his services to the English; harbouring British agents and giving them the means to spy in France; heading an émigré corps on the French border; trying to foment a revolt in the Strasbourg area; and being one of the ringleaders in a plot against the life of the First Consul.

D'Enghien did not deny his hostility to the current régime in France: like all exiled nobles, he had joined an anti-revolutionary 'crusade' and could scarcely have respected himself if he had not done so. But he did deny taking part in a plot and said that he had never even met Pichegru; he ended by requesting a personal interview with Napoleon, which was denied. After a very brief hearing the military tribunal condemned him to death. Again it is worth stressing that the tribunal had no juridical credentials. It was an *ad hoc* body which was not bound by any rules; the accused was not told the exact nature of the charges beyond the generalities in the counts of the indictment; no witnesses were called, no defence was allowed, and there was no possibility of appeal or judicial review, as guaranteed by a 1798 law. At 3 a.m. on the morning of 21 March, d'Enghien was taken out into the courtyard of the Château de Vincennes and executed by firing squad.

Two months later the other conspirators were disposed of. Their trial began on 25 May but almost immediately Pichegru was found to have 'hanged himself' in his cell. On 25 June twelve Chouans were executed as ringleaders in the plot. All aristocratic conspirators were pardoned and Moreau exiled. It hardly needs to be added that Bernadotte had been in on the whole project and was once again pardoned for Désirée's sake. The plot, which definitely existed, had been a shambles from the very beginning. The plotters were poor at planning and had not taken public opinion into account; in fact at this juncture there was no significant discontent against the régime, as both unemployment and the price of bread were low. Moreau ineptly played into Napoleon's hands. His banishment left the Army nowhere to go but into Napoleon's pocket.

The execution of the duc d'Enghien caused hardly a murmur in France at the time but, as the Bonaparte women saw clearly, it was an irremovable stain on Napoleon's escutcheon and has come back to sully his name ever since. Josephine pleaded with Napoleon for mercy for the young Bourbon, but he contemptuously dismissed this as a woman's weakness. Letizia told him bluntly that the execution of d'Enghien would be ascribed to his Corsican barbarism and blood-lust and that his reputation would suffer accordingly. The truth of the affair seems to be that Cadoudal and Pichegru took the prince's name in vain, that, although a deadly enemy of the régime, he had never been involved in a plot to assassinate Napoleon.

In the opinion of his enemies and of later critics Napoleon joined the regicides by this brutal and unnecessary murder of an unimportant enemy. So what were his motives and how do we assess his moral stature as a result? Napoleon himself mostly tried to brazen the scandal out and remained unrepentant even on St Helena. On 27 March 1804 he said to Le Couteulx de Canteleu, one of the leading senators: 'The circumstances we found ourselves in did not allow chivalry or mercy. If we acted like this habitually in affairs of state, people would legitimately call us puerile.' Seventeen years later, in his last testament on St Helena, he said he regretted nothing, as the security, interests and honour of the French people were at stake.

Yet there is evidence that Napoleon, possibly after listening to the entreaties of Josephine, realized how the affair might be perceived by posterity and accordingly prepared for himself a Machiavellian 'alibi'. On the one hand, he sent an express to Murat via his aide René Savary ordering him to make an end of everything that very night. On the other, he composed a note for Réal, asking him to hold d'Enghien over for further questioning. This note was written at 5 p.m. on 20 March but not sent until 10 p.m.; Réal was asleep when the courier arrived and did not open the letter of 'reprieve' until it was too late. It was the scenario famously described in *Richard III*:

> But he, poor man, by your first order died,
> And that a winged Mercury did bear;
> Some tardy cripple bore the countermand,
> That came too lag to see him buried.

Although Napoleon cannot evade the ultimate responsibility for an act of piracy and murder, he was singularly ill-served on this occasion by all his henchmen. He later claimed that even as he hesitated, Murat lost his head and spent the day panicking over imminent Bourbon counter-revolution. And, despite his later denials, Talleyrand was deeply involved in the assassination – for that is the only appropriate word. It was on his advice that the snatch squad was dispatched. Most of all, the evil genius of Fouché can be detected: Fouché's aim was to show the First Consul that his police force was indispensable and needed to be granted new powers and new funds; in a new Terror he would be the effective Robespierre. Savary, too, colluded to rush through the execution and overruled a twenty-four-hour delay in executing sentence asked for by the President of the Military Tribunal, General Kulin.

Napoleon's critics accuse him of playing up the d'Enghien affair so as to ascend the imperial throne more easily. Tolstoy even alleged in *War and Peace* that there was a pathological element in Napoleon's treatment of d'Enghien. Tolstoy's story was that the First Consul and d'Enghien at one time both shared the concurrent favours of Mlle George and that d'Enghien used to make frequent clandestine trips to Paris to see her. According to the story, on one occasion he found Napoleon in her boudoir at the mercy of one of his fainting fits and could have killed him as he lay helpless; his murder was the thanks he got for his magnanimity.

However, this argument is weak in that Napoleon did not need d'Enghien for his imperial purposes; he had what he needed in the genuine Cadoudal/Pichegru plot. As he himself said, if he were a convinced regicide he had had many chances and would have many more. If it was his policy to kill Bourbons he could have had Louis XVIII and his kinsmen the comte de Lille and the comte d'Artois assassinated with ease, and the same was the case when Ferdinand and Don Carlos of Spain were at Valençay in 1808. He claimed that several 'hitmen' had approached him over the years, asking for sums of two millions to eliminate his political opponents, but he always refused on principle. Part of this argument may be allowed to stand. He was not in the grand league of regicides: he had not overthrown the house of Saul like David, overturned the Roman Republic like Caesar, executed a Stuart king like Cromwell or a Bourbon monarch like the men of '93. Clearly Napoleon was in no sense a killer of princes or collector of Bourbon scalps and he had d'Enghien executed for misperceived reasons of state. There was a conspiracy and there were British intrigues that called for a vigorous riposte, but Napoleon's murder of d'Enghien was actually irrelevant to these rational aims. But, like all men, Napoleon was convinced that he never performed an evil action and once declared: 'I am not at bottom a bad sort.'

However, there can be no denying that Napoleon used the Pichegru/ Cadoudal plot, regardless of the reality of d'Enghien's actual involvement, to become Emperor. If he established a dynasty with hereditary succession, it would be pointless in the future for royalists to try to kill *him*. Moreover, the royalists in exile were genuinely cowed and terrified by Bonaparte's ruthless action against their prince. If the Concordat had given comfort to the right, the events of March 1804 silenced the outré Republicans who had suspected Napoleon of being soft on Bourbon aspirations. It also reassured the notables and the Thermidorians – all who had done well from the sale of national property – that their property and prosperity was safe with Napoleon: had he not now joined them in the ranks of the regicides? By becoming Emperor he had decisively rebutted the Jacobin canard that his role was to be that of General Monk to the restored king. He convinced both Jacobins and bourgeoisie that there could be no going back to 1789 and therefore that their interests were secure; the gains made by the Revolution were irreversible. Even the doomed Cadoudal realized he had played into Napoleon's hands. He remarked gloomily: 'I came to make a king and instead I have made an emperor.'

In May 1804, in the wake of general indignation about the plot, the Senate proposed that Napoleon be made hereditary Emperor of the French. On 4 May the necessary ratification took place, and ten days later a new 142-article Constitution was published, which allowed Bonaparte to nominate his successor as Emperor. Although Carnot was the only one to oppose this publicly, many of Napoleon's adherents and so-called supporters expressed doubts. Junot, an ardent republican, is said to have wept at the news. The response of the opposition was more predictable. Lafayette, who had fought a king in America, now found an emperor in his native land, while Germaine de Staël remarked disparagingly: 'For a man who had risen above every throne, to come down willingly to take his place amongst the kings!' Even more famous disillusionment was voiced abroad by those who had seen Napoleon as a radical figure. Byron was sadly disappointed, while Beethoven tore up his initial dedication of the 'Eroica' Symphony. Others predicted that everlasting war in Europe would follow as Napoleon would be bound to go in search of fresh thrones for his brothers. Only Fouché, inveterate foe of the Bourbons, seemed enthusiastic about the idea. As for his bickering siblings, Napoleon remarked sarcastically at dinner on the evening of his proclamation as Emperor (19 May): 'To hear my sisters, you'd think I'd done them out of the patrimony my father left them.'

A third plebiscite was held, this time to confirm Napoleon as Emperor. On 6 November 1804 the result was announced: 3,572,329 'yeses' and 2,569 'noes'. Napoleon could now nominate a successor by adoption from nephews or grand-nephews if he chose but, since he had no sons, he began by making Joseph heir apparent, with Louis next in line; Lucien and Jérôme were currently in disgrace. Joseph and Louis were made Princes of the Empire, at a salary of a million francs a year and in addition they received an annual one-third of a million francs in 'expenses' arising from these posts. On 18 May it was announced that the wives of Joseph and Louis would be created Princesses and addressed as 'your royal highness'. Predictably, this was construed as an insult by the Bonaparte sisters. Élisa and Caroline, furious that they were without titles, sulked and threw tantrums. Following a ludicrous *opéra bouffe* scene thrown by Caroline, complete with fainting fit, Napoleon relented and granted them the title of Princess. Letizia too wanted a title but was so outraged by

'*Madame Mère de Sa Majesté l'Empereur*' that she boycotted the imperial coronation in pique.

It was evident that now, above all, the turbulent Bonaparte family was a thorn in the emperor's side. Essentially the reason Lucien and Jerome were in disgrace was that they had married without their brother's consent. Napoleon suggested to Lucien a dynastic marriage with the widowed queen of Etruria (Parma and Tuscany) but Lucien would have none of it. He obtained the senatorship of Trèves (Trier) with a salary of 25,000 francs together with the castle of Poppelsdorf on the Moselle, which had its own theatre and art gallery. Lucien then went on a spending spree, piling up debt, to fill the gallery with Flemish old masters. But he refused the lucrative office of Treasurer to the Senate so as not to impair his rights to the consular succession.

On 26 October 1803, without consulting Napoleon, he married the widow of a bankrupt speculator, Madame Alexandrine Joubertuon. Napoleon exploded with rage at this blatant act of defiance and tried to enlist Letizia on his side to give Lucien a dressing down. But she sided with her perennial favourite, causing coolness between First Consul and mother; it was this, as much as anything, that lay behind the formal title '*Madame Mère*' awarded at the time of the imperial proclamation. Insult was added to injury when Madame Mère said that as Napoleon had not consulted the Bonaparte family about his marriage to Josephine, the same rule should hold good for his siblings. The imbroglio ended in a slanging match between the two brothers, after which Lucien stormed off to travel privately in Italy and Switzerland; he told Joseph he hated Napoleon and would never forgive him. According to one colourful version of the altercation between the brothers, Napoleon upbraided Lucien for marrying a 'whore', to which he replied forcefully: 'At least *my* whore is pretty!' It was Lucien, too, who was most assiduous in spreading the rumour that Napoleon had slept with Hortense de Beauharnais and that Louis's son was really Napoleon's.

Jérôme meanwhile gave offence in even more spectacular fashion. When war broke out again, Jérôme deserted his ship in the West Indies and made his way to the United States. There, as described above, he met and, on Christmas Eve 1803, married a Baltimore beauty, Betsy Patterson, the daughter of a wealthy shipowner. Husband and pregnant wife soon took ship for Holland, to find that the Empire had been declared and that 'a woman named Patterson' was not to be allowed to land on French soil or that of its allies (a euphemism for vassal states like Holland). The weaklivered Jérôme, faced with a choice between his wife or power and fortune, chose the latter. On a promise of a kingdom, he agreed to have his marriage annulled by one of the complicated provisions of the Concordat, allowing France to set up an 'Officiality of Paris'. The luckless Betsy Patterson found sanctuary in England, where she gave birth to a son and was fêted as a propaganda trophy – an example of what happened to those who trusted the Bonapartes.

Yet the most troublesome aspect of the Bonaparte family was their hatred of Josephine and their constant meddling in matters that had nothing to do with them. Instead of being stupefied with gratitude that their brilliant brother had raised them from poverty and obscurity to unimaginable heights of wealth and power, the Bonapartes seemed to take the line that this was their due anyway, and that the natural order of things, previously distorted by untoward circumstance, had now re-asserted itself. Their unrelenting hostility towards Josephine – who requited it with a dangerous alliance with Fouché – was actually counterproductive, for it nudged Napoleon closer to an official declaration that Josephine would be Empress – something he had pondered long and hard. Fury at the impudence of his family in presuming to dictate to him about Josephine was one motive in making him decide to proclaim her as an imperial consort. Another was simple human decency – not a quality usually associated with Napoleon. He told Roederer: 'My wife is a good woman . . . happy to play the role of the Empress, with diamonds and fine clothes. I've never loved her blindly. If I've made her Empress, it's out of a sense of justice. I am above all a just man. If I'd been thrown into prison instead of becoming Emperor, she would have shared my misfortunes. It's only right she should share my greatness . . . People are jealous of Josephine, of Eugène and of Hortense.'

There was further dithering about whether Josephine would actually be crowned. Here the problem was that the Empress had 'dared' to throw jealous scenes about Napoleon's numerous amours. By this time everyone was thrusting wives, daughters and sweethearts at him. It was known that he gave *douceurs* of 20,000 francs a night to those he spent the night with. Some women, hearing that he was highly sexed and with an insatiable appetite, went in for orgies and sexual perversions with members of his entourage, hoping he would hear about it and be lured by the lubricious attractions on offer. They misread their man: Napoleon was not a sexual extrovert and he disapproved of women acting in a 'loose' way unless he personally had commanded it.

Nevertheless, there were mistresses a-plenty. In 1804, while on tour in the Rhineland, he had a brief affair with one of Josephine's ladies-in-waiting named Elisabeth de Vaudey. Josephine was able to scotch that particular liaison but she had less power in Paris, where for a while Napoleon had a 'love nest' in the rue de Vennes. Here he fornicated and cuckolded with gusto until a particular incident made him rethink his amatory strategy. Slipping on the snow outside his secret trysting place one day, he caught the ironic gleam in his sentry's eye and realized that he was making a fool of himself in the eyes of his beloved Grand Army; thereafter he decided to confine himself to a circle of court *hetairae*.

The snag about infidelity at St-Cloud was that it was too close to Josephine for comfort. A more serious and long-term amatory adventure produced a succession of tempestuous rows in the palace. The Murats, insanely jealous of the continuing favour he showed Josephine, devoted themselves to finding women who might displace her in the Emperor's affections. For a time Adèle Duchâtel seemed the answer to their prayers. Madame Duchâtel was a twenty-year-old beauty, separated or divorced – it is not clear which – from the middle-aged Director-General of Records. Napoleon took the bait and Murat provided cover by pretending to be madly in love with Adèle. But Josephine was not fooled. A game of cat and mouse developed between Emperor and Empress. Josephine found out about the affair from her spies (possibly from Fouché) and tried to maintain surveillance on her husband in the palace, but he outfoxed her by creeping along to his mistress's room in his bare feet.

Noticing her husband paying unwonted attention to la Duchâtel at a party, Josephine next day summoned Madame Junot (Laure Abrantes as was), who had been near the couple, to find out what had transpired. Laure Junot claimed that she and the Emperor had recently gone to bed together, and that Napoleon had been as ardent as a young lieutenant. The arrival of her lover cut short the narration and, seeing Napoleon, Madame Junot hastily took her leave. Josephine repeated the substance of what her visitor had said, which sparked off a tremendous row. Napoleon ended it by saying he was the Emperor and no one should presume to give him laws or tell him what to do. He then smashed several plates, broke a water jug, tore a tablecloth and stormed out.

Yet Josephine could not be so easily swayed from her purposes. Her sights were set on Adèle Duchâtel. One evening at St-Cloud she saw Duchâtel leave the drawing-room and noticed that the Emperor was no longer present. She left the room and came back half an hour later in a state of high agitation to tell Claire de Rémusat what she had discovered. She had gone up the private staircase to Napoleon's bedroom and heard Adèle's voice inside. She demanded to be let in and, when Napoleon finally opened the door, she found him and Duchâtel in an advanced state of undress. The sequel was more outrageous than any jealous scene hitherto. Napoleon came storming back to the drawing-room, causing all his guests to decamp for Paris in terror. He began by smashing up the furniture in rage, then told Josephine to leave St-Cloud immediately, as he was tired of being spied on by a jealous woman who could not give him children. The story made the rounds of Paris. One wag remarked that the Emperor had neglected the campaign against England in order to smash Chinese vases in the Empress's bedroom.

As it happened, Josephine had panicked and overreacted, possibly even giving the affair a new lease of life. Although the affair with Duchâtel dragged on from late 1803 to early 1806 – she was often a concurrent mistress with several others – Duchâtel was scarcely his kind of woman. Despite being attractive and intelligent and able to play to perfection the part of the coquette, Duchâtel was at heart a cold and haughty woman, who gradually revealed the frightening scale of her ambition. If Madame de Rémusat can be believed, matters actually reached the stage in the end where Napoleon asked Josephine's advice on how to get rid of her. It was a pleasing characteristic of Josephine's that she was never vindictive: once she realized she had nothing to fear from her rival, she ceased to be angry and even kept Adèle on in her service. Duchâtel herself always remained loyal to Napoleon, even when fair-weather friends deserted him. Napoleon, characteristically, repaid her loyalty with slights and insults, cut her in public and refused to speak to her again: in short he behaved like the classical cad.

Meanwhile, however, in the short term Josephine was in deep disgrace. Too late she realized she had carried things too far. Faced with disgrace, she implored Hortense to use her well-known influence on Napoleon on her behalf, but Hortense cried off, on the grounds that Louis had forbidden her ever to interfere in his brother's affairs. Eugène de Beauharnais also refused to face the Emperor's wrath, though when Napoleon told him he was thinking seriously of divorcing Josephine, he elected to follow her into exile rather than accept dukedoms and fortunes from his stepfather; the moral contrast with Jérôme could hardly be clearer. It seems that it was his family's gloating triumphalism over the supposed imminent demise of Josephine that swung Napoleon back towards forgiveness. After further soul-searching he told Roederer he intended to see her crowned. 'Yes, she will be crowned, even if it should cost me two hundred thousand men!' he declared in a typically melodramatic flourish.

So Napoleon made final plans for his coronation. It was important to him that the Pope should come from Rome to officiate, for this would carry overtones of Charlemagne and the Holy Roman Empire, aside from convincing royalists and peasantry that the Concordat was holding and that the Empire would be a Catholic empire. Napoleon's correspondence for this period is full of letters about the necessity for the Pope's attendance and the protocol to be observed on his arrival. Pius VII was wary and did not accept the invitation without a great deal of heart-searching. Finally Caprara, the Papal nuncio to France, persuaded him of the possible benefits in terms of fresh religious concessions from the new Emperor, but it must be realized that Caprara was a slavish creature of Napoleon, who took his cue from Bonaparte rather than the Papacy. So the Pope made the famous journey. He arrived at Fontainebleau on 25 November, where Napoleon met him; then after three days of entertainment Emperor and Pontiff proceeded to Paris.

Right until the last moment, Napoleon continued to be plagued by his women. On 17 November there was a violent scene when the Emperor told his sisters they would be expected to carry the Empress's train. Then Josephine decided that she could hardly be crowned by the Pope if she had not been properly married in the eyes of Holy Mother Church; actually this was a transparent ploy to make it harder for the Emperor to divorce her. Napoleon, cynical as ever, always had it in mind to divorce Josephine when he found it convenient, and was undeterred by the idea of a religious ceremony to 'solemnize' his marriage. So, towards midnight on the first day of December, before an altar erected in the Emperor's study, Cardinal Fesch, who had come with Pius from Rome, conducted a brief marriage service. Josephine was satisfied, but in strictly legal terms her status was no more solid then before, since the service was not attended by witnesses and the regular parish priest was absent. For Napoleon the first of December was far more important as the day when a *senatus consultum* established the legitimacy of the succession and the rights of his brothers to succeed if he died without issue.

Coronation Day was 2 December 1804. A recent snowfall followed by rain left the city streets slush-ridden. Three rows of troops lined the route: crowds clustered behind them but seemed more curious than enthusiastic. First out of the Tuileries, at 9 a.m., was the Pope, escorted by four squadrons of dragoons and followed by six carriages full of cardinals and assorted clergy; it was observed that the crowd split about fifty-fifty in its reaction: the pious dropped to their knees and made the sign of the cross, while the Jacobin sympathizers defiantly declined to doff their hats. Then came the secular carriages. Driven at breakneck speed through the streets through fear of assassins, Murat led the way, followed by ministers, councillors of state, the diplomatic corps and the sullen Bonaparte princesses.

Napoleon made a very late start. Although the Empress's ladies-in-waiting had been ready since 6 a.m., the Emperor himself made a leisurely toilette. Before leaving the Tuileries at 10 a.m. Napoleon took Joseph by the arm, pointed at the two of them in the mirror and said: 'Joseph! If only our father could see us!' Then the imperial couple set out for Notre-Dame cathedral in a sumptuous coach of glass and gilt, with seven wide windows and four eagles on the roof bearing a crown.

All that sumptuary extravagance could do had been done. The Emperor had decided on a predominant bee motif, as the emblem of the new empire was to be stars, bees and laurel leaves in relief. Napoleon wore a purple velvet coat with a white and gold silk sash and a short purple cloak embroidered with golden bees; the ensemble was topped off with a floppy seventeenth-century hat with turned up brim, ostrich plumes and a plethora of diamonds. Josephine donned a gown of white satin embroidered with bees and a court mantle of purple velvet; she was ablaze with diamonds – in her tiara, her necklace, earrings and belt. The entire court was dressed in velvet cloaks embroidered in gold and silver. Just before entering Notre-Dame Napoleon put on a huge cloak of purple velvet, lined with ermine and embroidered with his motif of golden bees. On his head he had a wreath of gold laurel leaves, to make him appear like the portrait of an emperor on a Roman coin. Like most successful dictators, Napoleon was alive to the importance of pictorial imagery, symbolism and iconography. But his short stature was ill-suited to the multicoloured finery, and one wag said that the Emperor most resembled the king of diamonds in a pack of cards.

Just as his coach arrived at Notre-Dame the sun came out from behind the clouds. Always sensitive to signs and portents, Napoleon claimed this was a good omen. As he and Josephine stepped out of the carriage, cannon roared and bells pealed. They entered the cathedral after a further unconscionable delay, each under a canopy and followed by a procession. Pius VII, who had had to endure a wait of several hours in a freezing Cathedral, began to intone the Mass. He anointed Napoleon's head, arms and hands in accordance with the ancient tradition that, since Clovis in 496, all monarchs of France should undergo this ritual. Next Napoleon took the crown from the altar and placed it on his own head; he then crowned Josephine, who burst into tears. This self-crowning, one of the most famous of all Napoleonic gestures, has been much misunderstood. It was not an act of spontaneous improvisation or a calculated snub to the Pope, as in the legend, but a carefully rehearsed matter of protocol which had already been discussed with the Pope at great length. The personal crowning of Josephine which occasioned her tears is more problematical, for that gesture can be interpreted variously as caprice, love or political manoeuvre.

Having completed the Mass, which climaxed with a singing of *Vivat imperator in aeternum* (May the Emperor live for ever), the Pope then withdrew, leaving the principals to administer the imperial oath, designed to counterbalance the religious ceremony and satisfy the scruples of former revolutionaries. Meticulous care had been taken to see that nothing about the coronation ceremony could cause laughter or ridicule or give rise to jokes, lampoons or scurrilous cartoons. But once again Napoleon's best-laid plans were nearly undone by his family. At one point in the proceedings there was a near-affray at the altar between Josephine and her sisters-in-law who were supposed to be carrying the train. Pauline and Caroline were the culprits, and Napoleon had to hiss some words of ferocious warning at them before they desisted.

The wording of the oath is interesting, revealing as it does the mixture of motives animating Napoleon's supporters and representing the apotheosis of revolutionary principles (the practice was to be very different).

I swear to uphold the integrity of the Republic's territory, to respect and impose the laws of the Concordat and religious freedom, to respect and impose the respect of equal rights, political and civil liberties, the irrevocability of the sale of national property, to raise no duty and to establish no tax except through the law, to uphold the institution of the Legion of Honour, to rule only in the interests of the happiness and glory of the French people.

If we disregard the bromides and the pious obeisance to vague principles, we are left with only one solid idea: that the sale of national property was sacrosanct. As for raising no duties and taxes outside the law, Napoleon *was* the law, so that provision was meaningless. Nothing more clearly illustrates the bourgeois nature of the régime Napoleon presided over than the wording of the oath.

Shortly before three o'clock on a cold, wintry afternoon the imperial party began the return to the Tuileries, arriving there after dark by flambeau light. Napoleon was euphoric and insisted that his Empress wear her crown at dinner, as if it were a party hat. Despite the mischievous efforts of Pauline and Caroline, the coronation had been a fairly complete triumph. By getting Pius VII to officiate Napoleon had achieved a Canossa in reverse and made the Pope look foolish. As Pius now realized bitterly, he had been gulled: there would be no *quid pro quo* in the shape of religious concessions. As Pieter Geyl witheringly remarked: 'The Pope would never have left Rome merely to perform a consecration.'

So far Napoleon had cunningly navigated between a series of potential rocks: peasantry, bourgeoisie, urban proletariat, petit-bourgeoisie, Catholics, Jacobins and royalists had been silenced through indulgence, *carte blanche*, bread and circuses, intimidation or terror. There remained just one powerful vested interest to be dealt with: the Army. At the time his imperial status was proclaimed, Napoleon hit on an ingenious ploy for co-opting the generals: he would revive the ancient title of Marshal of France and make all significant military leaders marshals. By a *senatus consultum* of 19 May Napoleon made eighteen appointments to the marshalate; eight more were added in later years. The marshals were also *ex officio* senators and were supposed to represent the interests of the Army in the Senate.

Some of the eighteen appointments were made for obvious family reasons: Murat received his baton since he was married to Caroline and the ungrateful Bernadotte because he had married Désirée. Then there were Napoleon's personal favourites, those who had been associated with him since Toulon or had fought with him in Italy in 1796–97: Berthier, Masséna, Augereau, Brune, Lannes and Bessières. These were the men who considered themselves an élite within an élite; they were, so to speak, the first apostles. But just as a modern prime minister has to appoint to his cabinet individuals he dislikes personally in order to maintain party unity and maintain a balance of all shades of opinion within the party, so Napoleon had to humour all the factions in the Army.

The veterans of the Rhine campaigns were proud warriors who always took the line that they had fought the hardest campaigns against the toughest opponents. All who had served with Dumouriez, Kellermann, Moreau, Pichegru and Kléber regarded the Army of Italy with contempt and considered that they alone had been tested against first-class enemy commanders. So Napoleon was obliged to promote to the marshalate men who had no experience of campaigning with him but who could not be denied on the basis of their general prestige in the Army: Jourdan, Soult, Mortier, Ney, Davout, Lefebvre. To make sure the new promotions left no army corps feeling aggrieved, Napoleon also elevated Moncey and Perignon from the Army of the Pyrenees and for good measure gave the last two batons to representatives of the 'old Army', Serurier and Kellermann.

Of mixed social origins, but with a predominance of looters and glory hunters, the marshalate has been construed as either Napoleon's biggest mistake or his most ingenious piece of machiavellianism. The main aim was to divide and rule, to set one military faction against another so that the Army never united to attempt a political coup. Napoleon shrewdly calculated that once inside the web of honours, titles and riches, with their women as princesses and duchesses, few would want to give up such privilege for reasons of ideology. And he realized, as few rulers or ruling classes have since, that it is not wise to give supreme honours to people who already have great financial privilege. While making sure his marshals were the equivalent in our terms of millionaires, the Emperor kept them in their place by putting the marshalate only fifth in the pecking order of Court precedence, after the Emperor and Empress, the imperial family, the grand dignitaries of the Empire and the ministers. And, since their formal appellation was 'Monseigneur', they could receive the deference due to them only if they in turn acknowledged Napoleon as Emperor and addressed him as 'Sire'.

Napoleon easily achieved his aims of ensuring acceptance of the Empire by the 'top brass' and integrating military leadership into a new civilian aristocratic hierarchy. The individuals he elevated were a very mixed bunch. Some were meritocrats but most were purely political appointments; this partly explains the generally lacklustre performance of the marshals on the battlefield. It was, in mean terms, a body of youngish men, with an average age of forty-four; like Hitler's stormtroopers in 1933 or Mussolini's blackshirts in 1922 Napoleon's élite military class was drawn, in the main, from the youthful. Eyebrows were raised at the appointment of the thirty-four-year-old Davout, but Napoleon knew what he was doing, as Davout later proved himself the most talented of the original bunch.

The marshals were the 'share options fat cats' of their day. Each of them was given money and income drawn on French lands or, in the later period of the Empire, on conquered territory. Looked at from one perspective, the marshalate was little more than a racket and the marshals little better than mafiosi – scarcely an exaggeration on kinship basis alone, since no fewer than 240 of Bonaparte's top generals were related to each other. Berthier, for example, was later created Prince of Neuchâtel and Wagram and received 'endowments' (*donataires*) of the value of 1, 254,000 francs a year. Ney, who later bore the titles Duke of Elchingen and Prince of the Moskova, received 1,028,000 francs from eight awards, while

Masséna, soon to be Duke of Rivoli and Prince of Essling, had an annual income of 638,375 francs from five. Davout had six endowments producing 910,000 francs a year, while Lannes, on 328,000, looked positively indigent by comparison. But it must be emphasized that the big money came from attracting Napoleon's attention by signal services on the battlefield. Brune and Jourdan, for example, who were in the outer circles, received no endowments at all.

The marshals were themselves the tip of an iceberg of a rewards system that gradually reduced the higher command to the status of clients. Altogether Napoleon created twenty-three dukes, 193 counts, 648 barons and 117 knights and disbursed over sixteen million francs in 1,261 awards in favour of 824 generals. The military were the principal financial beneficiaries of the patronage system, since even the highest ranking civilian noble, such as Cambacérès, was on a maximum of 450,000 francs a year. Gaudin, his title of Duke of Gaeta notwithstanding, received no more than 125,000, which was about the usual mark for top-ranking civilian nobles; Maret, Duke of Bassano, had an annual salary of 118,000 and Regnier, Duke of Massa, was on 150,000.

The great advantage the military had was that they could make several more fortunes by looting in conquered territories. The most significant bifurcation in the marshalate was not that between the Army of Italy men and the veterans of the Rhine but between the men of honesty and integrity, like Davout, Bessières and Mortier (and later Suchet), and the looters, like Masséna, Soult, Brune, Augereau (and later Victor). Napoleon knew all about the depredations of the looters from his spies and usually connived at them, but just occasionally he would force them to disgorge, to show that he was still master. He was amusedly contemptuous of their venality and on St Helena once reproved his entourage for talking in glowing terms about Lannes and Ney: 'You are fooling yourself if you regard Lannes thus. He and Ney were both men who would slit your belly if they thought it to their advantage. But on the field of battle they were beyond price.'

Napoleon always had a soft spot for swaggering boasters provided they were courageous, as witness his attitude to Augereau, whom in general he disliked. Like so many of Napoleon's marshals, Lannes and Ney were brave and audacious but lacked real strategic or military talent. Of the original crop of eighteen only Davout and Masséna were in the first class as military commanders, and of the eight later additions only Suchet proved their equal. Partly this was Napoleon's fault, because he made political appointments, and because he did not encourage independence of mind nor school the marshals in the finer points of strategy and tactics.

Because the Emperor always demanded absolute obedience, they were hopeless when they had to exercise individual initiative, and in the later years grew lazy and ill-motivated.

Nevertheless, nothing infuriated the marshals more than the suggestion that they had been granted vast wealth for no good reason. Lefebvre once said to a man who had expressed envy of his wealth and status: 'Come out into the courtyard. I'll have twenty shots at you at thirty paces. If I don't hit you, the whole house and everything in it is yours.' When the man declined the offer, Lefebvre told him: 'I had a thousand bullets fired at me from much closer range before I got this.' The honest and punctilious Oudinot, created marshal in 1809 but a significant military presence long before this, fought in all major campaigns except the Peninsular War between 1800 and 1814 and was wounded thirty-six times on twenty-three occasions.

Always an advocate of 'divide and rule', Napoleon actively encouraged the many rivalries among his marshals. The nexus of intrigue and jealousy can be inferred from a simple recital. Davout, always close to Oudinot, loathed Bernadotte and Murat; there was a long running feud between Lannes and Murat. Murat and Ney were the most unpopular marshals with no friends among their peers, so it hardly needs to be added that the two of them were also at daggers drawn. Oudinot entertained a particular animus towards Ney, as did Masséna. Ney, indeed, seemed to have a talent at once for harbouring grudges and for getting other people's backs up. He first swam into Napoleon's ken in 1802 when the First Consul selected him as a suitable marriage partner for Hortense's close friend, Aglae Augure. Once married, Ney hit on the idea of getting his wife into bed with the First Consul so that he (Ney) would be the real power in the land. The scheme did not work, so that Ney nursed a grievance towards Bonaparte, presumably on the ground that the Corsican had not agreed to cuckold him.

Ney was simply the most difficult personality in the galaxy of prima donnas that was the marshalate. The most admirable of them was Davout, who had been a protégé of Desaix in Egypt, and had accompanied him on the brilliant campaign in Upper Egypt. Desaix and Davout were close friends, and since Napoleon was himself a sincere admirer of Desaix, Davout recommended himself by this connection, by his dislike of Kléber and by his great military talent. A true man of war, with little time for social life, Davout was scrupulously honest in financial matters and later made a bitter enemy of Bourrienne by revealing his smuggling activities in Hamburg. A hard taskmaster with phenomenal powers of concentration second only to Napoleon's, Davout did not suffer fools gladly and had an unrivalled eye for the spurious and phoney. He despised Murat and saw right through Bernadotte, with whom he had a memorable feud, and also had a long-running vendetta with the hyper-venal Brune.

Lannes, a hard driver like his friend Augereau, was a great favourite of Napoleon, who derived secret satisfaction from Lannes's bitter enmity with Murat. Despite his braggadoccio, Lannes was real, which is more than could be said for Marmont, a man of no military talent whatever, who owed his elevation entirely to Napoleon's favour and repaid it with treachery. Mortier, by contrast, was conspicuously loyal. Immensely tall (6'4"), he was the only English speaker among the marshals, and recommended himself to Napoleon by his efficient military occupation of Hanover in 1803. Uniquely, he managed to get on well with both the Emperor and his sworn enemy Bernadotte. Moncey, on the other hand, had not only never served under Napoleon but had been friendly with the disgraced Moreau and the executed Pichegru; his appointment was the clearest example of the political gesture or balancing act and, coming so soon after the d'Enghien affair, it was a shrewd move on the Emperor's part. But the more impressive balancing was the fact that Napoleon had promoted a man of integrity on both sides: Davout from his favourites and Jourdan from the Rhine army faction.

Of all the marshals the man closest to Napoleon personally was Bessières, who as long ago as June 1796 had been chosen to head Bonaparte's bodyguard, the 'Guides' – that nucleus from which the Imperial Guard would later come. Bessières made a mortal enemy of Lannes by siding with Murat against him in 1801. Lannes was Commander of the Consular Guard and thus the favourite to head up the new body formed by the merger of Guards and Guides. But Bessières revealed to Napoleon that Lannes had overspent the Guards budget for 1801 by 30,000 francs; the Consul therefore exiled Lannes as ambassador to Portugal and appointed Bessières instead. Bessières' wife Adèle Lapeyrière was a favourite with both Napoleon and Josephine, which did the Guard commander no harm at all. But the rumours continued, fuelled by a furious Lannes, that Bessières was a nonentity with no military talent whatever.

The marshals destined to play the biggest part in Napoleon's military exploits were Murat, Lannes, Ney, Davout, Masséna, Bernadotte, Berthier and Soult – significantly those associated with him from early days. Bessières oversaw the Guards, Kellermann and Lefebvre played no significant part in Bonaparte's life, Perignon and Sérurier were always political makeweights from his point of view, while Brune, Jourdan and

Augereau gradually lost their place as important military actors; Moncey and Mortier spent their later careers away from Napoleon in the Peninsular War. More puzzling than the appointments made out of political considerations were the ones not made, for several obvious candidates were in the ring. By all laws of friendship, Junot should have been promoted but his quick tongue had spoken out of turn once too often. Suchet, who would eventually be created marshal in 1811 and be acknowledged by Napoleon as the finest of all his commanders, was at this stage severely underrated by the Emperor. He had quasi-familial claims, having married the niece of Julie and Désirée Clary, but had two strikes against his record; he had fallen out with the influential Masséna during the second Italian campaign of 1800 and, more seriously, had declined an offer to accompany Napoleon to Egypt in 1798.

The creation of the marshalate was the most important, but by no means the only, stage in Napoleon's construction of a new nobility. The day after his coronation, a morose Emperor, depressed by anticlimax after the euphoria of the day before, said to his Navy Minister Décrès: 'I have come too late; there is nothing great left to do . . . look at Alexander; after he had conquered Asia and been proclaimed to the peoples as the son of Jupiter, the whole of the East believed it . . . with the exception of Aristotle and some Athenian pedants. Well, as for me, if I declared myself today the son of the eternal Father . . . there is no fishwife who would not hiss at me as I passed by.'

Alexander the Great was on his mind in more ways than one, for he now sought to emulate the great Macedonian conqueror by creating a new nobility, partly by fusion of the notables and the returned émigrés, partly by intermarriage between his family and other European potentates; Alexander had famously ordered the mass wedding of Macedonian soldiers and Persian brides. To an extent the reestablishment of monarchical forms of power in France entailed the formation of a concomitant nobility. A decree of March 1806 gave the title 'Prince' to members of the imperial family, and in March 1808 the former ranks of the nobility were restored, except for viscounts and marquises. Senators, Councillors of State, presidents of the legislature and archbishops automatically became counts; presidents of electoral colleges, the supreme court of appeal, audit officers and some mayors received the title 'baron'. By 1814 there were 31 dukes, 450 counts, 1,500 barons and a similar number of knights.

The new imperial nobility was recruited from the Army, from officialdom and from the notables, with the military most heavily represented. The titles were rewards for military or civil service but the perquisites attaching to them varied widely. An imperial nobleman had no feudal privileges, had to pay tax and was not exempt from the general law of the land. Some of the titles had no income or property appended to them, but in any case the perks of office depended on the financial health of the Empire, as they were paid out of a general imperial coffer. It was therefore in the interests of the nobility that the Empire should fare well. Titles were personal, but some had a benefice or *majorat* attached and in that case both title and *majorat* were transferable. The size of the benefice depended on the particular title and might be in the form of unmortgaged real estate, shares in the Bank of France or government stock. The life interest in landed property granted to senators (the so-called *senatoreries*), however, immediately raised fears of a return to a feudalism in all but name and was not as popular as it should have been even with the beneficiaries, as some were disappointed to find that their income came from widely dispersed lands and was thus difficult to collect.

Napoleon was determined that all power and wealth in France should either emanate from the imperial government or be in its gift. Fearful that left to their own devices the notables might form a powerful *de facto* aristocracy behind his back, he hoped to distract them with a new nobility, a kind of bribe which they were supposed to accept in return for loss of political liberty. He declared rousingly: 'The institution of a national nobility is not contrary to the idea of equality, and is necessary to the maintenance of social order.' His idea that the hereditary transmission of privilege did not work against social equality and meritocracy serves only to show how bastardized revolutionary principles had become. He claimed to have asked a number of ex-Jacobins whether a hereditary nobility was in conflict with the Revolutionary ideology of equality and they said no. One can only assume that these Jacobins were of the kidney of Bernadotte, who while still spouting radical Republican principles had by this time got his snout firmly into the trough.

Napoleon's aims in creating a new nobility were flawed at the outset. His intention to destroy feudalism by introducing a meritocratic élite would have been more convincing if he had granted no hereditary benefices and forbade bequests from the nobility to the next generation; but in that case he would have been a Jacobin and not Napoleon. In any case, the creation of the nobility made the peasantry fear that feudalism was about to be reintroduced. The attempt to close the ideological gap between France and the rest of Europe was also a dismal failure. Intermarriage between his family and *ancien régime* dynasties might be accepted by Europe's royal families under duress, but fundamentally they hated and despised Bonaparte. As Stendhal said of the Emperor: 'He had the defect of all parvenus, that of having too great an opinion of the class into which he had risen.'

Napoleon's third aim – reconciling the beneficiaries of the Revolution with the nobility of the *ancien régime* – rested on too optimistic a conception of human nature – a surprising blind spot for someone usually so cynical and sceptical. The two aristocracies looked at each other with a contempt that could not be assuaged even by intermarriage; because of the issue of national property the two groups were divided by irreconcilable differences. The notables and the Brumairian bourgeoisie resented the reintroduction of the aristocratic principle as it were by the back door. Banking and financial élites prided themselves on their meritocratic achievements and felt degraded by the new nobility; while the shopkeepers and petit-bourgeoisie, who had been deprived of political liberty, received nothing whatever in compensation. Until 1807 the notables still feared a royalist restoration if Napoleon were defeated in battle so they clung to him; they needed time to consolidate their gains from the Empire and to be sure they would retain them under a new régime before they could even contemplate abandoning Napoleon. But there was no deep love between Emperor and notables.

There was even less between Bonaparte and the returned royalists who, even as they accepted the titles, were simply biding their time, waiting for the Emperor to destroy himself. Finally, those who had genuinely risen from the ranks to ennoblement were the worst ingrates of all. Far from acknowledging the favour of their benefactor, they were forever on the look-out for fresh sources of money and loot. There is a clear correlation between Napoleon's looting marshals and humble social origin: Augereau, Duke of Castiglione, was an ex-footman; Masséna, Duke of Rivoli was an ex-pedlar; Lannes, Duke of Montebello, was a onetime dyer's assistant; Ney, Duke of Danzig, was the son of a miller and a washerwoman. Napoleon never grasped that there was a fundamental contradiction between raising men from the gutter to the aristocracy even as he hankered after the titles of the *ancien régime*.

Yet one undoubted consequence of the way Napoleon bound the notables to his imperial system through the nexus of his new nobility was that it enabled him progressively to dispense with the constitutional accretions from the Consulate that still clogged his power. In effect he reduced the government machine to an appendage: ministers were reduced to the role of simple executives, and henceforth all their correspondence passed across the Emperor's desk. The assemblies, a counterbalance to the executive during the Consulate, were whittled down; the troublesome Tribunate was abolished in 1807; the Senate rubber-stamped the Emperor's decisions. The Assembly of Deputies quickly declined to the level of farce, with a high level of absenteeism in the electoral college responsible for presenting candidates; the reality was that the electors were sulking about elections whose results were a foregone conclusion. The Council of State, important under the Consulate, lost much of its influence: Napoleon attended it irregularly and imposed decisions without listening to the Councillors; sometimes he would throw them a sop by bowing to their will on trivial matters.

Always a devotee of divide and rule, Napoleon complicated the administration of France by dividing it up into more and more units, appearing to devolve power even while he centralized it more rigidly. Local assemblies were phased out in favour of 'general directorships' based on *arrondissements*. But the heart of his centralizing policy was the administrative council. This was a kind of cabinet, which met for lengthy sessions (sometimes from 9 a.m. to 7 p.m.) on Mondays, Thursdays and Saturdays, to examine one particular matter – be it the state of the Navy, the military budget or the situation of French roads and bridges. To this council were summoned Councillors of State, departmental chiefs and functional experts; all were invited to give an opinion but only the Emperor decided. The notables disliked the administrative councils, for they made a mockery of local government: the budget for the city of Paris, for example, would be set by the council before it had even been seen by the Parisian municipal council where the notables held sway.

All other bodies were even more empty of real power and influence. The Council of Ministers, meeting on Wednesdays, quickly became a mere talking shop. If Napoleon ever sought the advice of experts it was for the Machiavellian purpose of modifying the draft of a *senatus consultum*, never to discuss matters of real substance, even when he was theoretically and constitutionally obliged to consult other opinions. Napoleon found it impossible to delegate and insisted on making decisions even on minor and trivial matters. His insistence on having his finger in every pie led to near breakdown in the machinery of government: the *reductio ad absurdum* came at the Battle of Leipzig in 1813 when, fighting for his life, he was asked as a matter of urgency to approve the expenses of the Commissioner of St-Malo.

For a time the underlying discontent with the imperial system of nobility did not manifest itself in opposition from the notables. The initial problem was that, as Napoleon moved to put favourite sons and daughters in positions of influence or dynastic marriages, other jealous members of the Bonaparte clan would clamour for more privileges for

themselves. The scale of this madness became apparent during Napoleon's triumphal procession through Italy in the fourteen weeks between
the beginning of April and mid-July 1805.

Departing from Fontainebleau, Napoleon made his way south through
Troyes, Mâcon and Bourg to Lyons, on the first stage of his project to
have himself crowned King-Emperor of Italy. After pausing for a week in
Lyons, he proceeded via Chambéry and Modane to Turin, where he
remained for two weeks before making a triumphal entry into Milan on 8
May. A second coronation ceremony followed, after which Napoleon
appointed his twenty-three-year-old stepson Eugène de Beauharnais as
his viceroy in Italy. This particularly infuriated the Murats, who had set
their sights on being overlords of Italy. The rapacity of this grasping
couple is hard to come to terms with. On New Year's Day 1805 Napoleon
gave Caroline a present of 200,000 francs, and when her second daughter
was born he gave her the Élysée palace, together with a further million
francs with which to buy out all existing tenants there. In addition
Caroline had an annual allowance of 240,000 francs from the Civil List
and Murat himself had an official income of 700,000 francs. Together
with their estates and investments the Murats were able to command a
total income of one and a half million francs in the first year of Empire.
Yet they were still dissatisfied, so the dangerous and indefatigable
intriguer Caroline set her mind to increasing her influence over the
Emperor.

The Empire and its consequences raised the old feud between the
Bonapartes and the Beauharnais to a new pitch. To get rid of the
termagant Élisa, whose hostility to Josephine was overt, the Emperor
made her hereditary Princess of Piombino in March 1805. This served
only to work her sisters up into a fresh lather of jealousy, complicated by
the fact that Caroline Murat also loathed Pauline Borghese. At a loss how
to deal with the women in his entourage, Napoleon decided to win over
Madame Mère by bestowing fresh honours on her. He provided her with
a lavish household of two hundred courtiers, with the duc de Cosse-
Brissac as chamberlain, a bishop and two sub-chaplains as her confessors,
a baron as her secretary, nine ladies-in-waiting and one of Louis XVI's
ex-pages as her equerry; the egregious Letizia responded by complaining
about the expense of her court. Aware that she was pathologically mean,
Napoleon gave her a sackful of money to purchase the Hôtel de Brienne
from Lucien as her Paris base. As her country residence she had a wing of
the Grand Trianon and, when she found fault with that, a huge
seventeenth-century château at Pont-sur-Seine near Troyes, with Napoleon footing the bill for all furniture and redecoration.

Madame Mère was also effectively Napoleon's viceroy in Corsica:

nothing happened on the island without her say-so. Legendarily stingy, Letizia was also, bizarrely, put in charge of the imperial charities. She still tried to rule her family with a rod of iron but at last, overcome by the Emperor's largesse, she joined his campaign to get Lucien to give up his wife. Napoleon always hoped to repeat the success he had gained with Jérôme and Betsy Patterson, but the defiant Lucien refused to bend the knee; not even pressure from his mother could sway him. Meanwhile Letizia still sniped away ineffectually at Josephine. The Empress, when she was not spying on her husband and having rows about his amours, sought solace in grotesque clothes-buying sprees and in horticulture. She turned the garden at Malmaison into a veritable botanical paradise and proved she was still a force to be reckoned with by her presence at the baptism of Louis and Hortense's second son, in March 1805. Christened Napoleon in a ceremony conducted by Cardinal Fesch and using the ritual once employed to christen a Dauphin, the child was the only ostensibly joyful sign in the disastrous loveless marriage between Louis and Hortense.

Of all the Bonaparte siblings, Pauline was the closest personally to Napoleon. She was the sort of woman he approved of: a sensualist who lived purely for pleasure, be it in the form of clothes, parties, balls or lovers. By common consent the Princess Borghese was a stunning beauty, whose eccentricities provided endless tittle-tattle for the gossip sheets. Like Nero's wife Messalina, she was said to bathe in milk and to be carried into the lactic bath by a giant black servant named Paul – inevitably rumoured to have been a 'king' in Africa. When remonstrated with for her familiarity with her male namesake, Pauline replied offhandedly: 'A negro is not a man.'

Her fat husband soon departed to be a colonel in the Horse Grenadiers of the Imperial Guard, so there was no obstacle to Pauline's life of hedonism and scandal. Lacking maternal feeling, she was absent from the bedside when her only son by Leclerc, Dermide Louis, died aged eight, so Napoleon, fearing for the image of the imperial family, had to repair the damage with lying propaganda about a tearstained matron keeping vigil. During 1805–07 Pauline was normally to be found at the Petit Trianon at Versailles, usually in the arms of her principal (but not sole) lover Count Auguste de Forbin, a dispossessed aristocrat who recommended himself, as Gibbon would say, *enormitate membri*.

Such was Pauline's reputation for sexual adventure that, Bonapartist propaganda notwithstanding, the inevitable happened and her name was linked with her brother's. Beugnot, Louis XVIII's Minister of Police in 1814–15, made widely known a rumour that had been going the rounds in imperial times, to the effect that Napoleon and Pauline had been incestuous lovers. The 'source' was allegedly Josephine, said to have blurted out such an accusation in 1806 to the French scholar Constantin Volney. We may confidently reject the assertion. Josephine was prone to hysterical exaggeration and may have mistaken a typically hyperbolic Corsican gesture of sisterly affection on Pauline's part. Circumstantial evidence is entirely against the canard. It was a peculiarity of Napoleon – his admirers say because he was generous, his enemies because he regarded all women as whores – to lavish money on any woman he had been to bed with. Yet in January 1815 he refused to pay a paltry bill of 62 francs for curtains which Pauline had incurred.

Yet perhaps there was a certain poetic justice in the slanderous rumour, for as Napoleon approached the mid-life he began to exhibit clear signs of a satyriasis to rival Pauline's nymphomania. To an extent the Murats made it easy for him by acting as procurers of beautiful and willing young women. By now Caroline had concluded that her alliance with Joseph was not paying off in quite the way she had hoped. She therefore persuaded an initially reluctant Murat to adopt a sycophantic line with the Emperor and to outdo the resident yes-men. The Murats threw lavish parties for the Emperor and his entourage and punctiliously observed his etiquette. Josephine, with her hypersensitive antennae, vaguely intuited the new influence of the Murats as being aimed at her, without as yet being able to put her finger on why.

As he approached his thirty-sixth birthday the Emperor was, sexually speaking, a ripe fruit to be plucked. His infidelities were becoming more and more overt and the rows with Josephine as a consequence more and more bitter. In April 1805, on his way to Milan for the second coronation, he had a brief fling with an unknown woman at Castello di Stupigini, about six miles outside Turin. But the next liaison was almost a calculated insult to the Empress, as the twenty-year-old blonde Anna Roche de La Coste was one of the ladies-in-waiting whose job it was to read to Josephine. Yet Napoleon did not have things all his own way during this tempestuous affair, since La Coste herself proved capable of running more than one lover at once.

Hearing rumours that La Coste had been the mistress of his chamberlain Theodore de Thiard, Napoleon went to great lengths to ensure he and his new conquest would not be disturbed. Having posted guards around her room, he was stupefied when he arrived to find her and Thiard *in flagrante*. After a furious but ignominious altercation with Thiard, Napoleon sent him off on a mission to the Vatican, then bought La Coste's loyalty by the gift of a priceless jewel. Still smarting from the

Thiard business, the Emperor seems to have displaced some of his hostility on to Josephine, for we hear of a scene at court where he publicly humiliated his wife by offering La Coste a ring. When Josephine threw another angry scene and demanded La Coste's banishment, Napoleon agreed – provided Josephine received his mistress at a state reception – an unheard of privilege for a woman whose official function was supposed to be limited by protocol to the Empress's bedroom. But in order to get rid of La Coste Josephine swallowed the bitter pill.

Napoleon still harboured feelings of resentment towards Thiard and, in Italy shortly afterwards, he found a means to strike back at him. After a month in Milan, Napoleon spent three weeks in Brescia, Verona, Mantua and Bologna before resting for the week of 30 June–6 July 1805 in Genoa. One day Talleyrand was singing the praises of the daughter of a dancer, called Carlotta Gazzani and mentioned that Thiard was her current lover. First Napoleon smashed a vase in rage at the mention of the name, then he thought more coolly. After Genoa he intended to head back to Fontainebleau by way of Turin, Lyons, Roanne, Moulins, Nevers and Montargis. It would be an arduous journey, and what more ingenious way to kill two birds with one stone than to take Carlotta Gazzani with him as his new mistress. At once he appointed Gazzani to fill La Coste's place as Josephine's reader. Talleyrand pointed out this would scarcely do since Gazzani spoke no French, but a court wit came to the Emperor's aid by remarking that since Italian was the language of love, Gazzani knew all she needed to.

A gleeful Napoloen summoned Thiard and sent him on another long mission, with orders to leave at once. When Thiard looked dismayed, Napoleon taunted him: 'Anyone would think you are in disgrace; perhaps there is some reason for it.' Thereafter he made sure Thiard never got near Gazzani again: the luckless chamberlain served first in Austria, then in Dalmatia and was finally required to accompany the Emperor on the protracted military campaign of 1806–07. Back at St-Cloud Josephine tried to catch her husband in the act with Gazzani in his famous alcove room, but this time the imperial valet Constant firmly barred the way.

It was on Napoleon's return from Italy, and even as he trysted with Gazzani, that the Murats played their master card. They introduced to the Emperor a tall, willowy black-eyed brunette called Éléonore Denuelle de la Plagne, an eighteen-year-old beauty with the status of 'grass widow' since her husband was in jail. A beautiful though not very bright woman, Denuelle was to be one of the most important of all Napoleon's mistresses. She was the daughter of shady adventurer parents and found a niche as personal secretary to the Murats. Later an absurd story was concocted that Murat had raped her, but the truth was that she became his lover willingly enough. The cynical Caroline was unmoved by this but saw potential in Éléonore as a real threat to Joséphine.

The Murats set about their stratagem with great ruthlessness. First the husband, Jean-François Honoré Revel, serving a prison sentence for forgery, had to be squared. The Murats told Revel he would be freed at once if he agreed to divorce his wife, but the obstinate Revel dug in his heels. He was then hauled before a tame judge, a creature of the Murats, who told him he would be deported to Guyana if he did not agree. Something about the demeanour of the Murats convinced Revel that they were in earnest and would stop at nothing. He agreed to the divorce (granted in April 1806) but later got a kind of revenge by publishing the story of the affair in a pamphlet.

Napoleon threw himself into the affair with Denuelle with avidity; she used to visit the alcove every day. After each session she would return to Murat for a bout of lovemaking and would pour out her alleged distaste for the Emperor. Finding that Napoleon liked to spend exactly two hours with her every day, she once moved the big hand of the clock in her room on thirty minutes with her foot as the Emperor caressed her; a little later Napoleon noticed the time, cut short his caresses, jumped up, dressed hurriedly and departed. He never suspected her duplicity and was so pleased with her that he took a house for her in the rue de la Victoire. In December 1806 she bore a son, whose paternity the Emperor at first accepted, until wagging tongues and Fouché's spies put him in the picture. While still accepting the theoretical possibility that he could have been the father, he suspected that the true impregnator was Murat. Caroline had been just a bit too clever. By this time not only did Hortense and Josephine know of Denuelle's duplicity with Murat, but the rest of the Bonaparte family did as well. Angry with Caroline's barefaced scheming they combined to have Denuelle edged out of favour; but for that, it is possible Josephine might have been replaced as consort.

Napoleon finally managed to dovetail his amorous pursuits and his ambition for dynastic marriages when he was forced to sublimate his passion for Josephine's niece, Stéphanie de Beauharnais. The Emperor's open lusting after her caused great embarrassment at court and infuriated Caroline Murat; even Josephine began to grow alarmed when she found her husband capering outside her niece's room and realized he had allowed Stéphanie the run of the palace. The Empress put it to Napoleon that as he had formally adopted Stéphanie as his daughter, to have intercourse with her was a kind of incest and would certainly be construed as such by his enemies. After a severe talking to from

Josephine about her behaviour, Stéphanie reluctantly accepted the dynastic marriage Napoleon had arranged for her with Charles Louis, Prince of Baden, but at first refused to consummate the union, vainly hoping that Napoleon would come to her. Fighting his own libidinous instincts, Napoleon reluctantly confided to Stéphanie that she could hope for nothing from him and should therefore be a proper wife to the Prince of Baden. To sweeten the pill he gave her the territory of Breisgau as a benefice, provided a necklace costing one and a half million francs for her dowry and paid an exorbitant price for her trousseau. There is some evidence that for Napoleon Éléanore Denuelle was simply a fantasy surrogate for the unattainable Stéphanie.

Since Charles Louis was the brother of the Czarina, by this marriage of his 'daughter' Napoleon had cemented his ties with the dynasties of the *ancien régime*. But the alliance caused uproar in the Bonaparte family, with Caroline and Madame Mère especially frothing at the mouth; to placate them Napoleon made another huge grant of money. In some ways even more offence was given the Bonapartes by Eugène de Beauharnais's marriage to the daughter of the King of Bavaria. According to a story told by Napoleon to Gourgaud on St Helena, the Bavarian monarch considered his daughter Augusta too pretty to be bartered away for dynastic convenience and to prove his point brought her, veiled, to a private conference with the French Emperor. When the king lifted the veil to reveal his daughter's charms, Napoleon became flustered and embarrassed, which the king read as *coup de foudre*. When both parties had recovered from their misreadings, Napoleon introduced Augusta to Eugène, who was a handsome and intelligent young man. Augusta took to him immediately and told her father she was keen on the idea of the marriage, which was celebrated on 14 January 1806.

Given the general loose morality at Napoleon's court – a tone he set himself and which was so much at odds with the official face presented to the world – it was not surprising that the imperial court quickly became a subject for ridicule in European capitals. German aristocrats who despised 'the Corsican' as an upstart, sniggered as they told stories of masked balls where the Emperor was supposedly incognito but instantly recognizable from his distinctive gestures and body language. A court where money-grubbers like Soult and Masséna rubbed shoulders with masters of duplicity like Fouché and Talleyrand, where malcontents like Bernadotte could be seen cheek-by-jowl with nymphomaniacs like Pauline Borghese, and where the Emperor himself alternated between lust and insult in his relation with the women, was never going to be the headquarters of a philosopher-king. The entire imperial style, whether in architecture or entertainment, reeked of vulgarity, ostentation, conspicuous consumption and chip-on-the-shoulder aping of the baubles and excesses of the *ancien régime*. There was something pathetic in the way pompous new rituals were introduced at court and about the huntin'-, shootin-' fishin' ethos Napoleon admired in the belief that it was 'chic' even though he himself was a very bad shot and was hard put to hit Josephine's sedentary swans at Malmaison. One critic described Napoleon's court as the sort of colourful shambles one might expect from an amateur theatrical company on rehearsal night. Only one thing prevented the first Napoleon from descending to the level later occupied by his epigone Napoleon III and his 'carnival empire': the military genius that was now to make him master of Europe.

CHAPTER FIFTEEN

For more than two years, from the outbreak of war in May 1803, Napoleon was intermittently obsessed by the invasion of England. His mood oscillated between euphoria and facile optimism on the one hand and gloomy despair and defeatism on the other. His frequent journeyings in these years are a good barometer of a restless soul, a man impatient with the many logistical frustrations of the steady build-up of men and matériel in the Channel ports. His day-to-day itinerary betrays the zigzag pattern of a man temperamentally incapable of, as well as prevented by circumstances from, concentrating on any single objective. A tour of ports in the Pas de Calais in June 1803 was swiftly followed by a trip to Belgium; he was back in Boulogne again for a fortnight in November 1803 and again for a further two weeks in January 1804. The d'Enghien affair and the imperial coronation occupied most of that year, but in July he was in the Channel ports for a month; then came two weeks in Aix-la-Chapelle at the beginning of September followed by a tour of the Rhineland during the last two weeks of the month. The coronation and its aftermath necessitated a lengthy stay in Paris, but in April 1805 the Emperor was off again, this time on a fourteen-week trip to Italy for his coronation in Milan. Scarcely pausing at St-Cloud, he was at Boulogne again for the climax of the invasion attempt in August 1805.

Since all gunboats and sloops prepared for the would-be descents on England in 1798 and 1801 were by now in an advanced state of disrepair or had simply rotted away, Napoleon had to start from scratch. Undeterred by the fact that he had just thirteen ships of the line against England's fifty-two, he took heart from the bold showing of his men during Nelson's raids on Boulogne in August and September 1801, when French marines repulsed a British commando assault on the port with heavy loss. He now conceived an elaborate plan whereby two fleets would be constructed secretly and simultaneously at Dunkirk and Cherbourg, ready for a final rendezvous at Boulogne, which the Emperor decided was the most feasible launching pad for an enterprise against England. Troops would be assembled at Boulogne at the last moment and there would be smaller bases at Wimereux and Ambleteuse; the four principal army corps, each with artillery park, would be held back at Utrecht, Bruges, St-Omer and Montreuil until the very last minute, to keep the enemy guessing, but a fifth corps would prepare only at Brest as if an invasion of Ireland was the real project.

Whereas the Cherbourg flotilla was to consist of twenty sloops and eighty gunboats, the much larger one at Dunkirk would comprise one hundred sloops and 320 gunboats. A variety of boats was used, but principally the *prames*, sailing barges one hundred feet from bow to stern, twenty-three feet in the beam, rigged like a corvette and armed with twelve 24-pounders. A smaller version of the *prame*, armed with three 24-pounders and an 8-inch howitzer, and rigged like a brig, was the *chaloupe canonnière*. For transporting horses, ammunition and artillery there were the three-masted *bateaux canonnières*, resembling a fishing smack, with stables in the hold, a 24-pounder in the bow and a howitzer at the stern. Then there were the *péniches*, undecked vessels, sixty feet long by ten wide, basically converted trading craft and fishing smacks. Finally, there were sixty-foot sloops propelled by lug sails and oars and used exclusively for troop transport.

In his early period of invasion euphoria Napoleon displayed an amazing concern for detail. Nothing seemed too small to be beneath his notice, and at St Omer Marshal Soult was astonished to receive a virtual manual of drill for soldiers operating the *péniches* which contained detail that would have occurred only to a cox of oarsmen. He squeezed Dutch, Spanish and Portuguese allies for money to finance the invasion but even so could not drum up enough to cover the huge expenses and was in the end forced to raise a loan at the prohibitive interest rate of 15%. Some idea of the cost can be seen from a shipowner's tariff at the time: a *prame* cost 70,000 francs; a *chaloupe canonnière* 35,000 francs, a *bateau cannonière* 18–23,000 francs and a *péniche* 12–15,000 francs.

Still hugely confident, he dubbed his forces 'the Army of England' and wrote to Cambacérès that he had viewed the English coast across the sea from Ambleteuse on a clear day and the Channel was merely 'a ditch will be leapt as soon as someone has the guts to try'. A week later he wrote to Admiral Ganteaume in Toulon: 'Eight hours of night in favourable weather would decide the fate of the universe.' By October 1803 Minister of Marine Décrès reported the flotilla in possession of 1,367 vessels of all types; all major embarkation ports had been improved by deepening; and the problem of getting an invasion off from Boulogne on a single tide, which had so bedevilled French invasion attempts in 1745, 1759 and 1798, was to be solved by building a breakwater and sluice.

Yet even at this stage Napoleon had not come to terms with the fundamental problem that would in the end bring all his grandiose plans to grief. In a word, he had not absorbed the lesson – a commonplace to professional sailors – that navies could not simply be switched from theatre to theatre, as could land troops in war gaming or actual operations. The Emperor had no real conception of the effects of winds and waves and, while he vaguely understood that the *péniches* could not stand up to a heavy Atlantic swell, he failed to realize that the *prames* also lacked the ability to withstand a heavy sea. The eight hours glibly referred to in the letter to Ganteaume presupposed an unlikely combination, especially in dark winter months: the absence of the Royal Navy and a Channel as calm as a millpond.

Another initial error – which he did later make good – was the assumption that a 2,000-strong invasion flotilla, containing 150,000 troops and 50,000 sailors and auxiliaries, could cross the Channel to a beachhead without the support of a covering fleet. When asked about this, Napoleon airily spoke about crossing in fog, apparently unaware of the chaos and near-certain disaster that would ensue if an uncoordinated armada tried to run the gauntlet in mutual invisibility. He tried to overwhelm well-grounded objections with an appeal to revolutionary zeal and French patriotism. 50,000 labourers were set to constructing berthing places in the Channel ports, in the process virtually constructing a new port at Ambleteuse, but the commander of the invasion flotilla, Admiral Bruix, nervously pointed out to the Emperor that such commendable zeal did not actually solve the outstanding problems.

The British, aware that Napoleon was in deadly earnest, raised militias, constructed beacons and Martello towers, and tried to dispose their fleet to cover any contingency: Nelson invested Toulon while Admiral Cornwallis blockaded Brest. The Emperor meanwhile showed himself once more a master of propaganda by arranging for the Bayeux tapestry, a reminder of an earlier, successful invasion of England, to be taken on tour. Yet the British were no slouches at propaganda and disinformation themselves, and spread panic through the French army at Boulogne in 1804 with a cleverly planted rumour that bales of cotton carrying a plague virus had been cast on to the beaches around Boulogne. The war of nerves seemed to be tilting Britain's way in the autumn of 1803 when news came in that Robert Emmet's pro-French coup in Dublin had failed dismally, making it now seem implausible that the corps assembling at Brest could be sent to Ireland.

By the end of the year Napoleon had been brought down to earth from his dream-castles. All his staffwork pointed to depressing conclusions: the flotilla was not 'weatherly' enough for a winter crossing of the Channel; the movement of shipping from the assembly ports to the concentration area had been badly affected by the weather and Royal Navy interceptions; a calculation of winds and tides threw up too many imponderables, including the nightmare scenario that the flotilla might be becalmed in mid-sea for three days or that it would take six days to get the entire armada out of Boulogne. In January 1804 Napoleon bowed to the inevitable and ordered the project shelved. This was an acute personal disappointment, for he had even chosen the boat (*Le Prince de Galles*) in which he intended to cross the Channel. But he stressed that his order meant postponement only, not cancellation; in March 1804 he wrote to his ambassador in Constantinople: 'In the present position of Europe all my thoughts are directed towards England . . . nearly 120,000 men and 3,000 boats . . . only await a favourable wind to plant the imperial eagle on the Tower of London.' A believer in bad omens, he made light of an incident in January when his horse tripped over a cable and threw him into the sea; laughing it off, but doubtless inwardly troubled, he said: 'It's nothing. It's only a bath.'

When he returned seriously to the invasion project in July 1804, he began by conceding that his earlier ideas were chimerical: he would have to use the French fleet somehow to hold the Royal Navy at bay, and he would have to make the attempt in fine weather in the summer. But an alarming incident on 20 July showed that he had still not completely absorbed the problems posed by the elements. That day a gale was blowing which threatened to develop into a full storm. Napoleon blithely insisted that a scheduled naval review go ahead, which drew vociferous protests from Admiral Bruix. When Bruix persisted, he was dismissed on the spot and later exiled. His successor, Admiral Magon, dared not risk the imperial wrath further and gave the order to put to sea. In the ensuing storm ships were wrecked and over 2,000 soldiers and sailors drowned. The Emperor strode up and down the beach in a fury but expressed no remorse for the lives he had lost by his folly.

The year 1804 saw Napoleon engaged in two major stratagems to outfox the Royal Navy as he strove to make good his oft-repeated dictum: 'Let us be masters of the Straits of Dover for six hours and we shall be masters of the world.' His first scheme depended on luring away the English under Admiral Cornwallis, who was then blockading Brest. Admiral Ganteaume would clear for Ireland with his squadron, tying down Cornwallis outside Brest; meanwhile La Touche-Tréville, the Admiral of the Fleet and by far Napoleon's best naval commander, would come up from Toulon with eleven ships of the line, link off Cadiz with the Rochefort squadron (Admiral Villeneuve in command of another five men o'war) and then fetch a wide compass into the Atlantic before looping round into the Western Approaches north of Cornwallis; La Touche-Tréville would then proceed to the Straits of Dover to cover the crossing of the flotilla from Boulogne. This was an ingenious plan on paper, but it did not explain how the Toulon fleet was to emerge safely and avoid Nelson's blockading squadron. La Touche-Tréville duly tried to come out but was driven back by Nelson. When the able French admiral died two months later, the project died with him. Napoleon, who had no great opinion of Villeneuve, considered the implementation of such an intricate plan beyond the man he reluctantly promoted to Admiral of the Fleet.

In September 1804 he tried again. This time his conception was even more elaborate and we can detect elements of a fantastic, Promethean self-delusion in his strategic imagination, which now bade fair to embrace the globe. The main thrust of the project was a revived invasion of Ireland, but this time to be attempted with forces greater than any yet landed on John Bull's other island. Marshal Augereau was designated commander of the 16,000 troops which Ganteaume was ordered to take to Lough Swilly or environs; the Emperor even gave details on the track to be adopted: a wide sweep into the Atlantic, an approach to the north of Ireland from the west, and a successful landfall. Once Augereau's troops were ashore, Ganteaume was to take his course back to Cherbourg to ascertain the situation in the Channel. If all was ready at Boulogne, and the winds favoured the crossing of the Grand Army, he was to fall on the British blockading squadron. If this were not possible, Ganteaume was to switch to Plan B, pass through the Straits of Dover to Texel to join seven Dutch ships of the line, and then transports and another 25,000 men would be taken to Lough Swilly as the second wave of a gigantic French incursion into Ireland.

The Emperor was pleased with the apparent mathematical cogency of his new plan. As he saw it, one of these scenarios had to work out, which meant that he would either have armies in both England and Ireland or would have over 40,000 men on Irish soil – an irresistible force for the permanent wresting of the island from the British grip. But there was an element of 'overegging the pudding' in the capstone Napoleon put to his grand strategy, which surely shows once again the Romantic vanquishing the Classicist and the poet *manqué* the mathematician. As if the orders to Ganteaume were not complex enough, he also ordered the Toulon fleet, now under Villeneuve, and the Rochefort squadron he used to command (and now under Admiral Missiesy) to sail in separate divisions for the

West Indies. The Toulon fleet was to recapture Surinam and the Dutch colonies and take reinforcements to Santo Domingo (where the struggle with Christophe was still going on); additionally, it was to detach a small contingent of ships and 1,500 men to capture St Helena (dramatic irony!) and cut the East Indies trade route. The Rochefort squadron meanwhile was to capture Dominica and St Lucia, reinforce the French position at Martinique and Guadalupe, and then attack Jamaica and the British West Indies. As a final piece of icing on the strategic cake, Villeneuve and Missiesy were to rendezvous in the West Indies and return together to Europe, there to raise the Royal Navy blockade on the ports of Ferrol and Corunna.

With these grandiose and rather absurd plans we see clearly Napoleon's Achilles' heel: the inability to concentrate on a single clear objective to the exclusion of all others. The thinking was that Missiesy and Villeneuve would decoy Cornwallis away to the West Indies – for the British would surely have to divert in strength to deal with the threat to their position in the Caribbean – thus allowing Ganteaume the freedom for his multifaceted mission. The orders concerning Ferrol and Corunna were meant to give a last nudge to Spain to declare war on Britain, with whom she had been teetering on the edge of hostilities for months. But it was all much too convoluted in conception and was vulnerable to the obvious objection that as each part of the plan connected with every other, the possibility of something going badly wrong increased exponentially.

The amazing thing was that Napoleon nearly pulled it off, only to be thwarted by the elements. Everything was against the grand design: no one had thought how to divert Nelson from the blockade of Toulon; security was blown almost instantly, and the ease with which British secret agents got wind of the stratagem has led some scholars to conclude that Napoleon had already abandoned serious hopes of an invasion of England and was feeding disinformation to the enemy. Yet, against all the odds, on 11 January 1805 Missiesy and the Rochefort fleet evaded its windbound blockaders and, even more incredibly, Villeneuve too escaped from Toulon while Nelson's ships were watering in Sardinia. Despite crowding on sail, Nelson was unable to catch up with or even locate Villeneuve and for the first time England's greatest sailor began to feel genuine alarm.

Yet Villeneuve, having momentarily outwitted the British, was laid low by the weather. After a terrible battering in the Gulf of Lyons, he lost his nerve and crept back into the safety of Toulon. When Napoleon heard of his admiral's humiliating failure, his rage was a sight to behold. The volcanic anger is still evident in his correspondence in February:

'What is to be done with admirals who allow their spirits to sink and determine to hasten home at the first damage they may receive? . . . A few topmasts carried away, some casualties in a gale of wind are everyday occurrences. Two days of fine weather ought to have cheered up the crews and put everything to rights. But the greatest evil of our Navy is that the men who command it are unused to all the risks of command.'

The Emperor's withering scorn was warranted. Villeneuve's self-serving justification for his actions is decisively refuted by the fact that Nelson rode out the selfsame storms without sustaining significant damage to his ships.

It should be stressed that the British by no means simply awaited Napoleon's next move; they made serious assaults of their own, and there was always the danger that one of these might make grave inroads on the invasion flotilla and so lead to the cancellation of the whole enterprise. In September 1803 the Royal Navy bombarded Dieppe and Calais from the sea, though without momentous result. Then, in March-April 1804 it attempted to block Boulogne harbour by scuttling a group of stone-laden ships at the entrance to the harbour; however, the attempt was bedevilled by incompetent planning and adverse weather and was finally abandoned in a welter of mutual recriminations. In October and November Boulogne was bombarded with rockets, and mines and torpedoes were used, though again without effect. But the British never gave up and another such vain attack was made as late as November 1805 when all danger of an invasion had receded. There were those in England who urged amphibious assaults by commandos and marines, but the experience of the Seven Years War and even more so 1798 – when 1,400 men were lost in a futile attempt to destroy Ostend canal – argued against such tactics. The defences at Boulogne and the other Channel ports were extremely strong and the risks in landing and reembarking troops, especially in bad weather, were deemed unacceptable.

In 1805 Napoleon made his final, and in many ways most determined, attempt to gain that crucial temporary superiority at sea that would allow the Grand Army to cross the Channel. But once again his strategy was the work of a Cartesian apriorist, a mathematician used to commanding land armies and with no real understanding of the minutiae of naval warfare. The one dubious card he held that was not available to him in 1804 was the Spanish navy, for Spain had finally entered the war in December 1804. But the Emperor's attempts to confront the Royal Navy with an equally large Franco-Spanish fleet simply meant that problems of logistics and coordination were compounded. The elements of the putative grand Armada were now dispersed in six different ports, the French in Toulon, Rochefort, Brest and Ferrol, the Spanish in Cadiz and Cartagena.

On 2 March 1805 Napoleon composed a memorandum setting out his grand naval strategy for that year. Villeneuve was ordered to find ways of breaking out of Toulon again and this time staying out until he had completed his mission; he was to pick up the Spanish in Cadiz and Cartagena and sail to Martinique for rendezvous with Missiesy and the Rochefort squadron (five battleships and three frigates). Since Villeneuve commanded eleven battleships, six frigates and two corvettes and the Spanish admiral Gravina had seven battleships and a frigate, at the rendezvous there should already be a powerful French fleet. Yet Napoleon's idea was that the greatest Franco-Spanish naval force ever seen should assemble at Martinique, for he also ordered Admiral Ganteaume to break out from Brest with his twenty-one ships of the line, defeat the blockading squadron at Ferrol and take the French and Spanish ships there to Martinique. A huge armada of more than forty front-line warships would then proceed to Europe, keeping away from land and shipping lanes. Since the British could not possibly know where the various French squadrons were, and still less that they had all united at Martinique, there would be only a token force on guard at Ushant and the Western Approaches. Brushing this aside, the Franco-Spanish fleet was then to make all speed to Boulogne to cover the invasion flotilla.

Napoleon envisaged the final act of the drama taking place some time between 10 June and 10 July. It is one of the great examples of wishful thinking in the history of warfare. It assumed there would be no problems from storm or high seas, that the Royal Navy would behave exactly as he predicted, and that Nelson would be toiling far in the rear when the Franco-Spanish fleet entered the Channel. It also assumed, despite the evidence of the previous year, that Villeneuve and Ganteaume would have no problem breaking the blockades at their respective ports. Most of all, it betrayed an ignorance of the elementary facts of navigation. Naturally, if an enemy army was investing French troops in a city, the blockade could be broken by sending a relieving force. Napoleon assumed the same held good at sea, but a moment's consideration should have shown him that his strategy was chimerical. If the wind was favourable for a rescue fleet sailing *from* the west to relieve a blockade, it could not at the same time be favourable for the blockaded fleet trying to escape *to* the west.

The writing was on the wall as Ganteaume failed to get out of Brest despite strenuous efforts on 26–28 March 1805, when the French admiral was stymied by the Emperor's orders that he should avoid giving battle to Calder's blockading fleet. The tight British blockade throttled a further escape bid in April. Villeneuve, however, against all the odds, did manage to get away, successfully picked up the Spanish at Cadiz and stood away for Martinique on 9 April. Sir John Orde, stationed off Cadiz, failed to take appropriate action. Nelson was left without any clear intelligence of the enemy. His guess this time was wrong, as it had been when Villeneuve first broke out in 1804 (Nelson thought the French objective was Egypt), for he thought the Toulon fleet was merely aiming to relieve Ganteaume at Brest prior to an invasion of Ireland.

Missiesy meanwhile raided throughout the West Indies, as ordered in the 1804 strategy. Too late Napoleon suddenly realized that he had not put Missiesy in the picture on his new thinking and sent him an express, with orders to await Villeneuve at Martinique and not to leave the Caribbean before the end of June. The ship bearing this message crossed with Missiesy who, finding no Villeneuve at Martinique, tried to second-guess Napoleon's intentions and decided to return to Europe. The fact was that he was in clear breach of orders, since he sailed for Europe before the last date set down in contingency instructions for the rendezvous with Villeneuve. For this he was justifiably dismissed by Napoleon, but the Emperor must share some of the blame for the confusion.

The comedy of errors continued. On 20 May Missiesy arrived at Rochefort to find that Villeneuve was trying to rendezvous with him in the West Indies. Six days earlier Villeneuve arrived at Martinique, well ahead of Nelson, who was still in Madeira, to learn that the Rochefort squadron had returned to Europe. Villeneuve's orders were to await Ganteaume in Martinique for five weeks. But on 4 June he learned that Nelson had arrived in Barbados in hot pursuit, so immediately cleared for Europe. Nelson himself, having gradually worked out the tortuous reasoning in the Emperor's mind, put about for Europe on 13 June. By now it was abundantly clear what the French strategy was.

Napoleon meanwhile was in Italy, absurdly boasting to his followers that Nelson was still in Europe, with badly damaged ships and exhausted crews. Such was his aplomb that he committed the cardinal error of trying to control a global strategy, meant to dovetail with an invasion of England, from Milan and Genoa. This was an endeavour beyond his powers even if he had been in Paris, but in Italy, where intelligence was hopelessly out of date by the time it reached him, it was pure cloud-cuckoo-land. It was almost as though the Emperor had reacted self-destructively to the manifold problems of an invasion of England by turning it into a part-time occupation. In any case, he severely underrated the enemy. It was true that for four months the British did not know where Villeneuve was, but they guessed what lay behind some pretty transparent naval posturing and simply strengthened their watch on the Western Approaches at Ushant. Napoleon could never realize that, no matter what elaborate feints and deceptions he attempted, the Royal Navy would never relax its grip on the mouth of the Channel.

But Napoleon for a time lived in a fool's paradise. Believing that Nelson had been successfully decoyed, he began to convince himself that England's downfall was now a matter of weeks rather than months. On 9 June 1805 he wrote in high euphoria:

> If England is aware of the serious game she is playing, she will raise the blockade of Brest; but I know not in truth what kind of precaution will protect her from the terrible chance she runs. A nation is very foolish, when it has no fortifications and no army, to lay itself open to seeing an army of 100,000 veteran troops land on its shores. This is the masterpiece of the flotilla. It costs a great deal of money but it is necessary for us to be masters of the sea for six hours only, and England will have ceased to exist.

Then came news of the true situation. Angry and frustrated at the unravelling of his plans, the Emperor tried to salvage something from the wreckage. Hearing that Villeneuve was returning to Europe, he sent a courier to order him to lift the Brest blockade and then proceed to the Channel – again the assumption that naval blockades were just like land sieges. He compounded this fatuity by ordering the still blockaded Ganteaume to meet him at Boulogne by the beginning of August; he omitted to tell his admiral how he was to achieve this.

On 19 July Villeneuve found himself toiling off Cape Finisterre, running in the teeth of a violent gale. The tempest gave way next day to a thick blanket of fog, which hid enemy movements; had he been able to see, Villeneuve would have observed the Atlantic fleet of Sir Robert Calder manoeuvring to tackle any French squadron trying to break Cornwallis's blockade of Brest. On 22 July the two fleets came in sight of each other. Villeneuve and Gravina engaged Calder and a four-and-a-half-hour pounding battle was the result. It was an indecisive clash, which both sides claimed as a victory, and the strategic results were also inconclusive. On the one hand, Villeneuve and Gravina were able to link with the Ferrol fleet, bringing their total strength up to twenty-nine ships of the line. On the other, Calder linked up with Cornwallis to tighten the noose around Brest.

This was the moment when a French admiral of genius might have acted decisively. If Villeneuve had headed back to Ushant immediately, he would have caught the Royal Navy between two fires, forced either to abandon the blockade of Brest or let the French into the Channel; the danger was particularly acute since an error by Cornwallis at one stage left just seventeen ships to dispute the entrance to the Channel. But he dithered in Ferrol, pointlessly having his ships repainted while complaining to all who would listen that French naval tactics were obsolete. Nelson meanwhile arrived at Gibraltar on 20 July and at once headed north to join his strength to that of Calder and Cornwallis. Thirty-six battleships now barred the entry to the Channel. The end result of all Napoleon's convoluted and serpentine global feints and stratagems was that the Royal Navy was present in strength at exactly the right point to destroy his invasion plans.

On 13 August Villeneuve learned of this new concentration of enemy forces and in despair sailed south for Cadiz, where he allowed his combined fleet to be bottled up by Admiral Collingwood with just three ships – a stunning demonstration of the moral and psychological advantage the Royal Navy enjoyed over its French counterpart. Unaware of any of these developments, Napoleon arrived at Boulogne on 3 August, imagining that the invasion launch was little more than twenty-four hours away. But when he reached his headquarters at Pont-de-Brigues he was alarmed to discover that all was not well even with the Boulogne flotilla.

There was no problem about transports: twelve hundred boats lay ready at Boulogne and another eleven hundred at nearby ports. The naval commissars in fact had done their work so well that there were more boats than soldiers to fill them. Only 90,000 of the expected 150,000 were ready to move at a moment's notice and only 3,000 of the expected 9,000 cavalry horses. And, despite the fact that they had had two years to solve the problem, Napoleon's marine engineers had not yet devised a way of getting the flotilla out to sea on a single tide; it would still take three tides to get the armada out on to the open Channel, thus lengthening the time it would lie vulnerable to devastating attacks from the Royal Navy. Morale was low among men who had been cooped up in barracks and cantonments for two years, waiting for the signal that never came. There were many altercations between bored and rampaging soldiers and local civilians, including a notorious pitched battle in 1805 between female camp followers and local women, which reads like the village affray in *Tom Jones* and produced more than fifty casualties.

However, none of this affected Napoleon's superb confidence. Constant records that Napoleon diverted himself with the charms of a beautiful Genoese courtesan. As late as the morning of 23 August he was still able to write that in his imagination he saw the tricolour fluttering over the Tower of London. Then a messenger arrived with news that Villeneuve had retreated to Cadiz where he was now bottled up. By all accounts, this time Napoleon completely lost control of himself and was frothing at the mouth like a madman. After an outburst of violent and unprecedented rage, which his followers thought would probably end in an apoplectic fit, Napoleon that night allowed himself a few snatches of sick frustration as he wrote: 'What a Navy! What sacrifices all for nothing! All hope is gone! Villeneuve, instead of entering the Channel, has taken refuge in Cadiz. It is all over.'

After 23 August 1805 the invasion of England was never again a live option for Napoleon. Blaming Villeneuve for the débâcle, on 18 September he sent Admiral Rosily to Cadiz as the new Admiral of the Fleet together with a letter of dismissal for Villeneuve. This turned out to be another of Napoleon's psychological errors. To forestall the shame of replacement, Villeneuve took the Franco-Spanish armada out of Cadiz and into the jaws of the powerful fleet Nelson had assembled on the Atlantic side of Gibraltar. The battle of Trafalgar, fought on 21 October, resulted in catastrophic defeat for Villeneuve and was one of the most glorious episodes in the history of the Royal Navy. Supremely important in the history and legend of England and Horatio Nelson, Trafalgar is a mere footnote in the story of Napoleon, who had already called off his invasion plans two months before the battle. Yet Trafalgar always haunted Napoleon. After 1805 he rarely risked his warships. Four more ships of the line were captured two weeks after Trafalgar, five were taken off Santo Domingo in February 1806, five destroyed by fireships in the Basque roads in April 1809 and two destroyed in the Mediterranean in October the same year. But that completes the tally in the Emperor's ill-fated attempt to wage naval warfare against England.

These were rare opportunities for the Royal Navy, since Napoleon after Trafalgar kept his squadrons in port as a permanent threat – one the British did not take lightly as he continually added to the number of his capital ships. A war of nerves developed, with the Emperor constantly fomenting rumours of invasion, particularly of Ireland or the colonies. He encouraged his privateers to prey on British shipping and tried to secure the fleets of neutral European powers. His clever policy of keeping warships in full readiness in French ports meant that the Royal Navy could never relax and, more importantly, that Britain had to maintain its

Navy on permanent red alert, with the astronomical costs this entailed. The British were also wrongfooted diplomatically, by being forced into illegal interventions against neutral shipping, as at Copenhagen in 1807.

Napoleon's ill-starred attempt to invade England in 1803–05 was essentially vitiated by his lack of understanding of the sea and the problems faced by mariners. He expected his admirals to move like generals, without regard to wind and wave, and was notably unforgiving when they failed to come up to the mark. To an extent he was unlucky, since the 'French Nelson', La Touche-Tréville, died unexpectedly and he was left with second-rate men. Bruix and Missiesy felt his wrath, but none more so than Villeneuve. Taken prisoner after Trafalgar, when his flagship *Bucentaure* was forced to strike colours, Villeneuve remained in captivity in England until April 1806. Returning to France and learning that he was still in deep disgrace with the Emperor, Villeneuve, aged just 43, stabbed himself to death at Rennes.

Ironically, it was to Villeneuve that Napoleon owed potentially his best chance of a successful descent on England. For six days in March 1805, while Villeneuve was luring Nelson away to the Caribbean, the Channel opposite Boulogne was virtually unguarded. But by this time Napoleon had convinced himself that a crossing could never be made except under cover of a fleet. In any case, he was not at Boulogne in March, and here we see clearly the gravest defect of the imperial invasion plans. Too often Napoleon's mind was on other things, when an invasion project required monomaniacal twenty-four-hour concentration. The enemy he should always have focused on was England. But he wasted his intellectual substance on a dozen other projects: making himself King of Italy, destroying the Holy Roman Emperor, founding the Confederation of the Rhine, reviving Poland, adding Illyria to his empire, colliding with Russia in the east. He should have grasped that England was the paramount problem and devoted all his resources to defeating her. Why, for instance, did he spend on his navy not even a tenth of the sum he lavished on continental warfare? Napoleon seems always to have underrated the problem of England, to have regarded her as a 'noise offstage', to have viewed her as an obstacle to his plans rather than as the one enemy above all others who had to be defeated. Yet concentrating on England required a different, more Fabian, cast of personality. Even his hero Hannibal was prepared to settle in for a fifteen-year war of attrition against Rome. But Napoleon was temperamentally too impatient: he always wanted spectacular results and he wanted them *now*.

This inability to concentrate and the hopeless failure of Napoleon's invasion plans in 1803–05 has tempted some historians, unwisely, to suggest that the projected descent on England was always a feint, designed to mask continental ambitions. According to this view, the huge army assembled at Boulogne was actually used against Austria and Russia, so this must have been the emperor's intention all along. Besides, he never abandoned his Italian ambitions and actively pursued them when he was supposed to be concentrating on the problem of England. And if he truly wanted to invade England, would he really have provoked Austria and Russia to the point where they were likely, had he crossed the Channel, to launch themselves on France's undefended flank? Moreover, Desbrière, the great student of Napoleon's invasion plans, detected a number of strange discrepancies and oversights in both the detailed planning at Boulogne and the overall strategy, leading him to doubt the seriousness of Napoleon's intentions.

The 'feint' view was always encouraged by Napoleon when Emperor, as part of the propaganda image of his invincibility and infallibility. Since he had failed lamentably at Boulogne in 1803–05, it was in his interest to pretend that he had never seriously intended to invade England. But on St Helena he finally admitted the truth: he was in deadly earnest but had bungled things. All relevant circumstantial evidence bears this out. Even if he had been willing to spend millions of francs on 2,500 invasion craft he knew would never be used, how do we explain the agonizing about the need for covering fleet action? A feint to deceive European powers would have worked perfectly well without ordering Villeneuve, Ganteaume and the other admirals to the West Indies to draw off defending squadrons. If Napoleon was merely feinting, he must have been the greatest actor of all time, and his terrifying rage when he learned of Villeneuve's retreat to Cadiz the cheap trick of a thespian and charlatan. Besides, if he was feinting, Napoleon was certainly playing with fire. It was certainly possible that Ganteaume and Villeneuve could have combined and entered the Channel while Nelson was still far away in the Atlantic. If that had happened, the alleged 'bluff' at Boulogne would have been called in truly spectacular fashion.

However, it is certainly true that the assembly of a huge army at Boulogne turned out to be an act of serendipity from the viewpoint of the general political and military crisis – one that Napoleon confronted in 1805 as the result of his centrifugal foreign policy, where no one clear aim was ever pursued to the exclusion of others. Even as he assembled the Grand Army at Boulogne, his thoughts often turned to the occupation of the Italian ports of Taranto, Otranto and Brindisi as springboards for an assault on Turkey. Was this the Promethean mind of a genius or simply a rational objective – the invasion of England – being overwhelmed by the 'Oriental complex'?

By 1805 the European powers had lost patience with Napoleon and English gold gave them the necessary push to go to war. Even so, the genesis of the third coalition was complex, with Austria and Russia actuated by very different considerations. Austria was furious with Napoleon for his annexation of Genoa, Piedmont and Elba, his conversion of the Cisalpine Republic into a kingdom (with himself as King), his occupation of Naples and his provocative aping of Charlemagne in May 1805, when he crowned himself Emperor of Italy in Milan cathedral, using the Lombardy crown. All of this was not only contrary to the Treaty of Lunéville but exposed the hollowness of Napoleon's assurances, given on each fresh annexation, that this was positively his last territorial ambition. Further offence was given by Napoleon's so-called 'mediation' in Switzerland, and this turned to outrage when the French Emperor proceeded to reconstruct Germany: he reduced the Holy Roman Empire from 350 princelings to just 39 and made himself the guarantor of this trivial remainder.

Talleyrand once more warned Napoleon that Austria would not stand idly by and see her spheres of influence in both Germany and Italy so blatantly truncated. He argued that peace with Austria was the lodestone by which the Emperor should steer his foreign policy; otherwise France would be involved in a never-ending cycle of European warfare. He proposed getting Austria to acquiesce in the loss of Italy by offering her Moldavia and Wallachia at the mouth of the Danube. This would have a twofold effect: it would detach Austria from Russia and link Vienna with France in the drive towards Turkey and the East. But Napoleon wanted none of it.

Russian feelings towards France were even more complexly layered by 1805. On paper the natural geopolitical impulse should have brought Russia and Britain to blows. The Russians coveted the Baltic states and wanted a sphere of influence in the Mediterranean from which to attack its traditional enemy, Turkey; there were persistent demands, which Napoleon encouraged, that Russia be allowed to occupy Malta. But Britain did not want the Baltic supplies of timber, tar and hemp, crucial for the Royal Navy, in Russian hands, and it was a tradition of British foreign policy to support the 'Sick Man of Europe'. Moreover, British commercial interests were adamant that Malta could not be given up.

Additionally, Czar Alexander I, on acceding in 1801, encouraged a culture of Anglomania and made it plain that he intended to fulfil the long-standing Russian desire to be a major diplomatic player in Europe; some said Alexander inherited an acute inferiority complex about the West. The murder of d'Enghien in 1804 finally tipped the balance against Napoleon, for Alexander considered it a personal affront: he had set himself up as self-appointed leader and spokesman for Europe's crowned heads. The British cunningly encouraged the Czar to shift his Mediterranean interest towards Italy, the Levant and modern Yugoslavia, which Napoleon regarded as his sphere of influence and where he was unwilling to make concessions. And money finally did the trick: Alexander could not resist the financial deal struck with Britain, whereby Russia received £1,250,000 a year for every 100,000 troops she put in the field.

Since the Third Coalition would start a process whereby Russia became virtually supreme arbiter in Europe by 1815, and since Napoleon is often facilely bracketed with Hitler, it is worth dwelling on the geopolitics of all this and separating fact from propaganda. Napoleon's foolish intransigence and his desire to have a finger in every pie in 1805 was rightly condemned by Talleyrand, who saw where it would all lead. But we should also be aware of the humbug and hypocrisy in the Third Coalition. Why was a simple demand like 'natural frontiers' by France regarded as unacceptable by Britain yet Russian meddling in the Mediterranean was justified? Why was Russian seizure of Corfu as a *pis aller* for Malta not portrayed as warmongering by a British press always so eager to detect all such manifestations. Horror was expressed when Russia made itself a European power in 1945 but the prospect was viewed with complacency in 1805–15. Special pleading was never seen to such good effect as in the justifications by Britain for Russian expansionism after 1805.

By April 1805 British diplomacy had smoothed away Russian distrust of London's intentions in the eastern Mediterranean and, after extremely difficult negotiations between Pitt (who had returned to office in 1803) and Novosiltsov, an Anglo-Russian alliance was completed on 11 April at St Petersburg. Austria, initially reluctant to join an anti-French coalition if Prussia remained neutral, was inveigled into Pitt's web after Napoleon's coronation in Milan. Many Austrians, including General Mack, were confident they could beat France in a new war, so in June Vienna's Aulic Council began making overtures to Pitt. In August 1805 Austria formally protested to Napoleon over his seizure of Savoy, and a treaty of alliance was then signed with Pitt and Alexander. Talleyrand performed sterling service in keeping Prussia neutral, which he did by making over Hanover. So the Third Coalition was in being. It was an unwieldy alliance, where all three partners were motivated by different *raisons d'état* and where personal feelings also entered into play: Pitt was involved in an anti-Bonaparte crusade, Czar Alexander was moved by megalomania and jealousy of Napoleon; and the Austrian aristocracy by a patrician distaste for the new upstart empire and its bogus nobility.

The overt aims of the Third Coalition, which was soon supplemented by Sweden and the Kingdom of Naples, were to expel France from Hanover, Holland and North Germany, to clear the French out of Switzerland, northern Italy and Naples. The covert aims, divulged only in secret clauses of the treaty of alliance, were to deny France the 'natural frontiers' and to restrict her to the borders as in 1791: the ultimate aim of course was to return Europe to the pre-1789 world of the *ancien régime*. On paper Napoleon faced a formidable array of enemies, since the Austrian army was 250,000 strong, the Russians were expected to put another 200,000 in the field, and incursions in peripheral roles could be expected from the Swedes, Neapolitans and British, perhaps providing another 50,000 troops in all.

Quite undaunted by the odds, Napoleon revelled in the prospect of new battles. On 25 August he sent Murat to Germany on a secret reconnaissance mission and the same day wrote to Talleyrand: 'The die is cast. The operation has begun. On the 17th I will be in Germany with 200,000 men.' But he had jumped the gun, for there were factors he had overlooked. The outbreak of a general European war provoked a crisis at the Bank of France. Rumours were rife that Napoleon had emptied the bank's coffers when he left on campaign. The ensuing panic increased the embarrassment of a bank which had already been compromised by an unwise speculation in Mexican piastres by the Ministry for the Treasury. A low tax yield in 1804 left the State unprepared for the heavy expenses of the Grand Army on active campaign. Moreover, the 1806 economic depression in France was widely blamed on the general crisis of confidence arising from the unpopular return to large-scale continental hostilities (the two-year struggle against England often seemed from France to be a mere 'phoney war').

Napoleon was caught in a dilemma between needing a quick military victory to restore public confidence and needing to return to Paris to put the economy on a proper footing before he could begin campaigning. He had an additional technical problem about conscription, since he intended to call up 80,000 men in advance of the legal age of twenty. Leaving Boulogne on 3 September, he arrived in Paris two days later and was obliged to spend three weeks there, passing emergency measures that would enable his military plans to mature. His conscription proposals were intensely unpopular both with the public and the Legislature and to get his way the Emperor had to rush through the necessary legislation by *senatus consultum*.

He was now ready for the campaign itself. He planned to hit the Austrians hard before the Russians had time to join them and to do this he needed to get 210,000 troops to the Danube as fast as possible. There would be seven corps, each of which originally contained between two and four infantry divisions, a brigade or division of cavalry, about 40 cannon, plus engineers and back-up troops. In addition to the seven corps, he would dispose of a cavalry reserve of two divisions of cuirassiers, four of mounted dragoons and one each of dismounted dragoons and light cavalry; altogether there would be 22,000 horsemen plus an artillery reserve of twenty-four guns, or a quarter of the total cannon in the army. Over and above this was the Grand Reserve, comprising the Imperial Guard and various detachments of élite grenadiers; including second-line troops the *Grande Armée* probably had a total strength of 350,000 in 1805.

Now was revealed the happy accident of the troop build-up at Boulogne for the invasion of England. This in itself should have alerted the Austrians, who continued to think, despite all the evidence, that the main theatre of operations for the coming campaign would be in Italy. They seemed to imagine that this was Napoleon's chosen terrain, overlooking or forgetting that in 1796 and 1800 it was pure force of circumstances that made Napoleon fight in Italy. In those campaigns there were rival generals like Moreau in the Rhine-Danube theatre, but in 1805 they were no more and the Emperor had a clear field to himself. Napoleon had anticipated that an Austrian strike would manifest itself either as an invasion of northern Italy or an attack on Alsace from the Danube; he had already decided to strike first and eliminate the danger on the Danube before the Russians could come up.

The initial attack by the Austrians in Bavaria gave Napoleon the perfect excuse to withdraw from Boulogne without losing face. Leaving Brune in charge of the camp at Boulogne, he ordered the Grand Army to cross the Rhine on 24–25 September; he himself left Paris on the 24th and, travelling via Nancy, was in Strasbourg on the 26th. The seven corps were commanded by Bernadotte, Marmont, Davout, Soult, Lannes, Ney and Augereau, with a cavalry reserve under Murat, and the entire force marched on the Rhine in well-planned itineraries which had been the object of Murat's secret mission the month before. The Austrians played into his hands by assuming that the main French effort would still come in Italy, and by miscalculating how long it would take the Russians to join them. In contrast to the streamlined efficiency of

Napoleon's army, the allied chain of command was poor. The Russian commander Kutusov was instructed by the Czar to take orders from the Austrian Emperor Francis but not from any other Austrian general. Even within the Austrian army the chain of command was unclear as the Emperor Francis left it vague whether General Mack or Archduke Ferdinand should have the final say.

Meanwhile everything about Napoleon's plans worked like clockwork. His strategy was to wheel south and envelop Mack's army, after which he would turn and deal with the Russians. Masséna would hold the ring in Italy, and there would be smaller armies in Naples and Boulogne to deal with any allied descents there. But the showpiece of the campaign was to be the lightning advance on the Danube. It should be emphasized that nothing like this had ever before been attempted in the history of warfare. The great French captain of the seventeenth century, the vicomte de Turenne, had an axiom that great strategic movements could be attempted with a maximum of 50,000 men only, and Marlborough's famous dash to the Danube in 1704 involved no more than 40,000. The originality of Napoleon's conception was to attempt the war of movement with large numbers. It was to solve this conundrum that he divided his army of 210,000 into seven independent corps.

The left wing of the Grand Army moved out from Hanover and Utrecht to the rendezvous at Württemberg, while the centre and right, from the Channel ports, converged on Mannheim and Strasbourg on the middle Rhine. The vast host made for splendid viewing, presenting a panorama of different units and a riot of corresponding colour. There were lancers in red shapkas and white plumes eighteen inches long; chasseurs in kolbachs with plumes of green and scarlet; hussars in shakos and plumes; dragoons in tigerskin turbans; cuirassiers in steel helmets with copper crests and horsehair manes; carabiniers in dazzling white with classically styled helmets. The grenadiers of the Old Guard were especially impressive in their long blue coats and massive bearskins with powdered coifs and gold earrings. The Grand Army was a gallimauffry of fringes, buttons, epaulettes, braids, stripes, leather and fur trimmings, all in a kaleidoscope of colours – scarlet, purple, yellow, blue, gold and silver.

The entire Army then crossed the river and, while Murat's cavalry feinted towards the Black Forest to bamboozle Mack, the seven army corps swept through Germany, for a final rendezvous on the Danube, aimed at cutting the Austrian communications. Each corps was routed along a separate line of march, thus avoiding congestion and pressure on food supplies. As always in the Napoleonic system, the corps were within one to two days' march of each other. Every day Napoleon liked to ride out on a tour of inspection, accompanied by his chief of staff Berthier, Caulaincourt, his Master of Horse, and Bacler d'Albe, the head of the Topographic Unit. Others in the immediate entourage were the duty marshal of the day, two aides, two orderly officers, an equerry, a page (carrying the Emperor's telescope), and a soldier carrying the portfolio containing maps and compasses. Also present were Roustam and an interpreter. Slightly ahead of the main party rode two more orderlies and an officer commanding a dozen cavalrymen. About a thousand yards behind the retinue lurked the main escort: four squadrons of Guard cavalry.

At first morale in his army was high, but it was dampened later when the weather broke. Performing prodigies of marching – some twenty miles a day – the Grand Army normally completed its day's trek by noon, having started at 4–5 a.m.; the afternoon would be spent foraging before the earliest of early nights. French staff work was brilliant and the enemy was left confused, unable to work out from the movements of discrete corps what was their likely ultimate objective. The speed and secrecy of the advance were such that within twenty days the Army was at Mayence and crossed the Danube without opposition. By travelling through the valley of the Main and via Donauwörth on the Danube, Napoleon cut off Mack's retreat. Beaten at Elchingen on 14 October and falling back generally after a few more sharp engagements, Mack realized too late that he was in a trap and would not be relieved by the Russians. He surrendered with 50,000 men at Ulm on 20 October, the day before Trafalgar.

At a stroke Napoleon was able to restore morale and business confidence in Paris. His bulletins, explaining and justifying the military operations, turned the Grand Army into a thing of legend and its exploits were read to spellbound audiences by actors, teachers, priests and town officials. The myth of a national army was born, but the *Grande Armée* was always the Emperor's personal instrument. Nor was the campaign as streamlined as in the Bonapartist propaganda version. The supply line held up well, there were ample boots and pay was prompt, but by November there were 8,000 soldiers on the sick list and large numbers of horses had perished because of the pace of advance. The men were tired, and Napoleon himself confessed to Josephine in a letter on 19 October that he had never been so exhausted. More worrying was the widespread theft and indiscipline in the army, which reached such proportions that by 25 November the Emperor was forced to set up military commissions with summary powers.

Napoleon's next objective was Kutusov and the Russians: by threatening Vienna he would force the allies to concentrate there. But Kutusov refused to be gulled into a defence of the Austrian capital that would hand the initiative to Napoleon and so retreated, forcing Archduke Frederick to go with him. For the first time Napoleon's well-laid plans began to go awry. Murat the glory-hunter set out with his cavalry to be the first in Vienna instead of harassing Kutusov, and earned the Emperor's angry censure. Bernadotte, whether through incompetence or conscious treachery, brought his corps across the Danube a day late, thus vitiating Napoleon's clever plan for the encirclement of Kutusov. French honour was restored by Mortier who, with General Dupont, fought a numerically superior Russian force to a standstill at Durrensten. But, as with all French battles with the Russians, this one was marked by its heavy casualties: 3,000 on the French side against 4,000 Russians.

On 12 November Murat and his riders reached Vienna; there was no resistance as the Austrians had declared it an open city. While the Grand Army took possession of 500 cannon, 100,000 muskets and a huge cache of ammunition, the Emperor, arriving on 15 November, amused himself by spending the night with an Austrian beauty; they conversed in the language of love, since she spoke no French and Napoleon no German. But by 23 November the Emperor was forced to rest the Grand Army: the troops who had campaigned non-stop for eight weeks were exhausted and on the point of cracking. The critical point of the entire strategic operation had now been reached. French lines of communication were stretched taut and likely to snap if the Russians retreated any farther. On the other hand, there was an abiding danger that the Archduke Charles might retreat from the Italian front and link up with the Russians on the Danube. There were also fears that Prussia was about to enter the war on the Allied side, and any retreat by the French, be it never so strategic, could be construed as a defeat and thus give Berlin the final nudge. Lacking the resources to envelop the enemy, Napoleon had to tempt them to attack by feigning weakness.

Learning that Kutusov had retreated north towards Olmutz, where he linked up with a second Russian army under General Buxhowden, Napoleon sent one-third of his army, under Soult, Lannes and Murat, to occupy the village of Austerlitz, east of Brunn in Bohemia (later Czechoslovakia), and the nearby Pratzen heights. Having thinned his army to 53,000 – a tempting target for the 89,000-strong allies – Napoleon laid plans for the rapid arrival of 22,000 reinforcements (under Davout and Bernadotte) who would come on the scene of the intended battle by forced marches. He gave every sign of being weak and having

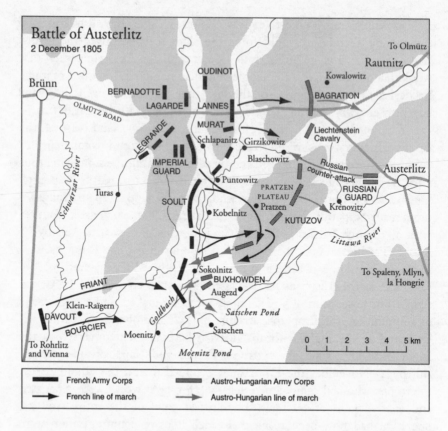

Battle of Austerlitz
2 December 1805

To Olmütz

Rautnitz

Brünn

OUDINOT

Kowalowitz

BERNADOTTE

BAGRATION

LAGARDE   LANNES

OLMÜTZ ROAD

MURAT

Liechtenstein
Cavalry

Schlapanitz   Girzikowitz

LEGRANDE

Blaschowitz

Russian
counter-attack

Austerlitz

IMPERIAL
GUARD

Puntowitz

PRATZEN
PLATEAU

RUSSIAN
GUARD

Schwarzar River

Turas

SOULT

Kobelnitz

Pratzen

Krenovitz

KUTUZOV

Littawa River

Sokolnitz

To Spaleny, Mlyn,
la Hongrie

FRIANT

BUXHOWDEN

Augezd

Klein-Raïgern

Satschen Pond

DAVOUT

Goldbach

BOURCIER

Moenitz

Satschen

0   1   2   3   4   5 km

To Rohrlitz
and Vienna

Moenitz Pond

French Army Corps   Austro-Hungarian Army Corps

French line of march   Austro-Hungarian line of march

overreached himself. When the Austrian Emperor Francis offered
an armistice on 27 November, Napoleon appeared almost pathetically
eager to accept. The French envoy to the parley in the Austrian camp
reported the Allies seriously divided, with the Emperor Francis and
Kutusov cautious but the Czar and most of the Austrian generals keen to
strike.

On 28 November Napoleon made the bait almost irresistible by
ordering Soult to pull out of Austerlitz and the Pratzen heights. Pursuing
his career as great actor, the Emperor next agreed to an interview with
the Russian emissary Count Dolgorouki (29 November) in which he
feigned confusion, uncertainty and an ill-disguised fear. So brilliantly was
he toying with the enemy and so confident of his own mastery that he had
actually chosen his battleground on 21 November. Since he lacked the
numbers to envelop the enemy, the final piece in his chessboard of
disinformation involved tricking the enemy into uncovering their rear.
He gambled that uncovering his own line of retreat by the withdrawal
from the Pratzen heights would lead the Allies to expose their rear. He

was in good spirits which not even terrible falls of snow and hail could dampen. His chamberlain Alexandre Thiard recorded that there was an enthusiastic dinner conversation about the Egyptian campaign.

Scenting victory, the allies advanced south-west towards Brunn and occupied the Pratzen heights unopposed on 1 December. That night both armies camped within sight of each other by the Bosenitz and Goldbach rivers. Unknown to the allies, Bernadotte's I Corps arrived on 1 December while the leading division of Davout's III Corps got to within striking distance that night by covering the sixty miles from Vienna in under 72 hours. Napoleon used his cavalry as a screen so that the enemy could not detect the arrival of these reinforcements. He drew up his army so that the allies would be tempted to attack him on the right. He placed most of the army, spearheaded by Lannes's V Corps, on his left and centre, with Bernadotte's corps concealed behind it; other units placed here were Murat's cavalry, Oudinot's grenadiers and part of Soult's IV Corps under generals Vandamme and St Hilaire. Strung out on the right, holding down very extended positions, were the men of Soult's third division under General Legrand, covered by Davout's unsuspected force. The bait was obvious, and perhaps too obvious, but the allies took it.

The night of 1–2 December was long, dark and cold. Few slept and Napoleon's men assuaged the boredom and waiting by holding a torchlight procession to commemorate the anniversary of his coronation. Thiard recorded that at dinner, which the emperor sat down to at 5 p.m. in the thickening gloom, Napoleon's conversation was the most animated he had ever witnessed. On the Pratzen the allies held their final conference; the elderly Kutusov took no part but slept right through it. Deprived of the support of the aged Russian general, the cautious Emperor Francis could make no headway against the hotheads led by the twenty-eight-year-old Czar Alexander and the Austrian general Weyrother. It was decided to make an all-out assault on the weak French right with 45,000 men under Buxhowden, detaching troops from the centre and the allied right for the purpose; the idea was to cut off the French retreat to Vienna. The Russian general Bagration was given the lesser task of pinning Lannes's V Corps in its defensive position on Santon hill. The enemy had thus fallen into Napoleon's trap: they would find the French right a tougher nut than expected and they had denuded their own centre.

Dawn broke on 2 December to reveal dense fog. Napoleon mounted his Arab horse and gave orders that every unit had to keep five spare horses ready in case the imperial staff needed them. It was one of those days when the weather dictated that all messages would have to be sent by horseback; under normal weather conditions a semaphore system conveyed intelligence at a rate of 120 m.p.h. The Russians began their great enveloping move at 4 a.m. and, after some confusion in the mist, attained their initial objectives by taking the villages of Sokolnitz and Telnitz. At 8 a.m. the surprise force of Davout's 7,000 men counter-attacked, causing a bewildered Buxhowden to summon reinforcements from the Pratzen heights. In response Napoleon ordered Oudinot's grenadiers to further strengthen the right, then checked that Lannes and Bernadotte were holding their own on the left. Satisfied on that score Napoleon next unleashed Murat's cavalry against the Russian horse. A massive encounter embroiling 10,000 horsemen ensued, from which Murat emerged triumphant.

Now seemed the moment to release Soult's two divisions (still concealed by the fog) against the Pratzen, but such was Napoleon's superb sense of timing and his sublime confidence, that he held off awhile. 'How long will it take you to storm the heights?' he asked Soult. 'Twenty minutes, sire,' replied the marshal. 'Very well,' said the Emperor. 'We will wait another quarter of an hour.' Napoleon's military genius was never more evident. By intuition he knew the exact equilibrium point at which the Pratzen would be sufficiently clear of allied troops to make Soult's task easy, but not yet so denuded that reinforcements from the heights were likely to overwhelm the hard-pressed French right.

At last, at 9 a.m. he gave the signal. The sun came out and out of the fog came Napoleon's trump card, their bayonets glistening in the sunlight. Too late Kutusov realized what was about to happen and frantically tried to recall his men from the left. To make absolutely sure there was no hitch, Napoleon called Bernadotte over from the left and sent him in Soult's wake. After heavy fighting the French were again in possession of the heights by midday, and had beaten off a succession of frenzied attacks from the Russians, commencing around 10.30. In desperation Kutusov asked his élite troops for one last effort. 1,000 men of the Russian Guard Corps streamed up the hill at 1 p.m. At first they made ground, but were soon outflanked by a combination of the cavalry of Bessières's Imperial Guard and one of Bernadotte's divisions. Crushed, the Russians scurried away down the hill, leaving Napoleon the master of Pratzen and the battlefield. He had effectively cut the Allied army in half.

As the shades of a winter evening began to appear, victory turned to rout. Napoleon moved the Imperial Guard on to the Pratzen and swung Soult's men south to the edge of the heights. He then brought up cannon and from 3.30 on began to shoot holes in the ice of the frozen lakes around the Pratzen, making great watery craters. Many of Buxhowden's men were drowned in them as the Russians attempted a panic-stricken escape. Bagration retreated ignominiously from his assault on the French left and the Allied monarchs left the field in despondency and confusion.

At Austerlitz Napoleon won his most perfect victory. This battle was to him what Gaugamela had been to Alexander, Cannae to Hannibal and Alesia to Julius Caesar. For the loss of 1,305 French dead and 6,940 wounded he had inflicted 11,000 Russian casualties and 4,000 Austrian, captured forty colours and taken 180 cannon. There was the same discrepancy in prisoners: 573 French as against 12,000 Allied captives. The superstitious Napoleon thereafter considered 2 December one of his lucky dates, but there are those who say that, consciously or unconsciously, he delayed the fighting of a battle which could have happened earlier just so that he could celebrate the anniversary of his coronation with a triumph. The 'sun of Austerlitz' also became an item in Napoleon's calendar of superstitions: he thought it significant that the sun had come out as his men surged on to the Pratzen just as it had shone through the mist on the day of his coronation.

Austerlitz confirmed that Napoleon was truly a great captain; before that it could have been claimed that he had met only second-raters. It should not be forgotten also that he had not been in a battle since Marengo five and a half years before, so that his talent for war was obviously innate and not something that needed constant practice. Writing to Josephine the day after the battle he was modest about his exploit: 'Yesterday I beat the Russians and Austrians. I am a bit tired. I have bivouacked eight hours in the open air, in very cold nights.' He complained of a stye in his eye which he was bathing with lotions of pure water mixed with hot rose water.

After their defeat the Russians retreated pell-mell to Poland. The day after the battle, Czar Alexander wrote to Savary as follows: 'Tell your master that I am going away. Tell him that he performed miracles yesterday; that the battle has increased my admiration for him; that he is a man predestined by Heaven; that it will require a hundred years for my army to equal his.' Napoleon thought this meant he could get a permanent settlement with Russia but Talleyrand, knowing the scope of the Emperor's ambitions and the geopolitical logic this involved, was always sceptical.

The Austrian Francis II asked for an interview with Napoleon and sued for terms. The dictated peace of Pressburg (signed 26 December

1805) was draconian. Austria ceded Venice, Istria, and Dalmatia to the Kingdom of Italy; Swabia and the Tyrol were given to the Electors of Württemberg and Bavaria; Austria undertook to pay an indemnity of 32 million francs in bills of exchange and eight million in cash. Even more momentous were the consequences in Germany. Napoleon rewarded his marshals by giving the Grand Duchy of Berg to Murat and Neuchâtel to Berthier; the award to Murat was in recognition of his excellent reconnaissance mission in August–September 1805 when he scouted suitable terrain under the nom-de-guerre of Colonel de Beaumont, not for his failure to intercept Kutusov.

As ever, the useless and treacherous Bernadotte was rewarded. Although Bernadotte had crossed the Danube a day late and had lacked energy in the pursuit of the enemy on the evening of Austerlitz, leading Davout to complain bitterly to the Emperor, Napoleon saw fit once more to promote him to higher office, this time making him Governor of Anspach and Prince of Pontecorvo, a tiny enclave within the Kingdom of Two Sicilies, between Sicily and Gaeta, but technically a sovereign state. Even though this donation brought Bernadotte a 200,000 franc lump sum and an annual income of 300,000 francs, Napoleon capped this by buying Moreau's house in the rue Anjou and giving it to Bernadotte as a present. The Gascon, who had plotted with Moreau against Napoleon, had no qualms about accepting the house of his erstwhile ally from the man he had wanted to overthrow.

But the perks to the marshals were the least of the ways in which Napoleon redrew the map of Germany. He promoted the Electors of Bavaria and Württemberg to crowns and fused the new kingdoms, Hesse-Darmstadt and all the principalities of south and west Germany into a Confederation of the Rhine, expressly designed as a vassal state of France. Based at Frankfurt, the Confederation left foreign and military affairs to Napoleon; he thus fulfilled a traditional aim of French foreign policy-building a buffer between France and central Europe. Naturally the immediate consequence of this new alignment was to destroy the Holy Roman Empire, since only Austria, Prussia and a few northern states were left. On 6 August 1806 the Holy Roman Empire officially ceased to exist when Francis II renounced his title of Emperor of Germany; as Francis I he retained the title Hereditary Emperor of Austria which he had assumed in 1804.

Elsewhere in Europe the consequences of Austerlitz were also groundbreaking. The Bourbons of the Kingdom of Naples were punished by expulsion for having backed the wrong horse. In their place Napoleon appointed his brother Joseph as King by simple decree on 31 March

1806. The month before, Joseph and Masséna had marched on Naples with an army of 40,000, forcing Ferdinand IV to flee to Sicily; the Neapolitan population itself reacted with indifference to the change of régime. On 15 February 1806 'King' Joseph made a triumphal entry into Naples. Napoleon meanwhile upgraded the Batavian republic to the Kingdom of Holland and put in Louis as the new King. These new kingdoms created out of nepotism created some ominous rumblings. Murat, jealous of any privilege that he himself did not possess, warned Napoleon that he was going too far, but the Emperor discerned his motive and ignored him; in retaliation Murat began to intrigue with Fouché and Talleyrand.

Napoleon himself did not return to Paris until 26 January, having spent the first three weeks of the new year in Munich and Stuttgart. He was greeted with enthusiasm by a Paris proud both of the great victory and the triumphalist peace that succeeded it. He was reasonably confident that the peace would hold, especially since he had placated Prussia by ceding Hanover to her. His most implacable enemy, Pitt, was dead. Allegedly he remarked on hearing of Austerlitz: 'Roll up that map of Europe. It will not be needed these ten years,' and there are even some who claim that he died of a broken heart after seeing his old enemy master of Europe. Pitt was replaced by Fox, well known for his French sympathies. Yet even a prime minister is the prisoner of entrenched financial interests, so it was not long before Fox was heard to say that he could not accept French suzerainty in Sicily. In Russia too after a brief struggle the Francophobe party regained the upper hand. It looked as though Talleyrand was right, and the fundamental logic of power politics would always prevail, no matter what the personal sympathies of foreign rulers.

The campaign of Austerlitz saw the *Grande Armée* in its first full appearance. It would grow in size until in 1812 some 630,000 men were mobilized, but by late 1805 Napoleon's military system was essentially what it would remain. The main features of his success were surprise, mobility, seizing and keeping the initiative and, above all, the flexibility of the corps system where each corps, in effect a miniature army 17–30,000 strong, was capable of living off the land and fighting superior enemy detachments. Clearly the personality of the Emperor himself was all-important: here was a man who lived for war and told Josephine, in a letter dated 9 February 1806, that reading an army list was his favourite occupation and gave him most pleasure when tired. But even a military genius needs a well-oiled machine and highly motivated soldiers to carry out his brilliant schemes. Both these assets Napoleon possessed.

The issue of morale is crucial. Some historians have overdone this and painted a picture of a citizens' army, fuelled by revolutionary élan, sweeping away the corrupt and demoralized armies of the rotten *ancien régime*. But the old cliché contains *some* truth. It has to be conceded that social mobility, such an important feature of the Revolutionary years, dried up under Napoleon. Under the Republic there had been 170 new appointments as general in a single year, but under Napoleon the highest number was thirty-seven. On the other hand, among those who would have blushed unseen in the pre-1789 system were Napoleon himself, eighteen of his marshals and generals like Junot, Friant, Vandamme, Montbrun and Delaborde. Half the generals in 1805 had been commissioned since 1789 though, as we have conceded, this hardly redounds to Napoleon's credit.

The impact of the French Revolution on the level of skills and talents in the Grand Army can scarcely be denied. Importantly, French generals were usually much younger than their enemy counterparts: in 1805 the average age of generals in the Austrian army was 63 and, in the war against Prussia in 1806, out of 142 Prussian generals 79 were over sixty and only thirteen under fifty. Moreover, French officers were there on merit, whereas enemy officers were often elderly, impoverished and lieutenants who had clawed their way up from the ranks or were 'silly ass' young noblemen. The contrast continued into the ranks. Most of the *Grande Armée*'s soldiers had at least a year's service to their credit; they were brilliant at living off the land; their morale was high as they thought themselves invincible and even, imbued as they were with the ideology of the French Revolution, superior to the benighted infantry of the *ancien régime* armies.

Another aspect of the Grand Army's success was its use of skirmishers, who were highly trained and invulnerable to all but other skirmishers. Although these were shock troops and did great damage in the 'softening up' phase of a battle, *ancien régime* armies were chary of using them, as they were thought too independent, too free-thinking and therefore prejudicial to discipline and a standing invitation to desert. Until the Spanish experience in 1808, aristocratic régimes feared to arm the masses for a popular war against Napoleon, lest the selfsame people turn their guns first against the native oligarchy.

Napoleon's military machine has provoked more argument, with some regarding it as a model of how army staffwork should be conducted and others finding it defective, overelaborate, needlessly complex and productive of errors, oversights, omissions and excessive duplication. As with all Napoleon's civil and military hierarchies, the devil was in the detail. The other problem was that hardy perennial of all bureaucracies: proliferation. Beginning with 400 officers and 5,000 men in 1805 the Imperial Headquarters swelled to 3,500 officers and 10,000 men by 1812. Apart from the personnel of the General Commissary of Army Stores, HQ housed the Emperor's personal staff and servants and the general staff of the *Grande Armée*.

The three key men were Alexandre Berthier, Minister of War and Chief of Staff of the Grand Army; Christophe Duroc, the Grand Marshal of the Palace, also in charge of the imperial household, family and servants and incidentally procurer of beautiful women for the Emperor; and the Master of Horse, General Armand de Caulaincourt, later Duke of Vicenza, in charge of stables, pages, messenger services and imperial escorts. Reporting to Duroc were Constant and the other three valets; the Mameluke bodyguard Roustam; the prefect of the Palace (also Duroc's deputy), plus secretaries, physicians, equerries, pages, butlers and servants. Because Napoleon esteemed Duroc and liked him more than any other man, he also put him in charge of liaison between the Emperor's personal staff and his planning staff. However, Duroc did not oversee Napoleon's private secretaries – the channel between the Emperor and his ministers – of whom the chief from 1796–1802 had been Bourrienne. Dismissed for peculation and larceny, he was replaced by Meneval. A much more long-running personality was Bacler d'Albe, who served Napoleon from 1796 to 1813 as head of his Topographical Office. He was in charge of all Napoleon's military maps, where he placed different coloured pins to denote battle positions. Bacler d'Albe was an invariable part of the retinue that accompanied the Emperor when he rode out to his vantage point to direct a battle or inspect individual units.

If the general staff presented a mixed picture to contrast with the great success of the corps system, the Imperial Guard itself remained the great unknown, since Napoleon consistently refused to send it into battle, even when its appearance would probably have won the day for him. In 1805 there was as yet only the 'Old Guard' – foot grenadiers, *chasseurs*, mounted grenadiers, dragoons, lancers, Mamelukes, *gendarmes d'élite* and *chasseurs à cheval*, but mainly grenadiers and élite cavalry, some 12,000 in all. The Guard was itself a growth industry. Formed from the core of bodyguards known as the Guides, added to successively by the Guards of the Directory, the Legislative Assembly and the Consular Guard, the reconstituted Imperial Guard of December 1804 contained 5,000 grenadiers and 2,000 cavalry (with artillerymen for its twenty-four guns, a total of 8,000). By mid-1805 alone there had been a fifty per cent increase in numbers and by 1812 there were 56,169 Guardsmen. The Old

Guard was supplemented in 1806 by the Middle Guard, formed from two fusilier regiments and added to in 1812–13 by two regiments of flankers, all crack shots. A third body, the Young Guards, was formed in 1809 from the choice recruits into the best regiments of light infantry, *voltigeurs* and *tirailleurs*.

By 1814 the strength of the three sections of the Imperial Guard totalled an incredible 112,482. The minimum entry qualification was five years' service and two campaigns. Guardsmen were paid on a differential scale: Guard privates were paid as ordinary sergeants, corporals as ordinary sergeant-majors, and so on; special rations, equipment and even special food completed the sense of being an élite formation. Until 1813 the Emperor would never send this crack corps into battle, and even then he held back his beloved Old Guard. Some said he thereby took the edge off the fighting calibre of the Guard, so that when it was finally called on to perform, it bore itself with lacklustre. Others complained that it was absurd to hold a huge, overmanned body in permanent reserve when the regiments doing the actual fighting had thereby been drained of their best manpower.

Such was the *Grande Armée* that won Austerlitz. Many students of Napoleon consider it a supreme irony that he should have brought his armies to such a pitch of perfection at the very time a misguided foreign policy meant that all their valour would ultimately be in vain. If there are those who think Napoleon began to go wrong at Lunéville and Amiens, there are many more who think that Austerlitz was the turning point, the moment when a traditional French foreign policy became a purely personal Napoleonic one. The key error was the construction of the Confederation of the Rhine, which meant that a lasting settlement with Austria and Prussia would never be possible. Sooner or later, given Czar Alexander's conception of his position, Prussia, Austria and Russia were bound to unite, in which case not even Napoleon would be able to resist them. It is thus that we may appreciate the truth of Pieter Geyl's words: 'Napoleon's wars were his own wars, made inevitable by his measureless greed for power, wars which never served the interest of France, wars for which the deceived and all too patient nation paid with the blood of its sons and in the end with the territorial gains won by the Republic.'

CHAPTER SIXTEEN

The afterglow of Austerlitz was ruined almost immediately by news of a financial crisis back in France. It must be stressed that at this point the crisis was financial only rather than economic in a general sense. A run on the banks had been triggered by the discovery that millions of government bonds had disappeared from the Treasury, bringing ruin to thousands of investors. The hubbub only subsided when the Emperor returned to France at the end of January 1806; after thorough investigation he suspended the Minister of the Treasury, Barbe-Marbois, on suspicion of embezzlement.

Until September 1806 Napoleon remained in Paris, dealing with a plethora of vexatious domestic affairs and disputes involving the marshalate. One of the first cases might have warned him that Naples was always going to be a thorn in his side. Gouvion St-Cyr was a highly talented general, uncorrupt, with a lifelong hatred of freemasonry, and an early protégé of Desaix's. A brilliant organizer, he had recommended himself to Napoleon by his dislike of Jourdan and Moreau. He was on the shortlist of possible marshals in 1804, but ruined his chances by refusing to sign a proclamation which congratulated Bonaparte on becoming Emperor. In Naples he clashed spectacularly with Murat and Masséna and in disgust with Masséna resigned in 1806 and left for Paris in January 1806. Napoleon convinced him to return only by threatening him with a firing squad for desertion if he did not.

The St-Cyr affair simply illustrated a general proposition: Napoleon's lieutenants rarely served him well. The Emperor set up an imperial university under the poet Louis de Fontanes, supposedly a body directing education throughout France: the idea was that the university would monopolize teaching and the Grand Master of the imperial university would be assisted by a council and a bureau of educational inspectors. But Fontanes subverted the intention of creating an imperial élite by stuffing the universities and lycées with ultramontane Catholics, thus producing the bizarre result that education under Bonaparte contained as much piety and religious indoctrination as under the *ancien régime*.

The fiasco over the imperial university was part of a more general power struggle with the Catholic Church. Napoleon suspected the hand of the Pope behind the riots in Parma which were bloodily suppressed at the beginning of 1806. Pius VII irritated him by refusing to annul Jérôme's American marriage, by declining to recognize Joseph as King of Naples, and by his political neutrality. During the struggle with the Third Coalition the Pope refused to garrison Ancona, which could have allowed the British to turn his flank in Italy. When Napoleon had defeated the Third Coalition he turned to settle accounts with the Papacy, complaining that Rome was a hotbed of British espionage and insisting that the Pope set his face against England; there should be a general treaty with Naples for the defence of Italy and the immediate closure of all Papal ports to British trade.

When the Pope demurred, the issue became one of credibility. Napoleon wrote angrily to Cardinal Fesch: 'For the Pope I am Charlemagne . . . I therefore expect to be treated from this point of view. I shall change nothing in appearance if they behave well; otherwise I shall reduce the Pope to be merely Bishop of Rome.' To Pius himself Napoleon wrote with a litany of complaints and reprimands: 'Your Holiness is sovereign of Rome, but I am its Emperor; all my enemies must be those of your Holiness.' The Pope replied curtly: 'There is no Emperor of Rome.' For the time being Napoleon had more pressing concerns, but he vowed that when Europe was more settled he would have a final reckoning of accounts with the Vicar of Christ.

To show his contempt for the Papacy, the Emperor had his tame nuncio Cardinal Caprara approve the publication of a new French Catechism, which ordained absolute loyalty to the Emperor on all French Catholics. In return for the outright purchase in his own name of his palace in Bologna, Caprara was happy to do Napoleon's bidding. The new catechism seemed at first merely to stress the age-old duty of Catholics to obey temporal rulers, but in the seventh lesson of the document the Emperor was mentioned by name:

'We in particular owe to Napoleon I, our Emperor, love, respect, obedience, loyalty, military service, the dues laid down for the conservation and defence of the empire and of its throne; we also owe him fervent prayers for his safety and for the temporal and spiritual prosperity of the State.'

Why do we owe all these duties towards our Emperor?

'Firstly because God ... plentifully bestowing gifts upon our Emperor, whether for peace or for war, has made him the minister of his power and his image upon earth. ... '

Are there not particular reasons which should attach us more closely to Napoleon I, our Emperor?

'Yes, because it is he whom God has sustained, in difficult circumstances, so that he might re-establish public worship and the holy faith of our fathers, and that he might be their protector. He has restored and maintained public order by his profound and active wisdom; he defends the State with his powerful arm; he has become the anointed of the Lord by the consecration he has received from the sovereign pontiff, head of the universal Church.'

What must one think of those who should fail in their duty to our Emperor?

'According to the apostle Paul, they would resist the established order of God himself, and would render themselves worthy of eternal damnation.'

Hubris after Austerlitz or the iron of despotism entering his soul? Certainly in 1806 there are many pointers to a new, harsher Napoleon, who would brook no opposition and whose attitude to dissent anticipated the dictatorships of the twentieth century. From Paris he wrote to Murat, now Grand Duke of Berg: 'I am astonished that the notables of Cleves have refused to swear allegiance to you. Let them take the oath within twenty-four hours or have them arrested, bring them to trial, and confiscate their possessions.' His attitude to Hesse was even more draconian. There was an insignificant, almost token revolt there while it was under military rule before being absorbed in a new kingdom of Westphalia. The general in command considered that a single exemplary execution was enough to assert French credibility, but Napoleon insisted that the village where the revolt started be burnt to the ground and thirty ringleaders shot *in terrorem*. When the general protested, Napoleon raised the number to sixty and finally two hundred.

As Talleyrand had predicted, for the Emperor to establish the Confederation of the Rhine and make himself arbiter of Germany was to embroil himself in a never-ending skein of problems and crises. It is extraordinary to follow the stages whereby the Emperor converted neutral Prussia into an enemy by the end of the year. Frederick William III was the least hostilely disposed of all European monarchs towards Bonaparte. He disliked the Bourbons, was in no way alarmed by Napoleon as First Consul and wanted only to steer clear of trouble and maintain the neutrality to which Prussia had adhered since 1795. Yet

Napoleon served him up affront after affront. In 1805 the *Grande Armée* blatantly violated the neutrality of the Prussian territory of Ansbach in violation of a promise France had just made to Berlin. Had the Allies won at Austerlitz, Prussia would certainly have entered the war on their side.

After Austerlitz Prussia was left out on a limb. Napoleon, knowing the contingency plans Frederick William had made to mobilize his troops, decided to cow him. He proposed peace terms to Berlin on a take-it-or-leave-it basis. Prussia was to lose territories which would be reconstituted as duchies for Berthier and the marshals; all Prussia's treaties were to be replaced by an exclusive accord with France; and Prussia was to pledge itself to take any and every economic measure against England that Napoleon proposed; as a *douceur* Prussia would receive Hanover. Frederick William meekly accepted, making himself a laughing stock in Europe. Then came the twin blows of the Confederation of the Rhine and the end of the Holy Roman Empire.

This was the moment Napoleon should have adopted Talleyrand's plan for a Paris-Vienna axis to dominate Europe and keep out Russia. The time was propitious, for Archduke Charles, restored to favour, was promoting a policy of military expansion in the east at the expense of Turkey, leaving Germany and Italy in Bonaparte's sphere of influence. But the Emperor believed in humiliating those he had defeated, not conciliating them. Having ensured by his contumacious behaviour that the spirit of *revanchisme* would live on in Austria, he then proceeded to alienate Prussia by three separate actions of gross insensitivity.

First, by insisting that Prussia join his proposed economic blockade of England, he forced her into war with Britain; seven hundred German ships were at once impounded in British ports and ruin stared the mercantile classes in the face. Secondly, he struck out vigorously at inchoate signs of German nationalism. He ordered Berthier to raid into neutral territory to seize a subversive Prussian bookseller named Palm. In a sordid rerun of the d'Enghien affair Palm was kidnapped and executed by firing squad for disseminating nationalist tracts prejudicial to the interests of the French Empire. Thirdly, Napoleon made a final attempt to secure terms with Britain by offering to let her have Hanover back. The offer was brusquely snubbed, but the proposal soon leaked, and infuriated the Prussians who realized that Napoleon had been quite prepared to sell them down the river. Napoleon's hamfisted attempts at personal diplomacy as usual ended up by securing the worst of both worlds: hatred and contempt from both Britain and Prussia.

Alarmed at the way the prestige of nation and army were being impaired by Frederick William's unwillingness to stand up to Bonaparte, a war party led by the formidable Queen Louise gained the upper hand in Berlin and forced the reluctant king to a declaration of war; the fiasco over Hanover had been an insult too far. Mobilization began on 9 August and on 26 August came the Prussian ultimatum: Napoleon was to take his troops back across the Rhine by 8 October or the two nations would be at war. Yet the decision for war was a disastrous one. Prussia was now fighting alone when a year ago she would have been in well-nigh invincible combination with Austria and Russia. Prussia, with an army ossified in the methods of Frederick the Great, was something of a museum piece, bedevilled by old and useless generals, excessive factionalism and negligible staffwork. And this was the force that would be taking on Napoleon's Grand Army, now at the very peak of its power in terms of numbers, equipment, efficiency and morale.

There was something comical too about the way the Prussian leadership dithered about their intentions, unable to decide between three different strategies. They compounded their error by not waiting for the Russians, who resumed hostilities with France once they heard of the Prussian ultimatum. So spectacular was Prussian incompetence that Napoleon spent nearly a month devising counter-strategies on the assumption Berlin must have some masterplan up its sleeve. Finally convinced that he confronted merely bumbledom and that Austria would not intervene, Napoleon set out for Mainz on 24 September, accompanied by Josephine and Talleyrand.

His aim was to destroy the Prussians before the Russians could arrive. To bring the enemy to battle he decided on a drive for Berlin, first concentrating the army in the Bamberg-Bayreuth area, then swinging north through the Franconia forest towards Leipzig and Dresden, with the Prussian capital always in his sights. He whipped up battle frenzy in his troops by telling them that they had already been recalled to victory festivities in Paris when Prussian treachery caused a change of plan.

Adopting his usual principles, Napoleon tried to foresee the unforeseeable and anticipate the unexpected. He put Brune on full alert at Boulogne against a possible British descent on the Channel coast and put Eugène de Beauharnais's Army of Italy on a war footing just in case Austria was tempted to enter the war. The final Prussian ultimatum, delivered on 2 October, reached the French just twenty-four hours before the deadline expired and allowed Bonaparte to present the Prussians to French public opinion as warmongers. Then he made final preparations. The Prussians seemed to be offending every canon of warfare by menacing Bavaria with three separate armies that could be caught and destroyed piecemeal. The Duke of Brunswick and Frederick William commanded 60,000 Prussians; another mixed force of 50,000 Prussians and Saxons were under the Prince of Hohenlohe; and a third force of 30,000 was under Rüchel. Napoleon planned to intercept the armies before they could unite. He began crossing the Franconian forest on 2 October with a 180,000-strong army drawn up in a square formation, ready to deal with an enemy attack from any direction.

By 8 October Napoleon was expecting an engagement on the Elbe near Leipzig. But as he emerged from the forest and began to move across Saxony towards Leipzig, intelligence reached him that the main Prussian army was at Erfurt, to the west. Mentally calculating march times, he estimated that he would be fighting a battle on the 16th and faced his army round towards the river Saale. On 13 October Lannes, commanding the advance guard, reported that the Prussians were present in strength at Jena on the Saale. During the night of 13–14 October Napoleon ordered 120,000 of his men to converge on Jena while I and III Corps under, respectively, Bernadotte and Davout, were to advance north to Auerstädt to cut off the Prussian retreat to the Elbe.

Once again Bernadotte elected not to obey his orders, peeled away from Davout and marched to Dornburg. But at Jena confusion was compounding uncertainty as the main Prussian army streamed away northwards, leaving Hohenlohe at Jena (supported by Rüchel at Weimar) to cover the retreat. Meanwhile Napoleon, expecting to encounter the main enemy army, caught up with Lannes on the evening of the 13th and next morning got 50,000 men on to the projected battlefield, with 70,000 more coming up fast. Around 6 a.m. Lannes, Soult and Augereau began by driving off the Prussian vanguard and enlarging the bridgehead on the west bank of the Saale. There was then a short pause to allow new formations to come up. Once Ney's VI Corps arrived, Napoleon sent him and Lannes in a two-corps attack on the Prussians. An outnumbered Hohenlohe fought back fiercely and called up reinforcements. The headstrong Ney attacked furiously but allowed himself to be cut off from Lannes and Augereau (this around 10 a.m.). Napoleon had to intervene in person with a massed artillery battery to rescue Ney.

By midday Augereau and Soult were in their proper positions on the flanks. An hour's slaughter took place as the Prussian infantry, in an exposed position, was cut to pieces. Napoleon ordered a general advance at 1 p.m.; the Prussians retreated and the retreat soon became a rout. By 3 p.m. the French had inflicted 25,000 casualties (including 15,000 prisoners) and sustained losses of 5,000 themselves. Although roughly equal in numbers of big guns (120), the two sides were otherwise ill-

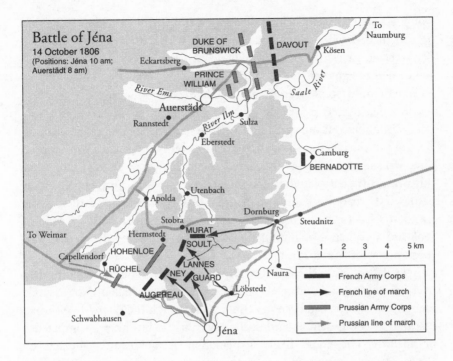

Battle of Jéna
14 October 1806
(Positions: Jéna 10 am;
Auerstädt 8 am)

To Naumburg

DUKE OF BRUNSWICK   DAVOUT   Kösen
Eckartsberg
PRINCE WILLIAM
River Ems   Saale River
Auerstädt
Rannstedt   River Ilm   Sulza
Eberstedt
Camburg
BERNADOTTE
Utenbach
Apolda
Stobra   Dornburg
To Weimar   Hermstedt   Steudnitz
Capellendorf   HOHENLOE   MURAT
RÜCHEL   SOULT
LANNES
NEY   GUARD   Naura
AUGEREAU   Löbstedt
Schwabhausen   Jéna

0 1 2 3 4 5 km

French Army Corps
French line of march
Prussian Army Corps
Prussian line of march

matched, for the French put 96,000 men on to the field against Hohenlohe and Rüchel's 53,000. Napoleon was content, for he was sure that Davout and Bernadotte would have reached Apolda and cut off the retreat.

But when he reached headquarters at dusk, he received the astonishing news that he had not after all been fighting the main enemy army. It fell to Davout to encounter that host, ten miles away at Auerstädt. Incredibly, with just 27,000 men and forty guns he routed the 63,000-strong army with 230 guns under Frederick William and the Duke of Brunswick. As Davout passed the Saale and the Kosen pass beyond, he collided with Brunswick's flankers. The divisions of Vandamme and Gudin under Davout performed wonders as more and more Prussian infantry and cavalry rushed to the spot, but things might have gone hard with them if Brunswick had not been wounded, throwing the chain of command into confusion. Davout faced odds of two to one but he remained calm and defiant as the Prussians grew ever more hesitant. Finally, Frederick William panicked at the thought that he was opposed by Napoleon in person. At 4 p.m. he ordered a retreat which also became a rout, for Davout counterattacked at the first sign of enemy withdrawal.

Davout's astonishing victory at Auerstädt was harder won than the Emperor's at Jena. He killed 10,000 Prussians and took 7,000 prisoners (21,000 casualties in all) while sustaining losses of 7,700 in dead and wounded himself. Napoleon at first found it difficult to acknowledge that he had made such a signal error and played this down in his bulletins. Privately he gave Davout full credit for his marvellous feat but showed some slight signs of jealousy by not giving him the Dukedom of Auerstädt until some years later. But if he felt some negative emotion towards Davout, this was nothing to the anger he displayed towards Bernadotte. Davout informed him that he had repeatedly sent for help to Bernadotte during the thick of the battle, but the Gascon had ignored him. Bernadotte, indeed, discovered the trick which at least one other third-rate marshal would later emulate, of not being present at either battle. If Bernadotte had reached the Apolda three hours earlier, as he was supposed to, he would have trapped the fugitives from the field of Jena and a Cannae-like annihilation would have resulted. Even as it was, Jena-Auerstädt was a great victory.

Speculation was rife in the army that this time Bernadotte had overreached himself and would surely be court-martialled. Not a single man in his I Corps had been in action, even though the *Grande Armée* had just fought two gruelling battles; the cause had to be either incompetence or malice. The most likely explanation is deliberate sabotage by Bernadotte, arising from his insane jealousy of Bonaparte. Napoleon certainly thought so and signed an order for his court-martial, to the great satisfaction of Davout. Then, to general consternation he tore it up. How could his marshals know that the Emperor was still thinking of Désirée Clary?

Bernadotte was given one last chance to retrieve his reputation. He, Lannes and Murat pursued the fleeing Prussians and this time the Gascon was on his mettle. Blücher, with 22,000 troops, headed for Lübeck, hoping to ship out for England with his men. But Bernadotte, in an unwontedly energetic pursuit caught up with him at the Baltic. Surrounded by Bernadotte and Soult, Blücher had no choice but to surrender. The French meanwhile won another victory at Halle and crossed the Elbe. There was a slight delay while gross indiscipline among drunken, marauding French troops was sorted out, but finally the *Grande Armée* entered Berlin on 25 October. In thirty-three days Napoleon had inflicted 55,000 casualties, forced the surrender of another 40,000 troops and taken 2,000 cannon. He had spent a lot of the campaign groping in the dark, but finally the combination of his famous intuition and his mathematical brain resulted in another memorable victory. It was a good result for the Grand Army too, for if Ney and Bernadotte had lost caste, Davout and Lannes had performed brilliantly.

The terms dictated by Napoleon after Jena were harsh. Prussia was to cede all territory between the Rhine and the Elbe, which meant the end for the Duke of Brunswick, the Prince of Orange and the Elector of Hesse-Cassel. A huge indemnity of 159,425,000 francs was levied (after Austerlitz Austria paid only forty millions in reparations) and Prussia was in effect turned into a French satellite. Napoleon pardoned Saxony on condition she joined the Confederation of the Rhine, along with Saxe-Weimar, Gotha, Meiningen, Hildburghausen and Coburg. Even though the army was shattered, 150,000 prisoners of war were in French hands and three-quarters of Prussia (including Berlin) was occupied, Queen Louise announced that the struggle would go on and put herself at the head of Prussian partisans who fled to the east to join the Russians. To Napoleon's consternation, he realized that the great victory of Jena-Auerstädt was not going to be a second Austerlitz and provide a knock-out blow.

To Josephine, whom he had left in Mainz when he began campaigning, the Emperor wrote with words of complaint about the Prussian Queen: 'How unhappy are those princes who permit their wives to interfere in affairs of state.' Josephine construed this as an attack on women in general and wrote back protestingly. Napoleon endeavoured to put her right: 'You seem displeased by my speaking ill of women. It is true that I detest scheming women. I am accustomed to ones who are gentle, sweet and captivating. It is your fault – it is you who have spoiled me for the others.' The tenor of this letter was of a piece with all his missives to Josephine that winter. He wrote tenderly, sometimes twice a day, invariably ending with the formulaic 'I love and embrace you' or 'I love and desire you.' The prevailing tone was very much that of an old married couple, with the Emperor complaining that he was putting on weight even though he rode up to seventy miles a day on horseback.

When Napoleon had written during the Italian campaign that he desired Josephine, it was literally true. Now the sentiment was a mere formal expression of regard, for the Emperor was used to satisfying his carnal appetites elsewhere. One such occasion was on the road to Berlin, on 23 October, when he took refuge from a hail storm in a hunting lodge and dallied with the young widow of an officer from the Egyptian campaign. On 27 October he entered Berlin, having spent the previous night at Sans Souci in Potsdam, where he visited the tomb of his idol Frederick the Great. Hearing that Mortier had successfully taken the port of Danzig, he wrote that he would be leaving for Poland in a few days. He was beginning to toy with the idea of a permanent occupation of the territory between the Oder and the Vistula and to this end asked Fouché to send him Tadeusz Kosciuszko and the other leaders of the Polish independence movement.

On 8 November Magdeburg capitulated and Murat wrote in triumph: 'Sire, the war is over owing to the lack of combatants.' But Murat was jumping the gun. Paradoxically, after a great military triumph Napoleon was on the defensive. As he saw it, a Russian counter-offensive could coincide with a British landing somewhere in Europe, and meanwhile the gold of London might have persuaded Austria to rise on his southern flank. Worst of all was the news from Paris. Where the French people had greeted Austerlitz with joy, they reacted to news of Jena with gloom; they wanted peace not a protracted struggle with Russia. But Napoleon refused to bow to public opinion. When the Senate sent a deputation to Berlin to urge him to make peace, he received it coldly and told the senators he would make peace only when Russia joined him in the great global fight against England.

He took vigorous action to make sure he retained the initiative. A judicious mixture of stick and carrot kept Austria quiet, so that the potential threat from the south never materialized during the 1807 campaign. He struck at England by announcing an economic blockade in his Berlin decree of 21 November 1806. And he headed off trouble in the army by ordering a cash bonus, doubling the commissariat supply, and issuing each soldier with a brand new set of clothes and several pairs of shoes. The more hardheaded and obdurate he was in military and political affairs, the more philosophical and detached from the world he seemed in his letters to Josephine. In a classic of compensation he wrote to her: 'Everything in this world must come to an end, wit, sentiment, the sun itself, but that which has no end is the happiness I have found with you – in the unending goodness and sweetness of my Josephine.'

Napoleon's analysis of the Russian army was that it was a very mixed bag. The infantry was usually poorly armed, trained and equipped, consisting of uneducated and unpaid peasantry, but it could fight with great stubbornness when cornered. If the rank and file were tough and brave, the officers were of very poor quality, often military dilettantes or men whose only professionalism was in gambling; and there were few generals of any calibre. The Russian army was hidebound by bureaucracy and suffocated by red tape, but could still not supply its fighting men adequately. On the other hand, its artillery was excellent in both quantity and quality, and the cavalry, especially the Cossacks, were as good as the French, if not better. Napoleon was under no illusions about the difficulty of the coming campaign.

The one card he could play was to win over Polish support by declaring for an independent Poland. He let it be known that he would make such a proclamation if the Polish leaders would put 40,000 good soldiers in the field. Meanwhile he sent Duroc on a mission to browbeat or cajole the Prussians into signing the proposed peace treaty. He began to proceed slowly through Poland. When the deputies of Poznan asked him (on 19 November) if he would declare Polish independence, he gave an evasive reply, stalling until he heard from Duroc. A week later he heard from Duroc that his mission had failed. But still there was no declaration. The Emperor finally revealed his hand to Murat on 6 December when he told his brother-in-law that he would not make such a proclamation until he was sure the Poles were prepared to do the hard work to sustain it. That meant 40,000 well-trained and organized men, fully armed, led by a mounted nobility ready to sacrifice their lives in battle instead of conspiring in coffee houses. Predictably, the leaders of the Polish independence movement were dismayed. Kosciuszko noted bitterly: 'He will not reconstitute Poland; he thinks only of himself and he is a despot. His only aim is personal ambition.' Kosciuszko was right: in his heart the Emperor had nothing but contempt for Polish national aspirations though he was prepared to pose as the deliverer of the Polish nation to win recruits for his armies.

Having convinced himself there was nothing substantial to hope for from the Poles, Napoleon began intriguing with the Turks. On 1 December he wrote to Selim III, Sultan of the Sublime Porte, suggesting that this was the moment to strike against Islam's ancient enemy (Russia) and so restore the former splendour of the Ottoman empire. This must be read as part of a continuing obsession with turning the Russian flank, manifest in the letters in this period from the Emperor to his marshals, and the frustration he felt, openly admitted in correspondence with Talleyrand, that the Russians were avoiding a battle. There is some anxiety just below the surface in some of his *billets doux* to Josephine, especially one on 2 December when he writes: 'It's raining but I'm all right. I love you and desire you. These nights are long, all alone.'

To forestall the Russians Napoleon decided to occupy Russia and sent instructions to Davout to meet him there with his corps. The Russian General Bennigsen, playing Fabius to the Emperor's Hannibal, decided not to oppose the French invasion of Poland and withdrew his army to the banks of the Vistula. The prize for entering Warsaw first went, as such prizes usually did, to the dashing Murat. But Napoleon was not yet finished with the Russians. In December he tried to cut the Russian communications by getting behind them to the river Narew. As a first step he sent forces to seize the town of Pultusk. But this was exactly where the Russian army had retreated to, so that the French crossings of the Narew river were hotly contested. A running battle developed from 22 December onwards, culminating in an indecisive battle at Pultusk on 26 December, which Napoleon was able to write up in his bulletins as a victory, since the Russians withdrew and allowed the French to occupy the town. The battle petered out mainly because the Russian commander Bennigsen decided to avoid a slugging match and because Davout, unwontedly off form, failed to support Lannes at the vital moment. Following another indecisive battle on 26 December between Davout and Augereau and Galitzin and Doctorov, the Russians withdrew to Rozan. Violently adverse weather forced Napoleon to break off pursuit and take the Grand Army into winter quarters. He wrote to Cambacérès on 29 December: 'I believe the campaign is over. The enemy has put the steppes . . . between us.'

On 19 December Napoleon arrived in Warsaw. There was much to ponder. In his heart he knew the Narew campaign had not gone well. He had failed to keep his corps within supporting distance of each other and thus could not bring the enemy to a decisive action. True, rapidity of manoeuvre was scarcely possible on fields that had become quagmires of mud, but the more worrying sign was gross indiscipline and desertion in the *Grande Armée* itself, with an astonishing 40% rate of absenteeism by the end of the year. But at least one of the Emperor's gambles had paid off. Against the odds Selim III declared war on Russia in December and followed it with a similar declaration against England in January. Encouraged by this, Napoleon, always lured by the East, began trying to encourage Persia to join in hostilities against Russia.

Meanwhile he faced the task of building up virtually a new army. Morale in the old *Grande Armée* was rock-bottom, for serving with the Emperor seemed like dealing with the Hydra's heads: each victory simply entailed yet another campaign. The actual physical conditions of marching and fighting in Poland were the worst yet encountered, with dreadful roads that disintegrated into mud paths when rain and snow fell. Indiscipline, desertion and looting were the inevitable result. One of the Emperor's first tasks in Warsaw was to work out how he could get his Army into shape for a possible spring campaign against the Russians.

He began by calling up the 1807 intake of conscripts a year early and followed up by a recruiting drive in Switzerland and Holland aimed at raising 35,000 men. Always allowing political considerations to be overridden by military necessities, he started bleeding Germany dry of money. He mulcted the conquered territories of 720 million francs, including 160 millions from Prussia; Hamburg bore a heavy toll.

Confiscated British assets in the Baltic ports increased the total. Not content with uplifting money, Napoleon imposed requisitions in kind, especially for military matériel such as 600,000 pairs of shoes. Coming on top of the Berlin decrees, these measures scarcely made the Emperor a popular man in Germany.

Napoleon did what he often did when confronted by titanic problems: he made a show of indifference and masked his anxieties by a riotous display of conspicuous consumption. Savary recalled in his memoirs that January 1807 in Warsaw was a virtually non-stop festival of concerts, balls, parties, fêtes and other spectacles. To Josephine the Emperor wrote offhandedly: 'I'm well. It's bad weather. I love you with all my heart.' Josephine, still in Mainz, had been plaguing him to let her join him, but Napoleon stressed that there was no point while his future plans were so uncertain. In a notably prophetic dream she saw Napoleon with a woman with whom he was in love. In what we may now see as dramatic irony Napoleon replied as follows: 'You say that your dream does not make you jealous . . . I think therefore that you *are* jealous and I am delighted. In any case you are wrong. In these frozen Polish wastes one is not likely to think of beautiful women . . . There is only one woman for me. Do you know her? I could paint her portrait for you but it would make you conceited . . . The winter nights are long, all alone.'

Only days after writing these words Napoleon met the woman who would be the second great love of his life. He had left Warsaw for a week on 23 December 1806 and was returning to the city on New Year's Eve in a six-horse carriage. At Bronie, the last post relay before Warsaw, as thick snow fell, the Emperor's carriage was mobbed by enthusiastic Poles, believing him to be the Messiah of Polish independence. What appeared to be a beautiful, blonde-haired peasant girl came up to the carriage and asked Duroc to present her to the Emperor. Napoleon was struck by her looks, her modesty, her ability to speak French and the simple adoration of a young woman overjoyed to see the man who had smitten Poland's three great historical oppressors: Russia, Austria and Prussia. He gave her one of the bouquets that had been thrown into his carriage when he lowered the window and thought about her all the way to Warsaw. Once there, he told Duroc to spare no measures to find the 'beautiful peasant'.

On 3 January Duroc told him the search had been successful. There was a problem, though: the 'beautiful peasant' turned out to be Countess Marie Walewska, the eighteen-year-old wife of an elderly Polish nationalist; though her husband was seventy-seven, she was supposed to have borne him a son. Further enquiries made the picture clearer. Marie had been married at sixteen and had indeed borne a son to Walewski, the *grand seigneur* of his district, even though he had a grandson of twenty-five! Marie herself had been strictly brought up, in the full piety of Polish Catholicism, and educated by a tutor who later became famous as the father of Frédéric Chopin.

Napoleon made plain to the Polish nationalists his desire for a liaison with Marie and told them bluntly he would not be attending the ball they were giving in his honour unless the young countess was there. Count Walewski, despite his age, did not take kindly to the prospect of being a cuckold and at first refused to procure his wife for the French Emperor, even though Prince Poniatowski argued that it would eventually redound to his prestige. But he was eventually browbeaten by a junta of leading Polish nationalists, who argued that Paris was always worth a mass. Marie, however, was not prepared to accept her husband's bidding in this matter and at first adamantly refused. She was appalled at what was being asked of her and thought it too high a price to pay for Poland; after all what were the male 'patriots' giving up for the cause? She later told how a deputation of patriots harangued her outside her bedroom door, then, when her husband admitted them to her boudoir, exhorted her to make this supreme sacrifice for the sake of Polish independence. After all, had not the biblical heroine Esther given herself to the Persian king Ahasuerus (Xerxes) to win liberty for her nation?

Marie responded with a kind of work to rule. She went to the ball dressed more like a nun than a great lady, swathed in tulle, wearing no jewellery and with her ball dress deliberately high-necked. Napoleon said to her: 'White on white is no way to dress, Madame,' an enigmatic statement sometimes read as the Emperor's customary derogatory remark when a woman was wearing clothes that displeased him, and sometimes taken to mean that he had penetrated her motives in appearing thus. But the fact that he spoke to her at all alerted a court sensitive to the slightest nuance. Clearly this was the coming woman. Marie was surrounded by fawning flatterers. She refused to dance, but two officers who flirted with her incurred the Emperor's displeasure and were dispatched to distant wintry outposts.

After the ball, Napoleon began the siege of her affections. He began with a letter: 'I saw only you, I admired only you, I desired only you. A prompt answer to calm the impatient ardour of N.' Marie was unimpressed and told the waiting courier: 'There is no answer.' Napoleon continued to press his suit and wrote passionate letters daily which she ignored. He also sent her jewels in a red leather box which she threw on the floor contemptuously, exclaiming that the Emperor must take her for a whore. He continued to bombard her with letters, including one which deserves a prize for its disingenuousness: 'Come to me; all your hopes will be fulfilled. Your country will be dearer to me when you take pity on my poor heart ... Whenever I have thought a thing impossible or difficult to obtain, I have desired it all the more. Nothing discourages me ... I am accustomed to seeing my wishes met. Your resistance subjugates me. I want to force you, yes, *force* you to love me. Marie, I have brought back to life your country's name. I will do much more.'

Under virtual siege from the all-powerful French Emperor while being constantly urged by the patriotic party, and even her own husband, to dispense with her absurd scruples, Marie finally cracked. She went to Napoleon's residence one night but when he began caressing her she changed her mind, provoking an angry outburst from the Emperor. He told her that if she resisted him, both she and her country would be ground under heel. He threw his watch on to the floor and ground it into pieces. What happened next appears to have been half rape, half seduction: on St Helena Napoleon said Marie put up merely token resistance while many years later in her memoirs she claimed she fainted clean away and awoke to find that he had had his way with her. At any rate, after the first act of sexual intercourse she burst into tears. Napoleon comforted her by vowing he would make good all his promises to her.

Gradually Marie, against her better judgement, found herself falling in love with him, responding warmly to his attentiveness, charm, gentleness – for he could lay it on with a trowel when he had a mind to. For his part he found himself enraptured by a woman as never since Josephine; like her, Marie was traditionally feminine, soft, gentle and unchallenging. But now he had the problem of Josephine to solve. Ever since Duroc first reported to him that he had found the mystery woman, Napoleon had been at pains to dissuade Josephine from travelling to Warsaw. Letters written on the third, seventh and eighth of January all said the same thing: the roads were bad and the countryside unsafe so the best course for the Empress was an immediate return to Paris. As the relationship with Marie moved towards consummation, he proved himself once more a Corsican master of duplicity: 'Paris claims you. It is my wish. I would have liked to share the long winter nights with you here.' By the end of January the tired phrases about 'long winter nights' and 'impossible roads' had become a meaningless litany. Contenting herself with a few jaundiced remarks about the military tasks ahead of her husband, she reluctantly commenced a long, slow journey back to Paris.

Napoleon's Warsaw idyll with Marie Walewska was meanwhile interrupted by news that Bennigsen and the Russians had launched an offensive. What happened was that Ney had winkled the Russians out of their winter quarters by an unauthorized plundering expedition in the Polish lakeland region – which he justified by pleading shortage of supplies. This hardened a resolve that been forming in Bennigsen's mind for some time: that he would thrust towards the French left, break through on the Vistula and open a spring campaign that would drive the *Grande Armée* back to the Oder. Napoleon decided on a countercoup by assaulting the Russian left as Bennigsen moved west; to lure the Russians into the trap he ordered French forces in the north to pull back, hoping ultimately to scythe through the Russian centre and bisect their army.

This promising plan miscarried when one of the French couriers got lost and delivered a copy of the Emperor's battle plans to the Russians. This mishap ruined Napoleon's entire winter strategy, for Bennigsen now realized to his horror the thin ice on which he had been skating and halted operations for a rethink. The Russian pause made Napoleon confused about their actions and it was 3 February before he realized the enemy must be aware of his intentions. His problem was that although 80,000 new troops had been levied, he barely had enough in hand for his immediate purposes. With insufficient forces he pressed forward and engaged the Russians at Lonkovo (3 February), but the battle was indecisive as night fell before the French columns could get into position. The warning signs were already there. The terrain in eastern Prussia did not suit the style of the *Grande Armée*, so that the rapid war of manoeuvre was not practicable. Cold, rain, snow, quicksands, inadequate supplies and guerrilla attacks by Prussian partisans all worked against Napoleon, and his supply situation was even further jeopardized by the scorched earth policy adopted by Bennigsen as he retreated.

However, when Augereau's Corps and the Guard arrived on 4 February, Napoleon was confident he would be able to beat the Russians next day. Once again, though, before he could complete his encirclement, Bennigsen retreated and again escaped the trap. Again it was the darkness that had thwarted the Emperor, for nightfall, occurring so early at this time of the year in these latitudes, came down just before he had got all units into position, so that by a hair's breadth he was robbed of the decisive victory he sought. He urged on his marshals to harry and pursue the fleeing Russians and it was nips and stings from these gadflies that finally made Bennigsen turn around and face his tormentors on 6 February 1807. Napoleon thought to surprise the Russians but it was they who surprised him, and in an inferior position.

The dreadful battle of Eylau began as an outpost skirmish. It was not fought in circumstances of Napoleon's choosing for, outnumbered as he was (initially 50,000 against 70,000) and outpointed in the artillery sphere (just two hundred big guns against the Russians), he wanted to wait until all his forces came up before giving battle. But the initial skirmish soon escalated into all-out, sanguinary conflict. Starting at 2 p.m. on 7 February, the battle raged on until 10 p.m., with artillery flashes lighting up the night sky. Each side sustained about 4,000 casualties but there was little chance of survival for the wounded on a night when temperatures plummeted to thirty degrees below zero. After spending a frightful night in the open, troops on both sides greeted the dawn, to find almost continual snowstorms driving into their faces. Squinting and blinking into the white hell, 75,000 Frenchmen prepared to do battle with roughly the same number of Russians: Bennigsen still had a marked superiority in artillery. Ever dreaming of a second Cannae, Napoleon ordered Soult to attempt the 'pinning' operation while Davout and Ney tried to work round the flanks; Augereau and Murat would be held for the decisive attack, with the Guard in reserve.

The Russians opened fire at 8 a.m. and soon a full-scale artillery duel was raging. At 8.30 Napoleon ordered Soult to attack the Russian right, to divert attention from the left where the decisive stroke would be delivered. But the Russians got their assault in first. Marching across the frozen lakes and marshes from about 9 a.m. on, they drove Soult rapidly back to Eylau, where a desperate struggle commenced. Even more menacingly, the Russians then started making inroads on the French left. Napoleon had neither anticipated this assault nor the speed with which Soult was driven back. He had no option but to order forward the reserve under Augereau with General St-Hilaire to contain the Russian left. This was risky and premature, for Davout was not yet on the scene, but Napoleon hoped he could stabilize the battle situation until he had his trump cards ready.

Proceeding in a heavy blizzard, Augereau's corps advanced deployed instead of in column. In the blinding snowstorm they quickly lost sight of their targets and blundered straight into the path of the Russian 70-gun battery, where they were cut to pieces at point-blank range. St-Hilaire's division did manage to reach its target but without their intended comrades in Augereau's corps could not effect a breakthrough. By 10.30 a.m. the battle appeared lost, with Soult driven back, Augereau's corps annihilated and St-Hilaire's division halted. An ominous gap appeared in the centre of the French line, and Bennigsen clearly held all the cards. Even while the remains of Augereau's corps were being slaughtered, some 6,000 Russians penetrated the town of Eylau. Napoleon, who had been using the belltower as his vantage point, would certainly have been killed or captured but for the heroism of his personal escort, who held the line until two battalions of Guards came up.

Napoleon could sense the extreme gravity of the situation, so ordered the second half of the reserve, originally designed to spearhead the final breakthrough, into the breach. At about 11.30 a.m. there occurred the most famous cavalry charge in history as Murat's horsemen hurled themselves upon the Russian centre. They smashed through and seized the guns that had annihilated Augereau's corps. For the loss of 1,500 men Murat saved the day for France, relieving Augereau, Soult and St-Hilaire at a stroke. Bennigsen, who thought himself on the brink of victory, became confused and felt he had underestimated the strength of the French centre. He hesitated and thus by midday had lost his chance of victory.

The obvious next ploy was for Napoleon to order the Guard into the centre to widen the gap made by Murat. Once again he manifested his extraordinary reluctance to use the Guard; the excuse he afterwards gave was that he was afraid a Prussian division under General Lestocq might appear on the field. He therefore ordered all his units – Murat's as well as Soult's and the remnants of Augereau's – to dig in and hold until Davout completed his encirclement. By 1 p.m. Davout was ready. He and St-Hilaire now pushed back the Russian southern flank until it resembled a hairpin. But just when victory was almost theirs, what Napoleon most feared came to pass: Lestocq arrived on the field at 3.20 p.m., having evaded Ney. The marshal later exculpated himself by saying he could hear nothing – neither guns nor the tramp of marching men – because of the howling din of the wind and falling snow.

By 4 p.m. Lestocq was easing the pressure on the Russians by falling on Davout's open flank. Step by step Davout's heroes were forced to relinquish the ground they had taken so painfully. Sensing that the pendulum in this see-saw battle was now swinging back to the Russians, Napoleon pinned all his hopes on Ney, for only he could turn the tide. Fortunately for him, Ney arrived on the Russian right around 7 p.m. and threw 15,000 fresh troops into the fray. By 10 p.m. the fortified French had fought the Russians to a standstill. In essence the Emperor's nerve held better than Bennigsen's. At a council of war Bennigsen overruled his generals who wanted to extend the fighting into a third day and at midnight began abandoning the field, screened by Cossacks. The exhausted French were in no position to follow.

After fourteen hours, tens of thousands of corpses littered the field, where the deep whiteness of the snow was stained, streaked and striated with blood. The French had taken casualties of one in three and had lost

25,000 men; the Russians lost 15,000 (the figures are disputed and some authorities are inclined to reverse these numbers). Napoleon was forced to crank his propaganda machine into top gear to disguise the scale of the disaster, using the dubious fact that he had been left in possession of the field to claim victory. About the scale of the casualties he lied barefacedly, admitting to only 1,900 dead and 5,700 wounded. Secretly glad the Russians had not decided to renew the conflict next day, he looked around for scapegoats. He found more than he was looking for, as, incredibly, Bernadotte had once again disobeyed orders. The Emperor had sent General Hautpol to the Gascon marshal with urgent orders to bring his corps to Eylau. Bernadotte claimed never to have received any such order, and as Hautpol was killed in the battle, there was no way to nail Bernadotte's transparent lie.

Next day Napoleon rode over the battlefield, gloomily inspecting the mounds of corpses. Later he wrote to Josephine: 'The countryside is covered with dead and wounded. This is not the pleasantest part of war. One suffers and the soul is oppressed to see so many sufferers.' That was an understatement. Percy, surgeon to the Grand Army, put it more vividly:

> Never was so small a space covered with so many corpses. Everywhere the snow was stained with blood. The snow which had fallen and which was still falling began to hide the bodies from the grieving glances of passers-by. The bodies were heaped up wherever there were small groups of firs behind which the Russians had fought. Thousands of guns, helmets and breastplates were scattered on the road or in the fields. On the slope of a hill, which the enemy had obviously chosen to protect themselves, there were groups of a hundred bloody bodies; horses, maimed but still alive, waited to fall in their turn from hunger, on the heaps of bodies. We had hardly crossed one battlefield when we found another, all of them strewn with bodies.

Appalled at the casualties, depressed by the mounds of dead and the huge task involved in burying them, and generally suffering from nervous exhaustion, Napoleon suspended military operations and took his depleted army back into winter quarters on 23 February. The Russians moved cautiously forward and retook the field of Eylau with its grisly heaps of frozen corpses. The most serious problem the Emperor faced was plummeting morale in the *Grande Armée*. The general atmosphere of chaos was compounded by a marauding army, a consequently hostile Polish peasantry and the implosion of the physical terrain, as a sudden thaw turned frozen rivers into oceanic surges and covered everywhere with a viscous, oozy mud. Worst of all, he had somehow to repair the damage to his personal prestige and to silence the 'I told you so' voices of the Talleyrands, who had warned of the hidden dangers of expansion into Germany. Jena was a great victory, but it did not knock out the Prussians, and Eylau seemed to be the end of the road. It was an object lesson against doubling one's stake.

Napoleon the military leader scarcely emerges with credit from the Eylau campaign and the myth of his invincibility was plain to see. To an extent the near disaster of the campaign was a testament to the breakdown of the French military machine. From top to bottom it had been inadequate, with marshals disobeying orders and rankers marauding, looting, indisciplined or deserting. Yet Napoleon could not put all the blame on the shortcomings of his collaborators and underlings. He broke his own rule that corps must always be within one to two days' march of each other, and he was much too slow to order up Ney's army, which should have received its instructions on the evening of the 7th, not the morning of the 8th. Beyond that, Napoleon blundered into a battle he had not expected and nearly brought disaster on his own head by being short of soldiers on the morning of the 8th. Once again he scrambled out of the jaws of defeat by a lucky gamble with Murat's charge; had that failed, his centre would surely have buckled.

The truth is that at Eylau Napoleon was saved more by his opponent's errors than his own skill. Bennigsen's cardinal error was to hesitate when Soult was repulsed instead of pressing on. When Davout appeared, he called off the attack against Soult but made poor use of his own right. Also, a determined attack against an exhausted French army at around 4 p.m., three hours before Ney arrived, would surely have brought victory. Until Eylau Napoleon had rarely put a foot wrong on a battlefield. After it, with some rare and brilliant exceptions, his touch was much less sure. It was a worried man who returned to the arms of Marie Walewska.

Napoleon moved his headquarters to the sumptuous Schloss Finkenstein in East Prussia, where Marie joined him for the resumption of an idyll cut short by the Eylau campaign. She was deeply in love with him, though aware that his attention span for women was not great, and therefore fearful that the affair would not last long. He certainly appreciated her more than any of his other mistresses: she seemed to have all Josephine's virtues plus special ones of her own. Where Josephine was silly, trivial and spendthrift, Marie was serious, bookish and frugal; she dismayed her lover by consistently turning down his offers of lavish presents. Her effect on him was certainly beneficial. During the sojourn at the castle of Finkenstein he displayed miraculous energy, giving detailed attention to all aspects of his Empire. It can hardly be a coincidence that the new surge of vigour and confidence was evident at the height of his liaison with Marie.

Among the detail Napoleon attended to was Josephine's daily life in Paris. To sustain the morale of Paris, which had been bowed down with horror stories about fields of mud into which entire divisions sank without trace and quicksands that swallowed an artillery park, Josephine held numerous state receptions for the Senate, the Legislature, the diplomatic corps and even the Church, while hosting lavish official dinners and gala nights. From Prussia the Emperor supervised her timetable to the smallest item, even specifying the days on which she was to be at St-Cloud, and those when she was permitted to relax at Malmaison. She expressed herself depressed at her husband's long absence and the virtual exile of her two children, Eugène as viceroy of Italy and Hortense as wife to Louis, the new King of Holland.

Gradually rumours about Marie Walewska reached her. She might already have suspected something from the mere fact that Napoleon had ended his ritual dirges about 'long, lonely winter nights'. She was particularly curious about what Napoleon was getting up to at the Schloss Finkenstein, which Napoleon did not leave from 1 April to 6 June, and expressed her misgivings in a letter. The Emperor's reply is vintage Bonaparte humbug: 'I don't know what you mean by ladies I am supposed to be involved with. I love only my little Josephine, good, sulky and capricious, who knows how to pick a quarrel with grace, as she does everything, because she is ever lovable, apart however from the times when she is jealous, when she becomes a demon. . . . But let us return to these ladies. If I needed to busy myself with one of them, I assure you I would wish her to have pretty pink nipples. Is this the case with those of whom you speak to me?'

Despite provocation, Josephine did not let him down and played the role of distant imperial benefactress superbly. She did not succumb to the temptation of returning to the fleshpots of the Directory or taking up with her raffish Thermidorian friends of yore. Napoleon, though, underrated her and gave many explicit warnings about that old hedonistic crew. There was a particularly splenetic outburst on the subject of Thérésia Tallien, now Princesse de Chimay, who had already notched up ten children by four fathers (including four to Chimay) which seemed to Napoleon to reduce her to the level of a beast in the field. He wrote to Josephine: 'You are not to see her. Some wretch has married her with her litter of eight bastards; I find her more despicable than ever. She was a nice enough trollop; she has become a horrible, infamous woman.' It is impossible here not to detect some displaced envy for Tallien's fecundity, with its obvious contrast to Josephine's barrenness.

The Emperor's correspondence from Finkenstein shows him indisposed to suffer gladly those he took to be fools. After some nagging from Fouché about the necessity of peace, he hit back irritably: 'Talking incessantly about peace is not a good means of getting it.' When Hortense sent him grief-stricken letters about the death from croup of her son Charles-Napoléon-Louis, he reproached her sharply for her 'excessive' lamentations: this was tantamount to letting death win, he chided, but as a soldier he knew very well that death was not that terrible an adversary. When Hortense unsurprisingly did not reply to this cold, unsympathetic 'condolence', Napoleon wrote in the tones of a stern but benevolent paterfamilias: 'My daughter . . . You have not written a word; you've forgotten everything. I'm told you love no one any more and are indifferent to everything; I can see this from your silence. This is not well done, Hortense . . . If I had been at Malmaison, I would have shared your pain.'

By early June 1807 Napoleon was ready to begin operations against the Russians. Herculean efforts saw the total strength of the *Grande Armée* – including units in Naples and Dalmatia and those guarding the coasts of France and Holland – raised to 600,000 by May. Six fresh divisions had been raised, two each from Italy, Germany and Poland. A particular feature of early 1807 was the appearance of an Army of Germany, 100,000 strong, recruited particularly from Saxony and Baden. Designed to make sure that Germany did not rise in his rear or Austria suddenly enter the war, the Army of Germany straddled Prussia, with Jérôme in command of the right wing in Silesia, Brune in the centre and Mortier commanding the left in Pomerania. To make sure that there was a firm hand on Warsaw, the Emperor summoned Masséna (to his disgust) from Italy.

By June Napoleon had 220,000 men in Poland and outnumbered the Russians two to one. The two heroes of Eylau, Davout and Murat, were with him, and Lefebvre, helped by Lannes and Oudinot, had just successfully completed a second siege of Danzig. The brimming magazines of Danzig eased the French supply problem, which had been acute in the winter of 1806–07, and encouraged Napoleon to cast envious eyes on the next such military cornucopia, at Königsberg. The only cloud over the Grand Army was the dissolution of Augereau's VII Corps, no longer viable after Eylau; the survivors were redistributed among the other corps. Napoleon felt confident that he could now cut Bennigsen off from his base at Königsberg, where the Russians kept their main stores and arms dumps.

But the Emperor's first efforts seemed to presage another Eylau. He engaged the Russians at Heilsberg on 10 June, but an indecisive, slugging battle resulted, lasting well into the darkness of a midsummer evening. By his inexplicable frontal assaults on well-defended positions Napoleon simply produced the consequence that the French lost 10–11,000 men (against Russian losses of some 8,000) without gaining any significant advantage. Finally Napoleon did what he should have done that morning instead of offering battle, and manoeuvred to threaten the Russian communications, forcing Bennigsen to withdraw from his strong defensive position on a hillside. As at Eylau Napoleon was left in possession of the battlefield and, also as at Eylau, he presented Heilsberg as a victory in his official bulletin.

Trying to read Russian intentions, Napoleon guessed that Bennigsen would cross the Alle on the left bank farther down river at Friedland. But Bennigsen's plans were more ambitious. Learning that Lannes's corps was marching in detachments on Friedland and was dangerously isolated from the rest of the French army, he gave orders to construct pontoon bridges so that his army could cross and wipe out Lannes. Unhappily for him, by the time he got the first 10,000 of his men to the far side of the river (13 June), Lannes had already received reinforcements, notably a large body of cavalry under Grouchy.

Bennigsen opened the battle just before dawn on 14 June with a huge artillery barrage but inexplicably did not press his great local superiority. By 9 a.m. the French still only had 9,000 infantry and 8,000 cavalry and there was a 45,000-strong Russian army on the other side of the river. Napoleon sent Lannes orders to lure this army over the river and pin it while the rest of the *Grande Armée* moved up. While Bennigsen dithered, more and more reinforcements reached Lannes. At 9.30 Berthier arrived to swell Lannes's numbers to 35,000 and half an hour later there was further stiffening from another 5,000 French troops.

Unaccountably Bennigsen still made no move. Soon after midday Napoleon arrived on the spot and assumed command. The consensus of his staff was that the best plan would be to wait until next day, for by then the heroes of Eylau, Murat and Davout, would be present and the French would have an overwhelming superiority in numbers. The Emperor demurred. Two factors weighed with him. Ever superstitious, and recalling how Austerlitz on 2 December had mirrored his coronation day a year before, he decided that 14 June, the date of Marengo, was a lucky date and he should give battle. More practically, he saw at once that Bennigsen had made an egregious mistake by deploying the Russians with their backs to the river. Furthermore, the Russian line was bisected by a millstream and a lake, which would make it very difficult for the Russian wings to support each other. By 4 p.m., with 80,000 men in position, Napoleon was convinced he had a glorious opportunity which would not present itself again.

His strategy was simplicity itself. He would attack the Russians in the right angle formed by the river Alle, where the millstream bisected the two wings. This would be done swiftly, immediately and without further artillery bombardment. Once at least two of the bridges over the Alle were destroyed, the remaining Russians could be driven north into the arms of Davout and Murat. At 5 p.m. he ordered Ney's corps to lead the onslaught. It was not a moment too soon. Napoleon's famous intuition had been right again; there would not have been such a unique opportunity on the morrow. By now Bennigsen had seen the danger and was just in the process of ordering a retreat when Ney attacked; he had to countermand his orders rapidly to deal with the sudden French incursion.

Bennigsen began by launching a cavalry counterattack, which was beaten off in heavy fighting. Gambling that the French could not sustain another massive cavalry attack, he ordered his élite horsemen in again, but this time they were taken in the flank by Victor's corps. Chaos ensued when the retreating Russian cavalry collided with their own infantry; the twisting confusion of cursing and panicky men gave the French gunners an unmissable target. Victor, as much the hero of Friedland as Davout had been at Auerstädt, saw his opportunity and moved up thirty cannon. Opening up successively from ranges of 600 yards, 300 yards and 150 yards, French artillerymen tore gaping holes in the Russian ranks. At point-blank range case-shot did terrible damage, and hundreds of Russians fell dead within minutes.

Bennigsen tried to relieve the shambles on his left by sending his reserve under Gortchakov against the key corps of Lannes, Mortier and Grouchy. The Russians would have been at their most effective south of the millstream, but superb work by the French cavalry kept them pinned to the north of it. In desperation Bennigsen ordered a massed bayonet charge on Ney's right flank, but this move too came to grief and thousands of Russians drowned in the Alle without getting to grips with the French. General Dupont then crossed to the north bank of the millstream and attacked the flank and rear of the exhausted Russian centre. With Ney already in the outskirts of Friedland, Bennigsen played his only remaining card and sent in the Russian Imperial Guard; these in turn were rapidly 'eaten up' by Ney's and Dupont's men.

By 8.30 p.m. Napoleon was in possession of Friedland. The Russian tactic of gutting the town literally misfired when the flames spread to the pontoon bridges and cut off further large numbers of Russian troops. Seeing that north of the millstream a series of desperate Russian attacks had been beaten off by Oudinot's and Verdier's corps, Bennigsen had to extricate his men fast or face total disaster. With three out of the four bridges destroyed, it was touch and go for a while but at last the Russians found a usable ford. This was the time when Napoleon to achieve total victory needed to unleash the forty cavalry squadrons on his extreme left. The ill-starred Grouchy, alas, was no Murat and muffed his chance. None the less nightfall did not slacken the French pursuit, which continued until well past 11 p.m.

For 8,000 casualties Napoleon gained a decisive victory, inflicted 20,000 casualties on the Russians and took eighty guns. It had been a grim six-month slog, but at last the French Emperor had the result he wanted. This was one of his great battlefield achievements, second only to Austerlitz, and there was some justification for the words he wrote to Josephine: 'My love, I can only write you a word because I am really tired . . . My children have worthily celebrated the battle of Marengo; the battle of Friedland will be just as famous and just as glorious to my people . . . It is a worthy sister of Marengo, Austerlitz, Jena.' On the other hand, Napoleon in this battle was not an initiator: he simply reacted to Bennigsen's moves. Bennigsen made many bad mistakes on 14 June 1807, of which two stand out: he should not have allowed the two sectors of his army to be bisected by an unbridged stream, and he should have worked out that in the event of a Russian retreat there would probably be only one bridge left over the Alle.

Friedland was in many ways the apotheosis of the *Grande Armée*. For once the marshalate had come up to Napoleon's expectations. General Victor won his baton as the nineteenth marshal after his brilliant showing; Ney had his finest hour in the battle; Oudinot, the most obviously rising star in the Bonapartist entourage, received an annual pension of 33,000 francs for his performance and was marked down by the Emperor as 'one to note'.

Yet for more thoughtful military observers there were some worrying omens and not just the fact that the Emperor, a notoriously bad horseman, had fallen from his horse no fewer than three times during the Friedland campaign. Napoleon, it was clear, habitually placed too much emphasis on the offensive. Clausewitz, the great Prussian military theorist who fought in this campaign, would later warn that offensives were always weakened by the very fact of advancing. In 1807 Napoleon had the numerical superiority to make his strategy work, but what would happen if ever he had to fight a campaign where he was outnumbered? This was an especially potent consideration, given that the Emperor evinced more and more impatience with the chessplaying aspect of his military craft. His ignorance of terrain and failure to scout ahead adequately put him in a false position at Eylau, and his disregard of climatic and geographical factors led him to cross the Oder without taking into account the ice, snow and mud. Remembering similar débâcles in Egypt and Santo Domingo which arose through a fundamental ignorance of climate and geography, the Emperor's more circumspect followers wondered how long it would be before he led them into a major disaster.

Yet for the moment Napoleon seemed invincible, not just in practice but in principle. Czar Alexander I, whose wildly fluctuating moods oscillated between elation and depression, decided after Friedland that negotiation was the only way forward. His peace feelers were received with secret relief by Napoleon, who was anxious to end the war before an increasingly fractious Austria was tempted to join in. The Emperor had hoped Turkey would be a trump card but a revolution on 27 May in Constantinople overthrew Selim III. And Napoleon was also aware that he had been away from Paris for far too long. Josephine was very good at showing the imperial eagle, but who would deal with the plots and conspiracies of the Fouchés and the Talleyrands?

A truce between the French and Russians was soon agreed and it was decided that the two Emperors would meet on a raft in the middle of the river Niemen near the town of Tilsit. The genesis of this famous meeting is interesting. The Niemen marked the western frontier of Russia and, since Alexander would not set foot on French-held territory nor Napoleon in Russia, an ingenious compromise was worked out. Napoleon ordered a huge barge-like raft to be built, on which was constructed an elegantly decorated apartment with a door on either side giving on to an antechamber; the two outer doors were crested with the respective national eagles. The two sovereigns then appeared at the same time on opposite banks of the river around noon on 25 June and got into their boats. Napoleon, with a crew of expert oarsmen, easily beat Alexander to the raft, boarded alone, walked through the apartment to the far antechamber and opened the door, waiting patiently while the Czar's less skilful oarsmen laboriously rowed him to the rendezvous.

Shortly after noon, one and a half hours of friendly discussion began. The two men got off on the right foot when Alexander allegedly greeted

Napoleon with the words: 'Sire, I hate the English as much as you do.' 'In that case,' replied Napoleon, 'peace is established.' The initial ease between the thirty-eight-year-old Emperor and the thirty-year-old Czar had deepened into something like friendship by the end of the interview. Quite apart from other considerations, each man was physically drawn to the other. Alexander fell under the spell of a charismatic Napoleon, exerting himself to exude all his well-known charm. Napoleon, as he later acknowledged, was much affected by the physical beauty of the Czar and described him as an Apollo: Alexander was tall and handsome, with blue eyes and blond curls. Both men later went on record that they 'loved' each other.

Napoleon also thought Alexander highly intelligent, but some nagging internal voice gave him pause. As he said later: 'There is something missing. I have never been able to discover what it is . . . a decadent Byzantine . . . a Talma of the north.' By referring to his favourite actor, Napoleon was actually revealing more about himself than the Czar. Alexander's problem was not histrionic but psychological. Debate has raged about his exact mental state. Some have thought him schizophrenic while others opt for 'depressive mania'. His frequent mood swings have even led some to posit the multiple personality model of 'dementia praecox'. At the very least, Alexander was disturbingly neurotic. He liked to think of himself as a simple soldier, but this was bunk. He was actually a physical coward who had stayed well clear of the fighting in the Austerlitz campaign and would do so again during the stirring days of 1812.

Next day, 26 June, the two sovereigns met at 12.30 and spent the day together until 9 p.m. Thereafter the protocol-conscious courtiers on either side devised an elaborately 'egalitarian' programme. On the 27th Napoleon visited the Czar for a review and dinner and next day the Emperor played host to Alexander. This was the day Napoleon chose for his elaborate 'Ottoman' charade. An obvious barrier to an accord between France and Russia was Napoleon's incitement of Turkey. The opportune removal of Selim III in the coup of 28 May gave Napoleon the excuse he needed: he could now pretend that his entente with Selim had been purely personal and that it lapsed with a change of Sultan. Although he already knew the news from Constantinople – as did Alexander – Napoleon pretended that his intelligence service was lackadaisical and had only just got word of the coup. As he sat with the Czar around four in the afternoon of 28 June, a courier arrived with an 'urgent' dispatch. Napoleon opened it, read it and jumped up with feigned astonishment. To Alexander he said excitedly that he no longer had debts of honour to

Turkey as Selim had been deposed. 'This is an act of Providence; it tells me that the Ottoman empire can no longer exist.' By all accounts Alexander swallowed this and hung on every word.

While the diplomats got down to the small print of the draft treaty, the tiring and stressful round of dinners and meetings between the two rulers went on daily until 5 July. Then Queen Louise of Prussia arrived. Using all her charm and cajolery, she made strenuous efforts to get the draconian terms of the draft peace treaty amended, but Napoleon could not forgive her for her obduracy after Jena, that had cost him so much blood and treasure. To Josephine he wrote: 'The Queen of Prussia is really charming, she is full of coquetry for me, but don't be jealous. It's water off a duck's back to me. It's too much effort for me to play the gallant.' Finally, the Tilsit agreement was ready for signature on 7 July. It was ratified two days later so that, at last, on 9 July, Napoleon bade farewell to the intriguing and enigmatic Alexander. A quite separate treaty with Prussia was signed on 9 July and ratified on the 12th.

The Treaty of Tilsit gave the Czar a free hand against European Turkey and Finland; Russia would join Napoleon's blockade of Britain (the 'Continental System'); the Russian navy would help France capture Gibraltar. In a secret protocol the Czar promised to raise no objections to Napoleonic interventions in Spain and Portugal, though this did not justify, as was later alleged, Bonapartist assertions that Alexander had formally connived at the expulsion of the Bourbons in the Iberian peninsula and their replacement by Napoleon's brothers. Alexander also agreed informally – this did not form part of the final protocol – that he would collaborate in a joint Franco-Russian project aimed at British power in India, initially by sending a 50,000-strong army into Persia. Napoleon's extreme duplicity here must be stressed, for before Friedland he had been encouraging the Persians to ally themselves with him and thus regain from Russia the lost province of Georgia. Napoleon was to mediate in the Russo-Turkish conflict and, if the new Sultan refused his mediation, the Ottoman provinces in eastern Europe were to be shared between the signatories. In return, Alexander was to mediate in the Franco-British war: if Britain refused, Alexander would bring pressure on the courts of Copenhagen, Stockholm and Lisbon to force them to close their ports to English produce.

The treaty with Prussia represented a humiliation for the Hohenzollerns. Prussia was restricted to her 1772 frontiers and the French held on to the fortress of Magdeburg. All Prussian possessions west of the Elbe and a part of Hanover were incorporated in the new kingdom of Westphalia, with Napoleon's brother Jérôme as king. All Prussian provinces in Poland were to be merged in a Grand Duchy of Warsaw, to be ruled by the King of Saxony. The Grand Duchy of Warsaw and the Kingdom of Westphalia in turn would form part of the Confederation of the Rhine, which became a colossus that swallowed up all Germany except Prussia and Austria. Danzig would be a free city but occupied by a French garrison. There would be a huge war indemnity, and French troops would remain on Prussian soil until it was paid. Finally, Prussia agreed to join the Continental System and to recognize the kingdoms of Westphalia, Holland, Naples and the Confederation of the Rhine.

The Treaty of Tilsit brought Napoleon close to total triumph in Europe. It was a particular blow to Britain because the Baltic was the primary source of supplies for the Royal Navy: the best timber for masts came from Russia; the best firs for ships' decks came from Russia; 90% of Britain's hemp came from Russia; and the best underwater planking was provided by Baltic oak. Russia also supplied most of Britain's tallow, half her linseed, half her pitch, tar and iron. The rest came from Sweden, which was now firmly in the Russian sphere of influence. It was not surprising that in 1807–08 the British were preoccupied with the Baltic and entertained particular fears about the Russian and Danish navies: the Royal Navy maintained a large fleet there in the ice-free summer months and after 1808 had twenty battleships and thirty-eight frigates on permanent station. Even though the Royal Navy gained a striking success in 1807 with the capture of the 69-strong Danish navy (including sixteen battleships and ten frigates), that year also saw Britain blundering to disaster in Buenos Aires, Egypt and the Dardanelles. Not surprisingly, after Tilsit both George III and Canning were in favour of an accommodation with Napoleon. For a long time he dithered, then turned down the offer in 1808 just before he launched into his Spanish adventure.

Tilsit also completed the alienation of Talleyrand from the Emperor. Two opinions are possible on this. On the one hand the treacherous and venal Talleyrand was now in the pay of Austria and actively involved in subverting Napoleon's designs. He surreptitiously urged Alexander to resist Napoleon 'for the good of all Europe' and advised him that the notables in France were happy with the natural frontiers and wanted no part of the Emperor's German adventurism. On the other, Talleyrand had long argued that even the 'natural frontiers' were an insuperable barrier to peace and that only a return to the 1792 frontiers would guarantee stability in Europe. In any case, he argued, weakening Austria and Prussia was wrongheaded as it meant destroying Europe's natural bulwark against Russia – and it was obvious that Alexander was merely playing for time.

After Tilsit Napoleon turned his face homewards and began a leisurely progress back to Paris. In Dresden on 19 July the Polish deputies for the new Duchy of Warsaw were presented to him, and he dictated to them the constitution of the new government. While in Dresden he found time for a brief affair with Charlotte von Kilmansegg. A week later he was back at St-Cloud, where Fouché and Talleyrand found him much changed. Talleyrand recorded that even his voice seemed different after Tilsit. Certainly the harsher side of his nature came to the fore, and after July 1807 his reflex action when faced with a problem was to use a heavy hand, be it military force, secret police or government censorship. Fouché reported that Parisians were becoming increasingly restless with his régime, the recent military and diplomatic successes notwithstanding. They sensed that the war with the Russians had been a near-run thing and dreaded the social and economic consequences if French society was to remain on a permanent wartime footing. Fouché indeed now concluded that the Emperor was incapable of dealing rationally with bad news. It was the generally received opinion in France, certainly with hindsight, that at Tilsit the Emperor crossed an invisible Rubicon. He thought himself poised on the cusp of permanent European hegemony but was about to start sliding down a slippery slope whose end would be disaster.

CHAPTER SEVENTEEN

Napoleon returned to Paris from Dresden on 27 July 1807. The next six weeks saw imperial triumphalism and conspicuous consumption at their apogee. First came the lavish preparations for the Emperor's thirty-eighth birthday on 15 August, which he celebrated with the most glittering fête seen since the days of the *ancien régime*. There followed a series of self-satisfied speeches to the Assembly, in which Napoleon assured his countrymen that the influence of England in Europe was a thing of the past; henceforth perfidious Albion would be confined to its island fastness, at least until the Continental blockade forced her to surrender. Finally, at the end of August, there was another coruscating round of celebrations, this time for the marriage of Jérôme, the new King of Westphalia, with Princess Catherine, daughter of the King of Württemberg.

It was his family in its narrowest sense that commanded the emperor's immediate attention on his return from Tilsit. Napoleon decided that he needed an heir and must therefore divorce the barren Josephine. Two factors seemed to have weighed with him. First, there was the fact of Éléonore Denuelle's son, which seemed to suggest that he would have no problem about begetting issue, even though his spies kept him informed and he realized that Murat could have been the father. Then there was the impact of Tilsit itself. He had discussed with Alexander I the possibility of a marriage to the Czar's sister to cement the alliance. Josephine's days seemed to be numbered.

On his return to Paris Napoleon also came under extreme pressure from both Talleyrand and Fouché, especially the latter. The two old rivals made common cause on the necessity for the removal of Josephine but differed on who should replace her. Talleyrand, secretly in the pay of Austria, wanted a Habsburg empress; Fouché vehemently opposed this and favoured a Russian alliance, both to prevent Bonaparte's useless brothers from succeeding to the purple and to preclude the return of the Bourbons. The Emperor's table talk convinced Fouché that he had *carte blanche* to resolve the matter, so one Sunday after Mass at Fontainebleau he took Josephine aside and suggested she should agree to a divorce in the interests of France and the dynasty. Josephine faced Fouché down by getting him to admit that the suggestion did not come directly from the Emperor himself, then reported the interview to her husband. Napoleon brushed it aside as an excess of zeal on Fouché's part, then asked his wife 'purely for the sake of argument' what would be her reaction to such a proposal. Josephine knew the card to play and said she was afraid that if she left him, all his good luck would go too. The superstitious Bonaparte was affected by the argument and let the matter drop.

A more intelligent woman than Josephine might have realized that Fouché would not have dared be so 'impertinent' had he not had the tacit support of his master. Although the immediate tearful sequel to the blundering intervention of the chief of police was a pledge of eternal devotion by the Emperor, the shrewdest observers concluded that it was only a matter of time before the Empress was jettisoned. Count Clemens Metternich, the new Austrian ambassador, reported to Vienna that Napoleon behaved in a cold and distant manner towards Josephine, but the truth was more complex. The Emperor infuriated his closest advisers by his constant dithering over a divorce, but in reality he was torn: he saw the urgent political case for a dynastic marriage and the begetting of heirs but was sentimentally attached to Josephine and genuinely believed she did bring him luck. When he was away from her, he could contemplate divorce with equanimity, but when in her company became strangely indecisive. Though no longer sexually besotted, he was excessively fond of her, and his later assessment of her to Bertrand is shot through with ambivalence: 'I truly loved her, although I didn't respect her. She was a liar, and an utter spendthrift, but she had a certain something which was irresistible. She was a woman to her very fingertips.'

It seems clear that marital relations between the two had all but ceased, apart from a few instances of sentimental dalliance. Instead Napoleon regaled her with details of his mistresses and described what they were like in bed, even asking her advice at times on whether he should continue a certain liaison. Josephine learned to ignore affairs like the brief one at Fontainebleau between the Emperor and the comtesse de Barral in September 1807. She could afford to connive at his infidelity, for she knew that far the greater danger came from the search for a suitable dynastic bride for her husband – a quest in which she knew Talleyrand, her old ally Fouché and the Murats were actively engaged.

By so acting Talleyrand unwittingly shored up Josephine's position, for she dreaded Caroline Murat's machinations more than any others. The crazed ambition of the Murat couple knew no bounds, and the interlocking cabals of intriguers at this juncture sometimes defy credibility. Caroline had numerous affairs with men of power and influence, culminating in a torrid romance with General Junot in 1806–07; her motive was to secure Junot's adherence (he was governor of Paris) in the event of a coup in which she planned to replace her brother with her husband. Junot was so sexually inflamed by Caroline that he wanted to remove Murat by challenging him to a duel, but Napoleon forbade it. When the affair ended, a broken-hearted Junot referred to Caroline as a new Messalina.

Murat, habitually unfaithful himself, took a detached view of his wife's adultery with Junot, for he knew her emotions were not fully engaged. Her next affair, however, was a very different matter, which made him angry and jealous. In the Austrian ambassador Metternich Talleyrand encountered a fellow spirit but a man of even more voracious sexual appetites. Metternich seduced Caroline with ease, and she very soon became infatuated with him. Not content with having one conduit to the very heart of Napoleon's decision-making, Metternich opened a second front by seducing Laure Abrantes Junot, to Caroline's stupefaction and consternation. Beside herself with anger, Caroline anonymously tipped off the equally insanely jealous Junot at a masked ball. Junot taxed Laure with her adultery and, receiving no satisfactory answer, stabbed her and nearly killed her; incredibly the couple were later reconciled.

Metternich apart, the Murats condoned each other's infidelities, since they were united by their vaulting ambition. In 1807 they were in particularly vengeful mood, brooding and resentful that Joachim had not been made King of Poland or even the Grand Duke of Warsaw. Since March 1806 they had been Grand Duke and Duchess of Berg and Cleves, enclaves on the right bank of the Rhine. Having taken the oath of sovereign in his capital at Düsseldorf, Murat was then made a knight of the Spanish Order of the Golden Fleece – one of the *ancien régime*'s highest distinctions – but this was not good enough for the Murats. Lacking a kingdom, they had to yield precedence to Camillo and Pauline Borghese.

Perennially fearful of Caroline Murat's mischief, Josephine tried to secure her position with Napoleon through her daughter Hortense. Napoleon returned to find Hortense still grieving over the death of Napoléon-Charles. Irritated, he asked if there was anything he could do to lift the pall of gloom, and the opportunistic Hortense suggested that he adopt her second son Napoléon-Louis as his heir apparent. The Emperor replied that to do that would be to confirm the scurrilous rumours that the dead Napoléon-Charles was really his son; credibility therefore stood

in the way of her proposal. Josephine began increasingly to be aware of
the thin ice on which she was skating, but calculated that to make scenes
would be counterproductive. When Napoleon left for an Italian tour in
November, she raised no objection when the Emperor did not invite her
to accompany him, even though it meant missing the chance of a reunion
with her son Eugène. Nor did she react noticeably when word was
received in the capital that Napoleon was consoling himself in Italy in the
arms of an old flame, Carlotta Gazzani.

Napoleon's trip to Italy was itself occasioned by a chance to view a
prospective bride, Princess Charlotte, sister of Princess Augusta of
Bavaria. Leaving Paris on 16 November 1807, he proceeded via Lyons
and Chambéry to the Mont-Cenis pass, where he encountered a terrible
storm, then descended into the plains of Italy and arrived in Milan on 20
November. To his annoyance, he found that Charlotte was an ugly
woman and had to concoct a hasty excuse for the King of Bavaria. He
rationalized his advent in Milan with a trip to Venice, taking in Monza,
Brescia and Vicenza on the way. En route to Venice he met his brother
Lucien, with whom he was still at daggers drawn. On the strength of a
loan to Pius VII Lucien had acquired the papal fief of Canino and exulted
in the title of prince. Once again Napoleon offered him a crown if he
would give up his second wife, but once again Lucien refused. Arriving
in Venice on 29 November, the Emperor made a triumphant entry up the
Grand Canal and stayed in the palace of the Doges until 8 December. He
opted for a leisurely progress back through northern Italy to Milan,
which he quit on Christmas Eve for another strenuous journey, via
Turin, Mont-Cenis, Lyons, Mâcon and Chalon. He arrived back in Paris
on New Year's Day 1808.

The contretemps with Lucien was not the only family disappointment
for Napoleon. Every single one of his siblings continued to disappoint
him. Perhaps the most successful, though the least close to the Emperor
personally, was Elisa. Even her liaisons, as with the master violinist
Paganini, were discreetness itself in comparison with her sisters'. After
making a success of the minor territories her brother threw her way – she
turned Lucca into a showpiece and revived the Carrara marble quarries –
she was rewarded in 1808, when Napoleon annexed Tuscany and Parma,
by being made Duchess of Tuscany. She was a superb administrator and
a shrewd politician who knew exactly how to play the Emperor. It was
her misfortune that he never liked her and she could never please him
whatever she did.

Louis Bonaparte had all but disgraced himself by his abysmal
performance in the 1806 campaign and Napoleon had sent him home in

disgust, giving out, for purposes of 'family honour', that his brother had had to withdraw because of broken health and, once recovered, would be 'inspecting' units in Antwerp and Amsterdam. As King of Holland he further enraged Napoleon by trying to evade implementation of the Continental blockade of England, thus winning great popularity in the Netherlands, by getting his brother to withdraw French garrisons and by commuting death sentences on 'patriots'. But he continued neurotic, melancholic and hypochondriacal, and his hatred of Hortense seemed to increase daily. Despite the virtual breakdown of the marriage and the ill omen of her first two sons (one dead, the other sickly and destined to die young), Hortense gave birth to a third son in 1808; this Louis Bonaparte would become Louis-Napoleon or Napoleon III, though grave doubts must be entertained as to whether Louis was really his father.

While Napoleon was always harsh in his dealings with Lucien and Louis, he was absurdly indulgent towards Joseph and Jérôme. In late 1805, while the Emperor was winning the great victory of Austerlitz, Joseph spent his time lolling in Flanders and the Rhineland, giving lavish dinner parties. When he was appointed King of Naples, he soon showed himself to be the prey of absurd delusions. Because he was modestly popular with the Neapolitan élite, he imagined himself to be a 'people's king'. Unable to see that he relied totally on his brother's bayonets, he tried to make himself more Neapolitan than the natives, ostentatiously refused to levy a 30-million-franc war tax demanded by the Emperor, and took a local mistress, Maria Giulia Colonna. Believing the grotesque lies told him by his circle of sycophants, he imagined himself as a second Philip II of Spain and toiled long hours over state papers.

Not even the frightful events of 1806 served to shake Joseph permanently out of cloud-cuckoo-land. In July that year a British expedition landed in Calabria and defeated a larger French force at Maida in a battle sometimes claimed as a classic of line versus column. Although the British soon withdrew to Sicily, southern Italy exploded in guerrilla warfare whose ferocity shocked good King Joseph. In panic he wrote to his brother for reinforcements. French troops suppressed the rising ruthlessly and it was contained by February 1807, but at the cost of forced loans and the sale of crown lands; moreover, the nobility's feudal privileges were abolished and martial law was imposed on Naples. The feckless Joseph stayed on in his capital and allowed the 50,000-strong French army of occupation a free hand, while still imagining himself to be the most popular monarch in Neapolitan history.

Jérôme cut an even more absurd figure as King of Westphalia – that artificial creation carved from Hesse, Brunswick, Nassau, Hanover and

Prussia west of the Elbe. The scandal of his first marriage and the fiasco of his naval career proved no barrier to an illustrious marriage with Princess Catherine of Württemberg, but when this compulsive woman-izer began neglecting Catherine just months after the wedding in order to flirt with Stéphanie Beauharnais, Napoleon dispatched him in disgrace to Boulogne. When he left Paris at the end of 1807 to assume direction of his kingdom, he left behind a mountain of debt (two million francs in Paris alone), which the Emperor had to pay for reasons of credibility and 'family honour'.

In Westphalia his rule was the predictable disaster. He bled the country dry with exorbitant taxes and the costs of French troops billeted there; his treasury was chronically in debt and his defence budget inflated. King Jérôme's grotesque extravagance and lavish consumption were compounded by a Nero-like penchant for acting on the stage. Habitually unfaithful to the luckless Catherine, he exhibited all the symptoms of satyriasis: it was said that he would sleep with anything in a dress, and simply bought off the outraged husbands and boyfriends with sackfuls of sovereigns. He even tried to trick his first wife Betsy into crossing from England to Germany so that he could seize his three-year-old son, but she outfoxed him and instead wrung compensation money from the publicity-conscious Emperor. For all Jérôme's incompetence and absurdity, Napoleon always forgave him, partly because he was the beloved Benjamin and partly because, unlike Louis, Jérôme was a genuine puppet ruler and allowed French recruiting sergeants and press gangs free rein in his domains.

Yet in many ways the most hyperbolic of all the Bonapartes was always the nymphomaniacal Pauline. Promiscuous, impulsive, capricious and arrogant, she showed her contempt for the fraternal gift of the tiny duchy of Guantalla near Parma by selling it on to the kingdom of Italy for six million francs. Yet Napoleon was always fond of her and was pleased with her husband Camillo Borghese's behaviour at Friedland. He even gave him the honour of taking the news back to Paris, but here Camillo was upstaged by the official imperial messenger who beat him to the capital with a duplicate set of dispatches. Camillo was then posted to Turin as governor-general, where Napoleon ordered Pauline to join him; she, however, claimed to be very ill so as not to have to return to Italy.

Yet Pauline's alleged malady may have had an organic basis, for around this time appeared the first signs of a breakdown in her constitution that would eventually consign her to an early death at forty-five. At the age of just twenty-eight she slipped into a cycle of illness and debilitation. Medical opinion is divided on the cause. Some say she suffered from salpingitis – an inflamed uterine tube – as a result of gonorrhea and therefore constantly suffered pain, exhaustion and depression. More salacious commentators allege that she had been damaged by the giant member of her old lover Forbin. It is certain that her physician advised her that sexual intercourse would exacerbate her problems and that she ignored him.

The string of lovers accordingly continued. First there was the musician Blangini then, in 1810, a twenty-year-old notorious military stud named Captain Canouville. Napoleon, who had increased her official allowance the year before to a million francs a year, took umbrage at the Canouville liaison. The reason was that the Emperor had given to Pauline, as a special mark of favour, a collection of the most expensive furs, which Alexander I had given him at Tilsit; Pauline then passed them on to her lover. An *opéra bouffe* episode ensued when Napoleon banished Canouville to Spain, whence he returned three times to Pauline only to be rebanished on each occasion. Napoleon finally solved the problem by sending Canouville to the Russian front in 1812.

The crimes, misdemeanours and peccadilloes of his siblings could be dealt with, at least in principle. The issue of Josephine was always more difficult, for Napoleon felt himself tugged two ways, towards a cosy, sentimental domesticity which he as a private person preferred, and towards the rupture with the Empress that his dynastic interests required. The ambivalence was reflected in even more severe mood swings which the imperial entourage came to dread. At balls or receptions he liked to upbraid the women for their alleged shortcomings, particularly over matters of dress.

At St-Cloud the greatest fear was that the Emperor would appear in the Yellow Salon after dinner. Apprehension quickened on those occasions when Napoleon took an early dinner then decided to play billiards with his generals or favourites, for he was known to be a very bad player but one who sulked when he lost. It was a source of mortification to Napoleon that he, the commander of genius, was a bad shot, a poor horseman, and an indifferent contestant in all ball or card games. Sometimes the session in the Yellow Salon would be followed by some tender moments with Josephine, when he would ask her to read to him, but more often he would go to bed or work in his study. Such was his restlessness that he often got up at night, took a steaming hot bath – one of his perennial obsessions – and then summoned Méneval for further dictation.

But it was Josephine who bore the brunt of the wild oscillations in mood that sometimes looked very like a manic-depressive cycle. There were still rows about her extravagance with money, but most of them were formulaic, for in his secret heart Napoleon thought that to be hopeless with money was to be truly feminine. At any rate he took no effective steps to curb his wife's spendthrift tendencies, so she simply carried on as before. The one area where he was a stickler concerned her clothes. He had pronounced views and often made her change her outfit several times. Once he took a dislike to a pink and silver lamé gown and threw a bottle of ink over it to make sure it could never be worn again. He particularly liked her in décolleté dresses and, if too much bosom was concealed by a shawl, he would tear it off and throw it into the fire. His attitude to clothes was in general bizarre, for if a jacket was too tight or a collar chafed at his neck his immediate instinct was to rip the offending apparel from his body and hurl it in fury on the floor.

Nothing was more evident than the total reversal of the balance of power between the couple as compared with the period of the late 1790s when Josephine had the whip hand. By now even her small acts of rebellion were stifled. While Napoleon was in Italy in November-December 1807 she allowed herself a brief liaison with the thirty-year-old Duke Frederick Louis of Mecklenburg, who had come to Paris for Jérôme's wedding, but Fouché alerted the Emperor. Hearing that she had been with the prince incognito to a 'low theatre', Napoleon warned that her behaviour was becoming as infamous as that of Marie Antoinette; he also took immediate steps to banish Frederick Louis from France. But not even this act of infidelity could turn him against Josephine. As he wrote to Talleyrand, in many ways she was still the perfect wife and divorce was not to be undertaken lightly: 'I would be giving up all the charm she has brought to my private life . . . She adjusts her habits to mine and understands me perfectly . . . I would be showing ingratitude for all she has done for me.'

Nevertheless, the Empress's sexual charms no longer had the potency of yore and, immediately on return from Italy, Napoleon summoned Marie Walewska to Paris. A separation was arranged between her and Count Walewski and she arrived from Warsaw at the end of January 1808 to take up her quarters at the Quai Voltaire. The idyll of Schloss Finkenstein was resumed. One of Napoleon's favourite pastimes was to imitate Henry V and take nightly strolls incognito, engaging shopkeepers in animated conversations about the Emperor or 'that devil Bonaparte'. As a variation on this practice, he and Marie liked to check in at some country inn in disguise and spend the night making love. Josephine was much alarmed at the resumption of this liaison and threw yet another attractive lady-in-waiting, Mlle Guillebeau, at him to try to break it up.

At first it seemed that Marie Walewska might be the catalyst that finally made Napoleon opt for a divorce. In March Talleyrand told the Rémusats that the Emperor was definitely going to ditch Josephine. Yet once again she made a comeback. One night the Emperor was preparing to host a grand reception at the Tuileries when he was taken violently ill with stomach cramps. Josephine, fully attired in ball gown and crown jewels, hastened to his bedside to comfort him, and a deeply touched Emperor was overcome with waves of sentimentality. He pulled her down on to the bed and exclaimed: 'My poor Josephine, I can't possibly leave you.' When he recovered, the two made love and spent the night together. Once again Josephine had been reprieved, to the fury of Talleyrand and Fouché. 'Why can't the devil of a man make up his mind?' Talleyrand fumed. Fouché remarked that the Empress would be better off dead, though he himself had unwittingly helped to secure a stay of execution for her; when he told Napoleon that there was massive opposition to the military draft and one-tenth of all conscripts had deserted, Napoleon concluded this was not a propitious moment for a divorce.

The interlock between military concerns and domestic matters is vividly illustrated by Napoleon's decision to set off for Spain on 2 April 1808 and to send Marie Walewska back to Poland. The affairs of the Iberian peninsula had begun to obsess the Emperor, as the logic of his blockade of England sucked him more and more into that theatre. The beginning of a long and ultimately fatal trail was his order to Junot to invade Portugal in October 1807, but as early as July he had told Talleyrand that no Continental Blockade of England would work unless Portuguese ports were closed. To him it was a simple matter: 'The English say they will not respect neutrals at sea; I will not recognize them on land.'

This was the point where Napoleon, master of Europe, should have devoted all his energies to a military solution to the problem of England. His plan for an economic strangulation of the British Isles was bound to fail, if only because it had global implications the Emperor had not thought through. A very good example was the way the logic of the blockade cut across his earlier hopes to inveigle Britain into a war with the U.S.A. On 2 July 1807 President Jefferson excluded British warships from U.S. territorial waters. Then Napoleon ruined things by authorizing his corsairs on 18 September to seize from merchant ships on the high seas any merchandise exported from England. In the circumstances Jefferson decided on a wait-and-see policy, ordered an act of embargo (22

December 1807) and kept all ships engaged in American commerce in U.S. ports.

With Russia, Austria, Prussia and Denmark cut off from trade with England, Napoleon sought to tighten the noose by denying Portugal to British commerce. He began in July 1807 by demanding closure of the ports, then followed up next month by insisting that Portugal declare war on England. The Portuguese were thus in an impossible position, for a war with Britain would mean the loss of its colonies and its global trade while a war with France would mean military occupation. While negotiations with Spain went on for a treaty to carve up a defeated Portugal, in September Napoleon sent Junot and a full army corps to mass at Bayonne on the Spanish border.

Tortuous negotiations proceeded with both Spain and Portugal. In September Junot's army was admitted to Spain, when the chief Minister in Madrid, Manuel Godoy, agreed to allow transit in return for receiving all Portugal south of the Tagus as his personal fief. France was to retain Lisbon and northern Portugal, which was to be given to the house of Etruria in one of Napoleon's bizarre swaps whereby Tuscany was made over to his sister Elisa. In Portugal the Regent John, deputizing for his insane mother, agreed to close the ports, declare war on Britain and seize her subjects, but jibbed at handing over confiscated property to France. Napoleon lost patience and on 12 October ordered Junot to invade Portugal.

The Portuguese, having dithered for months, were now galvanized into action and finally closed their ports. On 5 November their batteries actually fired on a Royal Navy frigate. Behind the scenes, however, it was a different story: on 22 October the Portuguese ambassador signed an Anglophile accord and pledged that the Portuguese royal family and fleet would flee to their colony in Brazil. The British did not trust Portugal and sent Admiral Smith and nine battleships to the Tagus to enforce the agreement. Smith invested Lisbon and prevented supplies arriving.

Matters were on a knife edge when the perennially impatient Napoleon decided he had had enough of Portuguese vacillation and declared the House of Braganza extinguished. This finally forced the hand of the Prince Regent (John VI of Portugal, João I of Brazil): the royal family and most of the fleet departed for Brazil. Junot's corps was meanwhile making very slow progress along the Peninsula's dreadful roads. He was in Salamanca on 12 November but it took him until 30 November to reach Lisbon. He arrived to find the entire Portuguese fleet gone and just one unseaworthy ship of the line at anchor. The British completed their triumph in the battle of wits by occupying Madeira on Christmas Eve.

Junot completed a lacklustre performance by failing to build an alliance with the liberal Portuguese bourgeoisie and introduce Enlightenment reforms – a mistake so egregious that Junot has been suspected of wanting to become King of Portugal himself.

Having dealt with Portugal in this rough-and-ready fashion, Napoleon turned his attention to Spain. His intention to bring the entire Iberian peninsula under the French aegis was clear enough from his actions in January 1808. First he rebuked Charles IV for conspiring to prevent the marriage of Prince Ferdinand and his niece Louise, Lucien's daughter. He then informed Charles that his son was plotting to depose him, which caused Charles to arrest Ferdinand for treason. Having set the Bourbons at each other's throats, Napoleon moved in for the *coup de grâce*: on 16 February 1808 he threw three army corps (180,000 men) into Spain and occupied all Spanish cities (including Barcelona) along a line from Pamplona to Figueras.

What was in Napoleon's mind when he took this extraordinary step? There can be many answers. He was always fundamentally contemptuous of the Bourbons, wherever they manifested themselves; having expelled them from France and Italy, he may have seen them as a dangerous rallying point against his own dynasty. Some historians have seen his decision as a mere 'bureaucratic reflex': since the Bourbons were laggardly in supplying men and money for his cause, he wanted to put in a Bonapartist administration that would do the job properly. He may also have intended to emulate Louis XIV, during whose reign France had effectively ruled Spain. He may have been trying to find more kingdoms for his siblings. And he may have been seduced by the golden legend of Spain, bedazzled both by the tradition of riches from the Indies and by the history of great armadas sent against the old enemy, England. Though all these factors doubtless played a part in his thinking, the fundamental determinants of his Spanish policy were twofold.

Partly he was motivated by opportunism, for diplomats' reports convinced him that Spain was in terminal decline and would welcome him as a saviour. Charles IV, on the throne since 1788, was presiding over the decline of a great mercantilist past, and in addition Spain was split both economically and ideologically. Economically the new bourgeoisie in ports like Cadiz and Barcelona had been the winners, at least until Napoleon's economic blockade, while the peasantry of Andalucia and Galicia were the losers. Ideologically, the nation was divided between devotees of traditional, ultramontane Catholicism and supporters of the Enlightenment. Spain looked like a fruit ripe for the plucking and, moreover, if Napoleon controlled Spain, it seemed to him he might control the wealth of Latin America too. On the Latin American front he was seriously misinformed, for the great days of bullion cargoes and galleons groaning with precious metals were long gone; moreover, a Latin America theoretically controlled by Napoleon would be easy prey for the Royal Navy.

Secondly, the occupation of Spain answered Napoleon's grand strategic design, which was supposed to drive England out of all its overseas possessions and bottle her up in her island home. The early months of 1808 saw Napoleon battling with a Promethean, some would say fantastic, plan. A joint Russo-French army would take Constantinople and cut the British lifeline to India while a French fleet carried the war to the Cape of Good Hope and the East Indies. Then there was Sicily. On 24 January 1808 Napoleon sent Joseph a detailed plan for the invasion of Sicily. Two years before, when the deposed Neapolitan Bourbons (Ferdinand IV and Maria Carolina) fled there, it had been Napoleon's intention to send French armies after them, but the British intervention in Calabria and subsequent revolt had aborted that plan. Now the time was ripe. Finally, a Spanish army was to march through Spain, take Gibraltar, defeat the Barbary kingdoms and thus seal the Mediterranean for ever against the British. England would thus be excluded from the Mediterranean, Africa, the Levant, the East and Latin America in addition to continental Europe.

Once again Napoleon's insights were confined to the surface. Had he studied Spain more closely, he would have seen some ominous pointers. On paper Spain had been France's loyal ally since 1796 and had even sent armies into Portugal to forestall British intervention. But Napoleon's policies, which involved war and more war, worked against Spanish interests, as he might have inferred from the joy with which the Latin American traders of Cadiz had greeted the peace of Amiens. The long interruption of colonial trade had brought them close to ruin, impoverished the Spanish state and led to a 70% depreciation of the paper money. When war was resumed in 1803, Manuel Godoy tried to stay out of it, but Napoleon bullied Charles IV into joining in; one of the first fruits was the destruction of the Spanish fleet at Trafalgar.

Godoy was always fundamentally antagonistic to Napoleon and on news of Trafalgar, thinking luck had deserted the French Emperor, he mobilized the Spanish army to deal with an unknown enemy (obviously the French). Austerlitz changed everything, but Napoleon was aware of Godoy's proposed treachery and stored it in his capacious memory as a salient fact. Godoy again revealed his hand in 1806, making it clear that he was hostile and expected the Prussians to win the war that year. After

Jena he quickly tried to backtrack and even sent a Spanish army corps to the Baltic, but the Emperor was not deceived. Charles IV was thus compelled to hold fast to the French alliance. The Spanish were forced to collaborate in Napoleon's schemes to bring Portugal under the umbrella of the Continental System, even though they were sceptical of the worth of Portuguese trade and argued that the occupation of Portugal would simply provoke England to seize Brazil and then proceed against Spain. Godoy went along with Napoleon's tough line towards Portugal, hoping that his royal master could emulate Philip II and annex it. The Treaty of Fontainebleau in October 1807, which divided the country, was therefore a severe disappointment to him.

Despite his many mistakes in Spain, Napoleon at least read Godoy's character correctly. Godoy, the royal favourite and the alleged lover of the Queen was at once the Rasputin and the Franco of his time, with the malign influence of the one and the dictatorial power of the other. He rivalled Pitt by becoming first minister of Spain in 1792 at the age of twenty-five, after promotion from Charles IV's bodyguard. Great things were expected of him and it was hoped he would revitalize Spain after the signal failure of earlier ministers, especially Floridablanca with his hostility to the French Revolution and Aranda with his bankrupt neutralism. Yet Godoy lacked the ability to be a statesman and perceived international relations purely in terms of how they could be used to defeat his enemies at court. Napoleon, who despised him and saw right through him, was always prepared to exploit this Achilles' heel. He intrigued against Godoy with the Infante Ferdinand, then set it up so that his young ally was arrested for treason, giving him the pretext to intervene.

By 1808 Godoy was universally unpopular and held to blame for all the symbols of Spanish decline: the economic depression, price inflation, dear bread, the loss of the American market, the unpopular war with Britain, which exacerbated the economic crisis, and most of all the scandalous disgrace of a royal family in which the Queen was believed to entertain this 'low born' impostor as a lover. Passions in Spain finally boiled over at Aranjuez on 17 March 1808. A mob of soldiers, peasants and palace grooms forced Charles IV to dismiss Godoy, who was found hiding in a rolled-up carpet; two days later another mob obliged the King to abdicate in favour of his son, the Prince of Asturias, who briefly became Ferdinand IV. Using this 'revolt' as a pretext Napoleon ordered Murat and a large body of troops to Madrid, where they arrived on 23 March.

This so-called 'Tumult of Aranjuez' was not the work of liberal opinion, but of a group of malcontent nobles in alliance with the court faction of the Prince of Asturias – using as their instrument the army and the mob. Historians have seen this as another manifestation of the hidalgo tradition: the grandees could stomach rule by bureaucrats but not by parvenu court favourites like Godoy. There was particular animus between Ferdinand and Godoy as the prince believed Godoy was aiming at a regency to exclude him from the throne, while Godoy was aware that the prince was intriguing against him with Bonaparte through the French ambassador. Godoy was shrewd enough to see that the Tumult of Aranjuez was not a spontaneous popular uprising, but the work of the exploited masses manipulated from above. In retrospect it looks like just another in the long line of demonstrations of political power by the alliance between the Army and the mob which habitually decided the fate of kings and ministers in nineteenth-century Spain.

The Spanish story abounds in ironies and none richer than the fall of Godoy. The first minister had just decided that Napoleon must be opposed before he took over Spain and to this end elected to remove the King to safety in Seville – a step which ironically triggered the 'Tumult'. Ferdinand was at this stage virtually a creature of Bonaparte, and by far Napoleon's wisest course would have been to set him on the throne as a puppet. But, showing the first clear signs of self-destructive behaviour, Napoleon set off for Bayonne in April with quite other ideas in his mind. Passing swiftly through Tours, Poitiers and Angoulême he stopped in Bordeaux for ten days, sightseeing and attending receptions. On 14 April he arrived at Bayonne and settled in for three months at the château of Maracq, ready to put the final touches to his Spanish policy.

His first action at Bayonne was scarcely an act of consummate statesmanship. The Bayonne decrees of 17 April declared all American ships entering European ports to be lawful prize. Napoleon argued that since the U.S.A. had embargoed its own ships, any vessels purporting to come from North America must be British merchantmen in disguise, bearing forged papers. This attempt to plug another hole in the Continental System simply increased friction unnecessarily with the U.S.A. But as a blunder it was a bagatelle alongside what was to follow.

On 18 April he offered to mediate between father and son and summoned both Charles IV and Ferdinand (also Godoy) to meet him. The deposed Charles was predictably keen to have Napoleon as a supposed champion, but Ferdinand was less certain of the wisdom of making the journey. To help him make up his mind the Emperor sent his favourite troubleshooter Savary to entice him to Bayonne with specious promises. The brutal Savary, whose destiny seemed to be to destroy young princes (he was principal agent in the execution of the duc d'Enghien), was the man of whom Napoleon once said: 'If I ordered

Savary to murder his wife and children, I know he would do it without a moment's hesitation.' This was the man whose blandishments Ferdinand was stupid enough to trust. He arrived at Bayonne on 20 April, ten days before his father.

It took a week for Napoleon to bend the Bourbons to his will. On 5 May there was a violent scene, which ended with the Emperor threatening to execute Ferdinand there and then if he did not abdicate in favour of his father. Already revealed as a fool, the prince proved himself a coward also. Without even trying to call Bonaparte's bluff he caved in and acknowledged Charles as King. Charles then immediately handed his crown over to Napoleon, who eventually gave it to his brother Joseph. A junta of Francophile Spaniards already summoned to Bayonne ratified the arrangement. Ferdinand and his brothers were held in France under house arrest, while Charles and Godoy were exiled to Compiègne. With a choice sense of irony Napoleon selected Talleyrand as the man who would have the 'honour' of offering Ferdinand hospitality on his estate at Valençay – irony because Talleyrand thought the Spanish adventure was the most disastrous aspect of a generally erroneous foreign policy. Some have argued that this was the one occasion when the Emperor clearly got the better of his vulpine Foreign Minister: that Talleyrand was playing a machiavellian game by enticing Napoleon into the Spanish quagmire while distancing himself publicly, but that Bonaparte outfoxed him and compromised him by thus openly associating him with the abdication of Ferdinand.

The bizarre events at Bayonne in April–May 1808 call for further comment. Even as the negotiations were taking place, Spain exploded into general revolution caused by the national humiliation implied by the conference. Napoleon thus directed the forces involved in the rising at Aranjuez against his own head. Why he did not use Ferdinand as a stooge is still slightly mysterious, for the forced abdication cannot be explained solely as a desire to find new thrones for his siblings. It seems that, Ferdinand's enthusiasm for his cause notwithstanding, Napoleon never trusted him. Having a very low opinion of his talents, the Emperor feared the prince would not be a reliable ally but instead would become the plaything of Court factions who would not necessarily be friendly to France.

The Bayonne manoeuvre was a disaster that would eventually involve Napoleon in five years of bloody fighting in the Spanish peninsula. The affront to Spanish pride was dual: the conference should have been held on Spanish soil, not French (preferably in Madrid) and Napoleon should have confirmed Ferdinand as King. Even those sympathetic to the

Emperor concede that his Spanish policy was one of his greatest errors. It has been described, not unjustifiably, as an 'ambush' and compared to the crimes of Tiberius. On St Helena Napoleon conceded his mistake and tried to rewrite history by producing a letter in which he rebuked Murat for having misled him over the true state of Spanish opinion. Even at the time he was aware of the propaganda gift he had made over to his enemies: 'My action is not good from a certain point of view, I know. But my policy demands that I shall not leave in my rear, so close to Paris, a dynasty hostile to mine.' On St Helena he was more frank: 'I embarked very badly on the Spanish affair, I confess; the immorality of it was too patent, the injustice too cynical.'

His 'solution' to the Spanish problem was also deeply flawed and his approach to it puzzling. Before giving the crown to Joseph he had offered it to Louis, although he, as King of Holland, had opposed his brother most strongly. Joseph was reluctant to take on the task and at first accepted only on condition he could also be King of Naples. Napoleon forced him to opt for the Spanish throne, though Joseph always hankered after his beloved Naples and always felt he had made a mistake.

Even more bizarre is Napoleon's penchant for arbitrary swaps. The obvious candidate for the Spanish throne was Murat, who openly lusted after it and had even made dispositions in Madrid as if the result was a foregone conclusion. As a consolation prize he was prepared to accept the throne of Portugal, but at first fumed with anger when Napoleon spoke of him as a necessary cog in his Italian policy. With extreme reluctance Murat took over Joseph's old role as King of Naples. Why, in any case, did Napoleon persevere with people who had already proved they were useless? Did he think that, because they were blood of his blood, his brothers 'must' have talent if they would only exert themselves? Or did he simply act from crude Corsican family feeling? Murat's form was fully exposed and Napoleon cannot have had a high opinion of him as an administrator, yet he used him for a post fraught with dangers and one, moreover, that held out myriad temptations for a man of Murat's overweening ambition. Beyond that is the glaringly obvious fact that the entire system of vassal kings contained irreconcilable contradictions. A credible monarch had to identify with the people and nation he ruled, yet Napoleon insisted that his brother kings be first and foremost loyal Frenchmen, ready to anticipate the Emperor's slightest wishes.

By becoming entangled in Spain Napoleon evinced pride, arrogance and lack of imagination: pride, because he could not believe that anyone would resist his will; arrogance, because he thought that even if armed opposition arose, the task of suppressing it would be a military walkover; and lack of imagination in that he could not understand that other peoples could be just as much motivated by national pride as the French were. He failed to see the quicksands yawning before him or to intuit the vibrancy of a nation of twelve million inhabitants in arms. By no stretch of the imagination did the Spanish adventure answer French national interests. It blew the notion of 'natural frontiers' skyhigh and emphasized the divide between genuinely French national needs and the purely dynastic ambitions of the Bonapartes. Economically, the chance for loot aside, the Spanish incursion made no sense: a few businessmen looked forward to seizing Iberian wool and Latin American silver, but even these hopes proved chimerical. France had been grudgingly behind Napoleon during the wars of 1805–07 but almost universally opposed this foray south of the Pyrenees; the opposition was perhaps especially marked in Bordeaux and the south-west of France. Above all, Spain drove a wedge between Napoleon and the notables – those bourgeois pillars of his rule.

From May 1808 the Emperor was on a downhill slide towards ultimate disaster. On the second of the month there was an uprising in Madrid, which Murat suppressed bloodily, and which has been immortalized in Goya's painting. But this was merely the first of many outbreaks. On 20 May the pro-French Governor of Badajoz was murdered by a mob; two days later the same fate overtook the Governor of Cartagena. On 23 May the province of Valencia rose, on the 24th Asturias, on the 27th Seville; Oviedo rebelled on the 24th, Zaragoza on the 25th, Galicia on the 30th, Catalonia on 7 June. By what seemed like chain reaction the splitting molecule of revolution produced a mighty holocaust. Napoleon should have realized the strength of feeling in Spain and cut his losses but, like a fanatic, redoubled his efforts when he had lost sight of his aim. Murat claimed that it was the Emperor's attitude that was the cause of the prairie-fire rapidity of the Spanish revolt. When Murat complained about the difficulty of getting supplies, Napoleon replied impatiently that he should live off the land and take by force whatever he wanted: he was tired of a general who 'at the head of 50,000 troops asks for things instead of taking them'. Murat claimed that he sat stunned when he read the letter as if a tile had fallen on his head.

Who, then, were these Spanish revolutionaries and what were their aims? At first the different risings were separate, manifestations of frustrated localism, using anger about Bayonne and Madrid on 2 May as pretexts; local grievances, expectations and disappointments found a focus in acute xenophobia and were legitimated in anti-French propaganda portraying Ferdinand as 'the Desired One'. Initial resistance was from local notables and commanders, since Ferdinand had instructed his junta in Madrid to cultivate the French at all costs. It was only much later, when the rising was in full swing, that Ferdinand rescinded his orders to the Madrid junta.

Historians differ on the nature of the Spanish rising. Some say the revolt was led by those implicated in the plot against Godoy and was thus a continuation of the Tumult of Aranjuez. Others hold that the tumult and the revolt are distinct – with the latter a mindless outburst of fanatical xenophobia led by the regular clergy, especially monks and friars. The second is the interpretation Napoleon himself always promoted, for obvious propagandist reasons – to portray the rising as benighted reaction against reform and the Enlightenment and to mask his own blunder at Bayonne – but it is not thereby fallacious.

One thing is certain: the rising initially found Spain as divided as ever it had been under Godoy. The middle and upper classes were circumspect, since they saw clearly that the price of defeating the French might be power to the people; having observed the French Revolution, they realized it might then be their turn to be overthrown. Also, the fact that Charles and Ferdinand had abdicated legally placed them in a quandary, since the only non-circular way to challenge Joseph's accession would be by appealing to popular sovereignty, with the same possible horrific outcome. There was therefore nothing for it but that judges, magistrates and officials should cooperate with the invaders, who formed the military arm of a legally constituted monarch.

In the occupied parts of Spain the propertied classes collaborated with the French, but in the unoccupied areas the xenophobic mob swept all before it, including vacillating local bureaucrats. Peasants, students and religious raided arsenals, erected gallows and instituted a reign of terror that made the propertied fear for their own skins; in panic they joined in and declared war on the French. Seeing that if they remained aloof, the result might be peasant anarchy, local notables and military officers joined the 'revolution' so as to control it. Napoleon, absurdly complacent, meanwhile basked in the illusion that the propertied would be bound to rally to him out of fear of the mob and that his only important task was to win over the Captains-General of the localities.

This was just one of a plethora of errors the increasingly accident-prone Emperor made in Spain. To an extent he was unlucky in that, having squared the Iberian bourgeoisie, he encountered wholly unexpected opposition from the Church, the peasantry and the urban proletariat. This was not so much patriotism (though often rationalized as such) but rather a twofold reaction against the economic depression resulting from Napoleon's Continental System and (particularly on the part of the Church and the landowners) resistance to the kind of socio-economic changes the pro-French faction wanted to introduce. The Bayonne coup, though often cited as *the* cause of the uprising, was the occasion rather than the deep motor of insurrection. Napoleon's lack of imagination was palpable. He seems to have assumed that 1808 in Spain could simply be a rerun of 1789 in France, with a nascent bourgeoisie eager to seize power; just a little social analysis would have revealed to him that this enlightened faction of Spanish bourgeoisie was too small to serve as the social basis of state power.

For anyone who cared to look at Spain with an unjaundiced eye there were clear and ominous signs of things to come. England's aim was to see that the insurrection did not splinter into warlordism, so London backed the formation of a national junta under Jovellanos, which issued *pronunciamentos* at Seville and Cadiz, declaring war on France in the name of Ferdinand VII. After some hesitation, the British also decided to send a 9,000-strong army to the Peninsula under General Arthur Wellesley and to supply the revolutionary juntas through Gibraltar.

Napoleon was soon disabused of his notion that pacifying Spain was a mere police operation. Bessières won a victory over the rebels at Medina del Campo in Galicia on 14 July, which allowed Joseph to enter Madrid, but the new king was taken aback by his icy reception and wrote about it in some alarm to his brother. But the French failed to take Zaragoza in Aragon; in Catalonia General Duchesne was bottled up in Barcelona; in the south-east, to Napoleon's fury, Moncy fell back from Valencia to Ocana.

Worse was to follow. Napoleon gave the task of conquering Andalucia to General Dupont and a corps of conscripts. Dupont moved down from Toledo, with Cadiz as his objective, and sacked Cordoba. But then everything went wrong. Half-starved after the severing of its supply lines, heavily outnumbered by the rebels and suffering the burden of Dupont's 'horrible generalship' (Napoleon's phrase), this 19,000-strong army surrendered to the junta forces under Castaños on 22 July at Bailén, at the foot of the Sierra Morena. This was the first defeat of the Emperor's troops in open country but it was scarcely a victory over the élite of Austerlitz, as the Spanish imagined. In panic Joseph quit Madrid and skulked on the French border.

Already the war was acquiring the savage character that would make it infamous in the annals of man's inhumanity to man. After Bailén the Spanish violated the terms of capitulation by leaving 10,000 troops to perish on a barren island because, as they put it, they saw no reason to obey the rules of war when dealing with a 'captain of bandits'. Zaragoza, having held out for two-and-a-half months against a large siege train, even though poorly fortified, was then the scene of sanguinary house-to-house streetfighting. French patrols were ambushed and cut down to the last man, if they were lucky. If they were unlucky, they were reserved for horrible deaths by mutilation, crucifixion, being nailed to trees, boiled in oil, drowned or buried alive. The crazed xenophobia of the juntas must bear some of the blame for the descent into barbarism. An inflammatory proclamation by the Valencia junta on 7 June 1809 said of the French: 'They have behaved worse than a horde of Hottentots. They have profaned our temples, insulted our religion and raped our women.'

It must be conceded that the French gave as good as they got. Dupont sacked Cordoba and elsewhere Spain was given over to the looting of a Napoleonic soldiery imbued with a spirit wherein a rational system of living off the land by military requisition had yielded to an anarchy of rapine and plunder. The French were devotees of mass execution, usually without trial. They dispatched hundreds by firing squad and hanged, looted and raped with gusto. Repression and backlash, atrocity and counter-atrocity plunged the country into an inferno of brutality and degradation. The breakdown of all social order had predictable results. Soon the country hovered on the brink of famine. The writer George Sand remembered vividly the terrible scenes in Spain in 1808 when she travelled there as a child with her father. She existed on raw onions, sunflower seeds, green lemons and soup made of candle-ends, which she shared with the soldiers. She remembered the noise of the wagon in which she lay as it crunched over the bones of corpses in the road, and recalled once clutching at the sleeve of a trooper only to find his arm missing.

The resistance on the peninsula spread to Portugal, where Wellington landed at Oporto and soon had an army of 16,000 behind him. The impulsive Junot foolishly attacked with inferior numbers and was defeated at Vimeiro. The Convention of Cintra, to Spanish fury, allowed for the repatriation of French forces in English ships, together with all their equipment and loot. Wellington was opposed to such liberal terms, but his last-minute supersession by General Burrard – reflecting infighting in London – took the shine off Vimeiro; and it was Burrard who let the French off the hook with the Cintra agreement. A disconsolate Wellington temporarily returned to the post of Irish Secretary in London. The British then marched into Galicia, where the locals welcomed them with open arms. The Vimeiro defeat was played up for its full propaganda worth in the London broadsheets, where it was claimed that Napoleon himself had been worsted.

A facile moment of opportunism by the Emperor had plunged the *Grande Armée* into the maelstrom. To an extent he was protected from the immediate consequences of his own error, for news of Bailen did not catch up with him until he was almost back at St-Cloud. After leaving Bayonne on 21 July he made the most leisurely progress back to Paris, visiting Toulouse, Montauban, Agen, Bordeaux, Rochefort, Niort, Nantes, Tours and Blois as if he were a nineteenth-century tourist of the most ambling sort. But the news of Bailén shook him from his torpor, for he immediately realized that he had plunged himself into a deadly struggle in Spain; the shock news of Bailén would give fresh heart to his enemies in Germany and perhaps even tempt the spirits of Prussian and Austrian revanchism.

Preoccupied with the thought of keeping Austria quiet, so that if necessary he could shift further corps of the *Grande Armée* to Spain, Napoleon at once made arrangements for another 'summit' meeting with Czar Alexander. Meanwhile he made contingency plans for transferring 100,000 men under Ney, Victor and Mortier from the Elbe to the Peninsula. Intense diplomatic activity then went on to set up the earliest possible reunion of the two most powerful men in Europe: a venue was agreed at Erfurt, a temporary French enclave in Thüringen. Napoleon set out from St-Cloud on 22 September for another encounter with the man he thought he had overcome with charm. He had two objectives: securing his rear against Austria and achieving a dynastic marriage with the Czar's sister.

The Erfurt conference was not destined to be a success. There were two main reasons: the parties had not been honest with each other at Tilsit; and since then clouds had gathered over the makeshift relationship. Both Napoleon and Alexander had always regarded the Tilsit treaty as a way of buying time; there is the clearest possible statement of Napoleon's position in a cynical letter he sent to his ambassador in St Petersburg, Louis de Caulaincourt, on 29 January 1808. But he saw the need to keep the Czar sweet and four days later (2 February) he sent Alexander a long letter offering to share a dismembered Ottoman empire with him. As he explained in a letter to his brother Louis a fortnight later, he was deeply influenced by the speech from the throne at the beginning of 1808 when George III made clear his determination to continue the war. Angered by Albion's intransigence, Napoleon tried to tighten up the plans he had laid with Alexander at Tilsit for a Franco-Russian pincer movement on India.

But, the insincerity of the two parties apart, events had already moved on since Tilsit. The Czar was increasingly convinced that even the stopgap accord at Tilsit had been simply one-way traffic in Napoleon's favour. He liked the Emperor personally, but his affection was not shared at the Russian court. When he returned home after Tilsit, he was alarmed to find how high feelings were running on the treaty. There were even whispers of a coup to replace him with a more Francophobe ruler. Remembering the fate of his father, who had been betrayed by his courtiers for precisely this reason, Alexander began to renege on Tilsit.

The anti-French party at St Petersburg certainly had a case when they argued that the entente with France worked against Russian interests. French hegemony in the Baltic stood in the way of Russian expansion into Finland. The Grand Duchy of Warsaw, a French vassal state in the Russian 'sphere of influence', especially rankled. In Prussia France had agreed to evacuate the country by 1 October 1808 but showed no signs of a phased withdrawal; Napoleon indeed was delaying the evacuation on the grounds that he had to have every last penny of the war indemnity before pulling out. And whereas Napoleon had agreed to a division of Turkey and often talked about it, he remained evasively silent on the key question of who would control Constantinople.

Most disadvantageous of all were the economic protocols agreed at Tilsit. Exports of corn, hemp and wood destined for England had been embargoed because of the Continental System; moreover, France made no offer of compensation but retained a favourable balance of trade with Russia, leaving her with a ruinous glut of hemp, wood, tallow, pitch, potassium, leather and iron. Of 338 ships recorded as leaving Russian ports in 1809, only one was bound for Bordeaux and meanwhile France exported to Russia luxuries like spirits, scents, porcelain and jewellery instead of the goods she really needed.

A gesture of goodwill in advance of the Erfurt conference was needed, so Napoleon announced he would evacuate Prussia immediately, provided the full reparations of 140 million francs were paid first and Prussia agreed to limit its army to 42,000 men. But even this concession did not seem to thaw the frosty relations between Paris and St Petersburg. Napoleon's secret instructions to Talleyrand were to secure a treaty that would tighten the screws on England and make Russia in effect Austria's gaoler while giving him a free hand in Spain. Since the duplicitous Talleyrand was already working against him, this seemed a forlorn hope, but the Emperor limited the foreign minister's scope for double-dealing by insisting on two clauses: that he, not Alexander, should determine the criteria for Russia's going to war with Austria, and that Russian troops should at once mass on the Austrian border.

Napoleon arrived in Erfurt on 27 September, welcomed the Czar and spent the rest of the day with him. The two men were together until 14 October. Immense efforts had been made to impress Alexander with French power, as Napoleon had explained to Talleyrand in his original letter of instruction: 'Before we begin, I wish the emperor Alexander to be dazzled by the spectacle of my power ... Use the language he understands. Tell him that the grand designs of Providence are evident in the benefits our alliance will have for mankind.' To this end he had summoned all the vassal kings of Bavaria, Saxony and Württemberg and all the dukes and princes of the Confederation of the Rhine to meet him at Erfurt. Sumptuous apartments were put at the disposal of Alexander and his retinue, all furnished with paintings, sculptures and tapestries sent from France as if they were a travelling museum exhibit; lavish banquets were prepared by French chefs; there were shooting parties and daily receptions, balls or fêtes; Napoleon's favourite actor, Talma, came from Paris with the Comédie-Française to perform.

The social round worked out magnificently. On 7 October Napoleon took Alexander on a tour of the battlefield of Jena and talked him through all the military manoeuvres; afterwards a 'hunt' (actually a mass slaughter) of hares and partridges was conducted over the terrain of the battlefield. The tenor of the day before can be gauged from a letter Napoleon sent to Josephine on the 6th: 'Emperor Alexander danced but I didn't. After all, forty years old is forty years old.' Another letter to Josephine hints at the repressed homosexual elements in the Emperor's makeup: 'I am satisfied with Alexander and he should be satisfied with me. If he were a woman I think I would make him my mistress.' The way they actually bonded was itself curious. In Napoleon's retinue was his old mistress Mlle Bourgoin, the woman he had stolen from Chaptal. When Alexander took a strong fancy to her, Napoleon tried to head off the liaison, fearing that she would reveal intimate secrets of the boudoir. But Alexander insisted he must have her, and so it transpired.

The talks themselves, by contrast, were a huge disappointment to Napoleon. This was hardly surprising, since Talleyrand was engaged in a daily game of sabotage. After being briefed by Napoleon and encouraged to see the Czar privately, he would visit Alexander and reveal every aspect of Napoleon's hand. On his very first meeting with the Czar, Talleyrand begged him to resist the Emperor with all his might, since Napoleon's foreign policy no longer answered French national interests.

Talleyrand told Alexander that the tacit social alliance between Napoleon and the notables was at an end, that the notables wanted nothing but the 'natural frontiers' and viewed with extreme alarm both Napoleon's German expansionism and his quixotic foray into Spain. The consequence was that the Czar refused to accept Napoleon's two extraordinary clauses. The highly unsatisfactory final protocol signed on 12 October dealt with marginal matters.

To secure a breakthrough at Erfurt Napoleon had to give Alexander a free hand in Poland and, especially, give him Turkey. For mysterious and unexplained reasons, Napoleon could not bring himself to do so; almost certainly the explanation is the 'Oriental complex', for such obstinacy has no rational basis. He did concede the Czar Finland and the Romanian provinces of Moldavia and Wallachia, but that was about the only significant content in the Treaty of Erfurt. All the concessions were on Napoleon's side: a reduction of Prussia's war indemnity by twenty million francs, a promise not to intervene in any conflict between Russia and Turkey, and the meaningless acceptance of Russia's 'mediation' in the conflict with England. Article 10 pledged the Czar to go to war if Austria attacked France, but the article was vaguely worded, allowing Alexander several loopholes. When Napoleon sent a minatory letter to the Austrian Emperor, designed to preempt any attempts at revanchism, Alexander refused to be a co-signatory.

The most signal failure at Erfurt was the farcical attempt to secure a dynastic marriage. Talleyrand pretended to be making strenuous efforts to this end but all the time was sabotaging his master's policy. Every time Napoleon complained about the Czar's evasiveness, Talleyrand would assure him that Alexander was as taken with him as ever. Then he would depart for a teatime rendezvous with the Czar and together they would plot a fresh item of verbal obfuscation with which to bamboozle Napoleon. Face to face with the Emperor, Alexander claimed to be enthusiastic for the idea of Napoleon's marriage to his sister, save only that he needed the consent of the Dowager Empress. In the end Napoleon grew so frustrated with Alexander's stalling that he stayed up late with Talleyrand, in a state of high agitation. 'Tell him I will agree with him on any of his plans for the partition of Turkey . . . Use any arguments you want. I know you favour the divorce. Josephine favours it too.'

There can be no question of Napoleon's sincere desire to marry the Grand Duchess Catherine. To Caulaincourt he wrote that he was making this union the acid test of the Czar's friendship, for 'it would be a real sacrifice for me. I love Josephine; I will never be happier with anyone else, but my family and Talleyrand and Fouché and all the politicians insist upon it in the name of France.' When the two autocrats parted on 14 October without agreement on this, or indeed anything of real value, Napoleon's dismay was palpable. One can almost sense the depression behind his laconic words to Joseph, in a letter on 13 October: 'I've finished all my business with the Czar of Russia.' Savary confirmed next day, when the Czar left, that the Emperor was in a sad and pensive mood, as if he knew the conference had been a failure.

It could scarcely have failed in a more spectacular way. Almost as if he were slapping his 'friend' in the face, a month later the Czar announced that his sister, Grand Duchess Catherine, would be marrying the Prince of Oldenburg. Since Alexander's other sister, Anna, was only fourteen and not yet considered of a marriageable age, it was clear that the Russians had slammed the door on dynastic union with France. Nor was this the worst of it. Talleyrand, already in the pay of the Austrians, leaked the treaty to Vienna, together with intelligence of Alexander's refusal to back Napoleon in any war with Austria. The Austrians at once took a secret decision for a spring offensive.

Pausing just a few days in Paris, Napoleon left for Spain on 29 October. With him he took 160,000 men divided into seven army corps under Lannes, Soult, Ney, Victor, Lefebvre, Mortier and Gouvion St-Cyr. Accompanied by the Imperial Guard, the Emperor made rapid southward progress via Angoulême and Bordeaux and arrived in Bayonne on 3 November. When he crossed the Spanish border next day, he met a deputation of Capuchin monks at Tolosa; angry at the role of the regular clergy in the Spanish insurrection, he warned them forcefully: 'If you monks have the effrontery to meddle in military affairs, I promise you I'll cut off your ears.'

After spending four days in Vitoria, on 9 November Napoleon opened his campaign proper. Since the Spanish armies were aiming to encircle Joseph's forces, the emperor decided to turn the tables by picking off each enemy wing in turn. Dividing his army into three, he opted for simultaneous flank attacks on the isolated Spanish wings while the remaining third pressed on for Madrid. The first of many disappointments in this Spanish campaign was the lacklustre performance of the marshals; Lefebvre and Victor, consumed by mutual jealousy, allowed the Spanish army of Galicia to escape. Lefebvre failed to cooperate effectively with Victor and jumped the gun, thus alerting the Spanish of the danger in which they stood and allowing them to retreat. The other Spanish army got clear away when Lannes and Ney also failed to spring the trap effectively. But this plan – to encircle the army of Castaños, with Lannes making a frontal attack while Ney worked round to the rear – was more controversial. While Napoleon railed at Ney for incompetence, accusing him of arriving on the scene three days too late, revisionist military scholars have fastened the blame on the Emperor himself for failing to calculate the marching distances correctly.

By the time Napoleon reached Burgos on 11 November, it was clear there would be no repeat of Austerlitz or Jena. He had to spend twelve days in Burgos whipping his own undisciplined and insubordinate troops into line, which he did by some exemplary hangings and other draconian punishments. After a further week's preparations at Aranda de Douro, the *Grande Armée* finally commenced its push on Madrid. On 30 November there was a bloody engagement in the Somosierra pass, which later critics adduced as yet another sign that the Emperor was losing his grip. Frustrated and irritated by the doughty resistance of the Spanish army in the pass, Napoleon ordered the 3rd Squadron of Polish Light Horse to make a frontal charge on the Spanish guns. It was a pre-echo of the charge of the Light Brigade nearly fifty years later, and the proportionate slaughter was as great. The Poles failed to reach their target and left sixty dead and wounded behind them, out of a total complement of eighty-eight. Napoleon then proceeded to defeat the Spanish by the patient, methodical, coordinated attack he should have employed earlier.

The vanguard of the *Grande Armée* was in the suburbs of Madrid on 1 December and all resistance in the capital had been mopped up by the 4th. Napoleon then spent two weeks in Madrid, usurping the functions of his restored brother King Joseph. The junta of nobles who had assembled in Bayonne earlier in the year to endorse Joseph had merely abolished torture and the *majorats* but had left many Bourbon institutions intact. Napoleon now went much further, by sweeping away all relics of feudalism, the Inquisition and the old Bourbon system of taxation. With winter descending fast, he again reorganized his army, ready for a rather different sort of campaigning. He managed to alienate *madrileños* by bombastic speeches about Spain's backwardness and his own role as liberator, of which the following is a fair sample: 'Your grandchildren will bless me as your redeemer. The day when I appeared in your midst they will count as the most memorable, and from that day Spain's prosperity will date its beginning.' He was also in womanizing mood in the Spanish capital and would often call for female company: 'I want a woman! Bring me a woman! A woman here and now!' But his highly developed sense of smell sometimes got in the way of his pleasures: a voluptuous sixteen-year-old actress had to be sent home because she reeked of perfume.

This was the moment when Napoleon should have moved south to deal decisively with the Spanish. Instead he opted to take out the British. Hearing that Sir John Moore had tried to fall on his isolated right flank under Soult at Sahagun, he marched north in person, aiming to get behind Moore and cut off his retreat to Lisbon; while Soult 'pinned' Moore the Emperor would execute a classic *sur les derrières* to annihilate him. But first he had to traverse the Sierra de Guadarrama in winter. This turned out to be an even more terrible exploit than the passage of the Alps during the 1800 Marengo campaign.

On 22 December the *Grande Armée* began the ascent of the Sierra amid motionless torrents of snow and silent cataracts of ice. A circumspect man would have drawn back, but Napoleon urged his veterans on, defying them to achieve the impossible. What on the Emperor's battle plans was a mere 'traverse' was in reality a white hell, a nightmare of slithering and crashing over precipices. On this march the Army came closer to mutiny than ever before or afterwards. The *poilus* called out for someone to have the guts to shoot the Emperor so they could all go home. Napoleon overheard the remark but, so fragile was morale in the ranks, he dared not punish the culprits and pretended he had heard nothing.

Finally the nightmare ended and the Army was through the pass. But the two extra days braving crevasses and avalanches had made all the difference: Moore had made good his escape and won the race to Astorga, which was where the Emperor had planned to encircle him. Since a completely satisfactory outcome was no longer feasible, Napoleon handed over the pursuit to Soult and Ney but not before he had reduced the size of the pursuing force and sent the balance back to help the hard-pressed Joseph in Madrid. Moore decided to evacuate his army at Corunna, using the Royal Navy, but the two marshals caught up with him before the evacuation was complete. Moore was forced to turn and deal with his pursuers. In a hard-fought engagement on 16 January 1809 he repulsed Soult and Ney, inflicting 1,500 casualties for the loss of 800; he himself was killed by a cannonball but the rest of the British army got off safely on to the waiting transports.

On 6 January 1809 Napoleon left Astorga for Valladolid, where he remained for eleven days, completing the military and administrative arrangements for the handover of power in Spain to Joseph and his marshals. It was in Valladolid that he made the fateful error of allowing the bickering marshals to become, in effect, warlords with semi-autonomous commands, only nominally under Joseph's suzerainty. This he did to palliate the growing unpopularity of the Peninsular War and to give his marshals bones to gnaw on, but the long-term effect was to vitiate central control from Madrid and play into the hands of the Spanish guerrillas and, later, the British army under Wellington.

Bonapartist propaganda again went into top gear to present the short imperial campaign of 1808–09 in Spain as an unalloyed personal triumph. Napoleon's mistakes were glossed over, and the incontestable fact that Napoleon had won three victories and chased a fourth army out of Spain duly played up. However, Moore's diversion was the really significant military event of 1808–09. By pulling Napoleon north of Madrid, he prevented the Emperor's intended southward sweep, which might have ended the war at a stroke. As it was, Moore's campaign bought Portugal and southern Spain a year's respite and meant the 'Spanish ulcer' would continue to suppurate.

Napoleon left Valladolid on 17 January and was in Paris on the 23rd. Accompanied by Duroc, Savary and an escort of the Guard, he rode at a fast gallop and ate up the seventy-five miles between Valladolid and Burgos in just five hours; Savary later claimed it was the fastest ride ever achieved by any monarch. From Burgos the imperial party pressed on to Tolosa and arrived in Bayonne in the small hours of the 19th, just forty-five hours after leaving Valladolid. Then it was on to Paris via Bordeaux and Poitiers; he arrived in the capital at 8 a.m. on 23 January. The Emperor's reasons for haste were twofold. First, he received definite intelligence in Valladolid that the Austrians were mobilizing for a spring campaign. Then came the in some ways even more disturbing news of a plot hatched in Paris by Fouché and Talleyrand to depose him and replace him with Murat. There was little time to lose.

CHAPTER EIGHTEEN

Joseph Fouché seems to have been the one man the Emperor genuinely feared, and with reason. The J. Edgar Hoover of his day, the atrocious chief of police had files on everyone, and at a moment's notice could send a legion of Bonaparte skeletons rattling out of the cupboard. Napoleon therefore ducked the task of tackling him head on and went for the softer option, Talleyrand. On 28 January 1809 he summoned his lame chamberlain, kept him standing for three hours, and tore into him with rare ferocity; the burden of his invective was that Talleyrand was an ingrate and money-lover who, in return for the wealth of Croesus lavished on him by the Emperor, had repaid him with bad advice – the d'Enghien fiasco was mentioned – and treachery. Doubtless remembering Mirabeau's famous quip about Talleyrand – 'the Abbé of Périgord would sell his soul for money; and he would be right, for he would be exchanging dung for gold' – Napoleon cast at him a famous insult: 'You are nothing but shit in silk stockings.'

Talleyrand made no reply but a bow, then, when the three-hour tirade finally blew itself out, went straight to the Austrian embassy and sold his services again for one million francs to the new ambassador, Clemens Metternich. This inflation-proofed equivalent of thirty pieces of silver seems on the generous side, for Talleyrand was sacked as Grand Chamberlain next day and was thus cast out of the inner circles. Besides, all that Talleyrand could tell him Metternich knew already. There was discontent in France in élite circles? Well, certainly, why else was Talleyrand in the Austrian embassy?

The Austrians had already taken this factor into account when making their decision for a war of revenge. Four principal considerations encouraged them to think that this time they could beat Napoleon. In the first place the French would be reluctant to engage with them, for they were already fully stretched in Spain and their crack units were in the Peninsula. Secondly, Czar Alexander had hinted strongly that, Erfurt or no Erfurt, he would not back Napoleon; when the French suggested a joint remonstrance to Austria, backed by the threat of a Russian declaration of war, Alexander declined to have anything to do with it. Thirdly, the Austrians knew, even before Talleyrand confirmed it, that France was war-weary and the necessary moral commitment for a major war was lacking. This in turn connected with the final consideration; that there was a new spirit of nationalism abroad in Germany and in Austria.

After Jena, Prussian intellectuals like Fichte, Arndt and Schlegel began campaigning for a unified Germany as the way to defeat Napoleon. Within the government reformers like Friedrich Stein had the upper hand for two years. They emancipated the serfs, founded universities, shook up the old bureaucracies and, most ominously, reformed the army with a unified Ministry of War and a Commission for Military Organization, which oversaw a new *Landwehr* militia (finally called up in 1813) and its Trojan horse, the *Krumper* system of short-service training. Stein eventually proved the truth of the proposition that the key to Napoleon's imperial power was his alliance with Europe's old élites. The landowning *Junkers*, fearing that they were the eventual target of Napoleon's reforms, divulged the scope of his ambitions to the French. Napoleon's reaction was swift. From Spain he imposed a new Convention on the Prussians, including an order to exile Stein; he backed this with an imperial edict declaring Stein to be an enemy of France and the Confederation of the Rhine.

Although the Prussian middle classes had originally welcomed the French Revolution, the trauma of Jena turned them into a curious hybrid, liberal reformers at home, rabid Francophobes in foreign affairs. Over and over again the soul-searching Prussians asked the same questions: how was it that in late 1806 large, well-provisioned garrisons surrendered to Napoleon without firing a shot? Why did German monarchs have no pride? William II of Prussia had emerged as a cowardly nonentity; the King of Saxony was a self-abasing French puppet whose palace at Dresden Napoleon used as a hotel; while the Emperor Francis was a pathetic figure who spent his time making toffee or endlessly stamping blank sheets of parchment with specimens from his huge collection of seals.

Something of this German *risorgimento* spirit was also evident in Austria. Despite a precarious financial base and Emperor Francis's dislike of anything that smacked of 'Jacobinism', Archduke Charles, appointed supreme Commander-in-Chief with powers superior to those of the Aulic Council, managed to reform the Army. Charles's methods involved wholesale imitation of Napoleon's: the army corps system, employment of sharpshooters and skirmishers, rigorous drilling, improved artillery and supply infrastructure. By early 1809 the Austrian commanders were itching for war.

The cautious Emperor Francis was doubtful. To the war party, who argued that England would help with troops and subsidies and there was a good chance that Prussia and Russia would be drawn in, the Emperor answered that Czar Alexander had made it plain he would not go beyond neutrality. As for England, she would consult her own interests as ever. The Emperor and his advisers had tried to drive a hard bargain with the British over subsidies for fighting Napoleon but, in financial terms, they had gone a bridge too far. London curtly refused the extravagant Austrian demand for a down payment of £2.5 million to cover mobilization and a further £5 million for each year her armies fought. Emperor Francis was finally 'bounced' into war in February 1809 when it was put to him that any further delay might enable Napoleon's Continental Blockade to work, in which case there would be no English subsidies.

As a result of the Austrian declaration of war Napoleon faced his most difficult military task since the Marengo campaign. The Austrian army was far better than in 1805, but his own Grand Army was far worse. Behind him was an insurgent Spain and a British presence in Portugal; ahead of him was an armed and restless Germany; and his home base was moody, uncertain and treacherous Paris, with men like Fouché and Talleyrand waiting in the wings. However, he was not entirely unprepared. At the back of his mind he had long been expecting this blow to fall and, in anticipation, had conscripted the necessary manpower to deal with the threat. In 1808 a *senatus consultum* called up 80,000 more conscripts from the classes of 1806, 1807, 1808 and 1809, and in December 1808 a further 80,000 from the class of 1810 were called up two years in advance. The unexpected losses in Spain meant that a further 110,000 of the class of 1810 were called up in the new year of 1809.

The original Austrian plan was for a surprise attack on the Rhine, hoping to spark a rebellion in the Confederation of the Rhine which would suck Prussia into the conflict. But Archduke Charles finally reverted to a more traditional strategy: there would be a three-pronged attack, with the main army punching through Bavaria, Archduke John invading Italy and Archduke Ferdinand taking out the Grand Duchy of Warsaw in the rear. The tripartite assault was the first Austrian mistake; the second was the assumption that Napoleon lacked the manpower to fight on all these fronts and continue campaigning in Spain. Perhaps Bonaparte encouraged the false optimism by an unreal, almost Neroesque, stance in early 1809. On 11 February Roederer recorded a conversation with the Emperor in which he stated: 'I have only one passion, only one mistress – France. I sleep with her, she never lets me down, she pours out her blood and treasure; if I need 500,000 men, she gives them to me.'

This was boastful self-delusion. His original aim was to have 260,000 troops in Germany and 150,000 in Italy by the time war broke out; in fact he managed a combined total of 275,000 in the two theatres. Already about a tenth of all conscripted Frenchmen deserted and hid in the mountains. In any case, about half the *Grande Armée* was non-French, being composed of Belgians, Italians, Dutch, Germans and special mixed units resembling the later French Foreign Legion. In Napoleon's army of 1809 could be found Swiss, Polish, Croat, Albanian, Greek, Portuguese, Spanish, Lithuanian, Dutch, Irish and even negro units. *Pace* Clausewitz, this was no longer a citizen army or a *levée en masse* but a professional army with interests distinct from those of the French nation or even the class (the peasantry) from which it was mostly recruited. Once it was possible for conscripted citizens to purchase substitutes, the Grand Army filled up with the dregs of society and became more like a traditional flotsam-and-jetsam host of the *ancien régime* type. Had Napoleon read his Machiavelli carefully, he might have spotted the danger. The one clear element of continuity with the past was the Guard, most of which was withdrawn from Spain in the spring of 1809.

Napoleon made three bad errors at the beginning of the 1809 campaign. He assumed that the Austrians would send large forces to Italy and make their main effort there, as in past wars. He appointed Berthier commander-in-chief, with Davout, Masséna and Oudinot immediately below him, and himself remained in Paris; this curious decision is usually interpreted as a desire to extract maximum propaganda advantage when the Austrian blow fell, by presenting it to the French people as a wholly unexpected sneak attack. Berthier, though, proved a disastrous choice as field commander and could not even keep abreast of the flow of orders from the Emperor. But Napoleon's worst mistake once again revealed his military Achilles' heel: failure to take the weather into account. Having campaigned on the Danube in autumn and winter, he was wholly unprepared for the weather-driven physical aspects of the battles he would face there in spring and summer.

On 9 April the Austrians began their invasion of Bavaria, without a formal declaration of war and six days earlier than Napoleon expected. At first Archduke Charles and his 120,000-strong army carried all before them: through Berthier's incompetence the French forces were hopelessly split, and disaster loomed. It was fortunate for Napoleon that heavy rain and inadequate supplies held the Austrians up, so that he was able to speed to the front and take personal charge. Leaving Paris at 4 a.m. on 13 April, and accompanied by Josephine as far as Strasbourg, he arrived at Donauworth on the 17th and at once realized that the price for concentrating his army would have to be the abandonment of Ratisbon. He then spent five days of continuous fighting, trying to regain the initiative.

He began his counterstroke by ordering Davout to make a fighting withdrawal from Regensburg and Ingolstadt, drawing the Austrians after him while Masséna and Oudinot struck east round the enemy left flank and cut communications to Vienna and the Danube. The battles of Thann, Abensberg, Landshut, Eckmühl and Ratisbon (17–23 April) saw Archduke Charles repulsed and his army badly mauled. But Napoleon was scarcely at his best at the climactic battle of Abensburg-Eckmühl on 20–22 April, where the Austrians brought Davout to bay. After much vacillation he finally decided to attack Charles there with his entire army instead of trying to encircle him. He therefore diverted Masséna from his outflanking movement and commanded him and Lannes (ordered north from Landshut) to attack the Austrian left before Charles could overwhelm Davout with superior numbers.

Eckmühl was a hamlet on the river Raaber, containing a huge baroque watermill. Napoleon ordered a frontal attack across the Raaber water-meadows, which eventually forced the enemy to retreat. But nightfall and general weariness in the ranks meant that the French did not pursue their foe to Ratisbon and, on advancing there next day, Napoleon found it grimly defended by Charles's rearguard. It was during the unsuccessful attempt to force this position that Napoleon sustained his one and only battle wound, being struck on the right foot by a spent cannonball. Eventually Lannes's division was able to take Ratisbon, but not before Archduke Charles made good his escape.

Although Charles retreated from Bavaria to Bohemia, Napoleon had hardly covered himself with laurels. The two decisions – to attack frontally instead of attempting encirclement, and not to press the pursuit from Eckmühl – were both contrary to his own military canons. The chance of a quick knockout blow, as in 1800, 1805 or 1806, was gone. Some have even precisely pinpointed Eckmühl as marking the decline of Napoleon as a great captain. Certainly he made a number of miscalculations and unwarranted assumptions and was so far from his usual form that one is tempted to adduce psychological reasons. It is known that Napoleon took one of his casual 'one night stand' mistresses during this campaign, which was not his usual practice. His defenders, however, claim that sending Masséna on a sweep of the Saale on the 20th was his real error, that his tactical handling of a week of battles was inspired and that the road to Vienna lay open – a not negligible achievement for a commander whose best units were in Spain. Most of all, Charles's 30,000 casualties and precipitate retreat removed all temptation from Saxony, Bavaria and Württemberg to throw off the yoke of the Confederation of the Rhine in the name of German nationalism.

Uncertain exactly where Charles had gone, but guessing somewhere between Vienna and Moravia, Napoleon advanced cautiously along the right bank of the Danube, uncomfortably aware that the enemy had broken down all the bridges across a river in full springtime spate. Learning finally that Charles was in Bohemia, the Emperor opted not to follow him there but to aim for Vienna and try to secure a negotiated peace. Yet time was not on his side. The Austrian corps under General Hiller fought several rearguard actions to delay the French advance on Vienna, to give the city time to prepare its defence adequately. Napoleon found himself held up not just by stubborn fights at Wels and Ebersberg but by the crossing of several flooded Danube tributaries. To make matters worse, news now came in that his viceroy Eugène de Beauharnais had been defeated in Italy.

Vienna surrendered on 13 May under threat of bombardment but the garrison withdrew to the north bank and destroyed all four bridges across the Danube. Napoleon entered the Austrian capital to an icy and sullen welcome. The problem of the Danube bridges obsessed him; as he wrote: 'To cross a river like the Danube in the presence of an enemy that knows the ground and has the sympathy of the inhabitants is one of the most difficult military operations conceivable.' Additionally, he was outnumbered. On 16 May Archduke Charles joined forces with Hiller, giving him a total strength of 115,000 against Napoleon's 82,000. Moreover, French forces were scattered, for Davout with 35,000 men was forty miles west of Vienna, putting down local uprisings, while Lefebvre's VII Corps was at Salzburg. The problem remained: how to strike fast at Charles, given that he was on the north bank and the Danube was engorged with heavy spring floods.

Napoleon now made another mistake. He decided to cross the Danube at Albern, six miles south of Vienna, where islands split the river into three streams. He intended using Lobau island, two-thirds of the way across, a lush, uninhabited place full of enormous poplar trees, as a jumping-off point, but he had not taken into account the difficulties of building bridges in these conditions. Lashed by torrential rains and assailed by Austrian commando raids, sometimes even having to endure violent storms and the attacks of fireships, French engineers and pioneers took a week to build a pontoon across the 825-yard stretch from the right bank to Lobau, using 68 pontoons and nine rafts. The first French units reached the island on 20 May and, after completion of the much shorter bridge across the third channel to the left bank, Masséna's and Lannes's corps crossed north to the mainland and established a bridgehead at the villages of Aspern and Essling.

By 21 May Napoleon had 25,000 men on the large open plain known as the Marchfeld, an arid and desolate spot on the north bank of the Danube. Timing his attack brilliantly, Archduke Charles then attacked with a huge army of 100,000 men and 250 guns; he quickly drove the French out of the villages of Aspern and Essling and back to the bridge. Once again, it turned out, Napoleon had miscalculated. He had not known that Charles was within striking distance on the bridgehead on the left bank and assumed he would be able to reinforce Lannes and Masséna easily. But now the news came in that the bridge from the left bank to Lobau had been breached, first by rising water and then by Austrian fireships and battering rams. By now the Austrians had perfected a technique of floating huge hulks and logs down river which smashed into the pontoons.

On the north bank an increasingly serious battle developed around Aspern; in the nick of time Napoleon got enough men across the repaired bridge to fight the Austrians to stalemate. But the French position remained grave, for Charles could easily get reinforcements and they could not. On the 21st 31,000 French troops had to confront more than 100,000 Austrians with 260 big guns at their disposal. On the 22nd, after makeshift repairs to the pontoons, Napoleon managed to ferry more men over; now he had 50,000 infantry, 12,000 cavalry and 144 guns to face the Austrian host. Ferocious streetfighting went on in Aspern and Essling on the morning of the 22nd, and then Napoleon ordered a strong attack on the Austrian centre.

At first Lannes seemed to carry all before him, but he was eventually forced to retreat by his own shortage of ammunition as much as an Austrian counterattack. In any case, Napoleon could not get Davout's corps across the river for the *coup de grâce*, as the bridge had broken once again. The hand-to-hand fighting of that morning in Aspern and Essling was repeated in the evening darkness; in one of these desperate encounters perished General St-Hilaire, on the point of receiving his marshal's baton. After murderous close combat General Rapp and the Young Guard managed to retake Essling but then came news that the bridge to Lobau was broken once again and the Emperor had ordered a general retreat to the island. In almost the last fighting on the mainland, Marshal Lannes had both legs smashed by a cannonball. His limbs were amputated but gangrene set in and he did not recover, lingering in feverish agony for eight days before succumbing on 31 May. Predictably, Bonapartist propaganda elevated his death into a 'glorious death for France and the Emperor' apotheosis.

The French withdrew to the island of Lobau, cut the bridge linking the mainland from its moorings and drew it back on to the island. Heavily outnumbered, Napoleon had been defeated – a fact his propaganda machine worked hard to conceal. But Austrian propaganda was just as mendacious: twenty-five French generals and Napoleon himself were said to have perished in a Cannae-style débâcle. Despite heroic deeds by Lannes, the *Grande Armée* had been worsted and the fault was the Emperor's. He made two bad mistakes: giving battle without knowing Charles's numbers, and failing to assemble his entire army on Lobau first. The Austrians sustained 23,340 casualties, the French probably in the region of 20–22,000; Napoleon, naturally, lied and claimed his casualty figures were 4,100.

At Aspern-Essling the Emperor lost his reputation for invincibility. For thirty-six hours after the battle he remained in an indecisive brown study, apparently stupefied by the setback. Fortunately, perhaps, the Austrians made no attempt, either then or later, to take Lobau; it was almost as though they could not believe their luck in having beaten the Corsican ogre. By 24 May Napoleon was himself again and next day the bridge from Lobau to the south bank was reopened, allowing the French finally to evacuate their wounded, who had lain in the open for forty-eight hours. Napoleon was aware that he faced one of the great crises of his life, for unless he retrieved his reputation with a great victory Germany would rise behind him.

It has to be conceded that Bonaparte recovered well from the initial paralysis after Aspern-Essling, for the gloomy news he received while on Lobau would have been enough to demolish a lesser man. Following the initial French setbacks in Italy, a serious insurrection broke out in the Tyrol, headed by the charismatic figure Andreas Hofer. There had been serious military stirrings in Germany, prompted by the new spirit of nationalism. In Westphalia Major Schill was attempting guerrilla warfare while in Saxony the Duke of Brunswick's son and his 'hussars of death' were on the rampage; this so-called 'black legion' cut a swathe through the cities of Dresden, Leipzig, Brunswick, Hanover and Bremen. In Paris there were rumours of popular discontent and plots, and hard news of a fall on the stockmarket. In Spain the military advantage the Emperor had secured a few months earlier was thrown away by the incompetence of his marshals, principally Soult, who remained inactive after capturing Oporto in March 1809, apparently in the quixotic belief that he might be proclaimed King of Portugal. His idleness and inactivity, and his jealousy of Ney, enabled the British to land large-scale forces under Wellesley in Portugal in April 1809.

Displaying nerves of steel, Napoleon ordered up reinforcements from Spain. Convinced that the Austrians would not attempt a landing in strength on Lobau but simply keep up a token bombardment from the north bank, he evacuated all the army except Masséna's corps, then turned the island into a fortress bristling with guns, one hundred of them trained on Charles's army. Then he painstakingly built proper bridges across the Danube, which would be invulnerable to anything but actual Austrian occupation. Isolated on Lobau for a month, by the end of June he had constructed five more bridges across the Danube, three of them to Lobau, and built stockades, piledriven into the river bed upstream, to block the passage of fireships or floating logs and hulks; additionally, he stationed a fleet of naval gunboats on the river.

Fortune favoured the brave. On 14 June Eugène Beauharnais and General MacDonald with the Army of Italy defeated Archduke John at Raab, then sent word they were on their way to the relief of Lobau. With their 23,000 men and the corps under Davout and Marmont he had also summoned, Napoleon had 160,000 men and 500 guns by the beginning of July. Amazingly, the Austrians remained inactive in face of this build-up, waiting for the general German uprising which never came.

On 4 July the Emperor was ready to strike. He began by throwing across three bridges from Lobau to Aspern-Essling, encouraging Archduke Charles to believe that he would be attempting his manoeuvre of six weeks earlier. His real objective with this feint was to put his army on Charles's left flank so as to get between him and the second Austrian army under John, which had retreated into Hungary after Raab but was now closing in again. He therefore landed an advance guard at Gross Enzerdorff, from which his engineers constructed seven pontoons to Lobau. He assembled his troops at the northern crossings to Aspern-Essling with great din and hubbub, then switched them at the last minute to the seven bridges east to Gross Enzerdorff. On the night of 4–5 July the French streamed across the Danube on the seven eastward pontoons, beset by torrential rain, yet buoyed up by the Emperor's inspired tactics.

His plan was indeed a brilliant one, requiring split-second timing and coordination. Amazingly, the diversionary feint and the actual crossing went off without a hitch; not a single man was lost and complete surprise was achieved when the French emerged at their new location on the north bank. But Charles was saved by his own lack of imagination. Hoping to repeat his success on 21–22 May he pulled his troops back to lure the French into Aspern-Essling instead of opposing the imagined crossing, as Napoleon had expected. The consequence was that the French outflanking movement was no longer feasible. But the Austrians were in a rare panic when they realized the true state of affairs and pulled their troops out of Aspern and Essling on the double.

By 9 a.m. on 5 July the three front-line corps of Davout, Oudinot and Masséna were moving forward to make way for the second line (Eugène and Bernadotte) and the third (Marmont's corps, Bessière's cavalry and the Guard. The general advance was sounded at noon. Everyone knew there would soon be a battle, for on the treeless plains of the Marchfeld there were now nearly 300,000 men and 900 cannon; the Austrians had 136,000 troops and 400 guns, Napoleon 156,000 and 500 guns. Charles drew up his army in a semicircle of fifteen miles running from Aspern through the villages of Aderklaa and Markgrafneusiedl with his centre resting on Wagram. Napoleon placed the bulk of his army – Davout, Oudinot, Eugène and Bernadotte (110,000 in all) on the right, leaving Masséna with just 27,000 on the left; in reserve he kept 11,000 Guard and 8,000 cavalry. The dispositions were classically Napoleonic, aiming for the 'centre position' or hinge between the two wings of the enemy army, and arranged so that he could transfer troops from one flank to the other faster than his opponent. But it was not a textbook formation, since Napoleon had no choice but to fight with his back to the Danube. The Emperor had three aims: to pierce the Austrian centre before it was reinforced; to gain a decisive victory so that Charles could not escape and to split the enemy before Archduke John could come to the rescue.

It was with John in mind that Napoleon ordered the attack at 5 p.m. on the 5th, despite the lateness of the hour. The first part of the Battle of Wagram was a near fiasco. Oudinot's corps withdrew after taking heavy losses, while Eugène's Army of Italy panicked and fled, having earlier mistaken the Saxons for the enemy and fired on them; they were forced to turn and face the enemy only when they nearly impaled themselves on the bayonets of the Guard in reserve. Both Davout and Bernadotte failed to make progress; the Emperor was forced to call off the attack and spend his third successive night without sleep.

Once again Bernadotte had failed at a crucial battle but this time he went too far. Attempting one of his gasconnades to conceal his failure to take the village of Aderklaa, he declared that Napoleon had botched things and that if he, Bernadotte, were in command he could have forced Charles to surrender without firing a single shot. He followed this up by abandoning his position outside Aderklaa at 4 a.m. on the 6th, pleading the necessity of shortening his line by linking with Eugène on the right and Masséna on the left. This was reported to Napoleon, who finally snapped after a decade of ingratitude and treachery from the Gascon. Furiously countermanding Bernadotte's movements, he ordered him and Masséna to take the village regardless of casualties.

Bernadotte then committed the error of galloping right into the Emperor's path. Napoleon raged at him. 'Is this the type of "telling manoeuvre" with which you will force Archduke Charles to lay down his arms?' he thundered. Seeing Bernadotte lost for words, he continued: 'I hereby remove you from command of the corps which you have handled so consistently badly. Leave my presence immediately, and quit the *Grande Armée* within twenty-four hours.' But the contumacious Gascon had not finished. Before he left for Paris he issued a bulletin, praising his men for their part in the battle and claiming they had stood 'like bronze'. The only thing brazen about Bernadotte's corps was its marshal's effrontery. Napoleon was obliged to publish an official rebuke, stating that Bernadotte's order of the day was contrary to truth, policy and national honour.

On the morning of the 6th Napoleon tried again. His tactics were for Masséna to hold while Davout and Oudinot made a frontal attack; the Army of Italy would be held back for the moment of breakthrough. But Charles upset the Emperor's plans by attacking first, aiming for a double envelopment of the French: with the anvil of his operations at Wagram, he sent his right wing to seize Aspern and cut Napoleon off from the Danube in that sector while his left threw the French right back against the river. Two Austrian corps accordingly attacked Masséna, hoping to roll him up and seize the Danube bridges in the rear.

By 11 a.m. things seemed to be going the Austrians' way: on their right they were forcing the French back to Aspern while in the centre they were forcing the Saxons to give ground. Fearing that Masséna's corps was on the point of buckling under the onslaught, and therefore that a gap might open up enabling Charles to use the 'centre position' against him, Napoleon ordered Masséna to disengage and shift to the left. This involved marching Masséna south across the front of the enemy lines, screened by cavalry. To take the pressure off, the Emperor ordered the cavalry reserve to charge and Davout to press his attack with even greater vigour. MacDonald and the cavalry performed brilliantly but took heavy losses. To some extent these were offset by the accuracy of the massed

French artillery on Lobau which, finding a perfect target in Charles's would-be enveloping forces, mowed them down in droves.

Next Napoleon filled the gap vacated by Masséna with massed artillery; one hundred cannon opened up on the Austrians at close range. For a while the battle settled down to slugging, bloody attrition, with Oudinot's men directing artillery fire on the Austrian centre at Wagram but not yet engaging it. By midday Masséna succeeded in reaching his new position and was poised for counterattack; the plan was that he would switch flanks at the decisive moment to aid Davout.

Meanwhile a titanic struggle between Davout's corps and the Austrian left was finally resolved in favour of the French, but not before Davout's first line was broken. Shortly after midday Napoleon saw through his spyglass that Davout's firing line was passing the church tower at Markgrafneusiedl, the prearranged signal that Davout had turned the Austrian left and was about to curve towards Wagram from the rear. It was time to move up the Army of Italy under MacDonald and Eugène.

Following a heavy, sixty-gun bombardment, the Emperor launched Oudinot, Masséna and the Army of Italy under MacDonald against Wagram and the enemy centre. MacDonald deployed 30,000 men in a gigantic hollow square, six ranks deep, with other infantry in column on either flank and 6,000 cavalry in the rear. Austrian cannonballs devastated the square but it still came on. MacDonald's force finally dug in at a sandpit and under this cover reinforcements were brought up. By now Napoleon had spotted a weakness on the Austrian left centre caused by having to reinforce their left against Davout. He ordered Davout to strike at this hinge while Masséna attacked the enemy right. But the Austrians continued to fight like dervishes and MacDonald's attack again seemed to be petering out when Napoleon finally broke the deadlock by committing all his reserves except two regiments of the Old Guard.

This was a crucial decision. Finally the Austrians broke and by 2 p.m. the French were advancing confidently on both sectors. Learning that his own reinforcements would not arrive until nightfall, shortly after 2.30 Charles was forced to order a general retreat to Bohemia; Napoleon's forces were too exhausted to pursue him. The Austrians had been beaten but by no means routed and withdrew in good order, leaving no guns or standards behind. This was no Austerlitz or Jena. Having fought six hours non-stop, the French were at the limits of endurance and could not be prodded to follow the enemy; in any case Napoleon still feared that Archduke John might arrive, in which case a third day's fighting was likely.

Wagram was Napoleon's last great victory on the battlefield but it had been a close-run thing and, had Archduke John appeared at the moment the Emperor committed his last reserves, a signal defeat would have followed. As it was, a greatly improved Austrian army had fought a below-par French army almost to a standstill, to the point where Napoleon lacked cavalry for pursuit operations. The *Grande Armée* had fired 71,000 rounds in a murderous, bludgeoning battle that seemed to usher in a new era of slaughterous warfare and anticipated the blood-letting of the American Civil War. French casualties were 32,000, Austrian 35,000; Napoleon, following his usual practice, toured the battlefield to inspect the piles of dead and wounded.

After further skirmishing at Zynam on 10–11 July, the Austrians suddenly threw in the towel and asked for an armistice, which was arranged on the 12th; Francis I at first refused to honour it but reluctantly ratified it on 17 July. A dispute between Francis I and Archduke Charles led the latter to resign and retire into private life. A tense three months of negotiations and bargaining ensued, with the likelihood of renewed hostilities ever-present. There were two main reasons for this: one was Napoleon's demand for the abdication of Francis I; the other was that Austria stalled, hoping that the military intervention of the British could save them from harsh peace terms.

The British had made some attempt to assist their ally. When Austria invaded Bavaria in April, Britain sent a subsidy of £250,000 and a further £337,000 a little later; by the time of Wagram, subsidies to Austria amounted to £1,185,000, even as London also committed substantial sums to the struggle in Spain. In April Admiral Gambier led a Royal Navy attack on the French Rochefort squadron. His deputy, Admiral Thomas Cochrane used fireships to burn three French ships of the line, made three more unfit for service and destroyed two frigates. The rest of the French squadron lay aground, waiting to be finished off, but Gambier refused to take his battleships into the roads, to the fury of Cochrane and other observers, including Captain Frederick Marryat. As Napoleon justly remarked: 'If Cochrane had been supported, he would have taken every one of our ships.'

But the great British enterprise of 1809 was an attack on Walcheren Island on 30 July, supposedly the opening of a second front to aid Austria. But in attacking Walcheren in the Scheldt the British were primarily consulting their own interests and pursuing their old obsession about Belgium: thoughts of the possible benefit to Austria came a long way down the list. The operation was feasible only because Napoleon had sent most of his troops eastwards, so that it was a case of Austria helping England, not vice versa. In any event, the landing on Walcheren quickly turned to débâcle, though it was a protracted one, since the British did not leave the island until 23 December, hoping the Austrians would resume hostilities. Bad weather, inadequate planning and incompetent leadership vitiated the expedition; the British took so long to take Flushing that the French were able to rush reinforcements to the ultimate target, Antwerp. Disease ('Walcheren fever') finished off the enterprise: 4,000 troops died and 19,000 were hospitalized.

The British incursion at Walcheren enabled the dauntless Bernadotte to make a temporary comeback. Put in command of the troops at Antwerp, waiting for the British thrust that never came, Bernadotte issued an order of the day boasting that his '15,000 men' could hold the city against all comers. When this order was brought to him, Napoleon was enraged: he pointed out that there were 60,000 troops at Walcheren, not 15,000 and that, whatever the numbers, it was simple professional incompetence for Bernadotte to reveal them to the enemy. He sent an order relieving the contumacious Gascon of command: 'I intend no longer to leave the command in the hands of the Prince of Ponte Corvo, who now as before is in league with the Paris intriguers, and who is in every respect a man in whom I can no longer place confidence . . . This is the first occasion on which a general has been known to betray his position by an excess of vanity.'

Meanwhile the Austrians dragged out the peace negotiations, hoping for a great British success or for intervention from the Czar, now widely known no longer to see eye to eye with Napoleon; the Russians, however, warned that they were not yet ready for a rupture with France. In Poland, after an initial victory by Archduke Ferdinand, the brilliance of Prince Poniatowski soon undid all the Austrian gains. The one possible bright spot for Austria was the Tyrol, where heavy fighting had been in progress since April: there had been two major campaigns and twice Napoleon's Bavarian allies had been thrown out of the region by the Tyrolese 'liberators', most recently on 13 August.

Napoleon decided that he could not return to Paris until he had a definite peace treaty with Austria, so in the summer of 1809 he ruled the Empire from Schönbrunn in the Austrian countryside. Here he resumed his affair with Marie Walewska, but it was no longer the grand passion of two years earlier, as the tone of his letter of invitation to her partly indicates: 'Marie: I have read your letter with the pleasure your memory always inspires in me . . . Yes, come to Vienna. I would like to give you further proof of the tender friendship I feel for you.' The imperial valet Constant's diaries show Napoleon and Marie spending every afternoon together, but Napoleon's attentions cannot have been fully engaged for, when he went to Vienna in August to consult the physician Professor Lanefranque about his indifferent health (he wrote to Josephine on 26 August that he had not felt well in years), he conducted a brief liaison with the nineteen-year-old Viennese Eva Kraus, who was said to have borne him a son. What is certain is that in September his regular mistress Marie Walewska announced that she was pregnant. Once it was demonstrated that the Emperor could indeed sire children, it was evident to all well-informed observers that Josephine's days were numbered.

Finally, in October, the Austrians accepted that they could stall no longer and signed the Treaty of Schönbrunn on 14 October. Napoleon imposed harsh conditions to assuage the shock of the 1809 crisis. Francis I was forced to cede Carinthia, Carniola and most of Croatia, including Fiume, Istria and Trieste. Bavaria was given Salzburg and the upper valley of the Inn, while the Grand Duchy of Warsaw got northern Galicia, Cracow and Lublin. Czar Alexander, who had played a double game throughout, ended up with eastern Galicia. Additionally, Austria had to pay a war indemnity of 85 millions, and agreed to abide by the Continental System, limit its army to 150,000 men, and recognize Joseph as King of Spain.

The humiliation to Austrian national pride found expression in a manifestation of the dark side of Austrian nationalism. At a military parade at Schönbrunn, two days before the signing of the treaty, a young Saxon student, Frederick Staps, tried to assassinate Napoleon while ostensibly presenting a petition; it was only a chance movement by General Rapp that diverted the would-be assassin's dagger. Napoleon was convinced Staps was mentally deranged, possibly from a childhood under the aegis of his father, a stern Lutheran minister, but Staps refused to accept this chance of a reprieve and insisted that his action was rational. 'Is a crime nothing to you, then?' Napoleon asked him. 'To kill you is not a crime, it's a duty!' Staps replied defiantly. He was executed a few days later and met his end exclaiming: 'Long live Germany. Death to the tyrant!'

Ever a man to turn any event, however untoward, to his advantage, Napoleon told Marie Walewska he was concerned at the possible shock to her unborn child and suggested she return to Poland. He himself left for Paris two days after the treaty, on 16 October. But he was shaken by the Staps incident and was convinced that if he had lost at Wagram, Germany would have flamed into rebellion. As he wrote to Rapp, who had intercepted the knife thrust: 'This is the result of the secret societies which infest Germany. This is the effect of fine principles and the light of reason. They make young men assassins. But what can be done? ... A sect cannot be destroyed by cannonballs.'

Once again he had escaped from a tight spot. Once the Austrians capitulated, the steam went out of the Tyrolean rising. On 25 October the Bavarians occupied Innsbruck for the third time, this time signalling the collapse of the Tyrolean rebels. It took some time before Andreas Hofer could be tracked down, so that he was not executed until 20 February 1810. Napoleon's way with this 'martyr' was as brisk as with Staps. There is a cold ruthlessness about the order he sent to Eugène Beauharnais, now back in Italy as viceroy: 'My son, I had commanded you to send Hofer to Paris, but since you have him in Mantua, give instant orders that a military commission be set up to try him on the spot. See that this takes place within twenty-four hours.'

On his journey back to Fontainebleau, where he arrived on 26 October, Napoleon had time to ponder the lessons of the 1809 campaign. He had shown himself resilient under pressure, especially when he had to correct Berthier's mistakes, and he had displayed tactical flair at Wagram. On the other hand, his blunders were many. He should not have appointed Berthier in the first place, he offended against his own military principles during the fighting on 19–25 April and even more afterwards, perhaps especially by pressing on to the symbolic goal of Vienna instead of seeking out and destroying the enemy on the north bank of the Danube. His famous opportunism descended into mere folly in May when he attempted a quixotic and unprepared crossing of the Danube and, all in all, the Emperor seemed to lack his old élan and brilliance; there were fits of lethargy and depression and vaguely worded orders. There is even some evidence that he had begun to lose confidence in his military abilities, for he wrote after Wagram: 'Battle should only be offered when there is no other turn of fortune to be hoped for, as from its nature the fate of a battle is always dubious.'

Just as worrying was the declining calibre of the Army, especially the allied contingents; the flight of the Saxons on the first day of Wagram did not bode well. There was a worryingly high level of officer casualties, and indiscipline in the ranks was so bad that Napoleon was forced to institute five courts-martial. The one bright spot, the removal of Bernadotte apart, was the distinguished showing of the marshals. MacDonald, Marmont and Oudinot all won their batons for their exploits in the toughest campaign so far. Oudinot, whose contribution at Wagram was decisive, received a further annual income of 60,000 francs and the dukedom of Reggio, which itself carried an annual endowment of 36,000 francs. But if Austria was pacified, there still remained the Spanish ulcer.

CHAPTER NINETEEN

By 1808 Napoleon controlled an army of 800,000 men and an empire that stretched from the Russian frontier to the Atlantic. In theory his ships had access to the Baltic and the North Seas, the Mediterranean and the Aegean. It has been customary ever since to make a threefold distinction in the Napoleonic Empire: there were the lands within the 'natural frontiers', the so-called *pays réunis*; the states ruled by other members of the Bonaparte family, otherwise known as the *pays conquis*; and the nominally independent satellite states or *pays alliés*.

This neat classification conceals many rough edges. In the first place, many lands annexed by Napoleon and ruled directly from metropolitan France were not within the natural frontiers. Whereas in 1803 Napoleon possessed Belgium, Nice, Savoy, Piedmont and the left bank of the Rhine – following the logic of a policy laid down by the Revolution – two years later he added Genoa, Parma, Piacenza, Guastalla and Tuscany. In 1808 he acquired Rome, in 1809 Holland, the Valais, parts of Hanover and Westphalia, plus the Hanseatic towns – Hamburg, Bremen and Lübeck; Oldenburg was added in 1810 and Catalonia in 1812. Ever the centralizer, Napoleon managed to increase the 1803 figure of 108 departments and 33 million people of his tightly administered domain to 130 departments and 44 million people by 1811.

The states ruled by other members of the Bonaparte family included the Swiss territory of Neuchâtel, ruled by Marshal Berthier; Tuscany ruled by Elisa Bonaparte; the Kingdom of Italy under the aegis of the Emperor's viceroy and stepson, Eugène de Beauharnais; Naples under the Murats; Spain theoretically ruled by Joseph; Holland under the benevolent sway of Louis Bonaparte; and the crossbreed kingdom of Westphalia, formed in 1807 from Hesse-Cassel, Brunswick and parts of Hanover and Prussia, which had the misfortune to have Jérôme Bonaparte as king. However, there was also a group of territories under military or direct Napoleonic rule that stopped short of formal annexation, such as Portugal, the Ionian islands, Slovenia, Dalmatia and parts of Croatia and Germany (Berg is a good example).

The most important satellite state was the Confederation of the Rhine, a league of states set up by Napoleon to replace the old Holy Roman Empire; in essence it comprised all of Germany except Austria and Prussia – not just Westphalia but Baden, Württemberg and Bavaria. Except for Westphalia and Berg, these satellite states in the Confederation were ruled by old-style legitimist princes who had opportunistically thrown in their lot with Napoleon. Other important satellite states were Switzerland and the Grand Duchy of Warsaw. Switzerland was technically neutral but in 1803 Napoleon had intervened there with his Act of Mediation, which renamed the country the Helvetic Confederation and provided a new constitution. Even more complicated were the arrangements governing the Grand Duchy of Warsaw, a buffer state created in 1807 from the Polish territories Prussia ceded at Tilsit. Theoretically ruled by the King of Saxony as Grand Duke – but Frederick Augustus never even bothered to visit his duchy – Warsaw experienced a 'dyarchy' of a so-called independent government and a powerful French Governor-General.

The Napoleonic Empire was thus bewilderingly heterogeneous, but uniformity was supposed to be provided by the Code Napoléon and the centripetal tug of Paris, the very symbol of European integration under Bonaparte. Napoleon's way with mystification and the way he liked to conceal autocracy under a show of pluralism was evident in the notional tripartite separation of powers, with the executive based at the Tuileries, the Legislative Assembly at the Bourbon Palace and the Senate at the Luxembourg Palace. Napoleon claimed in 1804 that he wanted to site his capital at Lyons, but this was obviously a sop to extra-Parisian feeling, for he made no serious attempt at relocation.

The Emperor wanted his capital to be a political, administrative, cultural and even religious megalopolis – a grandiose city full of palaces and public monuments. Napoleon had ambitions to make Paris both a fabulous, and a futuristic city. On St Helena he told Las Cases: 'I wanted Paris to become a town of two, three, four million inhabitants, something fabulous, colossal, unknown until our time.' Circumstances prevented this. Although the population of France's capital city rose from 500,000 to 700,000 under the Empire, a sober estimate must conclude that Napoleon pulled down more of the old city than he created of the new. His particular target seemed to be the architectural reminders of the Revolution: among the 'monuments' of 1789–94 he ordered destroyed were the Salle de Manège, where the National Assembly had met and the Marais Temple where Louis XVI and family had been imprisoned;

joining them on the rubble heap were the many ex-convents where the Jacobin and other clubs had convened.

Considerable improvements were made in sewage and drainage and the provision of an adequate urban water supply. But the overall appearance of Paris did not change much. There was the new Vendôme column, completed by Gondoin in 1810 with Chaudet's statue of the Emperor on top, the triumphal arch on the Place du Carrousel, the arcaded rue de Rivoli, named for his first great military triumph, and the church of the Madeleine. But otherwise the dream of a city of Xanadu palaces and Shangri-La monuments and fountains did not materialize. The planned Arc de Triomphe on the Étoile was still merely a makeshift wooden affair by 1814.

More significantly, perhaps, there were two new bridges over the Seine and no less than fourteen highways spiralling out from Paris to convey the *Grande Armée* rapidly to any emergency point. Particularly important, therefore, were the international thoroughfares. Route Two of the fourteen ran to Amsterdam via Brussels and Antwerp, Route Three to Hamburg via Liège and Bremen and Route Four to Prussia by way of Mayenne. Of the southerly routes, the road to Spain was Route Eleven (Paris-Bayonne) while Six, to Rome via the Simplon and Milan and Seven, to Turin via Mont-Cenis, linked Italy to the Empire. One of the ways in which the Emperor wished to emulate his Roman forebears was as a road builder. It was due to Napoleon's energy that the spectacular Simplon route across the Alps was opened in 1805 and the Mont Cénis pass in 1810. For all that, the new roads were not of high quality: it took 120 hours to travel by stagecoach from Paris to Bordeaux, and the simple fact that most people travelled long distances by foot was one of the factors in the endurance of the Grand Army.

Economically Paris benefited hugely from the Revolutionary and Napoleonic periods. The Continental System eliminated British competition and provided an internal market of 80 million people. Particular beneficiaries were the cotton, chemical and mechanical industries, where the impact of war stimulated new technologies also. The influx of foreigners to Paris in this period encouraged the manufacture of luxury goods. Another, less welcome, influx was the annual immigration of 40,000 seasonal workers, many of whom stayed on in the city in the dead season to form the kernel of the 'dangerous classes' that are such a feature of nineteenth-century French literature. This aspect of the economic boom worried employers and the authorities, who did not want a concentration of workers in the capital, fearing overcrowding, famine, disease, unemployment and riots.

Napoleon's ambition to make Paris a cultural capital suffered from the obvious drawback that his censorship policies and general philistinism did not encourage the arts to prosper, although it is true that his impact in this area has been overdrawn; after all, no one was executed in the Imperial period for services to literature, as André Chénier was during the Revolution. Only Madame de Staël and Chateaubriand, both opposition figures, are first-rank literary figures from this period, though we should remember that Balzac, Hugo, Musset and Vigny received their 'formation' during the Empire. The Napoleonic period was not a good one for literature: the Emperor himself ruefully remarked: 'The minor works of literature are for me and the great are against me.' The oft-cited vast increase in readership during the Empire is a red herring, unless we are to take seriously the idea of a 'trickle down effect'. There was a huge appetite among the literate for Gothic novels and tales of the supernatural, though whether readers of the translated versions of Horace Walpole, Ann Radcliffe or Monk Lewis were thereby led on to sample Rousseau or the Abbé Prévost is more doubtful.

It was in the visual arts that the Napoleonic period made its mark. All great dictators recognize the importance of visual media as propaganda: Lenin was among the first to spot the potential of the cinema. Similarly, Napoleon had a keen sense of the way an entire triumphalist imperial culture could be inculcated through great works of art that bore a tendentious or subliminal 'message'. He was always a propagandist of genius, and one proof of this is the subtle way he transmogrified the classical revival of the 1790s, originally intended to transmit Republican values of self-sacrifice, Spartan austerity and civic *virtu*, into a paean to his own achievements.

The *locus classicus* was the career of Jacques Louis David (1748–1825). David was an arch-Jacobin who had voted for the death of Louis XVI and narrowly escaped the guillotine after the Thermidorian counter-revolution of 1794. In his revolutionary period David took his models from ancient history and legend. The quasi-mythical figures of Horatius and Decimus Brutus were annexed to put across the moral that one's commitment to the Republic should transcend even the love of siblings, parents and children. But like many reformed Jacobins – Bernadotte is the best-known example – David, when 'converted' to the Napoleonic ideal, developed a huge appetite for money. He therefore took on blatantly propagandist commissions from Napoleon, stressing the continuity between the First Consul (and later Emperor) and the great leaders of classical antiquity. So, for example *Napoleon crossing the St Bernard* explictly stresses the parallels with Hannibal. And whereas the historical Napoleon crossed the Alps in 1800 on the Marengo campaign by mule – the only way to negotiate the icy passes – the mythical figure in David's painting is seen triumphant on a rearing horse.

Napoleon's favourite painting by David was *Napoleon in his Study*. There is a sword on the chair, the Code Napoléon is on the desk, and the clock shows the time at 4.31 a.m. The propaganda intent is obvious: here is the First Consul slaving away for the good of his people at an hour when they are all in bed. Yet for all that he was delighted with this work, and with the famous painting of the coronation in 1804, Napoleon was never entirely happy with David. He objected to his portraits of antiquity on the ostensible ground that David's classical heroes seemed too effete and weedy to wield modern weapons. But what really worried him was that the subject of David's studies of antiquity – concerned with Spartan austerity, Republican virtue, the Roman severity of Cato the Elder, the self-sacrifice of Brutus, etc – were at a deep level subtly subversive of the imperial ethos.

For this reason Napoleon always preferred the work of David's pupils, especially François Gérard, Antoine Gros and Jean-Auguste Ingres. Gérard specialized in paintings illustrating the exploits of Ossian, the hero of the controversial 'epic' by James Macpherson, Napoleon's favourite author; in battle scenes; and in motifs from Greek and Roman myths. Gros was the man for the outright propaganda. His *Napoleon at Arcole* helped to transform the hard-fought battles of the 1796–97 Italian campaign into an image of effortless triumph by a superman, while his celebration of the famous incident in Syria in 1799, *Napoleon visiting the plague victims of Jaffa*, turns Bonaparte into a Christ-like figure. Historical distortion reaches its apogee in Gros's *Napoleon at the Battle of Eylau*. Sober fact records that Napoleon's casualties at the dreadful and indecisive battle with the Russians fought in a snowstorm at Eylau in 1807 were horrific and that his generalship was not of the best. Gros, however, presents the Emperor as a kind of Florence Nightingale *avant la lettre*, comforting and blessing the dying. Ingres was not much better. His *Napoleon as First Consul* suggests that Bonaparte is primarily a civilian, an unwilling Cincinnatus pitchforked into politics by his country's pressing need. Ingres's *Napoleon on his Throne* goes completely over the top, portraying the Emperor as a combination of Jupiter, Augustus and Charlemagne.

Imperial fever in French painting probably reached its apogee around 1810. In that year the Paris salon was dominated by such entries as David's *Distribution of the Eagles*, Gérard's *Battle of Austerlitz*, Girodet's *The Revolt of Cairo* and Gros's *The Battle of the Pyramids*. Additionally, by this time Napoleon had under his wing as court favourites Pierre-Paul Prud'hon, whose sensual allegories were very much to his liking and who was the art director of the great fêtes given in Paris in the Emperor's honour, and the Venetian sculptor Antonio Canova, whose statue of Pauline Bonaparte, semi-nude, first suggested to the world the lubricious charms that had enslaved cohorts of men.

There was a neo-classical 'Empire style' too in sculpture, architecture, interior design and fashion where the inspiration was predominantly the art of antiquity or the Orient. Clothes followed the same pattern: colours were dark and materials heavy, partly to produce an impression of sumptuousness but also partly, said the cynics, to supply more work for the textile industry. Men's clothes were still influenced by the Revolution, while the frock-coat, tail-coat and straight waistcoat gave the connotation of military uniform. In some ways the military effect on fashion was even more noticeable with women's clothes: hair was piled up high in the form of a shako, skirts were straight and cut like a scabbard, and boots, epaulettes and crossbelts were worn.

Napoleon's taste was for the monumental and the classical as a conscious aping of the grandeur that was Rome, but the art of the Imperial period was nothing like so monolithic as this brief sketch indicates; the best known exception is the 'Romantic' work of Géricault, but there were other examples. It was in any case difficult to insist on a 'politically correct' art when Napoleon's own conception of Empire was so confused. His desire to be a Roman emperor was yet another in the long series of irrational and unintegrated urges to which there is no reason not to give the traditional name 'complex'. Thus, in addition to 'complexes' about his mother, his brother, his wife and the Orient, Napoleon had an attitude towards Empire that was irrational at many different levels.

Bedazzled by the great conquerors of the past, Napoleon could never quite decide which of them he wanted to emulate. When fusing the imperial and *ancien régime* élites in France he was Alexander the Great, when crossing the Alps he was Hannibal, when berating his family he was Genghiz Khan. Even as a strictly Roman Emperor there was confusion, with Napoleon caught between the perspectives of the Julio-Claudians and the Holy Roman Empire: so his campaign in Italy in 1796–97 was analogous to Caesar's campaigns in Gaul as a self-conscious prelude to supreme power, but the forms and traditions he worked with once he had attained that power were those of Charlemagne. He made this clear by visiting Aix-la-Chapelle, ancient capital of the Frankish Emperor, in September 1804, and by adding the iron crown of Lombardy (once more placed on his head with his own hand, this time in Milan Cathedral) to the imperial crown of France, just as Charlemagne had done. The abolition of the Holy Roman Empire, whatever the political imperatives, can also be seen as a desire, consciously or unconsciously to outdo Charlemagne.

Any critique of Napoleon's imperial conception is bound to fasten on the obvious point that this was the Emperor displaying delusions of grandeur and rationalizing a much more sordid quotidian reality. Charlemagne and Constantine had Christianity at the core of their systems; Napoleon did not. A cynic would say that the oft-cited names of Charlemagne, Diocletian and Constantine were simply names thrown out to camouflage a basic lust for power. In any case, there was a fundamental confusion at the heart of Napoleon's thinking. How could a man who aspired to be a Roman emperor even pay lip-service to ideologies such as equality or the rights of man – notions which would have been received with stupefaction by the emperors on whom he modelled himself?

Besides, the analogy between France and Rome will not hold, no matter which particular Roman empire we choose. Both the Western Roman Empire and the later Byzantine variety were ruled by men who set limits to their ambitions. These empires remained on the defensive behind carefully circumscribed frontiers, apart from exceptional moments, such as Trajan's conquest of Dacia or Justinian's invasion of Egypt. Until these empires fell apart from internal implosion and external pressure from Vandals, Huns, Saracens or Turks, their rulers pursued circumspect aims. Above all, they made a very clear distinction between empire and world domination. Napoleon, by contrast, had no one clear aim, pursued several (often contradictory) objectives simultaneously and vacillated between them. Already by 1812 he possessed an empire that extended farther eastward in Europe than the Western Roman Empire. Had he been successful in 1812, he would have made Russia an Asian power, seized Constantinople, pressed on to India, occupied Persia, conquered Spain and acquired its colonies in Latin America prior to applying the *coup de grâce* to England.

Yet in 1808 the French Emperor was blind to all this and continued in his 'Roman' fantasy world. The next obvious step in his imperial progress was to bind vassal kings to him in marriage – which he did. Logically, he would then have to downgrade Rome so as to make Paris the 'new' Rome; it is not surprising, therefore, that in 1809 he found a pretext to annex the Eternal City. The next step would be to destroy the tottering Ottoman Empire and attain Constantinople; some even allege that this was the

deep impulse behind the events of 1812. The problem about unassimilated 'complexes' like Napoleon's imperial idea is not just their
irrationality but the way they collide with other complexes. So, to the
rational aim of worldwide struggle with Britain for a global empire are
added the inherited imperative of 'natural frontiers', the Bonaparte family
complex, requiring him to find thrones for his siblings, the Oriental
complex and the Roman emperor complex. It is hardly surprising that the
foreign policy that emerged from this mess was itself a fiasco.

It becomes increasingly clear that Napoleon's expansionism was a
much more complex affair than, say, Hitler's push for *Lebensraum*. As a
result of his irrational motivation, Napoleon had been forced to create a
monster he could not control in the form of the *Grande Armée*. He could
direct its marches like a master and even knock sense into his recalcitrant
marshals but he could not control the inexorable factor of finance. Once
launched into his overseas adventures through a variety of confused
motives, Napoleon could not turn back. His ambitions collided with those
of the other great powers. Britain could not tolerate natural frontiers
which put Belgium and the Rhine in French hands, Prussia could not
abide the Confederation of the Rhine, Austria thirsted for revenge for the
loss of Italy, while Alexander wanted to play the role Napoleon was
playing and was thus in competition for the same space. Napoleon
therefore had a stark choice: he could disband his armies and return to
the 1792 frontiers – which meant in effect to negate himself and deny his
own identity – or, because of fears of backlash from his enemies, he had
to keep the Grand Army in being.

To keep it in being meant performing a juggling act as between foreign
and domestic affairs. On the one hand Napoleon had to satisfy the French
bourgeoisie and peasantry, to ward off Jacobins and royalists and prevent
army coups. On the other hand, having inherited a legacy of financial ruin
from the Revolution, he had to make sure the huge costs of the *Grande
Armée* did not fall on the French taxpayer. Meanwhile, feeling that his
family contained the only people he could trust and knowing of their
jealousy and megalomania, he had to provide them with thrones and
incomes. Napoleon's Empire, conceived in Roman terms in his own
imagination, thus became in reality a massive system of out-relief. This is
another way of saying that a would-be Emperor should not be a rootless
adventurer without a proper power base.

It was not in Napoleon's nature to proceed cautiously or to make real
concessions to his enemies. Unable to concentrate on any one aim, he still
wanted it all and he wanted it now. He would neither let the Czar have
Poland nor declare for an independent Poland. Aiming for 'credibility' he

achieved precisely the opposite – a reputation as a man you could not reason or do business with. Once again we see the contrast between the mathematician and the poet *manqué*: it was as if all his logical faculties were expended on means and all the mystical ones on ends.

As Napoleon saw it when he surveyed his Empire in 1808, his first task was to deal decisively with the Catholic Church. The Concordat quickly broke down when Pius VII refused to implement the Continental Blockade in the papal territories, on the ground that he must be above temporal disputes between 'his children'. By this time Consalvi was no longer at Pius's elbow, so that the Pope increasingly listened to the reactionary Cardinal Pacca. As a countermeasure, in January 1808 Napoleon ordered General Miollis to occupy the Papal states. A year later, during the war with Austria, he ordered them annexed; Miollis was instructed to incorporate the Vatican's troops into his command and take over the administration of the Papal states, simply paying the Pope a salary as a pensioner. Pius, believing that Austria would win the war, issued a bull of excommunication against Napoleon. In response the Emperor ordered his troops into the Quirinal Palace, where Pius was requested to renounce his temporal power. When the Pontiff refused, he was arrested (6 July 1809).

Napoleon always liked to play his old game of distancing himself from the actions of his subordinates, consciously muddying the historical record by pretending they had acted in certain key instances without his authorization. On 18 July 1809, accordingly, he wrote to Fouché: 'I take it ill that the Pope has been arrested; it is a very foolish act. They ought to have arrested Cardinal Pacca, and have left the Pope quietly at Rome.'

That this was pure humbug can be seen from a letter he had written to Murat a year earlier: 'I have already let you know that it is my intention that affairs in Rome be conducted with firmness, and that no form of resistance should be allowed to stand in the way ... If the Pope, against the spirit of his office and of his Gospels, preaches revolt and tries to misuse the immunity of his domicile to have circulars printed, he is to be arrested ... Philip the Fair had Boniface arrested, Charles V kept Clement VII in prison for a long period, and those popes had done less to deserve it.'

Yet Napoleon barefacedly insisted that the actual arrest of the Pope had taken place without his orders, and made sure that all policy documents bearing his signature were couched in vague and ambiguous language. This was of a piece with his general trend towards obfuscating the record in controversial areas; such 'mystification' enabled him to blame Savary for the d'Enghien affair, Murat for the imbroglio in Spain and Miollis for the arrest of the Pope. The obvious retort for Fouché to make was to ask why, in that case, the Emperor did not simply order Pius returned to Rome. In fact Napoleon ordered the pontiff removed to Florence, on the ground that tensions between French and papal troops had reached fever pitch; if it came to armed conflict, he said, he did not want to run the risk that the Holy Father might be snuffed out by a stray bullet. The true reason appears elsewhere in his correspondence: 'It was impossible to send the Pope back to Rome without incurring the risk of consequences still more vexatious than those that had already taken place. The Battle of Wagram was impending.'

The Pope was taken first to Florence, then to Grenoble, Avignon and Nice and finally back to Savona while Napoleon dithered about what to do with him. A *senatus consultum* of 17 February 1810 ratified the 1809 decree by which the Emperor, as the heir of Charlemagne, original donor of temporal power to the Papacy, abolished Vatican sovereignty over the Papal states and declared them annexed to the French Empire. Under house arrest in Savona until June 1811, Pius dug in for a long battle with the Emperor. He began by refusing to consecrate bishops nominated by Napoleon to the vacant sees, stating that he could no longer carry out any papal functions as he was a prisoner. This hobbled whatever was left of the Concordat, for it was a central plank of that agreement that the Pope should preside over canonical 'institution' of bishops nominated by the Emperor.

At first Napoleon tried to conciliate Pius. He proposed a compromise whereby his heir would be named King of Rome and would hold his court there; in return the Pope would spend part of the year in Paris with Napoleon, all expenses being met from the imperial treasury. But he abandoned belief in an amicable settlement of the dispute in 1810 when his police intercepted letters smuggled out of Savona telling Catholic canons not to cooperate with Napoleon. This destroyed Napoleon's second line of defence, which was to legitimate his nominations for the vacant dioceses by the backdoor of the Catholic vicariate. The idea was to get the chapters of the various French sees to legitimate his nominations to the bishoprics without reference to Rome – precisely the manoeuvre Pius expressly forbade.

Napoleon responded by handing out indefinite prison sentences to any canons who would not cooperate and intensifying the hardship of Pius's internment at Savona. It was now apparent that schism was imminent, as also the formation of a national church along the lines of Henry VIII's Church of England. To prevent this a delegation of French bishops travelled to Savona, with the Emperor's permission, to try to get a compromise. The Pope made a few concessions, which the bishops took down in writing, then changed his mind once they were gone and issued a letter of revocation. Things went from bad to worse at the ecclesiastical council called in Paris by the bishops loyal to Napoleon. The aim was to get a decree allowing French archbishops to do the 'instituting' if the Pope refused, but the assembled clerics, stiffened in their resolution by the Pope's disowning of the draft agreement of Savona, displayed unwonted backbone and refused to oblige; the Council therefore declared itself incompetent to resolve the issue of 'institution'.

The two sides now seemed to have settled in for a long war of attrition. A final attempt to secure what Napoleon wanted was made by Cardinal Fesch at a council in Savona in 1811, but this too was unsuccessful. In fury the Emperor removed the Pope to Fontainebleau. Essentially, though, he had lost the war. At first French public opinion was indifferent to the conflict, but the failure of the Savona council seemed to many to portend ultimate civil war. Rampant anticlericalism was the new ideological bearing of the régime, but the stark choice this posed between Church and State worried that essential pillar of the Emperor's support, the notables. They feared a new period of social instability, the resurgence of the Jacobins and possible armed insurrection in the old Vendée areas, but most of all they dreaded that the Pope would repudiate the Concordat in its entirety, including the vital clause where he recognized the legitimacy of the sale of Church property. The more ultramontane factions of the clergy were already urging Pius to rescind this, on the ground that the loss of Church property, benefices and livings discouraged the sons of the élite classes from entering the priesthood.

His personal struggle with the Pope apart, Napoleon's attitude to Catholicism was ambivalent. In his heart he hankered after a national church, where priests in the pulpit would dilate on his military victories as the work of God, and from some docile clergy he did indeed secure this reaction. But, recognizing the power of the Catholic Church to allay the fears and enhance the hopes of the uneducated and to provide a cosmology that made sense of a frightening world for the peasantry, he was largely content to leave it alone. His general policy was to encourage his proconsuls not to offend the religious susceptibilities of devoutly Catholic countries; the many instances of anticlericalism or sacrilegious behaviour were largely the function of other-ranks Jacobinism.

A less finely judged ambivalence was in evidence in the Emperor's attitude to the Jews. On the one hand, Jewish communities were officially liberated from the prison-like ghettoes to which the *ancien régime* had consigned them. After 1806, for example, Frankfurt's infamous *Juden-gasse* ghetto no longer resembled a gigantic Marshalsea, though Jews still paid special taxes and were banned from entering coffee houses or walking through the city squares. On the other, Napoleon was personally anti-semitic, as he showed at the grand Sanhedrin of Jewish leaders he convoked in April 1807. A number of discriminatory measures were ordained: Jews could practise their religion only under State supervision, they were denied recognition as a separate nation, one-third of their marriages had to be with non-Jews, and so on. These laws were supposedly to hold good throughout the extended Empire, though the fate of Jewish communities largely depended on the attitude of the local rulers or proconsuls. In Holland and Italy Jews fared badly, but in Westphalia Jérôme, a notable philosemite, admitted them to full citizenship, while in neighbouring Berg most of the restrictions against them were lifted. Nevertheless, in general the lot of Jews was harsh. They were robbed, swindled and unable to recoup debts owed them, while in Holland Louis became notorious for forming a Jewish regiment from boys taken from the poor or press-ganged from orphanages.

With a few exceptions, the rulers of Napoleon's empire were a mediocre bunch. Perhaps the most spectacularly incompetent were the Murats in Naples. Joseph, when King of Naples, had made a good start, aided by his excellent ministers Miot, Roederer and Saliceti. He deployed a force of 40,000 men to combat brigandage; set up a Ministry of the Interior and a provincial intendant system modelled on the French prefects; established a property tax, supervised the sale of Church property and reorganized the fiscal system. The Murats, even with what many claim were even more talented ministers – Zurco at the Interior and Ricciardi at Justice – undid much of the good work and required constant injections of French blood and treasure to maintain their position. Murat, fancying himself as an independent monarch fully the equal of Napoleon, was mortified when he discovered that the Army obeyed the Emperor, not him. Detesting his scheming wife Caroline ever more daily, Murat worked himself into such a state of nervous tension that, when not womanizing, he sat up all night reading police reports. He alienated the Emperor by blatantly infringing the Continental Blockade, allowing U.S. ships to smuggle British goods into Naples. His invasion of Sicily, finally attempted with Napoleon's connivance in the autumn of 1810, predictably ended in miserable failure.

Murat's lacklustre performance was thrown into relief by the generally good showing of the viceroy of French Italy, Eugène de Beauharnais, who presided in Milan over an area divided into twenty-four departments. In northern Italy Napoleon's innovations – which he claimed on St Helena were the groundwork for his aim of Italian unification – built on what had been done by the Austrians. There was little opposition to Bonaparte in northern Italy, and the great landowners accepted posts in the new administration, happy to further the Emperor's plan to use Italy as France's agricultural base, supplying sheep, rice, corn, cotton and sugar and providing a market for French manufactured goods. The real opposition to Napoleon was in Rome where he succeeded in alienating all vital social sectors. Quite apart from the kidnapping of the Pope, he upset the clergy by introducing divorce; he outraged the nobility by the treatment of Pius and the plans to remove the Vatican itself to Paris; by extensive conscription levies he failed to gain the love of the common people; and he alienated the bourgeoisie, mainly lawyers, by abolishing the Pontifical Tribunals; in any case this nascent middle class depended too heavily on the Church and the old nobility to be able to break with them.

Napoleon's popularity, evident in northern Italy if not Rome, seemed to have been an Alpine affair, for in Switzerland too he won golden opinions as the man who had swept away the unpopular Helvetian republic and protected the Confédération Helvétique. His 1803 act of mediation was widely perceived to have maintained a rough-and-ready form of social equality between Swiss citizens and to have preserved the autonomy of the cantons; additionally a treaty of alliance gave the Confederation a proper status within the Empire. But, here as elsewhere, it was the Continental System that lost the Emperor many erstwhile friends. The ranks of the anti-Bonapartists, originally confined to aristocrats who had taken the Austrian side, were swollen after 1807 by tradesmen and industrialists who suffered the consequences of the Blockade. The Swiss were further alienated when the French annexed the Valais in 1810 and when they occupied the Tessin. Then there was the issue of the Alps themselves. Napoleon favoured the Mont-Cenis route to Italy more than the Simplon as the axis of the route Paris–Turin–Genoa, so that by 1807–08 the traffic through the Mont-Cenis was four times that through the Simplon. In 1810 the annexation of the Valais made the Simplon even more important by simplifying the work of customs officers. It was only after the annexation of Illyria, that the Swiss retrieved their share of Alpine traffic. It became obvious that the traffic in Levantine cotton would soon bring the Mont-Cenis route to a standstill so, by a decree on 12 April 1811 the Emperor divided the traffic between the two routes and gave the same rights to the Simplon as to the Mont-Cenis.

Another success story in Napoleon's Empire was the fate of the nine Belgian departments, formerly in the Austrian Empire, which formed the nucleus of modern Belgium. Capital generated by the sale of national property and stimulated by Napoleon's huge internal market brought the beginnings of Belgian industrialization, especially in shipbuilding, coal mining and cotton manufacturing. It was the sale of national property and its consequences that kept the bourgeoisie loyal to Napoleon. Curiously, the Belgian peasantry were also pro-Bonaparte and this is something of an historical puzzle, since, ferociously pro-clerical, the peasants stayed loyal to the Church, did not buy its confiscated lands and were thus not coopted into the Bonapartist economic nexus.

Matters were otherwise in Holland, ruled by his brother Louis, which was as anti-Napoleon as Belgium was pro. Three things in particular led to the débâcle of King Louis's abdication in 1810. In the first place Louis tried to adapt the *Code Napoléon* to local laws and customs and for his pains was severely reprimanded by Napoleon, who wrote sternly: 'A nation of 1,800,000 inhabitants cannot have a separate legislation. Rome gave her laws to her allies; why should the laws of France not be adopted in Holland?' Even more seriously, Louis connived at contraband so as not to ruin Dutch trade, and thus made Holland the weak link in the Continental System. But what particularly infuriated Napoleon was Louis's seeming inability to deal with the ultimately unsuccessful invasion of Walcheren by British forces in July 1809. In March 1810 he ordered Louis to hand over to direct imperial rule all his lands south of the Rhine; Louis, unable to stomach such humiliation, beat Napoleon to the punch by resigning on 1 July.

Napoleon's dealings with Louis showed that, beneath the rhetoric about European integration, he ultimately believed in brute force to achieve his will. His correspondence, even when delivering justified rebukes, breathed a spirit of contempt. The Emperor was impatient with the fine points of Louis's arguments for moderation, and insisted that a true ruler knew how to *force* his subjects to come to heel. On one occasion when Louis appealed to the ideals of honour, justice and decency, Napoleon snapped back: 'You might have spared me this fine display of your principles.' He always believed in tough measures to cow a recalcitrant population, arguing that the alleged brutality saved lives in the long run, and even suggested that a little blood-letting was good for the body politic. One of his most revealing letters was to Joseph in early 1808, when his brother was still King of Naples: 'I wish Naples would attempt a rising. As long as you have not made an example, you will not be their master. Every conquered country must have its rising.'

Napoleon's authoritarian stance was in part a reflection of his natural way of looking at the world but was also designed to make sure his family did nothing without consulting him. The imperial correspondence contains dozens of missives sent out to his siblings which are often glorified nagging. During Joseph's two years as King of Naples his brother deluged him with advice on how to run the kingdom. The following, from 1806, is typical: 'Make changes if you must, but bring the Code into force nevertheless; it will consolidate your power and, once in force, all entails will vanish, with the result that there will be no powerful families except for those whom you choose to create as your vassals. That is why I myself have always . . . gone to such lengths to see that it is carried out.'

To Jérôme, as King of Westphalia, Napoleon gave detailed instructions:

Do not listen to those who will tell you that your people, used as they are to subjection, will receive your benefits gratefully. There is more enlightenment in the kingdom of Westphalia than you will be told, and only in the confidence and love of the population will your throne stand firmly. What is above all desired in Germany is that you will grant to those who do not belong to the nobility, but possess talents, an equal claim to offices, and that all vestiges of serfdom and of barriers between the sovereign and the lowest class of people shall be completely done away with. The benefits of the *Code Napoléon*, legal procedure in open courts, the jury, these are points by which your monarchy should be distinguished . . . your people must enjoy a liberty, an equality, a prosperity unknown in the rest of Germany.

But by 1809 the Emperor's patience with Jérôme was wearing thin, and the iron fist was increasingly evident: 'I think it is ridiculous of you to tell me that the people of Westphalia do not agree . . . If the people refuse what makes for their own welfare they are guilty of anarchism and the first duty for the prince is to punish them.'

Of the myriad issues thrown up by Napoleon's Empire we may select four as salient. Was the Empire run on homogeneous principles, as the Emperor boasted? Did it subscribe to Revolutionary or egalitarian ideals? Who supported it and who opposed it? Was it a pilot version of European integration or merely a gigantic spoils system?

The most seductive of all Napoleonic myths is the one he himself promoted: that his aim was the noble ideal of pan-European federation, with all nations linked in peace – a project he claimed was vitiated by twin evils: the hatred of reactionary monarchies and the envy of Britain, 'the pirate swayed only by low materialistic motives'. In fact Napoleon's Europe had nothing in common with true federalism: it was a collection of satellite states whose interests were always to be subordinate to those of France. This was the core 'contradiction' that explained all the rough edges in the Empire and all the passages of arms with his siblings. As rulers, they tried to stand up for the interests of their subjects but were crushed by Napoleon who had given them their thrones on the quite different understanding that they would always put France first.

The heterogeneity of Napoleon's Empire was thus a product of many things: the success of the kings in frustrating the Emperor; the need not to offend the interests and susceptibilities of Bonaparte supporters within the satellite nations; the obeisance paid to powerful local customs and folkways; and the military imperatives of the Emperor himself. The degree of harmonization and integration was greatest in the *pays réunis* and least in the *pays alliés*, with the *pays conquis* presenting a mixed and patchy picture. On paper, the Empire was supposed to be unified by the Code Napoléon and Enlightenment reforms, and it is true that some of Napoleon's prefects did carry out reforms, introducing new agricultural techniques, new crops, improved livestock, marsh reclamation schemes and the building of flood barriers. In Rome, for example, the comte de Tournon reformed prisons and hospitals, fostered a cotton industry and reclaimed part of the Pontine marshes.

Yet the administrative impact of France on the Empire was superficial. On the one hand, the satellite states mirrored the French model, with departments and prefects; the 'notables' system was also replicated, with landed property, not hereditary status, as the basis of political power. But by and large the local bourgeoisie resisted the full implementation of the Code; French officials in turn largely bent with the local wind and connived at infractions. In Westphalia Jérôme allowed entails to conciliate the nobility but, even when Napoleon forced him out, he did not replace his officials. In Naples there was only partial introduction of the Code because of the clash of French interests and those of the local bourgeoisie. The so-called uniform taxation system was regressive by necessity, as the local bourgeoisie would not tolerate anything else; when Louis tried to introduce a more progressive form of raising revenue he quickly had to shelve his plans because of opposition from the propertied classes.

The solution usually offered to 'integration' was to pay lip-service to the Code Napoléon and other shibboleths of unity while working out local solutions. Sometimes this resulted in a syncretism of old and new, as in Aragon, where the sub-prefects retained the old title of *corregidores*. More often the resolution was the one familiar from twentieth-century

Latin America: an elaborate formal constitution which was systematically disregarded. The Emperor made sure that the various elected assemblies created by the many different constitutions were just so many talking shops.

Napoleon's attitude to uniformity and integration was an odd mixture of dogmatism and flexibility. He was always impatient of cultural differences and as the years went on his determination to impose the Code and other monolithic reforms hardened. Illyria, for instance, was a deeply religious country still essentially in the Middle Ages, yet the Emperor tried to govern it without the help of the clergy and even in the teeth of their opposition. By 1810 scarcely recognizable was the man who had boasted to Roederer ten years before of his flexibility: 'It is by turning Catholic that I finished the war in the Vendée; by turning Muslim that I established myself in Egypt; by turning ultramontane that I won the Italian mind.'

Yet Napoleon was always prepared to be flexible when his military interests were at stake. The obvious example was in Poland where, needing the support of the traditional élite, he did not even attempt to abolish feudal privileges. In Spain, whenever reform clashed with military exigencies, it was the latter that won. One can even argue that the reforms themselves were anyway dictated by military considerations. Napoleon's aim was to mobilize resources for his campaigns more rapidly than his *ancien régime* opponents, who were constrained by restrictions which gave tax immunities and exemptions to the Church, the nobility, to city corporations and many other bodies. Reform in the Napoleonic Empire came about if it suited Napoleon's military purposes or if the bourgeoisie gave it their consent; where no economic interests were involved they often did.

The logic of integration led Napoleon towards annexation in the *pays réunis* and *pays conquis*. Lacking a system of direct rule through the prefects in the conquered territories, Napoleon tried to keep control by putting his siblings in as kings or rulers; the family courts were further shackled by the presence of loyal French officials: Roederer in Naples, Beugnot in Berg, Simeon in Westphalia. The Emperor particularly liked to impose his favoured generals as War Ministers, as in the case of Dumas in Naples and d'Ebbe in Westphalia. Another ploy was to use his marshals as *de facto* viceroys: Davout in Poland, Suchet in Aragon, Marmont in Illyria.

The problem of the *pays alliés* was more tricky, for there was little he could do except exert pressure through his ambassadors: notable in this

area were Hédouville in Frankfurt, Bourgoing in Dresden and Bignon in
Warsaw. Saxony displayed particular independence, with Frederick
Augustus taking a 'pick and mix' approach to the Napoleonic system: he
favoured centralization to increase the power of the State, but was
impatient with the bogus assemblies and the representative principle in
general. Saxony also retained the institutions of the *ancien régime*, though
elsewhere in Germany elements of the prefect/department system were
introduced. The real snag with Germany was that reform could not make
much headway in the teeth of opposition from local élites whose support
Napoleon needed.

The impression is sometimes given in Anglocentric histories that
Napoleon held down his Empire by main force, and that he had no
collaborators in the subject or satellite states. Nothing could be farther
from the truth. A wide spectrum of pro–Bonapartists is evident in the
extended Empire. In the first place, there were the old élites themselves,
who looked to Napoleon to sustain their power. Had they attempted
anything so quixotic as a 'people's war' against France, they would very
soon have seen their own privileges swept away in the whirlwind. This
explains why, even in Spain, there was support for the Bonapartes and
why the grandees backed Joseph; many *hidalgos* and *afrancesado* bourgeois
saw the rising as an assault on the Enlightenment as much as on
Napoleon. There was even a kind of ideological harmony between
Napoleon and the old élites, for the Empire represented a return to
monarchical absolutism and its centralism, even in its attack on the
Church. Politicians and bureaucrats associated with absolutism worked
happily on administration in the satellites. Napoleon particularly
welcomed such collaboration as it furthered his Alexander the Great
project of fusion between old and new élites.

But it was not just in Spain that the intellectual middle class supported
Bonaparte. In Bavaria there were influential bureaucrats and bourgeois,
notably Maximilian von Montgelas, who took the view that the rising tide
of German nationalism was simply an aristocratic ploy to restore their
privileges. Moreover, it would be simpleminded to think that nationalism
always worked against Napoleon. In Poland nationalists yearning for an
independent state backed him, as did those who wanted a united Italy.
There were close bonds linking Napoleon and those agitating for
Hungarian independence from Austria, while in Greece and Romania he
was something of a hero figure for the support he gave those striving for
independence from the Turks. One Italian officer summed up well this
process of liberation through collaboration: 'What does it matter whether

one is serving the ambitions of this or that man? The great aim must be to learn to make war, which is the only skill that can free us.'

Napoleon was also seen as a very useful partner by a rising capitalist class. For bourgeois entrepreneurs the Empire was a gold mine, which combined the maximum of opportunity with the minimum of risk. Quite apart from the myriad entrepreneurial opportunities created by an era of rapid change and the sale of national property, there were vast fortunes to be made from the Napoleonic wars themselves, in everything from armaments to military victualling. The centralized administration and the efficient police force combined to provide the certainty and predictability economic investors traditionally like. Freemasonry, the ideology of the rising capitalist class, was spread rapidly over Europe by the many Jacobins and freethinkers in Napoleon's armies.

However, the misleading traditional picture of an Empire that satisfied nobody contains *some* truth; of their very nature, acts of resistance and dissatisfaction tended to make more of an impact than active or passive acquiescence. But the level of armed resistance was low. Apart from Spain, there were only two revolts that seriously challenged French authority: in Calabria and the Tyrol. In both these areas, significantly there was a long-standing tradition of military mobilization and National Guard service. The trouble in Calabria, which eventually obliged Murat to use draconian measures, was a mixture of xenophobia by bands of brigands and pot-stirring by the British operating from Sicily; Napoleon's old nemesis Sir Sidney Smith was active in this process. The revolt in the Tyrol looked like a peasant *jacquerie*, but turned out to be more than just an insurrection on economic issues. It was a confused would-be-independence movement, harking back to an alleged golden age in the Tyrol, Catholic, xenophobic and anti-semitic – in a word, the classic counter-revolutionary movement. Sidney Smith's role as agitator was here played by Archduke John, who had not the slightest intention of accepting an independent Tyrol.

Elsewhere, discontent took the form of banditry, desertion, absenteeism or, at a lower level, grumbling, alienation and the occasional demonstration or riot. There were very many reasons why Napoleon's formal and informal subjects should have been discontented with his Empire. Perhaps the overriding grievance was his insatiable demand for manpower, which in turn led to tough conscription policies. At the beginning of his reign Napoleon boasted that demography was on his side, because in 1789 three-quarters of France's 28 million inhabitants were under forty, and therefore there was no limit to the numbers of men he could raise. In France only 7% of the male population was drafted (as opposed to 36% in 1914–18), but even this figure featured in popular perception as a universal call-up.

Elsewhere in the Empire the percentage was higher. All the allies were obliged to provide a contingent for the *Grande Armée* in proportion to population, but Napoleon continually increased his demand for troops between 1808 and 1812. The respective figures for Westphalia are instructive: 16 infantry battalions, 12 cavalry squadrons and 3 artillery batteries in 1808 but 29, 28 and 6 respectively in 1812. Similar figures from other parts of the Empire show the same trend. In 1808 the Grand Duchy of Warsaw provided infantry, cavalry and artillery in the amount of 36 battalions, 26 squadrons and 12 batteries, but by 1812 this had risen to 60, 70 and 20 respectively; for Württemberg the corresponding figures were 12, 12 and 3 in 1808 and 20, 23 and 6 in 1812. In addition to regulars, the Empire had to raise and supply militia and national guards. At the peak of Napoleon's campaigns, in 1812, Italy supplied 121,000 regulars, Bavaria 110,000 (as against the original promised levy of 30,000), Warsaw 89,000, Saxony 66,000, Westphalia 52,000 and Berg 13,200. The minimum total of foreign conscripts serving in the Grand Army (not necessarily all at the same time) was 720,000, but some experts believe the true figure may have been almost one million men.

Resentment at this huge level of conscription was both individual and collective. Individually, those who served realized that their chances of survival were not that great. Of the 52,000 Westphalians only 18,000 survived and only 17,000 out of a 29,000-strong contingent from Baden. Conscription also left the wives and families of these men in destitution. A vicious circle was set up whereby young men, criminalized by the poverty resulting from the drafting of their fathers, were themselves dragooned into the ranks as punishment. Collectively, each locality in the Empire had to bear the massive costs of keeping these armies in being. Napoleon promised France he would make his wars pay for themselves, but he made no such promise to the satellites, and anyway his tactic of self-financing campaigns did not always work, notably in Spain and Russia. Even conquered Portugal paid only seven millions of the one hundred million francs levied as reparations after the 1807 campaign.

To maintain his armies Napoleon was forced into deficit spending: military expenditure accounted for 40% of the total French budget in 1806 and 58% by 1813. In an economy where Napoleon opposed state borrowing on principle and imposed a rigid metallic currency, his campaigns were bound to have a serious deflationary effect, and this was indeed the deep cause of the economic crises of 1805–07 and 1811–14. To palliate likely internal discontent in 1805 he set up an Extraordinary

Fund, administered by La Bouillerie under the authority of Daru, the Intendant-General of the occupied countries; between 1805–09 this fund allegedly received 734 million francs. In 1810, as his wars created greater and greater demands for money, Napoleon put the Fund on an official basis. A *senatus consultum* of 30 January set up an Extraordinary Domain, which was to be used only by the Emperor and only by decree for subsidizing the expenses of the *Grande Armée*; to soften the blow, it was announced that the Extraordinary Domain would also be used to reward great military or civil services, for public works and to encourage the arts.

The financial situation was far worse in the satellite states, where expenditure on the Army reached the dizzy levels of 80% of the total budget. In Westphalia the economics of the madhouse finally took over: Napoleon imposed a contribution to the Army of 31 million francs, plus 11.5 millions for upkeep, when the total state budget was only 34 millions. The irony of this was that the rationalization of finance and the consequent increases in income were simply wasted on the Army. Heavy demands for taxes from Napoleon went hand in hand with more efficient land registers, collection methods and fiscal mechanisms. In Berg tax revenues tripled between 1808–13, while in Naples they rose 50% in the three years after Murat's accession; all this was while the Continental System was anyway biting deep into the local economies. In Holland tax revenues yielded about 30 million florins in 1805 but 50 millions in 1809, and in addition there was a quite separate forced loan levied in 1807. When Napoleon annexed Holland in 1810, he liquidated two-thirds of the national debt, leaving penniless the bourgeoisie who had been forced to buy government bonds.

The predictable result of having to pay for the total costs of an Army conscripted unwillingly in the first place and for the costs of any French troops billeted outside France was national bankruptcy in many of the satellite states. The debt of the Kingdom of Italy rose from one to five million lire in 1805–11; the Grand Duchy of Warsaw's national debt trebled in the years 1807–11; while luckless Westphalia, which enjoyed the additional 'privilege' of having to pay the costs of 35,000 French troops quartered there in November 1811, saw the national debt rise from sixty million francs to over two hundred million, for in addition to Napoleon's exactions, there was the lunatic prodigality of his brother, King Jérôme.

Napoleon did not mete out such severe financial punishments only to his 'favoured' allies. Those who made war on him paid through the nose with war indemnities. Austria was mulcted of 350 million francs for the two ill-judged campaigns of 1805 and 1809; Prussia had to disgorge 515 millions for the catastrophic mistake of Jena, and Hanover, Prussia's appanage, had to pay fifty millions. The extraction of funds from Spain after 1808 was big business, with western Castile 'contributing' eight million francs in just six months in 1810. Additionally, the conquered territories were stripped of other significant material resources: in 1806 the Prussians lost 40,000 horses while the Saxons had to abandon all cannon, munitions and military stores.

The twin evils of conscription and taxes to pay for the draftees did not end there. French soldiers in foreign territories lived off the land – a euphemism for large-scale looting. The costs of having French troops quartered on them were so great that many citizens preferred to abandon their homes instead. The brutal French soldiers, many of them rapists and murderers who had chosen the army instead of a prison sentence, took their pick of the local women. Feelings ran high over sex, which was a threefold source of anger and resentment. There was rape pure and simple; there was a high level of prostitution; and there was the phenomenon of peasant girls and others choosing to go off with officers and becoming camp followers. As one French soldier wrote of his experience among the Germans: 'They cannot forgive us for having for twenty years caressed their wives and daughters before their very faces.'

Conscription, taxes, forced levies, debts run up by the Bonaparte family as kings, looting by ordinary soldiers, economic disruption and dislocation, the Catholic backlash triggered by anticlerical and freemason soldiery, the affront to local cultures, traditions and folkways which engendered primitive nationalism – not even this long list of sources of discontent exhausts the alienating impact of Napoleon's Empire. Over and above all this was the crucial consideration that Napoleon ran his so-called integrated Europe as a gigantic spoils system. The exiguous revenue base in the hard-pressed satellites was shrunk still further by the estates set aside for the Emperor's *donataires*.

The titles and benefices Napoleon assigned to his marshals were always located in the satellite or annexed states, never in France itself, partly for prudential reasons so as not to alienate French taxpayers, partly to give his generals a strong motive for fighting campaigns beyond the 'natural frontiers', partly because all worthwhile national property had already been alienated. Never was there a more blatant example of the Emperor's boast that 'I have only conquered kingdoms ... to serve the interest of France and help me in all I am doing for her.' His barefaced exploitation of the satellite states emerges clearly from one salient fact: first charge on all state revenues went to the entailed incomes of his marshals and other *donataires*.

Also very clear is Napoleon's determination to run a personal Empire, for he rigidly controlled the system of entails and benefices himself. He kept two large account books on the corner of his desk, in which names and amounts were listed. In his memoirs Baron Agathon Fain, successor to Bourrienne and Méneval as the Emperor's secretary, relates how he got his share in the system of imperial rip-off. Napoleon ran his eye over the pages of the ledger, quickly reminding himself who had what. Then he stopped and looked hard at an entry. 'Aha, I've found you one. Here you are! 10,000 francs income in Pomerania! Let it not be said I've forgotten my secretaries.'

By 1814 Napoleon had made grants to 4,994 persons at a cost of nearly thirty million francs a year; in money terms half of this went to 824 generals. There was an inner circle of favoured recipients even among the lucky pensioners, for people like Pauline, Davout, Ney, Berthier and 486 other favourites (10% of the total) received 24 million francs or 80% of the total amount. Berthier, for example, was made Prince of Neuchâtel, never once visited the place, yet received half the gross revenue of the principality (610,000 livres) in the seven years 1806–13. After the decisive battle with the Austrians in 1809 he was made Prince of Wagram and added a further 250,000 francs to his endowment, making his total annual income 1.3 million francs.

Even these lavish sums did not satisfy the marshals' cupidity. The worst offenders were Augereau, Soult, Masséna and Victor. Augereau once strode into an Italian pawnshop and stuffed his pockets with jewels. When this was reported to Napoleon, he dismissed the objections cynically: 'Don't talk to me about generals who love money. It was only that which enabled me to win the battle of Eylau. Ney wanted to reach Elbing to procure more funds.'

The result of Napoleon's refusal to discipline his marshals was predictable. Art treasures were looted across an area stretching from Egypt to Spain and, although some of the paintings found their way into the Louvre, most were purloined for private collections. Soult acquired paintings worth one-and-a-half million francs, which he pocketed; Napoleon kept back a wealth of choice items for Josephine; many hundreds more precious artefacts were sold at State auctions. The plunderers habitually lied to the Emperor. In December 1806 General Lagrange, the French military governor of Hesse-Darmstadt, found the treasure of the Landgrave of Hesse, who had made the mistake of backing the Prussians. The total value of the haul, accumulated painstakingly over the years by the notably miserly Landgrave, was nineteen million francs. In return for a bribe of a million francs, Lagrange fabricated a report that only eight millions had been unearthed. The remaining ten millions, in bonds, bills, cash vouchers and mortgage documents were then smuggled out of the country for the exiled Landgrave's use.

Napoleon put his foot down only when the personal corruption of his acolytes put in jeopardy the Continental System. Bourrienne, as French representative in Hamburg sold over 150,000 authorizations for the export of illegally imported goods between August 1807 and December 1810, at rates of 0.25% and 0.5% the value of the merchandise. He made more than one million francs from this scam, which meant that goods worth between sixty and 120 millions were exported annually. It was hardly surprising that colonial cotton, sugar and coffee continued to circulate in Germany, Switzerland and Austria at prices lower than in Paris, even after the decrees of 1810. Recalled and fined for his corrupt practices, and heedless of the fact that Napoleon had already pardoned him once for embezzlement, the wretched Bourrienne complained of the Emperor's 'ingratitude' and became a secret agent for the Bourbons.

Many commentators have remarked on Napoleon's hubris in embarking on the adventure in Spain at the very moment his Empire looked rock-solid. Less attention has been lavished on the objective side of the picture, which shows Napoleon launching into new and quixotic adventures at the very moment the economic, demographic and psychological factors hitherto favouring him were undergoing a reverse. The ethos of the *Grande Armée* shifted from revolutionary virtue to personal gain and advancement, producing a catastrophic decline in morale and *esprit de corps*. After 1807 the once magnificent army was badly equipped, badly officered and frequently indisciplined. It became increasingly obvious that most of the marshals were of poor military calibre; Napoleon frequently rued the loss of the brilliant Desaix. The reservoir of men was beginning to run dry, and after 1807 the proportion of battle losses was no longer so favourable to the French. The inexperience and poor morale of conscripts after 1807 – at its simplest level a result of having to fight in wars far from France which did not seem to involve national interests – meant the army was not nearly so potent a weapon as in 1796–1805; consequently manoeuvres under fire became less plausible and therefore battle casualties greater.

Above all, the factor of money began to haunt the Emperor. An examination of Napoleon's accounts for the period 1 October 1806 to 15 October 1808 shows a healthy state of affairs. Extraordinary taxes raised 311,662,000 francs, property taxes 79,667,000 francs and the foreclosure of coffers 16,172,000. In addition, there was the huge war indemnity of 600 million francs from Prussia, including the remounting of 40,000 cavalry and other supplies. During the same period the expenditure of the *Grande Armée* was 212,879,335 francs. The protracted campaigns in Prussia and Poland had therefore cost the French taxpayer nothing, but this situation was about to change with a vengeance. At the beginning of 1809 Napoleon's Empire still looked secure, but in retrospect we can see him already at the edge of a precipice.

Perhaps unconsciously Napoleon even realized this for, as if by pre-established harmony, his health began to decline before his fortunes dipped, and this process can be dated to 1808. His features coarsened, his body grew heavier, his stomach protruded, his look grew less alert and his voice less commanding. The gastric attack at Bayonne in 1808 and the eczema at Vienna in May 1809 were pointers to a valetudinarian future. It was almost as though the colossus began to crack in anticipation of the unravelling of his life's work.

CHAPTER TWENTY

When he left Spain, Napoleon assured Joseph he would be back as soon as he had dealt with the Austrians. Furthermore, he made this grandiloquent announcement to the Corps Législatif: 'When I show myself beyond the Pyrenees the terrified leopard [England] will seek the Ocean in order to avoid shame, defeat and death. The triumph of my arms will be the triumph of the spirit of good over that of evil.' Yet he never went back to Spain and remained in France for over two years for no good reason while the military situation worsened. How is this to be explained?

The usual answer provided is that he thought the Spanish theatre secondary and considered that the war there could be won whenever he chose to return. Superficially, too, the situation in Spain in the spring of 1809 seemed much more promising: the English had been expelled, Madrid taken and the siege of Zaragoza successfully completed after 40,000 casualties among the defenders. Yet there are grounds for believing the real explanation is in terms of Napoleon's own credibility. It seems unlikely, to say the least, that the problems of his army in Spain appeared mysterious to him. But how could he pull his forces out now and risk an unacceptable loss of prestige?

Napoleon's problem was that he needed an immense army to subdue Spain, yet such an army could neither live off the land nor be supplied from France, because of the atrocious state of the roads across the Pyrenees. Even if he did manage to supply them, the drain on the French treasury would be unacceptable. Hitherto he had been able to pyramid his successes: blitzkrieg warfare was followed by an orgy of looting, which in turn paid for further armies, further blitzkriegs, further loot, and so to the continuance of the cycle. But in Spain the French, instead of gaining some 250 million francs per successful battle, began to pour out blood and treasure, gaining nothing in return. There was no possibility of an Austerlitz. Seeing all this clearly, yet unable to withdraw for reasons of pride and prestige, Napoleon simply distanced himself from the campaign, as he had with the Vendée in 1795 and Egypt in 1798; reasons of credibility ensured that the marshals would take the blame for a war that was in principle unwinnable.

Yet if Napoleon had no intention of returning to Spain, the British certainly did. Wellesley returned to Portugal in April 1809 and began by defeating Soult at Oporto on 11 May. On 28 July came the hard-fought battle of Talavera, where Wellesley defeated Victor but not without cost, sustaining 5,000 casualties to the French 7,000. When Wellesley moved back into Portugal to head off another thrust from Soult, his Spanish allies complained vociferously that the British were abandoning them, just as Moore had allegedly done the year before. London, though, upheld Wellesley and created him Viscount Wellington for the success at Talavera. The Spanish were obliged to accept Wellington grudgingly as an informal supremo of the allied forces. To deal with the triple threat of Wellington, Spanish regulars and the growing numbers of guerrillas, by the autumn of 1809 Napoleon had committed 350,000 troops to the Peninsula.

The Peninsular War has sometimes been written up as if it were an inevitable British response to Napoleon's Continental Blockade and his blundering into Spain. In fact the decision to intervene in the Iberian peninsula was a marginal one, for no vital British interests seemed involved there, unlike, say, the Baltic. Opponents of an expedition to Spain argued variously that the area did not pose an invasion threat, was not a source of vital imports, was not a link in the chain of command with other powers and offered no barrier to French attacks in the Middle and Far East. Others argued that there could be important economic benefits, that even if Napoleon bought off or suborned his opponents in northern Europe, Britain could still fight on in the south, and in sum that a Peninsular campaign made Britain independent of her allies.

Initially opportunism was the spur: it was an opportunity to strike at French naval power, for the six Franco-Spanish ships of the line that had huddled in Cadiz and Vigo since Trafalgar were taken out, as were all Portuguese warships; the Royal Navy also gained the use of the Atlantic ports of Lisbon and Oporto. Gradually, though, London became aware of other implications of the Spanish intervention. They could deny France the commerce of Latin America – which was why British policy shifted in these years from encouraging Latin American independence to keeping the colonies loyal to Spain – and by tying Napoleon up in Spain prevent him from making any moves against Canada and India. The conjectured economic benefits did materialize. In Spain British exports rose from £1.7 million in 1807 to just over £6.7 million in 1809, and by 1812 Spain was taking one-fifth of British exports. Latin America, too, proved a cornucopia. A commercial treaty with Dom João in 1810 threw Brazil open to British trade, so that British exports to South America rose from £1.2 million in 1807 to £2.7 million in 1812.

Most of all, the British could take independent action against Napoleon in Spain but not in the rest of the continent until 1813; this enabled them to allay the suspicions of nations like Russia, who feared that Britain wanted to conduct the war against Napoleon on their backs, and also to shrug off requests for military aid, as from Russia in 1812 and Austria in 1813. Not coincidentally, Spain made Wellington's fame and fortune, especially after he was formally given the title of Commander-in-Chief in 1812, for if he had been able to campaign with Britain's allies in northern Europe before 1815, he would have been merely another minor general. The Peninsular campaign gave Britain an independent voice at later peace talks – a voice that would probably have been drowned by the Russians and Austrians had she committed her forces to northern Europe.

This explains why the British were always more lavish with subsidies in Spain than in other theatres of war. They began by giving the five leading juntas £1.1 million, with a promise of more once a supreme junta had been set up. Once this was done, in September 1808, a British envoy was sent to the peninsula with £650,000 in silver and instructions to negotiate a commercial treaty covering Latin America. Altogether, £2.5 millions in arms and money was sent to Spain in 1808, leading to severe specie shortages in England. This shortage was the principal reason why Britain could not take maximum advantage of Napoleon's embroilment with Austria in 1809.

With the British fully engaged, the position of the French, committed to holding down all of Spain, quickly became untenable. To combat the threefold opposition of Wellington, the Spanish army and the guerrillas, the French could seldom field an army even 100,000 strong at the point of maximum danger, even with their vast numbers. Suchet commanded 80,000 in Aragon and Catalonia; Joseph's personal corps in Madrid numbered 14,000; another 60,000 were kept back to guard the Pyrenean passes and keep open the roads to Madrid and Salamanca; and a further 60,000 under Soult entered Andalucia in 1810 and became bogged down in a pointless siege of Cadiz.

There were three separate enemy forces facing the French and there were three distinct phases of the Peninsular War which roughly corresponded with them. In 1808 the Spanish army enjoyed its one great triumph at Bailen, in the wake of the nationwide spontaneous uprisings. In the second phase of the war, roughly from 1809 to 1812, the campaign was mixed, part regular engagements involving Wellington and the

British expeditionary force, part guerrilla warfare; in fact Wellington got better cooperation from the guerrilla chiefs, terrorists and brigands as they were, than from the regular Spanish commanders who showed a cynical lack of interest in anything from the British except cash and free weaponry and ammunition. It was only in the final phase of the war, in 1812–13 that Wellington was able to dovetail all three elements and use the guerrillas in a coordinated strategy.

The problem for the French was that they could have defeated Wellington on his own or the guerrillas on their own, but they could not defeat both. One hundred and fifty years later the Americans were to learn the same bloody lesson in Vietnam: that the combination of a regular army plus widespread guerrilla warfare and a hostile population made military occupation of a large country impossible. What did for the French was the deadly combination of Wellington and the guerrillas, and the key element was the guerrillas. This is a fact notoriously overlooked by British historians who treat the war solely as a series of set-pieces between Wellington and Napoleon's marshals.

The French were strong enough to occupy the main towns and strategic centres and thus contain the guerrillas provided they did not also have to fight Wellington. But the British were merely the necessary conditions for Spanish defeat; the guerrillas provided the sufficient conditions. The more intelligent French commanders saw that the requirements of military occupation in a hostile country contradicted the requirements for active campaigning. An exhausted Bessières wrote in 1811: 'If I concentrate 20,000 men, all my communications are lost and the insurgents make great progress. We occupy too much territory.' Jourdan agreed that the military occupation of Spain was not feasible and that any number of French set-piece victories would make no difference: the only solution was to hold a line north of Madrid.

Guerrilla warfare meant constant threats to an already tenuous supply line and the threat of starvation. Masséna was fond of quoting an old saying attributed to Henri Quatre: 'Spain is a country where small armies are defeated and large armies starve.' Another marshal, Marmont, wrote despondently in 1812: 'The English Army had its pay on time, the French Army received not a penny. The English Army had magazines in abundance, and the English soldier never needed to forage for himself; the French Army lived only by the efforts of those who comprised it . . . The English Army had 6,000 mules for its food supplies alone; the French Army had no other means of transport but the backs of our soldiers.'

This was the hidden subtext of Wellington's eventual triumph, which has been portrayed too often solely in terms of his peerless military talent. Supplied by sea by the Royal Navy, he could manoeuvre in Spain when and where he wished; the French troops had no regular supply and were too numerous to live off the land. Foraging parties, unless in brigade strength, would be taken out by the guerrillas, while a wholesale effort to supply the army from France would mean that Napoleon had no resources left over for adventures elsewhere in Europe.

Since the guerrillas were the rock on which Napoleon's Spanish adventure foundered, they merit more attention than they have received in most histories of the Peninsular War. Who were they, what were their aims and why were they so successful? Unfortunately, historians disagree on almost every aspect of the Spanish irregulars. Some say there were as many as 50,000, others that the figure may be as low as 30,000 – in contrast to an English army of 40,000 and 25,000 Spanish regulars. As for the casualties they inflicted, this too divides commentators. Although we may discount King Joseph's figure of 180,000 guerrilla-caused deaths out of a total French mortality of 240,000 in the years 1808–1813 as being absurdly high, some scholars opt for a high of 145,000. Others claim that many deaths through wounds and disease were attributed to the guerrillas, so that the true figure is in the region of 76,000 deaths. But at the very least the guerrillas must have accounted for thirty French deaths every day.

Another problem is that the Spanish guerrillas have been hopelessly romanticized as freedom fighters. There were a few idealists but mostly they were old-style bandit chiefs whose activities were legitimated by the struggle for Ferdinand, the 'desired one'. Spanish guerrilla warfare was overwhelmingly a rural affair, with undertones of social war, poor against rich, but it always tended to shade into tax-resistant brigandage. It was in almost every respect a retrograde and reactionary phenomenon which, with its ethos of partisan warfare, the cult of the leader, xenophobia and mindless hatred and atrocity, left Spain a baneful legacy which some say would eventually surface in the Spanish Civil War of 1936–39. By encouraging contempt for social norms, it encouraged Spaniards to live outside the law and accept the doctrine that power comes out of the barrel of a gun. By romanticizing revolution, glorifying insubordination and deifying violence and atrocity, it laid the foundations for a sea of troubles in later Spanish history.

No service is done to history by endorsing the legend of the Spanish 'guerrilla patriots'. But of their power of attrition there can be no doubt. Although difficult to use strategically in planned campaigns, they were invaluable in preventing French armies appearing in overwhelming force.

If the French did not occupy territory effectively, it fell into the hands of partisans, leaving the French the task of 'cleansing' the area with inadequate numbers and defective maps. They attacked regular troops only when in overwhelming numbers and largely restricted themselves to occupying areas evacuated by the enemy. But they struck terror into French soldier and *afrancesados* alike. Known never to take prisoners, they practised with gusto the arts of crucifixion, garrotting, boiling in oil and burning at the stake. In addition to the luckless hundred thousand French troops who died at their hands, another 30,000 Spaniards suspected of collaboration were put to death in extremes of cruelty; sometimes entire villages were wiped out.

The very geography of Spain favoured the partisans and worked against the French. The principal mountain ranges – Pyrenees, Cantabrians, Guadarramas, the Sierra de Guadalupe, de Toledo and the Sierra Morena – run east to west, as do the rivers Ebro, Douro, Tagus, Guadiana, Guadalquivir; guerrilla movement was easier that way, but the French needed good north-south communications to be supplied effectively. In their mountain fastnesses the guerrilla leaders ruled bands of warriors that could number anything from a few dozen to 8,000 – as in the case of Francisco Espoz y Mina. Active in Navarre and the most famous of the guerrillas, Mina was an authoritarian peasant responsible for many of the worst atrocities.

Other names that became familiar to French commanders were Juan Pilarea, 'El Medico', who operated over a wide area from La Mancha to Toledo and often menaced the environs of Madrid; Juan Diaz, 'El Empecinado' ('the stubborn'), who was active in Castile (Aranda, Segovia, Guadalajara) and boasted that he never lost a man in action; and Juan Diaz Porlier, estimated to have commanded 4,000 men by 1811 and particularly associated with Galicia and the Asturias. Bloodthirsty, ruthless and cruel men, they were, like sharks, not averse to devouring each other if French victims were lacking; Mina fought a campaign in 1810 against another bandit leader, Echeverria. Haughty and indisciplined, they disregarded any orders from the Cortés or the Junta or Wellington that clashed with their own interests and were thus a perfect analogue for Napoleon's marshals in Spain.

That the French held their own for so long, faced with a hostile population and desperate enemies, was largely because they enjoyed the support of local quislings or *afrancesados*. These pro-French collaborators have divided historians as strongly as the guerrillas. Some view them as naïve idealists, who believed that collaboration with Joseph was the way to preserve Spanish independence and annexation by Napoleon or who genuinely thought that Napoleon was the bringer of reform and enlightenment. Others take a more jaundiced view of the *afrancesados* as opportunists who, at least until 1812, thought that Napoleon was invincible or see them as a mixture of cynicism and inertia, wedded to a simple desire for salaries, places and privilege. In many cases, the question of to be or not to be a French collaborator was settled by geography, almost on the old principal of *cuius regio, eius religio* – yet another link between 1808 and the Civil War of 1936.

There is some evidence that Napoleon occasionally tried to pull out of the Spanish maelstrom, but each time he took a faltering step circumstances worked against him. By the end of 1809 he seemed to have become convinced that installing Joseph as King of Spain had been a mistake and that the best strategy was restoration of Ferdinand, provided he would agree to make common cause against England. While Joseph fortified himself with the illusion that he could conciliate the Spanish by reforms, a gentle forbearing rule and a show of independence from the Emperor, Napoleon decided to apply pressure on him.

An imperial decree of 8 February 1810 seemed like the prelude to yet another annexation. By the decree Napoleon lopped off a huge area of northern Spain from Joseph's domains and organized four independent military governments – Catalonia, Aragon, Navarre and Guipuzcoa – under direct French control. Naturally piqued, Joseph talked of abdication – which is exactly what his brother wanted. But in the end he decided not to abdicate, leaving Napoleon with the straight choice of dismissing him or sustaining him. The only way the Emperor could have winkled the firstborn of the Bonapartes out of Spain was by allowing him to return to his old kingdom in Naples, but this was politically impossible as it would mean ousting the Murats.

In April 1810 Napoleon gave the command of the Army of Portugal to Masséna but it was September that year before the marshal commenced a tortuous march on Lisbon with a 70,000-strong army. By this time Wellington had an army of 50,000, even though he could normally put only about two-thirds of this in the field because of garrison and other duties. But he had used the lull in fighting to good effect by planning and constructing the lines of Torres Vedras – a set of fortifications from the Atlantic to the Tagus, straddling the neck of land around Lisbon. Beginning in late 1809 Wellington built two fortified lines to defend Lisbon; the work was completed in the summer of 1810. The first line was twenty-nine miles long and ran from the coast to the Tagus at Alhandra; the second, six miles to the south and supposedly impregnable, stretched twenty-two miles from the coast to the Tagus, roughly parallel with the first line. These lines were a mélange of strong points, artillery positions, trenches, redoubts, ditches and palisades. The ground in front of the lines was cleared of all cover and a set of redoubts at the end of the second line gave crossfire with Admiral Berkeley's gunboats on the river. There was even a third line of fortifications at the mouth of the Tagus, designed to enable the Army to embark safely in the event of a disaster.

In September 1810 Masséna struck into Portugal and gained some initial success. At first Wellington retreated, then stood his ground at Busaco near Coimbra on 25 September. Bringing his strength up to 50,000 by herculean efforts, he posted them on a ridge, then lured Masséna to attack by disguising his numbers. In a frontal assault on the ridge lasting three hours the French were badly beaten, taking 4,600 casualties (1,000 dead) against Wellington's 1,200 (200 dead). In October Wellington withdrew behind the lines of Torres Vedras. Masséna, coming up behind him, probed and concluded that an attack on the lines would be suicidal.

The resulting stalemate until March 1811 saw Masséna's army wasting away through sickness and starvation. Foraging was impossible because the British had implemented a 'scorched earth' policy and any attempt to revictual the army had to run the gauntlet of Spanish and Portuguese guerrillas. In desperation Masséna finally pulled out of Portugal altogether, leaving behind thousands of non-battle casualties (some say the toll from disease and famine ran as high as 25,000). He made a vain attempt to reenter Portugal, which aborted because of opposition from two subsidiary marshals. Soult, who hated him, was supposed to coordinate a pincer movement from Seville and Badajoz but failed to do so; then Masséna quarrelled violently with Ney (who refused a direct order to take his corps into Portugal without supplies) and sent him back to France in disgrace. While Masséna was thus preoccupied around Salamanca, Wellington emerged to besiege Almeida.

Factionalism among the marshals, some of whom had been effectively turned into independent warlords by Napoleon's 1810 decree, was proving to be almost as much a headache for the French as the guerrillas. Despairing of cooperation from Soult, Masséna approached Bessières, now commanding the Army of the North, for reinforcements with which to relieve Almeida; the cynical Bessières sent him just 1500 men. Pressing on nonetheless, the intrepid Masséna was surprised by Wellington at Fuentes de Oñoro but nearly managed to turn the tables on him. Wellington won a hard-fought battle but admitted: 'If Boney had been there, we would have been damnably licked.' Masséna withdrew to Ciudad Rodrigo and claimed a victory; Napoleon, however, was not deceived and a week later recalled him to France, appointing Marmont in his stead.

Napoleon, though, owed Masséna a favour, after an incident at an imperial shooting party at Fontainebleau in September 1808. The Emperor, a famously bad shot, hit Masséna in the face with a bullet when aiming at a bird and destroyed the sight in his left eye. Masséna had done his best in Spain and Wellington testified that he could never rest easy while the one-eyed marshal was in the field. Marmont was scarcely an improvement. Destined to be the least successful of all the Peninsular marshals, he was a man of no military talent who owed his elevation to the marshalate entirely to Napoleon's favour and repaid him with treachery. The two most talented Peninsular marshals were Suchet and Mortier who, alone of his kind, managed to get on with Soult. This was in marked contrast to another marshal, Victor, who all but refused to serve under the rapacious Soult, but Victor was almost the quintessence of the marshalate in that, after the death of his one friend, Lannes, he declined to take orders from anyone but the Emperor.

Before Wellington and Marmont could cross swords, Soult had at last blundered into action in the south. He came up to relieve Badajoz, then under siege by General Beresford, forcing the English commander to break off and deal with the threat to his rear. The resulting battle at Albuhuera on 15 May was the bloodiest in the Peninsular War, with both commanders losing control of their forces. The nerve of the British infantry held better, so that it was Soult who finally disengaged. Casualties were terrific: there were 4,000 fatalities among the 7,600 British casualties, and Spanish and Portuguese losses topped 2,400 besides; the French sustained total losses of 7,000. Since Beresford had begun the battle with 32,000 against Soult's 23,000, it was disingenuous of the British to claim a great victory; at the very best it was pyrrhic.

Wellington's strategy was to take the fortress towns of Badajoz and Ciudad Rodrigo in order to be able to advance securely into Spain, but the junction of Marmont's and Soult's forces forced him to break off the siege of Badajoz. Another stalemate ensued as both sides eyed each other warily. With just 60,000 men the French did not feel confident enough to attack Wellington with his 50,000. Soon the unified French command disintegrated, as the familiar jealousies and fissiparous tendencies among the marshals took their toll: Soult marched away to Seville while Marmont withdrew to the Tagus valley. Marmont and Wellington continued to play cat and mouse. The British commander again moved out to threaten Salamanca, whereupon Marmont summoned four divisions from the Army of the North, giving him 60,000 men once more. At this Wellington once more withdrew into the Portuguese mountains.

The year 1811 was one of mixed fortunes in the Peninsula. On the one hand, Wellington had clearly asserted his military supremacy over the French commanders by demonstrating how the massed French columns could be defeated. His favourite device was to keep the bulk of his troops concealed behind reverse slopes so that enemy artillery and skirmishers could not get at them. This upset the calculations of French commanders who would keep their troops in column until reaching the brow of the defended hill, by which time it was too late to deploy. Raking volleys from the British, sometimes from three sides at once, would obliterate the head of the column and send survivors reeling back in confusion. Had Napoleon taken the trouble to study the Spanish battles closely instead of railing formulaically at his marshals for incompetence, he would have seen that the fluidity, speed, mobility and sheer aggression of the French column, which had overwhelmed opponent after opponent for ten years, was beginning to fail and that his battle tactics should be rethought.

Wellington meanwhile, though never the military genius his supporters claim, went from strength to strength. A thorough knowledge of his enemy's methods meant that he was never psychologically unhinged, or beaten before he began, as were so many allied commanders facing French marshals. His remarkably effective methods were in fact as predictable as Napoleon's came to be. Everything depended on an eye for terrain and a clever choice of battlefield, which allowed him to use his favourite method of concealing men behind reverse slopes, using riflemen to dominate no-man's-land. Time and again the peninsular marshals fell into the trap of sending their men to the summit of a ridge, only to be met by the massed volleys of the 'long red wall', followed by the much-feared British bayonet charge.

If Wellington as a battle commander was predictable, his real claim to a place in the universal military pantheon lay in his mastery of logistics. The way he organized five invasion routes between Portugal and Spain, ensuring a continuous commissariat system was masterly. His three-fold supply line – by barge from Lisbon to intermediate depots, by ox-wagon convoys to forward supply depots, and thence by divisional and regimental mule-trains to the individual units at the front – was an object lesson in how to organize a military campaign. As the great historian of the Peninsular War, Sir John Fortescue, remarked: 'Wellington's supplies were always hunting for his army; Joseph's army was always hunting for his supplies.'

For all Wellington's talents, the British position in Spain was far from secure. By the end of 1810 London was increasingly pessimistic about the prospects of being able to stay in the Iberian peninsula in force and toyed instead with the idea of converting Cadiz into a second Gibraltar, making it a heavily garrisoned enclave which would command the trade of Latin America. The problem was money. London had gambled its sterling reserves on a quick victory, but the gamble failed, and thereafter the problem loomed: how to get specie to Wellington? He needed ready cash precisely because he was in a friendly country and therefore could not live off the land. But this was at a time when the Bank of England's hard currency reserves were draining away; they sank from £6.4 million in 1808 to £2.2 million in 1814. The British were forced into increasingly desperate measures to obtain bullion from India, China and Mexico.

Wellington, who did not understand economics, began to complain vociferously to London about 'sabotage' and spoke in a quasi-paranoid way of deliberate treachery; these complaints reached a peak in 1811. But he had not grasped the scale of the problem. To keep an Army overseas was the most expensive option London could exercise; the costs of the Navy were far less, for sailors were virtually prisoners of war inside their wooden world and, on leaving the ships, were paid off in a British port. Maintaining an Army in Spain cost three times that of maintaining the same Army in Britain, for in the United Kingdom suppliers did not demand payment in bullion and troops could be paid in paper money.

The financial drain of the Peninsular War did not end there. In 1811 60% of grain imports from the U.S.A. went to the Peninsula. As far as possible the British tried to victual Wellington's army from the homeland: in 1808 4.4 million pounds of beef, 2.5 million pounds of pork, 3.3 million pounds of flour, 7.7 million pounds of bread and 336,000 gallons of spirit were sent out. By 1813 the average daily consumption in Wellington's army was 100,000 pounds of biscuit, 200,000 pounds of forage corn and 300 cattle; at Lisbon there was always a seven months' food supply. But to meet local expenses and Spanish demands to be paid in silver, Britain became a major arms dealer: by 1811 a total of 336,000 muskets, 60 million cartridges, 348 pieces of artillery, 100,000 swords and 12,000 pistols had been exported to Spain, and by 1813 the British began diversifying in the market for arms in Russia, Prussia, Austria and Sweden.

None the less, for a while the financial fate of Wellington's expeditionary force hung in the balance. By 1812 London could not meet his pay bills, troops had not been paid for five months and muleteers for thirteen, and the inevitable result was looting and alienation of the local population. London was reduced to borrowing cash from shady Maltese and Italian bankers at outrageously usurious rates in exchange for bills drawing on the British government. The breakthrough was achieved in 1812 by the Rothschilds. First Jacob Rothschild bought up many of these bills at a fraction of their price and took them to London where his brother Nathan cashed them at the Bank of England at a huge profit. Then Nathan obtained £800,000 in gold from the East India Company, sold it on to the British government for Wellington's use, and even worked out how to get it to Portugal.

Yet it was really Napoleon who won the Peninsular War for the British at the very moment fortunes were equally poised and there was some evidence that London was losing heart. Making a disastrous and ill-judged intervention in Spanish affairs, he ordered Marmont to transfer 10,000 men to Suchet's army in Valencia and Catalonia. This left Marmont at Salamanca inferior in numbers to Wellington at the very time the increasing size of the guerrilla bands meant that by the end of 1811 the French could never muster an Army of more than 70,000 to deal with Wellington. It was this that finally allowed the British Army to take the offensive and remain there.

Napoleon's mistakes in Spain were legion. A wiser man would have pulled out as soon as he saw the depth of the opposition or at least held a defensive line north of Madrid, possibly from Mediterranean to Atlantic on a Catalonia/Galicia axis. As it was, the Emperor seemed woefully ignorant of the real problems of campaigning in the peninsula. He provided insufficient resources to achieve total pacification – admittedly this would probably have entailed committing most of the *Grande Armée* to this one theatre – closed his eyes and ears to the truth, continued his ludicrous underestimation of Wellington and the British (even at Waterloo he regarded Wellesley as no more than a 'sepoy general') and seemed almost wilful in his refusal to make a close study of the politics and culture of Spain. Until 1812 he directed operations from Paris, invariably making the wrong decisions.

The most egregious of his errors was his failure to appoint a commander-in-chief in Spain until 1812. The disastrous decision to hive off four 'excepted areas' and give them to the marshals – a cynical short-term decision to palliate the unpopularity of Spanish campaigning – allowed the bickering marshals to become, in effect, autonomous warlords, and the consequent lack of central control from Madrid in turn aided Wellington and the guerrillas. Spain thus became what one observer has described as a 'training ground in disobedience' for the marshals; when Napoleon finally did the right thing and appointed Joseph as Commander-in-Chief in Spain, the four marshal-warlords simply ignored his directives. Elsewhere the Emperor never allowed the feuding of the marshals to interfere with military efficiency and endanger operations, but in Spain he condoned a situation where the jealous baton-toting prima donnas often refused to cooperate with each other.

Napoleon compounded his mistake in allowing the marshals a free rein by assigning some of the most rapacious of them to Spain. The one success story was Suchet in Catalonia, but this was because of his lack of rapacity. Where Soult and Masséna pillaged and looted high and low in their crazed quest for booty and ill-gotten gains – Soult indeed in his barely disguised ambition for the Spanish crown came close to treason – Suchet governed Catalonia benevolently, prevented looting and did not use the province as a mere milch-cow. The result was that he won considerable acceptance and support in the province and was never defeated in battle. Even here, Napoleon could not let well enough alone, for he prevented Suchet consolidating his grip on Aragon by ordering him to conquer Valencia. Having completed the conquest of Catalonia in 1811, Suchet received his marshal's baton, but not before his champion at court, Duroc, explained to the Emperor that the few setbacks he sustained were all the fault of Joseph's incompetence.

But the greatest of all Napoleon's errors in Spain was his loyalty to Joseph. Even when he finally saw sense and realized that the solution in Spain was Joseph's abdication and the restoration of Ferdinand, his brother managed to talk him round after a long interview when the 'King of Spain' went to France to plead his case in person. For Frédéric Masson it was in Spain above all that Napoleon showed himself as the 'victim of the family sense, of the Corsican spirit, or primogeniture'. Others, surely with justification, speak of a 'brother-complex', making Napoleon absurdly weak when it came to Joseph. On St Helena he saw the truth when he told Las Cases: 'I believe that had I been willing to sacrifice Joseph, I would have succeeded.'

It would not be fair to conclude on Napoleon's mistakes in Spain without mentioning an alternative view of Napoleon's involvement there, which is that he was better informed than he seemed to be but was in thrall to a 'domino effect' of his own imagination. According to this jigsaw puzzle view of the Napoleonic schema, the Emperor's credibility in Spain was on the line in a more systematic sense. Napoleon had always had a tendency to invade country X because his thoughts were really on country Y. So, for instance, Holland had to be invaded to secure Belgium, Germany to secure the Rhine, Naples and Rome to safeguard Piedmont and Lombardy, and so on. According to this view, the invasion of Spain was supposed to overawe Austria but, when it signally failed to do so in 1809, Napoleon was involved in a game of double or quits to show that he was irresistible anywhere in Europe.

A variant of this view is that if he withdrew *anywhere* in Europe, he would then be under pressure to withdraw elsewhere. So if he pulled out of Spain, the cry would go up for him to quit Poland; if he quit Poland, he would then come under pressure to relinquish Prussia, then Holland, then Belgium, until in the end he was back with the frontiers of 1792. This is ingenious but offends against Ockham's razor. The simple truth is that Napoleon thought he could close the last open door in the Continental System against England by a walkover campaign in the Iberian peninsula and when this proved illusory, lacked the mental concentration needed to get out. To humiliate Joseph, discipline the marshals and accept the military logic of an unwinnable military campaign would have been a tall order at the best of times. From 1810 onwards Napoleon's mind was no longer primarily on Spain, for he had found a new interest and a new wife.

CHAPTER TWENTY-ONE

As he sped back from Schönbrunn to Fontainebleau in the last week of October 1809, Napoleon realized that the moment he had long dreaded was at hand: he would have to divorce Josephine. Marie Walewska's pregnancy changed everything, but her reward for proving that the Emperor could indeed sire children was to be cast into obscurity. She returned to Poland to her complaisant husband Count Walewski, and when her son Alexandre was born in 1810 he took the count's name. Napoleon was never so duplicitous as when reacting to the pregnancy. 'The infant of Wagram will one day be King of Poland,' he announced bombastically, even as he wrote to Czar Alexander to allow him a free hand in Marie's country – in return for the marriage he confidently expected with Alexander's sister, the Grand Duchess Anne.

It was a characteristic of Napoleon's never to accept full responsibility for drastic action, whether it was d'Enghien's murder or the Pope's incarceration. He therefore allowed the record of his official correspondence to evince continuing devotion to Josephine while his actions argued otherwise. He wrongfooted her by summoning her to Fontainebleau when he knew he would be there before her, so that he could react with cold surprise when she arrived there on the evening of 26 October. Next Josephine discovered that the door between her apartment and the Emperor's had been sealed up. For three weeks she never managed to get a minute alone with him, for he insisted on inviting members of his family to all his meals. Every evening the vindictive Pauline held parties for her brother and threw Italian beauties at him, while pointedly not inviting Josephine. Projecting the guilt he felt about the intended divorce on to her, and therefore holding her in some sense to blame for the awkward position he was in, he declined to tell her what was on his mind but reacted to her presence with cold rage. He spent all his spare time hunting – an activity Josephine was known to detest – and visited his murderous fantasies on the dumb beasts; on one occasion he and his fellow Nimrods slaughtered eighty wild boar in a Roman-style arena.

Seemingly unable to bear the emotion that would surely follow once he told Josephine his decision, Napoleon at first tried to get his intimates to break the unwelcome news to her. He tried to enlist Hortense, then Eugène, even Cambacérès, but all declined the task. He finally broke the logjam by moving back to Paris and then brusquely announcing his decision to divorce after dinner on 30 November. The Palace Prefect Baron de Bausset later related the events of that traumatic evening. He heard screams coming from the imperial salon, and was then summoned to find Josephine stretched out on the carpet, moaning and shrieking; he then helped the Emperor to carry the prostrate Josephine down to her apartments.

She recovered quickly and displayed admirable stoicism. Nothing in her career as Empress became her like the leaving of it. For a fortnight she attended a round of official receptions and dinners as if nothing had happened, waiting for the final thunderclap to sound. Once he had taken the irrevocable step, Napoleon's sentimental fondness for Josephine reasserted itself and he was often to be found by his intimates in tears of regretful expostulation, especially when he learned that Hortense and Eugène were determined to resist the blandishments of the imperial world to follow their mother into internal exile. Once again Napoleon engaged in a favourite fantasy – that of being the victim of circumstance and the plaything of destiny; all his decisions always had to take on the hues of Hegelian necessity, he could never admit that the so-called 'necessity' was simply what he himself had decided. But he tried to soften the blow for Josephine by showering her with rewards and perquisites. He promised her she would keep the title of Empress, her château at Malmaison, her jewels and an annual income of three million francs in gold, as well as acquiring the honorary title 'Duchess of Navarre'.

On 14 December came the formal public announcement that the marriage was to be dissolved. In the Throne Room of the Tuileries, in what was presented as a glittering imperial occasion, Napoleon told his courtiers that he was acting against the dictates of his heart for the best interests of France. After expressing gratitude to Josephine for thirteen memorable years, he sat down in tears. Josephine replied by saying she was proud to show this ultimate proof of devotion, but then broke down and could not continue; the rest of her statement was read out by an aide. There were many crocodile tears from those courtiers who loved not Josephine, but the Bonaparte clan were almost publicly exultant – 'gloating' was the word used by the heartbroken Hortense. There was more emotion to come. Eugène fainted once he had left the Throne Room, while Josephine burst like a crazy woman into Napoleon's apartments that night and began kissing him wildly. Sobbing and tears followed, which Napoleon was unable to assuage with a promise that he would always protect her.

Disturbed by the emotional hyperbole of the scene, he made sure he was not left alone with her next morning when she and her retinue departed for Malmaison. For all the apparent coldness, he visited her at Malmaison next day and walked hand in hand with her in the garden in pouring rain. For a week he came for similar meetings, taking care never to embrace her or enter the palace. The two continued to correspond, for Napoleon seems genuinely to have been concerned that his ex-wife should adjust as painlessly as possible to her new sphere. Back at Versailles he snapped angrily at the triumphalist Bonaparte sisters and was gratuitously rude to the new Italian mistress Pauline had procured for him.

But soon his thoughts turned to Josephine's successor. His hopes of a marriage to the Russian Grand Duchess Anne were dashed by a less than tactful rebuff from the Czar, using the excuse that, not yet sixteen, his sister was too young for marriage; as yet, though, there was no formal repudiation of Napoleon's suit. Baulked of the Russian marriage he desired, Napoleon was forced back on his second choice, an Austrian match. Having made his decision, he acted in a quite extraordinary way. He sent Eugène de Beauharnais to the Austrian embassy to ask for the hand of Emperor Francis's nineteen-year-old daughter Marie-Louise, specifying that the proposal had to be accepted at once and the contract signed next day; there was to be no time for opinion in Vienna to be consulted. After trying vainly to prevaricate, the ambassador was forced to accept the proposal. Napoleon's tactless bullying was matched only by his equal insensitivity in using Josephine's son as the envoy to find a bride to replace his mother.

Once his suit was accepted, Napoleon sent two dispatches to the Czar: in the first he formally withdrew his petition for Alexander's sister's hand; in the other he announced his engagement to Marie-Louise. Much face-saving was involved on both sides, so that a legend later grew up that Napoleon's dispatches 'crossed' in the mails with a formal refusal of the suit from Alexander. The Czar's snub was actuated by many factors: the intense hatred of his court and the Empress Dowager for Napoleon; the realization that the logic of the Continental System would soon put the two nations on a collision course; and even the rumour, said to have been fomented by Josephine, that Napoleon was impotent. But the failed suit has a counterfactual attraction all of its own: would the 1812 campaign still have happened if the Emperor had married a Russian princess? Cold reason says yes, for the marriage to Marie-Louise did not prevent a war with Austria.

In these marriage negotiations in early 1810 Napoleon was at his most gauche, posturing and aggressive. He was scarcely in keen diplomatic form at this juncture, for the marriage to Marie-Louise was a mistake on many different fronts. To the French it seemed like the final abandonment of revolutionary principles, for what could be more blatant than another Austrian marriage, so obviously recalling the hated, doomed and much abused Marie-Antoinette? There was even a rumour that all who had voted for the death of Louis XVI and his wife were to be exiled. Meanwhile, Napoleon absurdly thought that a marriage with one of the great *ancien régime* families would win him acceptance among Europe's crowned heads and the old French oligarchy, so that his ambition of integrating old and new élites in France would be fulfilled. In fact, by casting Josephine aside, he alienated many of the old revolutionaries for whom la Beauharnais was 'one of us', without conciliating any of the old aristocrats or returned émigrés.

Further, many in France gloomily prophesied that Napoleon had put himself into a position where he could not win, since whichever power, Austria or Russia, he failed to yoke himself to dynastically would surely be at war with him within two years. He foolishly thought that Austria would have to support him politically from now on, which would force Russia into a league of three Emperors. Metternich, now Foreign Minister, advised Emperor Francis to sacrifice his daughter to gain Austria a breathing space but in a letter to his successor as Austrian ambassador in Paris showed how his mind was really working: 'We must continue to manoeuvre, to avoid all military action and to flatter . . . until the day of deliverance.'

Castlereagh remarked cynically that it was sometimes necessary to sacrifice a virgin to the Minotaur. This perception of Napoleon as monster was one the young Marie-Louise shared, and how could it have been otherwise when almost from birth she had had vitriolic anti-Bonaparte propaganda dinned into her? But she was a dutiful young woman, in awe of her father, who professed herself willing to make the supreme effort of self-abnegation if it meant saving her country. In personal if not diplomatic terms Napoleon had made a good choice, for Marie-Louise was not unattractive, even though critics said her face was high-coloured and that she looked a little coarse, with her popping eyes and ugly Habsburg lip. In compensation, she was a tall blonde with a good bust and a peach-blossom complexion. Moderately intelligent, she painted landscapes and portraits in oil, read a lot (with a fondness for

Chateaubriand) and was a talented amateur musician: she played the piano and harp and knew the works of Mozart and Beethoven well. Most pertinently for Napoleon, who regarded her before he met her as a mere 'walking womb', she was a virgin, never having been left alone with any man.

The Austrians were still anxious that Marie-Louise might end up not properly married to Napoleon in the sight of God, for the marriage to Josephine had not been properly annulled; the Pope alone could do that yet he was not only Napoleon's prisoner but had excommunicated him. Cardinal Fesch, the 'fixer' in matters religious, was wheeled in to find a solution. He quickly brought up the convenient issue of the absence of a parish priest and legal witnesses at Josephine's wedding, adding the new argument that Napoleon had not given his free consent to the religious marriage, having been 'bounced' into it by Josephine on the eve of his coronation to avoid a national scandal. This convenient fiction was accepted as removing the last obstacle to a full and proper marriage.

Lavish preparations were now made in France for the reception of the Austrian princess. Vast sums were spent on the wedding and the total refurbishment of the Château of Compiègne, where Napoleon had chosen to meet his bride. Caroline Murat was sent to Vienna to arrange Marie-Louise's trousseau. This was another inept choice, and not just because the Murats had thrown the Habsburgs out of Naples: Caroline hated to see any other woman getting preferment from her brother, especially one who, by producing an heir, would scotch all the wilder dreams of the Murats of possible future accession to the purple. Not surprisingly, Marie-Louise and Caroline took an intense dislike to one another when they met in Munich; of the two women, the Austrian was the shrewder, for she saw right through the Bonaparte woman while Caroline grossly underrated her.

Marie-Louise was married by proxy in Vienna on 11 March and commenced her progress to Compiègne, accompanied by Caroline as 'chaperone'. Caroline tried to bully her charge by sending all her entourage and even her dog back to Vienna. But she was discomfited by the daily arrival of letters from her brother to Marie-Louise, full of ripe sentiments of undying affection. In Compiègne Napoleon was as fretful and impatient as a young bridegroom, counting the days and hours until his beloved's arrival. Once he learned from Fesch that the proxy match in Vienna – with Napoleon represented by the bride's uncle Archduke Karl – was valid, he was determined to consummate the marriage as soon as possible. He did, however, keep on his Italian mistress until the night before he set out to meet his bride.

On the night of 2 April, in pelting rain, Napoleon set out to meet the coach which was reported on the road not many miles from Compiègne. After intercepting Marie-Louise and party, he jumped into the coach and embraced her. There was to be no disappointment with a previously unseen bride such as Henry VIII experienced with Anne of Cleves. Once back in the château at Compiègne he brusquely dismissed the crowds of well-wishers and, after an intimate dinner at which Caroline alone was allowed to be present, he took Marie-Louise to bed. Some would say this was no way to treat a nervous young virgin, and that this behaviour once again underlined Napoleon's fundamental misogyny, but Marie-Louise instantly proved to have a natural relish for sex. Napoleon's account of his honeymoon, given on St Helena, is justly famous: 'She asked me to do it again.' It was perhaps a choice irony for this misogynist to be surrounded by highly-sexed women: not just his bevy of mistresses but his sister Pauline and both his wives.

A week later, in a two-day ceremony on 1–2 April, the civil and religious marriages took place, the first at St Cloud, the second at the Tuileries; tactlessly Napoleon had decided that his own marriage would follow in exact detail the format of that between Louis XVI and Marie-Antoinette. The principal impression given onlookers at the first ceremony was that the bride was taller than the groom, but the glamour and ostentation of the drive through Paris and the religious ceremony swept aside cavils. Napoleon was dressed in white satin, Marie-Louise in white tulle embroidered with silver. The Emperor had once again dragooned his unwilling female connections into service. Walking in front and holding lighted tapers and insignia on tasselled cushions came Caroline Murat, Grand Duchess Stéphanie-Napoleone of Baden and the vicereine Augusta Amelia of Italy. Holding Marie-Louise's train were the Bonaparte Queens of Spain, Holland and Westphalia, plus Grand Duchess Elisa of Tuscany and Pauline Borghese who, as at the coronation six years earlier, complained that the task was beneath her dignity and tried to get out of it on grounds of 'illness'.

Throughout Paris splendid fêtes were given to celebrate the imperial wedding, including one hosted in the garden of his house by Prince Schwarzenberg, the Austrian ambassador. Intent on making a social hit, he had a vast ballroom erected in the garden but during the ball some gauze draperies caught fire, the flames spread and soon the entire house had gone up in an inferno. Napoleon and Marie-Louise escaped easily enough, but several people perished in the blaze, including the ambassador's brother's wife. The superstitious Napoleon regarded this as a very bad omen and recalled the fête in 1770, at the marriage of Louis

XVI and Marie-Antoinette, when 2,000 people died in the Champs-Elysées. His advisers tried to palliate the portent by alleging that it pointed to Schwarzenberg, not the Emperor, and Napoleon took heart from this. After the battle of Dresden in 1813 it was reported to him that Schwarzenberg had fallen, but he then became gloomy when it transpired that it was his old enemy General Moreau who had been killed.

Omens notwithstanding, the marriage initially turned out to be unexpectedly successful. Marie-Louise and Napoleon spent three months in honeymoon mode, even as France weathered a severe economic crisis and lost the initiative in Spain. The Emperor's apparent lack of interest in his Empire was universally remarked: he was often late for council meetings and kept postponing his promised departure for Spain. Indeed, right into 1811, he continued in uxorious and lovesick mood, frequently finding excuses for balls, fêtes, operas and hunts, and happily sitting through long banquets with his new Empress at his side. Even the cynical Metternich was forced to report to Emperor Francis that the couple were genuinely in love. Napoleon even seemed to be in awe of his wife, to the point where Marie-Louise confided to Metternich: 'I am not afraid of Napoleon, but I am beginning to think he is afraid of me.' The only criticism the Emperor ever made of her personally was that she was too fond of her food – an attribute he considered 'unfeminine'. Marie-Louise's one drawback as Empress was that she was never at ease with the French. Possibly because she could not forget that this was the people who had murdered her aunt, she appeared uneasy on public occasions; her shyness came across as coldness and hauteur, especially as she hated small talk and social chitchat. Josephine had managed to win Parisian hearts, but this was a trick the new Empress could never manage.

The marriage with Marie-Louise also exacerbated relations with the Church, for thirteen cardinals refused the urgent imperial summons to attend the wedding. These so-called 'black cardinals' – to distinguish them from the pro-Bonaparte 'red cardinals' – were then disciplined by Fesch and, when they proved intransigent, thrown into prison. Needing a break from the stresses of office, the Emperor decided on a showy imperial 'progress'. On 27 April 1810 Napoleon and Marie-Louise departed for a month-long tour of Belgium and northern France, taking in St-Quentin, Cambrai, Anvers, Breda, Bergen-op-Zoom, Middleburg, Ghent, Bruges, Ostend, Dunkirk, Boulogne, Dieppe, Le Havre and Rouen. The imperial couple were accompanied by thirty-five coaches full of princelings and puppet kings. Marie-Louise recorded in her diary the miseries of the long journey, the intrusiveness of protocol and her husband's irritation if ever she said she was hungry.

Back in Paris on 1 June, Napoleon decided to pay a visit to Josephine at Malmaison (13 June), where she had recently returned after a month's discreet exile at the château in Navarre while the marriage with Marie-Louise took place. Relations between Napoleon and his ex-wife remained cordial and they even continued to correspond, though Marie-Louise would become angry at any mention of Josephine or the Emperor's solicitude for her. 'How can he want to see that old lady? And a woman of low birth!' was one of her outbursts. At Malmaison Josephine devoted herself to her menagerie, especially the famed bird collection which contained swans and ostriches. She continued to run up enormous debts which Napoleon guiltily condoned, contrasting them with the austerity and financial prudence of Marie-Louise.

1810 was also the year Napoleon last clapped eyes on Bernadotte, who had still not been court-martialled or disgraced, despite the spectacular incompetence at Auerstädt and Wagram. After the fiasco at Walcheren Bernadotte, having learned nothing and forgotten nothing, continued to intrigue and was a frequent visitor at the salon of known enemies of the Emperor, such as Madame Récamier. But above all he was a man who proved the truth of the Napoleonic tag 'is he lucky?'

In 1810 there was a constitutional crisis in Sweden when Charles XIII died. The Swedes were adamant that they would not accept the return of his nephew Gustav IV, whom they had deposed two years earlier, nor would they accept his son. Arguing that, in a world where Napoleon was dominant, it made sense to have a Frenchman as their king, they approached Eugène de Beauharnais. He, however, was an ardent Catholic and refused the concomitant demand that he convert to Lutheranism.

They then approached Bernadotte who, gleaming with ambition, came to see Napoleon on 25 June for his reaction. So far from acceding, the Emperor should have remembered all the Gascon's past treacheries and sent him packing. Yet he lamely gave his consent and even, absurdly, gave him several million francs as a leaving present, so that he could appear in Sweden in suitable splendour. The upshot was that he had a powerful enemy as King of Sweden, commanding considerable military forces. Whatever possessed Napoleon to act with such consummate stupidity? The usual explanation is that, as always with Bernadotte, Napoleon's tender feelings for Désirée got the better of him. If this is true – and it appears to be – the judgement on Napoleon as misogynist should be tempered by a realization of the sentimental side of his attitude to women. Naturally, though, we should not forget that there were deep psychological drives behind his peculiar, complaisant attitude to both Josephine and Désirée.

There is no need to labour the contrast between Eugène de Beauharnais, always upright, loyal and a man of moral principle, and Bernadotte, who could switch religions and political principles like a change of clothes when it suited him. The new King Charles XIV of Sweden was the ex-Jacobin who had once had 'death to all kings' tattooed on his arm. When Bernadotte later, predictably, proved treacherous as King of Sweden, Napoleon reflected ruefully that there were three occasions when he should have had Bernadotte shot and spared him each time because of Désirée. His own explanation for letting this ingrate have a throne was as follows: 'I was seduced by the glory of seeing a Marshal of France become a king; a woman in whom I was interested as queen, and my godson, a prince royal.'

Yet Bernadotte was only the most spectacular disappointment of the nest of incompetents and schemers who formed the inner circle of Bonaparte's extended family. Lucien continued to resist all pressure to give up his wife and finally decided to make a new life in the U.S.A. He and his family had barely left France than they were captured by a British warship and taken to England. There the ruling élite made a point of lionizing him, for sheer propaganda advantage; what more signal proof of Bonaparte's tyranny could there be than that his own brother had fled from it? Lucien remained under very comfortable house arrest until 1814 at Ludlow and Thorngrove in Worcestershire. In terms of their own propaganda this was of course sheer illogicality on the part of the British élite: had they really thought Lucien was a refugee from egregious tyranny, they would surely have turned him loose to make trouble in Europe.

Louis Bonaparte's public career came to a humiliating close when Napoleon annexed Holland and forced him to abdicate the throne, while leaving him his income and honorary title. This was the chance Hortense de Beauharnais was looking for; deprived of the title of Queen, she no longer saw the need to put up with her sexually peculiar husband. In the late summer of 1810 she joined her mother on a leisurely trip in Savoy and took the comte de Flahaut as a lover.

In Westphalia the useless Jérôme felt himself to be on shifting sands but was uncertain whether the blow that would displace him would come from his brother or his subjects. There could be no doubting his unpopularity, since his kingdom was bowed down by taxation and united in loathing of the decadent court, the reckless rakes, libertines and adventuresses that swarmed there, and the Corsican playboy who had been set over them as monarch. Jérôme kept three horses permanently saddled and waiting in the courtyard, with three spares, in case he needed to flee his kingdom in a hurry. Meanwhile he continued his profligate *opéra bouffe* career. After one of his carouses he was so drunk that he was arrested in the street by his own police, who did not recognize him.

Napoleon could afford to treat his brothers with contempt, but the Murats were a more dangerous proposition. After Louis's downfall, Murat suspected that he was next on the Emperor's hitlist so opted for offence as the best form of defence. His minister Maghella advised that the card to play was to pose as the champion of Italian unity and to form a party which would back him if the French tried to dispossess him. While making secret contacts with anti-Bonaparte Italian nationalists, Murat tried to make his French officials put their loyalty to him and Naples above their oaths to France and the Emperor, and floated a scheme to make them all take out Neapolitan naturalization papers. The ingenious Napoleon stymied that by decreeing that *every* French citizen was also a citizen of Naples by virtue of that city's being part of the French Empire.

The noses of the scheming, unscrupulous Bonaparte clan were put out of joint by the news, in autumn 1810, that Marie-Louise was pregnant; an heir to Napoleon would end all their vague hopes of inheriting the wealth and power of Empire. But the birth of Napoleon's son, on 20 March 1811, was a close-run thing. As was usual in those days, a royal birth was a public event, with extended family, courtiers and ambassadors all present in the bedroom. Marie-Louise experienced a difficult and protracted labour, and her cries of pain caused Napoleon deep distress. The obstetrician told him that it would be a difficult breech birth and that both mother and child were in danger: it might be that he could save the mother only by killing the baby or vice versa; since the birth of an heir was the very point of the marriage with Marie-Louise, which was it to be? Without hesitation Napoleon replied: 'Save the mother.'

Marie-Louise's final agony lasted twenty minutes before a successful forceps delivery. The man who could look on scenes of battlefield slaughter unblinkingly could not take the blood and pain of childbirth and retreated to the bathroom near the end. When the child was born, it appeared to be stillborn and lay for seven minutes without signs of life. Napoleon looked at his son – for such it was – and was convinced he was dead. Suddenly the infant let out a lusty cry. Once the doctor assured him that the boy would live, Napoleon took him in his arms. Soon the cannon roared with the prearranged signal for the birth – twenty-one rounds for a girl, one hundred for a boy. At the twenty-second booming, the Parisian crowd went wild. Napoleon watched scenes of spectacular public drunkenness with tears running down his cheeks.

Napoleon's son was given the title 'the King of Rome'. At the age of three months, on 9 June 1811, he was solemnly baptized in Notre Dame. But immediately after the birth, observers noted a change in the Emperor's attitude to Marie-Louise. Whether it was because his cynicism reasserted itself once the 'walking womb' had fulfilled its biological function, or whether the gory scenes of childbirth had killed his appetite for his wife, he immediately seemed to resume the old pattern that had marked his life with Josephine. After a two-week tour of Normandy (Caen, Cherbourg, Saint-Lô, Alençon, Chartres) between 22 May and 5 June, he took his meals alone and spent most of the day in his office. He even resumed his liaisons with other women, and brought Marie Walewska and her son to Paris for another round of their on-off affair.

Marie-Louise began to grow disillusioned with her situation, especially since the Bonaparte set now loathed her more vehemently then they had loathed Josephine. She displayed an increasing tendency to withdraw into seclusion, confiding only in her lady-in-waiting Madame de Montebello. This woman was yet another in the long list of vipers Napoleon unwittingly clasped to his bosom, for the twenty-nine-year-old Louise, Madame de Montebello, was something of a female Bernadotte in her hatred for the Emperor; a Breton Jacobin of virulent anti-Bonaparte persuasion, she gradually poisoned Marie-Louise's mind against her husband.

Napoleon could therefore not look for much even in his own immediate family. Much more worrying in the long term was that in 1810–11 the social alliance between Emperor and bourgeoisie and between Napoleon and the notables began to break down. Superficially, this was because he appeared ever more despotic and demanding and thus alienated his power base. This was not a totally negligible factor, but this sort of analysis should be applied with care. The usual charge against Napoleon is that he introduced the first police state, and it is true that the heavy handed methods of Savary, the new chief of police, seriously enraged the bourgeoisie. Savary, a notorious bull in a china shop, finally replaced Fouché in 1810 after the sinister spymaster indulged in one intrigue too many: he sent a peace mission to England which proposed that the British abandon Spain in return for French help in reconquering the U.S.A. Since these quixotic proposals were made without the Emperor's knowledge and consent, he had no realistic option but to dismiss Fouché. Theorists of Napoleon as despot need to explain why he always took an unconscionable time to break with those who notably betrayed him: relations with Bernadotte, Fouché, Talleyrand and Murat all follow the same pattern.

But on the broader count of the indictment of introducing a police state, there is much to be said in Napoleon's favour. There had been 60,000 people in jail under the Directory but Napoleon boasted that at his peak there were just 243 prisoners in six state prisons. After all the chaos of the Revolution, and given the population of France (40 millions), this was a staggering figure. There was nothing of the modern dictator about Napoleon's treatment of prisoners. Most of the 9,000 imprisoned at the time of 18 Brumaire had been released, and the only political prisoners were either Chouans reprieved from the death penalty, British spies, royalists who had returned illegally, or émigrés who had violated the terms of the general amnesty by plotting and had then been caught by police surveillance. Apart from a handful of priests jailed after Napoleon's clash with the Pope, most of the prisoners in the cells were hardened criminals associated with organized crime, whom Napoleon had indeed arbitrarily – but some would say justifiably – detained when local juries were too fearful of reprisals to convict. Moreover, the police under Napoleon had no power to detain arbitrarily, in contrast to the situation in a totalitarian régime proper, while imperial attorneys had the power to release anyone imprisoned provided he was not jailed by a decision of the Privy Council. Although it would be absurd to claim that the imperial police and industrial conciliation boards were partial to labour, they did provide an appearance of fairness and made the point that employers were not the final court of appeal.

Nor was the bourgeoisie particularly upset by other manifestations of Bonapartist 'dictatorship'. His attempt to tighten his grip on national education by decreeing in 1811 that Catholic schools, hitherto independent, should be under the authority of Louis de Fontanes and the Imperial University, achieved little success; bishops frequently bypassed it with the collusion of Fontanes and his inspectors. The surprising thing about Napoleon's rift with the Pope and his apparently tough anti-Catholic stance was how little it changed. Napoleonic education was largely a process of inculcating the religious practices and pious observances he himself had learned under the *ancien régime*. The effect of the papal excommunication was negligible: it was notable that after this French bishops were still able to offer a *Te Deum* for the peace treaty with Austria in 1809 and for a valid religious marriage ceremony to be conducted for the Emperor and Marie-Louise.

Perhaps more irritation was caused by the confiscation of all independent Parisian newspapers in 1811; henceforth entirely in government hands, they became insipid and dull. Some said Napoleon was concerned at the poor image of his Empire presented by the independent newspapers and their scandal stories which pointed up the vulgar ostentation of the régime and even its quasi-gangsterism. Metternich's simultaneous affair with Caroline Murat and Laure Junot was the best known of these scandals, for when the jealous Caroline tipped off Junot about his wife's infidelity, and Junot found the incriminating evidence Caroline had guided him to, he attacked his wife with scissors, leaving her half dead, tried to challenge Metternich to a duel and insisted that the Emperor declare war on Austria. Readers of the scandal sheets particularly enjoyed the alleged riposte by Madame Metternich when Junot 'peached' to her: 'The role of Othello ill becomes you.'

The notables acknowledged, too, that Napoleon had not threatened their privileges with *carrière ouverte aux talents* meritocracy. The new administrative élite came from their ranks: sons and in-laws of ministers, senators, councillors of state, generals and prefects, provided they had an annual income of 6,000 francs, were the only ones eligible as auditors to the Council of State, as judges or as tax collectors, and the only ones who could afford the ill-paid posts anyway. The élitist nature of Napoleon's régime was also evinced by the Army, were nepotism and a caste mentality prevailed, and by the creation in 1808 of the Imperial University and the Grandes Écoles which established that the only route to a decent education was through parental wealth.

The administrative élite, in a word, was the preserve of the old aristocracy or the new plutocracy who had benefited from the spoils of the Revolution. Surprising numbers of landed proprietors had weathered the storms of 1789–94 to emerge as major real estate owners under the Empire; meanwhile the sale of national property had virtually dried up and the only entrepreneurial opportunity, apart from looting, was speculation in colonial products. The reality of negligible social mobility was obfuscated and 'mystified' in Napoleonic propaganda by constant emphasis on the careers of the handful, like Murat, who had made their way from the gutter to the top.

The traditional view is that the peasantry escaped their soil-bondage under Napoleon by military service, but this is largely a myth. It was just possible, but only just, for the average peasant to better himself by joining the Army and rising through the ranks. Every soldier may in theory have carried a marshal's baton in his knapsack, but the reality was that few peasants, however talented, could hope to progress beyond the rank of lieutenant; the most that could be hoped for was the salary attached to the *légion d'honneur*. As for loot from the conquest of Europe, again the reality was that only the already privileged really benefited, with gratuities and benefices for generals, highly placed officials and nobles or commercial profits for manufacturers and traders.

If France under Napoleon seemed at first blush like a paradise for the notables, why then were they so disenchanted with the régime by 1810–11? They disliked his foreign adventurism and would have been content with the 'natural frontiers'; they were suspicious of the creation of the new *noblesse de l'empire* and the Austrian marriage, both of which seemed to indicate a fondness for the old aristocracy; and they could see no point in the war in Spain, which simply looked like a crude attempt to seize a crown for Joseph. But they could no doubt have found a way to 'cohabit' with all this, had it not been for the severe economic depression of 1810–11 which was itself a consequence of the Emperor's Continental Blockade. The real sticking point for the notables, then, was the Continental System.

Napoleon's economic warfare against Britain began in earnest with the Berlin Decree of 21 November 1806, immediately after his victory at Jéna. Although the expression 'Continental Blockade' was first used in *Le Moniteur* on 30 October 1806, the idea did not originate with Bonaparte, but was one of many he inherited from the Revolution, since the Convention in 1793 announced the exclusion of British goods. According to Miot de Melito, in a speech on 1 May 1803 the First Consul vowed he would make the British weep for the coming war and tried to close Channel ports as far as Hanover to British commerce. Yet in the aftermath of Trafalgar it seemed as though the boot was on the other foot. On 16 May 1806 London announced its own blockade of the French coast – the so-called 'Fox blockade' whereby the Royal Navy closed ports from Brest to the Elbe – and began searching American ships.

Napoleon was attracted to the idea of economic warfare for several reasons but there are grounds for thinking that the worthlessness of paper money, which he had seen for himself in the form of the Revolutionary *assignats* and which he associated, not entirely logically, with the early financial struggles of the Bonaparte family, deeply impressed him. Since Britain by the outbreak of war in 1803 had a National Debt of over £500 million, forcing its leaders to issue paper money, Napoleon thought that a determined assault on her export trade would lead to economic collapse. This would have two effects: Britain would be unable to subsidize its continental allies; and revolution at home would force her to the peace table. In 1807 the Emperor wrote gloatingly of the prospect of 'her vessels laden with useless wealth wandering around the high seas, where they claim to rule as sole masters, seeking in vain from the Sound to the Hellespont for a port to open and receive them'.

The Berlin Decree established a notional blockade: any ship coming direct from a British port or having been in a British port after the decree came into effect, would not be permitted to use a Continental port; if such a ship made a false declaration, it was to be seized. All goods had to be accompanied by a 'Certificate of Origin' and all goods of British origin or ownership were to be confiscated wherever found. At first Britain affected to respond with incredulity and contempt. Comparisons were made with a Papal bull against comets and cartoons in London newspapers showed Napoleon blockading the moon. The general feeling was that the blockade would have little effect and, even if it did, trade could be switched to the U.S.A., Latin America and the colonies, which already took two-thirds of British exports.

Nevertheless, some anxiety was evident in the promulgation by London of the first Order in Council in January 1807, which prohibited trade 'between port and port of countries under the dominion or usurped control of France and her allies'. Napoleon hit back by extending his blockade to Turkey, Austria and Denmark, which prompted Canning's counter-stroke against the Danish fleet. July 1807 was a critical month for England for, even as Napoleon and Czar Alexander concluded their accord at Tilsit, a rash boarding of the U.S. frigate *Chesapeake* by the Royal Navy conjured visions of a war with the United States. If both northern Europe and the United States were closed to British trade, the consequences for English exports could be catastrophic.

In November and December 1807 London therefore issued the central Orders in Council, which required all trade with Napoleonic Europe to pass through British ports, where it would be licensed after paying a transit tax of 25% of the total intended transaction; failure to observe this procedure meant being seized as lawful prize by the Royal Navy. The consequence in this tit-for-tat battle was predictable: by the Milan decrees of 23 November and 17 December 1807 Napoleon ordered the seizure of all ships which had put into a British port and obeyed the Orders in Council. Caught in this damned-if-you-do, damned-if-you-don't crossfire, Americans and other neutrals complained that the only trade allowed them by the Royal Navy was precisely the kind Napoleon had forbidden them. President Jefferson tried to deal with this conundrum with his Embargo Act of December 1807, which banned American trade with Europe and embargoed the import of British manufactured goods. Far from putting pressure on the belligerents, the Embargo Act simply harmed American economic interests and was repealed in March 1809, to be replaced by a supposedly more nuanced Non-Intercourse Act.

The impact of the Continental Blockade on Napoleon's Empire varied enormously, not just over space but through time. Subject to later provisos, a risky generalization might be that in France itself the northern and eastern areas benefited while the southern and western suffered. This was part of a general process whereby the economy shifted structurally away from the Atlantic seaboard and towards the land markets of the Continent. All trade with a maritime or colonial component was hit hard: the manufacture of linen and hemp declined disastrously as a result both of the closure of colonial markets and the reduced demand from a mothballed and dry-docked Navy for ropes and canvas.

The mood in the northern departments from 1806–11 was notably pro-Bonaparte: brigandage declined; civic morale was high and there was a very low level of absenteeism and military desertion; cities like Lille, Amiens and Valenciennes did well. In the east, Alsace recovered under Napoleon and the blockade benefited the areas of the Haut-Rhin. It was noted that the four departments on the left bank of the Rhine particularly prospered, both because the abolition of tithes and seigneurial rights stimulated agriculture, and because the elimination of British competition benefited local textiles and metallurgy. In general, the growth of industry and trade in the Rhine area led to a strongly pro-Bonaparte commercial bourgeoisie. Almost overnight traffic on the river changed its character, as the upstream flow of raw materials from the Rhine basin exceeded the downstream dispatch of colonial produce from Holland, now choked off because of the blockade.

It was a very different picture in the west of France, where the ports were blockaded by the Royal Navy and the level of economic discontent accordingly very high. The west, where the tradition of the Vendée and the Chouans lived on, was always the weak point in the Napoleonic Empire. Royalist factions and English spies still had their networks here and banditry was rampant. Brigandage in the west under Napoleon has been much discussed and seems to have had many roots: the influence of the *petite église* – that part of the Church which opposed the Concordat; an indulgent magistracy; a chronic shortage of gendarmes; and an anti-Bonaparte tradition. The brigands themselves were a mélange of former Chouans, deserters and rebellious conscripts and ordinary criminals who spread a spurious political patina over their crimes. Napoleon thought it best to let semi-somnolent dogs lie, and softpedalled on the old Vendée areas, granting them low levels of conscription and a fifteen-year tax exemption (given in 1808) to all whose buildings were destroyed by civil war, provided they rebuilt them by 1812. These softly-softly measures largely worked, to the point where the gendarmerie brigades were reduced in number in 1810.

In central France there were many depressed areas too. Typical was the Auvergne, though here the problem was the breakdown of feudalism rather than the Continental Blockade. Breaking up the common pastures and woodland of the *ancien régime*, previously a haven for livestock, led to ecological disaster: the Auvergne became a gigantic goat sanctuary, against which possibility before 1789 there had been strict intendants' prohibitions. Tens of thousands emigrated from the Auvergne to Paris, swelling the throngs of unemployed and underemployed there; notable were the bands of children who became chimney sweeps and beggars in the capital.

But it was in the coastal areas that the worst effects of the blockade were felt. La Rochelle and Bordeaux, previously boom towns, became virtual ghost towns instead as the Atlantic ports collapsed through loss of neutral shipping. One statistic alone is eloquent: 121 American ships entered Bordeaux in 1807 but only six the following year. Any coastal merchant wishing to survive had to diversify into terrestrial industries such as sugar refining, paper milling or tobacco manufacturing. The Mediterranean coast presented the spectacle of British seapower at its most arrogant, with the Royal Navy often anchoring with impunity in the roads at Hyères. Toulon and Marseilles were the worst hit of the maritime cities as the factory owners of Carcassonne, the proprietors of the Nîmes silk industry and the Marseilles soap manufacturers themselves lost their markets in the East. The fundamental problem in the Mediterranean departments was that they had to import corn and cereals, but could do this only by the sale of goods for which the outlets had dried up. Morale plummeted and pro-British plots were rife. None the less, the decline in the Mediterranean relative to north and central Europe was not as catastrophic as on the Atlantic seaboard.

As always, there were winners and losers. Lyons experienced a boom in marketing because of new routes through the Alps, especially the Mont-Cenis tunnel; exporting books and cloth through this route, it received back Illyrian and Levantine cotton and Piedmontese rice. But the general trend was that industry suffered and agriculture gained. Vast amounts of land (but not 'national' property) came on to the market, allowing entrepreneurs to make huge profits from supplying food to the Army. Since investment in land seemed safer than industrial enterprise, the upshot was yet another reinforcement of the landed power of the notables.

The same general process was mirrored in the wider Empire, with some sections of the economy burgeoning and others plummeting. Those whose livelihood depended on ports or who were engaged in colonial trade had a thin time. Bankruptcy and ruin was the norm for all who based their fortunes in the great ports – Barcelona, Cadiz, Hamburg, Lisbon, Bordeaux, Nantes, Antwerp, Amsterdam – not just from the direct blockade but from the decline in colonial trade, affecting adversely ropemaking, linen, shipbuilding, sugar refining, distilling, provisioning and even some industries which throve elsewhere, such as cotton and tobacco. The Napoleonic years brought about a permanent transfer of social power away from the old élites in these ports, for even after 1815 most of these cities became thriving regional centres rather than the international entrepôts they had once been.

It will be clear that the economic blockade, originally designed to throttle England, took on a life of its own and produced a European economic bloc based on the Napoleonic Empire. This is why some historians prefer to distinguish the Continental Blockade proper, directed at British exports, from the more general notion of a Continental System which played a positive, if haphazard role, in European economic integration. In this system French production and, to a lesser extent, that of the satellites, was protected from British competition. The differing effects of the Continental System proper explain why the economic winners and losers under Napoleon were not merely regionally based but cut through the social strata.

The general picture of the peasantry until 1812 is one of reasonable contentment. In the early years of Empire the demands of conscription were more than offset by the abolition of tithes, feudal rights, the abolition of the ancient rights of the nobility and reassurances about the future of émigré property. But the Continental System drove a wedge between the upper peasants and their middle and lower cousins. Where big farmers benefited from price rises and increase in outlets, the small farmers suffered from rents that outstripped the price rise of staples like corn. Nine-tenths of the peasantry were share croppers and their marketable surplus was not large enough to enable them to benefit from the economies of scale in the Continental System.

It is generally agreed that living standards, as measured by diet, improved both in the countryside and in the towns in the Napoleonic period. One sociological curiosity of the era is the great popularity enjoyed by the Emperor among the urban proletariat, for this was not a vital element in his power structure, and the lot of city workers does not seem to have been particularly happy. Life expectancy was still only fifty and suicides were common; and the average Parisian worker earned 900 francs a year – not much when compared with the Councillor of State's annual salary of 25,000 francs. Indeed, by some indices the legal position of the worker worsened: all trade unions and labour combinations were forbidden, and Napoleon returned to the work permit or *livret* of the *ancien régime*, which allowed the police to control and supervise labour. None the less, it was notable that strikes tended to be apolitical and directed at particular grievances. The Emperor won points in the workers' eyes when his police sometimes prevented employers from lowering wages as part of a carefully calculated balancing act directed from the Tuileries. And the Emperor's wars concentrated minds: on the one hand, it was generally considered better to be a factory worker than to be cannon fodder; on the other, conscription produced a shortage of workers and forced wage rates up.

The Continental System, properly understood, had two main aims: to exclude British products from the Continental market and to provide a vibrant economy in the French Empire. It failed in the first aim and had only partial success in the second. As a corollary to this policy, the role of the State in the French economy was forced to increase by leaps and bounds. Napoleon is often compared to Hitler, but one of the few points of comparison usually not underlined is the similarity in both cases of the economic partnership between business and industry and the State.

Some would argue that Napoleon's economic blockade of Britain was doomed to failure, since one of the few clear lessons of history is that economic sanctions take generations to have any real impact. But in Napoleon's case there were more particular and specific reasons why the blockade was never likely to be successful. The three most salient considerations are that British seapower made strangulation of England impossible; that success depended on a number of factors that France could not control; and that the embargo of British goods worked against the self-interest of the blockaders themselves and thus in a sense ran counter to human nature.

Without control of the seas, France was always more likely to end up locked in than to lock Britain out. Apart from the fact that expeditions could be landed anywhere in Europe, as on the Iberian peninsula and Walcheren in 1808–09, there were three obvious economic advantages in the Royal Navy's maritime supremacy. First, Britain could conquer new territories, usually French and Dutch colonies, which would give her alternative markets and sources of raw materials; after 1808 by the same means she could control the trade of Latin America. Secondly, Britain could actually enforce its own blockade by Orders in Council and found it easy to clean out nests of French privateers, such as the one in Mauritius.

Statistics are eloquent on this point: France had over 1,500 ocean-going merchant vessels in 1801 but only 179 in 1812. Thirdly, as smuggling inevitably sprang up to fill the entrepreneurial gap left by the embargo, by controlling island entrepôts Britain could maintain a steady flow of colonial goods into Napoleon's Empire.

It was contraband that allowed the British economy to survive Napoleon's assaults. In the North Sea, Heligoland, occupied by the British in September 1807, became from the following April the centre of a connived-at trade with Germany which exchanged manufactures and continental produce for food and grain. In one seven-day period in 1809, £300,000 worth of goods was shipped out for European destinations, and by April 1813 2.5 million pounds of sugar and coffee was going to German ports. In the Baltic trade went on as normal under flags of convenience, either Swedish or Danish as circumstances dictated. In the Mediterranean, Trieste, Gibraltar, Salonika, Sicily and, above all, Malta, were the centres of contraband. The British followed a shrewd Mediterranean policy: after the abandonment of the ill-considered Egyptian expedition in 1807 to keep Turkey out of the French camp, they limited their ambitions to holding the islands of Malta and Sicily and threatening eastern Spain from there.

Nevertheless, it would be a mistake to write as some jingoistic British historians have done and insinuate the idea that the Royal Navy's triumph was cost-free. To maintain supremacy on the high seas often means literally that: to battle against the high seas themselves. Out of shipping losses of 317 in the period 1803–15, 223 were wrecked or foundered because of calamitous seas or freak waves. The worst storms took a frightful toll: in March 1810 winds of near-hurricane strength sank five Spanish and Portuguese ships of the line and twenty other craft; in December 1805 eight transports carrying troops to Germany went down in high seas, with the loss of 664 drowned and 1,552 others who were washed on to the French coast and made prisoner. Three Royal Navy ships lost in a storm in the North Sea in December 1811 accounted for more than 2,000 dead, more than the total losses in dead and wounded (1,690) sustained by the British at Trafalgar.

Among the factors over which France had little or no control were levels of corruption, levels of local resistance by allies and local populations and the impact of war on neutrals. Holland was a sore point with Napoleon while Louis was King, as he curried favour with his subjects by conniving at contraband with England. The smuggling trade between Britain and Holland was worth £4.5 millions in 1807–09, but when the Emperor ousted Louis and applied stricter controls, the trade slumped badly, being estimated at just £1 million for the years 1810–12. If Louis's complaisant policies in Holland played into British hands, Canning's aggressive foreign policy in 1807 gave the economic advantage to Napoleon, for the trade with Norway and Denmark before Britain seized their fleet was £5 million, but a year later had plummeted to just £21,000.

Because of the heterogeneous nature of local economies within the Napoleonic Empire, a given economic policy could produce skewed results. Among the unintended consequences of the protectionism of the Continental System were that German, Prussian and Austrian goods began to compete seriously with French ones in certain spheres. On the other hand, a state like Berg was particularly vulnerable to French protective tariffs, as its economy was like England's, concentrating on textiles; since the duties on these were threefold, the bankrupt Berg was soon reduced to appealing for absorption in metropolitan France to avoid them. Another problem was that Napoleon kept changing the rules of his own system. Bavaria was initially a beneficiary from the blockade of Britain and its products – sugar-beet, tobacco, optical glass, textiles, calicoes, ceramics, pins and needles – were in high demand, but this advantage diminished once Bonaparte extended his Continental System to Italy.

In short, the blockade distorted the normal flow of trade, diminished economic levels throughout Europe, diverted capital from industrial investment to trade and smuggling and jeopardized relations between France and her satellites. The customs barrier along the coast and the inland frontiers stretched French policing resources, tempted her into highhanded and illegal actions, and further harmed relations with the allied countries. Particular resentment was caused by the growing army of imperial customs officers, their arbitrary powers and their body searches; there had been 12,000 such officials in 1791 but by 1810 there were 35,000 of them. The ultimate absurdity was that this growing band of excise men was chasing a declining revenue from customs duties, at the very time Napoleon needed the funds to pay for the war in Spain which, unprecedentedly, was failing to pay for itself.

Yet the most telling reason for Napoleon's failure to blockade Britain effectively was that Napoleon's military interests did not square with the interests of consumers and entrepreneurs within his empire. All those who resented the lack of coffee, tea, sugar, cocoa and spices, the rises in the cost of leather and cotton, the high price of wool, linen and coffee, the official inspections of goods and the corruption of customs officers were bound together informally by a spirit of resistance to the System. It seemed absurd that England was crammed with surplus products while France languished through shortage of the selfsame products, especially raw materials and colonial produce, and could not work out an efficient method of import substitution. Whereas corn, fruit, wool, wood and wine had been sold to England before 1806, the peasants could not now export the surplus; this hit them particularly badly after the bumper harvest of 1808.

With industrialists, agriculturalists, shipowners, peasants and consumers all suffering from the blockade, it was not surprising that human nature asserted itself. Speculation in coffee, sugar and cotton led to high prices, inflated profits, stock exchange gambling mania and hence generalized corruption and cynicism. The blockade was evaded even by Napoleon's most senior lieutenants. Junior aides took bribes and traded on the black market, while the Bonapartist grandees indulged in corruption at a flagrant level. Masséna sold unofficial licences to trade with England to Italian merchants, thus swelling his already vast fortune. Bourrienne, French Minister at Hamburg in 1806–07, was ordered to find 50,000 greatcoats and cloaks for the *Grande Armée* for the winter campaign against Russia. He secretly purchased cloth and leather from England, claiming that the Army would have died of cold if the Continental System had been observed. In fact the inflow of British manufactures continued at such a rate that in the 1812 campaign soldiers in the Grand Army wore boots made in Northampton and greatcoats made from Lancashire and Yorkshire cloth.

But undoubtedly the great growth industry during the heyday of the Continental System was contraband, which was made easy by a combination of local demand, corrupt officials, lax surveillance and support from the British. Under Napoleon there were really only three ways to make a vast fortune if you were not a marshal: by supplying the Army, by speculation in national property, and by smuggling. With opportunities in the first two areas rapidly drying up, contraband beckoned as the future road to El Dorado.

It is hard to overestimate the rich pickings that could be made from smuggling. The Rothschilds, now coming to prominence after the pioneering labours of the dynasty's founder Meyer Amschel, made vast sums by financing illegal trading and made even more after 1810 by manipulating the British and French licensing systems simultaneously. One lace merchant, a certain M. Gaudoit of Caen, imported illicit British goods worth 750,000 francs between 1801–08, using the roundabout route London-Amsterdam-Frankfurt-Paris-Bordeaux. On the Rhine it was reckoned that a smuggler could earn 12–14 francs a night, when the daily wage for an agricultural labourer was $1-1\frac{1}{2}$ francs; in the Pyrenees the respective rates were ten francs and three francs. In Hamburg it was estimated that 6–10,000 people a day smuggled coffee, sugar and other comestibles, of which an absolute maximum of 5% was confiscated. Napoleon hit back with occasional exemplary punishments. In the Rothschilds' native city of Frankfurt, a sanctions-busting centre, French troops publicly burned £1,200,000 worth of contraband goods in November 1810. But such scenes were rare: even when French viceroys and governors found out about contraband they could usually be bribed to remain silent or simply go through the motions.

In the light of all this, the surprise is that the Continental Blockade worried the British as much as it did. The impact of the System on the British economy has been much disputed, and some indices seem to show an almost nil effect. Britain's merchant fleet rose from 13,446 ships in 1802 to 17,346; the rise in unemployment can be explained as a function of population growth in the U.K. from 15,846,000 in 1801 to 18,044,000 in 1811; the modest profits of industry can be interpreted as systematic tax evasion. But there are other figures that tell a different story, particularly in the early period of the blockade until 1808. Exports, which reached a peak in 1809 (£50.3 million) were only £9 million up on the peacetime figure for 1802. Continental trade, worth £22.5 million in 1802 fell to half that in 1808. The value of Britain's re-export trade in colonial produce declined from £14,419,000 in 1802 to £7,862,000 in 1808 and was still only at £8,278,000 in 1811; sugar, which sold for 73 shillings per hundredweight in 1798 fell to 32 shillings by 1807 and did not rise above 50 shillings until 1813. The stagnation of colonial produce on the market was matched by the crisis of British manufacturers; industrialists in Manchester could not liquidate their stocks of cotton; the price of flax rose; there was a grave crisis in the wool industry.

Matters were at an acute pass in early 1808. There was a serious drop in exports in the last six months of 1807 and the first six of 1808; exports to Europe sank to £15 million as compared to £19$\frac{1}{2}$ million in the twelve months before. The combination of Jefferson's embargo and Napoleon's blockade began to bite, and there were serious riots in Lancashire and Yorkshire in May and June 1808. Ex-Prime Minister Grenville was one of those in England who began to panic. It was precisely at that moment that Napoleon made his disastrous and self-destructive intervention in Spain. Ostensibly, he moved in to shut a door still open to British produce, but at a stroke he ruined the prospect of Spain as a market for French manufacturers and opened the trade of Latin America to the British. With justifiable irony the economist d'Ivernois remarked that the

Emperor's blockade would have been more effective if, at the same time as he was taking violent steps to close European markets to the British, he was not also taking even more violent ones to open South America to them.

The Spanish ulcer not only drained France of blood and treasure but saved the British economy. After 1809 the ports of Spain and, more importantly, of Latin America were open to them. When the *Grande Armée* was progressively switched from Germany to Spain in 1809–11, making contraband in northern Europe easier, British recovery was rapid. In 1809, at £50.3 million, British exports reached their peak during the Napoleonic years. Even though they declined again during the years of 'general crisis' from 1810–12, they never again descended to 1807–08 levels. When the North Sea became extremely difficult for the Royal Navy in 1810–12, the British switched the main thrust of their contraband efforts to the Balkans, Adriatic and Illyria; the Danube replaced the Rhine as the conduit for colonial goods.

If the Continental Blockade was a failure, the Continental System more widely considered was not an unalloyed disaster. From 1806 to 1810 French industry was bursting with confidence, with three industries particularly to the fore: cotton, chemicals and armaments. The great captains of industry enjoyed considerable prestige and were second only to the marshals and the Councillors of State in power and rank. Cotton – based in Paris, Normandy, Flanders, Picardy, Alsace, Belgium and the Rhineland – was the great success story and was the one area where France kept up with Britain technologically; in other spheres, where Britain had a commanding technical lead, the blockade made it difficult for her inventions to be copied and then remodelled in France. Silk was another success, especially in Lyons and St Étienne, as was wool in Verviers, Rheims, Aachen, Sedan, the Rhineland and Normandy. Agriculture did not fare so well, with sugar and tobacco on the decline, but viniculture did well.

It has often been asserted that Napoleon set back European economic life for a decade, because his troops, living off the land, destroyed a multitude of subsistence economies. But a strong argument can be mounted for a contrary point of view, according to which the Emperor was a vital motor in the promotion of French capitalism, and not just in the picayune sense that he suppressed the old guilds. Some economic historians make the case that the Continental System saved Europe from being swamped by British enterprise and thus that it enabled a European industrial revolution to take place; some go so far as to say that by 1800 Continental Europe was threatened by the fate meted out to India in the nineteenth century: forced pastoralization. The workings of the cotton industry in Catalonia provide an almost textbook example of how the Continental System worked: booming until 1808, it was then devastated by Napoleon's coup, six years of war and the British takeover in Latin America.

Summing up, then, on the wider impact of Napoleon's Continental System, it can be said that, although Europe's industrial revolution did not start under the Emperor, it was his policies, and especially the elevation of the bourgeoisie, that laid the groundwork. Europe, in a word, was given a breathing space that secured its future as an industrial society, the predominance of the nobility was ended, feudal guilds broken up, and the centre of gravity switched from the ports and seaborne trade to the heavy industry of the north and east and the coal and iron in north-east France and Belgium. It must be stressed that these were unintended effects. Nobody at the time really understood how international trade and the movement of capital worked, and Napoleon himself had old-fashioned ideas on economics – deflationary policies, suspicion of paper money, restrictions on credit, a balanced budget – without understanding the knock-on effects of such policies.

But it was always the Blockade, not the System, that obsessed him. Britain's chances of survival looked rosier than ever by the beginning of 1810, for the Royal Navy seized Cape Town and Java, Guadelupe and Mauritius from the Dutch and, by interposing the Royal Navy, detached Latin America from Joseph. Napoleon's only response to smuggling was to impose tighter political and military control on the allies, which meant annexation: Holland joined a long list that already included Ancona, Piacenza, Parma, Tuscany, the Papal States, Illyria (including Trieste) and was soon followed by most of Westphalia, the Tessin and the Valais in Switzerland and the Hanseatic towns of Hamburg, Lübeck and Bremen. Unfortunately for the Emperor, this remorseless policy of annexation simply increased the number of his enemies and critics, some of whom questioned his sanity and his judgement. All of Europe especially the Czar, was irritated by the annexations, and within France it reopened the debate about the desirability of resting content with the natural frontiers. To disarm his critics Napoleon thought of new economic devices, which merely exacerbated his problems.

1810 was the year when things began to go badly wrong with the French economy. Realizing that he could not close the coast of Europe to British products, and that French industrial production was impaired by the high price of colonial raw materials, Napoleon decided on a new tack. The decrees of St-Cloud, Trianon and Fontainebleau (3 July, 1 August,

10, 18 October 1810) introduced a new pattern of blockade which in many ways contradicted the old System. The July decree allowed France to trade with England while forbidding the Allies to do so; the first August decree stipulated that the entire maritime trade of the Empire was under his personal direction and that no ship could leave the Continent for a foreign port without a licence signed by him; the second August decree set out duties on colonial products such that the consumer paid the same as under the old smuggling régime, but the French Treasury not the smugglers made the profit; and the October decrees ordered all trading in colonial products in the Empire outside France to cease as it competed with French trade.

The St-Cloud, Trianon and Fontainebleau decrees had a threefold aim: to tighten the noose on the illicit trade in British goods and make London realize it could never win the economic war; to strengthen the privileged position of French manufacturing by raising the imperial and Italian customs tariff and thus to boost French industry by giving it a monopoly in industrial production and the distribution of colonial goods; and to destroy the point of smuggling by issuing licences for the export and import of necessary raw materials. Faced with a trade he could not stop, Napoleon in effect turned smuggler himself. French trade with England was *de facto* legalized by the imposition of tariffs as high as 40–50% – the equivalent of smugglers' premiums in the past.

The real question was whether allowing colonial goods to enter France from England while British manufactures were excluded would correct the kinks in the Continental System. But Napoleon's attempt at reforming a rickety blockade simply made everything worse. German traders were ruined at a stroke, creating an underground spirit of hatred and revenge. To enforce his monopoly Napoleon seized and destroyed huge stocks of contraband in Germany, Holland and Italy, ruffling national sensibilities in those lands. Authorizing the sale of prizes seized by privateers and corsairs together with a huge stockpile of confiscated goods in Holland weakened the market for French manufactures in the short term. The licensing system, which among other benefits was supposed to embroil the U.S.A. in conflict with Britain by accentuating American anger with the Royal Navy's searches and seizures, actually helped the United Kingdom by providing badly-needed wheat at a time of dearth; the war between Britain and the U.S.A. was provoked too late – in 1812. Meanwhile the 1810 decrees triggered a grave economic crisis in France. As for the efficacy of licences to deal with smuggling, the main effect of the 1810 decrees was to force contraband farther east, with the Danube taking the place of the Rhine.

The sustained economic crisis of 1811–13 in France was really a combination of three distinct factors: overproduction because of speculation; overproduction caused by loss of trade outlets; and bad harvests. The first two facets of the crisis were intimately intertwined and were direct consequences of Napoleon's decrees. Since many had speculated in colonial goods, general ruin ensued when French merchants were undercut by the new imports and foreign merchants deprived of their stocks. With speculation reaching its limit and stocks in France building up, a wave of bankruptcies and a credit squeeze ensued severely affecting industry, banking and trade. Industry was particularly badly hit as, with a general fall in prices, many manufacturers had to borrow heavily to survive.

Napoleon failed to understand that his decrees undid all the work of economic integration effected by his original Continental System. Once the assets of German firms were seized, nobody owed money by them could get it back. French importers who had made loans to firms in Amsterdam, Basle and Hamburg could not retrieve their assets; all those who had played safe by switching from speculation in *assignats* to colonial produce were now ruined. In September 1810 the firm of Rodde in Lübeck went bankrupt, dragging down with it the Parisian banks of Laffitte, Fould and Tourton. This in turn triggered further bankruptcies in Paris and eventually the rest of France.

1811 brought recession in the Lyons silk industry; the number of working looms was halved. Soon Tours, Nîmes and Italy were sucked into the slump and then it was the turn of the great success story, cotton. Contraction in that industry was dramatic: in Rouen the workshops used only a third of the raw materials they had used in 1810. Wool was the next to be hit, with a quarter of the nation's drapers ceasing payment. Although the depression was less serious in manufacturing, the pinch was felt from the Haut-Rhin to the Pyrenees. In May 1811, 20,000 out of 50,000 workers in Paris were unemployed. Napoleon was forced to respond by undertaking a programme of public works and giving loans to industry. Towards the end of the summer of 1811 the final blow fell as bad harvests exacerbated the crisis. The South was paralysed by drought while in the Paris basin violent storms wiped out most of the crops in the area.

Napoleon was immediately on red alert, for it was one of his axioms that bread shortages in Paris could lead to general revolution. His view was well known: 'It is unfair that bread should be maintained at a low price in Paris when it costs more elsewhere, but then the government is there, and soldiers do not like to shoot at women with babies on their backs who come screaming to the bakeries.' But like many absolute rulers, he found that economics was impervious to a dictator's wishes. The price of bread in Paris continued to shoot up, first from 14 sous to 16 and finally to 18 by March 1812, and even at that price there were no loaves to be had after the small hours of the morning. He tried to assuage anger by fixing maximum prices for bread and corn but the result was what it always is in such cases: the peasants responded by hoarding. Only in Marseilles where the free play of the market was permitted was there no bread shortage.

The situation was potentially explosive, but Paris did not after all rise in revolt, possibly because there was no shortage even after the 'exploitative' price was paid, because the price of a loaf did not go above 20 sous, and because Napoleon palliated matters with soup kitchens. It was a different story in the provinces, where there was either a shortage of bread or the price was too high. The death-rate rose, hospitals and charities were overwhelmed, and in some parts of France fully one-third of the population survived only through the soup kitchens. The consequences ranged from bread riots, beggary and Luddism to outright brigandage; many of the brigands tried to legitimate their actions by reference to the persecuted Catholic Church. There were serious riots in Normandy, particularly centred on Caen, Lisieux and Cherbourg. Emotions ran high and violent threats were uttered against notables, bourgeoisie and upper peasantry, based on suspicions of hoarding. Since these were the pillars of Napoleon's social support, he was forced to take tough measures: he sent the Grand Army to Caen and had six 'ringleaders' executed, including two women.

The combination of draconian action and the good fortune of a satisfactory crop turned the tide; by 1813, following a superb harvest, the internal situation was reverting to normal; agricultural depression returned to haunt the land only with the Emperor's military setbacks that year. But 1810 definitely marked the parting of the ways between Napoleon and his mainstay, the notables. Three black years dented business confidence and, particularly after 1812, the bourgeoisie no longer wanted to invest in the imperial enterprise that was showing spectacular losses. There was always a latent contradiction between the Emperor's military ambitions and the needs of his supporters in the social power base. Capitalists were used to taking risks, but the gigantic gambles of Napoleon's 'double or quits' military exploits were too much for them. The peasants meanwhile got tired of supplying manpower for wars which no longer had anything to do with guaranteeing the gains of 1789 but were about the ambition of a single man.

But the economic crisis of 1811 did not strike at France alone. The irony was that as Napoleon wrestled with a sea of internal troubles, he was probably closer to ultimate victory than at any other time. Britain, the subsidizer of Bonaparte's European enemies, was in a parlous state. In 1810 the country plunged into crisis on four different fronts, hit by a general monetary emergency, acute disappointment in the Latin American market, loss of exports because of the Continental System, and a rise in the cost of cereals. Trade was cut by a third and many speculators in government bonds were ruined. The causes of the crisis were various: the enforced participation of Sweden in the Continental System; Napoleon's determined attempt to break into colonial trade; the tightening of the U.S. trade embargo; disruption caused by a wave of revolutions in Latin America; and two bad harvests in 1809 and 1810 which necessitated wheat imports and hence inflation.

The most serious crisis in economic confidence began when British merchants could not get payment in money from their South American customers. Credit lines had been laxly extended to Latin America without a proper estimate of the capacity of the area to repay its debts. Elated by the apparent El Dorado provided by this new market, British entrepreneurs went overboard and flooded the old Spanish colonies with exports; the most famous story is of a London firm sending iceskates to Buenos Aires in the belief that it lay in polar latitudes. Then it transpired that Latin America could pay its debts only in colonial produce, of which there was already a glut in Europe. The knock-on effect was immediate: five Manchester houses went bankrupt in 1810; banks and industry came under pressure; the uncertainty affected the pound and sterling dropped 20% on the Hamburg exchange.

In 1811 the downward spiral continued; there were more bank failures and a general failure of economic confidence. The rate of bankruptcy doubled. There was a marked drop in the value of exports of metallurgy, cotton and shipbuilding; wage cuts and unemployment coincided with yet another harvest failure in 1811. Wool, hosiery, cotton and iron were the industries hardest hit, with 9,000 out of work in Birmingham, 12,000 in Manchester, handloom weavers turned into the street, and many Lancashire mills working a three-day week. Soon the convulsive events in France were being reproduced across the Channel. Anti-machinery riots broke out in Nottingham in 1811 and in Lancashire and Yorkshire the Luddites, with their hatred of modern technology, symbolized popular discontent. Unemployment and the rising cost of bread seemed to portend general social breakdown, at the very moment a political crisis with the U.S.A., leading to war in 1812, was distracting the attention of the political élite

The growing volume of peace petitions reflected a general feeling that the struggle with Napoleon was no longer worth the candle. The unpopularity of the Orders in Council reached a peak in 1811 and in July of the following year Lord Liverpool's government was forced to abandon them – too late, however, to prevent war with the U.S.A. By 1812 the Continental System was beginning to bite for the second time. Had there been prolonged famine, Luddism might have swept all before it, with incalculable consequences. In the short term it was Napoleon's very system of licences, allowing the export of cereals to perfidious Albion, that saved England from famine. That was one irony. Another was that in the long term, Napoleon's decision to invade Russia saved Britain in 1812, just as his incursion into Spain had saved her in 1808. The third irony is that Napoleon used his licence system to pay for the campaign in Russia. As the Emperor prepared for a final settling of accounts with the Czar, the fate of England hung in the balance. If he triumphed in Moscow, he would surely attain his dearest wish and celebrate a *Te Deum* in London.

CHAPTER TWENTY-TWO

From the beginning of 1811 it was clear to the shrewdest observers that France and Russia were on a collision course. Some have even antedated the process and claimed that the failure of the Russian marriage project at the beginning of 1810 and the subsequent match with Marie-Louise was the invisible Rubicon. But it is possible to go even further back and claim that the disappointing conference at Erfurt in October 1808 was the beginning of the end; the failure of the Russian marriage then becomes the occasion rather than the cause of a downward spiral in relations.

The Czar had both political and economic grievances arising from his entente with Napoleon. Politically, the Emperor refused to allow Alexander *carte blanche* in Turkey and kept postponing the promised division of the Ottoman Empire, on the grounds that possession of Constantinople would make Russia a Mediterranean power. He also irritated the Czar by enlarging the Grand Duchy of Warsaw, flirting with Polish nationalists and threatening to revive an independent Poland, something totally unacceptable to the Russians. In both cases Napoleon was being dog in the manger: he could not have a viable Polish kingdom or defeat Turkey without Russian support, yet he refused to collaborate with Alexander in seeking a rational settlement. Further political irritants in 1810 were French annexation of the Hanseatic towns and the Duchy of Oldenburg, to which the heir apparent was the Czar's brother-in-law, and the installation of Bernadotte as King of Sweden – which Alexander mistakenly thought meant an extension of French military power on his northern flank.

Lest all this should suggest an innocent, peace-loving Czar Alexander forced reluctantly into war by an expansionist Corsican ogre, it must be emphasized that Alexander was systematically duplicitous in his dealings with Napoleon and had Promethean ambitions of his own. Despite his professed admiration for the Emperor, the one and only significant reform Alexander took from Napoleon was to ape his method of modernizing the apparatus of repression and introducing a secret police force. Alexander managed to be both fool and knave. A coward who was unable to stand up to the Dowager Empress and feared that the fate he had meted out to his father would be visited on him, the Czar was an essentially stupid man masquerading as an intellectual. He had the besetting sin of indecisive tyrants, in that he agreed with the last person to speak to him; this explains why Talleyrand was able to twist him round his little finger. But there was another dimension to Alexander's essential stupidity: he was a religious maniac and, like later czars, easy prey for quacks, charlatans, gurus and 'perfect masters'.

Alexander was in any case scarcely master in his own house for, apart from pressure from the virulently anti-Bonapartist coterie around the Dowager Empress, he had to face the fact of the Army high command's hatred of Napoleon and the objective interests of the business community. Russia's economic interests were threatened both by the expansion of French influence to the Baltic and by the Continental System. The blockade of England destroyed the Russian export trade in corn, hemp, wood, tallow, pitch, potassium, leather and iron. France meanwhile was neither offering alternative outlets nor supplying Russia with the goods she needed; instead she sent luxury goods like spirits, perfumes, porcelain and jewellery. French traders in more basic necessities found it easier, cheaper and more predictable to find markets in Italy and Germany, where they had the might of the *Grande Armée* to back them. This was the context of the Czar's ukase in December 1810, when he effectively barred French luxury imports by imposing high tariffs and opened his port to neutral shipping.

By the beginning of 1811 relations between Czar and Emperor were tense. Prince Poniatowski, Napoleon's faithful Polish captain, warned the French that Alexander was preparing a pre-emptive strike against the small portion of the Grand Army that remained east of the Elbe. The intelligence was correct: Alexander had sounded his adviser Prince Adam Czartoryski about the possibility of suborning the Poles to his side, but Czartoryski replied that the price was an independent Poland. After a few tentative overtures to Austria, Prussia and Sweden which led nowhere, Alexander decided on a policy of 'wait and see'. A guarded correspondence with Napoleon ensued. On 28 February 1811 the Emperor wrote him a letter which was superficially cheerful and friendly but which contained a sting in the tail: referring to Alexander's virtual abandonment of the Continental System, he warned of terrible consequences if the Czar sought a rapprochement with the British. Alexander answered non-committally on 25 March, justifying his ukase by the crisis in Russia's maritime trade and the fall in the exchange rate of the rouble.

Napoleon decided that war with Russia was the only solution. It has sometimes been said that Alexander's duplicity, intrigues and expansionism forced conflict on an unwilling French Emperor but, the Czar's despicable nature notwithstanding, there is no warrant for this view in sober history. The truth is that Napoleon welcomed the looming clash of arms. From the beginning of 1811 the Ordnance Department, and especially Bacler d'Albe's Topography Department, was busy providing up-to-date maps of the terrain in western Russia. Danzig was made the centre of a gigantic collection of war matériel sent there from eastern France and the Rhineland. The Emperor showed the way his mind was working when he gave Kurakin, the Russian ambassador, the most ferocious dressing down in an audience at the Tuileries on 15 August 1811 which recalled the stormy scene with Lord Whitworth in 1803. The occasion was Alexander's suggestion that he be given part of the Duchy of Warsaw. 'Don't you know that I have 800,000 troops!' Napoleon yelled. 'If you're counting on allies, where are they?'

There is a slight hint of protesting too much in this imperial show of bravado. There is more than a little evidence that Napoleon felt he was pushing open the door to a dark room never seen before. His spies told him that Talleyrand openly predicted that France would fail in a war with the Russians. Captain Leclerc, his statistical expert, warned him of the dangers of campaigning in Russia and reminded him of the unhappy fate of Charles XII of Sweden, annihilated at Poltava in 1709 during an invasion of Russia. Bonaparte's ambassador in Russia, Louis de Caulaincourt, warned him several times in very strong language that he would be making a very serious mistake if he fought the Russians on Russian soil, and correctly conjectured that the Russians would employ the Fabian tactics used by Wellington in Spain. Tired of Caulaincourt's Cassandra-like prophecies, a tetchy Emperor finally recalled him in June 1811.

The indomitable Caulaincourt, one of the few people who emerges with unblemished credit from the saga of 1812, tried his utmost to preserve the Tilsit agreement, even when this meant falling foul of his imperial master. During a tense five-hour 'debriefing' interview when Caulaincourt returned from Russia in June 1812, the Emperor lost patience with his envoy when he kept insisting that Alexander wanted peace. All Caulaincourt's advice was shrewd but his master would not listen. Caulaincourt predicted with uncanny accuracy, what the impact of a Russian winter would be like and repeated the Czar's confident boast: that in a war the Russians would lose in the short term but win in the long, if only because Bonaparte could not afford to be absent from France for the two years it would take to subdue the warriors of the steppes.

Napoleon swept aside all these objections and continued to prepare for war.

But there was a significant lacuna in Napoleon's preparations from the end of August until mid-November 1811 while he mulled over all the implications of the proposed war. First he travelled to Compiègne for a three-week stay. Then on 18 September he followed a now familiar itinerary, through Wimereux, Ambleteuse, Calais, Dunkirk, Ostend, Flushing, Anvers and Gorkhum to Utrecht and Amsterdam. Anxious to see for himself this land from which he had expelled Louis he remained in Amsterdam for two weeks before setting out on 24 October for the completion of the journey. After visits to the Hague, Rotterdam, the château of Loo, Nijmegen and Arnhem, he crossed into Germany for stopovers at Düsseldorf, Bonn, Liège and Mézières before returning to St-Cloud on 11 November. His mind was now made up. The Continental System had to continue, and war with Russia was its logical expression.

Why did Napoleon embark on a course of action so fraught with danger and ultimately so fatal to his prospects? Not even Hitler made the mistake of fighting an active war on two fronts, since there was no war in western Europe when he invaded Russia in 1941. Yet Napoleon launched into the vast open spaces of the Russian interior at a time when he was already losing a major war in Spain. There was a rational element in his decision, but it seems to have been overwhelmed by multifarious slivers of wishful thinking, fantasy and self-destructive impulses. In his rational moments, Napoleon argued that a Russian campaign was necessary to maintain credibility and to extinguish British hopes. In the first place, if Russia was allowed to flout the Continental System, others would soon follow her example and the entire strategy for defeating England would be subverted. Secondly, England still sustained herself with the hope of another Continental coalition; with Prussia and Austria cowed, her only plausible potential partner was Russia. It followed that a military defeat of Russia would finally convince the British that Bonaparte was invincible and force them to sue for peace. Thirdly, Poland needed to be converted into a strong state, with a weak Russia on her borders, so that the French Empire could not be threatened from the east after Napoleon's death.

Many observers are convinced that even beneath this seeming rationality there lurked a second-order irrationality. Was it not almost suicidal to double the stakes just when the game seemed to be going against him? The Continental Blockade had not worked, and seemed unlikely to work. The attempt to close one door on England had led to the unforeseen débâcle in Spain. What might not invasion of Russia bring? This has led some historians to argue that Napoleon was once again engaged in 'double or quits'. On this view, his power base in France was becoming precarious, he was at loggerheads with the notables, and the economic crisis and continuing war in Spain had made him so unpopular that he needed a war to distract France from its internal woes and unite it behind a victorious Emperor.

But there is evidence of still deeper currents of irrationality and of self-destructive behaviour. It is unexpected to find, so late in his reign, the resurgence of the 'Oriental complex' yet it is clearly on show in the bizarre remarks made to the comte de Narbonne early in 1812 – an eccentric piece of behaviour explicable only because Narbonne was himself an oddity: a great noble, reputedly the illegitimate son of Louis XV and one time (1792) war minister to Louis XVI, who had fallen under the Bonaparte spell. This is Napoleon:

> The end of the road is India. Alexander was as far as from Moscow when he marched to the Ganges. I have said this to myself ever since St Jean d'Acre. . . . Just imagine, Moscow taken, Russia defeated, the Czar made over or assassinated in a palace plot. . . . and then tell me that it is impossible for a large army of Frenchmen and their allies to leave Tiflis and reach the Ganges. Essentially all that is needed is a swift stroke of a French sword for the entire British mercantile apparatus in the East to collapse.

Narbonne's private comment on this was: 'What a man! What ideas! What dreams! Where is the keeper of this genius. It was half-way between Bedlam and the Pantheon.'

The 'Oriental complex' was only one of many centrifugal fragments indicating a core personality under great strain, suggesting perhaps that things were falling apart and the Napoleonic centre could not hold. A host of psychological interpretations have been offered for Napoleon's state of mind on the eve of 1812. Those who see Bonaparte as the existentialist defying fate and declaring that nothing is written stress the way he liked to reinforce his identity through action and the challenge of an impossible adventure. This is plausible given that Napoleon himself admitted he had had a visitation from his familiar 'Red Man' who warned him not to invade Russia; to defy the Red Man would reveal the Emperor as a Prometheus, refusing to be bound by the iron laws of determinism.

Others see Napoleon as a self-doubting neurotic posing as a conqueror and trying to prove that his worst fears about himself were not true. In a similar vein Freud argued that 1812 was the ultimate self-destructive act in which Bonaparte, guilty for jettisoning Josephine, compassed his own downfall; consciously the divorce of Josephine signified to the superstitious Emperor the loss of his luck, and unconsciously triggered a need to be punished. It is tempting to dismiss this as fanciful, but there is the curious fact that, after a two-year absence, Napoleon suddenly visited Josephine at Malmaison on 30 June 1812, just days before setting out on campaign. Certainly the thesis of keeping depression at bay can be sustained circumstantially from the following remarks quoted by Roederer:

> I care nothing for St-Cloud or the Tuileries. It would matter little to me if they were burned down. I count my houses as nothing, women as nothing, my son as not very much. I leave one place, I go to another. I leave St-Cloud and I go to Moscow, not out of inclination or to gratify myself, but out of dry calculation.

If the disastrous decision to go to war with Russia was in some sense a symptom of Napoleon's declining psychological well-being, his physical health was also declining. 'After all, forty *is* forty,' was one of the Emperor's authentic remarks, perhaps indicating some alarm at his own rapid and premature decline. Those who had close contact with him in 1812 reported that he was woefully unfit and had grown fat from daily four-course meals. Méneval spoke of hypertrophy of the upper body, with a great head on massive shoulders, but small arms, no neck, a pronounced paunch and a lower body that seemed too slender to support the torso. One of the hidden factors working against the success of the 1812 campaign was the Emperor's ill-health. Loath to leave his carriage, he spent many hours on his couch undressed and came down just before the decisive battle of the war with a bad cold and dysuria. Throughout September he was like a skeleton on horseback, nursing a temperature, a constant cough, breathing difficulties and an irregular pulse, and suffering acute pain in emptying his bladder.

From early 1812 the drift to war was all but inevitable. Realizing that this time his forces would not be able to live off the land, on 13 January he ordered Lacue, his Director of War Administration, to supply enough provisions for an army of 400,000 men for fifty days. The basic provision was supposed to be twenty million rations of bread and the same of rice; additionally, 6,000 wagons, either horse or ox-drawn, were to carry enough flour for 200,000 men for two months, and for the horses two million bushels of oats, enough to feed fifty mounts for fifty days, were to be supplied. Needless to say, the Emperor did not say how such a vast commissariat was to be assembled in time for a spring campaign and seems almost to have believed that the resources could be conjured out of thin air.

Meanwhile the flower of the *Grande Armée* was earmarked for the coming campaign. The élite French battalions were all in I, II and III Corps, commanded respectively by Davout, Oudinot and Ney; together with the Guard and Murat's cavalry this made up the 250,000-strong First Army Group. Second and Third Army Groups (150,000 and 165,000 strong respectively) were to guard frontiers and lines of communication and provide reinforcements. IV Corps under Eugène de Beauharnais was basically the Army of Italy with a stiffening of French and Spanish regiments; the faithful Poniatowski led his Poles in V Corps while Reynier led the Saxons in VII Corps. Command of VI Corps went to Gouvion St-Cyr who, after near-disgrace in Spain, made a remarkable comeback in 1812 and ended with a marshal's baton; Victor, commanding mixed battalions of French, Germans and Poles in IX Corps, was another reprieved after less than satisfactory service in Spain. Yet another mixed corps (French, Italians and Germans) served under Augereau in XI Corps, while the Westphalians and Hessians in VIII Corps had Vandamme as their taskmaster. This by no means exhausted the units detailed for service in Russia, for there were also four cavalry corps, two of them led by Murat and a second Support Army under Jérôme. Finally, Napoleon himself would command the 50,000 'immortals' of the Old and Young Guards. The Corps were of widely differing manpower: Oudinot's had 37,000 men but Davout's was nearly twice as large with 72,000.

While these massive military preparations went on, a complicated game of diplomatic manoeuvring continued, in which Alexander won every round on points. On 26 February 1812 Napoleon sent the Czar's special envoy Tchentchev back to Russia with a threatening message for Alexander, but a police raid on Tchentchev's apartments threw up the alarming intelligence that the Russians had all along had a well-placed mole at the heart of Bonapartist decision-making, who had revealed all the most important intelligence about French military strength and troop movements. This development seriously harmed the valiant attempts of Caulaincourt to cobble together a compromise peace; caught between the giant egos of Napoleon and Alexander, he was the true unsung hero of 1812.

In any case, the Czar was intransigent in his reply on 27 April. His terms for Russia's return to the Continental System were impossibly steep: French evacuation of Prussia, compensation for the loss of the Duchy of Oldenburg and the creation of a neutral buffer zone between

Napoleon at his apogee:
the imperial apotheosis as seen by Ingres

Fouché:
the avatar of treachery and duplicity

Bernadotte:
Gascon windbag and mortal enemy

Murat:
a man of great courage but little brain

Talleyrand:
self-serving, Janus-faced spy and humbug

Alexander I of Russia:
he wanted to be Napoleon

Marie Walewska:
the only woman who truly loved him

Eylau, 1807: the bloodbath in the snow

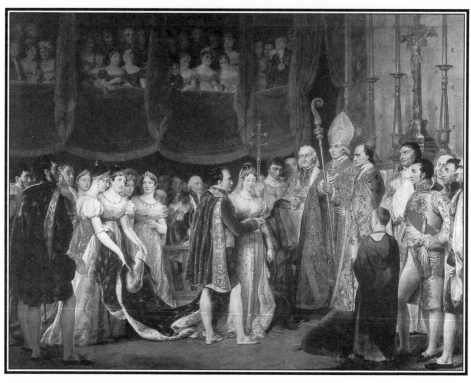

Napoleon as political simpleton: the marriage of Marie-Louise

The descent into barbarism: the first of the Spanish atrocities as seen by Goya

The killing fields of Russia: Borodino, August 1812

The decline and fall of the *Grand Armée*: the retreat from Moscow

Backs to the wall: the fighting retreat through northern France, 1814

The *grognards*:
'they grumble but they follow him always'

Hand-to-hand combat at La Haye Sainte: Waterloo, 18 June 1815

The charge of the Scots Greys at Waterloo

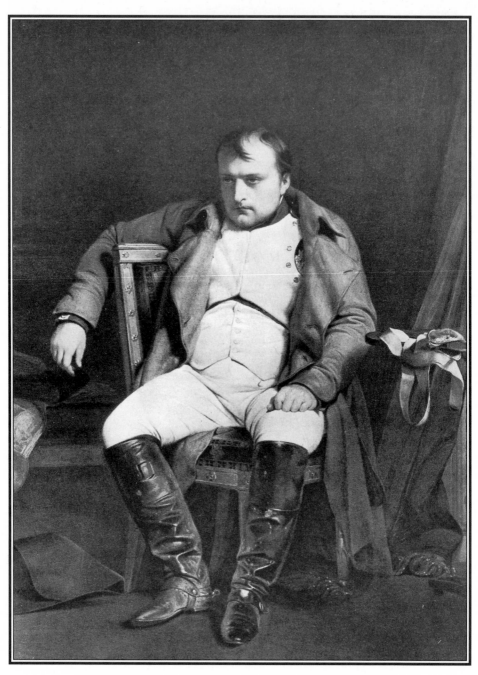

The end of a dream: Napoleon at Fontainebleau, 1814

the two power blocs. Napoleon regarded the answer as more of an insult than serious diplomacy. Some historians have claimed that, since Alexander was prepared to revoke his ban on French luxury goods, reimpose the blockade on British ships and withdraw his protest about the Duchy of Oldenburg, Napoleon was not justified in regarding the note as a *casus belli*, but this is naïve. Alexander had no qualms about war, for he thought he could win.

The screws were turned on the Prussians and Austrians to provide fighting men for the Russian front. They acquiesced and a 30,000-strong Austrian army under Schwarzenburg actually fought in the campaign after Metternich advised the Austrian Emperor that he had no choice but to comply. Frederick William of Prussia was forced to provide 20,000 troops and huge quantities of stores or face the occupation of Berlin by the French. But the Austrians and Prussians also secretly advised Alexander that they were simply acting under duress and would bide their time until they could openly proclaim an alliance with Russia.

Napoleon's overtures to Britain also ran into the sand. He proposed peace in Spain on the basis that Portugal would be restored to the Braganzas and Sicily given to Ferdinand, ex-King of Naples, provided Joseph remained as King of Spain. Since the British already held Portugal and Sicily, they could not understand what was supposed to be in the deal for them, and replied firmly that Ferdinand must be restored at once as King of Spain before negotiations could even begin. The truth is that they were beginning to grow confident that they could win the Peninsular War anyway, especially if Napoleon was busy in Russia.

Other diplomatic developments in the first half of 1812 were equally disastrous for France. Chafing under the Continental System and the insulting French occupation of Swedish Pomerania in January 1812, the Swedish nobility put pressure on their new King. With Bernadotte on the throne, they were preaching to the converted. At last he had the chance for revenge on the man who had humiliated him so many times. With singular relish Bernadotte brought Sweden over to the Russian side in April 1812, after securing a Russian promise to help him conquer Norway. Yet another body blow for Napoleon was the Treaty of Bucharest in May 1812, making peace between Russia and Turkey. In the space of a month Alexander had secured both his northern and southern flanks and could concentrate all his forces against Napoleon in the centre.

On 9 May 1812 Napoleon left St-Cloud with Marie-Louise and set out for Dresden, accompanied by three hundred carriages conveying an itinerant court. Travelling via Châlons and Metz he was at Mainz on 12 May, then proceeded to Dresden by way of Würzburg, Bayreuth and Freyberg, arriving there at midnight on 16 May in a triumphal procession, with the King of Saxony providing the honour escort. The poet Heine was one who witnessed the imperial passage through Germany and wrote of his first glimpse of Bonaparte: 'He was sending them to Russia, and the old grenadiers glanced up at him with so awesome a devotion, so sympathetic an earnestness, with the pride of death: *Te, Caesar, morituri te salutant.*'

Napoleon remained in Dresden for two weeks while his envoy Count Narbonne conducted futile negotiations at Vilna with the Czar's plenipotentiaries. On St Helena Napoleon described this fortnight in Dresden as the happiest time of his life, since all the rulers of Europe, except the Czar, George III and the Sultan, were there to pay homage to him. He took over the Saxon King's rococo palace and filled it with wagon trains of French tapestries, wines, porcelain, china, glass and furniture brought from Paris. Hundreds of French cooks worked on delicacies culled from all over the Empire for the delectation of Marie-Louise and the imperial nobility, now seemingly given the final seal of approval with the presence in Dresden of the great scions of the *ancien régime* nobility – the Turennes, the Montesquieus and the Noailles.

After leaving Dresden on 29 May the Emperor proceeded via Posan and Thorn to his main base at Danzig, where he arrived on the evening of 7 June. Almost his first encounter was with Murat, a man he had seen little of in recent years. The Emperor had not forgotten his disloyal intrigues in 1809 and often toyed with the idea of deposing him as King of Naples. On one occasion he had actually summoned him in order to dismiss him but Murat, tipped off by one of his spies (Fouché?), decamped for Italy to avoid the confrontation. By the time a lame excuse about crossed messages had been offered, Napoleon's mind was on something else and the Murat problem went into abeyance. But now, seeing again his disloyal brother-in-law, the Emperor greeted him coldly. He began with stern face and bitter words, then changed his tone to that of a man whose close friend has let him down badly. He finished with words so tender and affecting that Murat was deeply moved and near to tears. Once again it is worth stressing that Napoleon Bonaparte, his occasional harsh excesses aside, was a deeply human and forgiving man – too forgiving for his own good, some would say.

At Danzig Napoleon took stock of the situation on the eve of the Russian campaign. Altogether he had some 675,000 troops under arms, including reserves and those on supply and garrison duties. Aside from the French soldiers there were 40,000 Italians, 30,000 Portuguese and Spanish, Swiss, Dutch, Illyrians, Croats, Lithuanians and, above all, vast numbers of Germans. One corps was entirely Polish, another entirely Saxon, another entirely Austrian; yet another was Westphalian and Hessian, and still another largely Prussian. Morale in the polyglot army was high, and desertion levels low, partly because of the draconian punishments visited on those taking unauthorized furlough, but it was the local population who paid the price. In Prussia and Poland the French army exacted, commandeered and requisitioned without any regard to the fragility of local economies, behaved arrogantly and refused to pay for anything. Napoleon, exhibiting the insouciance with detail that was to mark him throughout 1812, did nothing to check these excesses.

There was another fortnight's delay at Danzig before Napoleon crossed the border into Russia. During these days the Emperor travelled for no discernible reason to Marienburg and Königsberg and on to Gumbinnen and Wilowski. This was the first of the many baffling delays he allowed himself in 1812, and the reason has always puzzled Bonaparte students. The most plausible conjecture is that he postponed the invasion until June because, with 110,000 horses and 90,000 draught oxen to feed, he needed to wait until the steppes were lush with grass. Another view is that he was concerned that the medical infrastructure was inadequate: expecting heavy casualties, he was alarmed to find at Danzig that the requisite surgeons, ambulances, medicines, bandages and stretchers were all lacking.

During this period of 'phoney war' the Emperor's thoughts often went back to Marie-Louise. It is curious how often this cynical man turned uxorious when campaigning, for the tone of his letters to his wife irresistibly recalls the correspondence with Josephine when he was conquering Italy in 1796–97. There was genuine regret in the letter he sent to her when he discovered she was not pregnant again, as he had hoped. And there was much more in the same sentimental vein. On 9 June he wrote to her from Danzig: 'My health is very good. Despite my cares and exhaustion, I feel there is something missing . . . the sweet habit of seeing you several times a day.'

But now he had to think seriously about his Russian strategy. His main aim was to prevent the junction of the army under Barclay in the north with that under Prince Bagration in the south. The idea was to push hard towards Moscow on the 'Orsha land-bridge' – the watershed between the Dnieper and Dvina which ran straight to the heart of Russia, interrupted only by the Beresina, one of the Dnieper's important tributaries. He calculated that he could achieve this end by crossing the river Niemen on a narrow front, with flanks protected by MacDonald's corps at Riga and Schwarzenberg's Austrian corps at Minsk; this would also allow him to cut off Bagration if the Russians took the offensive.

These were minimum aims, but there were also 'best-case scenario' maximum aims in the Emperor's mind. He planned to engage Barclay's army by pushing forward with the left flank while falling back with the right. Barclay would presumably then fall back and move south to avoid encirclement, but would be unable to link with Bagration, as he would be pinned by Jérôme and Schwarzenberg. Bagration would be forced to advance to attack Bonaparte's right, at which point the more powerful French left and centre would circle round and cut communications with Moscow. Both Russian armies would then be herded into a pocket around Grodno and 'eaten up', bringing the war to an end in twelve days.

It was a good plan but it depended on exact timing, close communication and secure lines. Most of all it envisaged *blitzkrieg* warfare. But Napoleon's previous victories had all been won with smallish armies operating over smallish spaces; he had never tried to coordinate vast armies over distances of hundreds of miles. Had he campaigned sustainedly in Spain he would have saved himself from this error. It was clear that too many things could go wrong – messages failing to get through, commanders failing to obey orders to the letter – and that execution could never match conception. The plan also assumed that the Russians would give battle as soon as the French crossed the frontier, whereas the Czar had already decided to make his stand 200 miles inland along the line traced by the rivers Dnieper, Dvina and Beresina.

In retrospect one can see that the Russian campaign was fatally flawed from the outset, and that Napoleon had not thought through most of the problems confronting him. His most straightforward blunders were political. He would not have had to face two armies in the first place if he had not allowed Alexander to outmanoeuvre him in Sweden and Turkey simultaneously. To turn the campaign into a crusade for liberty he should have given Poland its independence and freed the Russian serfs. The reluctance to turn the Duchy of Warsaw into an independent Poland is all the more surprising now that he no longer had to worry about giving offence to the Czar. As for his stated reasons for not freeing the Russian serfs, these seem almost fatuous. To state that manumission would have turned conservative Europe and the Right against him ignores the obvious fact that they already *were* against him, albeit mainly covertly. As for the argument that the ferocious and mindless *mujiks* would have committed terrible atrocities against their former masters, the only consequence of the Emperor's scruples in this regard was that the serfs visited atrocities on the French instead.

But perhaps more serious were the mistakes in the sphere where Napoleon regarded himself as a master: strategic planning and execution. Quite apart from his old fault of ignoring the seasons and the elements when drawing up his plans, the emperor proved singularly defective in logistics – an area where his mathematical ability should have come into its own. The preparations at Danzig were impressive, and the port held the desired 400,000 rations for fifty days, but no one had worked out how to get these supplies to a front that got more distant day by day. The factors of delay and distance meant that even if a food convoy got to the front, it was likely already to have consumed one-third of what it was transporting. Horses were a particular problem, for they needed nine kilos of forage a day each, including the oats they were pulling for the vast numbers (over 100,000) of cavalry mounts and artillery horses; when set to graze on unripe rye, they simply died in thousands.

Since the Army moved much faster than its supply convoys, it was constantly outstripping its own commissariat. The food wagons proved unsuitable to Russian roads – really no more than rutted tracks – and broke down in areas where there were no replacement horses or carts to hand. The consequence was not only that vast amounts of stores were dumped but that mills for grinding corn and ovens for baking bread could not keep up with the Army. It was not long before starvation loomed, for the initial twenty-day ration was consumed before the due date. For a while the troops were able to slaughter cattle, but then came the conundrum of living off the land where there was nothing to pillage. The lack of the firm smack of discipline from the Emperor did not help. Absurdly complaisant, he allowed his officers to bring servants and luxuries with them. The men in the ranks took their cue from their superiors, and the result was a huge subsidiary army of camp followers, themselves wasting the Army's substance. An army corps accompanied by hundreds of cattle on the hoof thronged the roads and blocked the progress of the food and ammunition convoys behind.

Both militarily and logistically Napoleon would have done better with an Army of half the size of the host he took into Russia. Hitherto, Napoleon's victories had been gained with an Army of maximum size of 100,000, which permitted the speed and flexibility that produced an Austerlitz. Significantly, the Emperor had never before commanded an Army of the size he led on to the steppes, and seems blithely to have thought he could achieve a sixfold increase in his strike rate. It never seems to have occurred to him that a sixfold increase in numbers would augment the problems of command and coordination *exponentially*. This applied particularly to logistics. In a nutshell, the *Grande Armée* was too big for the resources of Russia and its infrastructure. The problems of roads and food supply were so great that the most sober analysts have concluded that Napoleon's 1812 adventure was doomed from the start; it was an impossible dream, something impracticable before the advent of railways and the telegraph.

Since the problem of time was pressing, Napoleon should have crossed the Niemen in May. His failure to do so caused him problems which he, typically, attributed simply to bad luck. As the summer heats began, disease struck at the Army: 60,000 died from dysentery, diphtheria and typhus before ever a Russian was sighted or a shot fired. A believer in omens, Napoleon should have heeded the portents. But the superstitious Corsican did not even heed the 'warning' when he was thrown from his horse in the late afternoon of 23 June – a hare ran between the hooves of his steed – though privately he brooded on the conspiracy against him by paranormal forces. Yet there was still time to change strategy and save face. One possibility was to cross the Niemen for a massive raid in force and then return to the frontier for the winter: the Czar would then be informed that the same thing would happen every year until he came to heel.

It is impossible to avoid the comparison between the crossing of the Niemen by the *Grande Armée* on 23 June and the invasion of Russia by Hitler's *Wehrmacht* just one day earlier 129 years later. In both cases dictators had underestimated the enemy, failed to think their strategy through and started the campaign too late. But there the comparisons end, for the Germans in 1941 achieved striking early success with their *blitzkrieg*, while the Grand Army trekked for over a month before coming to grips with the enemy. And the five-day march to Vilna would have alerted a more circumspect commander of the possibility of ultimate disaster, for the warning signs were all there.

On the first day of the campaign 130,000 infantry and cavalry crossed the Niemen on three pontoon bridges; Napoleon himself crossed on the 24th and made his headquarters at Kovno, ready for the advance on Vilna. But on the march itself the poor organization of the Army was already apparent: the troops were indisciplined and consumed all four days' rations on the first day, so that long before they got to Vilna they were collapsing with hunger and exhaustion. Plodding along muddy tracks, past polluted wells, over collapsing bridges, maddened by lack of fresh meat and weakened by diarrhoea, the ravenous soldiers began to drop in their tracks; desertion and even suicide were common and losses ran at 5–6,000 a day. Even more seriously for the future of the campaign, the horses died in thousands; and between 10 and 20,000 perished on the Vilna road.

Arriving in Vilna on 28 June, Napoleon made another of his unaccountable long stopovers, apparently thinking he had penetrated far enough into Russia to defeat the armies of Barclay and Bagration piecemeal. As soon as he entered the city he sent Oudinot and Ney in pursuit of Barclay and Davout and Jérôme towards Minsk to intercept Bagration in a pincer movement. But the lightning manoeuvres of yore were not possible with exhausted men, exposed to huge variations of temperature between day and night, scarce local supplies and tortoise-like supply convoys. Davout did his best but Jérôme's ineptitude and slowness allowed Bagration to escape the forked trap being prepared for him. Davout raged at the incompetence of his 'colleague' and an angry Emperor wrote to his youngest brother on 4 July with a stiff reprimand and an order to come under Davout's command in future. The absurd and prima-donnaish King of Westphalia responded by throwing up his command and returning in dudgeon to his realm. Davout meanwhile dogged Bagration's heels through Minsk and Bobrusk but could not catch up with him.

The Russians were adopting a scorched-earth policy, withdrawing in face of the *Grande Armée*, but their later claims to have adopted this Fabian approach deliberately were mere rationalization. The plain truth was that they were afraid of meeting Napoleon in a pitched battle when he had such a marked superiority in numbers. Against the 450,000 Napoleon brought across the Niemen the Russians could initially pit only 160,000 men; this was yet another reason why Napoleon's vast host was too big for the job. The Czar had at first wanted to stand and fight by an entrenched camp at Drissa, but his advisers warned him that this would be playing to Bonaparte's strength. For the time being Alexander left the fighting to Barclay and Bagration.

While Napoleon remained in Vilna, his army staggered on towards the next objective: Vitebsk. They were soon caught up in another marching nightmare as the excessive heat of the day and the biting cold of night united with violent summer hailstorms to harass and lash the benighted French troopers. They trekked through dark pine forests or through foetid marshes, up to their waists in foul-smelling water; discipline collapsed and insubordination was rife. Another 8,000 horses died on this

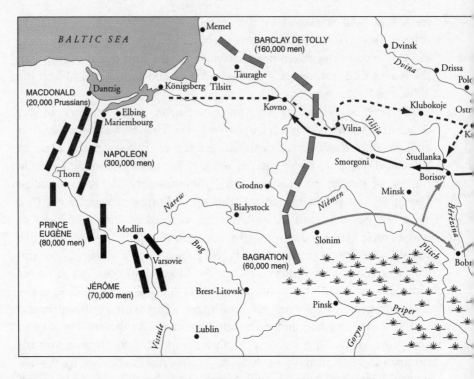

gruelling march between Vilna and Vitebsk: General Belliard, Murat's chief of staff, reported directly to the Emperor that he would soon have no cavalry left, since the horses were dying both from shortage of fodder and the violent oscillations in temperature between daytime heat and night cold. The cattle, too, lacked the stamina for such hard slogging and perished in droves, while the drivers in the supply columns found the going so tough they often sabotaged their wagons, thus reducing desperately needed food supplies.

The Emperor was not on hand to boost the morale of his men, as he remained in Vilna from 28 June to 16 July, displaying the same dithering mentality for which he had censured Jérôme. Foolishly he expected every day to hear from Alexander with his terms for surrender. The Russians were quite prepared to play along with this delusion, so that futile diplomatic representations and bogus peace missions shuttled between Vilna and Moscow. While in Vilna the Emperor came under renewed Polish pressure to proclaim an independent Poland but still he refused, on the ground that he had given his word to his ally Austria. Disillusioned both with Bonaparte's duplicity and his army's exactions on Polish soil, the patriots voted with their feet; the expected extra volunteer corps and guerrilla fighters for the Russian front did not materialize.

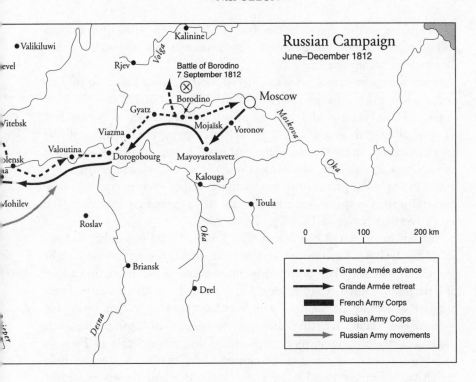

Leaving Vilna finally in mid-July, Napoleon with a few hard gallops soon caught up with his slow-moving army. Having failed to trap Bagration, he now made Barclay his target. On 25 July Murat caught up with the Russian rearguard and a sharp engagement took place at Ostrovno, a few miles west of Vitebsk, in which both Murat and Eugène performed impressively. Barclay, whose relations with Bagration had always been sour, was stung by the prince's taunts that he (Barclay) always ran away while ordering Bagration to hold fast. He therefore decided to stand and fight and drew up his army in battle order on 27 July. Napoleon, aware that he was between the two Russian armies, was overjoyed and looked forward to an easy victory. But he delayed going into action at once and waited for reinforcements to make the victory certain.

Next morning, however, there was no Barclay. Having learned that Bagration could not arrive to support him and was proposing instead to effect the junction of the two armies at Smolensk, Barclay slunk away in the night, leaving a disconsolate Napoleon empty-handed. The twenty-four-hour delay in joining battle, so untypical of the hero of Lodi, Marengo and Jena, meant that it was the second time in a month that French armies had failed to trap the enemy. Nothing had been achieved, Barclay and Bagration were now free to unite at Smolensk, and meanwhile a further 8,000 horses had died between Vilna and Vitebsk and 100,000 troops were absent from their units through illness, desertion or straggling.

It was a sombre Napoleon who entered Vitebsk at 8 a.m. on 29 July, to find a ghost town inhabited only by the sick and wounded and the local *canaille*. He at once held a council of war, where Berthier, Murat and Eugène all urged him strongly to halt the campaign in light of the enormous losses in men and matériel. At first he was inclined to acquiesce and again procrastinated, spending two weeks in Vitebsk and giving every indication of being prepared to winter there. Eugène was overjoyed to see him roll up his maps and declare that the 1812 campaign was over: 'We won't repeat Charles XII's folly,' he declared.

But this mood lasted just twenty-four hours. A cautious policy did not suit Napoleon's temperament and he was not the man to tarry eight months in Vitebsk when he could be in Moscow in twenty days. In vain did Berthier, Duroc, Caulaincourt, Eugène and all his intimates press him for a definite decision to winter either there or in Smolensk. He rounded on them, accusing them of being soft and pampered, with thoughts only of money, pleasure, hunting and the delights of Parisian social life. It was not for that, he chided them, that he had made them marshals of France. Besides, he knew Alexander and he was confident that he would not abandon either Smolensk or Moscow without a fight. 'The very danger pushes us on to Moscow. The die is cast. Victory will vindicate us.'

Once again (11 August) the *Grande Armée* resumed its reluctant march; the Emperor set out two days later. By this time the two Russian armies had united but the 'cold war' of mutual hatred between the two commanders undid most of the potential advantage of this. There was no question of a lightning strike towards Smolensk to catch Barclay and Bagration unawares, for such a step would simply mean the Army's outstripping its supply wagons. But the impatient Emperor still yearned to get behind the enemy so as to be between them and Moscow and thus force them finally to the battle they had so long avoided. Meanwhile Bagration and his circle, who had grown increasingly fretful at the constant retreating, taunted Barclay with cowardice and forced his hand. When the two Russian armies united at the beginning of August, making a force 125,000 strong, Barclay finally buckled under the pressure from his critics, who by this time included the Czar. He laid plans for a counterattack.

It has often been pointed out that Barclay had only two sensible options: either to turn Smolensk into an impregnable fortress or to advance to the Orsha gap. Barclay did neither, mainly because he feared Bagration was intriguing against him and would use any mistake he made to discredit him. He advanced cautiously. The first clash of arms, between the Cossacks and French cavalry, came at Inkovo to the north-west of Smolensk on 8 August. But when a further acrimonious clash of personalities led Bagration to withdraw cooperation, Barclay panicked at the thought of a possible ingenious Bonaparte counter-offensive and pulled back again. Napoleon, who had been hoping to lure Barclay into a trap, now opted for what he called the 'Smolensk manoeuvre': this involved a strategic envelopment which would place several French army corps in the enemy rear.

The Russians calculated that Napoleon would continue north of the river Dnieper along the Minsk-Smolensk-Moscow road, bypassing the city; he would cross the Dnieper only if he meant to attack Smolensk. The Emperor did the unexpected and crossed the river on a 15-mile front, using the unguarded bridge at Orsha and four pontoon bridges at Rosasna. At first things went well. Murat and Ney swept aside the single Russian division Barclay had stationed at Krasnoe, thirty miles from Smolensk, and moved in on the city, confident of being able to get round behind Barclay. By 14 August 175,000 French troops were south of the river. The envelopment would have worked, but for Barclay's panicky withdrawal, which once more took his forces out of range. The French began to encounter stiffer resistance than expected. At the approaches to the city the Russian defenders under Neveroski fought with ferocious courage while Murat wasted an entire day trying to smash through their lines with unsupported cavalry; but for this check the French would have reached Smolensk on the evening of 14 August. When Napoleon heard of Murat's failure, he ordered a 24-hour pause to regroup, losing the element of surprise and allowing Barclay and Bagration to pull back behind the defences of Smolensk.

The twenty-four hours should have given the Emperor pause for serious thought. The *Grande Armée* was losing 5–6,000 men a day from sickness and desertion; artillery horses had not been properly shod to deal with conditions on the steppes, so that large numbers of cannon were being left behind; the non-French troops were not performing well; the whole force was ill-equipped and in the rush to press men into service, large numbers of unfit men had been drafted. There was little versatility in the ranks, and Napoleon lamented the shortage of his old 'jack of all military trades' veterans. It now turned out that dragoons had been hurriedly transformed into lancers but did not know how to use their lances. The Army was down to 175,000 effectives in the central group and even while it shrank in size daily, the French army was dangerously strung out; what with Oudinot, who had defeated Wittgenstein at Polotsk, and MacDonald, who was besieging Riga, Napoleon's front extended 500 miles.

Moreover, if the Emperor had been honest with himself, he would have reflected that he was no longer the great captain of 1796 or 1805. The twenty-four hours stretched to thirty-six hours for it was only in the small hours of 16 August that French advance units began to probe the outskirts of Smolensk. Finally, the Emperor ordered a frontal assault, even though the city was well fortified and defended. It was to be a characteristic of the 1812 campaign that he tended to order frontal attacks of the kind he would have spurned in the days of his greatness. This time he justified his decision on the ground that, if he tried to ford the Dnieper to the east, he would be vulnerable to a Russian counterattack which could split his Army.

Accordingly, on 16 August, after a fierce bombardment of the city, he ordered the three corps under Ney, Davout and Poniatowski to take the suburbs of Smolensk. After grim hand-to-hand and building-to-building fighting, the French finally took possession of the outreaches but then found themselves faced by the fifteen-foot thick walls of the inner city. At dusk the Russians still held the old town, with the French firmly ensconced in the suburbs but with the prospect of a second siege of Acre before them. Next day there was more bloody fighting which barely altered the overall picture. At nightfall the Russians were still in possession of the city, having taken terrible losses but having also inflicted 10,000 casualties on the French in the two-day battle. Napoleon's critics are adamant that the battle was unnecessary, and that if he had crossed the Dnieper farther east he could have cut the Smolensk-Moscow road. It was the possibility of such a move that led the Russians to evacuate the city during the night of 17–18 August, following recriminations between Bagration and Barclay so vehement that relations between them finally and irretrievably broke down.

Once again it was Bagration's accusing Barclay of cowardice that caused violent antipathy. To Bagration, who wanted to stay and slug it out for a third day, the order to retreat came close to treason and was an insult to the patriots who fell in the defence of Smolensk. But Barclay had read his opponent better, and there is no doubt that if he had remained for a third day's fighting, he would have been surrounded. As it was, even when retreating fast he was nearly encircled. Ney and Junot got round behind him late on the 18th but the chance was lost when Junot refused to press the attack. When he heard the news next day, Napoleon was furious and told his aides: 'Junot has let them escape. He is losing the campaign for me.' Junot never recovered from the disgrace, went mad and finally threw himself out of a window to his death in July 1813. Perhaps his mind was already on the turn at Smolensk, for he was known to have brooded that he, alone of the Emperor's inner circle, had not received his marshal's baton, despite having started with Bonaparte at Toulon and been with him in Egypt and Austerlitz; in his own mind, too, he had been made the Duke of Abrantes for his 'sterling' services in Spain.

The main French Army began entering Smolensk at dawn on the 18th, to find it a smoking ruin and a charnel house of corpses; even hardened veterans vomited at the gruesome piles of dead and dying they saw. Napoleon meanwhile spent the day once again in inactivity and indecision, this time uncertain whether the Russians were retreating north or east and therefore reluctant to commit the bulk of his Army; yet again his inertia ruined the chance of finding the two enemy armies and splitting them. He was particularly at fault in not staying in close touch with Ney and Junot, whose timidity he might have been able to overrule; instead he returned from the front to Smolensk to rest at 5 p.m.

He was in vindictive mood that day. Fires were still raging through the battle-scarred city and the Emperor, with ill-judged levity, described the devastation as a second eruption of Vesuvius. Pointing to the inferno still raging, he nudged Caulaincourt: 'Isn't that a fine spectacle?' 'Horrible, sire,' Caulaincourt replied. Napoleon made a dismissive gesture. 'You should remember the saying of one of the Roman emperors: the corpse of an enemy always smells good.' It was noticeable that the Emperor, his keen sense of smell notwithstanding, was the only one who seemed unaffected by the stench of the dead and the scale of the suffering. In cynical mood he wrote to Mamet, his Foreign Minister, boasting that he had captured Smolensk without the loss of a single man. But he was not the only cynic. The Russians, in headlong flight, had the self-deceiving audacity to celebrate a solemn *Te Deum* in St Petersburg for the 'victories' of Vitebsk and Smolensk.

For another week Napoleon remained in Smolensk, seemingly still dithering, still undecided what to do next, but apparently hoping that the capture of the 'holy city' of Smolensk would make the Czar see reason and come to terms. While Murat was sent to dog Barclay's tracks, the Emperor brooded on his third failure to bring the Russians to a decisive battle. There seemed to have been a succession of errors: failure to scout Neveroski's defence force properly on the 14th, the day of inactivity on the 15th, underestimate of the fortifications of Smolensk which turned out to be much stronger than expected during the battle of 16–17th, the failure to cut the Moscow road initially and then the dispatch of the wrong commander (Junot) on the 18th to cut off Barclay's retreat.

But it seems that the week's delay in Smolensk was more a product of complacency than genuine indecision for, if we may believe Murat, the Emperor told him on the 17th that he was determined to pursue Barclay to the gates of Moscow if necessary; for that reason Murat felt suicidal and deliberately exposed himself to Russian shellfire that evening. If even a hard-driving hothead like Murat baulked at the idea of an advance on Moscow, it says much for the general mood in the French higher command. On St Helena Napoleon conceded that pressing on from Smolensk instead of wintering there was the greatest blunder of his life, but insisted there was more rationality in the decision than he had been credited with.

Time – and in Napoleon's mind it was always a question of time – was against him and so, knowing the risks, he committed the *Grande Armée* to a winter campaign for which it was unprepared. As he saw it, the pluses outnumbered the minuses. Russian morale was bound to grow with the propaganda advantage of an 'undefeated' army so that by 1813 they would be both materially and psychologically stronger while the French grew weaker; a six-month delay would enable Alexander to draw in his Moldavian and Finnish allies and press more men from the back country, to say nothing of the aid he might get from Britain. The canard that Napoleon had been halted in his tracks would give fresh heart to the Prussians and Austrians and might even persuade them to switch sides in the next campaigning season. An early offensive in 1813 against the overstretched French front would be 1807 all over again – and Napoleon had not forgotten Eylau.

On the other hand, Moscow was only 270 miles ahead, its inhabitants would panic if he advanced and, if the Czar would not fight for Smolensk, he would surely fight for Moscow. Napoleon still sought the decisive military victory that would bring Russia to the peace table, and his prestige and credibility demanded that he advance on Moscow; otherwise it could be said he had overreached himself and fallen short of his aims. But the overriding reason for Napoleon's decision was political rather than military. Aware of the depth of opposition to him in Paris, he could not afford to stay away for more than a year. So it was that the political tail, salted by the notables, wagged the military dog on the Russian front.

And so it was that Murat, Caulaincourt and all his marshals, with the single exception of Davout, urged him in vain to winter in Smolensk.

Their arguments were various: the Grand Army was now reduced to 160,000 effectives, many demoralized and exhausted, and would diminish further as fresh garrisons were left along the route; the problems of supply and horses were bound to multiply; if he lost a battle outside Moscow his plight would be desperate, but if he won he would be bottled up in Moscow for the six months of winter, unable to move against St Petersburg until spring and with an ever more tenuous supply line. Therefore he should dig in at Smolensk; both his flank armies had won victories, he still had time to capture Kiev and Riga this year and he could build up a new army behind the defensive screen at Smolensk by promising Polish independence. But Napoleon argued that there was a momentum in war which had to be seized. Excited by the news that Barclay was going to make a stand some fifty miles to the east, he exaggerated a skirmish fought at Valutino by Ney and Murat on 19 August (whose main result was another 6,000 French casualties), swept aside all objections and ordered an advance on Moscow. On 25 August the Grand Army left Smolensk.

Once again the soldiers suffered terribly on the onward march. Stifled by dust and pelted with rain, they used improvised masks against sandstorms and were reduced to slaking their thirst with horses' urine because of the shortage of water. Soon even that expedient became problematical, as the horses were dying in thousands from starvation: there were not enough fields for the horses to graze in and no time to let them eat their fill even if there were. One division which crossed the Niemen with 7,500 horses had just 1,000 left at the beginning of September. Yet another factor contributing to the wastage of horses was the cavalry tactics employed by the French. Alarmingly, Murat, the dashing cavalry commander, revealed on this campaign that he knew nothing whatever about the care of horses. Although the animals have about the same stamina as humans over long distances, they must be taken along slowly, alternating the walk and the trot, and fed well. At full gallop a horse could not cover more than three miles without great risk and could easily be killed by being forced to canter or slow gallop for five miles without rest.

Usually Napoleon was good at bolstering the morale of his men, but this time he remained aloof and did not share their hardships, choosing instead to travel in some style. His personal impedimenta included eight canteen wagons, a carriage for his wardrobe, two butlers, two valets, three cooks, four footmen and eight grooms. He himself usually travelled in a six-horse coach, sleeping on a makeshift couch if no suitable house or monastery was available when night fell. He worked all day long, even when in motion, since the carriage was fitted with a desk and lights. Such luxury might have been excusable in the Emperor but was barely tolerable in the case of the host of hangers-on who accompanied him: for their transport the huge imperial staff of aides and bureaucrats used up 52 carriages, 650 horses and innumerable carts.

On 5 September Napoleon found the Russians waiting in entrenched positions on the banks of the river Moskova, with their centre around the village of Borodino, and under a new commander. On 20 August the Czar had finally listened to the clamour against Barclay and the protests about continual retreat and appointed a new commander. General Michael Kutusov was a corpulent sixty-seven-year-old one-eyed womanizer and bon viveur but unquestionably the Russians' best captain. Lazy, lethargic, cautious, jealous of subordinates, reluctant to read or sign orders and generally wilful and unmalleable, Kutusov was none the less a soldier of deep cunning, shrewd intuition and keen instinct. Alexander, who blamed him for the débâcle at Austerlitz, never liked him, but was advised by his military council that no one else would do. A reluctant Czar made him Commander-in-Chief but with orders to abandon Barclay's Fabian approach and face the French in battle. Kutusov thought this was poor advice and, left to himself, would not have confronted Napoleon at Borodino. But faced with a direct order and under pressure of public opinion, he had no choice but to give battle.

He spent the 5th and 6th of September preparing his battle positions. The field of combat he chose was mainly open farmland from which the corn had just been harvested, with small copses of fir and birch dotted about. His right (under the demoted Barclay) was behind the river Kalatsha and his left on Borodino village astride the old post road between Moscow and Smolensk. In the centre was the Great Redoubt with eighteen big guns and flanking this the main army was drawn up on undulating countryside broken by streams and ravines which ran down to the new Smolensk-Moscow road. The Russian left-centre was deployed around the three redoubts of Semonovski and the left wing itself, under Bagration, covered the village of Utitsa. It was a very strong defensive position, manned by 120,000 Russian troops with 640 guns.

Napoleon took up station at the Schivardino redoubt (captured on 5 August), $1\frac{1}{2}$ miles west. He had fewer guns than the enemy (587) and his numbers were down to 130,000, less than a third of the front-line strength with which he had crossed the Niemen. Many of his men were sick, exhausted and half-starved by the endless marches that had outstripped convoy supplies. He needed all his ingenuity to overcome

Kutusov's clever dispositions, but astonished his marshals by opting for a direct frontal assault on the Russian right and centre, leaving Poniatowski to work round Bagration at Utitsa. Davout and Ney were to assault the redoubts of Semonovski while to Eugène de Beauharnais went the 'mission impossible' – a near-suicidal attack on the heavily armoured Great Redoubt. Junot's corps, Murat's cavalry and the Guard would be held in reserve. The battle plan was so unimaginative that Davout begged to be allowed to take 40,000 men and outflank the Russian left with an overnight march. A listless Emperor would not hear of it: 'Ah, you are always for turning the enemy. It is too dangerous a manoeuvre,' he told Davout.

This lacklustre response to an obvious suggestion has always puzzled military historians. It is well known that on 6–7 September the Emperor was ill, with a heavy cold and a bladder infection, and to this illness the many mishaps at Borodino are sometimes attributed. Others say that by now he was worried by the calibre of his cavalry and the morale of his infantry and that lack of numbers meant he had to rule out the idea of detaching a large corps. But the more likely explanation is that Napoleon was now desperate for a battle at all costs, having seen the Russians slip through his net three times already. An additional factor may have been that just before Borodino he received word that Wellington had won a great victory at Salamanca in Spain. Circumstantial evidence works in favour of this interpretation, for during the night of 6–7 September the Emperor constantly rose from his bed to reassure himself that the Russians were still there and had not once more melted away into the night. It was not until 2 a.m. that he felt confident enough to issue one of his famous bulletins.

The battle began with an artillery barrage at 6 a.m. on 7 September. Then Napoleon ordered his forces forward. Ney and Davout performed well but necessarily made slow progress over broken ground so, just two hours into the battle, the Emperor committed Junot's corps from the reserve. When Poniatowski attacked Bagration, Kutusov immediately transferred troops from his right to prevent breakthrough. The Russian commander then took the initiative, outflanking Borodino with his cavalry; while the French attended to this threat, the assault on the Great Redoubt was delayed. The marshals began to grow restive: the Emperor was not at the front of his army, inspiring and exhorting his men while watching minutely every nuance in the ebb and flow of battle; instead, he remained in the rear, ill, indecisive, listless and querulous, suspicious of the accuracy of every report brought to him. In frustration, Ney burst out with: 'Why is the Emperor in the rear of the army? If . . . he is no longer a general . . . then he should go back to the Tuileries and let us be generals for him.'

The first breakthrough for the French came with the fall of Utitsa, during which Bagration was mortally wounded. But a lull allowed the Russians to move men across and hold the line at prepared positions. Predictably, however, the centrepiece of the entire battle was the titanic struggle for the Great Redoubt, which went on in more or less intense form from 7 a.m. to 3 p.m. Eugène managed to take Borodino village but could make no headway against the Redoubt. During his first full-scale assault on it, a murderous struggle developed. Eyewitnesses said that cannonballs and shells fell like hail and the smoke was so thick that one could only rarely make out the enemy. Repulsed, the French fell back while the first massive cavalry battle of the day engaged attention. Napoleon decided to commit his penultimate reserves and unleashed Murat but he too failed to make a breakthrough. It was not until early afternoon that Eugène's second onslaught at last made some ground when a cuirassier division finally broke into the rear of the Redoubt. After a second great cavalry battle the French held on to their gains; the whole of the original Russian line was taken but Kutusov simply retreated to the next ridge and formed up again.

This was the moment when Napoleon could have won an outright victory by sending in the Guard. But, despite many urgent entreaties from the marshals he refused to do so. The usual explanation is his illness, but there was more to it than that. The Emperor *never* liked to use the Guard, whatever the circumstances, almost as though he were a Corsican peasant with one final secret hoard of gold that the tax collector knew nothing of. In this particular case, other considerations weighed. He felt that he was too far from his main base of operations to take any risks which was partly why he had vetoed Davout's flanking movement. And, knowing well that even victory now would be no Austerlitz or Friedland, he hesitated to commit the flower of his army, reckoning that there must be at least one more battle to come.

He may also have been appalled at the scale of slaughter he had already witnessed. Some authorities claim that Borodino was the worst single day's fighting in all history. The *Grande Armée* alone fired 90,000 artillery rounds and two million infantry cartridges. The Russians lost 44,000 dead and wounded and the French 35,000, though some military historians have claimed this is a conservative estimate and the true total for the day's casualties is 100,000; it seems that initial estimates of death rolls in Russian warfare are always timid, so that the higher figure is plausible. Even if we take the lowest possible figure, a modern observer has commented that this is the equivalent of a fully loaded Boeing 747 crashing with no survivors every five minutes for eight hours. Whenever the Emperor trained his field-glasses on the Great Redoubt, he was cast down by what he saw: the Russians fought with such fanatical stubborness that he remarked wearily to Berthier and Caulaincourt: 'These Russians let themselves be killed as if they were not human beings at all but machines; they are not taken prisoner . . . this is not helping us. They are citadels which only cannonballs can demolish.'

During the night of 7 September the Russians stole away from their second line of defence. No attempt was made to impede their departure, since the exhausted French army had been fought to a standstill. Kutusov took the difficult but heroic decision to abandon Moscow, arguing that as long as the Army continued in being Russia could prevail, despite the loss of its great city. Seven days of unopposed marching brought the Emperor within sight of the cupolas and onion-domes of Moscow which, despite its population of 250,000, retained its medieval look. But instead of the deputation of Muscovite nobles he had expected to 'wait on' him, he found merely another ghost town. Only 25,000 people were left in the deserted and eerie city and these, apart from foreigners and the sick and wounded, were the criminals that Kutusov would not allow to join in the mass exodus.

The day after Napoleon entered Moscow, a great fire engulfed the city and raged unchecked for three days. Properly speaking, several independent fires were started simultaneously by Russian arsonists under the orders of the Governor of Moscow, Count Rostopchin, who had distributed explosive fuses to groups of saboteurs. When the French tried to extinguish the flames, they discovered that Rostopchin had removed all fire engines and destroyed all other fire-fighting equipment. Napoleon expressed disgust at this action by the Russians: surely only barbarians would burn down their own cities: could anyone imagine him ordering the gutting of Paris? But the rankers in the Grand Army took advantage of the three-day confusion to loot and pillage with impunity, telling anyone who questioned their actions that they were 'salvaging' goods from the inferno.

It was 18 September before the Emperor managed to stop the looting, restore discipline and put his commissariat on a proper basis. Taking up residence in the Kremlin, Napoleon remained blithely confident that he had only to sit it out and Alexander would come begging to make peace. While he waited for emissaries to arrive, the Russians played him at his own game and so regained the initiative. Kutusov encouraged fraternization between his Cossacks and the French cavalry, insinuating the idea that peace was just around the corner. Meanwhile he steadily added to the 70,000 men he had been able to take away from Borodino. With local reinforcements and the arrival of two fresh armies (Wittgenstein's from Finland and Tornassov's from the south), he amassed a fighting force 215,000 strong; Napoleon's numbers had meanwhile shrunk to 95,000.

Frustrated at the non-arrival of Russian emissaries, Napoleon urged Caulaincourt to undertake a mission to St Petersburg, but the ambassador told his Emperor that all such overtures made to the stubborn Alexander would be in vain. In fact obduracy was not the only factor that limited the Czar's freedom of action; he was under constraints and if he had so much as bargained with the French he would undoubtedly have been deposed or assassinated. Moreover, he saw well enough the difficulty the French were in and realized he held all the cards. In the end Napoleon sent General Lauriston to treat with Kutusov, initially to secure a *laissez-passer* for an embassy to St Petersburg. Kutusov refused to allow Lauriston to proceed but agreed to take Bonaparte's letter, proposing a compromise peace to the Czar; he did so, but Alexander did not even deign to read it.

In the Kremlin, Napoleon was deluged with bad news. Communications with Smolensk were becoming increasingly difficult as the Spanish nightmare repeated itself, and semi-autonomous groups of peasant guerrillas sprang into existence. Soon their leaders' names became as well known as those of the *bandidos* in Spain: Davidov, Figner, Chetverakov. These men pioneered the atrocities that would make the 1812 campaign in Russia one of the most ghastly in all history. Davidov's method was to greet the French with exaggerated courtesy, offer them food and drink, then slit their throats when they were drunk or asleep. The bodies would then be burned in pigsties or deep in the forests, for French retaliation was swift if ever they discovered newly-turned graves near a village. Since so many patrols and supply convoys were cut off or ambushed by Russian partisans, Napoleon was forced to issue orders that no force less than 1,500-strong should ever leave Smolensk.

The Emperor knew from his Spanish experience that nothing demoralized his men more than a war where to be taken prisoner meant a far worse fate than a swift death in battle. He therefore tried to secure a guarantee from Kutusov that atrocities would cease. Kutusov sloughed off the responsibility and claimed that he could control only the troops in his army. When Napoleon sent a formal letter demanding that a code of behaviour be imposed on the peasants, Kutusov disingenuously replied as follows: 'It is difficult to control a people who for three hundred years have never known war within their frontiers, who are ready to immolate themselves for their country, and who are not susceptible to the distinction between what is and what is not the usage of civilized warfare.' Certainly a novel defence for war crimes.

As it became increasingly obvious that both Kutusov and the Czar were stalling and all hopes of a negotiated peace were vain, Napoleon's mood became increasingly uncertain and febrile. Unable fully to comprehend Alexander's 'unreasonable' stance, he clung to self-delusion and donned a mask of false optimism, in reality oscillating between inertia and anxiety. Louis-Philippe Ségur, whose diary is one of the most important sources for the campaign, wrote: 'He prolonged his meals, which had hitherto been so simple and short. He seemed desirous of stifling thought by repletion. He would pass whole hours half-reclined, as if torpid and awaiting, with a novel in his hand.'

Despite his previous scorn for novels, during the frustrating days in the Kremlin he would often take them up but found them impossible to read; he would stay on the same page for half an hour while his preoccupied mind drifted off elsewhere. Sometimes he would seek oblivion by playing *vingt-et-un* with Eugène de Beauharnais. More and more he seemed to be in a dream world. When told his troops needed winter clothing, he issued orders for their manufacture, but did not solve the question of who was to manufacture them and where in a deserted city. When informed that the artillery was short of horses, he at once authorized the purchase of 20,000 fresh mounts, though everyone knew there were no fresh horses to be had. Finally, at a war council on 30 September attended by Murat, Davout, Ney, Eugène and Berthier, he proposed marching on St Petersburg. This chimerical idea was at once howled down by the marshals and Napoleon may not have been wholly serious in suggesting it, but at least it held out the chance of activity rather than stagnation, which is what the Emperor most wanted.

Yet finally the nettle had to be grasped: was the *Grande Armée* to winter in Moscow, or was any other strategy feasible? Napoleon's increasingly neurotic state was a reflection of his dilemma: he knew that whatever course he opted for was fraught with risk and that he would never forgive himself if he chose wrongly. This is surely why he again delayed in a Russian city for no good reason, this time for a precious 35 days. It has been remarked wryly that it would have been better if the great fire of 15–17 September had completely destroyed Moscow, as the Emperor would then have been forced out. The options, repeatedly canvassed at war councils of the marshals, were essentially threefold:

remain in Moscow for six months; seek a second battle with Kutusov and then continue south to the pleasanter weather and richer landscape of Kiev and the Ukraine; or retreat to Smolensk prior to an advance on St Petersburg in the spring of 1813.

The second option, seeking a second battle and marching to Kiev, appealed to Napoleon, who was reluctant to retreat without winning a decisive victory over Kutusov. But the sheer volume of military, logistical and commissariat problems envisaged told against it in an army that could barely keep open its lines of communication with Smolensk. But Napoleon was unhappy about the prospect of a perilous 50-day retreat to the Niemen; contemplating his losses in the supposedly 'easy' season of summer, how could he view the prospect of a winter trek with equanimity? As Caulaincourt pointed out, the Grand Army lacked everything necessary to combat the winter: sheepskins, stout fur-lined gloves, caps with ear-flaps, warm boot-socks, heavy boots to protect the feet against frostbite; frost nails for the horses' hooves. On the face of it, then, there seemed much to be said for the idea of remaining in Moscow, especially since there was enough food in the city to feed the army for six months.

But Napoleon was still uneasy. It was true that his troops in Moscow had plenty of food, but if he tried to maintain the military *status quo* in Russia, his other far-flung units would starve. Kutusov would grow in numbers, resources and confidence all winter; what if the *Grande Armée* was beset by sickness, so that its numbers dwindled even further? There was assuredly no hope of reinforcements from the west until next spring, and what would happen if Kutusov launched another winter campaign, as the Russians had in 1806–07? The memory of the slaughter at Eylau, conflated with the recent bloodbath at Borodino, was enough to deter even the most reckless gambler. Yet possibly even more important than these weighty considerations, was the old political imperative: Napoleon could not afford to be away from Paris so long.

At last the Emperor ended his vacillation and, on 17 October, ordered that the retreat to the Niemen should begin two days later. Then came news of a near disaster to Murat's advance guard at Vinkovo. After three weeks of shadowboxing with the Cossacks, and becoming used to the presence of Kutusov's advance guard just an hour's march away, Murat grew careless. Kutusov, meanwhile, under intense pressure to take action instead of, as he advised, waiting for 'General Winter' to finish off the French, suddenly launched a surprise attack. Inflicting 2,500 casualties the Russian offensive came close to annihilating Murat who, however, managed to turn the tide at the eleventh hour. Furious with Murat for lowering his guard, Napoleon was none the less badly shaken and there was an air of panic about the announcement that the departure would be brought forward by twenty-four hours. Ahead loomed fifty days that would confirm Bonaparte's greatness or destroy his power forever.

CHAPTER TWENTY-THREE

Napoleon left Moscow with the aim of rejoining the 37,000 men of IX Corps at Smolensk, using the supplies and arsenals there, and thus appearing to good advantage at the end of the hitherto disastrous Russian campaign. He made yet another of a catalogue of mistakes in 1812 by failing to order his men to travel light and fast. Weakly he allowed them to take their immense hoards of booty with them, arguing that they needed proofs of their 'victory' in the campaign. The result was a tatterdemalion marching column well described by Louis-Philippe de Ségur, an eyewitness: 'It looked like a caravan, a wandering nation, or rather, like one of those armies of antiquity returning with slaves and spoil after a great devastation.'

The army marched in wide parallel columns towards Kaluga. Not even the regimental commanders were told the true destination of the once proud Grand Army. The seeds of a disaster were all there in the form of insufficient food and inadequate winter clothing; there was horse fodder for less than a week. As the man appointed 'Governor of Moscow' during the 35-day sojourn, it fell to Mortier and 8,000 of the Young Guard to remain behind in Moscow to set fuses, blow up the Kremlin and gut the city. Mortier, angry that one in seven of the Guard had succumbed on the march to Moscow through heat, starvation, fatigue and desertion, disobeyed his orders and spent the time trying to collect supplies for the perilous homeward march. It was not until 23 October that he finally quit Moscow. It was lucky for him, and the *Grande Armée* in general that Kutusov's military intelligence was so poor that he did not learn of the French retreat until the 22nd.

Napoleon had originally intended to strike south and west across country unravaged by war and therefore plentiful in supplies. Because of a signal failure of nerve, he instead directed his army on 26 October to follow the outward route – the post road leading north-west to Smolensk – terrain which had been devastated first by the Russian scorched-earth policy and then by the advancing French army. A crow flying over this barren area would have needed to carry its own provisions. The decision to divert from the south-westerly route meant that the destruction of the French army became inevitable. So what led Napoleon to yet another error of judgement, and this one the worst yet?

Moving swiftly in pursuit of the encumbered *Grande Armée*, Kutusov caught up with it at the river crossing at Maloyaroslavets on 23 October. Next day a ferocious battle for the town took place, during which it changed hands seven times before the Italian corps under General Pino rose to the occasion and drove the Russians out. Both sides withdrew, prior, so it seemed, to a second Borodino. But then both commanders dithered. Kutusov was shaken by the stirring performance of the Italians and broke off contact to lick his wounds. Napoleon's scouts reported Kutusov's army well dug in, too strong to attack. The Emperor was downcast and indecisive: he told Caulaincourt mournfully: 'I always beat the Russians but it never seems to solve anything.' He nearly had even more serious reason for depression: at 4 a.m. a Cossack patrol came within an ace of capturing him; it turned out that the Old Guard had unaccountably failed to place pickets.

Convinced that his famous luck had deserted him, Napoleon sought sanctuary in the known, however terrible, rather than in the unknown on the south-western route. Never had his gambler's instinct more obviously failed him; he did not even send out scouts on the Kaluga road, for had he done so he would have discovered it was clear and unopposed. Instead he called a council on 25 October, attended by Eugène, Murat, Davout, Bessières and Berthier, at which the reluctant decision was taken to follow the devastated road to Smolensk through Borosk, Mojaisk, Gzatsk and Viasma. The Emperor half-heartedly suggested a return to Moscow, but this was shouted down. Murat boldly opted to continue via Kaluga even if it meant risking another battle, but the other marshals fell in eagerly with the idea that a north-westerly retreat might drop Kutusov astern, especially as he seemed to be retiring southwards. When Bessières ventured to use the taboo word 'retreat', no one demurred.

Napoleon's panic – no other word will do – after the bruising encounter at Maloyaroslavets shows he was no longer the great captain he once was. The young Bonaparte would have seen the importance of Maloyaroslavets and secured it long before the Russians got there. Besides, the decision taken on 25 October evinces the utmost mental confusion. Once the possibility of retreating from Moscow loomed, the Emperor should have bent all his energies to gathering adequate supplies for the Army. Moreover, if, as he claimed, his purpose in taking the south-westerly route was to sweep Kutusov from his path, why did he shirk the challenge when it came? If the fear of further casualties deterred him, why had not similar considerations ruled out the march on Moscow after Borodino? As it was, the battle of Maloyaroslavets followed by the diversion in route to the outward itinerary meant that a week had been lost for no good reason; this lost week was to be crucial later on.

Having handed Kutusov a great strategic victory on a plate, Napoleon managed to coax his army to complete the fifty miles from Maloyaroslavets to Mojaisk in two days (27–28 October). Next day they marched through the village of Borodino, skirting the battlefield. Psychologically, this had a disastrous affect on morale. Although the men tried to shield their eyes they could not avoid the sight of the 30,000 corpses on which wolves had fed, the immense tomb-like open grave into which bodies had been shovelled, the wheeling of carrion crows in the sky or the stench of myriad rotting corpses. At 2 a.m. on 30 October Napoleon asked Caulaincourt for a prognosis. He replied that things could only get worse: the weather would grow colder and the Russians stronger. The self-deceiving Emperor argued lamely that the superior native intelligence of the French would allow them to prevail.

Kutusov's failure to move in with his vastly superior numbers and finish off the French has forever puzzled military historians. Kutusov has his claque of admirers who see him as a brilliant Fabius to Bonaparte's Hannibal, but there has always been a revisionist point of view that sees him as bumbling and inept, slow and ponderous by nature rather than design. The most interesting suggestion is that Kutusov believed the destruction of the *Grande Armée* would ultimately benefit England more than Russia and so, as an Anglophobe who suspected the British of being an ungrateful, unreliable and treacherous ally, he refrained from delivering the *coup de grâce*. Those who champion Kutusov sometimes advance the unlikely suggestion that he was so keen to avoid casualties among his own men that he preferred to allow starvation, panic, demoralization and 'General Winter' to do his job for him.

The most sinister interpretation is that Kutusov did not want to take prisoners so he allowed the peasant guerrillas to exact their own grisly revenge; it is significant that he remained insouciant when Lauriston complained to him about atrocities by the partisans. Russian cynicism has since been rewritten in the form of a myth about a 'people's war', supposedly analogous to that visited on the Germans by Tito's partisans in 1942–44. Nothing could be less historically sound. Class antagonism in early nineteenth-century Russia was so acute that the nobility would have been terrified of a genuine people's war, since they would, rightly, identify themselves as next in the line of fire after the French. The thing that most terrified the oligarchy of Moscow and St Petersburg in 1812 was the possibility that Napoleon might free the serfs, as they themselves urged him to. So fearful was the Russian élite of the peasantry that it armed most of the rural militias with useless pikes; near Moscow peasants who took up arms against French foragers were actually arrested as mutineers. The fear was well grounded: in December 1812 there were serious riots among Russian militia regiments raised in the province of Penza.

It cannot be stressed enough that the Russian peasants did not fight out of patriotic fervour but for loot, for self-defence and, most of all, for revenge. Napoleon could not have selected a worse itinerary, for the fury of the peasants on this route was incandescent; this was the third time in as many months they had been looted and despoiled by marauding armies. It was noteworthy that when they had a choice, the peasants kept out of the war and refrained from 'scorched earth' policies – for, after all, what did that mean but the destruction of their own flocks and produce without compensation. 'People's war' is a pure myth: the burned crops and poisoned wells were the work of the Cossacks and the army; when the French penetrated areas where the Russian army had never been, everything was intact and supplies were plentiful.

It is quite clear that the dreadful atrocities visited on French prisoners, stragglers or the wounded were the expression of a terrible displaced homicidal fury towards the Russian nobility: the peasants were doing with impunity to an invader what, but for fear of death, they would have done to their own masters. Displaced fury and rage projected on to their own kind goes far to explain the frightful tradition of cruelty in Russian peasant life. The peasants thought nothing of stripping adulterous wives naked and beating them half to death or tying them to the end of a wagon and dragging them naked though a village, or castrating horse thieves, branding housebreakers with hot irons or hacking other petty criminals to death with sickles. Gogol later spoke of the exceptional cruelty of the Russian people, and the peasantry in particular. Partly it was a function of a culture in which life was held cheap, partly a reflex action to a harsh environment, but mostly it was an internalization of the brutality to which the peasants had been subjected by their 'betters'.

But if the Russian nobility had sowed the wind, it was the luckless French Army in 1812 that reaped the whirlwind. The fortunate ones taken by the partisans would suffer a quick if agonizing death, being impaled on stakes or thrown alive into vats of boiling water. For the less fortunate more hideous ends lay in store. The peasants would offer large sums to the Cossacks to be able to take over their prisoners. Then they would subject them to stomach-turning tortures: eyes were pulled out, nails hammered into the body, legs and arms cut off to leave a bleeding torso, stakes driven down the throat. One of two particularly favoured methods was to wrap a naked victim in a wet sack with a pillow tied around the torso; villagers would then vie with one another to beat the stomach with hammers, logs and stones, so that the internal organs were crushed but no marks were left. Another was to raise the victim on a pulley with hands and feet tied together; he would then be dropped so that the vertebrae in his back were broken. The process was continued until the prisoner was reduced to a spineless sack.

News of the fate that awaited them if captured ran through the ranks of the *Grande Armée*, causing terror. Such was the soldiers' fear of the partisans that they would attempt suicide if taken prisoner, and the more humane Russian officers simply shot their captives out of hand to spare them the insane attentions of the peasants. Lest it be thought that stories of Russian atrocities lost nothing in the telling, it is worth citing three instances recorded by Sir Robert Wilson, a British observer with the Russian Army. After subjecting their prisoners to horrible tortures, the partisans first burnt a group of some fifty French troops alive; a second group of the same number was buried alive; while for the third group, about sixty strong, a kind of death by peasant bacchanalia was prepared. The prisoners were stripped naked, then spreadeagled across a large felled tree with their necks protruding as if on the executioner's block; peasant men and women then hopped about singing in chorus while they beat out the prisoners' brains with hoes and cudgels.

That large numbers of wounded were rounded up to share this gruesome fate was largely the fault of the callous French wagoneers. When carts jolted over rutted tracks, the wounded would naturally scream in agony. Exasperated by this, the drivers liked to crack the whip to accelerate, thus bouncing off their ululating charges; the lucky ones were run over by the carts following behind, and the unlucky ones left for wolves to devour or the partisans to execute in their frightful way. Sir Robert Wilson conveyed some of the flavour of the French panic-stricken retreat in a famous description:

> The naked masses of dead and dying men; the mangled carcasses of 10,000 horses which had in some cases been cut for food before life had ceased; the craving of famine at other points forming groups of cannibals; the air enveloped in flame and smoke; the prayers of hundreds of naked wretches flying from the peasantry, whose shouts of vengeance echoed incessantly through the woods; the wrecks of cannon, powder-waggons, all stores of every description: it formed

such a scene as probably was never witnessed in the history of the world.

Wilson makes the important point that, even without the presence of the murderous partisans, the Grand Army would have been in grave trouble from lack of equipment and horses. Soon the French discarded uniforms in favour of anything that gave a little warmth, be it stolen or looted merchants' winter coats, women's furs and even Chinese or Tartar apparel. The very appearance of the army worked against its morale, as it looked like a gigantic troupe of itinerant mountebanks or some Dantean version of a travelling circus.

Meanwhile the horses, which had died in tens of thousands on the outward march, succumbed in even larger numbers on the retreat. In the early days, on an inadequate diet of pine and willow bark, they were too exhausted to pull the artillery out of the mud and, when the snow and ice came, they could not walk at all. Not having been fitted with winter shoes (small iron spikes or crampons), they simply slithered helplessly on the snow and ice. Miraculously, almost until the end the French were still somehow able to mount cavalry charges, but mostly the horses simply dropped in their tracks. For hundreds of miles the *Grande Armée* lived mainly on horseflesh.

Napoleon's once proud host was on the verge of extinction even before it reached Smolensk. They had run out of provisions and there were no more to be had in the desolate and ravaged countryside. Mortier, who had hitherto survived with the Young Guard in the rear on an exclusive diet of brandy and biscuits, found himself by 8 November reduced to eating horse's liver washed down with snow. More and more men abandoned their booty, and then their weapons. When Napoleon reached Viasma, there was already a 50-mile column straggling behind him, with the rearguard looking like a rabble of refugees, with masses of starving camp-followers strung out behind it. As the Army approached Smolensk, attacks intensified: on 3 November I Corps was cut off near Fiodoroivsky and only narrowly rescued by the intervention of IV Corps. And now what Napoleon had most dreaded finally came to pass: the intervention of 'General Winter'. The first snow flurries fell on 5 November and by 7 November it was snowing heavily.

Napoleon reached Smolensk on 9 November to find that all his hopes of wintering in a secure base in the city were vain. No less than four items of depressing intelligence rained in on him and made him aware that he would have to retreat immediately all the way back to the Niemen. First, the city governor, General Charpentier, informed him that the stocks of food were not at the expected high levels, since Victor's and Oudinot's corps had taken most of it when they headed north. Secondly, his spies reported that the Russians were manoeuvring to cut off his escape. While Kutusov dogged his steps, moving parallel to the French column a little to the south, Wittgenstein was heading for the Beresina to seize the bridges there while on the other flank Tshitsagov threatened the great French supply dump at Minsk. Thirdly, word came of an attempted coup in Paris by General Malet (the Emperor first heard of this on 6 November). Finally, as the most pressing immediate problem, it was clear that French morale had collapsed completely. An entire division of reinforcements under General Baraguey d'Hilliers surrendered lamely to an inferior force south-west of Smolensk.

Napoleon remained in Smolensk for three days, trying vainly to instil order into chaos. As more and more intelligence reached him, it must have seemed to the Emperor that all the powers of heaven were conspiring against him. MacDonald, it transpired, had abandoned the siege of Riga and was currently lolling in inactivity, while Schwarzen-berger's corps to the south were also out of the picture. And by the time the rearguard entered Smolensk, there was no food for them. In a ruthless application of 'first come, first served', the vanguard ate up all the food stocks, gorging themselves with no thought of their fellow-soldiers toiling in the rear. At first quartermasters asked for chits and ration books, but the hungry men brushed them aside, took what they wanted, broke into the reserve warehouses and consumed everything there too.

Unable to control this rabble, Napoleon vented his fury on the governor, Charpentier, who explained meekly that he had had no power to countermand the orders of Oudinot and Victor, his superior in rank. The Emperor was reduced to watching helplessly while his men enjoyed the crudest form of 'rest and recreation' – huddling in improvised camps amid the rubble of the city they had destroyed three months earlier. The infuriated rearguard, finding all the food gone, sacked and looted whatever they could find in mindless acts of desperation. Cannibalism became rampant as men ate the charred flesh of fallen comrades.

On 12 November Napoleon and the vanguard moved out of Smolensk, now seriously concerned that the Dnieper crossing at Orsha and the Beresina crossing at Orshov might already be in enemy hands. His army was now a barely credible fighting force: a muster at Smolensk revealed that numbers were down to 41,000, as against the 96,000 present at Maloyaroslavets and the 65,000 left at Viasma. Even so, the survivors did not form a compact force but were still strung out: it was not until the 17th that Ney and the rearguard got clear of Smolensk.

Leaving Smolensk on icy roads, the *Grande Armée* literally slid and slithered the first 15 miles, which they covered in 22 hours. By now it was snowing heavily; visibility was severely limited in thick blizzards; the breath of the exhausted soldiers froze on their beards; the heavy weight of the snow on their boots made every step an ordeal. Some sank into crevasses formed by sunken lanes or excavated earth and never rose again. With temperatures ranging from a high of $-20°$ F to a low of $-30°$, frostbite was common.

Napoleon forced the pace, ordering fourteen hours marching a day, much of it in darkness since by now there was daylight only between the hours of 8 a.m. and 4 p.m. There was no shelter and little rest and their clothes, sodden with snow, froze on their bodies. The nights were if anything even worse. In the first place it was hard to light fires from frozen pine branches, and when the fires were lit places nearest the flames were sold to the highest bidder. Too far from the fire, and you risked freezing to death or being picked off by the lupine partisans who were attracted to the beacons of light. Too near, and you were in danger, when returning to the cold, of suffering gangrene on the extremities.

Food and drink could scarcely be had at any price. Many men were killed when they swallowed snow to quench their thirst. Steaks were cut from the haunches of horses on the hoof: numbed by the cold, the animals felt no pain and their wounds would congeal in sixteen degrees of frost, but they would die later from septicaemia. At dawn a line of ragged, bedraggled and increasingly shoeless men began dragging themselves through the snow, leaving behind a deserted camp-village of corpses, cannons and wagons. Many companies who managed to sleep in comfort around a roaring fire after dining on horseflesh lost the will to march on in the morning and were still apathetically sitting by their fires when the Cossacks or partisans caught up with them.

The languishing army struggled on until 17 November when Kutusov unexpectedly launched an attack. Six miles east of Krasnyi a force of 20,000 Russians under Miloradovich cut the road between Napoleon's vanguard and Eugène de Beauharnais's corps. Eugène resisted stubbornly and sent to the Emperor for reinforcements. Napoleon sent back Mortier and the Young Guard, whom after Smolensk he had switched to the van. The Young Guard acquitted themselves brilliantly and forced the Russians to break off the action. But if Eugène was now safe, Davout was not. Napoleon was finally forced to send his 16,000 'immortals' of the Old Guard into action. The Guard proved as good as their reputation and routed the Russians in short order. The Russian Colonel Davidov reported that the Guard scythed through the Cossacks 'like a hundred-gun warship through fishing boats'.

Napoleon now thought his rearguard was safe and was dumbfounded when the rescued Davout came to report that he had lost contact with Ney. Instead of leaving Smolensk together, Ney and Davout's corps had unaccountably left on separate days. Though the explanation was yet another mix-up in the imperial orders, Napoleon chose to fasten the blame on him for what seemed to be Ney's certain annihilation. It says much for Davout's moral fibre that he did not lose confidence in the Emperor from that moment; as for Davout himself, having alienated both Jerome and Murat on this campaign he was lucky to have the influential figures of Duroc and Bessières still speaking up for him.

Ney meanwhile experienced adventures that no historical novelist could cap. He left Smolensk with 6,000 men on the 17th and made rapid progress towards Krasnyi on the 18th only to find the defeated but still substantial forces of Miloradovich across the road that led to the rest of the Grand Army and safety. Undaunted by the thought that Kutusov had a total force of 80,000 somewhere ahead of him, Ney attacked and with just 3,000 effectives broke the Russians' first line. Driven back from the second line by artillery and the sheer weight of Russian numbers, he dug in at a ravine, expecting at any minute to be overwhelmed by Kutusov's hordes. Kutusov, however, had been badly shaken by the mauling encounter with the Old Guard, and hesitated to press home the attack. Dusk fell.

Under cover of darkness Ney found his way to the Dnieper where, incredibly, his men were able to 'island hop' from one ice floe to another and so gain the far bank. But the cost was high since only 2,000 men reached the far side of the Dnieper; another 3,000 troops and a further 4,000 stragglers and camp followers were abandoned. All next day, under heavy Cossack attack, Ney's men hugged the river and surrounding woodland while they covered the 45 miles to Orsha. By nightfall they were down to 1,500 men and had constantly to form square to fend off marauding Cossacks. At 9 p.m. Ney resumed the march and, gambling that Orsha was still in French hands, sent a courier ahead asking for help. The message was received by Eugène, who throughout the horrors had consistently enhanced his military reputation. He set out at the head of a rescuing force, and early next morning he and Ney embraced each other as heroes. At 5 a.m. on 21 November, to universal amazement and joy, Ney arrived to join the main army with just 900 survivors. Napoleon was overjoyed and dubbed Ney 'the bravest of the brave'. He added further plaudits: 'I would sooner have given 300 millions from my treasury than lose such a man,' he said.

Ney's totally unlooked-for arrival temporarily lifted morale, which had taken a battering at the Dnieper. The Grand Army reached Orsha to find the river bridges intact and a two-day supply of food for 40,000, but there were two pieces of devastatingly bad news. First, Minsk, with its store of two million individual rations, had fallen to the Russians. Secondly, and more immediately threatening, it now seemed certain that Tshitsakov would beat them to the Beresina crossings at Boritsov. 'This is beginning to be very serious,' Napoleon confided to Caulaincourt, before ordering the destruction of all surplus transport and impedimenta, preparatory to another gruelling forced march.

Beyond Orsha there was finally some relief for the beleaguered *Grande Armée*. The local people here, though not friendly, were not Russian and did not go in for massacres and atrocities. The worst of the ordeal from fellow-humans was over, and at first it looked as though the same might apply to the ordeal by element, for a thaw set in, so that the troops could sleep at night without fearing death. Ironically, the thaw also threatened the Army with total destruction, for the change in weather had turned a hard-frozen polar surface into a seething torrent. Normally in late November the river was frozen to a depth of several feet of ice, so that the Army could have crossed the river anywhere with complete safety. The same was the case in November 1812 until the last week of the month. Here was yet another fatal consequence of the Emperor's many unreasonable urban delays.

By 22 November Napoleon already knew from his spies that Tshitsagov had destroyed the Beresina bridges. This meant that the French were now virtually surrounded, with Wittgenstein's 30,000 men and Tshitsagov with another 34,000 ahead of them and Kutusov's 80,000 in their rear. With the bridges down and without bridging equipment of their own, the French seemed doomed as they had just 49,000 effectives (with 250 guns) and 40,000 militarily useless stragglers. Fearing the worst, Napoleon ordered all state papers and regimental tricolors burnt.

What saved the Emperor at this desperate juncture was a combination of Russian timidity and the most amazing good luck. Mindful of Borodino and Krasnyi, Kutusov kept at a safe distance, some thirty miles away. Then Oudinot came in to report to Napoleon what sounded like a miracle. General Corbineau, approaching the Beresina from Vilna and the west, found an unmarked ford near Studienka village, which he had bribed a peasant to reveal to him. Corbineau crossed the river on 23 November and reported that a traverse by the whole army was feasible.

But how to build the bridges? At this point it transpired that a certain General Eblé had taken the forethought the Emperor should have exercised. Against orders he had saved two field-forges, two wagons of charcoal and six of sapper tools and bridging equipment. If there was timber near Studienka, where the crossing was unopposed, and if the Emperor could distract the Russians on the far side who were guarding all the likely bridging places, a small miracle could yet be achieved.

Now, for the first time during the 1812 campaign, Napoleon returned to something like his best form. The task of crossing an icy river in full spate in the face of enemy forces appealed to his imagination. He ordered a number of feints to distract the enemy; the principal one was attempted by Oudinot at Uchlodi, some miles below Borisov, on 25 November. Tshitsakov took the bait and moved his forces southwards, leaving the Borisov-Studienka stretch of river unopposed. He then compounded his error by not destroying the causeway through the marshes on the other side which led from the west bank of the Beresina to Vilna.

Napoleon ordered Eblé to take his engineering force, demolish the houses in Studienka to get their wood, and then build two three-hundred-foot bridges over the Beresina, to be completed by the 26th. As soon as the first bridge was completed, Ney's and Oudinot's corps would cross and form up defensively on the far bank to deal with any counterthrust from Tshitsagov. The bulk of the Army would cross while Davout's I Corps and Victor's IX Corps held the eastern bridgehead; finally they too would cross. It was noteworthy that there was no place in this plan for the 40,000 stragglers.

There followed a samurai exploit by Eblé and his men, who worked all night in freezing water to put the trestles and planking in place; Oudinot at once got his men across to form the western defence. Later that afternoon a second, larger, bridge was completed, and the artillery rushed over to the far bank. So far there was no sign of the Russians, but three breaks were discovered in the bridges, which Eblé and his 400 heroes worked all night to put right. By early afternoon of the 27th the Guard and the imperial staff were also safely across. But around 4 p.m. three trestles on the artillery bridge collapsed. Those still on the eastern bank panicked, and a mad rush to the one remaining bridge ensued: order was restored with great difficulty, but by that time hundreds had been trampled to death or knocked into the river to drown. Eble repaired the other bridge and then had to hack a path through corpses on the smaller bridge to get I Corps and the rearguard across.

It was not until the 27th that the Russians realized what was happening and attacked on both sides of the bridge. All day Oudinot's and Victor's men fought valiantly and repelled attack after attack, so that the crossings went on without interruption until the afternoon's débâcle with the large bridge. Only at dusk did the sounds of battle fade away. The exhausted Eblé told the non-combatant stragglers to cross to the western bank under cover of darkness, but apathy won the day; they remained obstinately huddled round small fires on the eastern bank. Eblé could do no more. He and his 400 engineers were the great heroes of Beresina. Hardly any of them survived, for those who did not perish of frostbite, exposure and hypothermia were swept downstream in the ferocious current or were scythed down by enemy fire while they were repairing the bridge.

Thus far Napoleon could congratulate himself on a superb feat of ingenuity and courage. But the pendulum swung against him during the night of 27–28 November when General Partoneaux's division of Victor's corps lost its way in a heavy snowstorm and blundered into the Russian lines, where they had no choice but to surrender. This loss tore a gaping hole in Victor's thin defensive line in the rearguard. After an ominous lull, at about midday on the 28th the Russians on the east bank brought heavy guns to bear on the bridges, causing a panic-stricken repeat performance of the previous day. Once again terrified men fell to an icy death in the Beresina as the artillery bridge collapsed a second time, brought down by a combination of Russian shells and the sheer weight of fleeing soldiers. Once again the rearguard performed prodigies of valour, and the astonishing accuracy of their artillery at last pushed the Russians back out of range. For the second day the rearguard fought unaided, for on the western bank French units were engaged this day in a grim do-or-die struggle. Oudinot and Ney covered themselves in laurels by personal bravery. Oudinot by his personal charisma and courage prevented a rout, while Ney inflicted 2,000 Russian casualties by leading a charge by Dumerc's cuirassiers. It was a second Krasnyi: like Kutusov before him, Tshitsagov fell back in alarm at the ferocity of the French fightback.

The last stage of a brilliant operation was completed when the rearguard finally crossed to the western bank at 1 a.m. on 29 November but the stragglers still refused to follow them. Shellshocked and demoralized, the camp-followers seem in a very real sense to have been afraid of the dark. At any rate, they ignored warning after warning from Eblé that this was their last chance since in the morning he would be detonating charges to prevent a pursuit by Kutusov's contingents. At 9 next morning, as promised, Eblé blew up the bridges. Now at last, when it was too late, the non-combatants began to rush for the bridges, only to be consumed by an inferno. Some 10,000 perished, some in the flames but most of them in the river as the bridges sank under the waters of the Beresina, with a hiss like that of a gigantic ingot steeped in water by a blacksmith; the river was choked with corpses for a week. The 30,000 survivors who were left on the east bank were then cut to pieces by the Cossacks.

It had cost Napoleon 25,000 casualties in fighting men and 25 guns plus the loss of the non-combatants to cross the Beresina. By any standards the net result was a disaster but, playing up the miraculous aspects of the Army's escape and the 20,000 or so casualties inflicted on the Russians, he issued a communiqué and claimed a victory. At last the survivors could rest secure from partisan attacks and close pursuit by the Russian army, but now the real enemy was General Winter. The 160 miles to Vilna saw the cruellest December on record. Wilson spoke of 'a subtle, razor-cutting, creeping wind that penetrated the skin, muscle, bone to the very marrow, rendering the skin as white, and the whole limb affected as fragile, as alabaster.'

A week later the Grand Army was down to 13,000 effectives; thousands more had simply fallen asleep and died in the snow. Napoleon expressed no concern for the suffering, doubtless reckoning that in the circumstances it was a waste of emotion. Despite notable instances of great selfishness, discipline in the ranks was actually better now that Kutusov and the partisans had been dropped astern. Kutusov largely abandoned the pursuit at the Beresina, simply sending large squadrons of Cossacks to harry the French. At Molodetchno, where the main road from Minsk to Vilna joined them, there was a very sharp skirmish between the rearguard and the Cossacks. Napoleon dismissed it as a bagatelle and spent the 3rd of December composing his 29th bulletin, a précis of the campaign, which admitted some part of the disaster but played up Borodino, Krasnyi, Beresina, Ney's wanderings after Smolesnsk and all other heroic exploits of the *Grande Armée*.

This was the Emperor's last contribution to the 1812 campaign for, at Smorgoni at 10 p.m. on 5 December, he left the Army, pleading the necessity of getting back to Paris with all speed. For appearing to abandon his army he has been much criticized and shades of Egypt in 1799 have been invoked. The comparison will not really hold, as indeed has been pointed out by those of his critics who allege that it was even *more* reprehensible to quit the Army now than in 1799, for in that case he left shortly after a notable victory and in this he left after a disaster. On the other hand, what was left of his Army was now almost safe, as it had not been in Egypt, and Napoleon in self-defence cited the accepted practice whereby a general was usually ordered home if his army was reduced to a single corps. He also feared that if he tarried in Poland, Austria and Prussia would declare war and bar his passage back to France. Most of all, though, his departure was dictated by pure *raison d'état*. After the Malet coup, it could only be a matter of time before there was another attempted putsch; the Emperor could well arrive home to find he had been deposed in his absence.

Accordingly, Napoleon made preparations for the swiftest possible 1,400-mile journey. Since they were still in hostile territory, it was decided that the best method was to travel incognito in three coaches. With him in his own coach were Caulaincourt, Duroc, Lobau, Fain the Grand Marshal, the Mameluke valet Roustam and a Polish interpreter. Escorted by Polish and Neapolitan cavalry, he thought it best not to enter Vilna but met its governor, Maret, outside the walls while Caulaincourt went in to buy warm clothing. The coaches and their escort then proceeded through Kovno to Gragow where the Emperor decided to exchange the carriage for a sleigh.

Once Napoleon left, morale in the French Army plummeted; there was indiscipline and desertion even among the Guard. As if by some sort of pathetic fallacy, the day after his departure was the coldest day of all, with the temperature down to −36° F. Bonaparte's poor judgement of men was once again made manifest as command devolved on Murat, who began by inveighing against the Emperor, telling Davout they both served a monster; Davout, who despised Murat, replied coldly that he was a monster to whom Murat owed everything.

The death toll again began to rise. 20,000 men dropped away in the three days between Smorgoni and Vilna. In the extreme cold it was common for 400 men to cluster round a fire at night and in the morning for 300 of them to be dead. Soldiers started setting entire houses on fire and standing round the flaming ruins all night. On the march to Vilna the food shortage was so acute that some men ate their own severed fingers and drank their own blood. But the greatest killer was gangrene – an inevitable consequence of men trying to warm frozen limbs at the fire. Since at these temperatures water froze a mere three feet from the fire, one could only get warm by getting burnt; men became gangrenous simply because they had no sensation in their limbs and got too close to the heat. All who braved the horrors of that winter suffered frightfully, not just the French. Contrary to popular belief, the pursuing Russians were not well equipped against the winter. In recoiling in horror at the casualty list of the Grand Army, it is easy to forget that 100,000 Russians died in the snows in addition to battle casualties.

Poland and friendly territory lay tantalizingly close, but still the

Army's ordeal was not over. The force that entered Vilna on 8 December in temperatures of −26° F was no better than a rabble, as became clear by their actions on entering the town. Elaborate quartermastering arrangements had been laid down in a situation where there was enough meat and flour to feed 100,000 men for forty days, but the incoming soldiery simply ran amok, looting and pillaging. In an initial riot at the city gates many men were crushed to death. Others drank themselves into a stupor on the plentiful brandy, collapsed drunkenly on the sidewalk and died of exposure in the frozen streets. No attempt was made to post pickets, with the black comedy result that pursuing Cossacks actually came galloping into town while drunken French troops gorged and caroused. The mere sight of a handful of Cossacks threw Murat into wholesale panic. Even though he had express orders from Napoleon to hold Vilna for at least eight days and give his men adequate rest and recreation, Murat ordered a general evacuation just twenty-four hours after arrival. There were 20,000 wounded allied troops from all theatres in the town's hospitals, but they were simply left to the barbarous mercies of the incoming Cossacks. When he heard of this shameful retreat before a handful of Russian irregulars, Napoleon became incandescent with rage.

Only 10,000 men resumed the march with Murat on 10 December. As soon as they encountered the first steep hill, they abandoned all remaining carts, cannons and pay chests; with great reluctance they carried only the regimental eagles. At Kovno only 7,000 effectives were left, and at this town Ney had to turn and join with the rearguard, fighting for a day and a night (13–14 December) before the Russians broke off, allowing the French to cross the Niemen. Ney was the last Frenchman to leave Russian soil and, as he watched the Niemen bridges burning behind him, he at least had the satisfaction of reflecting that for him the 1812 campaign had been a personal triumph.

The Russians began their invasion of Poland in January 1813. Murat pulled back to Posan, then fled to his kingdom of Naples, leaving the Army in the more capable hands of Eugène de Beauharnais who, obeying his stepfather's orders, pulled his men back behind the Elbe. Once in Germany the handful of survivors from Russia dispersed to the various fortress towns. MacDonald had already retreated into Poland and eventually brought a force of 7,000 back to Königsberg via Riga and Tilsit; Schwarzenberger and Reynier took their corps into Austria. It was estimated that by New Year 1813 just 25,000 survivors from Central Army Group and 68,000 from the outlying corps had reentered Germany.

On leaving Gragow Napoleon travelled in disguise and took with him in his sledge only Caulaincourt as company and a small escort, for they were now in supposedly friendly territory. The temperature was −25° F and Napoleon, whose penchant for hot baths and roaring fires was well known, complained of the cold. Caulaincourt remembered how their breath froze on the lips and how small icicles formed under the nose, on the eyebrows and round the eyelids. The Emperor kept going over and over the details of the campaign he had just lost, wondering at what points he should have done things differently. Occasionally Caulaincourt would interrupt the litany of 'if onlys' to tell the Emperor a few home truths about the unpopularity of the imperial régime, the high taxes, suppression of liberties and general bitterness about nepotism and favouritism. Napoleon took the criticism well, smiled occasionally and, when Caulaincourt expressed himself forcefully, tried to pinch his ear; unable to find it under the snowcap, he tweaked his neck and cheek instead.

On 10 December they reached Warsaw, where the Emperor thought it safe enough to abandon his incognito. He summoned the French ambassador, the Abbé Pradt, and treated him to another sermon on the Russian campaign. He ended by asking Pradt sharply where were the 10,000 Polish cavalry he had been promised. Pradt replied that there was no money, whereat Napoleon lost his temper and accused him of defeatism. According to Caulaincourt he repeated obsessively the line about 'from the sublime to the ridiculous'. Continuing the journey that evening, he and Caulaincourt arrived in Posan on 12 December. This was the first town which had secure communications with France, so Napoleon was able to read a stack of letters. The ones that pleased him most were from Marie-Louise, reporting the progress of their son. He beamed, read some extracts to Caulaincourt and said: 'Haven't I got a good wife?'

The 13th of December, as he sped across northern Germany, saw Napoleon at his oddest. He discussed his career and personality with his companion as if they were talking dispassionately about a third party. Caulaincourt thought him a man who had lost touch with reality. He seemed unaware of the scale of his losses and full of self-delusion and unrealistic plans for the future. His mood swings were violent. One moment he would be complaining, rightly, that far too many people had taken advantage of him. Next moment he would be roaring with laughter at the conceit that the Prussians might ambush them and deliver them over to the British, to be exhibited in London in an iron cage. Those who hold that Napoleon was the great existentialist like to cite this sleigh-ride, which shows the Emperor unsurprised by anything, a man always ready for anything, however improbable, to happen.

They proceeded by sledge through Saxony to Dresden where they arrived at midnight on the 13th. The King of Saxony met them at 3 a.m. and made available his comfortable coach, in which they departed at 7 a.m. on the 14th. Changing vehicles several times, they took another three days to reach Verdun, travelling via Leipzig, Auerstädt, Erfurt, Frankfurt and Mainz. After a short stop at Meaux, they arrived in Paris at a quarter to midnight on 18 December and drove straight to the Tuileries. Caulaincourt reported that he had not slept properly for fourteen days and nights and could not reestablish his proper sleep pattern for another fortnight.

Once back in Paris, Napoleon ordered a round of balls, fêtes and receptions, acting as if nothing much had happened during his absence. But two days before his arrival the 29th Bulletin had been published in *Le Moniteur*. Even this heavily doctored version of the truth caused consternation among people grown used to the seeming inevitability of victory and the invincibility of the Emperor. As the scale of the losses became clear, Napoleon's propagandist attempt to put a brave face on things and, by the sumptuous balls and luxurious dinners, to pretend it was 'business as usual' seemed the crassest of insensitivity. It was fortunate indeed that General Malet had not staged his coup a couple of months later.

Napoleon now learned the details of what had happened on the night of 22–23 October 1812. Malet, who had been involved in the Fouché-Talleyrand plot in 1808–09 while the Emperor was in Spain, began by releasing the anti-Bonapartist generals Lahorie and Guidal and, together with his fellow plotters Boutreux and Rateau, announced that Napoleon was dead in Russia. The conspirators managed to arrest both the Minister and Prefect of Police but fell foul of General Hullin, commander of the Paris garrison, who refused to join them. Without his support, the conspirators were sunk: they and their accomplices were rounded up, tried on 28 October with a rapidity that recalled the d'Enghien affair and executed by firing squad on the 29th.

Although the imperial police had betrayed extreme incompetence in allowing themselves to be arrested, the plot was not the serious threat to Bonaparte it might have been. This time neither Fouché nor Talleyrand were involved nor, fortunately for the Emperor, were the notables. The coup was an *ad hoc* pact between royalists and extreme Republicans; the idea was that, with Napoleon out of the picture, a new assembly would decide later between a Republic or a Bourbon restoration. Napoleon's response on his return was to make Marie-Louise regent (with an advisory council of princes of the blood and grand dignitaries) against his likely future absences on campaign.

1812 was the beginning of the end for Napoleon. The miracle was that he was able to rally a reluctant French people at all after such a catastrophe. The total loss of human life on this campaign has been disputed and almost certainly underestimated. 370,000 French troops perished on the battlefield, of cold and exposure or disease. 200,000 more were taken prisoner or deserted and, in the light of what has been said about partisan atrocities, there need be no serious debate about their probable fate. The frightful loss of life can be gauged from one single statistic: the Guard, 47,000 strong, had not been involved in the heaviest fighting, but returned with just 1,500 men alive. Additionally, the French lost 200,000 horses – a loss that could never be made good and was to have devastating military consequences. The Russians lost at least 150,000 dead in battle, plus a huge but unknown number of civilians. Given the propensity of historians seriously to underrate casualties in Russian warfare (now apparent from the significant upward revisions in total fatalities for the 'Great Patriotic War' of 1941–45), it is not improbable that a million people died during the six-month campaign of 1812.

In retrospect, it seems that Napoleon made virtually every mistake in the book: failure to keep Sweden and Turkey in play as allies against Russia, failure to set out in May, to grant Polish independence, to free the serfs, to reach Moscow by early August if he was to go there at all. Then there were sins of commission: wasting time in Vilna, Vitebsk and Moscow, not sending in the Guard at Borodino, losing his nerve at Maloyaroslavets. But the worst mistake was the failure to think through logistical problems, admittedly almost insurmountable in an army of 600,000. Everything was underestimated: the speed at which armies could march, the amount of food that could be obtained en route, the poor state of the roads. The supply dumps at Danzig and Königsberg were too far behind the army and the mud roads could not take the convoy traffic, while those at Minsk and Vitebsk were not well enough guarded, so that they fell into Russian hands. There was no absolute shortage of supplies, but no proper infrastructure to get them where they were needed.

Additionally, by his gambler's ploy of doubling his bets each time the original wager failed, Napoleon ended up in Moscow when he had never considered this as a possibility in his original plans. If he was to invade Russia at all – a serious error while he was bogged down in Spain – he should have wintered in Smolensk. By marching so far into the heart of

Russia, he proved the truth of Clausewitz's observation that to advance deep into enemy country is itself a kind of defeat. By the time of Borodino the Emperor had lost so many men that he lacked the resources for decisive victory. Apart from losses through disease and starvation, another factor was at play. The longer his lines of communication, the more troops he had to detach for secondary roles – the protection of depots, internal security, the garrisoning of cities captured, the provision of escorts for couriers and envoys. To spend a month in Moscow waiting for the Czar to surrender made no sense; why did Bonaparte not remember that French possession of Vienna had not weighed with the Austrians in 1805 nor the loss of Berlin with the Prussians in 1806?

Napoleon's explanation of the disaster of 1812 was peculiarly disingenuous. He was right to be scornful of the Russian Army, since Kutusov's much-lauded strategy of trading space for time was a pure accident, not something he intended. Kutusov has often been claimed as 'the man who defeated Napoleon' but in fact his military calibre, both at Borodino and during the French retreat, was not impressive. But Napoleon in his own apologia quickly moved from a warranted proposition to pure fantasy. He claimed that his total numbers were 400,000 and that only 160,000 went beyond Smolensk; of this total of 400,000 half were German or Italian and only 140,000 members of the polyglot army spoke French. So, according to Bonaparte's numerical legerdemain, only 50,000 Frenchmen were lost in 1812 and the Russians lost four times total allied fatalities! This sort of cynicism gives powerful ammunition to those who claim that the Emperor never really thought of anyone but himself.

His further 'explanation' for 1812 was also mendacious. He claimed that he beat the Russians at all points but was then overcome by 'General Winter'. But winter was only a major factor in the latter stages of the retreat, more especially after Beresina. The sober facts are that the French lost more men – through starvation, exhaustion, sickness, capture, desertion and death in battle – on the advance to Moscow than on the retreat. The Grand Army suffered more from the heat of July and August, and the initial stages of the Russian winter in 1812 were mild. It was, after all, because of the thaw that Napoleon faced the great crisis at the Beresina. But the self-serving myth propagated by the Emperor – that he was defeated only by the weather – took hold, gained acceptance and is the received opinion today – surely the ultimate triumph for Bonapartist propaganda.

It is a clue to Napoleon's personality that his explanation for disaster always hinges on fate. The excuses are all 'ifs': if Moscow had not been burnt, the Emperor Alexander would have been forced to make peace (how?); if winter cold had not set in fifteen days earlier than usual; if Murat had not abandoned Vilna. There is no suggestion that the Emperor should have foreseen some of the obvious consequences of campaigning in Russia: he even absurdly claims that there was no reason to predict that the temperature might fall to six degrees below freezing in November! The objective nightmare suffered by half a million allied troops in the frozen steppes was itself the product of a mind that had ceased to function effectively and of an imagination that had gone into free fall.

CHAPTER TWENTY-FOUR

Napoleon's first military concern on return from the Russian fiasco was the war in Spain. From this theatre the news was mixed: in the short term the situation was satisfactory but long-term there were worrying trends. In Madrid King Joseph was reduced to raising money on his estates because of the dire shortage of funds, but he was still unable to command the obedience of those nominally on his side. When Napoleon sent him 500,000 francs in gold bullion, one of the French field commanders intercepted the convoy and requisitioned 120,000 francs to pay the troops under his command. 1812 was the year when both Joseph and Wellington were appointed Commanders-in-Chief of their respective forces. In Wellington's case this resulted in a cohesive military force; in Joseph's case it changed nothing, for the marshals continued to behave like provincial satraps and take notice of their 'King' only when they chose to.

Wellington's strategy for 1812 was to strike at Marmont and the Army of Portugal, with the intention of forcing Soult to abandon southern Spain. His intelligence sources revealed that Suchet, with 60,000 men in Aragon and Catalonia, never had the slightest interest in supporting his fellow marshals; most of Soult's 54,000 men in the south were engaged on the siege of Cadiz; Joubert's 18,000 in Madrid had their hands full with partisans and a hostile city population; and Caffarelli's Army of the North was fully occupied with keeping the Pyrenean passes open and containing the guerrillas in Navarre. By now, after Napoleon had withdrawn 30,000 men for the Russian campaign, Wellington's army was superior in numbers to any one French army. Just to make sure he would have no interference from the other marshals, he ordered all Spanish forces in the south to make a concerted effort against Soult; Suchet would be diverted by an Anglo-Neapolitan landing from Sicily; and the Royal Navy would disembark marines for irregular warfare against Caffarelli.

After his usual careful preparations, Wellington advanced with 42,000 men (most of them British) to besiege Ciudad Rodrigo. This time he was successful but, after storming the town in a bloody assault, his men went berserk, burning, looting and raping wherever they went. It took until the morning after the siege for order to be restored but London was unconcerned about war crimes and atrocities and awarded their general an earldom and an extra £2,000 in annual pension. In March he moved on to besiege Badajoz. This proved a tough nut, the British took heavy losses, and Wellington was about to call off the siege when he heard that his men had taken the citadel on the other side of the city. After a bitter battle on 6–7 April 1812, the British again ran amok in an orgy of rape and drunken pillage. On 8 April Wellington erected a gallows and threatened to hang his men by the dozen if they did not come to order.

Despite heavy casualties (5,000 in all, including 1,500 in the main breach), Wellington had taken 5,000 prisoners and demonstrated to his own satisfaction that he could proceed to destroy French armies piecemeal. The siege had lasted a month but none of the marshals, and especially not Soult who was nearest, had come to the aid of Badajoz. With the strategic advantage Wellington now proceeded to invade the heartland of Spain. He held the whip hand, especially as Marmont's forces, in obedience to explicit orders from the Emperor, were strung out in a huge arc stretching from Oviedo in the Asturias to Avila and the Gaudarramas.

Wellington and Marmont circled each other warily at first, then the marshal withdrew, leaving the British free to take Salamanca. Wellington then set off into Leon after the French, but Marmont doubled back, trying to beat the enemy to Salamanca. Marmont's strategy was clear: to keep Wellington forever doubling back to Portugal by hooking round his right and forcing him west. But in moving south-west towards Ciudad Rodrigo, Marmont mistook Wellington's main army for a baggage train and concluded that the British were retreating. He sent his divisions west to continue the hooking manoeuvre, leaving his army strung out with a weak centre. Wellington attacked there (22 July) and was able to destroy Marmont's army systematically, division after division. There could be no doubting the scale of the victory: the British lost 5,000 at Salamanca but of 48,000 French troops in the Army of Portugal, 14,000 were casualties (among the wounded were Marmont and his second-in-command General Bouvet) and 7,000 were prisoners. Once again Wellington was supremely lucky, for this was an untypical error by the talented Marmont. None the less it was a major setback for the French, and the news, reaching Napoleon just before Borodino, did nothing for the morale of the *Grande Armée* in Russia.

The Army of Portugal was forced to retreat north, first to Valladolid, then to Burgos. In Madrid on 5 August Joseph ordered Soult to abandon

Andalucia and bring his Army of the South to central Spain. Wellington entered Valladolid on 30 July. Worried about a long supply line stretching back to Portugal, he decided to move on Madrid; Joseph fled to Toledo and on 12 August Wellington entered the Spanish capital. His main fear now was that the four French armies might finally decide to combine, for to the south of him was Soult's Army of the South en route to Valencia, to the north was Clausel (Marmont's successor)'s Army of Portugal and to the east, in Catalonia, Suchet's Army of Catalonia. His concern was justified, for if the factionalist French had been able to combine, Wellington's position would have been supremely perilous. As it was, he decided to hit Clausel first, pursued him to Burgos and invested the city, but found that his siege-train was inadequate and drew off in late October.

Meanwhile Suchet and Joseph had linked up at Valencia, prior to marching on Madrid. Outnumbered, Wellington pulled his troops out of the capital and set up a defensive line at Salamanca, ready to engage with Soult. Predictably Soult baulked at tackling the British in such well-prepared defences, and fell back on the now tired ploy of trying to turn the British right by hooking past it to Portugal. Wellington retired to his starting place for the year – Ciudad Rodrigo – but not before his own army had given him a few nervous moments through loud grumbling at food shortages, indiscipline, looting, straggling and deserting. In the snow and rain of Ciudad Rodrigo the year's Peninsular campaign petered out. For his exploit at Salamanca Wellington was made a Marquess, but there was criticism in London for his failure to take Burgos or retreat to Portugal. Nevertheless, Napoleon was depressed that none of his Peninsular marshals had yet been able to beat this 'sepoy general' and that Wellington now held the strategic advantage through having forced Soult out of Andalucia.

In addition to the Spanish ulcer was the Papal headache. The struggle with the Pope had gone into abeyance during the Russian campaign but in the summer of 1812 Napoleon ordered Pius moved from Savona to Fontainebleau. Immediately on return from the icy nightmare the Emperor went in person to Fontainebleau to negotiate a new Concordat, in which Napoleon retreated from his hardline position and allowed the Pope to have unimpeded access to his cardinals. But no sooner did the 'black cardinals' arrive in Fontainebleau than they persuaded Pius that the new Concordat was a mistake. Pius loftily informed Napoleon that he was withdrawing his signature. Enraged at this treachery, Napoleon ordered a new round of arrests and conscriptions of priests and seminarists. At this even the venal Cardinal Fesch cried Hold! Enough!

After an acrimonious meeting Napoleon banished his uncle from Paris and confined him to his see. At his Archbishop's Palace in Lyons, Fesch supported the Catholic resistance to the Emperor and laid the foundations for the reactionary post-1815 French Church. But, being Fesch, he did not abate his love of money and luxury one whit.

Yet both Spain and the Papacy were subplots to the great drama beginning to unfold in Germany. After Murat's craven departure, Eugène de Beauharnais had done his best to stem the Russian advance, but by mid-January they were over the Vistula and on 7 February they occupied Warsaw. The sheer numbers of Russians meant they could outflank any defensive position, so that Eugène was forced back from the Oder to the Elbe. An even more sinister development was the convention of Tauroggen of 31 December 1812, when the Prussian general Yorck, whose corps had been part of the French Army, went over to the Russians. Eastern Prussia rose in support and the movement spread to Silesia and Brandenburg. On 28 February 1813, under pressure of fervently nationalistic public opinion, a reluctant Frederick William signed an alliance with the Czar to pursue a 'holy war' against the French. The Kaiser really had little choice for the Russian hordes swept into Berlin.

On 13 March 1813 Prussia declared war and put an Army of 80,000 into the field. There has been much discussion about the provenance of this force since Napoleon had previously limited numbers in the Prussian Army and taken many of them to Russia with him. The explanation appears to be twofold. Napoleon had incautiously authorized the Prussians to recruit so as to make up the losses sustained in Russia. Additionally, the Prussians had over the years been secretly building up their strength by retiring large numbers of regulars each year and then training others to take their place. The new Prussian Army was a more formidable instrument than the force that had failed at Jena; motives of civic *virtu* and German nationalism replaced the old feudal attitude of blind obedience. Since 110,000 Russians had already entered Germany, the allied force was considerable even before the treacherous Bernadotte entered the war on their side, adding 28,000 Swedes. By the time Napoleon entered the field himself, Eugène was entrenched in a strong position on the Saale, having been repeatedly forced to retreat.

To combat this menacing build-up Napoleon had to ask the French people for more sacrifices, more taxes and more manpower. 1813 was the year when he decisively lost the support of the two pillars of his régime, the notables and the peasantry. Napoleon tried to curry favour with the peasantry by putting up more common land for sale, but the recent recession meant the peasants had no money with which to buy it. As for the notables, the last straw for them was the *senatus consultum* of 3 April 1813, which raised guards of honour from the sons of all rich and noble families in the Empire; each son had to arm and equip his troop (it was envisaged there would be 100,000 in all), and anyone without a valid reason for avoiding military service had to pay a heavy tax. The response was patchy, with some noble sons serving and others resisting, but the main effect was to irritate both the notables themselves and the officer corps in the regular army, who resented the intrusion of the new upstarts.

This device was just one of many Napoleon employed in a desperate bid to raise the numbers needed to hold the Russians and Prussians at bay. His problem was that conscription demands had grown steeper over the years. Whereas in the years 1800–07 the average call-up total was 78,700, from February 1808-January 1809 alone 240,000 men were drafted. From then until 1812 another 396,000 were drafted, mainly for service in Spain: men were increasingly taken from age groups that had been previously balloted or were under age, in addition to the current crop. Military service also became harder to avoid, as its administration was taken out of the hands of local authorities, the right to use substitutes was restricted, the demand for a minimum height was waived, and efforts were made to end exemptions for married men.

Resistance to conscription reached unprecedented levels in 1812–13. Draft dodgers often joined the large gangs of deserters who roamed the hillsides in a life of petty crime, and in the north these bands became genuine 'primitive rebels' as their resistance took on a coating of political consciousness. Often these groups enjoyed widespread local support, from priests, peasants and even prefects who, aware how high the tide of local feeling was running, would keep the deserters informed of Army search parties. In some *départements* evasion and desertion was at epidemic level, and there was a departmental instance of a levy of 1,600 men where 1,000 decamped. The families of those who had taken to the hills to evade service were punished by hefty fines or by having troops billeted on them, while more and more troops were sent to scour the countryside for the estimated (in 1811) 139,000 missing draftees.

The attitude to the draft in 1813 showed just how low French morale had sunk. Those who served did so in an attitude of sullen resignation, but many others inflicted terrible injuries on themselves to avoid call-up. The married man's exemption was widely abused, with youths of seventeen 'marrying' ninety-year-olds to achieve the cherished status. All kinds of tricks were used to avoid being given a clean bill of health. Teeth were pulled or made to decay by using acid or chewing incense. Some men blistered themselves and then dressed the sores with water and arsenic to make them incurable; others gave themselves hernias and applied corrosive acid to their genitals. Napoleon retaliated by calling up the class of 1814 a year early, by a systematic sweep to find the draft dodgers of earlier years and by transferring 80,000 National Guardsmen to the Army. Once again the Emperor discovered the difference between paper numbers and reality, for it turned out that only four-fifths of the notional strength of the National Guard existed.

Napoleon's overall aim was to recruit 650,000 new soldiers by mid-1813. With the 137,000 conscripts just completing training and the transferred National Guardsmen he had less than a third of the total. He therefore called up the class of 1814 in February 1813 and demanded fresh troops from Germany and Italy. Mounted gendarmes were turned into cavalry and 20,000 sailors were retreaded into the Army. By also calling up 100,000 conscripts of 1809, 1810, 1811 and 1812 he somehow levied 350,000 men for the 1813 campaign. Further calls in April, August and October, including a levy on the 1815 class produced another 160,000 by the end of the year. But the calibre of the new Army was poor at every level, especially the officers. The top-class officers of the *Grande Armée* of the golden age were mostly dead, since good officers led from the front. And the Emperor suffered mightily from a shortage of mounts for his cavalry, since 250,000 had perished in Russia and most of the horse-rearing areas of eastern Europe were by now in enemy hands. Lack of horses meant that Napoleon would fight the 1813 campaign, in effect, with one hand tied between his back, as he could neither gather intelligence efficiently nor pursue a defeated enemy.

Napoleon's original strategy for 1813 had been to retake Berlin and fight the campaign between the Elbe and the Oder, using the fortresses of Torgau, Wittenburg, Magdeburg and Hamburg as pivots. This would enable him to relieve the 150,000 French troops bottled up in the Vistula fortresses – Danzig, Thorn and Modlin – thus forcing Prussia out of the war and turning Kutusov's flank. But Josephine's unfortunate son was constantly outflanked, to Napoleon's disgust, especially when Eugène abandoned Hamburg and concentrated at Dresden. In any case, this initial Bonaparte conception required an Army of 300,000 seasoned troops which the Emperor did not possess. At a pinch he could have put that number of raw levies in the field, but how would they stand up against Kutusov's veterans? And what of the Confederation of the Rhine? Would Saxony and Bavaria remain loyal?

After some dithering, the German allies reluctantly threw in their lot with the French. Napoleon's initial moves in the campaign were fumbling. He sent word to Eugène that Hamburg was more important than Dresden, so Eugène pulled out and occupied Magdeburg instead, leaving Field-Marshal Blücher and the Prussians to enter Dresden. Napoleon then announced his battle-plan: to open the offensive in May, retake Danzig and then throw the enemy back behind the Vistula. He therefore moved to link with Eugène so that he would have 150,000 men on the Saale; he then intended to advance on Dresden via Leipzig, seize the Elbe crossings in the allied rear and so cut them off from Berlin and Silesia. With any luck, this would lead to a battle and a quick victory. The revised plan did not mean that the Emperor had lost sight of his grand strategy in the north, but he needed a triumph in the south to retrieve his own reputation, restore morale in his Army and dissuade the waverers in the Confederation of the Rhine.

He spent much of March in painstaking preparations and pepping up the confidence of the marshals, from whom there was much muttering to the effect that the Emperor was over the hill as a military commander and now listened to court sycophants rather than them. A litany of complaints contained the following: the Emperor rarely visited battlefields any more, issued vague and impenetrable orders, and showed no concern for the increasing indiscipline and looting that was making the *Grande Armée* a byword for pillage and alienating support continent-wide. Informed of these canards, Napoleon decided to underline the fact that the marshals owed all their wealth and prosperity to him. Pointedly he created a new title for Ney, whose proper mark was as an unimaginative corps commander: the 'bravest of the brave' was now dubbed Prince of the Moskova, with a month's leave and a further annuity of 800,000 francs a year.

On 15 April 1813 Napoleon left St-Cloud, reached Mainz two days later and stayed there for a week, working on details of the campaign. Ney's III Corps had a strength of 45,000, Marmont's VI Corps 25,000 while the depleted IV Corps under Bertrand and XII Corps under Oudinot together barely mustered 36,000. The Guard had been brought up to a strength of 15,000. Additionally the Emperor could call on Davout's I Corps (20,000), II Corps (the Army of the Elbe) and units from V, VIII and XI Corps, plus Sebastiani's 14,000 cavalry.

His main worry was the severe shortage of horses, which deprived him of an effective cavalry arm, but he comforted himself with the thought that the Allies were overconfident and could probably be gulled into a battle. After all, was it not Russian veterans against raw French recruits? Napoleon therefore set out for Leipzig with a 200,000-strong army and was at Erfurt on the 25th. Heavy fighting began almost immediately, culminating in a French victory at Weissenfeld on 1 May, in which Marshal Bessières was killed. This was a severe blow to the Emperor: Bessières had been his comrade since 1796 and was one of the few marshals who could follow orders. Bessières was widely unpopular in the Army for having persuaded the Emperor not to send in the Guard at Borodino, but Napoleon felt his loss keenly: 'Bessières lived like Bayard; he died like Turenne.'

But Weissenfeld was simply the overture to a much more savage battle at Lutzen next day, when Napoleon tested the mettle of his new army against the Russian veterans under Wittgenstein. The battle was something of a textbook Bonaparte affair. Ney was ordered to occupy the town of Lutzen with III Corps while the rest of the army scythed through the Russian left. Predictably, Ney neglected to send out patrols, so the Allied commander Wittgenstein took the bait and sent the Prussians forward to wipe out what he thought was a single infantry brigade. Fierce combat began at around 11.45 a.m. and Blücher nearly achieved complete surprise against Ney, but the allies in turn had seriously underestimated the strength of their enemy.

Nevertheless, when Napoleon reached the battlefield at about 2.30 p.m. he found things going badly. At great personal risk he rode among the demoralized III Corps and got them back into fighting trim. He then stiffened Ney's defences with VI Corps, set the Prince of the Moskova's only friend among the marshals, MacDonald, to threaten the Russian right with IX Corps and began probing on the left with Bertrand. Both Wittgenstein and Yorck (who replaced a wounded Blücher in the afternoon) behaved obtusely and fell for all the Emperor's ruses. Yorck refused to heed advice from Czar Alexander and committed his reserves at 4 p.m.; they gained early success but were then driven back by the Young Guard and a revitalised III Corps. At 5.30 p.m., with the outflanking units of MacDonald and Marmont in place, Napoleon gave the signal for a general assault. Seventy cannon were moved up to point-blank range and both Young and Old Guards began advancing. Marmont and Bertrand swept in from the right and MacDonald from the left; the Allied line began to buckle.

By dusk both MacDonald and Bertrand had completed the necessary prelude to encirclement, but night fell and the French lack of horses really showed itself when shortage of cavalry prevented a decisive victory. With sufficient horse and two more hours of daylight Napoleon might finally have had his Cannae-style victory. The Allies were severely shaken and spoke of retiring to the Oder or even the Vistula. In terms of casualties honours were even at 20,000 apiece, but Lützen decisively salvaged the Emperor's reputation. The battle revealed him at the top of his form, brilliant in foresight and anticipation of enemy movements. In contrast to the Russian campaign, his orders were lucid, succinct and economical.

Napoleon, however, soon showed that he was not really the force of yore. He was depressed, justifiably, by the gap evident between his own talents and those of his mediocre corps commanders whose deficiencies, as he saw it, had prevented total victory. Once again he defended himself against critics who said that he should have sent in the Guard in the early evening to deal the *coup de grâce*.

Unexpectedly, it was the quality of the Prussians, rather than the Russians, which had most impressed him: 'These animals have learned something,' he remarked. It was also observable, particularly as the warfare of 1813 in Germany became protracted, that Napoleon was often fatigued and frequently ill, especially after battles, and even fell asleep at crucial moments.

The Allies withdrew to Bautzen, there to receive 13,000 Russian reinforcements under Barclay de Tolly. On 4 May Napoleon split his Army in two, sending half north under Ney to incorporate the Army of Saxony as VII Corps, advance on Berlin and perhaps force the Russians into suing for a separate peace; the rest of Ney's forces were to pursue Wittgenstein while to General Lauriston and V Corps fell the task of maintaining communication between the divided Army of the Elbe. Learning of Metternich's intrigues to suborn the Confederation of the Rhine and fearing that Austria would soon join a League of three Emperors against him, Napoleon sent Eugène back to Italy to distract the Austrians there. The overall plan now was that a divided French Army, with a northern wing of 85,000 under Ney, Victor, Reynier and Sebastiani threatening Berlin, and a southern wing under Napoleon himself aiming at Dresden, would force the Prussians to detach themselves from their Russian allies, so that Napoleon could defeat them piecemeal.

Unfortunately for best-laid Bonapartist plans, the allies did not split their forces but simply withdrew over the Elbe to Bautzen where they intended to stand and fight again. They quit Dresden on 7–8 May but neglected to blow up the bridges behind them. By 8 May Napoleon was in possession of Dresden and two days later had secured two bridgeheads on the east bank. Welcome news arrived that Eugène, before his departure, had badly mauled the Prussian rearguard at Colditz on 5 May. Most encouraging of all developments was that the King of Saxony had been forced off his perch and had committed fresh troops to the French army. Napoleon now set to work to devise a master plan that would suddenly unite the two wings of his army in a lightning stroke and pulverize the enemy.

Having sent orders to Ney to 'mask' Berlin and send part of his force south hidden from the enemy, Napoleon advanced across the Elbe. The Allies were slightly inferior numerically but had more seasoned manpower and a good defensive position, with the river Spree in front of them. Napoleon was trading on the confidence his enemy presumably felt to bring off a spectacular victory of the Austerlitz kind. His battle-plan was a strategic conception based on Alexander the Great's envelopment of the Persian flank at Gaugamela in 331 BC. He would begin by pinning the enemy – gradually committing more and more units in the centre. Ney meanwhile would proceed south by forced marches, ready to appear in the Allied rear and fall on the right flank. Once the Emperor was convinced that all enemy reserves had been drawn into the frontal engagement, the outflanking force would attack, forcing their opponents to switch forces from the centre to deal with the new threat; the French reserves would then deliver the *coup de grâce* in the centre.

Had the plan worked out, Bautzen would have been in the pantheon along with Friedland, Jena and Marengo. But, apart from his old fault of issuing imprecisely worded orders, Napoleon did not really have the generals for the job. This was a conception that required the skills of the late and lamented Lannes, of Masséna who was back in Spain, or of Davout who was on the lower Elbe. Instead, Napoleon had to use his worst marshals: Soult, Ney and MacDonald. Ney once again proved incapable of following orders. Instead of leaving a holding force at Berlin, he marched south with his entire army; he then failed to implement the clear order to wheel to the east of Bautzen to cut off the Allied retreat.

On 19 May Napoleon drew up his forces in battle order: Bertrand was on the left, Oudinot on the right, Marmont and MacDonald in the centre, with Soult's corps and the Guard in reserve. The initial French aim was to seize the village of Hochkirk and to wear out the enemy in the centre while Ney completed his outflanking movement on the right; Bertrand would then move across to deliver the knock-out blow. But Ney sent word that he would not be in position by the 19th; Napoleon therefore opted for a slugging match on the 20th, hoping to lull the enemy before the envelopment on the 21st. Facing him were the Prussians under Blücher and the Russians under Czar Alexander: their battle-plans were almost the mirror image of Napoleon's, since they intended to mass their attack on the French left and expected the main onslaught from the *Grande Armée* to come on their own left, where they kept their reserves.

Battle commenced on 20 May. After a cannonade from the French, their sappers bridged the Spree and the frontal assault by three French corps went well. Oudinot's corps performed valiantly on the right, reinforcing the Allied idea that their left was the real target. By nightfall everything had gone largely to plan and the French were in possession of Bautzen. But it soon became clear that Ney had bungled his part of the operation. Improvising swiftly, Napoleon ordered Ney to dig in and await the enemy while General Lauriston was detached with a separate task force to try to perform Ney's original task of appearing in the Allied rear.

Next morning the Emperor massed Soult's forces and the Guard ready for the knock-out blow. Despairing of his original outflanking plan, he now intended to punch right through the centre while holding on the flanks, in effect substituting Marlborough's tactics at Blenheim for Alexander's at Gaugamela. On the right Oudinot's conquering heroes of the 20th began to come under increasingly heavy pressure from the Allied left. Oudinot appealed for reinforcements, but Napoleon told him to hold until 3 p.m., noting that as the enemy sent more and more units after the slowly retreating marshal, they thinned their centre.

At 2 p.m. he ordered Soult and his 20,000 men of IV Corps forward for the masterstroke in the centre. IV Corps fought its way on to Bautzen plateau but then the assault faltered and gradually petered out. There were three main reasons: the Russians fought with all the tenacity of men determined not to be outdone by the 'new look' Prussians; Blücher spotted the danger and pulled back some of the units pursuing Oudinot; and Napoleon could not get his artillery forward because of the lack of horses. By late afternoon the two centres had fought each other to stalemate and Oudinot was still being pressed hard. The Emperor asked himself the question he had often asked in the past, and would again in the future: what is Ney doing?

The answer was that since 11 a.m. Ney had been bogged down in a pointless fight for Preititz village. Apparently unable to understand the import of the Emperor's commands, Ney failed to see that he should simply have 'masked' the village and pressed on into the enemy rear. Instead he insisted on costly attacks against the well-defended village, all of them repulsed; to make matters worse, his retreating troops collided with Lauriston's men, making even more hopeless the idea of outflanking the Allied army. Even when he finally managed to take Preititz, Ney compounded his previous errors by attacking Blücher head-on instead of manoeuvring behind him and forcing a Prussian withdrawal.

The struggle in the centre was bloody and protracted and the Emperor was again cast down by the fanatical fighting spirit of both Russians and Prussians. By 5 p.m. Oudinot had regained the initiative on the right, but both he and Soult were making very slow progress against a determined resistance. The Prussians were still holding Ney easily when the centre at last began to buckle, principally because the exhausted Russians were running low on ammunition. Finally sensing a definite weakening in the enemy pulse, Napoleon sent in the Guard. At this the Allies ordered a general retreat but were able to withdraw in good order with all guns thanks to the bungling of Ney and Lauriston. Around 10 p.m. that evening a violent thunderstorm ended the perfunctory French attempt at pursuit.

Both sides had lost about 20,000 men; the difference was that the Allies could afford to absorb these losses and the French could not. On points Napoleon had won another clear victory, but he could not fail to be cast down when he considered what might have been. Incompetent staffwork, Ney's stupidity, Lauriston's slowness, a poor supply system and some indiscipline in the ranks had contributed to the disappointing outcome, and malcontents whispered that the Emperor had been forced to send in his beloved Guard to win even a limited victory. But the most important factor in Napoleon's failure to achieve another Austerlitz was his shortage of horses, and this was a factor over which he had no control and which remained to plague him in the future. In his dejection he was not to know that the Allied commanders were beginning to lose confidence as they realized 'the ogre' was still a force to be reckoned with.

On 22 May the *Grande Armée* began a slow pursuit. Their wounded quarry showed how dangerous it still was during a violent clash at Reichenbach, where Napoleon lost a comrade even more dear to him than Bessières. A cannonball ricocheted off a tree-trunk, hit Duroc in the stomach, tore open his belly and spilled out his intestines in a gory mess over uniform, saddle and horse. Duroc was helped into a tent, where surgeons quickly concluded they could do nothing for him. Napoleon came to see his favourite friend as he lay dying. Duroc apologized to the Emperor for not being able to serve him further, asked him to be a father to his daughter, and then requested him to withdraw so that he was not present at the moment of death. Napoleon's grief at the death of his friend was like that of Alexander the Great for Hephaistion, or Achilles for Patroclus, but the inference of homosexuality is unjustified. Those, like Sir Richard Burton, who claim Napoleon as a bisexual Emperor, make unreasonably great play of the intense friendship with Duroc; but it is true that in some ways Napoleon never recovered from this loss.

It may well be that the balance of his mind at this juncture affected the entire course of the 1813 campaign, for the grief-stricken Emperor called off the pursuit, allowing the bickering Allies to fall back in disarray to Silesia. Although Napoleon now held most of the trumps, especially when Davout captured Hamburg, he gratefully accepted an offer of mediation from Austria. An armistice was signed at Pleschwitz on 2 June which had the effect of suspending the conflict for two months. Unaware of Metternich's intense animosity, Napoleon naïvely thought that his naming Marie-Louise regent would guarantee Austrian neutrality. In fact the Machiavellian Metternich was determined to bring Austria into the war, but needed a breathing space in which his dejected military partners could recover their spirits.

Although Napoleon has been severely criticized for falling into his enemies' trap by accepting the armistice, there were rational grounds for his decision. His army was already exhausted and had sustained 25,000 more casualties than the enemy in the campaign as a whole; there were 90,000 men on the sick list and desertion had reached epidemic proportions; additionally ammunition and supplies were scarce because of raids on lines of communication by Cossacks and German partisans. But, crucially, he lacked a good intelligence network, so did not realize the Allies were in a desperate position. After Bautzen there was acrimonious recrimination between Russians and Prussians; on the Russian side Wittgenstein resigned, to be replaced by Barclay de Tolly, who withdrew to Silesia. With enough horses to equip proper reconnaissance parties and cavalry pursuit, Napoleon would already have won total victory. This became clear when Oudinot's advance on Berlin ground to a halt because he had not enough horsemen to keep the harrying Cossacks at bay.

Each side regarded the armistice as a mere lull, each pinning hopes on Austria. It was clear that neither side could score a complete victory without the Habsburgs. Everything hinged on whether Austria would be most swayed by the matrimonial alliance with France or by the desire for revenge for humiliations extending from 1796 to 1809. This was the moment when Metternich came forward as mediator, on certain terms: Prussia was to be restored, the Confederacy of the Rhine dissolved, and France restricted to the 'natural frontiers'; Napoleon was to release Austria from any political or military obligations so that she could be an honest broker, and Prussia and Russia were to appoint Metternich sole agent, so that there was no possibility of a separately negotiated backstairs peace with France by either of them.

Napoleon agreed to recognize Metternich as mediator and to hold 'talks about talks' to resolve the substantive issues. One of the most famous meetings in history took place in the map room of the Mercolini palace (Elsterwiese Castle) in Dresden on 26 June, where the French Emperor made his base from 9 June to 10 July. But the Dresden conclave, where Metternich confronted the 'ogre' he so detested, was never a serious peace conference. Metternich went to the meeting in full cynicism, determined to buy time while Austria mobilized and the Prussians and Russians licked their wounds. Assured by his spies, including Talleyrand, that the French notables would accept the natural frontiers, and knowing that Austria was committed to enter the war on the Allied side if French agreement to peace proposals was not received by 10 August, Metternich was confident that he held all the trumps.

This most famous of meetings lasted from around noon to shortly after 8.30 p.m. There are two versions of the nine-hour Dresden conference, one from Metternich, the other from Napoleon. Both show the meeting as tempestuous and emotional. It was on this occasion that Napoleon made his famous weary remark, that even if he defeated the Kings of Austria and Prussia twenty times, they would still keep their thrones, whereas he needed the momentum of constant victory to survive at all. Metternich reported Napoleon's words thus: 'My reign will not outlast the day when I have ceased to be strong and therefore to be feared . . . I know how to die . . . But I shall never cede one inch of territory. Your sovereigns, who were born on the throne, can allow themselves to be beaten twenty times and will always return to their capitals. But I cannot do that – I am a self-made soldier.'

He accused Austria of going over to his enemies under a guise of neutrality and claimed that, but for Metternich's blundering intervention, he could already have made peace with Prussia and Russia. The so-called mediation was simply an excuse for all three Continental *ancien régime* powers to gang up on him. He upbraided Austria for treachery, naturally not revealing his own intended Machiavellianism, which was to buy Austria off, defeat the other two powers, then turn round and force Austria to disgorge the concession he had made. It was then a question of price. He was prepared to sacrifice Illyria to Austria. Would that be enough?

Metternich soon showed he was in no mood to compromise. Grimly he laid out the peace terms: Austria wanted the return of all former provinces in Italy, Russia required the dissolution of the Grand Duchy of Warsaw and Prussia demanded an end of the Confederacy of the Rhine. These were not so much negotiating overtures as a demand for France's unconditional surrender; Napoleon was being asked to give up all his conquests since 1796. As he gradually realized that Metternich had not come with genuine offers of mediation but simply to hold a gun to his head, the Emperor became more and more angry, and it is in this context that we should read the supposedly 'unbalanced' behaviour Metternich presents in his memoir as having occurred spontaneously. There is a circumstantial ring of truth about Metternich's narrative, but it is partial: it omits the provocation and the atmosphere of treachery that induced Napoleon's outbursts.

Napoleon asked how he could possibly be expected to accept such ludicrous terms after just winning two victories. He spoke of the martial tradition of the *Grande Armée*. Metternich replied: 'I have seen your soldiers. They are no more than children.' Then came the three-cornered hat incident. According to Metternich, Napoleon threw it into a corner of the room in a rage. According to Napoleon it 'fell to the ground', Metternich did not deign to pick it up for him, so in angry contempt he kicked it away from himself. He raged at Metternich: 'You know nothing of what goes on in a soldier's mind. I grew up on the field of battle. A man like me cares little for the lives of a million men.' Metternich replied caustically that he wished the windows and doors of the palace could be thrown open so that all Europe could hear what had just been said. He taunted Napoleon with sacrificing French lives to his own ambition and mentioned the Russian campaign. The Emperor replied that he had lost 'only' 300,000 in Russia and that 'less than a tenth' were French; he had spared the French by sacrificing Poles and Germans. At this even the icy Metternich lost his composure. 'You forget, sire, that you are addressing a German.'

The meeting quickly descended into a slanging match. 'I may lose my throne,' Napoleon exclaimed, 'but I shall bury the whole world in its ruins.' 'Sire, you are a lost man,' Metternich replied witheringly. Changing tack, Napoleon asked him scornfully how much England had paid him to play Judas. Metternich remained silent. He could scarcely admit that, in addition to the £2 million each Prussia and Austria had been given in the spring, the government in London had set aside a further million and £590,000 worth of supplies for Austria if she joined the Allied side. British aid in March–November 1813 came to a staggering £11 million – a figure equal to the total cost of all loans and subsidies during the wars of 1793–1801. This was excluding a further £2 million of arms and equipment provided during 1813, and other large sums paid to Denmark, Holland and Hanover.

The conference achieved nothing. Napoleon made it clear that he would concede on Illyria but not on Italy, the Grand Duchy of Warsaw or the Confederation of the Rhine. Metternich replied that in that case there was nothing to talk about. Angrily Napoleon flashed at him: 'Ah, you persist, you still want to dictate to me. All right then, war! But, au revoir, in Vienna!' Metternich shrugged. As he was leaving the conference chamber, Berthier took him aside and asked if things had gone satisfactorily. Metternich replied: 'Yes, he has made everything abundantly clear. It's all up with him.' Next day Austria signed the secret accord of Reichenbach with Prussia and Russia, agreeing to enter the war on their side if France would not accept Metternich's terms.

Immediately after the Dresden conference Napoleon had second thoughts, felt he had mishandled matters and arranged a further peace congress in Prague; the armistice was extended until 10 August. But in the immediate aftermath of Dresden there came news also of the sudden collapse of the French position in Spain. One immediate result of the 1812 débâcle was that Britain sent reinforcements to Spain. By the beginning of 1813 Wellington, recognized as Commander-in-Chief, Spain, by the Supreme Junta in November 1812, commanded 87,000 troops (56,000 of them British) and the number would top 100,000 by the spring. So far from reinforcing his armies in Spain, Napoleon was forced to recall 15,000 of them to serve in the 1813 campaign in Germany.

Sheer numbers now told against Joseph. With the increasing strength of the guerrillas, it took four divisions to keep open the route between Madrid and the Pyrenees and six weeks for a dispatch from Madrid to reach Paris. When Soult, to Joseph's relief, was recalled and replaced with Marshal Jourdan, Joseph's old friend, the two men took counsel on what they could achieve with their exiguous numbers. Jourdan advised that the south and north-west of Spain must be abandoned in favour of concentration in the key areas of Old Castile, Navarre, the Pyrenean routes, Santander and San Sebastian. Napoleon concurred and in March 1813 ordered Joseph to abandon Madrid and move his capital to Valladolid.

Joseph had long been preparing for Wellington's annual invasion of Spain but was sadly short of troops. Originally he had planned to deploy his forces in a great semicircle stretching from Leon, west of Burgos, to La Mancha, south of Madrid, but his brother's orders, finally realistic, at least enabled him to fight a defensive campaign. But he could neither persuade his brother the Emperor that Wellington outnumbered him, nor summon aid from Suchet, who had his hands full in Catalonia and Aragon with invaders from Sicily. Working with Jourdan, Joseph decided that Wellington would enter Spain via Ciudad Rodrigo and head north-east through Salamanca and Valladolid.

As expected, Wellington advanced on Salamanca in May. Concentrating his forces to meet him, Joseph discovered to his alarm that it was not the full 100,000 strong Allied force (80,000 British and Hanoverians, 20,000 Spanish) that had occupied the city but a much smaller force. Wellington had duped him by sending his main army under General Sir Thomas Graham to cross into Spain further north. Graham's six divisions emerged on to the plains of Leon from the Tras-Os-Montes mountains, where Wellington's decoy force from Salamanca joined them after forced marches. After concentrating at Toro, Wellington turned Marmont's old tactics back on the French by hooking ever north, threatening to get round the enemy and forcing the evacuation of Palencia and Burgos.

Continually outflanked, Joseph pulled his forces back to the plain west of Vitoria. Wellington realized that a victory here would not deliver the ultimate strategic objective of clearing the French out of Spain and that ideally he needed a battle farther west, but he had problems himself with long supply lines. Although he was being partially provisioned by Royal Navy vessels at Corunna, the main supply line ran back to Portugal, a ten-week journey away, and for five days he had had to live off the land.

The decisive clash came on 19 June. Joseph was expecting a frontal attack from the west but Wellington planned a two-pronged onslaught from the north. He observed that Joseph had made a bad error by drawing up his forces with a five-mile gap between the front-line Army of the South and the second-line Army of Portugal. To lull the French, Wellington sent General Hill through the pass of La Puebla on to the Vitoria plain, as Joseph had expected. Then he unleashed his main attack. Caught between two fires, the French attempted a fighting withdrawal, which quickly became a rout as they discovered, too late, that the British had come down behind them to seize the roads to Bayonne and Bilbao. Reduced to withdrawing along the rough track to Pamplona, the French army soon dissolved into a chaos of panicked men, frightened camp-followers and abandoned wagons.

Vitoria was a spectacular victory, as it severed the French retreat to San Sebastian and Bayonne, and made the French abandon all their artillery (150 guns), stores, ammunition and equipment, including paintings, money and other treasures evacuated from Madrid. The entire payroll of the French army was also captured, with the result that millions of gold francs disappeared into the pockets of British, Spanish and Portuguese soldiers. Joseph's army took 8,000 casualties (as against 5,000 in Wellington's army) and lost several hundreds more to guerrillas during the retreat. It was fortunate for the French that torrential rain and the state of the road led Wellington to call off the pursuit up the Pamplona track after five miles. The panic-stricken French did not halt their flight until the Pyrenean border and Joseph retired in disgrace to Paris.

Wellington was now the cynosure of Europe; he received his field-marshal baton and Beethoven composed 'Wellington's Victory' in his honour. But he was frustrated at not being able to press on into Aragon and Catalonia to deal with Suchet and Clausel. In a word, the discipline of his troops broke down completely; it was their crazed looting after Vitoria that drew from their commander the celebrated remark that his men were the scum of the earth. If Joseph had been able to regroup and counterattack, he would have found the entire British army roaring drunk. By the time Wellington had restored order with the gallows and the lash, Clausel had retreated into France, leaving only Pamplona and San Sebastian in French hands.

News of Vitoria reached Dresden on 1 July and simply hardened Austrian resolve to join the Allies. Even if Austria, Prussia and Russia had been willing to come to terms with Napoleon, this was not really an option now, for the British called in the *quid pro quo* for their subsidies, insisting that the Allies remain in the field lest Napoleon turn his full power against Wellington in Spain. Napoleon sent an unwilling Soult from Dresden to Bayonne to form a new army from the escapees of Vitoria and gave him a warrant for Joseph's arrest (which Soult tactfully did not use). For once Soult bestirred himself, retrained the scattered remnants of the former French armies in Spain and recrossed the border into the Peninsula with a force of 80,000 hoping to relieve Pamplona.

Soult contrived to delay Wellington's invasion of France for four months by launching a two-pronged attack on the besiegers of Pamplona. Defeated twice by Wellington and with dwindling food supplies, he managed to delay the fall of Pamplona and San Sebastian before withdrawing into France; he had done enough to escape the worst rages of the Emperor. The cautious Wellington was not the man to invade France with San Sebastian and Pamplona still untaken in his rear. In any case England's military hero had his own problems, for the United States was at war with Britain, and American warships and privateers made serious inroads on British shipping in the Bay of Biscay. And when San Sebastian did finally fall, on 31 August, there was the almost predictable orgy of rape, murder and pillage from the 'scum of the earth'.

In Dresden Napoleon awaited the results of the Prague conference, where Caulaincourt was his envoy. Historians divide on Napoleon's intentions at this time. Some claim that he genuinely wanted peace, foreseeing the outcome if he had to fight all three great European powers, but that he was overwhelmed by the sheer malice of his enemies, who never had any intention of offering him reasonable terms. Others claim that he was merely stalling for time, waiting until the harvest was in, hoping the Allies would have second thoughts once they realized France was not on its knees, but determined to fight to the end if that was necessary. Ever the opportunist, Napoleon was clearly hoping for something to turn up, but he refused to make the one concession that might have split the Allies: relinquishing the Confederation of the Rhine. This was the item that particularly exercised Prussia and Austria, who were fearful long-term of a permanent Russian presence in western Europe. Caulaincourt pleaded with him to bend on this point, but had to endure irate outbursts and slammed doors for his pains.

At Prague Caulaincourt went well beyond his instructions in an attempt to secure an accord with Metternich. Some French historians have even accused him of treason, but his action was surely simply the despair reasonable Frenchmen felt about the everlasting conflict with which their Emperor had landed them. Metternich unhelpfully repeated that Austria was committed to go to war on the side of the Allies if there was no agreement by 10 August. When Caulaincourt reported this to Napoleon, he once again stalled and disingenuously tried the ploy known to every roguish solicitor: he asked for further and better particulars. Metternich, tired of French procrastination and convinced there could never be an agreement, opted for a propaganda advantage by offering surprisingly mild terms. Nothing was said about Italy, but Prussia would have to be restored as far as the Elbe and the Duchy of Warsaw broken up; although Hamburg, Trieste and Lübeck were declared non-negotiable, the return of the western portions of Prussia, lost to the kingdom of Westphalia in 1806–7, were not demanded back. But Metternich was adamant that the Confederation of the Rhine would have to be dissolved.

Caulaincourt begged Napoleon to accept these terms. But the Emperor argued that the buffer states of the Confederation of the Rhine were the only way France could safeguard its natural frontier on the Rhine. Although the new conditions seemed more lenient than those offered at Dresden on 26 June, when their implications were teased out, it seemed that France was being asked to return, not just to 1796, but to 1792, before the decree of the Convention laid down the natural frontiers as an integral part of French sovereignty. Napoleon once again insinuated the idea that he was a mere plaything of history, a slave of destiny, not the purposive conqueror of the 'ogre' myth. In reply to Metternich's ultimatum, he asked for compensation in the form of Austrian and

Prussian territory for the King of Saxony, the partition of the Duchy of Warsaw and for Hamburg and Trieste. He told Caulaincourt he had to insist on this for, if he acquiesced in Metternich's terms, it would simply encourage the Allies to demand even more. The deeply disillusioned Caulaincourt commented: 'The cause of our disappointments is in the refusal to make timely concessions, and it will end by ruining us completely.'

On 11 August, true to her word, Austria declared war on France. The previous month Sweden, under Bernadotte, had joined in, animated by his hatred for Bonaparte. The Czar had made strenuous efforts to get him on the Allied side and, in an ironic gloss on *la ronde de l'amour*, even offered him as bride the very sister he had refused Napoleon – provided, of course, Bernadotte got rid of Désirée. The Allies could draw on enormous forces. Apart from Sweden's 40,000, Prussia was contributing 160,000, Russia 184,000 and Austria 127,000. Half a million men were ready to march and there was an estimated 350,000 more in the recruitment pipeline. There would be four separate Allied forces: the 110,000 Army of the North (Swedes and Russians) under Bernadotte, based on Berlin; the 95,000-strong Army of Silesia under Blücher at Breslau; the Russian so-called Army of Poland with a new commander, Bennigsen, the veteran of Eylau, and the main striking force, the 230,000-strong Army of Bohemia (Austrians, Prussians and Russians) based on the upper Elbe, under the command of the Austrian Schwarzenberg.

Czar Alexander insisted that the Austrian be the Allied Commander-in-Chief, in preference to the more obvious choice, Blücher; he thought he could dominate the Austrian but knew that the fiery Prussian would simply ignore him. The three allies, wary of taking on Bonaparte at anything like equal odds, had agreed on a Fabian strategy of attrition. If Napoleon threatened any of their armies, it was to retreat while the others manoeuvred to cut his communications. Relying on favourable elements of space and time, they would gradually wear the French down by avoiding battle with the Emperor while defeating his marshals.

On paper Napoleon could oppose these 800,000 Allies with 680,000 of his own, raised by titanic efforts. Most of these were raw and ill-trained recruits but 90% were French and the officer problem was easing, though the shortage of horses always remained his Achilles' heel. His strategy for the renewed campaign was to await the enemy at Dresden with his main force of 250,000 in seven corps, while 120,000 men in four infantry corps under Oudinot would advance on Berlin to deal with Bernadotte and the Army of the North; Davout's XIII Corps would defend Hamburg and the lower Elbe.

Dispersing his corps like this seemed an obvious mistake, not only because it vitiated the doctrine of concentration of force, but because it meant the Emperor would have to rely on the independent judgement of marshals, used simply to executing part of his grand battlefield conception. Moreover, it played right into the hands of the Allied strategy of attrition. It is hard to understand what lay behind this decision. The best guess is that he wanted to disguise his essential weakness from the Allies: since even if he won at Dresden he lacked the strength to follow them into Poland, a northern campaign would show evidence of the 'advance' he would need to claim in his bulletins. Even the marshals protested at the decision. Marmont said gloomily: 'I greatly fear that on the day we gain a great victory, the Emperor may learn he has lost two.'

If the early months of the 1813 campaign had seen Napoleon back to something like his best military form, the late summer and autumn found him back in his vacillating 1812 mood. From 17–21 August he dithered unconscionably. He advanced to Bautzen, learned the Russians intended to reinforce Blücher and decided to strike him before they could do so. Then he decided instead to intercept the 40,000 Russians. Next he changed his mind again and decided to assault Blücher at Breslau, only to fi d the Prussian withdrawing before him, in accordance with the Allied plan. While Napoleon was trying to pin Blücher down, Schwarzenberg advanced from Prague to threaten Dresden. It now seemed possible to strike Schwarzenberg's Army of Bohemia on a vulnerable flank, so Napoleon ordered Marshal Gouvion St-Cyr to hold out in Dresden while he got into position. But word came back that Dresden could no longer hold out. This put the Emperor in a dilemma. He hated to give up his idea for a flank attack but on the other hand could not afford to lose Dresden with its massed supplies of artillery, its ammunition dumps and food supplies.

In an unsatisfactory compromise Napoleon divided his forces and took most of them back to Dresden, leaving just a single corps under Vandamme to harry Schwarzenberg's flank. Some military historians have claimed that if the decision had been reversed, Napoleon would have won the victory he sought. The new French army bore itself in the great traditions of the *Grande Armée* by an astonishing 90-mile forced march in 72 hours. They arrived at Dresden on 26 August just in time to repel Wittgenstein's Russians, who had already reached the suburbs. Napoleon expressed contempt for his marshals, railing that he could not be everywhere at once. But his fury was matched by that of the Czar, who saw the prize snatched from him. None the less, Alexander was prepared to make the most of it and break off the action, in accordance with the general policy. It was the other two Emperors who insisted on a battle then and there.

All afternoon of 26 August the Allies tried to blast their way into Dresden, but the French held firm. At 5.30 Napoleon launched a counterattack and regained all the ground lost during the day. That night he brought up reinforcements. Both sides planned to go over on to the attack on the morrow. The Allies intended a mass assault in the centre, leaving the flanks weak, but it was there that Napoleon hoped for a double envelopment, using Victor on the left and the Young Guard on the right. He was confident that his centre, fortified by trenches and redoubts full of cannon, was impregnable.

Fierce fighting went on all day on the 27th. Although the Allied wings resisted strenuously, the French flank attack succeeded. The problems came in the centre where the French were hard put to it to hold their own. Napoleon expected a decisive third day of fighting, but the Allies had taken such a mauling (losing 38,000 casualties to the French 10,000), that they had lost heart. In a dramatic role reversal, the previously circumspect Czar found himself vainly arguing at a council of war for perseverance, but the unexpectedly unpliant Austrians overruled him. By dawn on the 28th the French were left in possession of the field and Napoleon could claim yet another points victory which essentially solved nothing. Moreover, the Emperor's health was again giving cause for concern. At the height of the fighting on the 27th, drenched with rain and shivering with fever, he had to return to the town and lie down. Conspiracy theorists believe that an attempt was made to poison the Emperor at this time, and some claim he was absent from the field at the precise time when his presence could have ensured a knock-out victory.

Any momentary euphoria was soon dissolved by bad news from all the other fronts. Oudinot had been defeated at Grossberen on the road to Berlin and MacDonald had lost 15,000 men and one hundred guns in a defeat by Blücher at Katzbach. Vandamme and I Corps, harrying Schwarzenberg were heavily defeated at Toplitz by the Russians and Prussians under Ostermann and Kleist. This was sheer bad luck. The enemy suddenly turned at bay to face I Corps and, just as Vandamme engaged them, another enemy column which had lost its way suddenly blundered into his rear. With 13,000 casualties I Corps was all but wiped out. This showed that the Allies' strategy was correct and that Marmont had been a true prophet. Napoleon should never have split his forces and never have entrusted these delicate operations to his lesser marshals.

After Dresden Napoleon had two choices: march on Prague or Berlin.

He opted for the Prussian capital but was unable to progress towards his objective because of constant Allied probes towards Dresden. First Blücher again threatened it, then he withdrew when he heard Bonaparte was still in charge. Next Schwarzenberg moved forward, only to retreat likewise when Napoleon appeared. While all this went on, there came news of Ney's defeat by Bülow and Bernadotte at Dennewitz (6 September). Napoleon had foolishly put Ney in over Oudinot and Oudinot, piqued and far the superior general, at once realized Ney's tactics were misguided. He therefore followed them to the letter, allowing Ney to discredit himself.

Ney, who rushed into the thick of the battle, when he should have been commanding from a hilltop, was not the only buffoon at Dennewitz that day. The absurd Bernadotte managed to arrive on the field of battle when the fighting was almost over. He then ordered Bülow to pull back and let him take over. The Prussians were infuriated at this arrogance: the people who had fought all day were to be forgotten while a Gascon popinjay with an army that had not fought at all coolly claimed the victory. Napoleon could have told the Allies what to expect from Bernadotte, had he space to consider the multitudinous nonsense emanating from the new King of Sweden. But he had more serious matters on his mind. When news of the defeat came in, the Emperor's public sangfroid was notable. He listened to the bulletin 'with all the coolness he could have brought to a discussion of events in China', as he himself boasted. But secretly he fumed against the fool he had made Prince of the Moskova.

The game of 'avoid Bonaparte' continued, with Bernadotte, Schwarzenberg and Blücher keeping up the pressure. As soon as Napoleon moved east from Dresden to deal with Blücher, the other two would close in and force him back. The Emperor was permanently off balance, forever rushing from one front to another to make good the errors of his generals. The Allied policy of avoiding him and picking off the marshals was proving a spectacular success. Already angry about this, Napoleon threw one of his pyrotechnical displays of rage when he learned by chance that Bernadotte had been corresponding with Murat, Berthier, Oudinot and MacDonald, trying to suborn them. He denounced Murat as a traitor and feelings ran so high that Murat was seen to grasp the hilt of his sabre. When Berthier tried to pour oil on troubled waters by speaking of his duty as a 'French prince' to explore all possible avenues for peace, Napoleon rounded savagely on him: 'You, too, old imbecile, what are you meddling in? Be quiet!'

The stress was showing. Since mid-August the Emperor had lost

150,000 men and 300 cannon, and there were a further 50,000 on the sick list. Food supplies were running out, and the whole of Germany except for Saxony had gone over to the enemy. To husband his resources Napoleon decided to shorten his front and was contemplating breaking off all contact with the enemy when they changed tactics. Leaving Dresden alone, they decided to concentrate at Leipzig to cut French lines to the Rhine. Napoleon moved swiftly to take up his favourite centre position around Leipzig, enabling him to move either against the combined forces of Blücher and Bernadotte (140,000) or Schwarzenberg and Bennigsen (180,000). But he made the bad error of leaving St-Cyr in Dresden with a large garrison, again offending against the principle of concentration of force. Hanging on to Dresden at this stage in the campaign made no sense militarily, though possibly politically, as it was the capital of Saxony, his one remaining ally. But the time for caution was long gone. The Emperor needed to assemble every available man for one last battle.

The game of military tag went on for three weeks, with Bernadotte, Blücher, MacDonald and Napoleon all chasing each other at various times: the French Army wore itself out with marching and counter-marching while achieving nothing. Napoleon's dilemma was that if he pursued Blücher and Bernadotte too far, he would leave Leipzig unguarded. At the same time, because the Allies always avoided battle with him, he could spend forever probing out of Leipzig without making contact. His one chance came on 5 October when Blücher and Bernadotte linked up. The Swedish monarch favoured withdrawal over the Elbe, but Blücher was adamant that they must join Schwarzenberg and the Army of Bohemia; the three armies therefore finally converged on Leipzig. Based at Duben from 10–14 October, Napoleon was once again sunk in the deepest gloom. Fain reported that he would sit at his desk with an abstracted expression, doodling on a piece of paper.

The French now faced the obvious danger of being trapped between three armies instead of being able to defeat the enemy piecemeal. Napoleon finally ordered a general concentration of his forces at Leipzig, but still kept a substantial garrison in Dresden. Once again it was the hard-driving Blücher who ultimately persuaded the Allies to take on Bonaparte in a final battle; both Bernadotte and Schwarzenberg were highly dubious. So it was that 160,000 French troops faced twice that number of Allies in a titanic three-day struggle that ever afterwards bore the title 'the Battle of the Nations'.

The geography of Leipzig determined the course of the battle. Napoleon had the advantage of interior lines to offset his numerical disparity, since he could fight with Leipzig at his back while the Allies had to enter combat on a wider front. Four rivers meet at Leipzig and in 1813 they divided the environs into the four points of the compass. Having destroyed most of the bridges, Napoleon could feel confident that the main fighting would take place to the east of the city, where a series of undulating ridges, harbouring many villages and hamlets, protected an otherwise flat plain; the terrain therefore uniquely combined strong defensive positions with a battleground where cavalry could be used. It seemed unlikely that the Allies could work their way round to the marshy south, so their only other option was to probe around the west or possibly try to break in via the flat and open north.

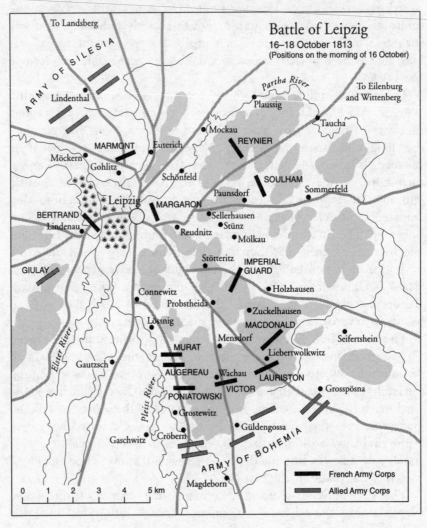

Battle of Leipzig
16–18 October 1813
(Positions on the morning of 16 October)

To Landsberg
ARMY OF SILESIA
Lindenthal
To Eilenburg and Wittenberg
Partha River
Plaussig
Taucha
Mockau
MARMONT
Euterich
REYNIER
Möckern
Gohlitz
Schönfeld
SOULHAM
Sommerfeld
Paunsdorf
Leipzig
MARGARON
Sellerhausen
BERTRAND
Stünz
Lindenau
Reudnitz
Mölkau
Stötteritz
IMPERIAL GUARD
GIULAY
Holzhausen
Connewitz
Probstheida
Zuckelhausen
Lössnig
MACDONALD
Mensdorf
Seifertshein
MURAT
Liebertwolkwitz
Gautzsch
AUGEREAU
Wachau
LAURISTON
Elster River
PONIATOWSKI
VICTOR
Grosspösna
Grostewitz
Pleiss River
Güldengossa
Gaschwitz
Cröbern
ARMY OF BOHEMIA
Magdeborn

0 1 2 3 4 5 km

French Army Corps
Allied Army Corps

Napoleon's idea was to fight a holding action in the north, using III, IV, VI and VII Corps, while the garrison troops of Leipzig secured the western routes to Lindenau. The decisive action would be in the east, with II, V, VIII and XI Corps; IX Corps and the Guard would be in reserve. The Allies initially planned to loop round through the marshes to the south but were intercepted by the French, so that the main battle took place in the south-east. Napoleon did not expect much fighting in the north and west, so was caught off balance when it happened. His inadequate preparations to deal with this contingency can be realized from two salient facts: he was utterly complacent about the west and had built no additional bridges across the river from Leipzig to Lindenau; and he was so confident that fighting in the north would be sporadic that he weakened the sector by withdrawing part of Marmont's VI Corps to the south.

When contact with the enemy was finally made and the Emperor realized his error, he drew up the bulk of his army south-east of Leipzig, planning to pin Schwarzenberg and the Allied centre while Augereau and IX Corps enveloped the right; Marmont and the others were to hold Blücher at bay in the north. But the Battle of Leipzig, which began at 6.30 on the morning of 16 October, soon became a murderous slugging match, a bloodbath of pure attrition which reached a peak between 9 and 11 a.m. On Napoleon's chosen terrain the Austrian attack was badly coordinated and a well-drilled defence could have annihilated it. Instead the French defenders fell into confusion, allowing the Austrians to press on, all the while taking dreadful punishment from 700 well-sited French guns. By mid-morning it was clear that the Allied offensive against the French centre had failed.

At this crucial moment Napoleon dithered. Not wanting to order Augereau's flanking movement until he was certain that Marmont had not been overwhelmed by Blücher, he opted instead for softening up the Austrian centre by wheeling up 150 guns and pounding them for an hour. At midday he launched his counterattack in the main sector; initially this went well, and the prospect of victory loomed. At 2 p.m. he decided to go for the knock-out punch, and for half an hour there followed the most vicious fighting any of the French veterans could remember. At 2.30 p.m. Murat and his 10,000 cavalry went into action. Thinking all was secure in the centre, Napoleon turned his attention to the north.

Here Marmont and VI Corps had been involved in fighting that was, if anything, even more sanguinary than the engagement in the south-east. Marmont's captaincy that day was inspired and he almost achieved a miracle like Davout's at Auerstädt against the Prussians. Two things worked against him. Once again Ney proved the French nemesis by his supreme idiocy: he continually recalled and re-recalled two divisions of Souham's III Corps, undecided whether to send them to Marmont, to Lindenau or the Emperor, with the result that the two divisions finally got into the battle (in the south-east) just half an hour before dusk. The other thing that prevented Marmont's miracle was the refusal by the Württemberg cavalry to charge when ordered; probably they were already planning the treachery that took place two days later. As in all battles, the vital moment came and went. By nightfall the Prussians had counterattacked and were getting the better of the engagement. However, Napoleon cannot escape censure for the failure in the north, as he had not expected heavy fighting there at all.

Since there was murderous fighting in both sectors, numbers told, and Napoleon was probably just a corps short of achieving total victory in both parts of the battle. The distraction in the north was probably crucial to French fortunes in the south too, for the Emperor was concentrating on Marmont's problems at the precise moment he should have been sending in infantry to support Murat in the *coup de grâce*. His failure to do this allowed Russian cavalry to countercharge, and by 3.30 p.m. the great opportunity had gone. By 4 p.m. the French were making ground steadily but had still not broken the Austrians. Then the arrival of Allied reinforcements allowed the Austrians to counterattack. By nightfall the French were back where they started.

When the fateful day of 16 October ended, the French had had slightly the upper hand in the south-east but slightly the worse of it in the north. Since French losses (25,000) nearly equalled those of the Allies (30,000) the result of the battle could only be considered a draw. But for Napoleon matters could only get worse, since he had no significant reinforcements to draw on, while Bernadotte and Bennigsen were drawing near with an extra 40,000 for the Allies. Grave and rapid decisions needed to be made next day, but Napoleon again spent the day in gloomy indecision. At first he ordered a general retreat to the Rhine, then countermanded this and decided to stay on in Leipzig, apparently hoping that the Allies would score some spectacular own goal. It seems that he could not quite accept that he had come so close to victory only to see it snatched away. This was his most grievous mistake over the three days. The Allies were quite content to wait until all their reinforcements had come up.

Too late Napoleon's intelligence agents brought word of the scale of the forces opposed to him. Whereas the initial numbers had been 260,000 to 200,000 in the Allies' favour, the figures were now 320,000 and 160,000 respectively. With six centripetal attacks planned for the 18th, it seemed that the Allies were preparing to crack him like a nut.

At the eleventh hour the Emperor finally bestirred himself and ordered more bridges to be built over the river Lindeman in case he needed to retreat. In torrential rain he pulled his men back, conscious that they were now outnumbered two to one.

On the morning of 18 October the Allies advanced confidently. Once again dreadful fighting took place, particularly in the afternoon, as more and more divisions on both sides were sucked into the conflict. Bennigsen and Bernadotte made significant inroads in the east against MacDonald and Sebastiani, and Napoleon had to order in both Young and Old Guards to prevent this sector collapsing altogether. Just when French fortunes were being restored, two brigades of Saxons and some Württembergers from Reynier's VII Corps – supposedly Napoleon's precious reinforcements – deserted to the enemy, leaving a gaping hole in the French line. By dusk Bennigsen and Bernadotte had dislodged Marmont and Reynier's corps from their positions, and both in the north and the east the French were being inexorably forced back into the suburbs of Leipzig.

With rising casualties and dwindling ammunition, Napoleon now had to accept that Leipzig was untenable. He ordered a phased evacuation, which began at 2 a.m. on the 19th. First out were the cavalry, then followed the infantry units. The Allies did not detect the withdrawal until 7 that morning but were held up by Oudinot's ferocious rearguard action, in which his men fought street by street and house by house until the army crossed the Elster river causeway to Lindenau. By 11 a.m. when Napoleon himself crossed over, all seemed to be working out well. All that now remained, once Oudinot's men had retired across the bridge, was to blow up the causeway, preventing Allied pursuit to Lindenau.

Now came utter disaster. In a classic of buck-passing, the general assigned to the actual demolition delegated the setting of charges to a Colonel Montfort. This worthy in turn decamped when the streetfighting came uncomfortably close and left the final job of demolition to a corporal. Unaware of the carefully scheduled timetable, the corporal ignited the fuses at 1 p.m. when the bridge was still crowded with French troops and Oudinot's rearguard was still in the city. The explosion and subsequent panic and rout led to the deaths of thousands of French troops and the capture of thousands more. Oudinot's heroes held out until late afternoon before surrendering, and Oudinot himself escaped by swimming the swollen Elster. Others were not so lucky, and among the celebrity prisoners were Reynier and Lauriston. The saddest fate befell the newest marshal, Prince Poniatowski. The Pole, who had been rewarded with a marshal's baton for his conspicuous gallantry the day before, enjoyed his rank less than twenty-four hours. As he spurred his steed across the engorged Elster, the horse lost its footing on the river bed, toppled over and pitched its master into the flood waters, where he drowned.

Leipzig was a catastrophe for Napoleon second only to 1812. Over four days he had lost 38,000 casualties and a further 30,000 taken prisoner as a result of the fiasco at the Elster bridge; in addition he had abandoned 325 cannon and been deserted by 5,000 Saxons. The Allies could make good their horrendous 54,000 casualty roll over the same period, but the French could not. Altogether in the 1813 campaign Napoleon had lost a further 400,000 men on top of the massive casualties in Russia in 1812, including 100,000 men in the scattered garrisons from Danzig to Dresden who were gradually forced to surrender, many of them by dishonest Allied promises which the victors later refused to ratify. The Confederacy of the Rhine was stone dead, as Bavaria and Saxony now made common cause with the Allies.

The demoralized French Army arrived at Erfurt like a pack of beaten curs and tatterdemalion beggars. Gloomily they retreated through Frankfurt and Mayence. But even at this stage the Army had teeth, as the incautious General Wrede, with a force of Bavarians and Austrians, learned to his cost in an utter defeat at Hanau on 30 October. Remaining at a respectful distance and hampered, like their opponents, by heavy rain and a typhus epidemic, the Allies took until Christmas to reach the east bank of the Rhine. By that time the prize for first to invade France had already gone to Wellington, who trod French soil for the first time on 7 October.

The reasons for Napoleon's failure in 1813 were several. The poor calibre of his men, the lacklustre performance of the marshalate, the dwindling enthusiasm at all levels in the French Army, all these played a part. Napoleon's performance as a captain was indifferent. He started well at Bautzen and Lützen but seemed to have run out of ideas by Leipzig, especially as it became clear that the enemy had learned their lessons well and were alive to all his tricks. Above all, though, the two things that sank Napoleon were the lack of horses, preventing him from campaigning properly, and the sheer volume of numbers on the Allied side. In all his career as a gambler the Emperor had never before had to confront the combined might of Russia, Austria and Prussia. In his heart he knew his chances were forlorn after August 1813, and hence the many interludes of almost catatonic depression. But now he needed to reach down into the bag in which he stored all his guile and experience, for by the end of 1813 his very survival was at stake.

CHAPTER TWENTY-FIVE

With his back to the wall, Napoleon was defiant. Having lost the military war against the Allies, he proceeded to lose the political war in Paris by refusing to conciliate the notables. He made an initial gesture towards them by ordaining that the Senate and Council of State should join the Chamber of Deputies in a joint session of the Legislature, but spoiled the effect by appointing one of his own placemen as president of the session. Bourgeois hostility was redoubled by emergency cuts in salaries, the collapse of the stockmarket, the acquisition by the Allies of frontier factories, as at Liège, and new taxes: the Emperor reintroduced the *droits réunis* on alcohol, tobacco and salt, doubled the *patente* and increased the normal rate of taxation by 30 centimes. To cap all, the French people were about to experience the horrors of war as French territory was invaded for the first time since 1792.

By the beginning of 1814 Napoleon no longer had significant support in France outside the Army. The propertied classes were angry that all their concessions to the Emperor had been in vain: they had had to see their sons serve in the wars, see all the money they had spent on substitutes in the draft in previous years spent for nothing, and now they faced business ruin. They were also under physical threat from a number of directions: from the Allied invaders, from peasants hungry for a redistribution of land, from the extraordinary commissioners (rather like the Revolutionary *députés en mission*) Napoleon threatened to unleash upon them, from the volunteer militias formed from the unemployed, and from the host of deserters, draft evaders and bandits who roamed the countryside.

The notables were angry that they were back with the disorder that had plagued them under the Directory. Was it for this they had made an Emperor? Bonaparte's blunders meant they were now back with the dilemma they sought to avoid by opting for the imperial 'third way'. They did not want the restoration of the Bourbons but they feared even more Jacobinism and the *levée en masse*. However, the Bourbons came to seem an increasingly attractive bet after Louis XVIII's decree of

1 February 1813, in which he declared that he would accept the Revolutionary and Bonapartist land settlements and not attempt to tamper with 'national property'.

It was therefore in an atmosphere of high tension that the Legislative Body met in plenary session on 19 December 1813. Apparently conciliatory, Napoleon promised to consult the Legislature on all peace proposals and two commissions were elected to study Allied overtures. The Senate gave the Emperor its full backing, but the Chamber censured him for continuing the war, and a charter incorporating the criticism was adopted by 229 votes to 31 – a clear warning to Napoleon had he been minded to heed it. He responded by declining to print the charter, refusing even to contemplate peace, and finally by dissolving the Legislature. 'You are not the representatives of the nation. The true representative of the nation is myself. France has more need of me than I have need of France.' On New Year's Day 1814 he made his intransigent attitude clear by hinting that, if the war effort was impeded by the notables, he himself would head a Jacobin revolution to sweep away all existing privilege in France.

Napoleon's position seemed hopeless, but the Allies were far from unanimous in their intentions after Leipzig. In November 1813 a conference at Frankfurt broke up in dissension. The stumbling block was the western European powers' increasing unease with the presence of Russia in the West; the sleeping giant that had been aroused from its slumbers on the steppes could turn out to be as great a threat to them as to Napoleon. Austria, having regained all her possessions, wanted to offer Bonaparte the natural frontiers, foreseeing that his downfall would benefit Russia and Prussia but not herself. Why should she collude in the Czar's dream of a triumphal entry into Paris, sweet revenge for Napoleon in Moscow in 1812? For balance-of-power reasons, too, Britain was inclined to go along with Austria, always provided France did not retain Antwerp and the Scheldt. The machiavellian Bernadotte, representing Sweden, had his own reasons for opposing an invasion of France: he actually hoped he would be summoned back as the next Emperor after a coup by the notables dislodged Bonaparte.

To save face, the feuding Allies offered Napoleon the natural frontiers in November 1813, imagining that the Emperor would refuse and that in the meantime they could hammer out a common policy. Napoleon dithered, then surprised everyone by accepting the terms though, oddly, he would not allow his acceptance to be promulgated in France. Meanwhile in Britain there were second thoughts, once it was understood that 'natural frontiers' must inevitably collide with British insistence on a neutral Belgium. Castlereagh, the British Foreign Secretary, travelled to Basle in some alarm. There he was able to make common cause with Metternich, who realized that he needed British support to counter the Czar and that the only way forward for Austria was to continue the war. The Allies therefore replied early in 1814 that the 'natural frontiers' terms were no longer on offer, that France would have to accept the pre-1792 boundaries. This enabled Napoleon to present the Allies in propaganda terms as ravening wolves, intent on destroying France. The hollowness of their claim to be waging war only on the Emperor of France, not its people, was now evident.

With Wellington advancing in the extreme south of France, Napoleon made an eleventh-hour effort to remove the Spanish piece from the board and get the Peninsular veterans to the eastern frontier by offering Ferdinand the throne of Spain. By the treaty of Valençay in November 1813 Ferdinand accepted these terms, though with Wellington advancing into France they were a pointless concession anyway. It did not suit Napoleon's enemies, internal as well as external, that Spain should be wrapped up so neatly. Ferdinand found himself unable to leave Valençay for the Pyrenees until March 1814.

Baulked politically at every turn, Napoleon determined to go down fighting. On paper his position was hopeless. He had 80,000 exhausted survivors of the grim campaigns of 1813 to set against an Allied force of 300,000, with tens of thousands being added to its muster rolls every week. In Italy Eugène was already hard pressed by the Austrians and in the Pyrenees Soult was retreating before Wellington. The Confederation of the Rhine was lost and both Holland and Belgium were on the point of rebellion. But Napoleon did not yet despair, fortified by the élan of his most loyal marshals, such as Mortier and the gallant Davout, who defended besieged Hamburg brilliantly against impossible odds during the winter of 1813–14. Napoleon drafted the National Guard, called up aged reservists plus policemen, forest rangers and customs officials and pressed into service a year early the 1815 class of conscripts. But there was still an acute manpower shortage, as the number of deserters and draft dodgers who had slipped through the net since 1808 now topped one million. Of the 300,000 men Napoleon was able to raise on paper, barely 120,000 actually served in the 1814 campaign.

Apart from shortage of numbers, two other factors told against the Emperor in January 1814. One was money, and in the light of this it was something of a miracle that a campaign was fought at all. The new taxation was systematically evaded and produced nothing worthwhile; army contractors had to be content with promissory notes. Since the

Domaine Extraordinaire had been used up by the disastrous 1812 and 1813 campaigns, Napoleon had to dig deeply into his private funds – the so-called *Trésor des Tuileries*; in January there were still 75 million francs left, but by April this had shrunk to 10 million. The other unfavourable development was the treachery of the marshals, with a few honourable exceptions. Victor began the new year by abandoning Strasbourg and Nancy, giving the Allies free passage over the Moselle and forcing the entire French line back.

Even worse was the perfidy of the Murats in Italy. With the support of his wife, in January 1814 Murat signed a treaty with Metternich which guaranteed that he would continue to be King of Naples, in return for his help in waging war on Eugène de Beauharnais. 'Caroline! Mine is a family of tramps!' Napoleon allegedly said, when told of his sister's treachery. But even in the sober columns of his official correspondence his deep anger is palpable: 'The conduct of the King of Naples and that of the Queen is quite unspeakable. I hope to live long enough to avenge for myself and for France such an outrage and such horrible ingratitude.' Once again the true man of honour was manifestly Eugène de Beauharnais, who fell back to Lyons with his forces in obedience to the orders of his ex-stepfather. Though offered the crown of Italy by the Allies if he would desert his master, Eugène refused. As he wrote to his mother: 'The Emperor's star fades, but that is simply a further reason to remain faithful to him.'

Napoleon's one hope was that the Allies might delay their offensive until the spring. But in January came news that the enemy was on the move. He therefore ordered Paris to be held and defended as a fortress. In one of his very worst errors, he appointed Joseph Lieutenant-General to the Empress's Council of Regency and *de facto* Governor of Paris. Since the other members of the Council were Cambacérès, who had no reason to love the Emperor, and Talleyrand, who was already actively intriguing against him, his only true supporter in the highest circles in Paris was his wife Marie-Louise, whom he respected as he had never respected Josephine – 'never a lie, never a debt' was how he characterized her, in pointed contrast to his first wife. Napoleon's 'brother complex' was alive and well in 1814, not just in the inexplicable decision to make the man who had failed so signally in Spain his Lieutenant-General, but in his ludicrous sexual jealousy of his elder sibling. Napoleon actually worried that while he was campaigning Joseph would try to seduce Marie-Louise.

The Allied plan for 1814 once again envisaged the operation of four armies. The Prussian Bülow would take half Bernadotte's Army of the

North and, together with an expeditionary force sent from Britain under Sir Thomas Graham, would occupy Holland and Belgium before moving into northern France; the other half of the Army of the North, under Bernadotte and Bennigsen, would divert to besiege Hamburg and Magdeburg. Meanwhile Blücher would cross the Rhine with 100,000 men of the Army of Silesia on a broad front between Coblenz and Mannheim and try to pin Napoleon frontally; and Schwarzenberg and the three emperors would advance via Kolmar with 200,000 men of the Army of Bohemia, fall on the French right and, depending on their progress, either make contact with the Austrians from Italy advancing from Lyons or with Wellington coming up from the Pyrenees. By February the Allies hoped to have 400,000 troops on French soil.

Schwarzenberg began by advancing cautiously to the Langres plateau where he waited until 23 January, having heard that new peace overtures were afoot. On 22 January Blücher crossed the Meuse, and advanced seventy miles into France; his vanguard established a bridgehead over the Marne. Napoleon made the salvation of Paris his prime aim in the 1814 campaign; to do this he had to prevent a junction of the two main Allied armies. Hearing that Blücher and Schwarzenberg were only two days march apart, he left Paris on 25 January and next day took up station at Châlons-sur-Marne, ready to occupy the 'centre' position and keep the two armies divided.

Since the area to the east of Paris is crisscrossed with numerous rivers and roads and Napoleon knew the geography intimately, he planned to fight an unorthodox campaign based on the advantage this gave him. His mode of fighting would be somewhere between regular and irregular fighting, as he could not afford the casualties he would sustain even in a victorious pitched battle. But he was gradually forced into orthodox warfare when the apathetic peasantry refused to heed the exhortation to take up arms against the foreign invader. Once again we may discern the level of cant in all the talk about a 'people's war'. The lesson of 1812 was that peasants would take up arms only when the enemy was already defeated or in full retreat. The obvious solution for Napoleon was to declare a *levée-en-masse*, as in 1793, and this was in fact what the Allies most feared. Although he toyed with the idea, he rejected it decisively, as it would transfer power to local Jacobin leaders. Napoleon was never more the man of the Right than when he declared: 'If fall I must, I will not bequeath France to the revolutionaries, from whom I have delivered her.'

First blood in the campaign was drawn by Mortier, with whom Blücher fought a sanguinary but indecisive battle at Bar-sur-Aube on 24

January. When the Emperor came on the scene at Châlons, with Ney and the Young Guard, he noticed Blücher's forces dispersed, so hatched a plan to pin him down while Marmont worked around his rear to launch an attack at Bar-le-Duc. Just in time Blücher managed to avoid the trap but on 29 January near Brienne (where he had been to school) Napoleon caught up with him and, using Ney and Grouchy effectively, badly mauled the Prussians, who left behind 4,000 dead and wounded. He then dogged the steps of the Prussians through heavy snowstorms but Blücher got away to link up with part of Schwarzenberg's army.

On 1 February Napoleon and 40,000 men waited for the Allies at La Rothière on the road to Brienne. The scouts he had sent out brought back poor intelligence, for it was difficult to make out anything in the blinding snow. When news came that an enemy army was on the march north from Trannes, Napoleon at once offered battle, unaware that Blücher had linked with Schwarzenberg and that he therefore faced an 110,000-strong army, nearly three times larger than his. There ensued a miniature version of Eylau, fought in a raging blizzard which soaked the ammunition and made it difficult to distinguish friend from foe. As night fell, Napoleon broke off contact, having suffered a tactical defeat, with 6,000 casualties and the loss of 50 guns (Allied losses were of the same order). Despite the wild disparity in numbers he had acquitted himself well.

Napoleon returned to Troyes, where he arrived on 3 February, having lost 4,000 men through desertion on the march. The citizens of Troyes gave him a very frosty welcome. For a few hours the Emperor brooded, idly pinning his hopes on peace talks which had opened at Châtillon-sur-Seine; according to his spies, Austria was still opposed to Prussia and Russia in not wanting *guerre à outrance*. If the war continued, his problem was how to fight the enemy in detail if they were already united. There seemed no other way, as guerrilla warfare was anathema to him. Then his scouts brought him some good news. The enemy had grown overconfident and once more divided their forces.

Blücher had decided to advance by way of the Marne while Schwarzenberg proceeded up the Seine. This gave Napoleon the separate targets he required, but first he needed to widen the gap between the two Allied armies so that they could not regroup by a rapid forced march. Then he intended to strike hard at the Army of Bohemia while Marmont and Oudinot contained Blücher. A number of small victories hastened the process: Marmont defeated the Bavarians at Arcis-sur-Aube, Grouchy and the Guards cavalry beat the Russian cavalry at Troyes, and there were successful skirmishes at Vitry and Sens. But while Schwarzenberg veered south, the effect of all this was to drive Blücher pell-mell towards Paris, and he was soon reported at Meaux, 25 miles from the French capital. Napoleon's strategy was now in ruins. After a brilliant feint that sent Schwarzenberg eastward, he doubled back for the defence of Paris.

The early days of February severely tested Napoleon's morale, for bad news rained in on him thick and fast. Paris was in a high state of panic over Blücher's advance, while Caulaincourt removed the last hope of a peaceful settlement by reporting from the Châtillon-sur-Seine conference that the Allies would offer only the 1792 frontiers. There was now fine detail on Murat's defection in Italy and news that Bülow had taken Brussels and was besieging Antwerp. The Napoleon of 1812 and 1813 would have sat brooding, but the man of 1814, displaying energies not seen since his heyday, not only put strong forces into Paris to restore morale there but, with just 30,000 troops made plans to defeat Blücher in detail before turning south to deal with Schwarzenberg.

Advancing cautiously and hampered by icy and slushy roads and food shortages, Napoleon took time to get within range of Blücher. Then, learning that the Prussian field-marshal had divided his forces, he struck hard. On 10 February he sent Ney and Marmont against the advanced Prussian positions at Champaubert, inflicting 4,000 losses on the enemy at cost of two hundred Frenchmen, and providing himself with an entering wedge between the corps of Yorck and Sacken which Blücher had foolishly separated. Too late Blücher ordered his two deputies to concentrate, but Napoleon got to Sacken first. On 11 February at Montmirail he brought off a textbook manoeuvre, pinning Sacken's Russian allies with artillery fire until Mortier arrived to deliver the knock-out blow. Timing his movements perfectly, Napoleon then sent in the Guard for the *coup de grâce*. Montmirail was one of the Guard's great moments and the victory was particularly to be savoured as the Emperor had once again defeated a numerically superior enemy (18,000 against 10,000), inflicting twice as many casualties (4,000) and hauling in 3,000 prisoners. Those who claim that the Napoleon of 1814 was the General Bonaparte of 1796–97 back to his best form are not exaggerating.

Flushed with victory, Napoleon seemed to gain a new lease of life; he was again the complete commander, full of energy, alert to the slightest battlefield nuance. In this mood he attacked Yorck at Château-Thierry on 12 February; the Prussians fought a desperate rearguard action before escaping north over the Marne to Soissons. Marching to Yorck's aid, Blücher sheered off once he heard the Emperor himself was commanding the French and then had to beat off assaults on his rearguard. In the fighting on 12–13 February the Prussians and Russians lost 6,000, the French no more than 600.

Once again it was bad news from other fronts that led Napoleon to break off the pursuit of his quarry. It was Victor who had let Blücher through the net to menace Paris earlier and it was again Victor who let the Emperor down. Napoleon had been reasonably confident about holding the Army of Bohemia at arm's length, for the key to Paris was the Nogent bridge over the Seine and he had left clear contingency plans to blow it up if it could not be defended. However, the Austrians found another bridge at Bray, ten miles west, and crossed there. Victor abandoned the Nogent bridge to avoid encirclement, thus precipitating another panic in Paris. But Schwarzenberg did not take the gleaming opportunity apparently offered him. He was afraid of being caught between Napoleon's force and the other army Augereau was supposed to have raised in Lyons. Moreover, he was finally running into partisan resistance as the French peasants, enraged by Allied looting, at last began showing signs of the guerrilla spirit.

When Blücher heard the news from the Seine, he naturally calculated that Napoleon would be forced to go to the help of his capital, giving the Prussians the opportunity to take them in the rear. The Emperor was keen to encourage this thinking and laid out a decoy for the Prussians, using the small forces of Marmont's corps, Grouchy's cavalry and the Guard as bait. Blücher fell for the trap and came within an ace of being surrounded; he was saved only because the roads, muddy after melted snow, prevented Grouchy from bringing up the horse artillery to finish the Prussians off. Nevertheless at Vauchamps on 14 February Napoleon inflicted 7,000 casualties for the loss of just 600.

In the so-called 'Six Days Campaign' of February 1814, Napoleon returned to his peerless best as a commander, inevitably recalling his successes in 1796–97. He could probably have finished off Blücher and the Prussians on 13 February but for the hiccup caused by the news from the Seine front. As it was, he caused Allied losses of 20,000 and seized a large number of guns. The key to his success was that he had a small army (30,000) under his personal direction, much as in the Italian campaign of 1796–97. A generalization becomes inevitable: Napoleon was a brilliant commander of small armies which he could mould to his will as a conductor moulds an orchestra, but the huge armies of 1812 and 1813 spiralled out of his control; the Emperor had in a sense promoted himself to his own level of incompetence. The irony of the 'Six Days' was that all Napoleon's brilliance availed him nothing. Within days Blücher had received 30,000 Russian reinforcements, more than making good his lost numbers. It was as if Napoleon's victories had never been achieved.

Reasonably confident that Blücher would take time to lick his wounds after such a mauling, Napoleon left Marmont and Mortier in a holding position at Vauchamps, and swung away south-east in pursuit of Schwarzenberg, whose cavalry patrols were already probing Melun and Fontainebleau. After marching 47 miles in 36 hours, he hurled his forces, now 60,000 strong, against the Austrians. In engagements at Mormant and Valjiouan the French generals carried all before them. For the fourth time on this campaign the supremely useless Victor ruined things. Commanded to march through the night to catch the enemy at Monterreau, he disobeyed orders, thus allowing the Austrians to dig in behind strong positions. Napoleon angrily dismissed him, replaced him with General Gérard, then brought off another superb victory by sending in his cavalry at just the right moment. For the loss of 2,500 the French inflicted casualties of 6,000.

Yet another French success at Méry-sur-Seine on 21 February left the Allies demoralized and in disarray. Having won seven battles in eight days, Napoleon was again offered the 1792 frontiers as the basis for peace but, flushed with his string of recent successes, turned the offer down. He intended to pursue Schwarzenberg to Troyes, forcing him to make a stand there, but learned to his dismay that Blücher had managed to link up with him there. Disheartened, Napoleon sent word through his envoys that he would accept the 1792 frontiers, only to be told that the offer was revoked. Even so, had the Allies stood to face him at Troyes, Napoleon, with 70,000 against 100,000 might have won a great victory. But at a council of war between Blücher and Schwarzenberg in Troyes on 22 February, the Allies agreed to withdraw: Blücher would head north to the Marne to link up with Bülow and divert attention from Schwarzenberg, who would retire to Langres. Consequently, Napoleon entered Troyes to a greeting far warmer than his last one; the burghers had had enough of Germanic depredations.

From a military point of view Napoleon's position at the end of February looked promising. But the apparent situation masked a host of problems: the Emperor had reached the end of his ingenuity, his armies were exhausted, there were no recruits, France seemed sunk in apathy and morale in the army failed to pick up. Ominously, too, the Allies' political will was growing stronger. After conferences between Castlereagh, Czar, Kaiser and Austrian Emperor at Bar-sur-Aube on 25 February and again at Chaumont on 1 March, it was agreed that Britain would commit another £5 million in subsidies so that the war could continue for another twenty years if necessary.

In the last week of February Blücher again began advancing on Paris. Napoleon ordered Marmont and Mortier to block his advance at all costs; meanwhile, leaving Oudinot, MacDonald, Kellermann and Gérard to face Schwarzenberg, he set off after the Prussians, hoping to take them in the rear. Oudinot engineered a deception whereby Austrian spies would think the Emperor was still in Troyes; he held noisy reviews, with the air full of cries of '*Vive l'Empereur!*' But Schwarzenberg caught them off balance by suddenly ordering a general advance and defeating Oudinot at Bar-sur-Aube on 27 February.

Napoleon's daring plan to catch Blücher also failed. Once again Blücher escaped the trap in the nick of time and crossed to the north bank of the Marne, before withdrawing north to Aisne with Napoleon on his heels. Because of cowardice by the commandant of Soissons and the tardiness of Marmont and Mortier, who were supposed to head the Prussians off there, Blücher made good his getaway, met his reinforcements under Bülow and emerged from the chase with an army of 100,000 Prussians and Russians. Just then word came in that MacDonald had retreated and allowed the enemy to occupy Troyes; once again the Emperor was stupefied at the incompetence of his marshals. Undeterred he hurried on to engage Blücher, whom he found on the plateau of Craonne on 7 March.

With just 40,000 men, Napoleon was again facing impossible odds, especially with 25,000 fresh Russian troops in the field. It was the Russians who caused the French the heaviest losses, including both Grouchy and Victor wounded, but finally they gave ground and retreated to Laon; casualties were about 5,000 either side. Even at these odds Napoleon might have scored a complete victory but for the idiocy of Ney, who attacked prematurely before the artillery had been brought up. Lacking cavalry for reconnaissance, Napoleon concluded from the enemy withdrawal that he had defeated Blücher's rearguard and was astonished to run into the main army at Laon on 9 March.

A grim struggle on 10 March saw the French unable to make progress against superior numbers; Blücher fought defensively, fearing a trap. That night Yorck probed and found Marmont's VI Corps, coming up as reinforcement, in an exposed position. He unexpectedly counterattacked and routed Marmont's corps; another 4,000 men were lost that Napoleon could ill afford. Napoleon heard the bad news at 5 a.m. and decided to stand his ground and deflect the Prussians on to himself. It was fortunate for the Emperor that at this point Blücher fell ill and handed over to his deputy. Gneisenau was overawed by the responsibility of facing the Corsican ogre, so failed to move in to finish the French off, as a good commander could have done. After a day of skirmishing, Napoleon concluded that success against such superior numbers was impossible, so withdrew across the Aisne to Soissons. In the fighting around Laon and Craonne he had lost 6,000 men to the Allies' 2,000.

Events were turning away from Napoleon in every theatre. Caulaincourt got an extension of the offer of the 1792 frontiers until 17 March, but Napoleon still refused to consider this a basis for peace. For a month he had been vainly urging Augereau to appear in the field with the new Army he was supposedly gathering at Lyons: at one point he exhorted Augereau 'to forget his 56 years and remember the great days of Castiglione'. Now word came in that Augereau had given up and there would be no second Army. Next he heard from Marie-Louise that Joseph was trying to organize an address to the Emperor from the Council of State and National Guard in favour of peace. Angrily he exploded, and made his dark suspicions of his brother overt: 'Everyone has betrayed me. Will it be my fate to be betrayed also by the King? . . . Mistrust the King; he has an evil reputation with women, and an ambition which grew upon him while he was in Spain.'

The Emperor was still full of fight. When the Allied General St Priest incautiously ventured ahead of the main army to take Rheims, Napoleon fell on him and inflicted 6,000 Russian casualties for 700 French losses. But he was still no nearer shaking off the tentacles of the two armies under Blücher and Schwarzenberg. He made a final attempt to break the impasse by marching on Troyes, keeping Schwarzenberg pinned there while he cut Blücher's communications with Strasbourg and made contact with the strong French garrisons at Metz and Verdun. At first Schwarzenberg seemed to be retreating, but suddenly changed tack and concentrated his vanguard at Arcis-sur-Aube. There the two armies collided on 20 March. The French took the town, only to come under very heavy enemy counterattack.

The engagement with Schwarzenberg at Arcis-sur-Aube miscarried when the Emperor was unable to deploy the numbers he needed as Blücher had meanwhile defeated Marmont. Napoleon, victorious against the Bavarians on the Allied right, was nearly killed when a shell exploded directly under his horse. Some describe the incident as a suicide attempt or manifestation of death wish for, seeing a howitzer shell just about to explode, the Emperor deliberately rode his horse over it. The animal was killed instantly, but Napoleon got up without a scratch. Many times later he would regret that he had not died on the field of Arcis.

The French had the better of a nocturnal skirmish with Schwarzenberg's vanguard, but next day the entire 80,000-strong Army of Bohemia appeared. Having only 28,000 to pit against them, Napoleon withdrew, leaving Oudinot to cover the retreat. From 3–6 p.m. on the 21st a grim battle raged around Arcis in which the French rearguard was badly mauled before getting away. This time the French managed to complete an evacuation by bridge and then blow it up. Losses at Arcis were 3,000 French and 4,000 Austrians. Undaunted, Napoleon did not do the obvious thing and march for Paris but made for St Dizier, hoping to cut off Allied supply lines.

At first the Allies seemed likely to fall for this decoy and began pulling their forces back from the advance on Paris. But then a letter from Napoleon to Marie-Louise was intercepted. Talleyrand had for some time been advising the Allies that the Emperor was deeply unpopular in Paris and there was a strong royalist party there, but the Russians, particularly, were not convinced, suspecting machiavellianism on Metternich's part – for Talleyrand was Metternich's creature. Now in the clearest possible terms they found Napoleon admitting to his wife the truth of this and, incidentally, revealing his own strategy: 'I decided to make for the Marne and his line of communication, in order to push him back further from Paris and draw nearer to my fortress. I shall be at St Dizier this evening.' After reading this, the Czar, on the advice of Bonaparte's oldest enemy, Pozzo di Borgo, changed his mind and argued strongly for an advance on Paris.

The Allies united both armies and, 180,000-strong, advanced smoothly down the Marne towards Paris. Marmont and Mortier tried to bar the way but were swept aside at La Fère-Champenoise on 25 March. Napoleon meanwhile spent four days in a fool's paradise at St Dizier, vaguely wondering whether he dared call a 'people's war'. He was aroused from his fantasy on the 27th by news that the enemy would be in Paris before him. Marmont and Mortier fought the last battle at the foot of Montmartre on 30 March, the National Guard defended courageously at Belleville and the Charonne heights, as did Moncey at the Porte de Clichy, and made the Allies take significant losses as they fought their way into the suburbs. In the end, though, they were simply overwhelmed by superior numbers, and on the evening of the 30th Marmont signed the capitulation of Paris.

Elsewhere in France resistance had collapsed. Lyons, from which so much had been expected, fell on 21 March, joining a long list of important provincial cities that were in hostile hands. In mid-February Wellington commenced his advance from the Pyrenees. He defeated

Soult at Orthez on 27 February, as a result of which Bordeaux rose against Bonaparte and opened its gates to the English on 12 March. On the 24th the hopelessly outnumbered Soult abandoned field operations and took his army inside the walls of Toulouse. Three days later Wellington began besieging it, forcing Soult to withdraw after a sanguinary encounter on 10 April. The venal marshal actually achieved his finest hour in the last days of the 1814 war by trying to link up with Suchet, who had at last been forced out of Catalonia. Soult was still in the field when Toulouse declared for the Bourbons and on 12 April Wellington entered the city in triumph, to learn of the amazing dénouement in Paris, six days earlier.

On learning that the Allies had stolen a march, Napoleon set out for Paris with a small force, hoping to marshal the city's defences. He got as far as Fontainebleau before he heard of Marmont's surrender. His response was stupefaction. Could it really be true that Joseph had done nothing to fortify the city and had then bolted in a blue funk? Sadly, this turned out to be the case. Joseph had not raised the numbers of defenders Napoleon expressly asked him to, had no gunners to service the artillery park at Vincennes, and spent most of his time conferring with Talleyrand on the best terms he could obtain from the Allies for himself. Napoleon raged impotently: 'It is the first time I have heard that a population of 300,000 men cannot survive for three months,' he said of the inexplicable failure of Paris to survive even one hour of siege. It is said that the city did not fight because all *quartiers* save the working-class suburbs hated Napoleon, that Parisians feared it would be sacked and gutted if they resisted, and because Joseph had left them without fortifications, but none of these alleged reasons convinces.

For once the age-old French cry of *nous sommes trahis* expressed the plain truth. The most culpable of those who failed Napoleon was his brother Joseph, whose incompetence was so spectacular that one is justified in suspecting deliberate sabotage. Marmont has been identified as the prime villain by the influential historian Henry Houssaye, on the grounds that supply lines and logistics would have forced the retreat of the Allies if Paris had held out for just another twenty-four hours. But the worst of all villains was the venal and treacherous Talleyrand who, with Fouché and other inveterate plotters, remained in the capital to welcome the Allied 'deliverers' while Joseph and Jérôme rode hell-for-leather for the Loire. Joseph persuaded Marie-Louise that the Council of Regency and the Court must leave the capital but ignored Napoleon's explicit instruction that nobody must be left in Paris who could legitimate a transfer of power to an Allied nominee. Talleyrand managed to stay on in Paris by the simple ruse of appearing at the barrier at the city exit without a passport authorizing him to leave.

Talleyrand, together with Chabrol, prefect of the Seine and Pasquier, prefect of police, were therefore on hand to welcome the Czar and the King of Prussia when they entered the city with their troops on 31 March. But he was nearly beaten at his own game when a little-known assembly jumped the gun. The Council of the Seine – an assembly so despised by Napoleon that he habitually drew up the budget for Paris without consulting it – in a proclamation by its councillors called on Parisians to repudiate Napoleon and petition for a Bourbon restoration; it was the notables on the Council, not the aristocracy who were the prime movers. Talleyrand, fearful lest this premature proclamation provoke a backlash, banned it from *Le Moniteur* and quickly formed a provisional government on 1 April. Two days later he persuaded the Senate to vote for Napoleon's deposition. With deeply researched malice he had already packed off Marie-Louise and her son, using Joseph, moronic or treacherous according to interpretation, as frontman in persuading her. The upshot was that it was no longer feasible for anyone in the government to suggest a transfer of power to the Regency and the abdication of Napoleon in favour of his son.

Nevertheless, this was the option Caulaincourt held out for in negotiations with Czar Alexander. At Fontainebleau meanwhile Napoleon had assembled 60,000 troops and was prepared to fight on. But on 4 April a delegation of marshals, headed by Ney, Moncey and Lefebvre, told him this was no longer an option. 'The Army will not march,' said Ney. 'The Army will obey me,' said Napoleon indignantly. 'The Army will obey its chiefs,' came the uncompromising reply. Opinion is divided as to whether Ney, Berthier or Lefebvre was most responsible for the revolt of the marshals, but Napoleon then had no choice but to write out a conditional abdication, provided the Allies recognized his son as his successor. Caulaincourt, Ney, Marmont and MacDonald formed the delegation that took this offer – the so-called 'Brumaire in reverse' – back to Paris.

Alexander vacillated, fearful that if he did not accept a Regency of the King of Rome, fighting might break out again. But Talleyrand had not finished spinning his web of intrigues. He flattered the gullible Marmont that he could be a second General Monk and worked on him to betray his colleagues. While Caulaincourt and the others got into tough negotiations with the Czar about Napoleon II, a message was dramatically delivered to Alexander, stating that Marmont had signed an agreement with Schwarzenberg and that his corps were even then fraternizing ·with their new allies the Austrians. The marshals now had no option but to return to the Emperor with the bad news and ask for his unconditional abdication. On 6 April Napoleon signed the deed, and on the very same day Talleyrand nudged the Senate towards his final goal: the restoration of the Bourbons.

Three things strike the Bonaparte student as salient about the dramatic first three months of 1814. First is the brilliance of Napoleon's campaigning. Second is the astonishing level of treachery towards the Emperor. Third is the affectionate relationship between Napoleon and Marie-Louise. Of these the first largely speaks for itself. As Wellington commented later after a close examination of the northern campaign: 'The study of it has given me a greater idea of his genius than any other. Had he continued that system a little while longer it is my opinion that he would have saved Paris.' On the second, the only surprise is that the dreadful Talleyrand still finds his supporters. Even the great Pieter Geyl displayed naïveté in thinking Talleyrand had the interests of France at heart, rather than his own, in 1814. Talleyrand's apologists appear to work from a false syllogism: Napoleon's interests and those of France were different; Talleyrand's interests and Napoleon's were different; therefore Talleyrand's interests and those of France were identical.

Marie-Louise's conduct and support for her husband during these trying three months were irreproachable. She was the only one on the Council of Regency who fully supported the Emperor and was continually thwarted by Joseph and Talleyrand. Despite the danger that the Paris mob, enraged by the Allied siege, might in exasperation visit on her the fate it had meted out to Marie-Antoinette, she wanted to stay and fight and was overborne only when Joseph produced a letter from Napoleon written on 8 February. This contained the following: 'If I lose a battle . . . get the Empress and the King of Rome to leave for Rambouillet . . . Never let the Empress and the King of Rome fall into the hands of the enemy . . . I would prefer my son to be killed rather than see him brought up in Vienna as an Austrian prince.'

Marie-Louise made it plain in a letter to Napoleon on 29 March that she thought this was bad advice:

They insist on my going . . . I should have been quite brave enough to stay, and I am very angry that they would not let me, especially when the Parisians are showing such eagerness to defend themselves . . . But the whole lot of them have lost their heads except me, and I believe that in a day or two you will tell me I was right in not wanting to evacuate the capital for a mere 15,000 cavalrymen who would never have got through the streets. I am really angry at having to go, it will have terrible disadvantages for you, but they pointed out to me that my son would be running into danger, and that was why I dared not gainsay them once I had seen the letter you wrote to the King [sc. Joseph].

In further letters she revealed the true calibre of Joseph: he had asked her to intercede with her father, the Austrian Emperor, to make sure the Bonaparte family did not suffer from France's humiliation.

Yet most of all, Marie-Louise's correspondence in early 1814 reveals a woman still very much in love with her husband. She may not yet have been a woman of the world – she would come to that later – but she had no doubts about her heart. Two letters in particular show something of the inner woman. On 2 February she wrote: 'I myself am growing very brave since your latest successes, and I hope I don't deserve to be called a child any longer – that's what you used to like to call me before you went away.' And on 10 March she wrote, to commemorate the anniversary of the birth of her son in 1811: 'I have been thinking about you so much today, it is three years since you gave me so moving a proof of your love that the tears come whenever I think of it, so it's an exceedingly precious day to me.' It was Napoleon's misfortune that, sunk in self-pity and depression, he seemed unable to respond to her once he had abdicated. In more ways than one, it now appeared, he seemed ready to give up on life.

CHAPTER TWENTY-SIX

On 11 April 1814 the Allies signed the Treaty of Fontainebleau, which was meant to settle the fate of the Bonapartes. Napoleon was granted the title of Emperor and given sovereignty over the island of Elba, where he was to receive a stipend of two million francs from the French Government; the rest of the Bonapartes were given pensions, while Marie-Louise received the Duchy of Parma with reversion to her son, the King of Rome. It was a dismal end to a dynasty that once bestrode Europe.

It was Czar Alexander who originally proposed Elba to Caulaincourt, at the time when the provisional abdication was being discussed. Caulaincourt loyally nudged Alexander to keep the offer on the table even when the abdication became absolute. The other allies thought the proposal too generous – Metternich considered Elba was too close to Italy while Castlereagh thought it too close to France. In the end they reluctantly acquiesced for fear of offending the Czar, who was known to despise the Bourbons; if he suddenly recanted on a Bourbon restoration and opted instead for the King of Rome, Europe would face another crisis.

Yet Elba was chosen only after a host of other candidates had been considered and rejected. Fouché urged the Allies to deport the 'ogre' to the United States, but this was considered mere extremism. Corsica and Sardinia were thought dangerously large – Napoleon might be able to turn them into formidable strongholds – while Corfu was too small, distant and unacceptable to Napoleon. Most of the proposed sites for the Emperor's exile were British possessions – Gibraltar, St Helena and even Botany Bay were mentioned – but Tory backbenchers argued that Bonaparte would sully these places by his presence. Castlereagh came up with the ingenious idea of keeping Napoleon under a form of house arrest on the British fort of St George on the Beauly Firth, where Dr Johnson and Boswell had dined with the garrison in 1783. But his Cabinet colleagues objected that if Napoleon was there, Whig opposition leaders would serve a writ of habeas corpus, forcing the government either to free him or bring him to trial. And trial for what? Waging war to retain the natural frontiers could by no stretch of the imagination be considered a crime.

Elba, then, was the Czar's choice. Some residual regard for the man he once briefly called his friend may have entered into the choice, but mostly it was sheer machiavellianism: on Elba Napoleon was a constant thorn in the side of Austrian Italy, so the Habsburgs could be kept occupied while Alexander gave himself a free hand in Poland. Neither Metternich nor Castlereagh liked the idea of Napoleon as sovereign of Elba and partly discerned the Czar's motives; in the end Castlereagh refused to sign the treaty, though Metternich reluctantly did.

There were six days between Napoleon's abdication and the arrival of the draft treaty of Fontainebleau, which he would have to sign. Once again he was sunk in gloom, immobilized by depression. He seemed unable to decide whether he wanted Marie-Louise with him or not. There was something inherently absurd about the events in the week after his abdication, with him in Fontainebleau and his wife in Blois, just one hundred miles to the south-west. She very early threw out a broad hint that she wanted to join him: 'I would be braver and calmer if I were sharing your fate and consoling you for all your setbacks,' she wrote. But the reply was a somewhat charmless directive to pay out money from the Treasury to his grasping family: a million francs each for Madame Mère, Louis, Jérôme, Pauline and Élisa; once they received their money, the Bonapartes decamped, unconcerned about the Empress. But still there was no definite word from the Emperor: 'I am sorry to have nothing left but to have you share my evil fortunes,' he wrote on 8 April.

When they arrived in Blois, Joseph and Jérôme tried to persuade Marie-Louise to surrender to the first Austrian patrol. She resisted the pressure and, once Joseph had got his share of the Treasury handout, he departed for Switzerland. On 8 April she made her position explicit: 'I am awaiting orders from you, and I do beseech you to let me come.' Napoleon's answer was disappointingly offhand: 'You can come here if you like . . . or you could stay there.' In the light of this incoherent, muddled and evasive advice, it seems bizarre that Napoleon was able to write to Méneval, the Empress's secretary, on 10 April: 'Try to find out the real intentions of the Empress and to discover whether she prefers to follow the Emperor . . . or to retire, either to a State which would be given to her, or to the Court of her father, together with my son.' The answer was clear enough in all her daily letters: 'You must send someone to tell me what to do . . . No one loves you as much as your faithful Louise.'

By 11 April – the date of the Treaty of Fontainebleau – he seems to have assumed she would be accompanying him to Elba. 'You are to have at least one great country house and a beautiful country when you tire of my island of Elba, and I begin to bore you, as I can but do when I am older and you still young.' This crossed with a letter in which Marie-Louise asked his permission for her to interview her father, with a view to being assigned the Grand Duchy of Tuscany. Soon she was on her way to Rambouillet to meet her father, and sent him a letter through the Polish officer who was acting as go-between. Napoleon finally bestirred himself and decided to send a troop of cavalry to bring her back to Fontainebleau. Somewhat complacently he wrote on 15 April: 'You must have met your father by this time. I wish you to come to Fontainebleau tomorrow, so that we may set out together for that land of sanctuary and rest, where I shall be happy – provided you can make up your mind to be so and forget worldly greatness.'

He was too late. His vacillation had forced Marie-Louise to take decisive action on her own, but as soon as she crossed Austrian lines she found she was no longer a free agent. There can be no mistaking the genuine sorrow with which she announced that seeking her father's help had been a grave error: 'You will know by now that they have made me leave Orléans and that orders have been given to prevent me from joining you, and even to resort to force if necessary. Be on your guard, my darling, we are being duped. I am in deadly anxiety on your behalf but I shall take a firm line with my father. I shall tell him that I absolutely insist on joining you, and that I shall not let myself be talked into doing anything else.'

The 'firm line' produced no results, nor was it likely to even if Marie-Louise had had the courage to oppose her father's will, when she had been brought up to think such conduct unnatural. Soon she was writing dolefully again to Napoleon: 'He will not allow me to join you now, or see you, or travel with you to Elba . . . He insisted on two months first in Austria and then in Parma and that I could see you there.' She was escorted to Compiègne, where she met the Czar and the Kaiser. All who talked to her were astonished that she would hear no ill of her husband, and even refused to be swayed when Napoleon's old associates detailed his many affairs and infidelities. Forced back to Austria against her will, she was still at this stage determined to be reunited with Napoleon on Elba.

But Napoleon was beginning to suspect that Metternich's malice would ensure that he never saw his wife and son again – a suspicion confirmed by the arch and disingenuous letter he received from Emperor

Francis before he left Fontainebleau. 'I have decided,' Francis wrote, 'to propose that she should pass some months in the bosom of her family. Her need of rest and quiet is paramount, and Your Majesty has given her too many proofs of real attachment for me to doubt that you will share my wishes on the subject and approve of my decision. Once she has regained her health, my daughter will proceed to assume the sovereignty of her country and this will naturally bring her near Your Majesty's place of abode. I assume it is unnecessary to assure Your Majesty that her son will be accepted as a member of my family, and that during his residence in my dominions he will enjoy his mother's constant care.'

By his paralysis of will during the week after his abdication, Napoleon lost the chance of reunion with his wife. But he seems to have been in the state of mind during this period when rapid decisions were beyond him and his will to live at all was faltering. He was in the grip of the dislocating effects of anomie – too great a change in circumstances in too short a time. The obvious cliché – how are the mighty fallen – was put more trenchantly by Hegel, not normally a writer associated with clarity. It was Hegel who had recorded this impression of Napoleon after Jena: 'I saw the Emperor – this world-soul – riding out of the city on reconnaissance. It is indeed a wonderful sensation to see such an individual, concentrated here at a single point, astride a horse, reach out over the world and master it . . . It is only from heaven, that is, from the will of the French Emperor, that matters can be set in motion.' But on the fall of Napoleon he wrote gloomily: 'It is a frightful spectacle, to see a great genius destroy himself. There is nothing more tragic in Greek literature. The entire mass of mediocrity, with its irresistible leaden weight . . . has succeeded in bringing down the highest to the same level as itself.'

Doubtless revolving similar thoughts in his own mind, the Emperor thought of suicide, as he had often done in an abstract, Werther-like way. But did he go further this time? There seem to have been two attempts to poison himself, one on 7 April and one on the night of 12–13 April, but everything about these incidents is mysterious, including the method Napoleon used, why it failed, and who witnessed the botched bids for self-slaughter. It is also impossible to establish what kind of poison was used. The accounts given by Constant, Méneval and Laure Abrantès can be dismissed as mere fantasy and rumour-mongering, but the narrative by Caulaincourt, usually an unimpeachable source, commands our attention.

Caulaincourt's version is that, ever since his narrow escape from the Cossacks at Maloyaroslavets in 1812, Napoleon carried a small bag around his neck, containing a suicide pill – a tiny pouch of black taffeta containing a mixture of belladonna, white hellebore and opium. When Caulaincourt brought the draft treaty of Fontainebleau for him to sign on 12 April, he remarked cryptically: 'I shall not need anything; a soldier does not need much space to die in.' After dining with Caulaincourt, when he again behaved as on the sledge to Warsaw in 1812, talking about himself and his reign as if of a third person, he complained of the base ingratitude of all who had known him and said that life had become intolerable.

At 3 in the morning of the 13th, Caulaincourt was summoned to the Emperor's bedside. Napoleon told him he had taken poison and made a fond and tearful farewell. Caulaincourt implies that he was alone with his master, but Constant claimed he and a valet named Pélard were also in attendance; this seems more plausible, as someone must have woken Caulaincourt from his sleep. Then Napoleon began vomiting and suffered convulsions. Grand Marshal Bertrand and the military physician Dr Yvan were summoned and told to administer another dose and finish him off; allegedly Yvan refused, saying that he had taken the Hippocratic oath and was no murderer. After suffering great pain for four hours, Napoleon found the pangs easing at 7 a.m., to the point where he was able to show himself in public next day. As to why the poison had failed to take effect, two theories were offered. One was that Yvan, following orders after Maloyaroslavets, had mixed a double dose of poison that turned out so powerful that the Emperor's system could not absorb it and so it was vomited up. The other was that the poison had lost its potency over nearly two years.

There is something very unsatisfactory about the traditional accounts of this entire incident. We may reject at the outset the story that Dr Yvan prepared a double dose of poison, for this is internally inconsistent with other parts of the tale. Yvan could scarcely claim he had taken the Hippocratic oath and was no murderer if he had already prepared a deadly concoction. As to the suicide pill 'losing its potency', one can only conclude that whoever devised it must have been supremely incompetent, as there were extant at the time many deadly poisons, arsenic most notably, from, which death would have been instantaneous. Moreover, most people, having taken a near-lethal dose of poison, are not up and about next day.

What, then, is the explanation? The key seems to be the failure of the first attempt, on 7 April, which Caulaincourt mentions without giving details – he was not at Fontainebleau on this date. Had Yvan given the Emperor a placebo in 1812 to reassure him? Did a puzzled Emperor, having taken the phial without effect on 7 April, try again on the night of 12–13 only to be visited, quite coincidentally, with a genuine case of food poisoning? Was an attempt made by person or persons unknown to murder him by poison? Or is Caulaincourt's account unreliable? Scholars have from time to time raised doubts about the authenticity of his memoirs, or parts of them at any rate, and suspicions have arisen that they might have been doctored by later hands. To a large extent we are in the realm of circumstantial evidence. Napoleon's state of mind was certainly such as to predispose him to suicide at this juncture, but he was to survive worse ordeals and far more dark nights later without turning to suicide. It is still possible that Caulaincourt's version of events is true but, if so, a more systematic reinterpretation of Napoleon's character is called for than historians have been willing to provide.

Certainly Napoleon's emotions at the time were helter-skelter. After signing the deed of abdication on 6 April, he thought of recanting and trying to lead a war of national liberation, Spanish-style, or of escaping to join Eugène, who did not surrender until 17 April. After initially bowing his head under the Treaty of Fontainebleau, he decided not to sign it, then finally gave in. But he drove a hard bargain, determined not to let Castlereagh off the hook. He insisted that the British guarantee the treaty, both to guarantee his own safety on the way to Elba and to guarantee his person against abduction by Maltese, Sicilian or Barbary pirates once he was there; as an earnest of British intentions, he asked for a commissioner who would reside with him in Elba. Castlereagh was forced into the absurd situation of having to guarantee the independence of a sovereign whose formal title he refused to recognize.

The man chosen as Commissioner was Colonel Sir Neil Campbell, a Highlander who had fought at Bautzen. On arrival in Fontainebleau on 16 April, Campbell recorded his first impressions of Napoleon: 'I saw before me a short, active-looking man, who was rapidly pacing the length of his apartment, like some wild animal in his cell. He was dressed in an old green uniform with gold epaulets, blue pantaloons, and red topboots, unshaven, uncombed, with the fallen particles of snuff scattered profusely upon his upper lip and breast.' The arrangement was that Napoleon would travel to Elba with Campbell and three other Allied Commissioners, together with Bertrand and detachments of the Guard under General Drouot.

On 20 April a convoy of fourteen carriages escorted by 62 Polish lancers set off for Elba; 600 Guardsmen would eventually follow the Emperor to his island. Before he left Fontainebleau, Napoleon made an emotional farewell in the courtyard of the Château to those Guardsmen he would not be seeing again. There is no reason to doubt that he reduced them to floods of tears by his sentimental oratory. The moment was one of the great setpieces of Napoleonic iconography, a famous inspiration to poets and painters of the Romantic movement, and the speech, possibly reported apocryphally, contained all the well-known elements of Bonapartist rhetoric:

> Soldiers of my Old Guard, I bid you goodbye. For twenty years I have found you continuously on the path of honour and glory . . . I have sacrificed all my rights, and am ready to sacrifice my life, for my one aim has always been the happiness and glory of France . . . If I have chosen to go on living it is so that I can write about the great things we have done together and tell posterity of your great deeds . . . Goodbye, my children! I should like to press you all to my heart; at least I shall kiss your flag.

The convoy set out southwards, following the road through Nemours, Montargis, Briare, Nevers and Roanne to Lyons. Then the imperial party headed down the Rhône Valley. With hindsight, in the knowledge of the White Terror that swept through Provence after 1815, it was ill-advised to proceed through this fanatically royalist territory. As they trekked through Vienne and Orange there were hostile demonstrations, hangings of the Emperor in effigy and finally, in Avignon, physical violence when the coaches were stopped by a mob and an attempt made to take him out and lynch him. On his own admission, Napoleon, who had always feared and loathed the vulgar crowd, lost his nerve. He said to the Austrian Commissioner, General Koller: 'As you know, my dear General, I showed myself at my very worst.'

He insisted on going in disguise after that, and refused to eat in local inns for fear of being poisoned (strange behaviour, for a man who had allegedly tried to kill himself by the same means two weeks earlier). His physical cowardice was noted with disdain by Campbell, who wrote: 'It was evident during his stay at Fontainebleau and the following journey that he entertained great apprehension of attacks upon his life, and he certainly exhibited more timidity than one would have expected from a man of his calibre.' After staying overnight with his sister Pauline at Le Luc, Napoleon's party reached Fréjus. Still disguised, this time in a servant's blue livery with a tiny round hat on his head, he flatly refused to cross to Elba on a French warship, knowing the particular animus French naval officers felt for him. Instead, he embarked on 29 April on the British vessel HMS *Undaunted*.

Whenever he encountered ordinary British serving personnel, especially naval officers, Napoleon always impressed them mightily. Captain Ussher of the *Undaunted* was no exception and he always remembered the Emperor's 'unfailing cordiality and condescension'. On 3 May the vessel anchored at Porto-Ferraio in Elba, where legend credits Napoleon with having won over the hostile Elbans in a single hour. This was necessary for, by an irony of ironies, in mid-April 1814 the Elbans, still ignorant of developments in Paris, revolted against Bonapartist rule and were put down with much bloodshed. Because of plague in Malta, Elba was quarantined at about the same time, so that it was just a day before the Emperor's arrival that the 12,000 inhabitants of the island learned that their new ruler was to be Napoleon Bonaparte.

The polyglot population of Elba – Tuscans, Spaniards, Neapolitans – were either employed in lead or granite works or in the iron mines of Rio Marina; apart from fishing, these were the only sources of the island's wealth. On this unpromising base Napoleon erected the panoply of a court, with all the expected accoutrements. He established his palace at I Mulini, a modest house built by the Medicis in the eighteenth century for the governor's gardener. His court contained a Grand Marshal of the Palace, a Military Governor, a Treasurer, four chamberlains, two secretaries, a doctor, a chemist, a butler and a chef with seven assistant chefs, two valets, two equerries, a Mameluke servant called Ali, two gentlemen-ushers, eight footmen, a porter, a director of music, two female singers, a laundress and a washerwoman; 35 men worked in the stables which housed 27 carriages and his favourite horses.

For the first few months Napoleon enjoyed playing ruler of his miniature kingdom. He reorganized administration, planted vineyards, even started to build a theatre. He poured out a stream of decrees covering all aspects of the island's agriculture: the harvest, irrigation, forests, olives, mulberries, chestnuts, potatoes – nothing was too trivial to escape his attention. Campbell reported: 'I have never seen a man in any situation of life with so much activity and restless perseverance.' Napoleon had grandiose ambitions for new roads, a new hospital, a military school. But all these plans came to nothing, for two main reasons. As rumours spread of tax increases and forced labour through *corvée*, initial Elban inclination to give their new sovereign the benefit of the doubt turned to sullen passive obedience. And, more to the point, there was no money to implement these schemes as it gradually became apparent that the Bourbon government had no intention of honouring its commitment to pay the annual two-million-franc subvention.

Moreover, it soon became clear that Caulaincourt's portrait of Elba as an island made prosperous by commerce, and an important stopping point for ships from the two Sicilies and the East, was wide of the mark. Gradually Napoleon lost interest in his kingdom and rarely emerged from his two-storey palace, to the intense discomfiture of the scores of sightseers, adventurers, mercenaries and spies who thronged the island. Disappointed, too, with the standard of his court, he soon gave up holding receptions, preferring to play *vingt-et-un* and dominoes with his immediate circle of intimates. He was so bored that he started taking up practical jokes: once he slipped a fish into Bertrand's pocket, then asked him for the loan of a handkerchief, so that fish came slopping out on to the table.

The Emperor was left with much time on his hands to reflect on the past and mull over the news from France, with which he kept in constant touch through his secret agents. He was clearly a man fated to be betrayed by all those he had helped and protected. Even his valet Constant and the faithful Mameluke Roustam, who used to sleep outside his door, abandoned him when he went to Elba. Then there were the great betrayals: by Fouché, by Talleyrand, by Murat and by Bernadotte. Murat's treachery had been decisive in 1814 for, if he had remained loyal, a large Austrian army would have been pinned down in Italy, and the Allies would not have had the numbers necessary to invade France until May. As for Bernadotte, the man's ability to survive scandals that would have disgraced anyone else and to continue to be taken seriously by the Allies was nothing short of astonishing. One single statistic is eloquent on Bernadotte, a Walter Mitty who became a King. Of the lavish subsidies provided by the British in 1812–14, Prussia received £2,088,682, Austria £1,639,523 and Russia £2,366,334. These were the three nations whose forces tore the heart out of the *Grande Armée*. Yet Sweden, headed by a king who did little more than find excuses not to take action, received £2,334,992 in the same period.

A great man is bound to be surrounded by jealous nonentities, just as the shark swims surrounded by remora fish. To an extent, then, the Murats, Bernadottes, Fouchés and Talleyrands could be understood if not forgiven. But scarcely to be borne was the treachery of his own brothers and of his sisters Élisa and Caroline. It is in this context that the sublimely immoral Pauline finally appears to advantage. Unconcerned in her featherheaded way about the great crisis faced by the Bonaparte dynasty in 1812–13, Pauline lolled in the flesh pots of Aix-les-Bains, fending off the advances of François-Joseph Talma, the great French tragedian of the day, and taking as her latest lover instead an obscure soldier, Colonel Antoine Duchard. But when Napoleon was exiled to

Elba she followed him there and never ceased to urge him to return to the mainland to regain his throne.

Pauline had written to Madame Mère in the spring: 'We must not leave the Emperor alone. It is now that he is unhappy that we must show our attachment to him.' So Letizia came too and sat with Pauline playing cards with her son, while the Emperor cheated shamelessly. Yet another faithful woman was Marie Walewska, who brought her son to Elba for a secret visit of a few days. Napoleon's attitude to Marie was always curious; he was forever blowing hot and cold as if he genuinely could not decide what his feelings for her really were. Caulaincourt related that in 1812, on the sledge to Warsaw, the Emperor toyed with the idea of diverting to spend a night with Marie at Walewice castle and was dissuaded only when Caulaincourt pointed out he would almost certainly be captured by Cossacks. Unfortunately for Marie, the Elba visit coincided with the down cycle of his feelings for her. Although he met and spoke to her, he did not take her to his bed. He kept her waiting all night and did not send for her, then, when she had gone, expressed bitter regret.

One alleged motive in his turning away Marie Walewska was the desire not to give Marie-Louise any excuse not to come to him in Elba. It may have been so, but the evidence shows Napoleon on Elba turning away in his thoughts from his second wife and back to Josephine. Even before he left Fontainebleau there are signs that he blamed Marie-Louise (unfairly) for the débâcle that had left him without wife and child, for he wrote to Josephine: 'They have betrayed me. Yes, all of them except our dear Eugène, so worthy of you and me ... Adieu, my dear Josephine. Resign yourself as I am doing and never forget one who has never forgotten and will never forget you. P.S. I expect to hear from you when I reach Elba. I am far from being in good health.'

Josephine's financial position was assured by Talleyrand and the new government, and she was even visited at Malmaison by Czar Alexander, who showed her every courtesy. Yet she refused to be an apostate where her ex-husband was involved. The verbatim comments jotted down by her attendants in 1814 all point in the same direction. Typical is the following: 'Sometimes I feel so melancholy that I could die of despair; I cannot be reconciled to Bonaparte's fate.' In the last week of May she caught a chill while out driving with the Czar, caught pneumonia and died on 29 May. Allegedly her last words were: 'Bonaparte ... Elba ... the King of Rome.' Napoleon first learned of her death from a newspaper and was so shocked that he stayed in his room for two days. His final judgement on her was written as if she were still alive: 'I have not passed a day without loving you. I have not passed a night without clasping you in my arms . . . No woman was ever loved with more devotion, ardour and tenderness . . . only death could break a union formed by sympathy, love and true feeling.'

Napoleon spent a lot of time on Elba brooding on where he had gone wrong. He had certainly not been defeated by a people in arms, as romantic nationalists were starting to claim. Even in the alleged fervour of German nationalism in 1813, the sober truth was that resistance inside Prussia to conscription was still widespread. No, surely the truth was that he had rated human nature too highly, had been deceived by Metternich and Emperor Francis and thus been faced by a coalition of four powers (Britain, Prussia, Russia and Austria) no one nation should contend against. Sheer weight of numbers had beaten him in the battlefield, but by this time his Empire had already collapsed from within. The implicit 'social contract' of 1799 was that foreign policy should never harm the interests of the notables. This meant, as a minimum, that he had to avoid conflict with the Catholic Church, maintain living standards and keep taxation and conscription to a reasonable level. As he now ruefully realized, he had failed in all three areas.

Alongside the notables, the peasantry, too, had been alienated. His imperial policies demanded mass conscription, but the peasantry had never known the draft before 1793 and hated it with a rare fervour. Napoleon could have no defence on this issue, for the warning signs were there for all to see, even in the consular period, with an estimated 250,000 draft dodgers even in the comparatively quiet military period of 1799–1805. One study finds no less than 119 riots occurring between Napoleon's coronation and the 1806 campaign against Prussia on this one issue alone. Although conscription did not fall on the notables before 1813, even they felt its consequences in the gangs of criminalized deserters roaming the countryside, looting the substance of the bourgeoisie and threatening their physical security.

Napoleon also meditated long and hard on the present political situation in France. Talleyrand and his supporters in the Senate offered Louis XVIII Bourbon restoration on the understanding that the clock would be put back to 1791 rather than 1798. The offer to Louis was always a *pis aller*. There was no enthusiasm for Bernadotte as a 'saviour', no real support for the duc d'Orléans and a regency under Marie-Louise would have allowed Napoleon to direct matters from afar and settle accounts with his betrayers. The worry for Talleyrand and his minions was whether Louis XVIII would accept a conditional restoration.

Early signs were not propitious. Louis reached Compiègne on 29 April and, in the declaration of St-Cloud on 2 May, repudiated constitutional monarchy and popular sovereignty. But in a Charter on 4 June he guaranteed the position of the Constituent Assembly and the freedoms of the Revolution, thus ensuring there would be no return to absolutism. Crucially, too, he recognized all the financial arrangements entered into by the Bonapartist régime, thus giving the notables what they wanted. A new constitution would give executive power to the King, legislative power to a chamber of deputies (which he could dissolve) and a chamber of peers (to which he could nominate an unlimited number).

As for the general European settlement, by the Treaty of Paris on 30 May 1814, only the frontiers of 1792 were restored, so that Savoy, Avignon and Montbeliard were the sole residue of all the wars fought between 1792–1814. Belgium was annexed to Holland; Venetia and Lombardy returned to Italy; many fortified towns, notably Hamburg and Antwerp were restored to their owners and refortified; and the fate of the rest of Europe was held over for a general congress to be held in Vienna. Napoleon realized that this was a grievous blow to French pride and wondered how the French people would react once it sank in that the loss of all his conquests to the Allies was the price for having the Bourbons restored. In propaganda terms there was a glaring contrast between Napoloen Bonaparte, defender of an invaded France, and Louis XVIII, brought back in a foreigner's wagon and imposed at the point of Allied bayonets.

By the winter of 1814 Napoleon was seriously thinking of raising his standard again on the mainland. The primary spur towards renewing the struggle with the Allies was financial. The Bourbons had not paid the two million francs pledged by Article Three of the Treaty of Fontainebleau and showed no signs of ever doing so. There was no money to be had on Elba, which could not export its iron because the Napoleonic wars had created a glut on the market. Raising fresh taxes on the island was also not an option. When the people of Capoliveri in the south refused to pay their normal taxes, the Emperor had to send in his lancers. The taxes were then paid, but out of the receipts Napoleon had to pay bonuses to his faithful Poles, so he was back where he started.

The perfidy of the Bourbons was particularly reprehensible since Napoleon had accepted the 'annuity' of two million francs in return for the 160 million francs of real estate and other property he had left behind on the mainland. By the end of 1814 the four million francs he had taken with him in cash to Elba was exhausted. He would therefore not be able to pay the 400 members of his Old Guard or the squadron of Polish cavalry and would thus be wide open to assassination attempts which were constantly threatened. Campbell wrote to Castlereagh: 'If pecuniary difficulties press on Napoleon much longer, I think he is capable of crossing over to Piombino with his troops, or of any other eccentricity.' The Foreign Office in London made light of Campbell's fears, but Castlereagh raised the issue of non-payment with Louis XVIII. The bloated Bourbon monarch made no direct reply, but suggested Napoleon should be removed to the Azores.

This talk of the Azores deeply worried the Emperor, and there were other possible future places of exile mentioned, among them St Helena and the West Indies. Once the future of Europe was settled by the peace talks in Vienna, might not Britain, Russia and the German allies lose interest in him, thus giving the vengeful Bourbons their chance for a final settling of accounts? Were they not being urged on by Fouché, who said that Napoleon on Elba was to Europe as Vesuvius to Naples? Given the extent of murderous hatred towards him by Louis XVIII's brother, the comte d'Artois, Bonaparte might even count himself lucky if he got as far as the Azores. An assassin's dagger or a hit man's bullet would be a more likely fate.

There were other reasons for the Emperor's extreme frustration on Elba. The extent of Metternich's double-cross over Marie-Louise became clear when Napoleon heard the full story. In September, still hoping to rejoin her husband, she set out to take the waters at Aix-les-Bains. Metternich, reading her mind, sent with her as aide-de-camp a man sometimes described as his physical double, the one-eyed Count Adam Albrecht von Neipperg, a man with a reputation as a ladykiller even greater than Metternich's. Marie-Louise, whose appetite for sex was not far short of Josephine's or Pauline's, soon succumbed to his subtle charms. Chateaubriand cynically described Neipperg as 'the man who dared to lay his eggs in the eagle's nest', but the eagle was by this time wounded and flightless. Marie-Louise eventually bore Neipperg two children, the first in 1815. Apart from a formal New Year's greeting in 1815, Napoleon never heard from her again.

If the need for money and the desire for revenge were powerful personal motives for a return to the mainland, Napoleon was also greatly encouraged by all he heard from his spies there. Particularly encouraging was a visit in February 1815 from Fleury de Chaboulon, former sub-prefect of Rheims, who reported his eyewitness impressions and brought confirmation in a letter from former minister Maret, the Bonapartist Duke of Bassano. Both spoke of dissension among the Allies and huge levels of discontent in France.

There were rumours that Austria, France and England were bound by secret convention against Russia and Prussia, whose ambitions they feared. France was supporting Austria against Prussia in its claim to Dresden, but Austria made a poor requital by failing to agree to a Bourbon restoration in Naples; she was actuated partly by jealousy of the House of Bourbon and partly by loyalty to Murat, whose abandonment of Napoleon in January 1814 had in some ways been the crucial military event in the entire campaign. Most of all, there was considerable personal animus between Czar Alexander and Louis XVIII. The Czar was furious when he heard the portly Bourbon tell another ruler known for his corporation, the Prince Regent, that he owed his restoration to the British; the Czar took the view, rightly, that it was the Russians who had done most of the fighting to topple the Corsican ogre. With a strong visceral dislike of Louis XVIII, Alexander also felt he had been insulted when Louis served himself first at a state banquet and refused to spend the night under the same roof. It was reported that Alexander remarked indignantly: 'One would think that it was actually *he* who put *me* on *my* throne.'

If there were doubts about how far the Allies would go to support Louis XVIII, it was very clear the Bourbons could look for little from the French people themselves. The demobilized soldiers already hated him and pined for the good old days of the Emperor. Tens of thousands of undefeated veterans who had been cooped up in the besieged fortresses, returned home, when these were surrendered, fully convinced that they had been sold down the river. They joined the throng of disgruntled Napoleonic officers and further tens of thousands of returning prisoners of war, who found that there was nothing for them in France as Bourbon placemen had taken all the good things. The result was an ex-army thrown on the scrapheap and abandoned, but bitter, brooding and eager for revenge.

The notables too were becoming concerned by the Bourbons' new bearing. They resented the dismantling of the Concordat and the assumption of their sees by the ultramontane bishops, for if Catholicism was restored to a dominant position in the state, it would not be long before the issue of confiscated Church property was raised. Indeed, there were worrying signs that Louis XVIII was about to go back on his word concerning national property in general. All other classes suffered too, and not just from an ending of all hope of careers open to talents. The peasantry were afraid that national property would be taken from them and feudal tithes reintroduced; urban workers were hit hard by unemployment as British goods came flooding in and they remembered with fondness Napoleon's cheap bread policies; while all who had had

Prussians, Russians and Austrians billeted on them were deeply resentful at the waste of their substance and the national humiliation.

Napoleon consulted his intimates on whether he should make a landing on the mainland. General Drouot advised against, but Pauline and Madame Mère were enthusiastic. Letizia's alleged advice was: 'Go, my son, fulfil your destiny. You were not made to die on this island.' On St Helena Napoleon revealed that he had not really had any option: if he had stayed on Elba while France was in turmoil and suffering under the Bourbon yoke, his veterans could rightly have accused him of cowardice. Given the refusal of Louis XVIII's government to pay him the agreed annuity, it is hard to see what realistic alternative he had. Chateaubriand claimed that the events of 1815 revealed Napoleon as an egomaniac without any real feeling for France and its suffering, but this is not really a plausible interpretation. More feasible is the idea that Austria and England colluded to set things up so that Napoleon would return; in order to send him to a distant island, they needed an excuse to convince the Czar, prime mover in the Elba idea, that none of them could ever rest easy while Bonaparte was in Europe.

Napoleon chose carefully the moment when he made his bid. On 16 February Campbell left Elba for a medical consultation in Florence on board the Royal Navy brig *Partridge*, which normally invested the island. Next day the Emperor ordered the brig *Inconstant* to be fitted out for a voyage. Men, arms and ammuniton were loaded on to six smaller craft. On 26 February Napoleon bade farewell to Elba. He took with him 650 men of the Guard, just over a hundred Polish lancers and some Corsican and Elban volunteers. The journey across the Mediterranean was risky, for with favourable winds the *Partridge* could have got back from Leghorn in time to intercept the *Inconstant*. But Napoleon's usual luck when at sea held. The only encounter with hostile shipping was with the French brig, the *Zéphyr*. The two ships hailed each other, but the *Zéphyr*'s captain was lacking in curiosity and was satisfied with the casually imparted news that the 'great man' was still on Elba.

On 28 February, Napoleon landed at Golfe Juan near Antibes with just 1,026 men, forty horses and two cannon. Nothing daunted, he addressed his comrades in arms: 'I will arrive in Paris without firing a shot.' In a further amazing prediction, he declared they would all be in Paris in time for the King of Rome's birthday on 20 March. To avoid the White Terror of Provence he proposed to head through the Basses-Alpes to Grenoble. This involved a gruelling march after Grasse on a winding, single-file track, made treacherous by ice. The early days were depressing, for two mules bearing one-tenth of his money plunged over a precipice, and so far only four recruits had come in: two soldiers from the garrison at Antibes, a policeman and a tanner from Grasse.

Leaving Grasse on 2 March, the tiny army proceeded to trek thirty miles through the snow over a rough mountain track, passing through Sermon, St Vallier, Barrème and Digne. The Emperor's health, which had been excellent on Elba, held up well through this ordeal. On 4 March his advance guard took Sisteron and on 5 March reached Gap. Two days later came the moment of truth. At Laffrey, 25 miles south of Grenoble Napoleon's forces met a slightly smaller detachment under Major Delessart, sent to intercept them by General Jean Marchand, comman-dant at Grenoble. Ever the gambler, Napoleon decided on a bold stroke. He might have been able to sweep Delessart's men of the 5th Regiment from his path, but that would mean bloodshed which he was anxious to avoid. He knew from his spies that one of his former aides commanded a regiment at Grenoble, and it was possible that imperial sentiment was still thriving in the 5th. It was worth the risk.

After telling his band to play the *Marseillaise* and getting his men to slope arms ostentatiously, he set off alone on horseback towards Delessart's infantry. At gunshot range he dismounted and, in his familiar grey greatcoat, began to walk towards the lines where several hundred muskets were trained on him. His histrionic talents had always been superlative, whether before the Pyramids or in the courtyard of Fontainebleau. Now he gave his greatest performance. He opened up his coat to expose the white waistcoat beneath, then called out in a loud voice: 'Here I am. Kill your Emperor, if you wish.' He then added, falsely: 'The forty-five best heads of the government in Paris have called me from Elba and my return is supported by the three first powers of Europe.' He was just a single bullet away from oblivion, but instead of a fusillade of shots there came back a mighty roar: '*Vive l'Empereur!*' The soldiers crowded around him in high emotion, pledging eternal love and support.

On the crest of this wave Napoleon swept into Grenoble on 8 March after a 240-mile march through icy mountains that had lasted six days. The garrison at Grenoble refused to open fire and instead opened the gates to him. 2,000 peasants with flaming torches lined the route for his triumphal entry, yelling 'Long live the Emperor!' In euphoria Napoleon acknowledged that he had easily won the opening round of the contest: 'Before Grenoble I was an adventurer; at Grenoble I was a reigning prince.' On 9 March the Army that continued the march north was 8,000 strong, with 30 guns. Proceeding via Rives and Bourgoin the Army's vanguard reached Lyons at 10 p.m. on the 9th. When Napoleon came in on 10 March he was received rapturously by throngs of Lyonnais silk workers. Napoleon learned that Louis XVIII's brother, the comte d'Artois, had come to Lyons to organize resistance but had found imperial sentiment so strong that he had decamped back to Paris.

On 13 March Napoleon left Lyons and headed north-west through Tournus, Chalon, Autun and Avallon to Auxerre. There he was joined by Marshal Ney, who had earlier boasted to Louis XVIII that he would bring Bonaparte back to Paris in an iron cage. Ney had taken an oath of loyalty to the King and did not change his loyalty without heart-searching, but three factors seem to have weighed with him. One was the obvious fact that the Bourbons had no popular support, and Ney could not even be sure of his troops' loyalty if he ordered them into battle against the Emperor. Secondly, Ney and his wife, who was known to be an ex-chambermaid, had been snubbed once too often by the royalist snobs at the Bourbon court. Thirdly, Ney, an unbalanced and emotional man, had been genuinely moved by the simplicity of the note the Emperor sent him from Lyons, in which Napoleon took his fidelity for granted: 'I shall receive you as I did on the morrow of the battle of the Moskova.'

Ney's defection swayed other waverers. Proceeding from Auxerre via Joigny, Sens and Pont-sur-Yonne, Napoleon reached Paris at 9 p.m. on 20 March. He was carried up the steps of the Tuileries by a crowd that seemed almost crazed with excitement. Incredibly, the Emperor had made good all his boasts. He had reached Paris in time for his son's birthday and he had done so without shedding a drop of blood. By any reckoning, the twenty-day march from Antibes to Paris was one of the high points in his life. As Balzac later wrote incredulously: 'Before him did ever a man gain an Empire simply by showing his hat?'

In his sensational triumph Napoleon had made just one mistake, but it was to prove costly. He did not wait until Europe's ministers and sovereigns had dispersed after their conclave in Vienna before crossing from Elba. Consequently they were all still together when news of his return came in. As soon as he got back to Elba, Campbell sent news of the Emperor's flight to the Austrian consul at Genoa, who in turn sent the message to Vienna by swift courier. Metternich's valet brought in the letter and woke him at 7 a.m. on 7 March, but the minister, who had been working until 3 a.m., put the envelope on the table and tried to go back to sleep. Unable to do so, he then opened the letter, sprang out of bed and was with Emperor Francis by 8 a.m. Fifteen minutes later Metternich was in conversation with the Czar and at 8.30 with the Kaiser. At 10 a.m the plenipotentiaries to the Conference met, and couriers were dispatched to mobilize the Allied armies. In this way war was declared in less than an hour.

Six days later Congress went to the limits of international law and beyond by declaring Bonaparte an outlaw. Wellington put his signature to the communiqué and was at once attacked by the Whig opposition in London for seeming to have called for Napoleon's assassination. On 25 March the four principal Allies each agreed to provide 150,000 men in the first instance to destroy the 'monster'; the British would make up any shortfall in manpower by appropriate subsidies. The ultimate strategy was to provide a *cordon sanitaire* around France from the Alps to the Channel.

Within France events moved at an even faster pace. Paris learned of Napoleon's landing on 5 March. Soult, now Minister of War, began by proclaiming Bonaparte outlaw and organizing an army of defence under the comte d'Artois. Louis XVIII received the support of the Legislature and the National Guard and took comfort from the rebuff Antibes had given Napoleon. The marshals seemed to be holding firm too, for Masséna in Marseilles and Oudinot in Metz proclaimed their royalist sympathies. Initially the only sign of nervousness was the fall in government stock from 81 to 75 francs. The turning point was Ney's defection at Auxerre on 16 March. This opened up the floodgates, so that almost instantly the entire Army seemed to go over to the Emperor. Ironically, stung by Allied taunts that he dared not raise an army in his own country, Louis XVIII had mobilized 60,000 men and put them on the march at the very time Napoleon landed; as a result of this coincidence, Soult was wrongly accused of collusion and treason. On the night of 19–20 March a panicky Louis XVIII fled from the Tuileries and took the road to Ghent.

Before putting France on a war footing, Napoleon made a final, futile attempt to come to terms with the Allies. They responded by reiterating that he was now outlawed as an enemy of humanity and would be banished from Europe forever if captured; in theory the sentence of outlawry also implied that the Emperor could be summarily executed if taken. In vain did Napoleon recognize the Treaty of Paris and the 1792 frontiers and send envoys to the Czar and the Austrian Emperor. The Allies were after his blood and would brook no compromise. It would be another fight to the finish. But first the Emperor had to put his domestic house in order.

All Napoleon's advisers had warned him that this time round he would have to rule France on liberal principles. Accordingly, as early as Lyons he proclaimed a reform of the Constitution and the summoning of an electoral college. And his first appointments in Paris seemed to breathe the spirit of reconciliation: Carnot, an opponent of the Empire, was appointed Minister of the Interior; Lafayette returned as part of the 'loyal opposition' in the Chamber; even Lucien Bonaparte was reconciled. As part of the balancing act, in which he tried to reassure both royalists and Jacobins, Napoleon recalled Fouché as Minister of Police; this was a bad mistake for Fouché, as always, was acting as the Allies' double agent.

Napoleon's greatest catch was probably the 47-year old Benjamin Constant, a disciple of Germaine de Staël and admirer of Madame Récamier. Just days before the Emperor arrived in Paris, Constant recorded a typically jaundiced opinion: 'He has reappeared, this man dyed with our blood. He is another Attila, another Genghiz Khan, but more terrible and more hateful because he has at his disposal the resources of civilization.' But when Napoleon invited Constant to the Tuileries and asked him to frame a new Constitution, which would avoid the mistakes of his old imperial system and the excesses of the Bourbons, Constant accepted.

Napoleon's first act on restoration was to issue the decrees of 21 March, in which he attempted to win over the bourgeoisie. The decrees abolished feudal titles, banished returned émigrés and expropriated their land. But the response to these 'generous' measures disappointed the Emperor, and it gradually dawned on him that his only real way forward was to promise to lead the Revolution in the direction it was headed when halted by the reaction of Thermidor in 1794. A great demonstration of workers and ex-soldiers filed past him on 14 May, urging him to head a war of liberation against *all* oppressors and to return to the principles of 1793. This was not only unacceptable to his bourgeois supporters, who wanted neither the *ancien régime nor* 1793 – and certainly not the *levée en masse* – but also to him personally: 'I do not want to be king of the Jacquerie,' he declared. This was shortsighted: he should have seized the moment, especially since it was self-defeating folly to try to appease the very faction (the bourgeoisie) that had ditched him in 1814.

The consequence was that the new régime was soon threatening to collapse under its own contradictions. The peasantry became disillusioned when it was a question of dipping into pockets to pay war taxes; there were riots in Paris, Lyons, Dunkirk, Nantes, Marseilles and elsewhere; while Carnot's purge of the prefects provoked a conservative and clerical backlash. Napoleon also became aware that French cities were forming federal pacts on the Swiss model, simply adding his name as a legitimating device but making it clear where their real sympathies lay. When he heard the details of the first such pact, between Nantes and Rennes, he sighed and said: 'This is not good for me, but it may be good for France.'

There was also great hostility to the *Acte Additionel*, promulgated on 22 April, by which Constant reformed the Constitution. Constant retained the Council of State and the plebiscite based on universal suffrage; there were guarantees of civil liberty, press freedom, an enlarged electoral college, an hereditary upper house, a lower chamber based on a restricted suffrage. But in the May plebiscite to confirm the *Acte Additionel* Napoleon received just 1,532,527 'yeses' and 4,802 'noes' – as compared with the 3.7 million affirmative votes he had received in 1802 and the 3.6 million in 1804. In the elections to the chamber only about a hundred of the 629 legislators were fully committed to a war against the Allies.

Napoleon's constitutional reforms were a failure on just about every front. It was a mistake for a ruler who professed liberal principles to retain hereditary peers. It was a mistake to call the constitutional refurbishment an 'Additional' Act, as this implied that the old unpopular imperial system was still in being. It was also an error to reveal the country hopelessly divided as in the past, with massive absentions in the referendum from the south, west and the urban regions, and enthusiasm only in evidence in the east, north and rural areas. Most of all, the reforms were misconceived because Napoleon's heart was not in them; he admitted to Bertrand that as soon as his position was militarily secure, he intended to rescind the more liberal concessions he had been forced to make. But for the present he played along with the new image of a man who had learned from his past mistakes: 'My system has changed – no more war, no conquests. Can one be as fat as I am and have ambition?'

The conflict between Napoleon's real and apparent intentions was perhaps revealed by some (surely unconscious) slips at the ceremony of the *Champ de Mai* on 1 June, when the 'Additional Act' was formally adopted. In a combined civil, military and religious ceremony, which yoked together proclamation of election results, speeches, signatures, a solemn Mass and *Te Deum*, and the distribution of eagles to the Army and National Guard, Napoleon chose to appear, for the last time, in the velvety Roman Emperor's robes he had worn at the Coronation in 1804. And when he addressed both houses of the Legislature on 7 June the Emperor, angered by the way the lower chamber had passed over Lucien as their president and refused an oath of loyalty to the Empire, spoke these ominous words: 'Let us not imitate the example of the later Roman Empire which, invaded on all sides by the barbarians, made itself the laughing-stock of posterity by discussing abstract questions when the battering-rams were breaking down the city gates.'

Napoleon had a point, for the Allies had no interest in the supposedly liberal, Jacobin or even royalist credentials of Bonaparte's Ministers and legislators as long as the man they had outlawed remained Emperor of France. And the 'liberal' legislators in the Chamber of Deputies were in any case being cynically manipulated by Fouché, who planned to deliver France to the Bourbons. The crucial question for Napoleon was whether he could raise enough troops to deal with the million troops the Allies intended to pour into France. He began by raising 40 million francs in ready cash by trading four million of the Sinking Fund bonds at 50% for credits on the National Forests. He ordered 250,000 stand of weapons, and French arms factories were geared up to turn out 40,000 new firearms a month, while the Ministry of War assured the Emperor that 46,000 horses would be ready by 1 June. On 28 March all non-commissioned officers who had left the Army were recalled and by 30 April four armies and three observation corps were in being.

Napoleon planned to have 800,000 men fully trained and armed by October 1815. But could he hold out until then and keep the massive Allied armies at bay? His first idea was to fortify Paris and Lyons heavily, hoping to tempt the enemy into protracted sieges which would gain him the time he needed. On 8 April he ordered mobilization, but delayed conscription for another three weeks. By his old measures of encouraging veterans to return to the colours, incorporating National Guardsmen, drafting sailors, policemen, customs officials, etc, he quickly raised 280,000. But it would be autumn before the 150,000 draftees from the class of 1815 would be ready, and meanwhile draft evasion continued at the high levels of 1813–14. But the worst blow was a fresh outbreak of the Vendée in mid-May, which required the diversion of significant bodies of troops.

As for officers and generals, Napoleon might have been well advised to follow his own advice on Elba, when he regretted using the marshals in 1813–14 and reflected that he should have promoted able generals with their batons still to win. This was an especially cogent consideration, since those marshals who remained loyal were not keen to fight again; it was the career officers and the old sweats of the *Grande Armée*, attracted by loot, promotion and meaningful employment, who were most eager for the adventure of the Hundred Days. The Emperor's staunchest support among the marshals came from Lefebvre and Davout, but Napoleon wasted Davout's great military talents by appointing him Minister of War. So many of his marshals were either dead (Lannes, Poniatowski, Bessières) or had defected to the enemy (Bernadotte, Victor, Oudinot, MacDonald, Marmont, Masséna) that, with a few notable exceptions, the Emperor was left with the dross (Ney, Soult, Grouchy).

Nothing more clearly shows the foredoomed nature of the Hundred Days than Napoleon's failure to use the few military talents available to him; though loyal, Davout, Suchet and Mortier all played no part in the events of June 1815. One who did, albeit indirectly, was the dreadful Murat. As soon as he heard of the Emperor's entry into Lyons, Murat feared that the colossus might soon be bestriding Italy once more. To preempt this Murat decided to raise Italy against the Austrians himself, under a banner of unification, but was swiftly defeated by the Austrian army, which entered Naples on 12 May. According to Henry Houssaye, Marmont was the villain of 1814 and Fouché of 1815, but Napoleon himself thought that it was Murat who was his double nemesis in both years; he had aggravated matters twice, by declaring against France in 1814 and Austria in 1815.

As his enemies began assembling their armies – Blücher at Liège with 117,000 Prussians, Wellington at Brussels with 110,000 Anglo-Dutch, Schwarzenberg with 210,000 Austrians on the upper Rhine, Barclay de Tolly with 150,000 Russians in the central Rhine area and Frimont with 75,000 Austrians on the Riviera – Napoleon had to decide his strategy.

There were only two realistic options: either to preempt the Allies by defeating the Prussian and Anglo-Dutch armies before the Russians and Austrians could join them, or to remain on the defensive. The latter seemed the better policy, as it would buy time in which the French themselves could build their planned force of 800,000; even if the Allies advanced on Paris in the summer, he would have 200,000 men to defend the capital as against a mere 90,000 in 1814. There was the additional advantage that the advancing enemy would have to leave significant detachments behind as each successive fortress was taken; the disadvantage was that large tracts of northern and eastern France (the very areas where Napoleon enjoyed most support) would have to be abandoned to the enemy.

If, on the other hand, he went for the preemptive strike option and it failed, this would precipitate a much more rapid Allied descent on Paris. It was a tall order to pit just 140,000 men against 224,000 of the enemy (his latest intelligence estimates put the Anglo-Dutch at 104,000 and the Prussians and Saxons under Blücher at 120,000), but Napoleon consoled himself with the thought that in 1814, with just 40,000 men, he had won a string of victories against enemy forces six times as large. The main advantage of a successful preemptive strike was likely to be political: Napoleon gambled that if Wellington was defeated, the Liverpool government would fall and the incoming Whig administration would make peace. Aware, too that the British and Prussians were poles apart in their political aims and did not have a unified military command, he thought there was a good chance of driving a wedge between them and vanquishing them by local superiority of numbers. Above all, though, the political tail wagged the military dog. Napoleon had had to make concessions to get even grudging and qualified support from the notables; they would certainly not support anything more than a short campaign, and to maintain himself in power thereafter his only option would be the Terror of 1793. He therefore decided to go for the preemptive strike.

Yet even before he set out for Belgium, Napoleon made three bad errors of judgement. Even at this late stage he could have had the erratic Murat on his side to command his right wing. Instead he had the newest marshal, Grouchy, whose incompetence and lack of imagination had ruined Hoche's 1796 descent on Ireland. As his principal field commander he had the headstrong and unreliable Ney, when he could have had the brilliant Suchet. Davout, too was wasted in a purely administrative capacity at the Ministry of War, also doubling as Governor of Paris. A further blow fell on 1 June when his peerless chief of staff Berthier threw himself (or was he pushed?) from a window in the

Bamberg palace in Bavaria. His place was taken by Soult, whose speciality was to issue opaque or sibylline orders that required an expert on hieroglyphics to decipher. This meant that instead of a top-flight winning combination of Suchet, Davout, Murat and Berthier, he had the three greatest duds among the marshalate as his aides: Soult, Ney and Grouchy.

After saying goodbye to Marie Walewska, who had rejoined him in Paris for their final period together as lovers, Napoleon left for the north. Already his health was giving cause for concern. Everyone remarked that he was obese, with a puffy face, greenish complexion, dull eyes and a heavy walk. He seemed to need far more sleep than in his vintage years and could not keep awake at night, no matter how much coffee he drank. Throughout the short Belgian campaign he was fatigued, needed lots of sleep, was lethargic and indecisive and generally prone to inertia. The omens for success were not good.

The Emperor left Paris at midnight on the evening of 11–12 June, lunched at Soissons, slept at Laon and arrived at Avesnes on the 13th. Roll-call next day established the Army's strength at 122,000. When Napoleon crossed into Belgium by the Sambre at Charleroi on 15 June, his spies placed Wellington in Brussels with a mixed force of British, Dutch, Belgians and Hanoverians and Blücher at Namur with his 120,000 Prussians. The Grand Army was a better fighting force than in 1814. This time it included a credible cavalry army, the Guard and five army corps under Generals Drouet d'Erlon, Reille, Vandamme, Lobau and Gérard (one of Napoleon's favourites). It was singularly unfortunate that the Emperor had had to deploy troops in five other main theatres: the Vendée (under General Lamarque), the Var (under Marshal Brune); the Alps (under Suchet), the Jura (under General Lecourbe) and at the frontiers of the Rhine under another old favourite, General Rapp. Had even one of these 8,000-strong forces been available for the campaign in Belgium, their presence might have made all the difference.

Napoleon's strategy was to get between the two enemy armies and then destroy each in turn. He decided to attack the Prussians first since Blücher was restless and mercurial where Wellington was cautious and slow-moving; it was therefore likely that Blücher would move faster to Wellington's aid than vice versa. On the other hand, alive to contingency, he realized his plan might miscarry so put out patrols on both left and right as 'antennae', ready to deal with whichever enemy first appeared; as soon as either one was 'pinned', Napoleon himself with the centre would move in for the *coup de grâce*.

Both Wellington and Blücher were taken by surprise by the speed of the Emperor's advance. Wellington was obsessed with the idea that the movement towards Charleroi was a feint preparatory to an attack on Mons. He responded by concentrating on his outer, not his inner, flank, thus increasing the gap between him and Blücher. Military historians have severely criticized Wellington for fastening on this unlikely scenario, as a French attack on the open flank would simply have driven the two Allied armies together. So it was that by the evening of the 15th Napoleon had successfully interposed himself between the two enemy forces. Returning that night from the Duchess of Richmond's reception in Brussels – 'the most famous ball in history' as it has been called – Wellington finally realized he had been gulled: 'Napoleon has humbugged me, by God!'

But the Emperor's plans were also going awry. He gave the simple task of capturing the crossroads at Quatre Bras (an important road junction uniting main routes north-south and east-west) to Ney and Grouchy, who predictably made a mess of the task. Consumed with lethargy the two marshals halted that night before achieving their objective. Their excuse was that the enemy was in possession of Quatre Bras. The reality was that just 4,000 troops, mainly Dutch, were ensconced there under Prince Bernhard of Saxe-Weimar. An energetic commander with the huge superiority in numbers enjoyed by Ney could simply have swatted such a small force aside. But when the Dutch beat off Ney's skirmishers, the 'bravest of the brave' allowed himself to be deceived into thinking there was a considerable Allied force there; apparently the shoulder-high rye grass had successfully concealed the exiguous numbers of the Dutch. So egregious was Ney's incompetence on this occasion that some of his biographers have speculated that he was suffering from moral paralysis, still brooding on the conflict between his fidelity to Bonaparte and the oath of loyalty he had taken to Louis XVIII. This would be more convincing had not Ney displayed similar folly on numerous other occasions.

Next day he proved the point that he was always singularly useless unless some daredevil escapade was called for. When Napoleon learned at 2 a.m. on the 16th that Quatre Bras was still in enemy hands, he had to shelve his plan to press on to Brussels to attack Wellington (once again he had changed his mind). He decided to make a virtue of necessity and attack Blücher at Ligny, using Ney's forces for the *coup de grâce*. While Grouchy engaged the Prussian left and Napoleon hurled the bulk of his troops at the centre, Ney was to complete the 'mopping up' operations at Quatre Bras, then swing right to Ligny and fall on the Prussian right flank.

It must have been obvious that speed was essential if this operation was to be successful. But Ney compounded his tardiness of the 15th with lethargy on the 16th, and made no move until the early afternoon. His inactivity allowed Wellington, who arrived at Quatre Bras at 10 a.m., to ride eight miles for a conference with Blücher; he advised him not to offer battle if Napoleon appeared. The incredible French sloth was later blamed on a confusing order from Soult which read: 'the intention of His Majesty is that you attack whatever is before you and after vigorously throwing them back, join us to envelop this corps.' Crucially the orders did not make it clear that the Ligny operation was at all times to have priority and that Ney should not commit himself at Quatre Bras to the point where he could no longer take part in the main battle. But a good general understands his commander-in-chief's intentions and grasps strategy as a whole; this kind of intellectual grip was quite beyond the Prince of the Moskova.

Finally Ney bestirred himself. If he had launched an attack at any time before 2 p.m. on the 16th, he would easily have wrested the crossroads from the Allies. Then for an hour 8,000 Anglo-Dutch (there had been reinforcements) held 40,000 French troops at bay while Ney advanced with exaggerated caution, terrified that the enemy might have extra men in concealed positions. By 3 p.m. the defenders were on the point of cracking when suddenly General Picton's 8,000-strong division arrived. For a while the two forces fought a furious seesaw engagement but then around 4.30 further large-scale reinforcements arrived under the Duke of Brunswick and tipped the scales in the Allies' favour.

A furious Ney, seeing victory snatched from his grasp, lost control of himself and ordered Kellermann's cavalry to charge the British infantry unsupported. At around 5 p.m. the dauntless horsemen formed up for what looked like a suicide mission. Against all the odds, they nearly succeeded, but then the British brought up heavy guns; the combination of artillery and packed infantry devastated the heroic French cavalry. By 6.30 p.m. the race to get reinforcements to Quatre Bras had been easily won by Wellington. With 36,000 men he felt confident enough to order a large-scale counterattack, and by 9 p.m. he had regained all the ground taken by the French during the day. The French had taken 4,000 casualties, the Allies 4,800 (half of them British).

With Ney's non-appearance at Ligny, the French did not achieve their aims there either. On the morning of the 16th Napoleon wrote: 'In three hours the fate of the campaign will be decided. If Ney carries out his orders thoroughly, not a man or gun of this army in front of us will get away.' At first the battle went according to plan. French cannonades devastated the exposed Prussian infantry – for the arrogant Blücher had waved away Wellington's suggestions for placing them in more hidden positions. If Ney had appeared on the flank as planned, the result would have been a crushing victory. When there was no sign of Ney and instead there came news that he was meeting stiff resistance at Quatre Bras, Napoleon decided to call up Ney's reserve under General d'Erlon to provide the knock-out blow at Ligny. What followed was one of the great fiascos in military history.

D'Erlon's I Corps began the day on 16 June on the road to Quatre Bras, where Ney planned to use them as a surprise reinforcement thrown into the fray at the last moment. But when Napoleon realized that Ney would not be appearing at Ligny, he himself sent orders to d'Erlon to march there to play the role originally to have been acted by Ney. His courier, General de la Bedoyère, found d'Erlon's corps toiling north to Quatre Bras and at once rerouted them east to Ligny. In one of the many misunderstandings that bedevilled this day, I Corps arrived on the French flank instead of the Prussian at around 6 p.m., causing momentary panic in the Grand Army, as it was thought that there were 22,000 enemy troops on their flank. Napoleon was just about to send in the Guard when this news arrived. He was forced to suspend the operation for an hour, wasting critical time, while the confusion was sorted out. Consoling himself with the thought that at least he could now use d'Erlon's men for the *coup de grâce*, he sent word to d'Erlon to alter course so as to come in on the Prussian flank. To his stupefaction he was informed that I Corps had disappeared.

The villain was once again Ney, who spent the day in one towering tantrum after another. When he learned that the Emperor had ordered I Corps to Ligny, he lost his temper and raged. Then came an imperial aide with a message from Napoleon to take Quatre Bras without delay. Again Ney lost his temper and raged. He told the aide caustically to report to the Emperor that he could hardly take Quatre Bras 'without delay' when Wellington's entire army was there and the Emperor was ordering his best units to Ligny. When Wellington counterattacked, Ney began to panic. At risk of grave displeasure from the Emperor, he overruled de la Bedoyère's orders to d'Erlon, making it a court-martial offence if I Corps did not respond. D'Erlon was actually in sight of Ligny when he received Ney's final orders and turned back. The upshot was that 22,000 crack French troops spent all day pointlessly marching between Ligny and Quatre Bras but seeing action in neither place.

At Ligny Napoleon ended the day far short of the sweeping victory that could have been his. Further time was lost between 6.30 and 7.30

that evening by a Prussian counterattack. Rain was already falling heavily and darkness coming down fast when the Guard finally went into action and cut a swathe through the Prussians. At 8 p.m. Blücher's counterattack with cavalry was easily beaten off. Napoleon had smashed the Prussian centre but the two wings got away intact under cover of darkness. If Napoleon had had two more hours of darkness, or if d'Erlon's corps had not been withdrawn, he would have won a total victory even without Ney. This would have doomed Wellington and possibly even swung the balance of the entire war in Napoleon's favour. As it was, he had sustained 12,000 casualties and caused Prussian losses of 16,000 men and 21 guns; there were also 9,000 Prussian deserters. Blücher himself was thrown off his horse and narrowly escaped being trampled to death by French cuirassiers.

Quatre Bras and Ligny should have taught Napoleon that he could never win while he used Soult and Ney as his chief agents. Ney's timidity on the 15th, his inactivity on the morning of the 16th, his inability to grasp the overall strategy at Ligny and his recall of d'Erlon were matched only by the impenetrability of Soult's orders and the incompetence of his staffwork. But the ultimate responsibility for appointing both these men rests with Napoleon – they were far from being the only senior individuals available. Perhaps Napoleon knew in his heart that the game was already up, for he went down with incapacitating illness, did not order a pursuit of the Prussians and so lost contact with them, with ultimately disastrous results. Medical historians of Napoleon claim that he was suffering from acromegaly – a disease of the pituitary gland among whose symptoms are tiredness and overoptimism – but a more likely diagnosis is a psychogenic reaction to excessive stress and extreme frustration.

Napoleon still expressed himself confident of total victory next day, since two corps (d'Erlon's and Lobau's) had not been in battle at all while the Guard had suffered only light casualties. But on the 17th, still suffering from a heavy cold and bladder problems, he fell back into lethargy. Nothing excuses the fact that he issued no orders until noon, thus losing the advantage he had gained by Ligny. Some military historians go further and claim that the twelve hours between 9 p.m. on the 16th and 9 a.m. on the 17th were the critical period when the Belgian campaign was lost. Ney, too, was his usual incompetent self. It is clear in retrospect that if Ney had attacked Wellington at Quatre Bras on the morning of the 17th he could have pinned him there while Napoleon moved round the exposed flank on the Anglo-Dutch left, where the Prussian withdrawal had left them vulnerable.

By the time Napoleon girded himself for action, the moment of advantage was past. After Quatre Bras, Gneisenau, taking over command from the injured Blücher, wanted to retreat north but Blücher recovered sooner than expected and overruled this. Wellington, meanwhile, elected for a perilous withdrawal from Quatre Bras to the prepared positions he had earlier identified at Mont St Jean as being the best place to make a stand. Napoleon's expectations for the morning of 17 June were that Blücher would have retired to Liège, Ney would be in possession of Quatre Bras and Wellington would be scurrying along the road to Brussels. When he learned the truth, he had to rethink his battle plans.

There seemed to be three obvious choices, in descending order of desirability. He could leave Ney to keep Wellington occupied while he pursued Blücher; he could send Grouchy with a skeleton force to dog Blücher's steps while he himself fell on Wellington with superior numbers; or he could divide his force, sending Grouchy with 33,000 men after Blücher while he himself attacked Wellington with the balance of the Army (69,000 men). It was typical of this ill-starred campaign that he went for the third, and least desirable, option. Having wasted five hours of daylight doing nothing, he sent Grouchy after Blücher and moved against Wellington at Quatre Bras.

At noon Wellington ordered a retreat from Quatre Bras to the positions at Mont St Jean, near the village of Waterloo. If Napoleon had been on top form, this would have been the moment when he caught Wellington in a position where none of the Duke's normal tactics would have worked. But meanwhile another contretemps supervened to buy the Anglo-Dutch force precious time. At 1 p.m. Napoleon, finally on the move towards Quatre Bras, found Ney's force bivouacked and eating lunch as if they were on a leisurely picnic. Angrily he got them on the march but it was 2 p.m. before the chase after Wellington commenced in earnest. Ney tried to retrieve his reputation by an energetic pursuit of the duke's rearguard but he did not discomfit the enemy to the point where Wellington was forced to turn and face him. Even so, the French might yet have overhauled him but for the outbreak of a violent afternoon thunderstorm which turned the ground into a quagmire of mud and ruled out further effective pursuit. By 6.30 p.m. Wellington reached Mont-St-Jean. Napoleon raged that he did not have two more hours of daylight so that he could attack at once but, having thrown away nearly seven hours of daylight at the beginning of the day, his railing against fate had a hollow ring.

From Mont-St-Jean Wellington sent a message to Blücher that he was confident of holding his position if he could have just two Prussian corps as reinforcement. By yet another of the twists that made the Belgian campaign a chapter of accidents for Bonaparte, the Prussians were that evening mustering at Wavre; ironically the net effect of Ligny and Quatre Bras was to push the two Allied armies closer together. Grouchy, supposedly in hot pursuit of Blücher, had not only failed to interpose himself between the two Allied armies, but at 6 p.m. stopped for the night at Gembloux, twelve miles south of Wavre; incredibly, his corps had covered just six miles in the whole of that day. Had Blücher gone anywhere but Wavre, or if anyone but Grouchy had been pursuing him, Wellington's position at Waterloo would already have been hopeless.

At 11 p.m. at his base at the farmhouse of Belle Alliance, two miles south of Mont-St-Jean, Napoleon received the astounding news that Grouchy was nowhere near Wavres but was complacently ensconced at Gembloux; the marshal actually had the stupid effrontery to send a reassuring message that he would be advancing on Wavres at first light, so nothing was lost. Scarcely able to believe his eyes when he read the dispatch, the Emperor sought confirmation. Aware that if, after all his efforts, the two Allied armies managed to combine, the tables would be turned on him, he went for a walk at 1 a.m., accompanied only by the Grand Marshal. The torrential rainfall had eased off, and in the clear light the forest of Soignes looked as if it were on fire, lit up as it was from the glow of myriad bivouacs. At 2.30 a.m. the rain began to pelt down once more. Napoleon grabbed some fitful sleep, only to be awakened at 4 a.m. by a dispatch confirming Blücher's presence at Wavres. This was the point where he should have sent an express to Grouchy, ordering him to break off the pursuit of the Prussians to Wavre and instead station himself between Waterloo and Wavre to prevent the Prussians moving west. In yet another fateful decision he delayed sending this crucial message until 10 a.m. on the 18th.

On the morning of Sunday 18 June Napoleon was once again unwell. He had slept less than four hours and before daybreak rode his horse in teeming rain to inspect his advanced posts. The deluge-like precipitation in the early morning was to have important effects: not only did the waterlogged ground make it impossible for the French to manoeuvre their superior artillery but the lethal impact of their cannonballs was reduced; since round shot would not ricochet in these conditions, the artillery would not be able to tear holes in the dense British squares. When he had completed his tour of inspection, the Emperor again felt tired. So fatigued was he that between 10 and 11 a.m. he fell asleep while seated on a chair on the Brussels road.

In his preparations for the battle of Waterloo Napoleon contrived to produce a grand slam of mistakes. It is surprising that his great name as a captain has survived the lengthy checklist of errors he committed that day, or that Wellington should have gained such a great reputation for taking advantage of opportunities that were virtually handed him on a plate. The Emperor seemed pleased that Wellington had the forest of Soignes at his back, making retreat impossible, but he showed consummate folly in allowing the Duke to fight on ground of his own choosing. It almost passes belief that Wellington was yet again allowed to implement his favourite ploy of sheltering troops on reverse slopes. Surely after the Peninsular War the French were alive to this tired old dodge? Even Soult was worried about the concentrated firepower of the British squares but Napoleon reacted to his chief of staff's warnings with arrogance and contempt: 'Just because you have been beaten by Wellington, you think he's a good general. I tell you, Wellington is a bad general, the English are bad troops and this affair is nothing more than eating breakfast.'

In his tactics for the day's battle, Napoleon could think of nothing more original than an unimaginative frontal assault. His idea was to turn Wellington's left rather than his right, both because it was weaker and to cut the Duke off from any hope of aid from the Prussians at Wavre. Moreover, if he attacked Wellington's right, there was a danger that he might lose touch with Grouchy's detachment. But – to anticipate a question the Emperor was to ask himself repeatedly on this Sunday 18 June – where was Grouchy and what were his intentions? Had he received the Emperor's latest orders and was he even now, as Napoleon hoped, doubling back to take part in the battle?

Grouchy was to be the greatest single failure in the Battle of Waterloo, so it is not surprising that the issue of his culpability has exercised military historians ever since. His defenders point to the impenetrability – gibberish would be a better word – of the orders received from Soult, which were worded as follows: 'His Majesty desires that you will head for Wavre in order to draw near to us, and to place yourself in touch with our operations, and to keep up your communications with us, pushing before you those positions of the Prussian army which have taken this direction and which have halted at Wavre; this place you ought to reach as soon as possible.' Since Wavre lay to the north of Grouchy and the Emperor to the west, the orders were nonsensical; moreover 'pushing' the Prussians before him, in the context of 'drawing near' could mean only driving Blücher to the field of Waterloo – the exact opposite of Napoleon's intentions. Grouchy solved the conundrum by fastening on the three words 'head for Wavre' and ignoring everything else. ·

It must have been obvious to the merest lieutenant in Grouchy's corps that the Emperor's overall intention was to impede a junction between the two Allied armies and that preventing this had to be Grouchy's main aim. At Wavre Blücher sent Bülow on a flank march west to Waterloo; if Grouchy had used even moderate intelligence and sent just part of his force west, they would have come upon Bülow and prevented his rescue mission. But Grouchy's idiocy did not end there. Having assured Napoleon that he would be setting out at first light for Wavres, he delayed departure from Gembloux until 10 a.m. When firing was heard from the direction of Waterloo after midday, Grouchy's senior generals, Gérard especially, urged him to turn round and march to the sound of the guns. Grouchy refused.

There can be no excuses or exculpation for this clear dereliction of duty. A marshal of France was supposed to be a man of initiative and intelligence, not an automaton blindly obeying orders; it was Grouchy's clear duty to head in the direction of the fighting, as the great Desaix had done at Marengo. When he heard that the plodding Grouchy was determinedly heading towards him at Wavres, Blücher sent word to Bülow on no account to be swayed from his mission. Grouchy deserves every syllable of the scathing judgement Napoleon eventually passed on his incompetent subordinate: 'Marshal Grouchy, with 34,000 men and

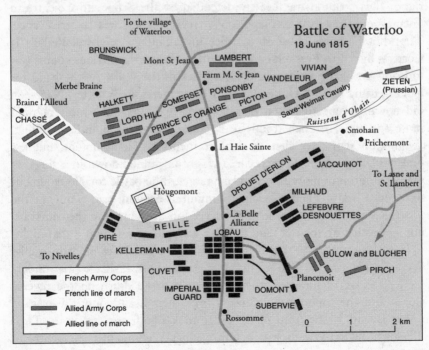

108 guns, discovered the secret, which seemed an impossibility, of being neither on the field of battle at Mont-St-Jean, nor at Wavres during the day of the 18th . . . Marshal Grouchy's conduct was just as unpredictable as if his Army had experienced an earthquake on the way which had swallowed it up.'

On the field of Waterloo Napoleon began the battle supremely confident, with 72,000 men against the Anglo-Dutch 68,000: 'We, have ninety chances in our favour and not ten against.' The peculiarity of the Battle of Waterloo was its narrow compass, with 140,000 men crammed into three square miles; the front was only four kilometres wide, as against ten at Austerlitz. Wellington had his men deployed along the 2½-mile ridge of Mont-St-Jean, with 17,000 sent to the west near Hal to stymie any French outflanking movements. His main strength was concentrated on his right, doubtless because he expected the advancing Prussian corps to safeguard his left. He established forward strong points at the hamlets of La Haie and Papelotte, the large sprawling farm known as La Haie Sainte on his left and the château of Hougoumont on his right.

The opening salvoes from the artillery took place at around 11.35, then Napoleon made yet another of his many mistakes this day by allowing his brother Jérôme to assault the château of Hougoumont on Wellington's right. This position was heavily defended by the Scots and Coldstream Guards and, in terms of Napoleon's overall tactics, was an irrelevance. The idiotic Jérôme chose to sacrifice his infantry – General Reille's II Corps – by a direct assault on Hougoumont when the obvious course was to bring up heavy artillery and blast holes in the walls. As the hand-to-hand fighting around Hougoumont became increasingly bitter, Napoleon did not intervene to halt it or take decisive action but simply allowed more and more French troops to be sucked into the pointless conflict. Wellington sent only slender reinforcements to Hougoumont, but the best part of an entire French corps was soon pinned down in a slugging match for an unimportant secondary target. The battle for Hougoumont went on all day. Flames began to engulf it around 3.30 p.m. but the fortress never fell; the French did succeed in breaking into the courtyard but were soon driven out, and fighting was still going on at 9 that night.

It was not until 1.30 that Napoleon finally ordered a cannonade against Wellington's centre with eighty big guns. This fusillade was largely ineffective, as Wellington ordered his men to lie down on the reverse slopes and the cannonballs whizzed over their heads; only the brigade under Bylant in the front of the ridge took significant casualties. Then d'Erlon's I Corps went into action against Wellington's left centre at around 2 p.m. Napoleon left the conduct of the battle in this sector to Ney, for reasons that are not entirely clear; some say he was too ill to assume direction himself, others that he was now preoccupied with the Prussian threat. Certainly the first sighting of Bülow's Prussians came around 1.30 p.m. when a column was spied some miles off near Planchenoit, moving towards the French right; the Emperor was forced to detach Lobau's VI Corps and two brigades.

Ney and d'Erlon advanced with 18,000 men, one brigade veering off at the last moment to attack La Haie Sainte. The battle for La Haie Sainte was another murderous affair and soon turned into a second Hougoumont. Meanwhile in the centre two of d'Erlon's four divisions advanced in a compact formation – the result it seems, of yet more botched orders – and presented unmissable targets to the British gunners. Had Ney supported the infantry with cavalry, the Allies would have been forced to form square, which could then have been decimated with case-shot from the horse artillery. Raked by devastating volleys, d'Erlon's men still came on and were soon engaged in murderous combat with Picton's 5th Division, the best infantry on the Allied side. Picton was killed by a musket ball, but his men held firm and gradually pushed the French back. Although the flanking divisions from d'Erlon's corps had fared better than the central two, largely because they were faced by Bylant's already weakened brigade, they bore the brunt of the British counter-attack when General Lord Uxbridge ordered a cavalry charge. Lord Anglesey's Household Cavalry and Somerset's Horse Guards cut through the French left flank like a knife through butter, while Ponsonby's Union Brigade, including the 2nd North British Dragoons (the Scots Greys), charged through the centre.

In the ecstasy of the moment the Scots Greys and other cavalry in the centre continued their charge towards the French guns. Taking charge of the battle for a while, Napoleon waited then timed a countercharge by his lancers to perfection. Jacquinot's lancers took the Greys in the flank from right and left, causing severe casualties; of 2,500 horsemen who charged, more than a thousand were killed or wounded. However, Wellington's main aim of buying time by repulsing d'Erlon's I Corps had been achieved and in the meantime the first French attack on La Haie Sainte had also failed.

At 3 p.m. came another of the great blunders of the day. Preoccupied with the Prussians, Napoleon ordered fresh attacks on Hougoumont and La Haie Sainte, hoping to roll up Wellington's advance posts and move in for the kill before Blücher's men could intervene. At this moment Ney inexplicably ordered the entire French cavalry to charge the ridge at

Mont-St-Jean without infantry back-up; it has been conjectured that he mistook a redeployment in Wellington's lines for a general retreat or that he misread the withdrawal of some ambulance wagons towards Brussels as a sign that the Allies were wavering. Ney thus managed in one and the same battle to send in infantry unaided by cavalry and cavalry unaided by infantry. At all events, the result of this folly was predictable: the unsupported horsemen were cut to pieces by British squares using case-shot.

Ney tried again. He called up Kellermann's division of cuirassiers and the heavy squadrons of the Guard. Once again the French were funnelled into a narrow 1,500-metre-wide front between Hougoumont and La Haie Sainte, but still the valiant cavalrymen came on. The British line at last showed signs of buckling, and if the French had thrown in infantry at this point, they would have won the day; as it was Wellington had to use up most of his infantry and cavalry reserves in order to achieve the final repulse of the French. The battered survivors of Ney's hare-brained assault were extricated from the firestorm of the British squares only with great difficulty by General Kellermann.

Around 4 p.m. came two sombre items of news, which made Napoleon revise his earlier estimate of the odds down to 60–40 in favour. Grouchy sent word that he was heavily involved in fighting with the Prussians around Wavre and would therefore be taking no part in the battle at Waterloo; and Bülow's relieving corps reached the wood two miles from the French right flank. Here they were met by Lobau's corps. The French defence against a force three times numerically superior was so skilful that they delayed the Prussians in and around the village of Placenoit for two hours. When the Prussians finally drove them out, Napoleon sent in the Young Guard to force them back again. Although Bülow played no part in the main battle, he forced the Emperor to divert 14,000 men away from Wellington at a critical time.

By this time Napoleon was making the capture of La Haie Sainte a priority. The French attacked with three battalions of infantry and some engineers. The heavy doors of the farm were battered in, the defenders ran out of ammunition, and at last La Haie Sainte fell, just after 6. p.m.; less than fifty of the original 900 defenders of the King's German Legion survived. Ney then wheeled up big guns to almost point-blank range of Wellington's centre and pounded away. This time he sensed a definite wavering and sent to the Emperor for the Guard to make the final breakthrough. This was yet another moment when Napoleon by swift action could have won the day. But he was still obsessed by the Prussians and reacted to Ney's request with bluster: 'Troops? Where am I supposed to get them from? Do you want me to manufacture some?' But some military historians think the true reason Napoleon did not indulge Ney was that the marshal had lost credibility and had cried 'wolf' once too often.

It took until 6.45 p.m. for the Guard to stabilize the front facing Bülow. By then Wellington had used the slight lull in fighting to stiffen the centre by throwing in his last reserves of foot and horse. As Napoleon's confidence rose, the Duke's dipped: 'God bring me night or bring me Blücher,' Wellington was heard to remark. Then at around 7 p.m. Napoleon decided to send in the Middle Guard to finish the business. French spirits rose as Napoleon led forward eleven battalions of his crack troops and handed them over to Ney at the smoking ruins of La Haie Sainte, and morale soared even higher as Ney spurred on the 'immortals' of the *Grande Armée*, resplendent in their columns seventy to eighty men wide. Ney was not a bit cast down when, for the fifth time that day, he had a horse shot from under him. He simply drew his sword, and joined the front ranks of the Guard.

Soon the Guard came under fire from British guns at Hougoumont. But initially they made good progress, overran the Brunswick brigade on the forward slope of Mont St Jean and captured two artillery batteries. Then they attacked and drove back the left-hand square of Halkett's brigade. Unexpectedly, the Belgians counterattacked, forcing back one battalion of the Guard with a barrage from horse artillery on the crest of the ridge, firing grapeshot, and following with a bayonet charge. By this time the French grenadiers were engaged in furious combat with the 69th Foot and the 33rd Foot, Wellington's old regiment from India. None the less, two battalions of the Chasseurs were on the point of gaining the crest when Wellington played his only remaining card. He ordered the 1st Foot Grenadiers, who had been lying hidden on the reverse slopes, to rise up and confront the enemy.

A scorching volley from the 1st Foot stopped the Guard dead in their tracks. As they hesitated, losing men all the time, they made the fatal mistake of deploying under fire. Taken in the flank by more British infantry, the Guard fell into confusion. The 1st Foot advanced with bayonets drawn and drove Napoleon's crack troops down the slope towards Hougoumont, where they collided with the still advancing rear columns of the Guard – the 4th Chasseurs and the remainder of the 4th Grenadiers. The 1st Foot retreated to the foot of the ridge and turned to face the hastily reassembled Guard. On came the French again and this time they seemed likely to overwhelm the opposition. Suddenly a fresh British force, the 52nd Foot under Sir John Colbourne, appeared over the crest of the ridge on the left flank of the Guard and began to pour volleys into the massed columns of the 4th Chasseurs. When they followed with a bayonet charge, the Chasseurs wavered, then slowly gave ground. Up went the cry no member of the Grand Army ever thought to hear: '*La Garde recule!*' ('The Guard is retreating!')

Almost by a magical preestablished harmony at this very moment the Prussians finally broke through on the French left. 33,000 fresh troops came flooding on to the field. Napoleon had been bolstering the spirits of his men by the blatant lie that the men they could see on their right were Grouchy's 33,000, not the Prussians. When they realized the awful truth, the men became demoralized and panic-stricken. 'Treason,' came the cry. 'We are betrayed.' Some still thought that the Prussians who opened fire on them were Grouchy's men, now suborned by the Bourbons. But whether they thought of them as Prussians or renegade Frenchmen, the effect was the same: first a catastrophic plummeting of spirits, then panic and finally rout.

It was not more than ten minutes after the arrival of the Prussians that Wellington rode to the crest of the Mont-St-Jean ridge and waved his hat three times in a prearranged signal to order a general advance. The entire Allied army descended from the ridge like a torrent. Napoleon ordered his veterans of the Old Guard to form square and try to rally the fleeing troops, but they were swept aside in the mêlée. Three battalions of the Old Guard then took up station at La Belle Alliance, covering the flight of their Emperor and their comrades. Their commander, General Cambronne, was called on to surrender but refused, according to the legend with one word: *Merde*. The Allies brought up big guns and mowed down the valiant Guard where they stood.

There was now no possibility of rallying the army. Scenes of the utmost chaos were witnessed as the defeated Grand Army streamed away southwards. Lobau's men fell back in good order from their position on the right, avoiding encirclement by the Prussians. *Sauve qui peut* was the watchword as Prussian cavalry pursued the vanquished throughout the night. At 9 p.m. Wellington met Blücher at La Belle Alliance, and both hailed each other as the victor. '*Quelle affaire!*' Blücher remarked (the only French he knew). Wellington's comment as he surveyed the heaps of dead is well known: that next to a battle lost the saddest thing he knew was a battle won. The day after the battle he wrote: 'It was the most desperate business I was ever in: I never took so much trouble about any battle, and never was so near being beat. Our loss is immense, particularly the best of all instruments, the British infantry. I never saw the infantry behave so well.'

The French lost 25,000 in dead and wounded at Waterloo plus some 8,000 prisoners; Wellington's casualties were 15,000 (including more than fifty per cent of his officers) and the Prussians' 7,000. Altogether during the three days of 16–18 June the Allies had lost 55,000 against 60,000 of the French. Wellington went on to fame and immortality on the strength of this victory, but he could not have won without Prussian intervention, which was only the most signal of Napoleon's blunders throughout the day. A fair non-Anglocentric judgement would be that Napoleon lost the battle through his own multiple errors rather than that Wellington won it by singular military genius. It is doubtful that the Emperor's illness made any real difference, though his arch-defenders claim that this resulted from a poisoning attempt or that his plans had been betrayed to the British by a spy. The plain truth seems to be that Napoleon performed far below his best form, and that something happened to his martial talents in general during the lacklustre four-day Belgian campaign.

Napoleon rode away from the battle towards Charleroi, tears coursing down his cheeks, his face described as a mask of pain and exhaustion. Next day he made a partial recovery as he reassessed the situation. On paper his fortunes after Waterloo were by no means so desperate as they are usually presented. Given that Grouchy had disengaged at Wavre with most of his corps intact, the Emperor still had 117,000 men available for the defence of Paris to face roughly the same number under Blücher and Wellington. By 1 July he would have another 120,000 men plus 36,000 National Guardsmen, 30,000 sharpshooters, 6,000 gunners and 600 artillery pieces for the defence of Paris. The Allies could not cross the Somme with much more than 90,000 men while the Austrians and Russians could not be on the Marbe before 15 July, by which time the Emperor calculated he could have 80,000 sharpshooters in position, doling out unacceptable casualties on the advancing enemy columns. As he remarked to Joseph, what was needed now was the spirit of Rome after the disaster of Cannae, not the defeatist spirit of the Carthaginians after the battle of Zama.

What was missing was his own energy and commitment. France could be mobilized to fight for the Emperor only if he showed the face of a fighter who would never give up. But Napoleon was depressed, ill, suffering from lack of sleep and, above all, indecisive. When he conferred with his generals, there were divided counsels. Davout urged him to return to Paris, prorogue the Senate and the Chamber, and set himself up as a dictator. Others urged him to ignore constitutional niceties altogether, ignore Paris and remain in the field with his Army. But as he did so often during the Hundred Days, Napoloen chose a third option, less satisfactory than either: he decided to return to Paris and work within the context of constitutional niceties. This was such a gross error that it is hard not to see him at this juncture unconsciously willing his own destruction. Later he himself admitted his decision was an act of consummate folly and could scarcely give a rational account of it.

The situation in Paris was parlous, as everybody knew; indeed it had been emphasized again and again by those of his supporters who urged him to remain in the field. During the Hundred Days, as part of his new liberal image, Napoleon had officially shared power with his Ministers and the two chambers. To prevent Ministers and Assembly from making common cause, he ordered a total separation of powers, forbidding his Ministers to have any contact with the Legislature. But in his absence Fouché campaigned tirelessly against him. Once news of Waterloo came in, Fouché bent all his energies to fomenting panic in Paris, stressing that the Grand Army had been totally destroyed and that Bonaparte was returning to make himself a dictator. Fouché had long been plotting for the contingency of the Emperor's military defeat, when he thought the hour of Fouché would come at last. The question is why Napoleon, as usual, did nothing about him. He threatened to hang him after his first victory in Belgium and later remarked ruefully: 'If I had just hanged two men, Talleyrand and Fouché, I would still be on the throne today.' There is a continuing mystery about his weakness when faced with the treachery of the trio of Bernadotte, Talleyrand and Fouché, which no student of Napoleon has ever satisfactorily explained.

Given all this, it was absurd for Napoleon to return to Paris and play by the constitutional rule-book. He should have seized control and dissolved the Legislature as Davout urged, relying on the loyalty of the garrison and people of France. When he reached Paris at dawn on 21 June, he still had powerful cards up his sleeve. He had plenty of support, for his lucid way with statistics persuaded wavering Ministers to give him their backing, while even Carnot joined Lucien, La Bedoyère and Davout in pleading for the immediate imposition of martial law and the removal of the fractious Legislature to Tours. They pointed out that the people were on his side – a fact evident when the crowd acclaimed him in front of the Élysée. Once again Napoleon dithered. But if he was lacking in energy, the diabolical Fouché was not. On 21 June, at his instigation, the two chambers declared themselves in permanent session, indissoluble except by their own will, and called in the National Guard for protection.

Repeatedly urged to use force against the Chamber of Deputies, Napoleon refused, on grounds of refusal to shed blood and unwillingness to head a 1793-style revolution. Foolishly he declared he would never become an 'Emperor of the rabble' and claimed that to harness the people to his cause would simply plunge France into civil war even as the Allies began their invasion. His continuing loyalty to the interests and principles of the bourgeoisie who had betrayed him is more than just strange, and suggests a kind of morbid, even pathological, political conservatism that transcended his own self-interest. He was also confused, indecisive, unrealistic and out of touch, and irritated his supporters by claiming that such-and-such a thing was 'impossible' when it was already an accomplished fact. Instinctively, the hyenas seemed to sense that the lion was wounded, for when Lucien went to the Chamber to try to talk the Deputies round, he got nowhere. Lafayette, in particular, played a leading role in stiffening the resolve of his colleagues against a possible second Brumaire, and outpointed Lucien in the debate, winning an ovation for his charge that since 1805 Napoleon had compassed the deaths of three million Frenchmen. The debate ended with an explicit demand for the Emperor's abdication and the appointment of a provisional government under Fouché.

With tension running high, it was largely a question of whose nerve would crack first. In private Napoleon raged to Benjamin Constant that the demand for his abdication – which would have as one of its consequences the disbandment of the Grand Army while the enemy were at the gates of Paris – was peculiarly absurd and gutless: if the Assembly did not want him, they should have made this plain when he was marching from Antibes to Paris or before he set out on the Waterloo campaign; to do so now was tantamount to betraying France to her enemies. But in public he bowed his head: on 22 June he formally abdicated in favour of his son the King of Rome. Disgusted and disillusioned, Davout began to think of his own future and allowed himself to be become a pawn in Fouché's devious game.

Fouché sent Davout to the Emperor on 24 June, urging him to leave Paris at once to avoid bloodshed; Fouché's real fear was that his own plans might still be scuppered by a spontaneous popular uprising in favour of the Emperor or by a pro-Bonaparte military coup by one of the marshals; it was known that the 70,000 men who had rendezvoused with Grouchy at Laon were angry at news of the abdication. The passive and flaccid Napoleon fell in meekly with his plans and departed for Malmaison on 25 June, but not before he had expressed anger that Davout was doing Fouché's dirty work for him. The transparent story that the Emperor was leaving the capital because of assassination fears fooled nobody.

At Malmaison Napoleon was the guest of his stepdaughter Hortense de

Beauharnais, who had inherited on Josephine's death. There was some consolation in being with his extended family. Marie Walewska, who had been with him throughout the Hundred Days except on the four-day Belgian campaign was there along with an early and a late Bonaparte mistress, respectively Madame Duchâtel and Madame Pellapra; also there were his two natural sons, Alexandre Walewski and Comte Leon. Once at Malmaison, a depressed Emperor, convinced that his star had deserted him and that his public life was over, considered his options. Where should he go and with what aim? Surrender to the Allies was not feasible, given that they had outlawed him. The Prussians reiterated that they would execute him if they caught him, and even though the Austrians and Russians were unlikely to mete out such a fate, there were special reasons why he could not consider surrendering to them. To bow the head to Alexander, the man he patronized at Tilsit, was too much for pride to bear, while Napoleon could never forgive Emperor Francis for his treachery in respect of Marie-Louise and his son.

He therefore decided to make his home in the U.S.A. He asked for two frigates to be put at his disposal and for passports and safe conduct to Rochefort, where he intended to embark for America, routing his request through General Beker, commander of the Guard at Malmaison, to Fouché (now head of the new 'Executive Commission') via Davout. Fouché authorized the frigates but ordered them not to leave until the safe-conducts had arrived; this was an obvious trick to remove the Emperor from the Paris area and keep him immobilized at Rochefort while he negotiated to hand him over to the highest Allied bidder. Even in his torpid and debilitated state, Napoleon was able to guess Fouché's intentions and checkmated them by refusing to leave for Rochefort until he possessed signed orders to the captains of the two frigates there, requiring them to sail for America immediately.

At Malmaison Napoleon put his financial affairs in order. Distributing largesse to his family, he gave Joseph 700,000 francs, Lucien 250,000 and Jérôme 100,000. He gave Hortense one million francs in timber shares and entrusted to the banker Jacques Laffitte his personal fortune of 800,000 francs in cash and three million in gold. Then he burnt his papers, still steadfastly continuing to refuse the option of armed insurrection. Benjamin Constant, who three months earlier had compared him to Attila and Genghiz Khan, notably changed his tune and wrote: 'The man who, although still strong in possession of the remains of an army that had been invincible for twenty years and a name which electrified the multitude, set aside power rather than dispute it by means of the massacre of civil war, has on this occasion deserved well of mankind.'

On 27 June Fouché stopped stalling and decided to let the Emperor go on his own terms. Perhaps he wanted him out of the way while the motion to restore the Bourbons was put to the Chamber, or perhaps he feared the Allies might seize him anyway. But no sooner had Fouché taken this decision than he learned from his envoys that the Allies were making the settlement of Napoleon a precondition of peace. He now had to force the Emperor out of Malmaison without giving him a safe-conduct. He therefore informed him that if he remained there he would be put under house arrest. Again Napoleon checkmated him by saying that he refused to travel to Rochefort without safe-conducts and was prepared to take his chances at Malmaison.

As the Prussians began to close in on Malmaison, Fouché saw his bargaining counter in danger of being whisked away from him. Fouché sent the necessary orders, permitting an immediate sailing from Rochefort. Napoleon, salving his pride, offered to lead the French armies defending Paris as a mere general; unsurprisingly, Fouché indignantly turned him down. Then it was time for final farewells at Malmaison. The Emperor said goodbye to Madame Mère, then spent his last moments in silent meditation in Josephine's room, before donning the garb in which he was to travel incognito as Beker's secretary.

The imperial party departed Malmaison on 29 June and travelled in three coaches, at first via Rambouillet and Chartres, with a diversionary convoy travelling by way of Orléans and Angoulême. From Chartres Napoleon's coaches proceeded through Vendôme to Tours and then through Poitiers to Niort. They entered Rochefort on 3 July, with the Emperor all the time awaiting a call from Paris to return. He spent the entire journey in an agony of uncertainty about whether he was doing the right thing, a few crests of optimism always sinking into the deeper troughs of pessimistic inertia. At Rochefort he discovered that a British squadron was blockading the port; this development was hardly surprising, as on 25 June Fouché had alerted Wellington that the Emperor intended to sail to the U.S.A.

On the very day Napoleon arrived in Rochefort, Paris surrendered to the Allies and Fouché put the final touches to his master-plan to restore the Bourbons. On 3 July he, a famous regicide, went with Talleyrand to St-Denis to 'wait on' Louis XVIII. Of this scene, a byword for humbug and hypocrisy, even Chateaubriand, no friend of Bonaparte's, wrote in his *Mémoires d'outre-tombe*: 'Suddenly the door opened; and silently there entered vice leaning on the arms of crime, M. Talleyrand supported by

Fouché. The infernal vision passed slowly in front of me, went into the King's study and disappeared. Fouché was coming to swear faith and homage to his lord. The trusty regicide, kneeling, put the hands which had made Louis XVI's head roll in the hands of the martyr king's brother; the apostate bishop stood surety for the oaths.'

In Rochefort the prefect, following Fouché's secret orders, stalled and prevaricated, pleading the impossibility of running the British blockade. In fact in these early days of July it was perfectly possible for the two frigates, *Méduse* and *Saale*, to have evaded the blockade, for most of the time only the *Bellerophon* was on station. But because of Fouché's treachery five precious days were wasted while the Royal Navy tightened its grip on the port. None the less, Napoleon himself must again be censured for vacillation. He received a good offer from an experienced sea captain for a mass breakout in small ships from the Gironde, using so many vessels that the Royal Navy would not know which one to chase, and then heading for America in the two corvettes *Bayardère* and *Indéfatigable*. Napoleon, foolishly, decided to 'wait and see'. Once again his mental processes remain a mystery. Why did he wait for five days in Rochefort, from 3–8 July, when he must have known that speed was essential? Perhaps he thought a safe-conduct might still arrive or that a mass demonstration in the Army would call on him to return. Joseph was still urging him to link up with the Army of the Gironde under Clausel.

On 8 July Louis XVIII reentered Paris after an absence of exactly one hundred days, having guaranteed the property of those who had benefited from the Revolution. Napoleon meanwhile, learning that word had come in from Paris that he must depart at once from Rochefort, set off in a rowing boat for the Île d'Aix but decided to spend the night aboard the frigate *Saale*. But a fresh set of orders arrived from the Commissioners in Paris: Bonaparte must embark for the U.S.A. *at once* and would not be allowed back on French soil; anyone abetting him to do so would be guilty of treason. Napoleon was given twenty-four hours to comply with this order, and the implicit threat was that if he did not do so, he would simply be handed over to the mercies of the incoming Bourbon government.

The Emperor returned to the Île d'Aix to ponder his choices. Apart from sailing out to almost certain capture, there only seemed two options: either return, put himself at the head of the Army and head a revolutionary movement, or surrender to the British and take his chances. Still indecisive, on 10 July he sent his aides Savary and Las Cases to negotiate with Captain Maitland of HMS *Bellerophon* and see what terms were available. They bore a letter written by Bertrand, asking if the

British would give a safe-conduct to the Emperor or whether they were determined to block his passage to the U.S.A. Maitland knew how the wind blew from London but could not resist the opportunity of landing such a prestigious prize. He therefore dissembled and, without committing himself overtly, hinted that asylum in England would be possible. He stalled until he could get instructions from the Admiralty; as expected, these were uncompromising. Maitland therefore suggested that while London took time to come to a final decision (he disguised from the French the fact he had already received his orders), Napoleon's entourage should think carefully about the question of asylum. It was pure machiavellianism on the part of an ambitious man.

Later on 10 July Napoleon called a council to discuss what to do. Bertrand, Las Cases, Gourgaud and Savary argued for seeking asylum in England; Montholon and Lallemand urged a return to the Army. Never a believer in democracy, the Emperor went with majority opinion this time as it accorded with his own secret wishes: he reiterated that he would not be the cause of a single cannon-shot in France. But what finally clinched matters was when the desperate option of trying to run the blockade was also ruled out. The captain of the *Méduse* sent a message that he was prepared to engage the *Bellerophon* in close combat. Naturally the Royal Navy ship would be victorious, but in the meantime the *Saale* could have cleared for America. Napoleon was initially excited by the proposal, but Philibert, captain of the *Saale* and senior to Captain Ponée on the *Méduse* refused to have any part of the plan, fearful of what the Bourbons might do to him afterwards.

Angered by Philibert's attitude, Napoleon left the *Saale* again and landed on the Île d'Aix. There a new idea was hatched. It was suggested that six naval officers should put to sea with Napoleon in a whaleboat, hail the first merchant ship they encountered on the high seas, and charter it to go to the U.S.A. This seemed too far-fetched to the Emperor, but he was running out of maritime options, as Baudin, the captain who had offered to take him from a Gironde port, responded to further overtures by saying he would take the Emperor alone and not his court. The dismayed courtiers, fearful of Bourbon revenge, pleaded with Napoleon not to abandon them. He therefore turned down the Baudin idea, as also a last minute plea from Joseph, who arrived at the Île d'Aix on the morning of 13 July, that he return and put himself at the head of the Army. Joseph in his very last interview with his brother played a truly fraternal role by urging him to get away to America and offering to impersonate him until he was safely at sea.

At midnight on 13 July Napoleon finally made his decision to seek asylum with the British. Next morning his envoys returned to the *Bellerophon*. Maitland said he would willingly take Napoleon to England, but could take no responsibility for what happened there; nevertheless, determined to have the kudos of taking this fabulous prize, he insinuated to the envoys that all would be well. It was only after hearing a highly favourable report from his envoys that the Emperor decided to trust his person to the British; Maitland later dishonestly claimed that the envoys had come to him with the formal offer of surrender, without any pre-conditions.

A final council met to approve the Emperor's decision. He was supremely ill-advised on this occasion. Gulled by Maitland's honeyed words, his followers also grievously underrated British rancour towards the 'ogre' and imagined they would be bound by the 'sacred laws of hospitality'. From London's vantage point things looked very different. Here was the man who had forced them to rack up the National Debt almost to ruinous levels so as to raise Europe in arms against him. Expenditure to the Allies during the Hundred Days had rocketed sky-high, with a £5 million flat payment to the Allies, plus a further £1 million to get the Russians to march west and an extra £280,000 to induce Austria to campaign in Italy. Altogether Britain disbursed £7 million for what turned out to be a four-day campaign, a ruinous rate of money-for-armies exchange.

On 13 July Napoleon wrote a famous letter to the Prince Regent, in which he expressed his naïve hope that, at worst, he would be subjected to English civil law:

> Your Royal Highness,
> Exposed to the factions which distract my country and to the enmity of the greatest powers of Europe, I have ended my political career, and I come, like Themistocles, to throw myself on the hospitality of the English people; I put myself under the protection of their laws, which I claim from Your Royal Highness as the most powerful, the most constant, and the most generous of my enemies.
> Napoleon.

On 15 July the Emperor travelled out to the *Bellerophon* on the brig *Épervier*. On the seven-day voyage to England, Maitland treated Napoleon with every courtesy and consideration, never revealing the true attitude of the British government, which he knew to be harsh and unyielding. Both on the *Bellerophon* and on the flagship *Superb*, commanded by Maitland's superior officer Admiral Hotham, the Emperor was treated like royalty. He won the respect and affection of the crew, though his prodigious need for sleep was much commented on. On 23 July he saw the last of the European mainland off Ushant, and remained for seven hours from dawn until noon on the poop deck observing geographical features with his spy-glass.

When the *Bellerophon* anchored at Torbay, boatloads of sightseers came alongside to try to catch a glimpse of the sensation of the hour. Napoleon was encouraged by his reception, but would have been deeply despondent had he known of the fate being prepared for him by a deadly triumvirate of his enemies. The three men who decided his future were the Prince Regent, the Prime Minister Lord Liverpool, and Lord Bathurst, Secretary of State for War and the Colonies – all men who hated Napoleon for the vast sums he had cost the exchequer, the fear he had caused them and the knowledge that he had been very close to victory. Liverpool's attitude is very clear in a letter to Castlereagh on 15 July: 'We wish that the King of France would hang or shoot Bonaparte, as the best termination of the business . . . if the King of France does not feel himself sufficiently strong to treat him as a rebel, we are ready to take upon ourselves the custody of his person.'

By legal sleight of hand this unsavoury British trio declared the Emperor a prisoner of war, although no state of war existed between France and Britain and Napoleon could not be considered a prisoner anyway, since he had embarked on the *Bellerophon* freely. Liverpool's tame lawyers were in a quandary, since they could never quite decide whether Napoleon was an enemy alien or an outlaw and pirate, outside the scope of the law of nations. Their problem was that, if he was not an enemy alien, he could not be detained as a prisoner of war. But how could he be an enemy alien if he was not the subject of any ruler (France had disowned him)? And how could somebody legally be treated as an enemy alien if England was not at war with any other country? If, on the other hand, Napoleon was a pirate, the situation was clear: he must be executed. The middle solution, adopted in a later era at Nuremburg, would have been to put the Emperor on trial for war crimes, but such a conception, even with its notorious inability to transcend mere 'victors' justice', did not yet exist.

When the *Bellerophon* departed from Torbay to Plymouth, Napoleon began to suspect he had a fight for survival on his hands. His one card was public opinion and the legal skill of his British supporters. Everything depended on getting Napoleon on to land by a writ of habeas corpus and an ingenious stratagem devised to this end. A former judge from the West Indies accused Admiral Cochrane of having failed in his duty by not having attacked Willaumez's squadron off Tortilla and demanded that Napoleon Bonaparte appear as a witness. A writ of habeas corpus was obtained, requiring Napoleon's presence in court on 10 November.

But while the *Bellerophon* was anchored off Plymouth, Lord Keith, Commander-in-Chief of the Channel fleet, was sent to the Emperor with the British government's answer. On 31 July Keith informed Napoleon that he was to be exiled to St Helena, where he would be treated, not as an Emperor, but as a retired general on half pay. Napoleon protested bitterly against this sentence, pointing out that he had come on board the *Bellerophon* voluntarily and that Britain's perfidious action would destroy her reputation in the civilized world. If he was a prisoner, he wanted to know the basis for this in international law, and if Britain assumed legal rights over him, it followed that he was entitled to due legal process. He wrote a formal protest: 'I am not the prisoner but the guest of England. If the government, in ordering the captain of the *Bellerophon* to receive me, as well as my suite, desired only to set a trap, it has forfeited its honour and sullied its flag.' As for the insult in addressing him merely as 'General Bonaparte', he remarked: 'They may as well call me Archbishop, for I was head of the Church as well as the army.'

But events were moving away from Napoleon and his supporters. On 2 August, the Allies rubberstamped the British action in the Convention of Paris. Later an Act of Indemnity was passed through Parliament, in which the government virtually admitted it had no legal basis for detaining Napoleon on St Helena. The Admiralty, warned that Bonaparte's supporters were trying to serve a writ of habeas corpus, ordered Maitland to put to sea from Plymouth and cruise off Start Point, where he was to rendezvous with the ship taking the prisoner to St Helena. Maitland sailed on 4 August and after three days at sea transferred the Emperor to the *Northumberland*, under the command of Admiral Cockburn, which was to make the long run to St Helena. On 9 August the Prometheus of the age began the voyage to the lonely rock where he was to be chained for the rest of his life.

CHAPTER TWENTY-EIGHT

As Napoleon was borne southwards by his British captors, he had plenty of time to take stock of the motley crew of adventurers who had chosen to accompany him and who would form his tiny court on the distant island of St Helena. Only three of the fifteen officers (plus a chamberlain) who were with him on the *Bellerophon* were allowed to transfer to the *Northumberland*, and Generals Savary and Lallemand had been expressly excluded as being on the Bourbon government's 'most wanted' list. First in rank was General comte Henri-Gratien Bertrand, an aide since 1807 and successor to Duroc as Grand Marshal of the Palace. Four years younger than the Emperor, Bertrand had served him faithfully but relations between the two were poor, mainly because of the behaviour of Bertrand's problem wife, Fanny. An unregenerate royalist, who frequently angered Napoleon by her unpunctuality and lack of deference, Fanny showed her true calibre by throwing an hysterical fit and trying to hurl herself from a cabin window on the *Bellerophon* when her husband announced he would be sharing the Emperor's exile.

General baron Gaspar Gourgaud, aged thirty-two, the first orderly officer, was always Napoleon's favourite of the St Helena entourage, but the obstinate and unbalanced Gourgaud remains an enigma to this day; some say he was a Judas, others that he was merely the St Peter who temporarily denied his master. He had not originally been on the St Helena shortlist, but when he threw a scene of hysterical jealousy, a complaisant Emperor allowed him to be substituted for the original choice, Colonel Planat. As Chamberlain there was appointed comte Emmanuel-Joseph de Las Cases, a civilian nobleman, formerly chamberlain and *maître des requêtes* in the Council of State, who was accompanied to St Helena by his young son, Emmanuel. Las Cases scarcely knew Napoleon but he was to develop a close friendship with the exiled Emperor.

The most controversial appointment, and in many ways the key to the entire St Helena episode, was a relative unknown who had wormed his way into the Emperor's good graces during the Hundred Days. The thirty-three-year-old Marquis Charles Tristan de Montholon was always an unlikely Bonapartist. So far from being a distinguished soldier, he was a coward who habitually shirked military service under the pretext of various 'illnesses' and managed to avoid the sound of gunfire entirely during the Hundred Days. But Montholon had an attractive wife who was quite willing to live on St Helena and that may have been the main reason Napoleon chose him; he was not a man to live for long periods without female company, and at Malmaison he had already turned down the offer by the gallant and loyal Marie Walewska to share his fortunes wherever he went.

Napoleon also had permission to take twelve servants with him to the South Atlantic. As chief valet he chose a young man named Louis Marchand, just twenty-four, who turned out to be discreet, adroit, shrewd and observant. A kindly soul, gifted with abundant commonsense and refined feelings, loyal, devoted, modest and disinterested, Marchand was the living refutation of the old saw that no man is a hero to his valet; he idolized the Emperor. His assistant St-Denis was a kind of lesser Marchand. Cipriani the butler was another who won golden opinions from Napoleon. Another valet, the Switzer named Noveraz, Santini, factotum and keeper of the purse, Ali a Mameluke bodyguard, three footmen (Gentilini and the brothers Archambault), a pantryman (Pierron), a cook (Lepage) and a lampman (Rousseau) completed the complement of Bonaparte's retainers.

A further addition to the Emperor's personal staff was Dr Barry O'Meara, a ship's surgeon on the *Bellerophon*, who was appointed the Emperor's physician when Dr Maingault refused to accompany Napoleon to St Helena. O'Meara was given permission by the Admiralty to take the position provided he acted as a spy within the imperial household. But it appears that O'Meara soon 'went native': he became a double agent at best, but the intelligence he provided the British was worthless and the advice he gave Napoleon was good. Out of the sixteen souls accredited to Bonaparte's 'court' in St Helena, no less than seven left memoirs of varying worth (Bertrand, Montholon, Gourgaud, Las Cases, Marchand, St-Denis and O'Meara). Since British official records draw heavily on what was told to the Governor of St Helena by these eyewitnesses, the unenviable task for any historian of Napoleon on St Helena is to make sense of their conflicting accounts.

The *Northumberland* slowly made its way south on the great Atlantic swells. Napoleon's usual luck aboard ship held, for there were no storms in the expected latitudes, and the voyage was uneventful. The ship was off Funchal on 24 August and three days later Gomera in the Canaries was sighted. Napoleon spent most of his time playing *vingt-et-un* with his courtiers or whist with the British officers, but liked to be sociable and on 12 September took part in landing a shark from the ocean. Admiral Cockburn, who bridled at the Emperor's habit of leaving the dinner table as soon as he had bolted his food, nevertheless conceded that he was a great favourite with all ranks and 'had descended from the Emperor to the general with a flexibility of mind more easily to be imagined than described'.

Doubtless thinking this would seem to his superiors in the Admiralty as though he had fallen under the Bonaparte spell, he laced his reports with uncomplimentary remarks about the ogre's intellect and intelligence. Colonel Bingham wrote that 'General Bonaparte' asked questions which revealed a depth of ignorance a cultivated Englishman would have blushed to admit to, while Cockburn himself added that Napoleon's ignorance was so prodigious that it took a kind of perverted genius to remain so intellectually benighted. Another focus for deprecatory remarks was the Emperor's (admittedly very poor) linguistic talent and his inability to learn English: 'He was on board six weeks and at the end could not even pronounce our names correctly.'

The *Northumberland* crossed the Equator at longitude 3°36' on 23 September, and on 16 October anchored at St Helena, a bastion of black basalt – all that remained of an extinct volcano. Used as a watering place by ships of the East India Company and a base from which to dominate the South Atlantic by the Royal Navy, the island boasted a mixture of inhabitants from all the races of the earth: Europeans, blacks, Malays, Indians, Chinese. Its society was dominated, if not governed, by an aristocracy composed of high officials from 'John Company' and great landowners whose estates were still worked by slaves. To keep Napoleon there the British government had earmarked 2,280 soldiers, 500 guns and two brigs on constant patrol around the rocky coast. The total cost of maintaining the covering squadron and the near 3,000 military and civilians on the island was estimated at £400,000 a year.

Napoleon was cast down by his first sight of the volcanic island, just twenty-eight miles in circumference, and apparently as escape-proof as Devil's Island. He is said to have remarked that he would have done better to stay in Egypt in 1799. His first night on the island was spent in a boarding house in the port of Jamestown. The East India Company had retained all the best houses when they handed St Helena over to the British government, so there was a dire shortage of suitable accommodation. Accordingly, for two months the Emperor lived in a pavilion in the garden of 'The Briars', where resided William Balcombe, the East India Company agent.

At The Briars Napoleon amused himself by a bizarre, half-flirtatious, half-facetious teasing of the two Balcombe daughters, Jane, sixteen and Betsy, fourteen. Betsy was a particular favourite, for with the lack of self-consciousness of youth, she treated Napoleon as an equal in hoydenish practical jokes and pointed out loudly, with the innocence of adolescence, that the Emperor cheated at cards. It was a sad moment for Napoleon when the Balcombes returned to England in 1818, by which time Betsy had emerged from the tomboy chrysalis into the butterfly colours of a pretty young woman. She was always very fond of Napoleon, remembered him with great affection and, many years later, recalled these times in conversation with Louis Napoleon (then Emperor Napoleon III), who rewarded her with an estate in Algeria.

In December Napoleon moved to Longwood, formerly the summer seat of the Lieutenant-Governor but really little more than a very large bungalow. Although it was said to contain 44 rooms, many of them were no bigger than cramped cells or outhouses, and the sheer physical proximity of so many people produced its own problems. For his own use Napoleon reserved a study, drawing-room, an antechamber with a billiard room, a crepuscular dining-room, a bedroom and a bathroom. On a plateau at 1,700 feet, Longwood was supposed to have a healthier climate than Jamestown, five miles away. But St Helena was in general an unhealthy spot, where amoebic dysentery, caught from a parasite, was an endemic problem; no less than 56 men out of 630 in the 2nd Battalion of the 66th Regiment, doing garrison duty on the island, succumbed to it in these years. Everyone in the Bonaparte household except Bertrand caught the disease at one time or another. The problem was augmented by lack of sanitation, and all fresh water had to be brought to Longwood from a well three miles away. The other notorious problem with Longwood was that it was infested with rats, which were so bold that they would even run between the legs of diners when they were at table.

Nevertheless, Napoleon made the best of an unpromising situation and went riding over a twelve-mile area without supervision. Bertrand issued dozens of passes for visitors, and there were frequent excursions with friends like the Balcombes or Dr Warden, the surgeon from the *Northumberland*. Napoleon continued to learn English from Las Cases, though he was an atrocious linguist, as the following attempt, dated 7 March 1816 shows: 'Count Lascasses. Since sixt wek, y learn the english and y do not any progress. Sixt wek do fourty and two day. If might have learn fivty word, for day, i could knowm it two thousands and two hundred.' Soon he decided to cut his losses, and after October 1816 there were no more English lessons.

Although the Emperor would sometimes snub Admiral Cockburn, just to make clear their respective stations, the rapport built up over the two months at sea saw them through temporary difficulties. But the halcyon days came to an end on 14 April 1816 with the arrival as Governor of Sir Hudson Lowe, a creature of Lord Bathurst's, who brought new instructions concerning 'General Bonaparte's' enforced stay on the island. A career officer without private means, and with the crippling legacy of an unhappy childhood, Lowe was a narrow, humourless, by-the-book martinet, who lacked the social ease and innate confidence to make a success of a job calling for self-reliance and the broadest human sympathies. No more disastrous choice as Napoleon's gaoler can be imagined, and his appointment prompts obvious questions about the British government's motivation. It has been suggested that London declined to appoint an aristocrat or true grandee to the post, as such men were susceptible to charm and thus liable to be won over by Bonaparte's charisma. Others speculate that because Lowe for many years commanded the Corsican Rangers and spoke Italian he was thought suitable but, if we take this seriously, it bespeaks staggering ineptitude in London. The Corsican Rangers were Corsican exiles, deserters and royalist émigrés who hated Napoleon. The commander of such men was no more likely to commend himself to Napoleon than the comte d'Artois to Robespierre.

Two days after arriving, Lowe tried to see Napoleon but the Emperor was angry with Admiral Cockburn, who had recently insisted that a British officer should accompany 'General Bonaparte' on his rides round Longwood. He therefore declined to see the two men together. On 17 April 1816 Lowe insisted on an interview and arrived at Longwood in company with Cockburn, who was to introduce him to Napoleon in accordance with normal protocol. The ingenuity that had served him through fifty battles had not deserted the Emperor. He had the footman show Lowe into the drawing-room, then shut the door in Cockburn's face when he tried to follow. The first interview went well enough with some inconsequential talk about Corsica and Egypt, where Lowe had served. Lowe was pleased with his own performance and in this mood of initial euphoria invited him to the Governor's mansion and put the library at his disposal.

But things turned sour – and as it turned out, irretrievably so – at the next meeting at Longwood, on 30 April. Emboldened by what he took to be the success of the first meeting, Lowe got down to business and divulged the new instructions from Bathurst, a man who was as much his alter ego as Neipperg had been Metternich's. These turned out to be draconian in the extreme: Napoleon's household was to be reduced from fifteen to eleven; those who elected to remain had to sign a document guaranteeing they would remain indefinitely; the new annual expenditure was limited to £8,000; no correspondence was allowed except through the Governor and only he could issue passes to visit Longwood; no gifts could be delivered to him if they contained any mention of imperial or sovereign status; riding without limits and without supervision was to be curtailed; the presence of the prisoner at Longwood was to be checked twice daily; and much more in the same vein. The instructions breathed a spirit of pure, vindictive spite, of a piece with the state-sanctioned kidnapping by which the British had brought Napoleon to St Helena in the first place. One of Napoleon's (British) biographers has commented: 'It is impossible for an Englishman to read the Lowe-Bathurst correspondence without blushing for his country.'

On 16 May there was a further meeting at Longwood. By this time Napoleon had had time to digest the full implications of Bathurst's instructions and was very angry. He accused Lowe of persecuting him and of causing him far more heartache in one month than Cockburn in six. He charged Lowe with being a little man interested only in the exercise of petty power and told him that his behaviour would become a source of scandal which would besmirch his reputation, that of his children and of England in general. Lowe stormed out angrily. Napoleon who had earlier declared in a *cri du coeur*: 'I want my liberty or I want a hangman,' now found that his cry had been answered though hardly in the sense he intended. He told Las Cases: 'They've sent me more than a hangman. Sir Lowe is a hangman.'

Lowe's final interview with Napoleon was on 18 August 1816. As a witness to the 'intolerable rudeness' he had to put up with, the Governor took with him to Longwood Admiral Malcolm, Cockburn's successor as commander of the squadron of frigates on constant patrol around St Helena. They found Napoleon in the garden in a towering rage. Lowe started to talk about the necessity of reducing expenditure, but Napoleon, pointedly addressing his remarks to Malcolm, launched into a tirade about the way Lowe, a commander of cutthroats in the Corsican Rangers, treated a real general like Bertrand. Lowe tried to cut across by talking of his duty. He claimed he had not sought the job, but said nothing about why he had accepted it and, while drawing a hefty emolument of £12,000 a year, tried to get the entire Longwood entourage to subsist on two-thirds of that sum. Not surprisingly, Napoleon became agitated and spoke of begging his bread from the British garrison, as one soldier from others. Then he and Lowe became involved in a heated slanging match about the merits of Lord Bathurst. Finally, the Emperor turned on him with withering contempt: 'I've never seen you on any battlefield. You were only good for hiring assassins.' Once again Lowe lost his composure and stormed away angrily.

Napoleon and Lowe now settled in for a protracted cold war, the latter determined to stick to the letter of every nugatory regulation that came from the dreadful Bathurst, the former determined to extract the maximum propaganda advantage from Lowe's mindless foibles. When, in October 1816, Lowe informed Montholon that French credit was exhausted in Jamestown and in future the inhabitants of Longwood would have to pay for their food supplies from their own pockets, the Emperor pounced. In a tremendous propaganda coup Napoleon had his silver plate broken up and sold to a jeweller in Jamestown, raising nearly £250 on the first sale and roughly equal sums on two subsequent occasions. The jeweller, Gideon Solomon, ostentatiously weighed the silver fragments in a public display witnessed by British officers embarking for England.

There was a similar incident involving supplies of wood. Napoleon, with his mania for roaring fires and anyway combating excessive damp at Longwood, complained about the niggardly ration of coal and wood. So as not to be wrongfooted, Lowe doubled the allowance of coal but stated that he could do nothing to increase the wood ration, as lumber was scarce on the island. Napoleon then had some of his furniture, including a bedstead and some shelves, broken up and used as firewood; he made sure the story lost nothing in the telling in the hostelries of Jamestown. But Lowe was guilty of his most spectacular idiocy over a marble bust of Napoleon's son secretly sent out to St Helena. Lowe got to hear about the clandestine import and impounded it, on the absurd grounds that a marble bust might contain (where?) a secret message. O'Meara, in his capacity as double agent, told Lowe that Napoleon knew about the bust, was angry that it had been kept from him, and intended to turn the affair to propaganda advantage. The wretched Lowe, fearful that he might have done the wrong thing and be reprimanded by Bathurst, sent the bust up to Longwood, where Napoleon gave it pride of place in his bedroom.

The conditions in which Napoleon was held on the island, the decaying state of Longwood, infested with rats and plagued by dysentery, the meanness and petty spite of Lowe and Bathurst, all these became the subject of a public outcry in England in 1817. Despite all Lowe's precautions, dozens of messages and bulletins reached the Fox family at

Holland House and the many other powerful Bonaparte supporters in England. In March 1817 articles appeared in *The Times*, clearly insinuating that the British government was trying to hasten Napoleon to an early death. A censure was moved in the House of Lords, when Lord Holland signally got the better of Bathurst in debate. Although the government easily defeated the motion in the Lords, they were rattled by the adverse publicity. Bathurst was forced to instruct Lowe that the allowance at Longwood was to be restored to the full £12,000.

Another bone of contention was Lowe's refusal to address Napoleon as Emperor and his continuing use of the title 'General Bonaparte' which was calculated to turn the person referred to splenetic. Lowe invited 'General Bonaparte' to dine at Plantation House and meet the Countess of Loudon and seemed surprised and put out when he received no reply. Apparently unable to take a hint, he persisted in his asinine conduct with another invitation to the 'General' to attend a party at Plantation House for the Prince Regent's birthday. Napoleon suggested that since recognition of the historical reality that he actually had been an Emperor appeared to stick in Lowe's craw, a solution might be for him to go under an alias; he suggested Colonel Muiron or Baron Duroc, after two of his beloved officers. Lowe refused, on the grounds that an assumed name was the prerogative only of sovereigns; evidently in his time with the Corsica Rangers he had never heard of a *nom de guerre*.

When in doubt, Lowe always did the wrong thing. A Bonaparte admirer tried to get round the problem of nomenclature by inscribing a book to *'Imperatori Napoleoni'*, since the golden age Latin translation of this would be 'General Napoleon'; Lowe, however, learned from the pedants on his staff that in silver Latin this could be translated as 'Emperor Napoleon' and confiscated the book. Such was Lowe's paranoia that he suspected a code or cipher in the most unlikely places. When Montholon gave the French Commissioner, Montchenu, some white and green beans to plant in his garden, Lowe suspected that the different colours of the beans had a semiotic significance. Even more fatuously, when Napoleon tried to order a new pair of shoes from the cobblers, Lowe intervened to say that the old pair of shoes had first to be sent to him and he would commission their replacement.

From time to time certain English 'my country right or wrong' Bonapartophobes have tried to rehabilitate Lowe's reputation and assert that he was simply a rather naïve dupe of Napoleon's well-oiled propaganda machine. Unfortunately this argument falls foul of all the extant independent evidence. When the three Allied Commissioners, charged with observing that the treaty relating to Bonaparte was being carried out, arrived on the island, they too found Lowe a sore trial. The French Commissioner, the marquis de Montchenu, he who had been given the beans by Montholon, found Lowe constantly trying to censor his small talk and malicious gossip, even the absurd canard he tried to spread that the Emperor and Betsy Balcombe were lovers. The Austrian Commissioner Balmain felt that Lowe treated the Allied observers with scant respect, reported back examples of his egregious rudeness to Vienna, and complained at the paranoid system of espionage with which Lowe oversaw every trivial detail of life on the island. The Russian Commissioner Sturmer was even more forthright: 'It would be difficult to find a man more awkward, extravagant and despicable . . . The English fear and avoid him, the French make a mock of him, the Commissioners complain of him, and everybody agrees that he is touched in the head.' Admiral Malcolm had nothing good to say of a man who became insanely jealous because Napoleon enjoyed good relations with Malcolm and confided in him. Even the Duke of Wellington, who had sacked Lowe from his staff before Waterloo, recorded that he was 'a damned fool'.

The long feud took its toll on both men. Though Lowe was consistently outwitted and outpointed intellectually, he had the consolations of power and the solace of a huge salary. Napoleon was dragged down by the intrinsic stress of his impotent position, by the internecine conflict between his 'courtiers' and by the unhealthy climate itself. His dreary life of reading, walking, pottering in the garden, dictating memoirs and staging dramatic readings from Corneille, Racine and Molière was made more tedious by the foggy, rainy climate of the volcanic island, the decreasing opportunities for physical exercise resulting from Lowe's strictures and the constant threat from amoebic dysentery. Whereas Napoleon's external conflict in these years was with Lowe, his internal battles concerned disease and the prima donnas in his household.

Almost from the moment of Lowe's advent, Napoleon was frequently, though intermittently, ill. In May 1816 he complained of weakness in his legs, headaches, abnormal sensitivity to light and a feeling of perpetual chill; his courtiers noticed that his speech was slurred, he had a gloomy air and seemed to be drugged. In July he was complaining of a pain in his side like a razor. In September the same year he had a week-long illness, of which the symptoms were insomnia, fever, headaches, colic and bad temper. Then, from 1 October to 9 November 1816, he had his most serious bout of illness yet, with headaches, swelling of the gums, looseness of the teeth, persistent coughing, shivering fits, trembling sensations, feelings of intense cold and weak and swollen legs; he alternated insomnia at night with drowsiness by day. He told O'Meara he suspected the British of poisoning him.

The curious cycle of good health and sudden illness continued throughout 1817: he was ill with the same symptoms in February and March, then had six weeks of health, and then relapsed with the same old maladies. Two months of rude health in July and August were followed by a further valetudinarian period in September. It was remarked that he was frequently thirsty and was forever drinking lemon juice; the intake of vitamin C meant that his symptoms could not have indicated scurvy, with which all his ailments were otherwise compatible. Other medical observers are positive that he suffered from amoebic dysentery, that an abscess formed on his liver – a not uncommon consequence of the disease – and that this drained into the lungs, chest, stomach and peritoneum, causing secondary problems in those areas. This would explain *some* of the symptoms – shooting pains, coughing, nausea, vomiting – but by no means all of them. Whatever the explanation, after 1817 the Emperor's health gradually worsened.

For other reasons, too, Longwood was a 'restless house' – the cockpit of bitter intrigues and jealousies among the members of Bonaparte's 'court'. The patient, tireless plotter who took the long view, the Aramis of the piece, was Montholon, but in the early years he bided his time, allowing the mercurial Gourgaud the centre stage. In the first year of exile on St Helena Las Cases was so obviously the Emperor's favourite that Gourgaud fumed and sulked; there was clearly a homosexual element in Gourgaud's feelings for Napoleon, for in his journals he refers to him as 'she'. But Las Cases was arrested by Hudson Lowe in November 1816 when it was discovered that he had smuggled secret correspondence out of the island; deportation swiftly followed. Some observers have suspected Las Cases of 'setting up' his own apprehension, as he was tired of exile; it is certainly striking that he refused to return to Longwood on a promise of good behaviour, as offered by Lowe.

Las Cases's departure partly answered Lowe's demand for a reduction in the staff at Longwood, but further dismissals were necessitated by Bathurst's imposed quota, and among the first to depart was Santini. On arrival in London Santini went to Lord Holland and gave him a full picture of life at Longwood, as well as a smuggled copy of Napoleon's *Remontrance*, which Holland worked up into a very effective pamphlet entitled *Appeal to the English Nation*. Napoleon consoled himself, on the departure of his favourite Las Cases, that he too would be effective in the propaganda effort being mounted on his behalf in Europe.

With Las Cases gone and Bertrand, to Napoleon's annoyance,

spending too much time with his wife and family, Montholon was put in charge of the household. Bertrand felt this an infringement of his prerogatives and brooded, but Gourgaud was more of a fighter. By this time it was obvious that Napoleon had made the pert and pretty Albine de Montholon his mistress, with Montholon himself as pander. Scholars have sometimes objected that there is no direct evidence of this liaison but, even if Napoleon was not a compulsive womanizer and we could in all seriousness imagine him content with a sexless, monastic existence, there is much at Longwood that cannot be explained otherwise. In his diary entry of 15 December 1816 Gourgaud unwittingly provided clear evidence of the affair. And it was Albine's hold over the Emperor that provoked Gourgaud to challenge Montholon to a duel. Montholon, a noted physical coward, ducked the challenge but complained to the Emperor that Gourgaud was unbalanced. He instituted an effective whispering campaign against Gourgaud, just as he had done earlier with Las Cases, but showed his moral imbecility by also disparaging the Emperor behind his back to Gourgaud.

By the end of 1817 Napoleon had had enough of Gourgaud. His follower's easy relations with Hudson Lowe, the constant battling with Montholon and his jealous rages pushed the Emperor to snapping point. Gourgaud himself records a dressing-down he received when his hero accused him of sulking like a woman. Napoleon said if he had known what life at Longwood was going to be like, he would have brought only servants, for talking to a parrot was preferable to dealing with his temperamental courtiers. Poignantly he expressed to Gourgaud some of the anguish that usually lay hidden: 'Don't you think that when I wake in the night I don't have dark moments, when I remember what I was and what I am now?' But Gourgaud threatened to leave his service once too often, and finally Napoleon took him at his word.

Once in London, Gourgaud acted the role of great betrayer. He met Bathurst and the French and Russian ambassadors and popularized three blatant lies. He asserted that Napoleon had an immense treasure of gold and silver at Longwood and could escape from St Helena whenever he chose. Even worse, although he had himself been ill on the island, he claimed that St Helena had a healthy climate, and that Napoleon's illnesses were purely diplomatic, an obvious ploy to gain sympathy in Europe. Bathurst pounced on these admissions and used them to persuade the Allies at the Congress of Aix-la-Chapelle to confirm the conditions of Napoleon's detention. Although Gourgaud later recanted and wrote high-flown appeals to the Czar and Marie-Louise to get the

Emperor released, the damage was done. Not surpisingly, Gourgaud was not mentioned in Napoleon's will.

Having seen the back of both Las Cases and Gourgaud, Montholon felt confident that there was now no impediment to his dominance at Longwood. Unexpectedly Napoleon turned to the butler Cipriani as his confidant. Suddenly Cipriani too was gone, dying in agony on 26 February 1818 from a mysterious and undiagnosed complaint. A few days later, again for reasons unexplained, his body was exhumed and never found again. This is an incident historians have never cleared up satisfactorily, and is especially murky when one considers that Cipriani had served with Hudson Lowe on Capri in 1806, but was at the time one of Saliceti's double agents. The more one penetrates the arcana of the world of Longwood, the more it appears like one of the darker chapters in Balzac or Alexandre Dumas.

However, Montholon could never have things entirely his own way at Longwood. The next complication came from Dr O'Meara. Finding a swelling on the Emperor's right side in the region of the liver, O'Meara diagnosed hepatitis and treated him with mercury. But Napoleon, possibly primed by Montholon, suddenly broke off the treatment and accused O'Meara of making reports to Hudson Lowe. This was true enough, but there was increasing concern in the Governor's mansion at Plantation House that O'Meara's intelligence did not square with that being passed (for money) by Montholon to the French Commissioner, Montchenu. Lowe, however, got O'Meara to return to Longwood and give his word of honour that he would make no more reports, while secretly insisting that he do just that. Napoleon, who seems to have been fond of O'Meara, took him back.

However, Lowe soon determined to be rid of O'Meara, for two reasons. It came to his attention that O'Meara was corresponding directly to the Admiralty, bypassing him; and in Europe the returning Gourgaud alleged that O'Meara was the secret channel by which the Emperor communicated with his supporters in Europe. Once again Lowe and Bathurst proved to be men of like mind. Lowe wrote to request O'Meara's dismissal, but Bathurst had always decided independently that he should be removed. O'Meara departed St Helena on 25 July 1818, still on cordial terms with Napoleon. Once in England he made public his opinion that the Emperor's health was suffering because of the unhealthy climate on St Helena, and was court-martialled and dismissed from the Navy for his pains. It is difficult to feel much sympathy for O'Meara, who seems to have been a likeable rogue. Without telling Napoleon, he passed on the gossip of Longwood to the Admiralty, who in turn circulated it to the Prince Regent and his rakish circle; meanwhile he accepted money from Napoleon without telling Lowe or the Admiralty. Even his skills as a doctor are open to question: some allege that Napoleon's robust health during the second half of 1818 was attributable to his no longer ingesting the mercury and calomel prescribed by his Irish quack.

By 1818, fortified by the endorsement of the Congress of Aix-la-Chapelle for the terms of 'General Bonaparte's' detention, and tired of the remorseless bad publicity he was receiving, Bathurst decided to relax the conditions he had previously described as 'essential'. The regulation that Napoleon had to show himself twice a day to the orderly officer had never been enforced anyway, as the Emperor threatened to shoot on sight anyone invading his privacy. Now Bathurst formally waived it and even suggested that if Napoleon was prepared to show himself twice a day, he might have the freedom of the island. But by this time Napoleon's health was such that he no longer had any interest in roaming the not extensive length and breadth of the island. Besides, he was still engaged in a battle of wills where he refused to compromise.

This was the context in which yet another physician made his appearance at Longwood. In accordance with the new post-1818 relaxed policy towards 'General Bonaparte', it was agreed that his household could be expanded. Madame Mère set about finding reliable servants who could be sent out to St Helena, but in the meantime Napoleon was without a personal physician for six months. Only when his old symptoms returned at the beginning of 1819 did he allow Bertrand to go to Hudson Lowe and engage the naval surgeon Dr John Stokoe, who had come out with Admiral Plampin in 1817. Plampin proved more biddable by Lowe than his predecessors, as he gave hostages to fortune in a singularly inept way. Contrary to Admiralty regulations, Plampin had brought with him a young woman not his wife. This placed him at Lowe's mercy, for if he did not toe the governor's line he was likely to be recalled at once.

Stokoe went out to Longwood and treated Napoleon for six days. Napoleon made him swear he would not report on the medical condition of his patient to Hudson Lowe. Stokoe agreed, but promptly issued three bulletins. These, however, enraged Lowe as they confirmed O'Meara's diagnosis of hepatitis; the implication was that Napoleon would recover if removed from the debilitating climate of St Helena. Stokoe was yet another who fell under the Emperor's spell, and felt well enough disposed towards him to tell him that people with his symptoms often lived to the proverbial old age. 'In the tropics as well?' Napoleon prompted. Stokoe shook his head. Then Napoleon exclaimed angrily: 'I would live to be eighty if I had not been brought to this damned island.'

On 21 January 1819 Stokoe came to Longwood to tell the Emperor he could not continue as his physician. Political imperatives meant that his honest diagnosis of hepatitis would have to be 'doctored' in another sense, and Stokoe felt unable to continue in these circumstances. His real fear was that he would be punished for a political gaffe, as there were just nine months to go before he retired on a pension. His fears were justified. The details of the hepatitis diagnosis leaked out, and Stokoe was court-martialled. In a particularly vindictive show of teeth by the British élite, Stokoe was dismissed the service and lost the full pension he had striven so hard to achieve. For Lowe, who now habitually got round problems of nomenclature by referring to 'the person now residing at Longwood', Stokoe's greatest crime was that he had referred to Napoleon as 'the Emperor' or, in the pompous officialese of the court-martial, 'knowingly and wilfully designating General Bonaparte in the said bulletin in a manner different from that in which he is designated in the Act of Parliament for the better custody of his person'.

The year 1819 initially saw Napoleon in good health, and much exercised with the departures and arrivals on the island. In September that year the supplementary staff sent by Madame Mère arrived. Two servants were a welcome addition, for one of them, Coursot, had worked for Duroc and Madame Mère, and Chandellier had trained as a cook in the Tuileries before entering Pauline Borghese's service. The two Corsican priests sent out by the increasingly devout Letizia seemed to have been handpicked as an odd couple: one was very old and almost incapable of speech as the result of a stroke; the other was very young but barely literate.

Opinions are violently divided on the doctor chosen by Fesch. Thirty-year-old Francesco Antommarchi was headstrong and boorish and never popular with Napoleon, who described him as an ignorant and unreliable bungler. Antommarchi fell foul of Napoleon even before the first interview on 21 September 1819 by going to see Lowe before travelling up to Longwood. An irate Emperor kept him waiting and then made him promise never to divulge any confidential medical details to the British. Next there was a period of entente until Napoleon again lost patience with him. Antommarchi then went to Lowe and requested repatriation, which the Governor granted. At one time, during the brief period of favour, Napoleon promised Antommarchi 200,000 francs in his will but then cancelled the bequest. Since there is something histrionic and even absurd about some of Antommarchi's coxcomb antics, there has been a tendency to conclude that he 'must have been' a poor doctor. This *non sequitur* is not borne out by the evidence. Antommarchi had never practised as a physician, but was a skilled anatomist, with long experience of dissecting corpses; he had more knowledge of post-mortem procedures than all other physicians on the island put together.

In the late months of 1819 (spring in the southern hemisphere) Napoleon temporarily developed a craze for gardening and used to roust out both old and new servants at first light in his desire to turn Longwood into a botanical garden. But this craze soon faded, especially when his health worsened. By 1820 there was abundant evidence of the dark side of the Bonaparte psyche, which seems to have been triggered by the departure of Albine de Montholon on 1 July 1819. Albine had given birth to a daughter the year before (26 January 1818), of doubtful paternity since, in addition to sleeping with her husband and Napoleon, she also had a British officer as her lover – one Major Jackson who passed on her pillow talk about Longwood to Hudson Lowe. She so far prevailed on the Emperor with her charms that she left St Helena with a 'handshake' of 200,000 francs in cash, an annuity of 20,000 francs and a gold snuff box set with a portrait of Napoleon surrounded with large diamonds. There was something very unsatisfactory about the explanations given for her departure, officially because of 'broken health' – not least the fact that her supposedly devoted husband did not accompany her.

Whether it was because Albine's departure left him without sexual gratification, or because he found out about Major Jackson, or whether on reflection he considered he had been gulled by her, the Napoleon of late 1819 and early 1820 was a man in strongly misogynistic frame of mind. On 29 September there was an embarrassing scene between him and Fanny Bertrand, caused, some said, because Napoleon made advances to her. Evidently, they were rebuffed, for the Emperor thereafter made Mme Bertrand a target for his rage. He described her as 'a whore, a fallen woman who slept with all the English officers who passed her house . . . the most degraded of women'. He even raised the subject with Bertrand himself and told him he should have put Fanny on to the streets as a common prostitute.

Some say that Napoleon finally became disillusioned with women when he learned that his faithful Marie Walewska had remarried in 1816. With consummate irrationality Napoleon was extremely annoyed by news of the marriage, and expressed no sorrow when he heard that Marie, having failed to recover from the after-effects of childbirth, died in 1817. But the signs are that it was simple sexual frustration that gnawed at him.

During a walk on Sandy Bay in March 1820 he met Hudson Lowe's wife and was surprised to find her very pretty – he had not lost his interest in feminine beauty. As a 'reward' for this vision of the female form, he laid aside his hatred of the Governor sufficiently to allow Mrs Lowe's daughter to visit Longwood.

In many ways Napoleon was at his most admirable while stoically enduring the unendurable at Longwood. Gradually it bore in on him that there would be no release from a life sentence on the rock. For a long time he fastened his hopes for release on a change of government in England or pressure of public opinion throughout Europe. His family lobbied assiduously on his behalf: Eugène de Beauharnais interceded with the Czar while Jérôme and Madame Mère wrote impassioned letters to the Prince Regent. The saintly Pius VII wrote a masterpiece of redemptive forgiveness, saying he pardoned Napoleon for everything and that it was now time to release him from a cruel fate. This letter too winged its way to the detestable 'Prinnie' but the fat hedonist did what he did with all letters urging compassion for Napoleon: he refused to answer it.

A reading of Hume's *History of England* gave Napoleon new insight into the mentality of his captors. Although he admired the bravery of the British soldier and the longevity of its Parliament, he found the British 'a ferocious race'. Here was a people, after all, who had transported 78,000 of their own kith and kin to Australia during nine years of the Napoleonic wars, many for faults no more serious than the abstract advocacy of political radicalism. He never lost the sense of France versus England being in some sense civilization and barbarism. A misogynist himself, he still had a tender, sentimental regard for women, which he found absent in English culture. What kind of mores were those that expelled women after dinner so that the men could quaff port? As for Henry VIII's egregious insensitivity in marrying Jane Seymour the day after he had had Anne Boleyn beheaded, in point of barbarism this went beyond anything Nero had achieved. For this reason, although he was agog at the arrival of each new ship from England, he lived on hope rather than expectation. Aware of the grim, unforgiving and ruthless nature of the English ruling class, he once upbraided his courtiers for their pious hopes: 'We are behaving like grown-up children and I, who should be giving an example of good sense, am as bad as any of you. We build castles in Spain.'

All the news from the outer world tended to depress him rather than buoy him up, and he concluded that pessimism was the only recourse of the sane man. 1816 was a particularly bad year when he finally pieced together the news from Europe from the preceding year. Apart from the executions of Ney in France and Murat in Italy, there was the humiliation of the *patrie* itself. The victorious Allies had rampaged through France like Huns or Vandals, looting the treasury at the Tuileries with fixed bayonets, billeting one million occupiers on the provinces and levying ten million francs war indemnity. Blücher, whose sole reaction to a visit to London was to remark what a pleasure it would be to sack it, headed the first of several brutal German occupations Paris was to experience in her history. Exploitation was the only appropriate term for the orders for compulsory billeting, whereby each householder had to take in a minimum of ten soldiers, each of whose beds had to have a pillow, a mattress, a blanket and two linen sheets and each of whom had to be given a daily ration of one pound of meat, two pounds of bread, butter, rice, a bottle of wine, brandy and tobacco.

Outwardly, Napoleon seemed to accept the hand dealt by Fate with resignation, but the anger evident in his dealings with Hudson Lowe was also in part an anger directed at the tormenting Furies generally. Did he never think of escape? Various plans for getting to America were discussed, and some very serious snatch attempts were devised in the United States. It is sometimes said that as there were only a few beaches where landings could be attempted, and the Royal Navy squadron patrolled them ceaselessly, all hopes of escape were chimerical. But it is by no means certain that an assault in strength by a number of American privateers, under cover of night, could not have succeeded. The main obstacle was Napoleon himself. He always refused to countenance any such attempt and explained why in a dictated letter to Montholon on 1 November 1820: 'I would not survive six months in America before being assassinated by the comte d'Artois's contract killers. In America I would be either assassinated or forgotten. I'm better off in St Helena.'

Eighteen months of good health and new-found energy came to an end in July 1820, when a fresh cycle of illness began. Once again Napoleon suffered headache, nausea, fevers, shivering fits, a dry and troublesome cough, vomiting of bile, pain in the liver, painful breathing and swollen legs and feet. He seemed to be recovering, then relapsed in September 1820 and remained on a plateau of invalidism for five months, complaining of exhaustion and permanently cold feet. These months saw his last real encounters with the external world. On 20 September he composed a letter to Lord Liverpool, requesting a period of recuperation at a spa in England or some other part of Europe; the request simply brought another clash with the implacable Hudson Lowe. On 4 October he ventured outside the grounds of Longwood for the last time, when he had an *alfresco* lunch with his neighbour Sir William Doveton.

Throughout his time at Longwood he never went outside after dark, so as not to see the sentries Lowe insisted on posting there at night.

On 17 March a serious deterioration was noticed in the Emperor's condition. Fearing that the end might be near, he told Bertrand that he hoped the English would not use him as a prize exhibit by burying him in Westminster Abbey. Although he spent much time on St Helena musing on religion and its psychology, he told Bertrand that he did not want the bogus consolations of Catholicism when the time came. 'I am quite happy not to have religion. I do not suffer from chimerical fears.' His fears seemed to be of another kind. On 15 April he added new codicils to his bequests and signed his last will and testament, of which Paragraph Five read: 'My death is premature. I have been assassinated by the English oligarchy and their hired murderer. The English people will not be long in avenging me.'

The course of Napoleon's illness throughout April 1821 may be briefly charted. On the fourth of the month his symptoms were a steeply rising and falling temperature, profuse sweating, coughing, a slow pulse, blackish vomit and a distended abdomen which suggested perforation. After five days of remission between 6–11 April, the symptoms recurred, with vomiting, nausea, copious sweats and high temperature at night. On 25 April his medical attendants noted flecks of black, like coffee dregs streaked with blood, in the substance coughed up. On 1 April Napoleon, who had no confidence in Antommarchi, consented to see Dr Archibald Arnott, a British army surgeon. Arnott, mindful of Lowe's standing instructions that no diagnosis of Bonaparte's ailments could be allowed to redound to the discredit of the British, and remembering the fate of O'Meara and Stokoe, reported that he could find nothing wrong and that Napoleon was faking. As late as 23 April Arnott reported: 'Convalescence will be long and difficult, but he is not in danger.'

On 27 April the fever got worse and Napoleon became delirious, with a rising temperature, shivering fits and a convulsive hiccup. He refused to see any more doctors, saying he had had enough of the pain that resulted from their treatments. By the 29th he could no longer recognize those at his bedside. He asked for Bertrand, not realizing he was standing there. Bertrand wrote in his journal: 'Tears came into my eyes when I saw this man – who had been so feared, who had so proudly commanded, so absolutely – beg for a spoonful of coffee, ask for permission to have it; not obtaining what he had asked for, but asking for it again and again, always without success but also without any display of bad temper. At other times in his illness he had sent his doctors packing, ignored their instructions and done what he wished. At present he was as docile as a little child.' Bertrand was also involved in a tussle with the two Corsican priests, who wished to give the Emperor the last rites. Bertrand was adamant that the freethinking Emperor should not die 'like a Capuchin monk', but, whether by prearrangement with the Emperor or on his own initiative the younger cleric, Vignali, administered extreme unction on 2 May.

By 3 May it seemed obvious the end could not be long delayed. By now the Emperor seemed to have lost his memory completely, his mind was addled and his speech confused. Montholon alerted Hudson Lowe to the fact that Napoleon was close to death, so Lowe, who had consistently maintained that 'General Bonaparte' was faking his illnesses, ordered the two most senior medical officers on the island, on the admiral's staff, to go to Longwood. The doctors Shortt and Mitchell arrived at the bedside and recommended a dose of calomel to produce a bowel movement. Since Arnott was junior in rank he did not dissent, but Antommarchi did, pointing out the danger to a man who had eaten nothing for six days, only to be overruled by Montholon. At 5.30 p.m. a dose of 0.6 grammes of calomel was administered by Marchand, with extreme reluctance. When told by the physicians that this was the only way to save his master, he mixed the calomel in a drink. Napoleon noticed something was wrong and mumbled to Marchand: 'You're deceiving me, too.'

When this concoction failed to produce the required bowel movement, the English doctors decided to dose their charge with a massive ten grammes of calomel. Antommarchi protested violently that this would surely kill the patient, but once again Montholon took the side of the British. At 11.30 p.m. the Emperor passed a 'very abundant stool' – in reality the matter from a massive haemorrhage of the stomach. Next day he had four more 'abundant stools' and on one occasion fainted eight times in succession. His mind was wandering, and on one occasion he asked Bertrand what was the name of the King of Rome. 'Napoleon,' Bertrand replied. At 8 p.m. the Emperor had a fifth evacuation; the calomel had obviously produced a violent haemorrhage. Then at 2 a.m. on 5 May he spoke his last words: *France, armée, tête d'armée, Joséphine.*

All next day the entire household of Longwood, including the children, clustered round the bed, watching the unconscious Emperor slowly drift away. At 5.49 p.m., he was seen to breathe his last, having heaved three sighs in his last three minutes. Bertrand noted in his journal: 'At the moment of crisis there was a slight flicker of the pupils; an irregular movement from the mouth and chin to the brow; the same regularity as of a clock.' Antommarchi officially pronounced him dead at 5.51 p.m. An autopsy, performed by Antommarchi in the presence of five

British surgeons, produced an official post-mortem report stating that Napoleon had a 'cancerous ulcer'. Antommarchi indignantly refused to sign the report. Napoleon was then buried with full military honours in Geranium Valley in a nameless tomb. The anonymity arose because even after the Emperor's death Hudson Lowe could not stop his petty bickering. A dispute between him and Montholon about the lapidary inscription led to the 'compromise' whereby nothing was inscribed at all.

The notion that Napoleon died of cancer is still widely accepted by those who are unaware of the perfunctory nature of the post-mortem, the dissenting opinions of those who conducted the autopsy, the implausibility of the verdict in view of the anamnesis, and the sheer convenience of the judgement on cause of death from the point of view of Lowe and the British government. Working back from the general to the particular, the most salient fact is that all five British surgeons who signed the report – doctors Shortt, Arnott, Mitchell, Livingstone and Burton – were under severe political restraints. They knew well enough what had happened to O'Meara and Stokoe and what would probably happen to them if they recorded any verdict that implied that the death had been caused by British negligence or callousness or by the unhealthy climate of St Helena. Cancer was the one diagnosis that would be totally satisfactory to Lowe and his superiors, and it had a superficial plausibility, because Napoleon's father had died that way. The one diagnosis not allowed was hepatitis, as this would immediately be connected with the endemic amoebic dysentery on the island. Not surprisingly, therefore, death by cancer was the verdict returned.

It is worth taking a closer look at the autopsy findings as contained in the minority report written by Antommarchi. Let us remember also that Antommarchi had infinitely greater experience in corpse dissection and autopsy than any of the others present. Antommarchi found that Napoleon's liver was abnormally large – indicating either hepatitis or poisoning – and that there were adhesions of the liver and the stomach. Shortt agreed with Antommarchi's findings and strongly dissented from his colleagues' opinion that there was no abnormality in the liver. In his private papers he made a note that the detail of the enlarged liver and the adhesions was omitted from the majority report on the express orders of Hudson Lowe. The best way to deal with Antommarchi's damaging findings, therefore, was to attack the man rather than his skills – which is what so many historians have done since.

What of the credentials of the other British doctors? It seems that the dominant spirit at the autopsy was that of an Assistant Surgeon, Walter Henry, who witnessed the operation and wrote up the report for the others to sign; because he lacked seniority, his own signature did not appear on the document. Henry was the man who first divulged (in a private report for Hudson Lowe in 1823) the story that Napoleon had abnormally small genitals, and the idea has proved remarkably popular since, answering as it does a bastardized conception of the idea of compensation – great man, small member, etc. But Henry had a pronounced animus against Napoleon and, in any case, strangely finds all Bonaparte's organs small – hands, feet, bladder, heart. Since this is the man to whose report the British surgeons appended their signature, it is not surprising that there is no mention of a large liver.

Many later writers have soared away into the empyrean of the imagination on the basis of Henry's 'observations' and found evidence for sexual infantilism, pituitary failure and much else. But, unlike the situation with Hitler's monorchism, it is improbable that rumour and reality coincide on this issue. As a man who liked to portray himself as a rough and ready soldier, Napoleon several times appeared in the nude in the presence of his troops, most recently in the 1814 campaign. His frequent smutty talk and general sexual profile scarcely suggest a man with a shameful secret to hide. Gourgaud records in his diary for 26 October 1817 that Napoleon said: 'If ever O'Meara writes a diary, it will be very interesting. If he gives the length of my – , this would be even more interesting.' This hardly sounds like a man worried that posterity would laugh at him, and indeed O'Meara did produce a journal and made no use of this 'astounding revelation'. Besides, even if we could imagine a substantially underendowed man as a compulsive womanizer – which Napoleon was – his bedmates would surely have spoken of this interesting aspect of his anatomy. Josephine and his mistresses did on occasion complain about his sexual performance, but only because he insisted on completing the act at such astonishing speed – expeditiously, is the standard euphemism.

Since the British surgeons' observations were either distorted or constrained by political expediency, the verdict of death by cancer hardly convinces in terms of the calibre of the alleged witnesses. What of the case history itself? Here the great stumbling block to the cancer theorists is Napoleon's obesity, since it is well known that death from this disease is almost invariably preceded by extreme emaciation. Yet both post-mortem reports (Antommarchi's and that signed by the British surgeons) speak of a layer of fat covering the entire body, with particularly large amounts around the chest and heart. This in turn has suggested to certain medical observers a quite different explanation for Napoleon's illness and death.

Since Napoleon's body was plump and round, like a woman's, with breasts like a woman and small, delicate, feminine hands, some have speculated that he suffered from hyperpituitarism – excessive activity of the pituitary gland – which may have accounted for premature 'burn-out' on the onset of middle age, with excessive tiredness, lethargy, obesity and even change of personality after 1808. Others advance the idea of 'hypogonadism' – a condition affecting one in five hundred male births where, instead of the normal XY (male) and XX (female) chromosome pattern, an XXY paradigm can occur, where the Y competes with the XX. The obesity and part of the post-1815 illnesses should, on this view, be separated from the hepatitis that (allegedly) killed him. Then there is controversy about whether the liver failure was a result of amoebic dysentery or whether chronic liver failure, antedating St Helena, could simply have combined with gynaecomastia (womanly breasts), constipation and digestive disorders to produce the valetudinarian Emperor of Borodino, Dresden and Waterloo.

Other suggestions for Napoleon's maladies and possibly for his death also include bilharzia, picked up in Egypt in 1798–99 – which would have accounted for the urinary malfunctions, Frohlich's disease or adiposo-genital dystrophia, caused by the defective functioning of the hypophysis – the organ of internal secretion – dysentery, scurvy, appendicitis, epilepsy, malaria, tuberculosis and gastric ulcers. Most of these seem no more convincing than the official verdict of death by cancer, but they do account for the obesity at death and they do explain the periodicity of Napoleon's illnesses, which the cancer theory cannot. However, by far the most convincing explanation for Napoleon's death is arsenical poisoning. This not only clears up all the puzzles over aetiology and symptoms but makes sense of so much else at Longwood which must otherwise remain a dark mystery.

Napoleon exhibited all the symptoms of a person poisoned by arsenic: heart palpitations, weak and irregular pulse, very severe headaches, icy chills in the leg extending to the hips, back and shoulder pain, a persistent dry cough, loosening teeth, coated tongue, pain in the liver, severe thirst, skin rash, yellowed skin and whites of eyes, shivering, deafness, sensitivity of eyes to light, spasmodic muscle contractions, nausea, difficulty in breathing. His fat, glabrous body (even after months of illness), with an absence of fine hairs on the surface, is another indication. When the body becomes toxic, it is apt to clothe itself in fat as a kind of armour against poisons. But perhaps the most telling piece of indirect evidence for arsenic poisoning is that when Napoleon's body was about to be transferred from St Helena to its final resting place at Les

Invalides in 1840 and his coffin was opened, it was found to be perfectly preserved. Since this outcome is yet another consequence of arsenic poisoning, and other attempts to explain the phenomenon simply result in absurdity (vacuum sealing in an era that did not possess the technology), the theorists of cancer have yet another mountain to climb. In the words of Conan Doyle, 'when you have eliminated the impossible, whatever remains, however improbable, must be the truth'.

Yet there is nothing improbable about the hypothesis of arsenic poisoning. Not only does it fit all Napoleon's symptoms, but science gives it rather more than warranted assertibility. Hairs from Napoleon's head, preserved by the valets Marchand and Noverraz and with an impeccable provenance and pedigree, have been tested for arsenic content and found to be abnormally high in the substance. Napoleon was found to have between 10.38 and 10.58 parts of arsenic per million in two hair samples, whereas in the early nineteenth century – an era of low pollution – the normal level would be between 0.5 and 0.65; even today, in a world of high pollution, the norm is only 0.86. Neutron irradiation tests conducted at Harwell Research Centre showed that the Emperor had ingested 600% of the levels of arsenic normal in the early nineteenth century.

One possible explanation was that Napoleon died of accidental arsenic poisoning, having taken in lethal amounts from his wallpaper or from hair creams or medications he took to improve his appetite. In that case, scientific tests would show that there was a regular ingestion of arsenic. The breakthrough came in 1975 when the Department of Forensic Medicine at Glasgow worked out a technique for dating the various doses of arsenic ingested. It was shown that the Emperor had taken in toxic doses of arsenic on forty different occasions and the periodicity of the doses correlated uncannily with the irregular pattern of his illnesses during 1816–21 – an irregularity which alone should have disposed of the cancer theory.

If Napoleon was the victim of arsenic poisoning, and if the poisoning was not accidental, the conclusion was obvious: he was the victim of assassination by person or persons unknown. Only one person had means and opportunity to preside over a slow poisoning and only one person was always present during all the acute troughs of Napoleon's periodic illness: the comte de Montholon. The motive is more elusive. The Montholons were unscrupulous adventurers and they may have been actuated by simple mercenary considerations: it is known that in April 1821 Montholon got the Emperor to destroy an earlier will in which he gave the bulk of his money to Bertrand. This he did by successfully hinting that the Bertrands intended to decamp to Europe and abandon him, and indeed it was well known that Fanny Bertrand had long been wanting to take her children back to France. Napoleon, whose dislike of the Bertrands increased during the last year of his life, amended his will so as to give Montholon two million francs, over and above what he had already given to Albine; Bertrand's legacy was reduced to 500,000 francs, only slightly more than Marchand, with 400,000, who, as a valet should have received only about a third the amount given to the Grand Marshal.

Certainly the financial factor was never far from Montholon's mind. The furtive way in which the last sacrament was administered to Napoleon by Father Vignali shows the hand of Montholon once more. Montholon feared that because the Emperor's will said he died as a Catholic, if he did not receive Extreme Unction, the will might be declared invalid and thus the financial provisions benefiting him would be set aside. But for him to have been able to administer arsenic surreptitiously over five years, he had to be far more than a mere fortune hunter. On the basis of *cui bono*, the only hypothesis that makes sense is that Montholon was a Bourbon agent who had been trained in those black arts of slow poisoning that were a special feature of this era, and are preserved for posterity in the pages of Balzac and Alexandre Dumas.

Despite Montholon's close ties with Hudson Lowe, it is a moral certainty that he was not working for the British on this diabolical scheme. Quite apart from the peculiar horror evinced for poisoners in the English culture – a statute from the reign of Henry VIII ordained a penalty of death by immersion in boiling water – it made no sense for Britain to murder Napoleon. If he died in suspicious circumstances, Britain would be the world's pariah, which was why Lowe was so adamant that the only possible cause of death allowed to be declared by the doctors under his jurisdiction was cancer. Besides, the British Foreign Office, famous for taking the long view, would have preferred to keep the ex-Emperor on St Helena indefinitely. By so doing they could, at the limit, bring recalcitrant European powers to heel by threatening to release the ogre.

That leaves the Bourbons as the most likely assassins. The most likely transmission belt for orders from the comte d'Artois, Montholon's presumed paymaster, was the French Commissioner Montchenu, who may not have been the bumbling idiot he pretended to be. The Bourbons' motive, as Napoleon knew well enough, was vengeance, not just for the general humiliation of their family but particularly for the murder of the duc d'Enghien. It would not be beyond the bounds of the plausible if the loathsome Talleyrand was also involved. Having established the correlation between Montholon's presence at Longwood on each occasion

Napoleon fell violently ill, one can heap up the circumstantial details that seem to incriminate him. If Montholon was a Bourbon agent, as seems probable, the periodicity of the poisoning could be convincingly correlated with events in France. The cessation in poisoning in 1819–20 could have mirrored the uncertain political situation in France, with the Decazes administration a liberal interlude between the reactionary governments of Richelieu and Villèle. And the trigger for final orders sent to Montholon could have been the murder of the Bourbon heir apparent, the duc de Berry, in 1820 by a Bonapartist; subsequent rioting revealed the formidable dormant strength of crypto-Bonapartism.

The most convincing aspect of the Montholon case is the number of mysterious incidents that would otherwise have to be written off as mere, and sometimes singularly fortunate (for Montholon) coincidences. Perhaps the most striking is the sudden death of Cipriani in 1818 and the disappearance of his body. A few days later a maid and a young child, who came in on a daily basis to assist him, also died suddenly of the same symptoms. Had they also eaten or drunk something the poisoner had prepared for Cipriani? Again, in 1821, Montholon, who in the past had managed by expert manipulation and his contacts with Lowe to have Las Cases, Gourgaud, O'Meara and Stokoe removed, contrived to be the Emperor's *de facto* night nurse. On 24 March 1821 the Swiss valet Noverraz fell violently ill and was out of action for six weeks. When Antommarchi stood on his dignity and petulantly refused to take his place, Montholon eased himself into a position where he could work largely unobserved. Dr Arnott, coming in on 1 April, was clay in his hands, as he spoke no French or Italian and understood nothing of what the Emperor said to him except through the garbled (and presumably censored) translations of Montholon.

But the masterpiece in the assassination plot was the manipulation of the British doctors into giving two different medications, one to relieve thirst, the other to assuage constipation (both were symptoms of chronic arsenic poisoning). The terrible beauty of the black art of slow poisoning was that arsenic was not used to kill victims outright, but merely to break down their health by destroying the immune system. When Montholon overruled Antommarchi to get the dose of calomel administered to Napoleon on 3 May, this was tantamount to signing his death warrant. Having given the patient calomel to relieve constipation and orgeat to relieve thirst, the doctors in effect created a lethal cocktail: the two medications would have combined in the stomach to create mercury cyanide, thus doing what bullets and bayonets in fifty battles had not been able to do and putting an end to Napoleon Bonaparte.

Such was the probable fate of Napoleon on St Helena. Unless an authenticated confession from Montholon is unearthed (some have claimed to have found it, only to have opponents declare the document a forgery), one can never really advance beyond the realm of probability into absolute truth, and one's judgement must always be predicated on likelihood rather than propositions beyond a reasonable doubt. It must be said in passing that champions of the orthodox theory – that Napoleon died of cancer – require from proponents of rival theories criteria for verification that their own hypothesis could never meet. And British culture, justifiably suspicious of 'conspiracy theory', has parlayed reasonable scepticism into the dogmatic assertion that conspiracies *never* take place. But perhaps in a wider sense the determination of the exact cause of Napoleon's death scarcely matters. The hero chained to the rock of St Helena was a mere ghost of the once all-conquering Emperor. Napoleon Bonaparte R.I.P.

CONCLUSION

Napoleon's death on St Helena initially passed almost unnoticed. By a bizarre correlation, which would set those of a Jungian frame of mind thinking, all those who were most devoted to him died young and all who had betrayed him or let him down enjoyed longevity. Of the marshals, apart from those who had predeceased 1815 or were swept away that year (and almost all of those were loyal Bonapartists – Berthier, Bessières, Poniatowski, Lannes, Ney), the faithful Davout, Suchet and Mortier died young or prematurely. All the marshals who had betrayed him (except for Murat who had virtually self-destructed in 1815) lived on to the fabled old age: Soult died only in 1851, Grouchy in 1847, Bernadotte in 1844, Marmont in 1852, Oudinot in 1847, MacDonald in 1844.

The same pattern can be discerned in the lives of Napoleon's family and intimates. His favourite sister Pauline died at 45, Élisa Bonaparte at 43, Eugène de Beauharnais at the same age, and Marie Walewska at 28. It is yet another strike against the death-by-cancer theory that in the Bonaparte family the sisters seemed to have inherited the paternal gene that determined a short life while the males inherited Letizia's biological factor of longevity (she died at 86): Joseph was 76 at death, Jérôme also 76, Lucien 75 and Louis 68. It need hardly be reiterated that this quartet of sibling ingrates owed everything to their brilliant brother and requited his favour with incompetence, defiance and treachery. The saddest fate was that of Napoleon's son, the 'King of Rome' who, after years as a virtual prisoner of his Austrian grandfather at Schönbrunn, died of tuberculosis at 21 in 1832.

Although she had been under duress in 1814, the weak-willed Marie-Louise owed more than the grudging tribute she paid him when news of his death on St Helena reached her: 'Although I never entertained any strong sentiment of any kind for him, I cannot forget that he is the father of my son, and far from treating me badly, as most people believe, he always manifested the deepest regard for me – the only thing one can expect in a political marriage. So I am very affected. Although I ought to be pleased that he has ended his miserable existence, I could have wished for him many years of happiness and life, as long as it would have been far from me.'

Given that all Napoleon's most deadly enemies – Wellington, Talleyrand, Metternich and Bernadotte – lived well into their eighties, the case for Napoleon as an ill-starred individual would seem to be clinched. But the man who died almost friendless on a rocky island in the South Atlantic won a final victory in death. The power of the myth he had created on St Helena affected most of the greatest writers of the period immediately after his demise – Balzac, Stendhal, Vigny, Victor Hugo, Chateaubriand, Byron, Hazlitt, Walter Scott. In the 1840s, after the Emperor's body was brought back to Paris and entombed in Les Invalides, a veritable Bonaparte craze developed, which was the most important factor in Louis-Napoleon (supposedly Louis's son)'s accession to power in the Second Empire.

If Napoleon became a mythical figure, this was because for once the cliché was true, and the whole was greater than the sum of the parts. If aspects of Napoleon's career and personality are scrutinized one by one, it is possible to mount a devastating critique. But what remains overall defies such a reductive analysis. Even Talleyrand, no friend of the Emperor, conceded this in a famous assessment made to the pro-Bonaparte Lord Holland: 'His career is the most extraordinary that has occurred for one thousand years ... He was certainly a great, an extraordinary man, nearly as extraordinary in his qualities as in his career ... He was clearly the most extraordinary man I ever saw, and I believe the most extraordinary that has lived in our age, or for many ages.' Another harsh critic, Chateaubriand, summed him up as 'the mightiest breath of life which ever quickened human clay'.

The greatness of Napoleon was that he tried to transcend human limitations and nearly succeeded; this is why his real magic is in the mythical realm rather than actuality. At a mundane level it is easy to tear Bonaparte to pieces. The pretence he made on St Helena – that his life's work was directed towards the unification of Europe – has been taken seriously by enthusiasts for a European Union who should know better. He claimed that, but for his own (admitted) mistakes in Poland, Italy and above all Spain, he would have solved the problem of nationalities and cultural differences: 'Europe thus divided into nationalities freely formed and free internally, peace between States would have become easier: the United States of Europe would become a possibility ... I wished to found a European system, a European Code of Laws, a European judiciary; there would be but one people in Europe.'

This is cunningly devised *ex post facto* rationalization. There is nothing here about the rape of Europe by the Grand Army, the thrones illicitly grabbed for the useless Bonaparte siblings, the huge handouts and benefices given to the venal marshals, the exploitation (no other word will do) of the satellite states for the sole benefit of France. On St Helena Napoleon defended his autocracy by saying that it was a regrettable temporary necessity. This reminds one only too forcibly of the equally 'regrettable' need for the dictatorship of the proletariat in Russia in 1917, pending the coming of the communist utopia. For Napoleon, as for Lenin, the time was not ripe, but for such men it never would be. The imperatives of charismatic leadership do not permit a benign abdication of such men in face of an era of peace and pluralistic democracy. This is *not* to concede the ludicrous claims of his opponents that they were fighting for 'freedom' against tyranny. The only possible rational response when faced with the blinkered and mindless reactionary fanaticism of Alexander I, Metternich, Louis XVIII – to say nothing of the unsavoury political trio of Liverpool, Castlereagh and Wellington – ranged against Napoleon and his money-grubbing acolytes is 'a plague on both your houses'.

The legend of Napoleon as political saviour can be safely laid to rest. A close analysis reveals that he has also been severely overrated as a military commander. There is much hyperbole of the 'greatest captain of all times' variety, but this cannot survive critical scrutiny. He had two great victories, at Austerlitz and Friedland, but otherwise his record was not outstanding. He won Marengo only because of Desaix and achieved a great victory at Jena-Auerstädt only through Davout. He scraped through Wagram by the barest of margins, was fought to a standstill by the Russians at Eylau and Borodino, and lost badly at Leipzig and Waterloo. He was at his best when commanding smaller armies: it is significant that his best campaigns overall were those of Italy in 1796–97, Egypt in 1798–99 and France in 1814, when he fought a series of smaller engagements against an enemy not present in overwhelming numbers.

There can be no denying that Napoleon occupies a high rank in the military history of the ages, but he cannot be counted among the handful of peerless commanders. There is nothing in his record to compare with Alexander the Great's undefeated record in the four battles of Granicus, Issus, Gaugamela and the Hydaspes, or with Hannibal's amazing quartet of victories over the Romans at Ticinus, Trebia, Trasimene and Cannae. Nor can he compare with a commander like Genghiz Khan's Subudei, who was undefeated in a thirty-year career of battles in Mongolia, China, Persia, Russia and Hungary. At his peak Napoleon never faced another commander who was nearly his equal in talent. Compare this with

Tamerlane, who at Angora in 1402 overwhelmed the Ottoman Turks under Bayazid, fresh from his triumph over the flower of Christian chivalry at Nicopolis.

Paradoxically, Napoleon often failed in his endeavours because he was not ruthless enough. When *raison d'état* demanded it, or seemed to, he could be almost monstrously cold-blooded, as in the notorious cases of the Chouan leader Frotte, the Jacobins unscrupulously sent to Devil's Island after the *machine infernale*, the duc d'Enghien and the Tyrolean leader Andreas Hofer. But a Stalin, a Hitler or even a Franco would not have wasted five minutes pondering what to do about the intrigues of Bernadotte, Fouché, Talleyrand or Murat. Napoleon responded to the almost invariable base ingratitude of his followers with a stoical shrug or a homily on the baseness of human nature. His story is the catalogue of an endless list of ingrates: all his family, almost all the marshals, including many pro-Bonaparte figures like Augereau, Ney and Berthier, childhood friends like Bourrienne, valets like Constant, physicians like Dr Yvan and even personal servants like the Mameluke Roustam.

Napoleon can be convicted on the count of callousness, rather than cruelty or ruthlessness. He was an autocrat but not a totalitarian dictator; he could not be that as he lacked the necessary technology. Napoleon had many blemishes, but he did not cause the loss of millions of his people through famine, as Mao did in China; he did not kill off hundreds of thousands of prisoners in a sadistic régime of 'redemption through suffering' as Franco did in Spain; he did not liquidate his peasants as Stalin did his kulaks, and he did not consign the Jews to genocide through holocaust. Even when it came to his treacherous and venal followers, Napoleon was forgiving: there is no 'Night of the Long Knives' or 'Great Terror' in his biography. He was unmoved by the human cost of his campaigns, though he sometimes shed crocodile tears about the loss of favourites or about the Army as an abstraction.

Into any moral scale when judgement on Napoleon is entered must be placed the huge death toll from his wars. Historians always tend to underestimate this and some have put the numbers of dead resulting from his wars as low as one million. This will not do. Napoleon lost half a million men in Russia in 1812 and almost the same number in Germany in 1813, while the Peninsular War cost France 220,000 men. Civilian casualties in these wars are unknown, but must have been enormous. The war dead in the Haitian campaign alone amounted to 55,000 Frenchmen and 350,000 of the island's blacks and mulattoes. If we estimate the loss to France between 1796 and 1815 as a million killed in battle and a further two million who died from disease, cold and hunger, the correct figure for total deaths caused by Bonaparte's campaigns must be four million at the very least, and this is likely to be a considerable underestimate.

Everything about Napoleon generates its own paradox. On the one hand, he can be viewed as the man who set back European economic life for a generation by the dislocating impact of his wars; on the other, he can be seen as the man who secured the final triumph of capitalism over feudalism and who protected nascent French industry from the devastating competition of the British. On the one hand, he can be seen as the most titanic figure in the long line of 'Caesarism' that disfigures French history, beginning perhaps with Louis XIV and stretching beyond Napoleon to include Louis-Napoleon, Thiers, Clemenceau, Poincaré, Pétain and De Gaulle. On the other, he can be viewed as a mere plaything of historical inevitability, a puppet of ineluctable social and economic forces – the version portrayed in Tolstoy's *War and Peace*. He is an inspiration to both the Right and the Left in their detestation of liberalism and the simple pieties of pluralistic democracy. Napoleon was the hero of Hegel and Nietzsche; he is also the patron of Irishmen struggling under the yoke of England and the inspiration of all who are 'agin' things.

Both these groups perceive what it is that makes Napoleon great: his Promethean ambitions and abilities. He was an astonishing phenomenon, a man often compared to Stalin and Hitler but one who, unlike them, had no party machine or mass movement to back him. If ever a man lived on his wits, it was Bonaparte. He detested the French Revolution but was in many ways the greatest revolutionary voluntarist of them all: in this sense his true twentieth-century heirs are Mao and Castro rather than Hitler and Stalin. The deepest paradox about Napoleon was that this deeply superstitious man, who professed an almost Oriental belief in Fate, again and again tried to prove that nothing is written. Dreaming the impossible dream, he attempted to fulfil it, and for a time the impossible was granted him.

An introvert by nature, Napoleon turned into an extravert in the Jungian sense, where the world of objects and the external world is the only true reality; this is why critics say that the mature Napoleon possessed almost no inner life. The age-old debating question – did Napoleon represent the triumph of the Classical or the Romantic – could be answered if we embrace this view, for the implication would be that Napoleon spurned Romanticism's elevation of the individual ego and its thoughts and feelings in favour of the project of mastering the woodenheaded world. Another gloss on this is that Napoleon could no longer be a Romantic figure once he had broken with Paoli and Corsica and thereafter had to play roles which he derived from his reading of the ancient classics; thus was born the ultimately fatal idea of making himself an Emperor. But the Tolstoys would reply that the classical sensibility implies the recognition that events make men, not vice versa and that Napoleon tried to achieve by willpower what can only be achieved by technology. There is accordingly no solution to the introvert/extrovert or Classical/Romantic antinomy in Bonaparte's case.

But Napoleon's role in myth can perhaps be established by a Jungian fable, emphasizing the mystical powers of quaternity. Born on one island (Corsica), he was exiled to a second (Elba) and died on a third (St Helena). Just as Jung insists the shadow side of the Trinity must be completed by a fourth to achieve integration, so may we see a fourth island, England, as Napoleon's nemesis and (from his point of view) bringing about a horrific closure. When he spoke scornfully of a 'nation of shopkeepers', Napoleon was really expressing his contempt for all who live by the laws of reality and conduct politics by the art of the possible. The traditional hero, like Hercules, harrows Hell, as Napoleon did in Russia in 1812. And Prometheus himself, who gave Man fire, was chained forever to a rock, where a vulture gnawed unceasingly at his entrails. Chained to a rock on St Helena, Napoleon became the sacrificial victim who in French cultural mythology more than any other man represents the nation and *la gloire*.

SOURCES

CHAPTER ONE

The most fundamental work for Napoleon's early life is F. Masson & G. Piaggi, *Napoléon Inconnu, papiers inédits 1769–1793* (Paris 1895), a priceless collection of primary sources. This can now be supplemented by the brilliant monograph by Dorothy Carrington, *Napoleon's Parents* (1988), based on an exhaustive trawl through Corsican sources. H. Larrey, *Madame Mère* (Paris 1892) contains invaluable recollections by Letizia. Joseph Bonaparte, *Mémoires et correspondance politique et militaire du roi Joseph*, ed. A. du Casse, 10 vols (Paris 1855) has to be approached with circumspection in general but can be relied on in the main for the early years. The memoirs of Antommarchi, Montholon and others from the St Helena period are examples of Napoleon the mythmaker at work but yield nuggets for the early life when used with caution and buttressed by other sources. See especially François Antommarchi, *Mémoires du docteur F. Antommarchi, ou les derniers moments de Napoléon*, 2 vols (Paris 1825)

Of the secondary works, A. Chuquet, *La Jeunesse de Napoléon* (Paris 1897–99) is outstanding. Also worth taking on board are T. Nasica, *Mémoires sur l'enfance et la jeunesse de Napoléon* (Paris 1852), P. Bartel, *La Jeunesse Inédite de Napoléon* (Paris 1954), A. Decaux, *Napoleon's Mother* (1962), J.B. Marcaggi, *La Genèse de Napoléon* (1902), M. Mirtil, *Napoléon d'Ajaccio* (1947) C. Iung, *Bonaparte et son temps 1769–1799*, 3 vols (1880–81), though all of these contain serious errors.

On Corsica two important contemporary sources are J.J. Rousseau, *Du Contrat Social* (1762) and James Boswell, *An Account of Corsica, the Journal of a Tour to that Island and Memoirs of Pascal Paoli* (1768). Cf. also Frederick Pottle, *James Boswell, The Earlier Years* (1966). G. Feydel, *Mémoires et Coûtumes des Corses* (1799) is good on the vendetta. Daily life is well summed up in Paul Arrighi, *La vie quotidienne en Corse au 18ᵉ siècle* (Paris 1970). For Paoli and the complex politics of eighteenth-century Corsica, Dorothy Carrington, *Sources de l'Histoire de la Corse au Public*

Record Office (London) avec 38 lettres inédites de Pasquale Paoli (Ajaccio 1983) is fundamental. Thad E. Hall, *France and the Eighteenth-Century Corsican Question* (NY 1971) provides a useful overview. The first volume of Dumouriez's memoirs, *La vie et les mémoires du général Dumouriez*, 4 vols (Paris 1823) deals with the French invasion of Corsica in 1768, and a good supplement is Christine Roux, *Les Makis de la résistance Corse 1772–1778* (Paris 1984)

Chateaubriand's eccentric view of Napoleon can be found in *Mémoires d'outre-tombe* (Paris 1902) and Taine's in *Les origines de la France contemporaine* (Paris 1890). For other far-fetched and mythological views of Napoleon, especially after 1815, see J. Deschamps, *Sur la légende de Napoléon* (Paris 1931): J. Lucas-Brereton, *Le Culte de Napoléon, 1815–1848* (Paris 1960); A. Guérard, *Reflections on the Napoleonic Legend* (1924); P. Gonnard, *Les Origines de la légende napoléonienne* (Paris 1906); M. Descotes, *La Légende de Napoléon et les écrivains français au XIXe siècle* (Paris 1967) and Jean Tulard, *Le Mythe de Napoléon* (Paris 1971).

For the views on Napoleon of psychoanalysis and depth psychology see C.G. Jung, *Collected Works*, eds Fordham, Adler, McGuire (1979), vols 3, 6, 7, 8, 10, 17, 18; A. Brill, *Fundamental Conceptions of Psychoanalysis* (1922); Wilhelm Reich, *Character Analysis* (1950); Freud to Thomas Mann, 29 November 1936. Useful pointers to the Napoleon-Joseph relationship can be gained from Alfred Adler, *Problems of Neurosis* (1929) which deals in general with the problems of the second son. For the likelihood of Letizia's infidelity see (apart from Carrington, op. cit) *Revue des Deux Mondes*, 15 September 1952; *Figaro littéraire*, 1 May 1954.

CHAPTER TWO

Jean Colin, *L'Éducation militaire de Napoléon* (Paris 1900) is a good starting place and can be supplemented by Harold de Fontenay, *Napoléon, Joseph et Lucien Bonaparte au College d'Autun en Bourgogne* (Paris 1869). Other pointers can be found in Anatole de Charmasse, *Les Jésuites au College d'Autun, 1618–1763* (Paris 1884); C. Gaunet, *Le Collège d'Autun sous les Jésuites (1618–1763) et après eux* (Autun 1940) and Bernard Nabonne, *Joseph Bonaparte: Le roi philosophe* (Paris 1949).

For Brienne the following are useful if used with care: A. Assier, *Napoléon à l'école de Brienne* (Paris 1874); A.N. Petit, *Napoléon à Brienne* (Troyes 1839); Albert Babeau, *Le Château de Brienne* (Paris 1877); François Gilbert de Coston, *Biographie des premières années de Napoléon Bonaparte* (Paris 1840) and A. Prévost, *Les Minimes de Brienne* (Paris 1915). Two journal articles on Napoleon's stay at the École Militaire are excellent: R. Laulan, 'La chère à l'École Militaire au temps de Bonaparte', *Revue de l'Institut Napoléon* (1959) pp.18–23 and General Gambier, 'Napoléon Bonaparte à l'École Royale Militaire de Paris', *Revue de l'Institut Napoléon* (1971) pp.48–56. On the reliability of Des Mazis see R. Laulan, *Revue de l'Institut Napoléon* (1956) pp.54–60.

The general military context is established in Albert Bâteau, *La vie militaire sous l'ancien regime*, 2 vols (Paris 1890) and Spenser Wilkinson, *The French Army before Napoleon* (1830). The fortunes of the Bonaparte family while Napoleon was at school can be followed in L. de Brotonne, *Les Bonaparte et leurs alliances* (Paris 1901) and François Collaveri, *La franc-maçonnerie des Bonaparte* (Paris 1982) – on which subject see also J.M. Roberts, *The Mythology of Secret Societies* (1972) and J.L. Quoy-Bodin, *L'Armée et la Franc-Maçonnerie: au declin de la monarchie sous la Revolution et l'Empire* (Paris 1987).

Those interested in more detail on Napoleon's unprepossessing father should read Xavier Versini, *M. de Buonoparte ou le livre inachevé* (Paris 1977). His mother has attracted more attention, and estimates of her vary wildly. Apart from Larrey already mentioned there are the following: Clement Shaw, *Letizia Bonaparte* (1928); Augustin Thierry, *Madame Mère* (1939); Gilbert Martineau, *Madame Mère* (Paris 1980); Clara Tschudi, *Napoleon's Mother* (1900); Alain Decaux, *Letizia mère de l'empereur* (Paris 1983); François Duhourcau, *La mère de Napoléon* (Paris 1921); Monica Stirling, *A Pride of Lions* (1961); Lydia Peretii, *Letizia Bonaparte* (Paris 1922). The generally unfavourable consensus is contested in Marthe Arrighi de Casanova, *Letizia mère de Napoléon a été calomniée* (Brussels 1954). Lucien, Napoleon's bane but occasionally his unwitting salvation, left some partially reliable memoirs: *Mémoires de Lucien Bonaparte, Prince Canino, écrits par lui-même* (Paris 1836). For Cardinal Fesch there is J.P.F. Lyonnet, *Le Cardinal Fesch*, 2 vols (Paris 1841) and Hélène Colombani, *Le Cardinal Fesch* (Paris 1979).

On the more general culture that helped to form Napoleon see Norwood Young, *The Growth of Napoleon, A Study in Environment* (1910) and F.G. Healey, *The Literary Culture of Napoleon* (Geneva 1959). His personality is studied in J. Holland Rose, *The Personality of Napoleon*; David Chandler, 'Napoleon as Man and Leader', *Consortium on Revolutionary Europe Proceedings* (1989), I, pp.581–606; Harold T. Parker, 'The formation of Napoleon's personality; an exploratory essay', *French Historical Studies* 7 (1971) pp.6–26. Adler's views are in *Social Interest* (1938).

This may be the place to mention the often highly unreliable memoir literature which starts to be a 'source' for Napoleon's life at this point.

Bourrienne's, *Memoirs of Napoleon Bonaparte* (1923), mostly ghosted by Maxime de Villemarest, are mainly transparent nonsense and provoked a 720-page rejoinder when first published in French: Boulay de la Meurthe, *Bourrienne et ses erreurs* (Brussels 1930); Laura Permon Junot, later duchess of Abrantes, is not far short of Bourrienne on unreliability. The Abrantes *Memoirs* (1929), which could be subtitled 'The Memoirs of an Opium Addict' both on account of their fantastic, pipe-dreaming quality and because Laura became such an addict, won for her the nickname Abracadabrantes. Peter Gunn, *Napoleon's Little Pest* (1983) is a lively account of her. Roederer, *Bonaparte me disait* (Paris 1942), on the other hand, is a genuine memoir and testifies to the influence of Rousseau on Napoleon. Cf. also Roederer's *Journal* (1909). Chaptal, *Mes Souvenirs* (Paris 1893), unreliable for the Empire period after 1804, are sound enough here.

CHAPTER THREE

In addition to works already cited, the following deal with the formative early years: Bertram Ratcliffe, *Prelude to Fame, an account of the early life of Napoleon up to the battle of Montenotte* (1981); Spenser Wilkinson, *The Rise of General Bonaparte* (1991); Jean Thiry, *Les années de jeunesse de Napoléon Bonaparte 1769–1796* (Paris 1975); Dimitri Sorokine, *La jeunesse de Napoléon* (Paris 1976); H. D'Estre, *Napoléon, les années obscures* (Paris 1942).

Jean Tulard, *Itinéraire de Napoléon* (Paris 1992) is invaluable for establishing the exact dates of the various comings and goings between Corsica and the mainland. Eleven letters from Napoleon in the years 1789–92 were printed in *Revue des Deux Mondes*, 15 December 1931. See also J. Savant, *Napoléon à Auxonne* (Paris 1946); M. Bois, *Napoléon Bonaparte lieutenant d'artillerie à Auxonne* (n.d.) For the important relationship with du Teil there is J. du Teil, *Napoléon Bonaparte et les généraux du Teil* (1897). For the financial aspect there is B. Simiot, *De quoi vivait Bonaparte?* (Paris 1952). For the impact of the flight of Louis XVI to Varennes see Marcel Reinhard, *La chute de la Royauté* (Paris 1969).

The principal works influencing Napoleon the artilleryman were: Jean de Beaumont du Teil, *L'Usage de l'artillerie nouvelle dans la guerre de campagne* (Paris 1778); Jacques de Guibert, *Essai général de tactique* (Paris 1772) and *Defense du systeme de guerre moderne* (Paris 1778); Pierre Bourcet, *Principes de la guerre des montagnes* (Paris 1786). The importance of artillery in this period can be followed in B.P. Hughes, *Firepower;*

Weapons' Effectiveness on the Battlefield, 1630–1850 (1974); G. Rouqerol, *L'Artillerie au début des guerres de la Revolution* (Paris 1898) and B.P. Hughes, *Open Fire! Artillery Tactics from Marlborough to Wellington* (Chichester 1983).

Napoleon's juvenilia is conveniently collected in *Oeuvres littéraires*, ed. Tulard (Paris 1968). Napoleon the writer is dealt with in N. Tomiche, *Napoléon Écrivain* (Paris 1952). Works on Rousseau which shed light on his influence on the young Napoleon include Carol Blum, *Jean-Jacques Rousseau and the Republic of Virtue* (Ithaca, NY, 1986) and D. Mornet, *Les sentiments de la Nature en France de J-J Rousseau à Bernardin de Saint-Pierre* (Paris 1907).

The complicated activities and travels of Napoleon's siblings are dealt with in Desmond Seward, *Napoleon's Family* (1986). The basic source for this and other such accounts (e.g. Theo Aronson, *The Story of the Bonapartes* (1967)) is F. Masson, *Napoléon et sa famille*, 13 vols (1897–1919). See also J. Valynseele, *Le Sang des Bonaparte* (Paris 1954); Hervé Pinoteau, *Vingt-cinq ans d'études dynastiques* (Paris 1982). For Louis there is F. Rocquain, *Napoléon I et le Roi Louis* (1875) and Labarre de Raillecourt, *Louis Bonaparte* (1963). Background on the Palais-Royal, where Napoleon had his first sexual encounter, is available in François de Saint-Paul, *Tableau du Nouveau Palais-Royal*, 2 vols (Paris 1788) and Robert Isherwood, *Farce and Fantasy: Popular Entertainment in Eighteenth-Century Paris* (Oxford 1986). The relationship with Ceracchi is dealt with in Hilaire Belloc, *Napoleon* (1932).

CHAPTER FOUR

The memoirs of Bourrienne and Joseph are useful for this period. *Napoleon's Memoirs*, ed. S. de Chair (1948), shed light on the complex activities in Corsica. Lucien Bonaparte's *Memoirs* (1836) denote the point at which Lucien became a significant figure in the story. On Lucien see also François Pietri, *Lucien Bonaparte* (1939); Napoleon's own testimony also appears in Tulard, *Œuvres littéraires*, op.cit. Vol.2

For the political situation in Corsica D. Perelli, *Lettres de Pascal Paoli*, 6 vols (Bastia 1889) is an obvious source. Paoli should also be studied in Peter Thrasher, *Pasquale Paoli, an Enlightened Hero, 1725–1807* (1970); Dominique Colonna, *Le Vrai Visage de Pascal Paoli en Angleterre* (Nice 1969) and René Emmannuelli, *Vie de Pascal Paoli* (Lumio 1978). On the tangled politics of Corsica see also L. Villat, *La Corse de 1768 à 1789* (Paris 1925); F.R.J. de Pommereul, *Histoire de l'Île de Corse*, 2 vols (Berne 1779); Jacques-Maurice Gaudin, *Voyage en Corse et vue politique sur l'amélioration de cette isle* (Marseilles 1978); Pierre Antonetti, *Histoire de la Corse* (Paris 1973); François Pomponi, *Histoire de la Corse* (Paris 1979); Jose Colombani, *Aux origines de la Corse française. Politique et institutions* (Ajaccio 1978); Antoine Casanova, *Peuple Corse, révolution et nation français* (Paris 1979). But two studies in particular stand out: Thad Hall, *France and the Eighteenth-Century Corsica Question* (NY 1971) and Jean Francesci, *La Corse française (30 novembre 1789–11 juin 1794*, (Paris 1980).

Napoleon's enemy Pozzo di Borgo has inspired a number of studies: P. McErlean, *The Formative Years of a Russian Diplomat* (1967); P. Jollivet, *Paoli, Napoleon, Pozzo di Borgo* (Paris 1892); P. Ordioni, *Pozzo di Borgo* (Paris 1935) and an outstanding article by Dorothy Carrington, 'Pozzo di Borgo et les Bonaparte', *Problèmes d'Histoire de la Corse* (1971) pp.101–129. The events at Easter 1792 are studied in F. Chailley-Pompei, 'Troubles de Pâques', *Problèmes d'Histoire de la Corse* (1971) pp.179–89. For the Maddalena affair see E.J. Peyrou, *L'Expédition de Sardaigne, Le Lieutenant Bonaparte à la Maddalena* (Paris 1912); G. Godlewski, 'Bonaparte et l'affaire de la Maddalena', *Revue de l'Institut Napoléon* (1964) pp.1–12 and M. Mirtil, *Napoléon d'Ajaccio* (Paris 1947).

For Paris in the turbulent year 1792 see R.B. Rose, *The Making of the Sans-culottes* (Manchester 1983). For Louis XVI consult John Hardmann, *Louis XVI* (1993). The best book for the dreadful day, 10 August 1792, is Marcel Reinhard, *10 Août 1792: La Chute de la Royauté* (Paris 1969). The coming of war that year is discussed in T.C.W. Blanning, *The Origins of the French Revolutionary Wars* (1986). Since the Army was to loom so large in Napoleon's life and there is debate about the continuity (or lack of it) between the revolutionary armies and Napoleon's *Grande Armée*, this may be the place to cite J. Bertaud, *The Army of the French Revolution: from Citizen Soldiers to Instrument of Power* (Princeton 1988). See also J. Lynn, 'Towards an Army of Honour: the moral evolution of the French Army, 1789–1815', *French Historical Studies* 16 (1989) pp.152–82.

The severe economic crisis that made '92 such a traumatic year is ably trawled through in Florin Aftalion, *L'Économie de la Révolution Française* (Paris 1987). The depreciating currency is the particular focus of S.E. Harris, *The Assignats* (Cambridge, Mass. 1930). A massive work which enables one to follow Parisian politics almost day by day is Fritz Baesch, *La Commune de Dix Août, 1792: Étude sur l'Histoire du Paris de 20 juin au 2 décembre 1792* (Paris 1911). A traveller's tale, enabling one to appreciate Paris exactly as it would have appeared to Napoleon is J. Moore, *A Journal during a residence in France* (1793).

Remarks on Napoleon's personality are scattered throughout the psychoanalytical literature, with Ernest Jones and Freud himself especially prominent. Jung's views on 'enantiodromia' can be found at CW. 7 pp.111–113.

CHAPTER FIVE

The siege of Toulon ushers in the most important source of all for Napoleon's life: *Correspondance de Napoléon 1*, 32 vols (Paris 1858–70). Other valuable primary sources are F.A. Doppet, *Mémoires* (Paris 1797); *Mémoires du maréchal Marmont, duc de Raguse, de 1792 à 1841*, 9 vols (Paris 1857); Claude-Victor Perrin, *Extraits des Mémoires Inédites de feu* (Paris 1846); J. Barrow, *The Life and Correspondence of Sir Sidney Smith* (1848). For Junot at Toulon see Marie-Joseph Emmanuel de las Cases, *Mémorial de Saint-Hélène ou journal où se trouve consigné . . . tout ce qu'a dit et fait Napoléon . . . du 20 juin 1815 au 25 novembre 1816*, ed. M. Dunan (Paris 1822).

For Toulon see also Paul Cottin, *Toulon et les Anglais* (Paris 1893); C.J. Fox, *Napoleon and the Siege of Toulon* (1902); D.J.M. du Teil, *L'École d'Artillerie d'Auxonne et le siege de Toulon* (Paris 1897). For the dithering commander-in-chief consult A. Chuquet, *Dugommier* (Paris 1904). The careers of those Napoleon met at Toulon can be followed in C.H. Barault-Roullon, *Le Maréchal Suchet, duc d'Albufuera* (Paris 1854); François Rousseau, *La Carrière du maréchal Suchet, duc d'Albufuera* (Paris 1898); R. Christophe, *Le maréchal Marmont, Duc de Raguse* (Paris 1968).

For Napoleon's life immediately before and after Toulon, as also the progress of his family see Paul Gaffarel, *Les Bonaparte à Marseille, 1793–1797* (Marseilles 1905); P. Masson, *Marseille et Napoléon* (Paris 1920); O. Lemoine, *Le Capitaine Bonaparte à Avignon* (1899); O. Connelly, *The Gentle Bonaparte; a Biography of Joseph, Napoleon's Elder Brother* (NY 1968). For Joseph's relations with the Clary family see F. Vérang, *La Famille Clary et Oscar II* (Marseilles 1893).

Napoleon's plans for operations in Italy are analysed in C. Camon, *La Première Manoeuvre de Napoléon* (Paris 1937) and L. Krebs & H. Moris, *Campagnes dans les Alpes pendant la Révolution 1792–1793* (Paris 1893). See also J. Godechot, *La Grande Nation* (Paris 1936). The political commissars are convincingly treated in H. Wallon, *Les Représentants du Peuple en Mission* (Paris 1899). Napoleon's private life is difficult to pin down at this period, but A. Thierry, 'Un amour inconnu de Napoléon', *Revue des Deux Mondes*, 15 November 1940, is useful.

Thermidor, the fall of Robespierre, and the consequences of both can be followed in Richard Bienvenu, *The Ninth of Thermidor; The Fall of Robespierre* (1968) and Gerard Walter, *La Conjuration du Neuf Thermidor* (Paris 1974). For Robespierre there is, additionally, J.M. Thompson, *Robespierre*, 2 vols (Oxford 1935); George Rudé, *Robespierre: Portrait of a Revolutionary Democrat* (1985); David Jordan, *The Revolutionary Career of Maximilien Robespierre* (N.Y. 1985) and Norman Hampson, *The Life and Opinions of Maximilien Robespierre* (1974). Carnot is a key figure in Napoleon's early life and is interestingly treated in Marcel Reinhard, *Le Grand Carnot*, 2 vols (Paris 1950–52).

CHAPTER SIX

By now the sources for Napoleon's life are becoming copious, not to say multitudinous. On Désirée alone there is Napoleon's own correspondence (e.g. *Correspondance* 42, 45, 47), the letters from the Swedish Royal Archives reproduced in Evangeline Bruce, *Napoleon and Josephine* (1995), the Abrantes memoirs and Napoleon's *Clissold et Eugénie* (in Tulard, ed. *Œuvres littéraires*, op. cit. ii. pp.440–53). The fundamental work for Désirée is Gabriel Girod del'Ain, *Désirée Clary d'après sa correspondance inédite avec Bonaparte, Bernadotte et sa famille* (Paris 1959).

For Napoleon in Paris in 1794–95 there is a wealth of memoir material. Apart from the memoirs of Joseph, Marmont, Victor, Bourrienne, Abrantes already cited there are: Victorine de Chastenay, *Mémoires* (Paris 1896); Paul Barras, *Memoires de Barras*, 3 vols (Paris 1895) – to be used with extreme care because of the violent anti-Bonaparte bias; G.J. Ouvrard, *Mémoires sur sa vie* (Paris 1826); Louis Amour Bouille, *Souvenirs pour servir aux mémoires de ma vie et mon temps* (Paris 1911); Chancelier Pasquier, *Mémoires*, 2 vols (Paris 1894); L.M. de La Révèlliere-Lépaux, *Mémoires* (Paris 1893) – almost as hostile as Barras. There are biographies, of varying worth, of most of the leading figures in the 'Chaumière' circle. Jacques Castelnau, *Madame Tallien* (Paris 1937); Princesse de Chimay, *Madame Tallien* (Paris 1936); Fernando Diaz-Plaja, *Térésa Carbarrus* (Barcelona 1943); André Gayot, *Fortunée Hamelin* (Paris n.d.); Françoise Wagener, *Madame Récamier* (Paris 1986).

The classic account of France after Thermidor is in Jules Michelet, *Histoire du XIX siècle* (Paris 1875). Some would also claim the title of 'classic' for the work of Georges Lefebvre, *Les Thermidoriens* (1937) and *Le Directoire* (1946). For the period 1794–96 consult also: A. Mathiez, *La Réaction thermidorienne* (Paris 1929); A. Meynier, *Les Coups d'Etat du Directoire* (Paris 1929); J. Godechot, *La Contre-Révolution* (Paris 1961). Some of the best recent works on this period are in English: Denis

Woronoff, *The Thermidorean Regime and the Directory 1794–1799* (1984); Martin Lyons, *France under the Directory* (1975); M.J. Syndenham, *The First French Republic 1792–1804* (1974). For 13 Vendémiaire see Henri Zivy, *Le 13 Vendémiaire An IV* (Paris 1898). Murat's crucial role is examined in A.H. Atteridge, *Joachim Murat, Marshal of France and King of Naples* (1911) and H. Cole, *The Betrayers: Joachim and Caroline Murat* (1972). See also Jean Tulard, *Murat* (Paris 1985).

The relationship with Josephine is central to an understanding of the flesh-and-blood Napoleon. There are many editions of Napoleon's letters to Josephine but the most scholarly is Jean Tulard, ed. *Napoléon: Lettres d'amour à Joséphine* (Paris 1981). Hortense de Beauharnais, *Mémoires de la reine Hortense, publiés par le prince Napoléon* (Paris 1928) is another essential primary source. There is a vast literature on Josephine, of which Evangeline Bruce (cited above) is the best in English. Other indicative titles are Louis Hastier, *Le Grand Amour de Joséphine* (Paris 1955); André Gavoty, *Les amoureux de l'impératrice Joséphine* (Paris 1961) and André Castelot, *Joséphine* (Paris 1964). Jung's remarks on the 'mother complex' are at CW. 9 i. pp.161–62.

Paul Barras is of prime importance to the story of both Napoleon and Josephine, but there is as yet no first-rate book on his life. J.P. Garnier, *Barras, roi du Directoire* (Paris 1970) is best supplemented by the Barras memoirs and the general histories of the Directory. On Kellermann and the Italian front see David Chandler, ed., *Napoleon's Marshals* (1987).

CHAPTER SEVEN

The first three volumes of Napoleon's *Correspondance* are fundamental for the years 1796–97. Other invaluable primary sources for the campaigns include M. Reinhard, *Avec Bonaparte en Italie d'après les lettres inédites de son aide de camp Joseph Sulkowski* (Paris 1946); J. B. Marbot, *The Memoirs of Baron Marbot* (1892); General Koch, ed. *Mémoires de Masséna*, 7 vols (Paris 1850).

The Italian campaign has been studied exhaustively, as in J. Colin, *Campagne de 1796–1797* (Paris 1898); C. von Clausewitz, *La campagne de 1796 en Italie*, trans J. Colin (Paris 1899); Gabriel Fabry, *La Campagne d'Italie*, 3 vols (Paris 1901); J. Thiry, *Napoléon en Italie* (1973). Napoleon's military debut is studied in Gabriel Defosse, *Montenotte, la première victoire de Napoléon, 12 avril 1796* (Paris 1986). The usual view of the Italian campaign is that it reveals Bonaparte's peerless military genius, but this view was strongly challenged in the iconoclastic book by Guglielmo Ferrero, *The Gamble* (1939).

The Austrian side of the story, including the campaigns on the Rhine can be followed in: S. Biro, *The German Policy of Revolutionary France 1792–1797* (Harvard 1957); Mallet du Pan, *Correspondance inédite avec la cour de Vienne, 1794–1798* (Paris 1884); G. Rothenberg, *Napoleon's Great Adversaries: the Archduke Charles and the Austrian Army, 1792–1814* (1982).

Biographies of the principal characters involved in the Italian campaign include G. Derrecagaix, *Le maréchal Berthier, Prince de Wagram et de Neuchâtel*, 2 vols (Paris 1905); Sydney J. Watson, *By Command of the Emperor: A Life of Marshal Berthier* (1957); Z. Zieseniss, *Berthier* (Paris 1985) Charles Thoumas, *Maréchal Lannes* (Paris 1891); Luc Wilette, *Le maréchal Lannes, un d'Artagnan sous l'Empire* (Paris 1979); André Laffargue, *Jean Lannes, maréchal de France* (Paris 1981); Édouard Gachot, *Histoire Militaire de Masséna*, 5 vols (Paris 1908); James Marshall-Cornwall, *Masséna* (Oxford 1965). Saliceti and Garrau are dealt with in J. Godechot, *Les Commissaires aux armées sous le Directoire*, 2 vols (Paris 1937). Henri Clarke comes to life in A. Dry, *Soldats Ambassadeurs sous le Directoire* (Paris 1906).

Bernadotte really merits an extended bibliography of his own. Surprisingly the best work on him has been done by British historians. Fundamental is Sir D.P. Barton's three volumes: *Bernadotte, the First Phase 1763–99* (1914); *Bernadotte and Napoleon 1799–1810* (1921) and *Bernadotte, Prince and King 1810–44* (1925). There is also Lord Russell, *Marshal of France and King of Sweden* (1981). The best modern biography is A. Palmer, *Bernadotte: Napoleon's Marshal, Sweden's King* (1990). Some idea of the Gascon windbaggery of the man can be got from the letters and dispatches collected in John Phlipart, *The Memoirs and Campaigns of Charles John, Prince Royal of Sweden* (1814).

The complex relationships between Napoleon, the Directory and their victims are laid out in R. Guyot, *Le Directoire et la Paix de l'Europe* (Paris 1911); P. Rain, *La Diplomatie Française de Mirabeau à Bonaparte* (Paris 1950); B. Nabonne, *La Diplomatie du Directoire et Bonaparte* (Paris 1952); E.Y. Hales, *Revolution and Papacy* (1960); G. MacLellan, *Venice and Bonaparte* (Princeton 1931); P.J.M. du Teil, *Rome, Naples et le Directoire* (Paris 1902).

Josephine's four months without Napoleon in March–July 1796 are covered in Antoine Arnault, *Souvenirs d'un sexagénaire* (Paris 1933). The milieux in the Serbelloni and Mombello palaces are well conveyed in Comte A.F. Miot de Melito, *Mémoires du Comte Miot de Melito*, 3 vols (Paris 1873). The Marmont memoirs are particularly good for the Milan period. See also the fragments of autobiography from Antoine Hamelin,

Douze ans de ma vie in *Revue de Paris*, November 1926, January 1927. Josephine's extended affair with Hippolyte Charles can be followed in Louis Hastier, *Le Grand Amour de Joséphine* (Paris 1955). See also André Gavoty, *Les Amoureux de l'impératrice Joséphine* (1961) and André Castelot, *Joséphine* (Paris 1964).

CHAPTER EIGHT

Napoleon's military genius is exhaustively analysed in David Chandler, *The Campaigns of Napoleon* (1966). This is highly laudatory and can usefully be contrasted with Owen Connelly, *Blundering to Glory. Napoleon's Military Campaigns* (Wilmington, Delaware 1987). On military strategy, tactics and technology there is a plethora of works: G. Rothenberg, *The Art of Warfare in the Age of Napoleon* (1977); M. Glover, *Warfare in the Age of Napoleon* (1980); R. Quimby, *The Background to Napoleonic Warfare* (N.Y. 1957); R. Johnson, *Napoleonic Armies: a Wargamer's Campaign Directory, 1805–1815* (1984); O. von Pivka, *Armies of the Napoleonic Era* (Newton Abbott 1979); G. Jeffrey, *Tactics and Grand Tactics of the Napoleonic Wars* (NY 1982).

On the looting in Italy Charles Saunier, *Les Conquêtes artistiques de la Révolution et de l'Empire* (Paris 1902) is useful, and even more so is F. Boyer, 'Les responsabilités de Napoléon dans le transfert à Paris des Œuvres d'art de l'étranger', *Revue d'Histoire moderne et contemporaine* (1964) pp.241–62. On Napoleon's plans for Italian confederation and unity see P. Gaffarel, *Bonaparte et les Républiques italiennes 1796–1799* (Paris 1895) and J. Godechot and G. Bourgin, *L'Italie et Napoléon* (Paris 1936). Godechot's article, 'Les Français et l'unité italienne sous le Directoire', *Revue Politique et constitutionelle* (1952) pp.96–110, 193–204 is particularly good on the knotty subject of whether Napoleon really intended Italian unification. Other monograph studies of central importance are E.Y. Hales, *Revolution and Papacy* (1960) and G. MacLellan, *Venice and Bonaparte* (Princeton 1931).

The struggle with the Directory is covered in Albert Sorel, *L'Europe et la Révolution française* (1903), Vol.5; R. Guyot, *Le Directoire et la paix de l'Europe, 1795–1799* (Paris 1911) and B. Nabonne, *La Diplomatie du Directoire et de Bonaparte* (Paris 1951). On the complex skein of events leading to Fructidor see Léonce Pingaud, *Le comte d'Antraigues* (Paris 1931); J. Godechot, *La Contre-Révolution* (Paris 1961); G. Caudrillier, *La Trahison de Pichegru et les Intrigues royalistes dans l'Est avant Fructidor* (Paris 1908); A. Meynier, *Les Coups d'État du Directoire. Vol. 1. le 18 Fructidor an V* (Paris 1928).

Talleyrand and Madame de Staël are important characters in Napoleon's story. Biographies of Talleyrand include Jean Orieux, *Talleyrand* (Paris 1970); G. Lacour-Gayet, *Talleyrand*, 4 vols (Paris 1934); A. Duff Cooper, *Talleyrand* (1932). These can be supplemented by his *Mémoires*, ed. de Broglie (1892) and the *Correspondance*, ed. Pallain (Paris 1891). To a large extent all existing biographies have been eclipsed by the exhaustive three-volume life by Michel Poniatowski, of which the relevant volume for these years is *Talleyrand et le Directoire* (Paris 1982). Germaine de Staël has also attracted biographers, as with Christopher J. Herold, *Mistress to an Age: A Life of Madame de Staël* (NY 1958); Henri Guillemin, *Madame de Staël, Benjamin Constant et Napoléon* (Paris 1959).

The continuing saga of Josephine is best followed in the works of the memoir writers, especially Abrantes, Rémusat, Miot de Melito, Marmont, Barras, Bourrienne and Antoine Arnault, *Mémoires d'un Sexagenaire* (Paris 1833). The classic work for Napoleon's invasion schemes is the multi-volume work by E. Desbrières, *Projets et Tentatives de débarquement aux Îles britanniques, 1793–1805* (Paris 1912). This can be supplemented on the British side by Norman Longmate, *Island Fortress. The Defence of Great Britain 1603–1945* (1991). Hoche is dealt with in Albert Sorel, *Bonaparte et Hoche en 1797* (Paris 1897). Hoche's one-time comrade Wolfe Tone has also attracted many biographies of which the most recent is Marianne Elliott, *Wolfe Tone* (1989).

CHAPTER NINE

Nobody can write about Napoleon's time in Egypt without consulting the massive study by C. de la Jonquière, *L'expédition de l'Égypte*, 5 vols (Paris 1900–1907). Indispensable too is Jean-Joël Bregeon, *L'Égypte française au jour le jour, 1798–1801* (Paris 1991). The Egyptian adventure is so compelling by its mixture of the rational and the irrational that it has always been a favourite subject for historians. So, among a host of volumes one might mention Jean Thiry, *Bonaparte en Egypte* (Paris 1973); J.C. Herold, *Bonaparte in Egypt* (1963); Michael Barthorp, *Napoleon's Egyptian Campaigns, 1798–1801* (1978); J. Bainville, *Bonaparte en Egypte* (Paris 1936); F. Charles-Roux, *Bonaparte: Governor of Egypt* (1937).

On Napoleon's 'Oriental complex' the following are indispensable: Jacques Benoist-Mechin, *Bonaparte en Egypte et le rêve inassouvi* (Paris 1966); G. Spillman, *Napoléon et l'Islam* (1969); Henri d'Estre, *Bonaparte, le mirage oriental, L'Egypte* (Paris 1946); Pierre Vendryes, *De la probabilité en histoire, l'exemple de l'expédition d'Égypte* (Paris 1952); also the classic study by Émile Bourgeois in *Manuel de politique etrangère*, vol. 2 (Paris

1898). On the other hand, F. Charles-Roux, *Les Origines de l'expédition d'Égypte* (Paris 1910) is a good summary of the 'rational' motives for the expedition.

Of the many offshoots and implications of Egypt in 1798–99 the Tippoo Sahib issue is best followed in Joseph-François Michaud, *Histoire de Mysore sous Hyder-Ali et Tippoo Sahib* (Paris 1899); L.B. Bowring, *Haidar Ali and Tipu Sultan* (1899) and the article by Saint-Yves, 'La Chute de Tippo', *Revue des Questions historiques* (1910). For the life of Desaix see A. Sauzet, *Le Sultan juste* (Paris 1954). This should be supplemented with Desaix's own *Journal de Voyage*, ed. Chuquet (Paris 1907) There is a fascinating discussion of Desaix's adventures in Upper Egypt in Alan Moorehead, *The Blue Nile* (1962). Kléber receives detailed treatment in Lucas-Dubreton (1937) and G. Lecomte, *Au chant de la Marseillaise . . . Merceau et Kléber* (Paris 1929) His 'Carnets' were printed in *La Revue d'Egypte* (1895). Pauline Fourès's story is told in Léonce Deschamp, *Pauline Fourès, Notre Dame de L'Orient* (Paris n.d.). For another significant personality from Napoleon's Egyptian period see E. d'Hauterive, *Le General Alexandre Dumas* (Paris 1897) and André Maurois, *Les trois Dumas* (Paris 1957). For the aftermath consult Robert Anderson & Ibrahim Fawzy, *Egypt in 1800* (1987).

For the naval side of 1798 there is Tom Pocock, *Nelson* (1988) and Oliver Warner, *The Battle of the Nile* (1960). R. Cavaliero sums up Malta usefully in *The Last of the Crusaders: the Knights of St John and Malta in the 18th Century* (1960) but the indispensable modern scholarly study is Desmond Gregory, *Malta, Britain and the European Powers, 1793–1815* (1996) For the wider context of the Egyptian adventure see Thomas Pakenham, *The Year of Liberty* (1969); John Ehrman, *The Younger Pitt: The Consuming Struggle* (1996) and Piers Mackesy, *War without Victory: the downfall of Pitt, 1799–1802* (1984). For the Turkish side of things consult W. Johnson & C. Bell, *The Ottoman Empire and the Napoleonic Wars* (Leeds 1988) and S. Shaw, *Between Old and New; the Ottoman Empire under Sultan Selim III, 1789–1807* (Cambridge, Mass. 1971).

On the wider cultural implications of the Egyptian adventure see Peter Clayton, *The Rediscovery of Egypt* (1982); James S. Curl, *The Egyptian Revival* (1982); Ibrahim Ghali, *Vivant Denon, ou la conquête du bonheur* (Cairo 1986); Pierre Lelièvre, *Vivant Denon* (Paris 1993); J.M. Humbert, M. Pantazzi, C. Ziegler, eds, *Egyptomania. Egypt in Western Art, 1730–1930* (Ottawa 1994).

There is a positive cascade of memoir literature relating to Egypt. R.N. Desgenettes, *Souvenirs d'un médecin de l'expédition d'Égypte* (Paris 1893) the memoirs of Napoleon's 'difficult' head of the medical corps – is clearly of the first importance. Another first-rate source is François Bernoyer, *Avec Bonaparte en Egypte et Syrie, 19 lettres inédites*, ed. Tortel (Paris 1976). Among the other 'first-division' memoirs are J.B.P. Jollois, *Journal d'un ingénieur attaché a l'expédition française, 1798–1802*, ed. Lefèvre-Pontalis (Paris 1904); Geoffroy Saint-Hilaire, *Lettres écrites d'Egypte* (Paris 1901); Alexandre Berthier, *Relation des campagnes du général Bonaparte en Egypte et en Syrie* (Paris 1901); Vivant Denon, *Voyage dans la Basse et la Haute-Egypte* (Paris 1802). But such a list, while containing the really important sources, barely scratches the surface of the embarrassment of riches provided by the memoir literature for this period; clearly it was not just Napoleon who was bedazzled by the lure of the Orient.

CHAPTER TEN

Albert Vandal's *L'Avènement de Bonaparte* (Paris 1907) is the classic study of 18 Brumaire. Other studies can only dot the 'i's and cross the 't's. So, for example, Jacques Bainville, *Le dix-huit Brumaire* (Paris 1925), A. Ollivier, *Le dix-huit Brumaire* (Paris 1959), Gustave Bord and Louis Bigard, *La Maison du dix-huit Brumaire* (Paris 1930) and D.J. Goodspeed, *Bayonets at Saint-Cloud* (NY 1965). The most recent account is J.P. Bertaud, *Le Dix-Huit Brumaire* (Paris 1987). For the technical legality of the coup F. Pietri, *Napoléon et le Parlement* (1955) is particularly valuable. On the issue of continuity and change there is L. Sciout, *Le Directoire* (Paris 1897); M. Reinhard, *La France du Directoire* (Paris 1956); A. Soboul, *Le Directoire et le Consulat* (Paris 1967); D. Woronoff, *La République bourgeoise* (Paris 1972). For the key element of propaganda see R. Holtman, *Napoleonic Propaganda* (Baton Rouge 1950). For military aspects of the decline and fall of the Directory consult Steven T. Ross, *Quest for Victory: French Military Strategy 1792–1799* (Cranbury, N.J. 1973).

As is to be expected, memoir literature is particularly valuable for 18 Brumaire. Apart from Bourrienne's, the evidence of Jérôme Gohier, *Mémoires* (Paris 1824), Pierre-Louis Roederer, *Journal*, ed. Vitrac (Paris 1909) and A.C. Thibaudeau, *Mémoires sur le consulat et l'empire de 1799 à 1815* (Paris 1827) and *Mémoires* (Paris 1913) are salient. Joseph Fouché, *Mémoires* ed. L. Madelin (Paris 1945) is as unreliable as one would expect from that prince of liars.

Biographical detail is particularly important for the host of personalities jostling for power and position at this conjuncture. Jean-Denis Brédin, *Sieyès, la clé de la Révolution française* (1988) is the latest on the man who played Volpone to Napoleon's Mosca. P. Bastid, *Sieyès et sa pensée* (Paris 1939) concentrates on his role as constitution maker. See also R. Marquant, *Les Archives Sieyès* (Paris 1970). For Lucien, in addition to works already cited, F. Pietri, *Lucien Bonaparte* (Paris 1939) is particularly good for his role on 19 Brumaire. Cambacérès has attracted a lot of interest: there is comte de Lamothe-Vangon, *Les après-diners de Cambacérès* (Paris 1946); François Papillard, *Cambacérès* (Paris 1991); Richard Boulind, *Cambacérès and the Bonapartes* (1976); P. Vialles, *L'Archichancelier Cambacérès d'après des documents inédits* (1908). Stefan Zweig, *Fouché* (1930) is the most probing psychological study of the loathsome chief of police, on whose activities further light is shed in L. Madelin, *Fouché* Paris 1901), Jean Rigotard, *La police parisienne de Napoléon* (Paris 1990) and E.A. Arnold, *Fouché, Napoleon and the General Police* (Washington DC, 1979).

The important women of this period are dealt with in Michel Lacou-Gayet, *Marie-Caroline reine de Naples, une adversaire de Napoléon* (Paris 1990) and Henri Guillemin, *Madame de Staël, Benjamin Constant et Napoléon* (Paris 1959). For women in general see Jean Tulard, *La vie quotidienne des Français sous Napoléon* (Paris 1978); Linda Kelly, *Women of the French Revolution* (1987). For the Jacobins see X. Biagard, *Le Comte Réal, ancien Jacobin* (Paris 1937) and I. Woloch, *Jacobin Legacy: The Democratic Movement under the Directory* (Princeton 1970).

The overthrow of the Directory raises the thorny question of the entire relationship of Napoleon to the men of Thermidor and to the French Revolution in general. Although this subject is briefly mentioned in the main text of the next chapter, it will be convenient to provide here the most relevant titles for this never-ending debate. So: Joe H. Kirchberger, *The French Revolution and Napoleon* (1989); Stephen Pratt, *The French Revolution and Napoleon* (1992); John Brooman, *Revolution in France, the Era of the French Revolution and Napoleon, 1789–1815* (1992); Martyn Lyons, *Napoleon Bonaparte and the Legacy of the French Revolution* (1994); Owen Connolly, *The French Revolution and Napoleon Era* (Fort Worth, Texas 1991); R. Holtman, *The Napoleonic Revolution* (Philadelphia 1967), L. Bergeron, *France under Napoleon* (Princeton 1981).

CHAPTER ELEVEN

For the military campaign of 1800 see Jean Tranie, *La Deuxième Campagne d'Italie, 1800* (Paris 1991). G.M.J.R. Cugnac, *Campagne de l'armée de Réserve en 1800*, 2 vols (Paris 1901); Édouard Driault, *Napoléon en Italie* (Paris 1906); Édouard Gachot, *La Deuxième Campagne d'Italie*

(Paris 1899) and E. Gachot, *Le Siège de Gênes* (Paris 1908); André Fugier, *Napoléon et l'Italie* (Paris 1947); R.G. Burton, *Napoleon's Campaigns in Italy* (1912). For particular aspects of the Marengo campaign see H. de Clairval, *Daumesnil* (Paris 1970) and David Chandler, 'To lie like a bulletin: an examination of Napoleon's rewriting of the history of the battle of Marengo', *Proceedings of the Annual Meeting of the Western Society for French History* 18 (1991) pp.33–43. For the war on the Rhine front see Jean Picard, *Hohenlinden* (Paris 1909) and for the last days in Egypt consult François Rousseau, *Kléber et Menou en Égypte* (Paris 1900) More generally A.B. Rodger, *The War of the Second Coalition, 1798 to 1801* (N.Y. 1961) sets the context.

There is a wealth of material on foreign policy and Napoleon's diplomatic aims. Albert Sorel's monumental multivolume *L'Europe et la Révolution française*, of which the relevant volume is VI (Paris 1903), is fundamental. Also important are Édouard Driault, *Napoléon et l'Europe*, again a multivolume monument, of which Vol.ii (Paris 1912) is the relevant one for these years. Later works include André Fugier, *La Révolution française et l'Empire napoléonien* (Paris 1954).

Fully to understand foreign policy in the Napoleonic period one needs a detailed knowledge of his opponents. So, in this case, Austria is best studied through a general history like C. Ingrao, *The Hapsburg Monarchy, 1618–1815* (Cambridge 1994). More general context is provided by R.A. Kann, *A History of the Hapsburg Empire, 1526–1918* (LA 1974); V. Tapié, *The Rise and Fall of the Hapsburg Monarchy* (1971) and C.A. Macartney, *The Hapsburg Empire, 1790–1918* (1969). The best study from the English viewpoint is Piers Mackesy, *War without Victory; the Downfall of Pitt, 1799–1802* (Oxford 1984). See also J.H. Rose, *William Pitt and the Great War* (1911).

Biographical studies once again prove their worth in this period. K. Roider, *Baron Thugut and Austria's Response to the French Revolution* (Princeton 1987) reveals the intransigence of Thugut. For Pitt there are the volumes by Ehrmann, for Addington there is Philip Ziegler, *A Life of Henry Addington, First Viscount Sidmouth* (1965) and for Grenville P. Jupp, *Lord Grenville, 1759–1834* (Oxford 1985). The key figure in 1800–1801 was Czar Paul I, so we are fortunate to have a number of articles by H. Ragsdale: 'A Continental System in 1801: Paul I and Bonaparte', *Journal of Modern History* 42 (1970) pp.70–89; 'Russian influence at Lunéville', *French Historical Studies* 5 (1968) pp.274–84; 'The case of Paul I: an approach to psycho-biography', *Consortium on Revolutionary Europe Proceedings* 1989 pp.617–24. See also the volume by H. Ragsdale, ed., *Paul I. A Reassessment of his Life and Reign* (Pittsburgh

1979). The most recent discussion is R. McGrew, *Paul I of Russia, 1754–1801* (Oxford 1992).

There is an ongoing (never-ending?) debate about the responsibility for the renewal of war. A. Lévy, *Napoléon et la Paix* (Paris 1902), P. Cassagnac, *Napoléon pacifiste* (Paris 1932) and J. Deschamps, 'La rupture de la paix d'Amiens', *Revue des Études napoléoniennes* (1939) pp.172–207 sum up the (surely incontestable) short-term case in Napoleon's favour. P. Coquelle, *Napoléon et l'Angleterre, 1803–1813* (Paris 1904) puts the hostile case. The key figure in diplomacy is Talleyrand, for whom see (apart from the works already cited) Louis Greenbaum, *Talleyrand, Statesman, Priest, the Agent-General of the Clergy* (1970); Michel Poniatowski, *Talleyrand aux États Unis* (Paris 1967); L. Noel, *Talleyrand* (1975), M. Misoffe, *Le Coeur Secret de Talleyrand*. On his systematic duplicity see E. Dard, *Napoléon et Talleyrand* (Paris 1937); L. Madelin, *Talleyrand* (Paris 1944) and the exhaustive four-volume study by G. Lacour-Gayet, *Talleyrand* (Paris 1934).

For the global context of Napoleon's wars see A. Harvey, *Collision of Empire: Britain in Three World Wars* (1992) and P. Fregosi, *Dreams of Empire: Napoleon and the First World War, 1792–1815* (1989) Colonial affairs are dealt with in G. Hardy, *Histoire de la Colonisation française* (Paris 1943); J. Saintoyant, *La Colonisation française pendant la période napoléonienne* (Paris 1931). The fascininating events in Haiti are dealt with by C.L.R. James, *The Black Jacobins* (1949), Hubert Cole, *Christophe, King of Haiti* (1967); Robert Cornevin, *Haiti* (Paris 1982); Martin Ross, *The Black Napoleon and the Battle for Haiti* (1994) and Antoine Métral, *Histoire de l'expédition des Français à Saint-Domingue sous le consulat de Napoléon Bonaparte* (Paris 1985). On Louisiana consult Michael Garnier, *Bonaparte et la Louisiane* (Paris 1992); E. Wilson-Lyon, *Louisiana in French Diplomacy* (1934); I. Murat, *Napoléon et le Rêve américain* (Paris 1976) and Villiers du Terrage, *Les Dernières Années de la Louisiana française* (Paris 1904). A general overview of Napoleon's policy in the Americas is provided by Jacques Godechot, *L'Europe et l'Amérique a l'époque napoléonienne* (Paris 1967) and Alexander de Condé, *The Quasi-War: the Politics and Diplomacy of the Undeclared War with France, 1797–1801* (NY 1966). Jefferson's role in the Louisiana purchase can be followed in Dumas Malone, *Jefferson the President. The First Term 1801–1805* (Boston 1970) and Alexander de Condé, *This Affair of Louisiana* (NY 1976).

CHAPTER TWELVE

For Napoleon's domestic reforms in the years 1800–04 memoir literature constitutes an essential source. Apart from the works already cited by Miot, Roederer and Thibaudeau, the following are essential: Baron Despatys, *Un ami de Fouché d'après les Mémoires de Gaillard* (Paris 1911); Martin Gaudin, *Mémoires* (Paris 1826); Mathienu Molé, *Souvenirs d'un témoin 1791–1803* (Geneva 1943); Pierre-François Réal, *Mémoires*, ed. Musnier-Desclozeaux (Paris 1835).

For internal order and pacification the following are useful: Émile Gaboury, *Les Guerres de Vendée* (Paris 1989); Philippe Roussel, *De Cadoudal à Frotté* (Paris 1962); G. Lewis, *The Second Vendée* (Oxford 1978); Richard Cobb, *The Police and the People: French Popular Protest, 1789–1820* (Oxford 1970). See also Clive Emsley, 'Policing the streets of early nineteenth-century Paris', *French History* I (1987) pp.257–82; E. Daudet, *La Police et les Chouans* (Paris 1895).

Plots against Napoleon were legion in this period and have spanned a huge number of books and articles. Indicative titles are H. Gaubert, *Conspirateurs au temps de Napoléon I* (Paris 1962); L. de Villefosse and J. Bouissounouse, *L'Opposition à Napoléon* (Paris 1969) (both general overviews); G. Hue, *Un complot de police sous le Consulat* (Paris 1909) (on the 'dagger' plot); E. Guillon, *Les Complots militaires* (Paris 1894); G. Augustin-Thierry, *La mystérieuse affaire Donnadieu* (Paris 1909); C. Rinn, *Un mystérieux enlèvement*; Ernest d'Hauterive, *L'Enlèvement du Sénateur Clément de Ris* (Paris 1926). For the royalists see L. Pinguad, *Le Comte d'Antraigues* (Paris 1894); G. Penotre, *L'Affaire Perlet* (Paris 1923); T.H.A. Reiset, *Autour des Bourbons* (Paris 1927); E. d'Hauterive, *Figaro policier* (1928) and *La Contre-Police royaliste en 1800* (Paris 1931); J. Vidalenc, *Les Émigrés français* (Paris 1963) and René Castries, *La Vie quotidienne des Émigrés* (Paris 1966).

The various Jacobin and royalist plots, some extraordinarily violent in intent, have spawned a wealth of journal articles, notably the following: J. Gaffard, 'L'opposition républicaine sous le Consulat', *Revue française* (1887) pp.53–50; Frédéric Masson, 'Les complots jacobins au lendemain de Brumaire', *Revue des Études napoléoniennes* (1922) pp.5–28; Masson, 'La contre-police de Cadoudal', *Revue des Études napoléoniennes* (1923) pp.97–112.

From a vast bibliography on the Concordat the following may be selected: V. Bindel, *Histoire réligieuse de Napoléon* (Paris 1940); A. Latreille, *L'Église catholique et la Révolution française* (Paris 1950); Jean Leflon, *La Crise révolutionnaire* (1949); S. Delacroix, *La Réorganisation de l'Église de France après la Rèvolution* (Paris 1962); Boulay de la Meurthêe, *Histoire de la Négotiation du Concordat* (Paris 1920); Owen Chadwick, *The Popes and European Revolution* (Oxford 1981); Margaret O'Dwyer, *The Papacy in the Age of Napoleon and the Restoration* (1985). For Pius VII see Ludwig Pastor, *History of the Popes* (1949).

For economic policy M. Marion, *Histoire finançière de la France depuis 1715* (Paris 1925) is the fundamental work. Further detail is provided by René Stourm, *Les Finances du Consulat* (Paris 1902); R. Bigo, *La caisse d'escompte et les débuts de la Banque de France* (Paris 1929). The central biography here is Fr.La Tour, *Le Grand argentier de Napoléon, Gaudin, duc de Gaète* (Paris 1962). Two recent works are valuable: Louis Bergeron, *Banquiers, négociants et manufacturiers parisiens du Directoire à l'Empire* (Mouton 1978) and G. Thuillier, *La Monnaie en France au début du 19e siècle* (Paris 1983).

The opposition to Napoleon in the legislature can be traced in A. Gobert, *L'Opposition des assemblées pendant le Consulat, 1800–1804* (Paris 1925); F. Pietri, *Napoléon et le Parlement* (Paris 1955); C. Durand, *L'Exercise de la fonction législative de 1800 à 1814* (Paris 1956); L. de Villesfosse and J. Bouissounouse, *L'Opposition à Napoléon* (Paris 1969); J. Vidalenc, 'L'Opposition sous le Consulat et L'Empire', *Annales Historiques de la Révolution française* (1968) pp.472–88; A. Guillois, *Le Salon de Mme Helvétius, Cabanis et les Idéologues* (Paris 1894); Irene Collins, *Napoleon and his Parliaments* (1979).

On the Code Napoléon consult P. Sganac, *La Législation civile de la Révolution française* (Paris 1898); André-Jean Arnaud, *Les Origines doctrinaires du Code Civil* (1969); R. Martinage-Baranger, *Bourjon et le Code Civil* (Paris 1971); R. Savatier, *Bonaparte et le Code Civil* (Paris 1927); R. Garaud, *La Révolution française et la famille* (Paris 1978).

Napoleon's centralized administration has spawned a plethora of studies. In a crowded field one might point to A. Edmond-Blanc, *Napoléon Ier. Ses institutions civiles et administratives* (Paris 1880); J. Savant, *Le Préfets de Napoléon* (Paris 1958); C. Durand, *Quelques aspects de l'administration préfectorale sous le Consulat et de l'Empire* (Paris 1962); Noel Whitcomb, 'Napoleon's Prefects', *American Historical Review* 79 ii. (1974) pp.1089–1118; Jean Tulard, *Paris et son administration* (Paris 1976).

For the notables see L. Bergeron and G. Chussinard Nogaret, *Les 'masses de granit'. Cent mille notables du Premier Empire* (Paris 1979); Jean Tulard, *Napoléon et la noblesse de l'Empire* (Paris 1986); L. Bergeron and G. Chaussinard-Nogaret, *Grands Notables du Premier Empire* (Paris 1978); R. Forster, 'The French Revolution and the "new" elite, 1800–1848', *The American and European Revolutions Reconsidered 1776–1848* (Iowa 1980).

For the related subject of 'national property' see M. Marion, *La Vente des Biens nationaux pendant la Révolution* (Paris 1908) and J.C. Perrot and S.J. Woolf, *State and Statistics in France 1789–1815* (1984).

CHAPTER THIRTEEN

For tourist impressions of France during the peace years there is a considerable literature, as for example: Henry Redhead Yorke, *Paris et la France sous le Consulat* (Paris 1921); Bertie G. Greathead, *An Englishman in Paris, 1803* (1953); Auguste Kotzebue, *Souvenirs de Paris en 1804*, 2 vols (Paris 1805); Mary Berry, *Voyages de Miss Berry à Paris, 1782–1836*, traduits par Mme la Duchesse de Broglie (Paris 1905); Countess Bessborough, *Letters to Lord Gower*, ed. Castalia Granville (1917); J.F. Reichardt, *Un hiver à Paris sous le Consulat* (Paris 1896); Elizabeth Mavor, *The Grand Tours of Katherine Wilmot: France 1801–03* and Russia *1805–07* (1992) John B. Trotter, *Memoirs of the latter years of C.J. Fox* (1811); Dawson Warren, *The Journal of a British Chaplain in Paris* (1913). An overview is provided in J.G. Alger, *Napoleon's British Visitors and Captives* (1904).

The outbreak of war in 1803 has already been touched on in the bibliography for Chapter Eleven. The titles mentioned there may be supplemented by O. Browning, *England and Napoleon in 1803* (1887); H.C. Deutsch, *The Genesis of Napoleonic Imperialism* (Cambridge, Mass. 1938); P.W. Schroeder, 'Napoleon's foreign policy: a criminal enterprise', *Consortium on Revolutionary Europe Proceedings* (1989). Pieter Geyl's classic *Napoleon: For and Against* has the outbreak of war in 1803 as its core theme. Not to be discounted is the anger Napoleon felt about his scurrilous portrayal in the British press, a subject dealt with in: D. George, *English Political Caricatures* (Oxford 1959) and F.J. McCunn, *The Contemporary English View of Napoleon* (1914).

This is the place to add further titles to the introductory volumes already cited on Napoleon's siblings. So: M. Weiner, *The Parvenue Princesses: Élisa, Pauline and Caroline Bonaparte* (1964); P. Marmottan, *Élisa Bonaparte* (Paris 1898); J. Turquan, *Caroline Murat* (Paris 1899); J. Bertaut, *Le Ménage Murat* (Paris 1958); M. Gobineau, *Pauline Borghese, soeur fidèle* (Paris 1958); B. Nabonne, *La Vénus imperiale* (Paris 1963); Paul Fleuriot de Langles, *Élisa, soeur de Napoléon I* (Paris 1947); Bernadine Melchior Bonnet, *Jérôme Bonaparte ou l'envers de l'épopée* (Paris 1979); M.A. Fabre, *Jérôme Bonaparte, roi de Westphalie* (Paris 1952); J. Bertaut, *Le Roi Jérôme* (Paris 1954); G. Girod de l'Ain, *Joseph Bonaparte, le roi malgré lui* (Paris 1970); Owen Connolly, *The Gentle*

Bonaparte; a Biography of Joseph, Napoleon's Elder Brother (NY 1968); M. Ross, *The Reluctant King: Joseph Bonaparte, King of the Two Sicilies and Spain* (1976); B. Nabonne, *Le Roi Philosophe* (1949), Paul. Marmottan, *Joseph Bonaparte à Mortefontaine* (Paris 1929); F. Rocquain, *Napoléon I et le Roi Louis* (Paris 1875); Labarre de Raillecourt, *Louis Bonaparte* (Paris 1963); Hubert Cole, *The Betrayers; Joachim and Caroline Murat* (1972); Jean Tulard, *Murat* (Paris 1985); Marcel Dupont, *Murat, cavalier, maréchal de France, prince et roi* (Paris 1980); J.P. Garnier, *Murat, roi de Naples* (Paris, 1959).

The principal source for the anecdotes illustrating Napoleon's personality is the memoir literature. See especially the splendid 'dual memoir', incorporating both Constant's and Méneval's accounts, published as Proctor Paterson Jones, ed. *Napoleon: An Intimate Account of the Years of Supremacy 1800–1814* (San Francisco 1992). Frédéric Masson, *Napoléon chez lui* (Paris 1911) is the classic summary. More probing and psychological accounts of Napoleon's personality are to be found in Jean Raymond Frugier, *Napoléon, essai médico-psychologique* (Paris 1985) and Frank Richardson, *Napoleon: Bisexual Emperor* (1977). Since many of Napoleon's psychological quirks are held by some to be explicable in purely organic terms, reference should be made to his medical history and the career of his doctor Jean Corvisart. So: P. Hillemand, *Pathologie de Napoléon* (Paris 1970); J. Kemble, *Napoléon Immortal* (1959); J. Bourguignon, *Corvisart* (Lyons 1937); P. Ganière, *Corvisart* (Paris 1951).

For Napoleon's superstitions see G. Mauguin, *Napoléon et la Superstition* (Rodez 1946). For the 'Red Man' see Sir Walter Scott, *Napoleon* (1827) and *Paul's Letters to his kinsfolk* (1816). On the question of his 'Italian' nature see Jones to Freud, 30 October 1912 in R. Andrew Paskauskas, ed. *The Complete Correspondence of Sigmund Freud and Ernest Jones 1908–1939* (Harvard 1993). For the views of Thiers and Quinet on the essential Italian formation of Napoleon see Adolphe Thiers, *Histoire du Consulat et de l'Empire* (Paris 1862) and Edgar Quinet, *La Révolution* (Paris 1965).

CHAPTER FOURTEEN

The best study of the d'Enghien affair is by Maurice Shumann, *Qui a tué le duc d'Enghien?* (Paris 1984). Yet many excellent books have been written on the subject: Jean-Paul Bertaud, *Bonaparte et le duc d'Enghien* (Paris 1972); Marco de Saint-Hilaire, ed. Poniatowski, *Cadoudal, Moreau et Pichegru* (Paris 1977) and J.F. Chiappe, *Cadoudal et la Liberté* (Paris 1971). But there are so many angles to this *cause célèbre* that the books can be usefully supplemented by a number of journal articles: J. Dontenville, 'La Catastrophe du duc d'Enghien', *Revue des Études napoléoniennes* (1925) pp.43–69; G. Caudrillier, 'Le Complot de l'an XII', *Revue Historique* 73 (1900) pp.278–86; 74 (1901) pp.257–85; 75 (1902) pp.45–71; J. Durieux, 'L'arrestation de Cadoudal de la Legion d'honneur', *Revue des Études napoléoniennes* (1919) pp.237–43. Other useful contributions to a still only partially solved mystery are: A. Maricourt, *La Mort du duc d'Enghien* (Paris 1931); J. Picard, *Bonaparte et Moreau* (Paris 1905); F. Barbey, *La mort de Pichegru* (Paris 1909); M. Dupont, *Le Tragique Destin du duc d'Enghien* (Paris 1938); H. Lachouque, *Cadoudal et les Chouans* (Paris 1952); B. Melchior-Bonnet, *Le duc d'Enghien* (Paris 1954).

Two interesting articles chart the passage from consulate to empire: P. Sagnac, 'L'avènement de Bonaparte à l'Empire', *Revue des Études napoléoniennes* (1925) pp.133–54 and 193–211 and G. Mauguin, 'Le plébiscite pour l'hérédité impériale en l'an XII', *Revue de l'Institut Napoléon* (1939) p.5–16. For the year 1804 the memoirs by Hortense and Roederer are especially revealing. The coronation itself is dealt with in Frédéric Masson, *Le Sacre et le Couronnement de Napoléon* (Paris 1925); José Cabanis, *Le Sacre de Napoléon* (Paris 1970) and Henri Gaubert, *Le Sacre de Napoléon I* (Paris 1964).

Eugène de Beauharnais becomes a significant figure around this time. His career can be followed in: Arthur Levy, *Napoléon et Eugène de Beauharnais* (Paris 1926); Carola Oman, *Napoleon's Viceroy: Eugène de Beauharnais* (1966); F. de Bernardy, *Eugène de Beauharnais* (Paris 1973); Jean Hanoteau, *Le Ménage Beauharnais* (Paris 1935). The contrast between the able Eugène and the useless 'Benjamin' Jérôme Bonaparte is one that constantly impresses the student, and there is a vivid account of Jérôme's spinelessness in S. Mitchell, *A Family Lawsuit: The Romantic Story of Elizabeth Patterson and Jérôme Bonaparte* (NY 1958).

Napoleon's marshals have spawned an industry all of its own. Apart from Chandler's edited volume *Napoleon's Marshals* (1987) already cited, there are L. Chardigny, *Les maréchaux de Napoléon* (Paris 1977) (concentrating on social origins); J. Valynseele, *Les maréchaux du Premier Empire, leur famille et leur descendance* (Paris 1957) (for the genealogy of the marshalate); George Six, *Les Généraux de la Révolution et de l'Empire* (Paris (1947); E.F. Delderfield, *The March of the Twenty-Six* (1962) and A. MacDonell, *Napoleon and his Marshals* (1934). For individual marshals see (in addition to the titles cited in the bibliography for Chapter Seven): John G. Gallagher, *The Iron Marshal: A Biography of Louis N. Davout* (Carbondale, Ill. 1976); H.F.G.L. Hourtoulle, *Davout le terrible* (Paris 1975); John T. Foster, *Napoleon's Marshal: the Life of Michel Ney* (N.Y.

1968); John B. Morton, *Marshal Ney* (N.Y. 1958); H. Bonnal, *La vie militaire du Maréchal Ney*, 3 vols (Paris 1914); S. de Saint-Exupéry & C. de Tourtier, *Les Archives du Maréchal Ney* (Paris 1962); L. Morel, *Le Maréchal Mortier* (Paris 1957); P. Saint-Marc, *Le Maréchal Marmont* (Paris 1957); R. Christophe, *Le Maréchal Marmont* (Paris 1968); R. Lehmann, *Augereau* (Paris 1945).

The Imperial Guard is an important subject to which the best guide is Henri Lachouque and Anne S.K. Brown, *The Anatomy of Glory: Napoleon and his Guard* (1961). Its relation to the Grande Armée in general is explored in J.R. Elting, *Swords around a Throne: Napoleon's Grande Armée* (NY 1988); Georges Blond, *La Grande Armée* (Paris 1979); H.C.B. Rogers, *Napoleon's Army* (1974) and J. Bertaud, *The Army of the French Revolution: from Citizen Soldiers to Instrument of Power* (Princeton 1988).

For Napoleon's new nobility memoir literature is important, especially Chancelier Pasquier, *Mémoires*, 2 vols (Paris 1894); Louis de Caulaincourt, Duc de Vicence, *Mémoires* (Paris 1933); Mathien Molé, *Souvenirs d'un témoin 1791–1803* (Geneva 1943); Victor, duc de Broglie, *Souvenirs 1785–1870* (Paris 1886); Baron de Frenilly, *Souvenirs du Baron de Frenilly* (Paris 1909) and the already cited memoirs of Roederer and Miot de Melito. Important secondary works include E. Pierson, *Étude de la noblesse de l'Empire crée par Napoleon 1er* (Paris 1910); Émile Campardon, *Liste des membres de la noblesse impériale dressée d'après les régistres de lettres patentes conservées aux Archives nationales* (Paris 1889); Jean Tulard, ed. *Armorial du Premier Empire* (Paris 1974); Labarre de Raillecourt, *Armorial des Cent Jours* (Paris 1961); J. Valynseele, *Les Princes et Ducs du Premier Empire non maréchaux, leur famille et leur descendance* (Paris 1959).

The benefices, *sénatoreries* and *majorats* of the new nobility are best approached through a series of articles in learned journals. E.L'Hommède, 'Les sénatoreries', *Revue des études historiques* (1933) pp.19–40; M. Reinhard, 'Élite et noblesse', *Revue d'Histoire moderne et contemporaine* (1956) pp.1–37; M. Bruguière, 'Finance et noblesse, l'entrée des financiers dans la noblesse d'Empire', *Revue d'Histoire Moderne* (1970) pp.664–79; P. Durye, 'Les Chevaliers dans la noblesse impériale', *Revue d'Histoire Moderne* (1970); E.L'Hommède, 'La question des majorats', *Revue des Études historiques* (1924) pp.45–70; G. Senkowska-Gluck, 'Les donataires de Napoleon,' *Revue d'Histoire Moderne* (1970) pp.680–93. See also L. de Brotonne, *Les Sénateurs du Consulat et de l'Empire* (Paris 1895); J. Bertaut, *Le Faubourg Saint-Germain* (Paris 1949); G. de Broglie, *Ségur sans ceremonies* (Paris 1977); J. Stalins, *L'ordre impériale de Réunion* (Paris

1959). The imperial court occupies much of Philip Mansel, *The Eagle in Splendour: The Court of France 1789–1830* (Cambridge 1988).

CHAPTER FIFTEEN

As might be expected, memoir literature comes into its own in the campaigns of 1805. For the projected invasion of England those of Hortense and A. Bigarré, *Mémoires* (1898) are particularly relevant. On Austerlitz the great memoir source is Auxonne Théodore Thiard, *Souvenirs diplomatiques et militaires de 1804 à 1806* (Paris 1900) which would be supplemented by Paul Thiébault, *Mémoires publiés sous les auspices de sa fille Mlle Claire Thiébault et d'après le manuscrit original par F. Calmettes* (Paris 1910); Capitaine Coignet, *Les cahiers du capitaine Coignet, publiés d'après le manuscrit original par Lordéan*, ed. Mistler (Paris 1968); Baron de Marbot, *Mémoires du Général Baron de Marbot*, 3 vols (Paris 1898). But this by no means exhausts the memoir literature for 1805. In this heyday of the *Grande Armée*, Napoleon's *Correspondance* needs to be supplemented by E. Picard and L. Tuetey, eds, *Correspondance inédite de Napoléon conservée aux Archives de la Guerre 1804–1810* (1913).

Fundamental for an understanding of the naval campaign of 1805 is Arthur T. Mahan, *The Influence of Seapower upon the French Revolution and Empire* (1892). See also his *Life of Nelson* (1898); J.S. Corbett, *The Naval Campaign of 1805* is a clear guide. A. Thomazi, *Napoléon et ses marins* (Paris 1950) underlines the problems Napoleon faced. The multivolume work by Desbrières already cited is fundamental for an understanding of Napoleon's (changing) naval strategy, as is Longmate (op. cit) for the English side of things. See also Peter Lloyd, *The French are coming: The invasion scare of 1805* (1991); Jean-Carlos Carmigniani and Jean Tranié, *Napoléon et l'Angleterre 1793–1815* (Paris 1994); Richard Glover, *Britain at Bay. Defence against Bonaparte, 1803–1814* (1973); Jeremy Black and P. Woodfine, eds. *The British Navy and the Use of Naval Power in the Eighteenth Century* (Leicester 1988) and C.N. Parkinson, *Britannia Rules: the Classic Age of Naval History, 1793–1815* (1977). Trafalgar, tangential to Napoleon's story, has been overwritten: René Maine, *Trafalgar* (NY 1960); Alan Schom, *Trafalgar* (1990) and David Howarth, *Trafalgar: the Nelson Touch* (1969) and D. Pope, *England Expects: Trafalgar* (1959) are the best-known titles in English but are merely the tip of an iceberg.

The genesis of the Third Coalition can be followed in: J. Holland Rose, ed., *Select dispatches from the British Foreign Office Archives relating to the third coalition* (1904); Talleyrand, *Lettres à Napoléon, 1800–1809*, ed. Bertrand (Paris 1889); E. Kraehe, *Napoleon's German Policy: the Contest with Napoleon* (Princeton 1963); Édouard Guillon, *Napoléon et la Suisse* (Paris 1910); M. Dunan, 'Napoléon et les cantons suisses', *Revue des Études napoléoniennes* (1912) pp.190–218; P.K. Grimsted, *The Foreign Ministers of Alexander I: Political Attitudes and the Conduct of Russian Foreign Policy, 1801–1825* (LA 1969); N. Saul, *Russia and the Mediterranean, 1797–1807* (Chicago 1970). Since Russia now enters the story in a big way, the two dominant Russian personalities at Austerlitz need to be studied. For Kutusov the best guide is Serge Nabokov, *Koutousov, le vainqueur de Napoléon* (Paris 1990). On Alexander I there is a wealth of material: J. Hartley, *Alexander I* (1994); M. Dziewanowski, *Alexander I: Russia's Mysterious Tsar* (NY 1990); A. McConnel, *Alexander I; Paternalistic Reformer* (Arlington Heights, Ill. 1970); Alan Palmer, *Alexander I, Tsar of War and Peace* (1974).

Austerlitz has also understandably attracted a lot of attention. The starting place is the six-volume *La Campagne de 1805 en Allemagne* (Paris 1902) by Jean Colin & Alombert. How the Grande Armée got there is explained in R.G. Burton, *From Boulogne to Austerlitz* (1912); Albert Chatelle, *Napoléon et la Légion d'honneur au camp de Boulogne* (Paris 1956); Henri Bonnal, *De Rossbach à Ulm* (Paris 1903), Colin and Alombert, *Le corps d'armée aux ordres du maréchal Mortier* (Paris 1897). There is a good interlinking account of the three great engagements of 1805 in Jean Thiry, *Ulm, Trafalgar, Austerlitz* (1962) Napoleon himself is put under the microscope in Henri Lachouque, *Napoléon à Austerlitz* (Paris 1960), Claude Manceron, *Austerlitz* (Paris 1960) and Jean Vachee, *Napoléon en campagne* (Paris 1913). Christopher Duffy's *Austerlitz 1805* (1977) is particularly lucid and H.T. Parker, *Three Napoleonic Battles* (Durham, N.C. 1983) puts the battle in a wider context. There are some important journal articles: J. Fufestre, 'La Manoeuvre de Boulogne', *Revue des Études napoléoniennes* (1922) pp.81–109; P.A. Wimet, 'Napoléon a-t-il dicté à Daru le plan de la campagne de 1805?', *Revue de l'Institut Napoléon* (1971) pp.173–82.

Next, consequences of Austerlitz. There is a very full bibliography on Naples. Apart from the general survey by A. Fugier, *Napoléon et l'Italie* (Paris 1947) and the many biographies of Joseph there are the following: E. Gachot, *La Troisième Campagne d'Italie 1805–1806* (Paris 1911); C. Auriol, *La France, l'Angleterre et Naples de 1803 à 1806* (Paris 1911); J. Rambaud, *Naples sous Joseph Bonaparte* (Paris 1911); R. Johnston, *The Napoleonic Empire in Southern Italy and the Rise of the Secret Societies* (1904). The impact on Sicily is explored in Dennis Mack Smith, *Modern*

Sicily after 1713 (1968). The consequences in Switzerland can be followed in J. Courvoisier, *Le Maréchal Berthier et sa principauté de Neuchâtel* (Paris 1959).

But by far the greatest changes took place in Germany with the formation of the Confederation of the Rhine. Representative titles are M. Dunan, *L'Allemagne de la Révolution et de l'Empire* (Paris 1954); A. Rambaud, *L'Allemagne française sous Napoléon I* (Paris 1897); C. Schmidt, *Le Grand Duché de Berg* (Paris 1905). Pointers can also be extracted from H.A.L. Fisher, *Studies in Napoleonic Statesmanship – Germany* (Oxford 1902); J.J. Sheehan, *German History, 1770–1866* (Oxford 1989); H. Kohn, *Prelude to Nation States; the French and German Experience, 1789–1815* (Princeton 1967) and H. Schmitt, 'Germany without Prussia: a closer look at the Confederation of the Rhine', *German Studies Review* 6 (1983) pp.9–39. The last days of the Holy Roman Empire are described in J. Gagliardo, *Reich and Nation: the Holy Roman Empire as Idea and Reality, 1763–1806* (Bloomington, Indiana 1980).

CHAPTER SIXTEEN

Important printed primary sources for the years 1806–07 include the Savary memoirs: Jean François Boulart, *Mémoires militaires* (Paris 1892); Guillaume Lorencez, *Souvenirs militaires* (Paris 1902); Étienne Pasquier, *Mémoires* (Paris 1895); P.G. Levasseur, *Commentaires de Napoléon* (Paris 1851); A. Saint-Chamans, *Mémoires* (Paris 1896); Choderlos de Laclos, *Carnets de marche* (Paris 1912); Louis François Lejeune, *Mémoires* (1895); Pierre François Puffeney, *Souvenirs d'un grognard* (Dole 1891); Jean-Marie Putigny, *Putigny, grognard d'empire* (Paris 1950).

The outbreak of war with Prussia and the Jena campaign are comprehensively covered in Jean Tarnie and Jean Carlos Carmigniani, *Napoléon et l'Allemagne: La Prusse 1806* (Paris 1984); P.N. Maude, *The Jéna Campaign 1806* (1909); E.F. Henderson, *Blücher and the Uprising of Prussia against Napoleon, 1806–1815* (1911); F.L. Pètre, *Napoleon's Conquest of Prussia, 1806* (1972); David Chandler, *Jena 1806: Napoleon destroys Prussia* (1993). There is good background in C.E. White, *The Enlightened Soldier. Scharnhorst and the Miltarische Gesellschaft in Berlin, 1801–1805* (NY 1989). Clausewitz's views are contained in Michael Howard, *Clausewitz* (Oxford 1983) and R. Parkinson, *Clausewitz. A Biography* (1971) and Davout's heroic action at Auerstädt is analysed in Daniel Reichel, *Davout et l'art de la guerre* (Paris 1975). See also Pierre Foucart, *Campagne de Prusse, 1806*, 2 vols (Paris 1890); Henry Houssaye, *Jena* (Paris 1912): Jean Thiry, *Iéna* (Paris 1964); Henri Bonnal, *La*

Manoeuvre de Jena, 1806 (Paris 1904); Henri Lachouque, *Iéna* (Paris 1964); Alfred Guy, *Le Bataillon de Neuchâtel au service de Napoléon* (Neuchâtel 1964). For the triumphant aftermath there is G. Lacour-Gayet, 'Napoléon â Berlin', *Revue des Études napoléoniennes* (1922) pp.29–48.

The 1806–7 campaign against the Russians has also attracted a plethora of studies: Jean Tranié and Jean-Carlos Carmigniani, *Napoléon et la Russie. Les années victorieuses 1805–1807* (Paris 1984); F.L. Pètre, *Napoleon's Campaign in Poland, 1806–7* (1901); Pierre Foucart, *La Campagne de Pologne, 1806–1807*, 2 vols (Paris 1882). For a view of the two great battles see Pierre Grenier, *Les Manoeuvres d'Eylau et de Friedland* (Paris 1901) and Jean Thiry, *Eylau, Friedland, Tilsit* (Paris 1965). For the military opposition see Philip Haythornthwaite, *The Russian Army of the Napoleonic Wars* (1988) and J. Keep, *Soldiers of the Tsar: Army and Society in Russia, 1462–1874* (Oxford 1985). For the role of Jérôme one can consult Bernardine Melchior-Bonnet, *Jérôme Bonaparte* (Paris 1979).

For Napoleon at Castle Finkenstein with Marie Walewska see Christine Sutherland, *Marie Walewska: Napoleon's Great Love* (1979); C. Handelsman, *Napoléon et la Pologne* (Paris 1909) and S. Askenazy, *Napoléon et la Pologne* (Paris 1925). On the new states consult C. Schmidt, *Le Grand Duché de Berg* (Paris 1905); A. Martinet, *Jérôme Bonaparte, roi de Westphalie* (Paris 1952); A. Fabre, *Jérôme Bonaparte, roi de Westphalie* (Paris 1952); Jules Bertaut, *Le Roi Jérôme* (Paris 1954); Alfred Ernouf, *Les Français en Prusse en 1807 et 1808* (Paris 1875). On the Grand Duchy of Warsaw see André Bonnefons, *Frédéric-Auguste, premier roi de Saxe et Grand-duc de Varsovie* (Paris 1902) and P. Wandycz, *The Lands of Partitioned Poland, 1795–1918* (Seattle 1974).

Turkey was an important factor in Napoleon's thinking during 1806–7. For this aspect see B. Mouravieff, *L'Alliance russo-turque au milieu des guerres napoléoniennes* (Paris 1954) and N. Saul, *Russia and the Mediterranean, 1797–1807* (1970). Two particularly important studies are S. Shaw, *Between Old and New: the Ottoman Empire under Selim III, 1789–1807* (Cambridge, Mass. 1971) and W. Johnson & C. Bell, *The Ottoman Empire and the Napoleonic Wars* (Leeds 1988).

The classic and fundamental study of Tilsit and its aftermath is Albert Vandal's *Napoléon I et Alexandre* (Paris 1893). This should be supplemented with Édouard Driault, *Tilsit* (Paris 1917); S. Tatistcheff, *Alexandre I et Napoléon* (Paris 1891) and L.I. Strakhovsky, *Alexander I of Russia: the Man who Defeated Napoleon* (1949). Further light is shed on Alexander's ditherings in foreign policy in W.H. Zawadzki, *A Man of*

Honour: Adam Czartorysky as a Statesman of Russia and Poland, 1795–1831 (Oxford 1993). For the important figure of Czartoryski see also M. Kukiel, *Czartorysky and European Unity, 1770–1861* (NY 1955) and a series of journal articles, viz: W.H. Zawadzki, 'Prince Adam Czartorysky and Napoleonic France, 1801–1805: a study in political attitudes', *Historical Journal* 18 (1975) pp.245–77; C. Morley, 'Alexander I and Czartorysky: the Polish Question from 1801 to 1813', *Slavonic and East European Review* 25 (1947) pp.405–26; W.H. Zawadzki, 'Russia and the reopening of the Polish questions, 1801–1814', *International History Review* 7 (1985) pp.19–44.

CHAPTER SEVENTEEN

It is probably true to say that there is more memoir literature relating to the long (1808–13) French involvement in Spain than any other episode in his life and reign. Apart from the important memoir contributions from Savary, Bigarré, Talleyrand, Thiébault, Miot de Melito, Marmont, Masséna and, by no means least, 'King Joseph' himself, all previously cited, the following are particularly important: J.B. Jourdan, *Mémoires militaires*, ed. Grouchy (Paris 1899); Martin Pamplona, *Aperçus nouveaux sur les campagnes des francais au Portugal* (Paris 1818); A. de Laborde, *Voyage pittoresque et historique en Espagne* (Paris 1818); Alphonse Beauchamp, *Mémoires relatifs aux Révolutions d'Espagne* (Paris 1824); Manuel Godoy, *Mémoires du prince de la Paix*, trans. Esmenard (Paris 1836).

The early years of Spanish involvement are discussed in André Fugier, *Napoléon en Espagne, 1799–1808* (Paris 1930); G. de Grandmaison, *L'Espagne et Napoléon* (Paris 1931); G. Grasset, *La Guerre d'Espagne* 3 vols, (Paris 1932); J. Lucas Brereton, *Napoléon devant l'Espagne* (Paris 1946). Important background material, crucial for an understanding of the Iberian cauldron, is contained in: John Lynch, *Bourbon Spain, 1700–1808* (Oxford 1989); R. Herr, *The Eighteenth-Century Revolution in Spain* (Princeton 1958); E.J. Hamilton, *War and Prices in Spain 1651–1800* (Cambridge, Mass. 1947); R. Herr, *Rural Change and Royal Finances in Spain at the End of the Eighteenth Century* (LA 1989). Spanish motivations are examined in J. Harbron, *Trafalgar and the Spanish Navy* (1988). For the key figure of Manuel Godoy and his double game see: D. Hilt, *The Troubled Trinity: Godoy and the Spanish Monarchs* (Tuscaloosa, Ala. 1987); J. Chastenet, *Godoy: Master of Spain, 1792–1808* (1953).

The events at Bayonne and the issue of the pro-French nobles who rallied to Napoleon there are discussed in A. Savine, *L'Abdication de*

Bayonne (Paris 1908); P. Conard, *La Constitution de Bayonne* (Paris 1909); M. Artola, *Los Afrancesados* (Madrid 1953); A. Derozier, *Manuel Josef Quintana et la naissance du libéralisme en Espagne* (Paris 1968); M. Defourneaux, *Pablo de Olavide ou l'afrancesado* (Paris 1959); A. Fugier, *La Junte supérieure des Asturies et l'Invasion des Français* (Paris 1930). The beginnings of the uprising are traced in Perez de Guzman, *El 2 de Mayo, 1808* (Madrid 1908). The role of the Church can be followed in W. Callahan, *Church, Politics and Society in Spain, 1750–1854* (1985).

The immediate (1808–9) military aftermath is covered in X. Balagny, *Campagne de l'Empereur Napoléon en Espagne*, 5 vols (Paris 1907); R. Dudorff, *War to the Death; the Sieges of Saragossa, 1808–1809* (1974); R. Parkinson, *Moore of Corunna* (1976); Carola Oman, *Sir John Moore* (1953). The controversial battle of Bailen is covered in A. Titeaux, *Une Erreur historique: le général Dupont*, 3 vols (Paris 1904) and M. Leproux, *Le Général Dupont* (Paris 1934).

There is a wealth of journal articles on French intervention in Spain, of which only the very important can be mentioned. A very good overview of the crisis of 1808 can be obtained from R. Herr, 'Good, evil and Spain's uprising against Napoleon', in R. Herr and H. Parker, eds, *Ideas in History* (Durham, NC 1965) pp.157–81. For Joseph as King of Spain there is: P. Gaffarel, 'Deux années de royauté en Espagné', *Revue des Études napoléoniennes* (1919) pp.113–45. For the Savary mission there is G. de Grandmaison, 'Savary en Espagne', *Revue des questions historiques* 68 (1909) pp.188–213. For Ferdinand's intrigues consult: H. Castro Bonez, 'Manejos de Ferdinando II contra sus padres y contra Godoy', *Boletin de la Universidad de Madrid* 2 (1930). The decline of Spain's position in Latin America, which led to Godoy's uncertain policy and hence the Napoleonic intervention, can be followed in John Lynch, 'British Policy and Spanish America, 1783–1808', *Journal of Latin American Studies* 1 (1969) pp.1–30. The role of the clergy is examined in W. Callahan, 'The origins of the Conservative Church in Spain, 1789–1823', *European Studies Review* 10 (1980) pp.199–223. The subject of J. Barbier and H. Klein, 'Revolutionary wars and public finances: the Madrid treasury, 1784–1807', *Journal of European History* 2 (1981) is self-explanatory.

CHAPTER EIGHTEEN

The subject of the Napoleonic empire has attracted some indispensable works: Stuart Woolf, *Napoleon's Integration of Europe* (1991); G. Ellis, *The Napoleonic Empire* (1991); Owen Connelly, *Napoleon's Satellite*

Kingdoms (N. Y. 1965); J. Godechot, *La Grande Nation: L'Expansion
révolutionnaire de la France dans le monde de 1789 à 1799* (Paris 1983);
Charles J. Esdaile, *The Wars of Napoleon* (1995). For the individual
countries of the empire, in addition to works already cited, the following
should be consulted: S. Balau, *La Belgique sous l'Empire* (Paris 1894);
Henri Pirenne, *Histoire de la Belgique*, vol. 6 (Paris 1926); P. Verhaegen,
La Belgique sous la domination française, 5 vols (Paris 1929); Lanzac de
Laborie, *La Domination française en Belgique*, vol. 2 (Paris 1895); Simon
Schama, *Patriots and Liberators: Revolution in the Netherlands 1780–1813*
(1977); J.M. Diefendorf, *Businessmen and Politics in the Rhineland,
1789–1834* (Princeton 1980); A. Pisani, *La Dalmatie de 1797 à 1815* (Paris
1893); M. Pivec-Stelle, *La Vie économique des provinces illyriennes,
1809–1813* (Paris 1931); H. Bjelovic, *The Ragusan Republic: Victim of
Napoleon and its own Conservatism* (Leiden 1970); F.W. Carter, *Dubrovnik
(Ragusa): a Classic City State* (1972); J. Baeyens, *Les Français à Corton*
(Paris 1973); J. Savant, *Napoléon et les Grecs* (Paris 1945); Auguste Boppe,
L'Albanie et Napoléon (Paris 1914).

Italy really requires extensive coverage of its own. A. Fugier, *Napoléon
et l'Italie* (Paris 1947); Jean Borel, *Gênes sous Napoléon* (Paris 1929); J.
Rambaud, *Naples sous Joseph Bonaparte, 1806–1808* (Paris 1911); J. Davis
and P. Ginsborg, eds, *Society and Politics in Italy in the Age of the
Risorgimento* (Cambridge 1991); W.H. Flayhart, *Counterpoint to Trafal-
gar: the Anglo-Russian Invasion of Naples, 1805–1806* (Columbia, SC
1992); D. Gregory, *Sicily, the Insecure Base: a history of the British
Occupation of Sicily, 1806–1815* (Rutherford, NJ 1988); J.H. Roseli, *Lord
William Bentinck and the British Occupation of Sicily, 1811–1814*
(Cambridge 1956) and *Lord William Bentinck: the Making of a Liberal
Imperialist, 1774–1839* (1974).

For the quarrel with the Pope see, additionally to the titles cited with
respect to the Concordat, Cléron Haussonville, *L'Église et le Premier
Empire* (Paris 1870); H. Welschinger, *Le Pape et l'Empereur* (Paris 1905);
A. Latreilla, *Napoléon et le Saint Siège, 1801–1808, l'Ambassade du
Cardinal Fesch à Rome* (Paris 1935); V. Bindel, *Histoire réligieuse de
Napoléon* (Paris 1942); Daniel Robert, *Les Églises reformées en France,
1800–1830* (Paris 1961); Maurice Guerrini, *Napoléon devant Dieu* (Paris
1960); H. Auréas, *Miollis* (Paris 1960). For Napoleon and the Jews see F.
Pietri, *Napoléon et les Israélites* (Paris 1965); R. Anchel, *Napoléon et les
Juifs* (Paris 1928); S. Schwarzfuchs, *Napoleon, the Jews and the Sanhedrin*
(1979); F. Kobler, *Napoleon and the Jews* (NY 1976); Z. Szajkowski,
Agricultural Credit and Napoleon's Anti-Jewish Decrees (NY 1953); F.

Malino, *The Sephardic Jews of Bordeaux; Assimilation and Emancipation in Revolutionary and Napoleonic France* (Birmingham, Ala. 1978).

For the visual arts under Napoleon there is Timothy Wilson-Smith, *Napoleon and his Artists* (1996); Albert Boime, *Art in an age of Bonapartism 1800–1815* (Chicago 1987); J.J. Draper, *The Arts under Napoleon* (NY 1969); Colombe Samoyault-Verlet, *Les arts à l'époque napoléonienne* (Paris 1969). On the individual painters see H. Lemmonier, *Gros* (Paris 1904); K. Berger, *Géricault et son oeuvre* (Paris 1968) Anita Brookner, *David* (1980); Antoine Schnapper and Arlette Serullaz, *Jacques-Louis David* (Paris 1989); Étienne Delecluze, *Louis David, son école et son temps* (Paris 1857); Robert Herbert, *David, Voltaire, Brutus and the French Revolution* (NY 1972); Warren Roberts, *David and the Revolution* (Chapel Hill, N. C. 1989). On literature the two most informative works are J. Charpentier, *Napoléon et les hommes de lettres* (Paris 1935) and Alice Killen, *Le Roman terrifiant* (Paris 1967).

For the Empire style in general and, more broadly, the role of Paris in diffusing a homogeneous imperial culture the following should be consulted: Louis Bergeron, *France under Napoleon* (Princeton 1981); M.L. Biver, *Le Paris de Napoléon*; Émile Bourgeois, *Le style empire* (Paris 1930); G. Janneau, *L'Empire* (Paris 1965); P. Francastel, *Le style empire* (Paris 1939); Madeleine Deschamps, *Empire* (1994); Alvar Gonzalez-Palacios, *The French Empire Style* (1970); Maurice Guerrini, *Napoleon and Paris* (1970); Le Bourhis, ed. Katell, *Costume in the Age of Napoleon* (NY 1990); Aileen Ribeiro, *The Art of Dress: fashion in England and France, 1750–1820* (1995); Michel Delon and Daniel Baruch, *Paris le jour, Paris la nuit* (Paris 1990). This might also be the place to mention two stimulating but marginal contributions: R. Hodges, *The Eagle and the Spade: the Archaeology of Rome during the Napoleonic Era, 1809–1814* (Cambridge 1992) and J.K. Burton, *Napoleon and Clio: Historical Writing, Teaching and Thinking during the First Empire* (Durham, NC 1979).

For conscription as the major source of discontent in the empire see the articles by G. Vallée, 'Population et Conscription de 1798 à 1814', *Revue de l'Institut Napoléon* (1958) pp.152–59, 212–24 and ibid. (1959) pp.17–23 and the various regional studies, as for example, R. Legrand, *Le Recrutement et les Désertions en Picardie* (Paris 1957) and G. Vallée, *La Conscription dans le département de la Charente, 1798–1807* (Paris 1973). Sources in English include A. Forrest, *Conscripts and Deserters: the Army and French Society during the Revolution and Empire* (Oxford 1989); G. Lewis and C. Lucas, eds, *Beyond the Terror: Essays in French Regional and Social History, 1794–1815* (Cambridge 1983); I. Woloch, 'Napoleonic Conscription: state power and civil society', *Past and Present* 111 (1986) pp.101–29; E.A. Arnold, 'Some observations on the French opposition to Napoleonic conscription, 1804–1806', *French Historical Studies* 4 (1966) pp.453–62. On the behaviour of the Grand Army see J. Bertaud, *The Army of the French Revolution; from Citizen Soldiers to Instrument of Power* (Princeton 1988); J. Bertaud, 'Napoleon's Officers', *Past and Present* 112 (1986) pp.91–111; J. Lynn, 'Towards an army of honour: the moral evolution of the French army, 1789–1815', *French Historical Studies* 16 (1989) pp.152–182.

CHAPTER NINETEEN

Apart from Napoleon's *Correspondance* see the supplementary *Lettres inédites de Talleyrand à Bonaparte*, ed. P. Bertrand (Paris 1891). Nearly all the major participants in the 1809 campaign left memoirs. See, of the memorialists already cited, Eugène de Beauharnais, Jérôme Bonaparte, Masséna, Marmont, MacDonald, Oudinot, Talleyrand and Metternich. Additionally, there are the accounts by Jean François Boulart, *Mémoires militaires* (Paris 1892); Charles Louis Cadet de Gassicourt, *Voyage en Autriche* (Paris 1818); Jean Roch Coignet, *Les Cahiers du capitaine Coignet, 1797–1815* (Paris 1883); Georges Chevillet, *Ma vie militaire* (Paris 1906); Comeau de Chavry, *Souvenirs de guerres d'Allemagne* (Paris 1900); Capitaine Gervais, *À la conquête de l'Europe* (Paris 1939); Guillaume Lorencez, *Souvenirs militaires* (Paris 1902); Jean Baptiste Marbot, *Memoirs*, 2 vols (1892); Denis Charles Parquin, *Amours de coup de sabre d'un chasseur à cheval: Souvenirs, 1803–1809* (Paris 1910) (1812); Pierre François Percy, *Journal des campagnes* (Paris 1904); François Pils, *Journal de Marche, 1804–1814* (Paris 1895); Jean Rap, *Mémoirs* (1823); Théodore Seruzier, *Mémoires militaires 1769–1823* (Paris 1894).

On the vast secondary literature on the 1809 campaign, working back from the most modern to the most dated, we find: Jean Tranié and Carpigani, *Napoléon et l'Autriche: la campagne de 1809* (Paris 1984); J.R. Arnold, *Crisis on the Danube: Napoleon's Austrian Campaign of 1809* (1990); Marcel Dunan, *Napoléon et l'Allemagne, le système continental et les débuts du royaume de Bavière* (Paris 1942); W. de Fedorowicz, *1809. La Campagne de Pologne* (Paris 1950); Hubert Camon, *La Manoeuvre de Wagram* (Paris 1926); F.L. Petre, *Napoléon and the Archduke Charles; a History of the Franco-Austrian Campaign in the Valley of the Danube in 1809* (1909); G.G.L. Saski, *La Campagne de 1809*, 3 vols (Paris 1900); C. de Renemont, *Campagne de 1809* (Paris 1903); E. Gachot, *Napoléon en Allemagne* (Paris 1913); Edmond Bonnal, *La Manoeuvre de Landshut*

(Paris 1909); Edmond Buat, *De Ratisbon à Znaim* (Paris 1909); C. Ferry, *La marche sur Vienne* (Paris 1909).

German nationalism and its upsurge is a well-trawled subject: W.C. Langsam, *The Napoleonic Wars and German Nationalism in Austria* (N.Y. 1930); J. Droz, *Le Romantisme allemand et l'État* (Paris 1966); S. Musulin, *Vienna in the age of Metternich: from Napoleon to Revolution, 1805–1848* (1975); S. Winters & J. Held, eds, *Intellectual and Social Developments in the Hapsburg Empire from Maria Teresa to World War I* (N.Y. 1975); J.R. Seeley, *Life and Times of Stein* (1878); E.N. Anderson, *Nationalism and the Cultural Crisis in Prussia, 1806–1815* (N.Y. 1939); G.S. Ford, *Stein and the Era of Reform in Prussia, 1807–1815* (Princeton 1922); W.M. Simon, *The Failure of the Prussian Reform Movement, 1807–1819* (N.Y. 1971); M. Gray, *Prussia in Transition; Society and Politics under the Stein Reform Ministry of 1808* (Philadelphia 1986). The countervailing trends in German society are analysed in R. Berdahl, *The Politics of the Prussian Nobility: the Development of a Conservative Ideology, 1770–1848* (Princeton 1988); F.L. Carsten, *A History of the Prussian Junkers (Aldershot 1989)*; C.E. White, *The Enlightened Soldier: Scharnhorst and the Militarische Gesellschaft in Berlin, 1801–5* (N.Y. 1989); W. Shanahan, *Prussian Military Reforms, 1786–1813* (N.Y. 1945); P. Paret, *Yorck and the Era of Prussian Reform, 1807–1815* (Princeton 1966); G.A. Craig, *The Politics of the Prussian Army, 1640–1945* (Oxford 1955).

The British intervention in the war of 1809 is exhaustively covered in Gordon Bond, *The Grand Expedition: the British Invasion of Holland in 1809* (Athens, Georgia 1979); Theo Fleischman, *L'expédition anglaise sur le Continent en 1809* (Paris 1973); A. Fischer, *Napoléon et Anvers* (Paris 1933); C. Hall, *British Strategy in the Napoleonic Wars, 1803–15* (Manchester 1992); J. Sherwig, *Guineas and Gunpowder: British Foreign Aid in the Wars with France, 1793–1815* (Cambridge, Mass. 1969).

The Tyrolean revolt is traced in F.G. Eyck, *Loyal Rebels: Andréas Hofer and the Tyrolean Revolt of 1809* (NY 1986) and C. Clair, *André Hofer et l'insurrection du Tyrol en 1809* (Paris 1880); Victor Derrecagaix, *Nos campagnes au Tyrol* (Paris 1910). The indispensable book for Frederick Staps is Jean Tulard, *Napoléon. 12 Octobre 1809* (Paris 1994). See also E. Gachot, 'Un régicide allemand, Frederic Staps', *Revue des études napoléoniennes* (1922) pp.181–203.

CHAPTER TWENTY

Fundamental are the memoirs of the French marshals already cited: Soult, Masséna, Moncey, Marmont, Suchet. Spanish monographic studies of Joseph's reign also come into their own here: J. Riba Mercader, *José Bonaparte, rey de España, 1808–1813: Historia externa del reinado* (Madrid 1971) and *José Bonaparte, rey de España 1808–1813: Estructura del estado español bonapartista* (Madrid 1983). The Spanish contribution to the historiographical debates about the Peninsular War seem particularly fascinating when set alongside British and French accounts. Sir William Napier's *History of the War in the Peninsula and in the south of France from the year 1807 to the year 1814*, 6 vols (1886) can be usefully contrasted in its emphases with Maximilien Foy, *Histoire des guerres de la Peninsule sous Napoléon*, 4 vols (Paris 1827) and with José Gomez de Arteche y Moro, *Guerra de Independencia: Historia militar de España de 1808 a 1814*, 14 vols (Madrid 1903) and J.R.Aymes, *La Guerra de la Independencia en España* (Manchester 1988).

More modern histories of the Peninsular War, all with a distinctive angle, are Sir Charles Oman, *A History of the Peninsular War*, 7 vols (1930); David Gates, *The Spanish Ulcer: A History of the Peninsular War* (1986); G. Lovett, *Napoleon and the Birth of Modern Spain* (NY 1965); Jean Tranie & J.C. Carmigniani, *Napoléon et la campagne d'Espagne, 1807–1814* (Paris 1978); M. Glover, *Legacy of Glory: the Bonaparte Kingdom of Spain, 1808–1813* (NY 1971); J. Read, *War in the Peninsula* (1977); J. Lucas-Dubreton, *Napoléon devant l'Espagne* (Paris 1946); C. Grasset, *La guerre d'Espagne* (Paris 1932); Jean Thiry, *La Guerre d'Espagne* (Paris 1966). Valuable studies of particular incidents or areas include Don Alexander, *Rod of Iron: French Counterinsurgency Policy in Aragon during the Peninsular War* (Wilmington, DE 1985); D.D. Horward, *Napoleon and Iberia: the Twin Sieges of Ciudad Rodrigo and Almeida, 1810* (Tallahassee, Fla. 1984); R. Rudorff, *War to the Death: the sieges of Saragossa, 1808–1809* (1974); P. Conard, *Napoléon et la Catalogne* (Paris 1909).

Wellington has naturally attracted biographers and historians by the score, most of whom tend towards hagiography. In a variable field one should mention Elizabeth Longford, *Wellington: The Years of the Sword* (1969); Philip Guedalla, *The Duke* (1946); Laurence James, *The Iron Duke: A Military Biography of Wellington* (1992); Arthur Bryant, *The Great Duke* (1971); P. Griffith, ed., *Wellington, Commander: the Iron Duke's Generalship* (Chichester 1986). Different aspects of Wellington's army are dealt with in Philip Haythornthwaite, *The Armies of Wellington* (1994); A. Brett-James, *Life in Wellington's Army* (1972); F. Page, *Following the Drum: Women in Wellington's Wars* (1986); C. Oman, *Wellington's Army, 1809–1814* (1913); G. Davies, *Wellington and his Army* (Oxford 1954); N. Glover, *Wellington's Army in the Peninsula, 1808–1814*

(Newton Abbot 1977); J. Weller, *Wellington in the Peninsula* (1962). An allied subject is overall British policy in the peninsula, which closely involved the Wellesley family. See J.K. Severn, *A Wellesley Affair: Richard, Marquess Wellesley, and the Conduct of Anglo-Spanish Diplomacy, 1809–1812* (Tallahassee, Fla. 1981) and Rory Marir, *Britain and the defeat of Napoleon, 1807–1815* (1996).

Pro-French Spaniards (*afrancesados*), patriots and guerrillas have not been so extensively studied but the following are useful: J. Polt, *Gaspar Melchor de Jovellanos* (N.Y. 1971); A. Demerson, *Don Juan Melendez Valdes et son temps* (Paris 1962); A. Derozier, *Manuel Josef Quintana et la naissance du libéralisme en Espagne* (Paris 1968); M. Defourneaux, *Pablo de Olavide ou l'afrancesado* (Paris 1959); F. Solano Costa, *El guerrillero y su trascendencia* (Zaragoza 1959); C.J. Esdaile, 'Heroes or Villains? The Spanish Guerrillas and the Peninsular War', *History Today* (April 1988); A.D. Berkeley, ed. *New Lights on the Peninsular War* (Lisbon 1991). See also the 1975 edition of *Consortium on Revolutionary Europe Proceedings*.

CHAPTER TWENTY-ONE

For Josephine's replacement as Empress by Marie-Louise see Frédéric Masson, *Joséphine Repudiée* (Paris n.d.) and *L'Impératrice Marie-Louise* (Paris n.d.). For Metternich's key role in the marriage negotiations see R. Metternich, ed., *Memoirs of Prince Metternich, 1773–1815* (1880); E. Corti, *Metternich und die Frauen* (Vienna 1948) and C. de Grunwald, 'Le Mariage de Napoléon et de Marie-Louise', *Revue des Deux Mondes* 38 & 41 (1937). For the psychology of the new empress see Gilbert Martineau, *Marie-Louise* (Paris 1985) and Geneviève Chastenet, *Marie-Louise: l'impératrice oubliée* (Paris 1983). 'L'Aiglon', the Emperor's son and heir, is comprehensively dealt with in Jean Tulard, *Napoléon II* (Paris 1992).

The most fundamental work for the Continental System is F. Crouzet, *L'Économie britannique et le Blocus continental* (Paris 1958). E.F. Hecksher, *The Continental System* (Oxford 1922) is still the most accessible general work in English. Cf. also Bertrand de Jouvenel, *Napoléon et l'économie dirigée: Le Blocus continental* (Paris 1942) These three should be supplemented by some notable monographs dealing with particular aspects of the system: G. Ellis, *Napoleon's Continental Blockade: The Case of Alsace* (1981); Marcel Dunan, *Le Systeme Continental et les débuts du royaume de Bavière* (Paris 1943); E. Tarle, *Le Blocus Continental et le royaume d'Italie* (Paris 1928); D. Heils, *Les Rapports économiques franco-danois sous le Directoire, le Consulat et l'Empire* (Paris 1958); M. Cerenville, *Le Système continental et la Suisse, 1803–1813* (Lausanne 1906); F.L.

Huillier, *Étude sur le Blocus continental: La mise en oeuvre des décrets de Trianon et de Fontainebleau dans le Grande-Duché de Bade* (Paris 1951); G. Sevières, *L'Allemagne française sous Napoléon I* (Paris 1904).

From these books one can make one's way to cited journal articles which would have remained unknown otherwise. So: Roger Dufraise, 'Régime douanier, Blocus, Systeme Continental', *Revue d'histoire économique et sociale* (1966) pp.518–543; M. Dunan, 'Le Systeme Continental, Bulletin d'histoire économique', *Revue des Études napoléoniennes* (1913); P. Butel, 'Le port de Bordeaux sous le régime des licences, 1808–1815', *Revue d'Histoire Moderne et Contemporaine* 17 (1970); R. Dufraise, 'Blocus et systeme continental. La politique économique de Napoleon', *Revue de l'Institut Napoleon* 99 (1966) and F. Crouzet, 'Wars, blockade and economic change in Europe, 1792–1815', *Journal of Economic History* 24 (1964) pp.567–90; E. Tarle, 'Napoléon et les intérêts économiques de la France', *Revue des Études napoléoniennes* (1926) pp.117–37; M. Dunan, 'Napoléon et le système continental en 1810', *Revue d'Histoire diplomatique* (1946) pp.71–98; R. Dufraise, 'La politique douanière de Napoléon', *Revue de l'Institut Napoléon* (1974) pp3–25; Jean Tulard, 'La contrebande au Danemark', *Revue de l'Institut Napoléon* (1966) pp.94–95; F. Ponteil, 'La contrebande sur le Rhine au temps de l'Empire', *Revue Historique* (1935) pp.257–86; J. Bertrand, 'La contrebande à la frontière du Nord en 1811, 1812 et 1813', *Annales de l'Est* (1951) pp.276–306; R. Dufraise, 'Contrabandiers normands sur les bords du Rhin', *Annales de Normandie* (1961) pp.,209–31.

The Continental System and accompanying blockade were really a contest of strength between the French and British economies in this period. Much light is therefore shed incidentally by more general economic studies. In the case of France there is P. Crowhurst, *The French War on Trade; Privateering, 1793–1815* (1989); F.E. Melvin, *Napoleon's Navigation System: a study of Trade Control during the Continental Blockade* (1919); S.E. Harris, *The Assignats* (Harvard 1950); M. Marion, *Histoire Financière de la France* (Paris 1925), Vol.4; O. Viennet, *Napoléon et l'industrie française* (Paris 1947); H. See, *Histoire Économique de la France* (Paris 1942); A. Milward & N. Saul, *The Economic Development of Modern Europe, 1780–1870* (1979); P. Boussel, *Napoléon au royaume des vins de France* (Paris 1951); L. Bergeron, *Banquiers, Négociants et Manufacturiers à Paris* (Paris 1975); J. Labasse, *La Commerce des soies a Lyon sous Napoléon et la crise de 1811* (Paris 1957).

For the English side of the Continental Blockade the following should be consulted: W.F. Galpin, *The Grain Supply of England during the Napoleonic Period* (N.Y. 1925); M. Olson, *The Economics of Wartime*

Shortage: a History of British Food Supplies in the Napoleonic Wars and World Wars One and Two (Durham, N.C. 1963); H.T. Dickinson, ed., *Britain and the French Revolution* (1979); C.N. Parkinson, *The Trade Winds; a Study of British Overseas Trade during the French Wars, 1793–1815* (1948); D.C. M. Platt, *Latin America and British Trade, 1806–1914* (1972); M. Edwards, *The Growth of the British Cotton Trade, 1780–1815* (Manchester 1967); A. Cunningham and J. Lasalle, *British Credit in the last Napoleonic War* (Cambridge 1910); A. Hope Jones, *Income Tax and the Napoleonic Wars* (Cambridge 1939); S. Cope, *The Goldsmids and the development of the British money market during the Napoleonic Wars* (1942); J. Winter, ed., *War and Economic Development* (Cambridge 1975).

For the impact on the USA of the Anglo-French economic struggle and its ultimate detonation in the War of 1812, see Ulane Bonnel, *La France, les États-Unis et la guerre de course 1797–1815* (Paris 1961); P.A. Heath, *Napoleon I and the origins of the Anglo-American War of 1812* (1929).

CHAPTERS TWENTY-TWO AND TWENTY-THREE

There is a huge memoir literature on 1812 of which Caulaincourt's *Mémoires* (Paris 1933) are by far the most important. Other highly valuable eyewitness reports include General Levin Bennigsen, *Mémoires* (Paris 1908); J.W. Fortescue, ed & trans, *Mémoires du sergent Bourgogne, 1812–13* (1985); Philippe de Ségur, *Histoire de Napoléon et de la Grande Armée en 1812* (Paris 1824); see also the English edition, published as *Napoleon's Russian Campaign* and edited by J.D. Townsend (1959); Agathon J.F. Fain, *Manuscrit de 1812* (Paris 1827); Sir Robert Wilson, *Journals 1812–14* ed. Brett-James (1864); R.E.P. Fezensac, *Journal de la campagne de Russie en 1812* (Paris 1850); Pion de Loches, *Mes campagnes* (Paris 1889); Chambray, marquis de, *Histoire de l'expédition de Russie* (Paris 1859); D.P. Boutourlin, *Histoire militaire de la campagne de Russie en 1812* (Paris 1824); Georges Bertin, *La campagne de 1812 d'après des témoins oculaires* (Paris 1895); C. de Grunwald, *La Campagne de Russie* (Paris 1963) Louise Fusil, *Souvenir d'une femme sur la retraite de Russie* (Paris 1910);). A. Brett-James, ed. *Eyewitness Accounts of Napoleon's Invasion of Russia* (1966); N. Milhailovitch, ed., *Alexandre I – Correspondance avec sa soeur la grande-duchesse Catherine* (St Petersburg 1910). K. von Clausewitz, *The Campaign of Russia in 1812* (1843) almost counts as an eyewitness history as does Antoine H. Jomini, *Précis politique et militaire des campagnes de 1812 à 1814* (Paris 1886); A. Chuquet, *Lettres de 1812* (Paris 1911).

There is a wealth of secondary literature: L.J. Margueron, *Campagne de Russie: Préliminaires, 1810–1812* (Paris 1906); Gabriel Fabry, *Campagne de Russie: Operations*, 5 vols (Paris 1903); Cate Curtis, *The War of the Two Emperors: the Duel between Napoleon and Alexander; Russia 1812* (N.Y. 1985); George Nafziger, *Napoleon's Invasion of Russia* (1988); Nigel Nicolson, *Napoleon. 1812* (1985); R. Riehn, *1812: Napoleon's Russian Campaign* (N.Y. 1991); Christopher Duffy, *Borodino and the War of 1812* (1973); E. Tarle, *Napoleon's Invasion of Russia, 1812* (1942); Alan Palmer, *Napoleon in Russia* (N.Y. 1967); Arthur Chuquet, *1812: La guerre en Russie* (Paris 1912); Jean Thiry, *La Campagne de Russie* (Paris 1969); Paul Britten Austin, *Napoleon in Moscow* (1995) and *Napoleon. The Great Retreat* (1996).

Many monographs have been written on particular incidents in this famous campaign: B. de Faye, *Smolensk* (Paris 1912); Van Vlijmen, *Vers le Beresina* (Paris 1908); R. Soltyk, *Napoleon en 1812* – medical aspects – (Paris 1936); T. Fleischmann, *Napoleon au Bivouac* (Brussels 1957). For the Moscow period Abbé Surrugues, *Lettres sur la prise de Moscou en 1812* (Paris 1820) is valuable, as is F. Pisani, *Con Napoleone nella Campagna di Russia, Memorie inedite di un ufficiale della Grande Armata* (Milan 1942). See also D. Olivier, *L'Incendie de Moscou* (Paris 1964).

Particular personalities are dealt with in the following: M.A. Fabre, *Jérôme Bonaparte, roi de Westphalie* (Paris 1952); Abel Mansuy, *Jérôme Bonaparte et la Pologne en 1812* (Paris 1931); Michael and Diana Josselson, *The Commander: Barclay de Tolly* (N.Y. 1980); Serge Nabokov, *Koutouzov, le vainqueur de Napoleon* (Paris 1990); F.D. Scott, *Bernadotte and the Fall of Napoleon* (Cambridge, Mass. 1935); E. Dard, *Narbonne* (Paris 1943); M. Jenkins, *Arakcheev: Grand Vizier of the Russian Empire* (1969); M. Josselson, *The Commander: a Life of Barclay de Tolly* (Oxford 1980); Sophie de Ségur, *Rostopchine* (Paris 1873); Roger Parkinson, *The Fox of the North. The Life of Kutusov* (1976).

The considerable role of non-French troops in the French army emerges in Jean Sauzey, *Les Allemands sous les aigles françaises* (Paris 1912); Paul Boppe, *Les Espagnols à la Grande Armée* (Paris 1899); M. Holden, *Napoleon in Russia* (1974); Le Gall-Torrance, 'Mémoires russes sur l'époque napoléonienne', *Revue de l'Institut Napoléon* (1979); R. Bilecki, 'L'effort militaire polonais, 1806–1815', *Revue de l'Institut Napoléon* (1976). Poland is particularly important in this story, especially during the retreat and is the subject of J. Mansuy, *Jérôme Napoléon et la Pologne en 1812* (Paris 1931) and B. Dundulis, *Napoléon et la Lithuanie en*

1812 (Paris 1940). See also Dominique de Pradt, *Histoire de l'ambassade dans le grand-duché de Varsovie* (Paris 1815).

Wider foreign policy implications appear in Alan Palmer, *Russia in War and Peace* (1972); A. Lobanov Rostovsky, *Russia and Europe, 1789–1825* (Durham, N.C. 1947); P.K. Grimsted, *The Foreign Ministers of Alexander I: Political Attitudes and the Conduct of Russian Foreign Policy, 1801–1825* (L.A. 1969); V. Puryear, *Napoleon and the Dardanelles* (Berkeley 1951); M. Raeff, *Michael Speransky, Statesman of Imperial Russia, 1772–1839* (The Hague 1957); A.C. Niven, *Napoleon and Alexander I: a Study in Anglo-Russian Relations, 1807–1812* (Washington DC 1978); H. Ragsdale, *Detente in the Napoleonic Era: Bonaparte and the Russians* (Lawrence, Kansas 1980).

Other aspects of 1812, a true *annus mirabilis*, include the question of Napoleon's motivation, for which clues can be picked up in his letters to Marie-Louise. Freud's wild (or inspired?) guess comes in a letter to Thomas Mann, 29 November 1936, in Ernst Freud, *Letters of Sigmund Freud 1873–1939* (1961) p. 430. See also H. Parker, 'Why did Napoleon invade Russia? A study in motivation, personality and social structure', *Consortium on Revolutionary Europe Proceedings* (1989) pp.86–96. Britain's war with the United States is dealt with in Harry Coles, *The War of 1812* (Chicago 1965) and Donald R. Hickey, *The War of 1812: a forgotten conflict* (Urbana, Ill. 1989). The Malet conspiracy has, strangely, attracted dozens of studies but there is no need to go beyond the following: B. Melchior-Bonnet, *La conspiration de Général Malet* (Paris 1963); J. Mistler, *Napoleon et l'Empire* (Paris 1968) and G. Artom, *Napoleon is Dead in Russia* (NY 1970).

CHAPTER TWENTY-FOUR

The years 1812–14 in Spain yield some specialized monographs of great interest: Jean Sarramon, *La bataille des Arapiles, 22 juillet 1812* (Paris 1978); Peter Young and J.P. Lawford, *Wellington's Masterpiece: the Battle and Campaign of Salamanca* (1973); Philip J. Haythornthwaite, *Die Hard: Dramatic Action from the Napoleonic Wars* (1996); F. Rousseau, *La Carrière du maréchal Suchet* (Paris 1898); P. Conard, *Napoléon et la Catalogne* (Paris 1910); C. Clerc, *Campagne du Maréchal Soult dans les Pyrenées occidentales en 1813–14* (Paris 1894); L. Batcave, *La Bataille d'Orthez* (Paris 1914); Henri Geschwind and François Gelis, *La Bataille de Toulouse* (Paris 1914); Jac Weller, *Wellington in the Peninsula* (1962); Michael Glover, *Wellington's Peninsular Victories* (1963).

The great upsurge of German nationalism in 1813 has produced a vast literature of its own. Representative titles include: G.P. Gooch, *Germany and the French Revolution* (1920); H. Kohn, *The Idea of Nationalism* (N.Y. 1945); C. Langsam, *The Napoleonic Wars and German Nationalism in Austria* (N.Y. 1930); A. Robert, *L'Idée nationale autrichienne et les guerres de Napoléon* (Paris 1933); E.N. Anderson, *Nationalism and the Cultural Crisis in Prussia, 1806–1815* (N.Y. 1939); M. Boucher, *Le Sentiment National en Allemagne* (Paris 1947); G.S. Ford, *Stein and the Era of Reform in Prussia, 1807–1815* (Princeton 1922); J. Droz, *L'Allemagne et la Révolution Francaise* (Paris 1949); Vidal de la Blanche, *La Regénération de la Prusse après Jéna* (Paris 1910); W.M. Simon, *The Failure of the Prussian Reform Movement, 1807–1819* (N.Y. 1971); G. Cavaignac, *La Formation de la Prusse Contemporaine* (Paris 1891); R. Ergang, *Herder and the Foundations of German Nationalism* (N.Y. 1913); R. Berdahl, *The Politics of the Prussian Nobility; the Development of a Conservative Ideology, 1770–1848* (Princeton 1988); W. Shanahan, *Prussian Military Reforms, 1786–1813* (N.Y. 1945); P. Paret, *Yorck and the Era of Prussian Reform, 1807–1815* (Princeton 1966); H. Kohn, *The Mind of Germany* (1961).

In many ways the key figure in 1813 was Metternich, and his attitudes have been exhaustively studied. Apart from the biographies already cited, the following are useful: Henry Kissinger, *A World Restored* (Boston 1957); Bertier de Sauvigny, *Metternich et son Temps* (Paris 1959) E. Kraehe, *Napoleon's German Policy* (Princeton 1963); C. Buckland, *Metternich and the British Government from 1809 to 1813* (1932); E. Gillick, *Europe's Classic Balance of Power; a Case History of the Theory and Practice of One of the Great Concepts of European Statecraft* (Ithaca, N.Y. 1955); M. Paléologue, *Romantisme et Diplomatie* (Paris 1924). The famous interview in Dresden has to be pieced together from a number of primary sources, many of which contradict each other, as, e.g. A.J.F. Fain, *Manuscrit de 1813* (Paris 1824); Clemens Metternich, *Memoirs* (1880); J. Grabowski, *Mémoires Militaires* (Paris 1907).

A number of the primary sources listed with reference to the Russian campaign of 1812 continue the story into the debacle in 1813. Other first-hand accounts include O. von Odeleben, *A Circumstantial Narrative of the Campaign in Saxony* (1820); A. Brett-James's collection of eyewitnesses in *Europe against Napoleon; the Leipzig Campaign 1813* (1970); Georges Bertin, *La Campagne de 1813 d'après des témoins oculaires* (Paris 1896); Erckman Chatrian, *Un Conscrit de 1813* (Paris 1977); Denis Charles Parquin, *De la Paix de Vienne à Fontainebleau: Souvenirs 1809–1814* (Paris 1911); Planat de la Faye, *Souvenirs* (Paris 1895); Eugène Vitrolles, *Mémoires* (Paris 1883); C.L.M. Lanrezac, *Mémoires: Lutzen* (Paris 1904); Jomini, *Précis politique et militaire des campagnes de 1812 à 1814* (Paris

1886); Jacques Norvins, *Le Porte-Feuille de 1813* (Paris 1825). To these should be added a number of excellent secondary narratives: J. Tranié and J.C. Carmigniani, *Napoléon 1813*, Campagne d'Allemagne (Paris 1987); F.L. Petre, *Napoleon's Last Campaign in Germany, 1813* (1912); Marcel Dupont, *Napoléon et la trahison des maréchaux, 1814* (Paris 1970); Frédéric Reboul, *La Campagne de 1813* (Paris 1912); J. Clément, *La Campagne de 1813* (Paris 1904); Lefebvre de Behaine, *Napoléon et les Alliés sur le Rhin* (Paris 1913); Ernest F. Henderson, *Blücher and the uprising of Prussia against Napoleon* (1994).

For individual studies of the four great battles in the 1813 campaign, see the following: Paul J. Foucart, *Bautzen, 20–21 Mai, 1813* (Paris 1897); R. Tournes, *La campagne de printemps en 1813: Lützen* (Paris 1931); Jean Thiry, *Lützen et Bautzen* (Paris 1971); George Nafziger, *Napoleon at Dresden* (Chicago 1995); Jean Thiry, *Leipzig* (Paris 1972); George Nafziger, *Napoleon at Leipzig* (Chicago 1996); F.N. Maude, *The Leipzig Campaign, 1813* (1908); Paul Foucart, *La Poursuite* (Paris 1901).

CHAPTER TWENTY-FIVE

There is a wealth of primary sources for the campaign of 1814, not least Napoleon's own letters to Marie-Louise. A.J.F. Fain's *Le Manuscrit de 1814* is as important as the corresponding document for 1813, Caulaincourt's previously cited memoirs come back into centre stage. Madame de Marigny's *Journal* (1907) gives many details unavailable elsewhere. Other fundamental sources include Volume 2 of Prefect of Police Pasquier's *Mémoires* (Paris 1893), Augustin Belliard, *Mémoires* (Paris 1842); A.G.P. Barante, *Mémoires* (Paris 1901). Also to be classed as primary sources are Clausewitz's *La Campagne de 1814* (Paris 1900), Georges Bertin, *La Campagne de France d'après les témoins oculaires* (Paris 1897) and Baron Vincent's *Le Pays Lorrain* (Paris 1929). How reliable Chateaubriand is as an observer of this period is disputed. See Beau de Lomenie, *La Carrière politique de Chateaubriand de 1814 à 1830* (Paris 1929) and H. Guillemin, *L'Homme des Mémoires d'outre-tombe* (Paris 1964).

The military campaign of 1814 has been exhaustively studied – some would say written into the ground. The classic account is Henry Houssaye's *1814* (Paris 1888) but there are other good monographs: A. Chuquet, *L'Année 1814* (Paris 1914), Jean Thiry, *La Campagne de France* (Paris 1938); F. Ponteuil, *La Chute de Napoléon I* (Paris 1943); F.L. Petre, *Napoleon at Bay 1814* (1914); Marcel Dupont, *Napoléon et la Trahison des Maréchaux* (Paris 1970); F.D. Scott, *Bernadotte and the Fall of Napoleon* (Cambridge, Mass. 1935). Modern perspectives, including the possibility of betrayal, are examined in David Hamilton-Williams, *The Fall of Napoleon: The Final Betrayal* (1994) and Jean Tulard, *Napoleon at Bay.* (1977). All these contain some political analysis, but for an emphasis on military technicalities see also the following: J. Tranie & J.C. Carmigniani, *Napoléon 1814: La campagne de France* (Paris 1989) Lefebvre de Béhaine, *La Campagne de France* (Paris 1935); Henry Lachouque, *Napoléon en 1814* (Paris 1960); M.R. Mathieu, *Dernières Victoires, 1814: La Campagne de France aux alentours de Montmirail* (Paris 1964); H. de Mauduit, *Les derniers jours de la Grande Armée* (Paris 1847) and Jean Colin, 'La bataille de Montmirail', *Revue des Études napoléoniennes* (1914) pp.326–58.

The military side of things can be supplemented by a huge literature on the experience of the provinces during the Allied invasion. Representative titles include: François Steenackers, *L'Invasion de 1814 dans la Haute-Marne* (Paris 1868); P. Gaffarel, *Dijon en 1814–1815* (Paris 1897); A. Chuquet, *L'Alsace en 1814* (Paris 1900); F. Borrey, *La Franche-Comte en 1814* (Paris 1912); P. Fauchille, *Une Chouannerie Flamande 1813–1814* (Paris 1905); R. Perrin, *L'Esprit public dans la Meurthe de 1814–1816* (Paris 1913); J. Vidal de la Blanche, *L'Évacuation de l'Espagne et l'Invasion dans le Midi* (Paris 1914); H. Contamine, *Metz et Moselle de 1814 à 1870* (Paris 1932) and A. Voyard, 'Les Anglais à Bordeaux en 1814', *Revue des Études napoléoniennes* (1914) pp.259–85. For the defence of Paris itself it is instructive to turn to the biographies of the principals and their controversial role: H. de Clairval, *Daumesnil* (Paris 1970); Duke of Conegliano, *Moncey* (Paris 1901); M. Morcel, *Le Maréchal Mortier* (Paris 1957).

For the war effort itself see L. Girard, *La Garde nationale* (Paris 1964); Eugène Lomier, *Histoire des Régiments des Gardes d'honneur, 1813–1814* (Paris 1924); J. Vidalenc, *Textes sur l'histoire de la Seine-Inférieure à l'époque napoléonienne* (Paris 1976); J. Durieux, 'Soldats de 1814', *Revue des Études napoléoniennes* (1933) pp.202–211. The purely political aspects of 1814 in France appear in Bertier de Sauvigny, *Le comte Ferdinand de Bertier et l'énigme de la Congrégation* (Paris 1948); F. Berry, *L'esprit public chez les prêtres franc-comtois pendant la crise de 1812–1815* (Paris 1912); Lefebvre de Behaine, *Le Comte d'Artois sur la route de Paris en 1814* (Paris 1921); L. Madelin, *La Contre-Révolution sous la Révolution, 1789–1815* (Paris 1935); E. de Perceval, *Un Adversaire de Napoléon, Laine* (Paris 1926); C. Pouthas, *Guizot pendant la Restauration* (Paris 1923); J. Bury, 'The End of the Napoleonic Senate', *Cambridge Historical Journal* (1948) pp.165–89.

1814 also saw the final collapse of the Napoleonic Empire and although the global ramifications of this cannot be followed in a biography, it does no harm to cite the relevant publications, which are largely self-explanatory: R. Rath, *The Fall of the Napoleonic Kingdom of Italy* (N.Y. 1941); R.M. Johnston, *The Napoleonic Empire in Southern Italy* (1904); H. Weil, *Joachim Murat, roi de Naples: la dernière année du règne* (Paris 1909); J. Rossetti, *Lord W. Bentinck and the British Occupation of Sicily, 1811–1821* (1956); G. Renier, *Great Britain and the Establishment of the Kingdom of Netherlands, 1813–1815* (1930); Caumont de la Force, *L'Architrésorier Lebrun, gouverneur de la Hollande, 1810–1813* (Paris 1907); C. Parkinson, *War in the Eastern Seas, 1783–1815* (1954); H. Prentout, *L'Île de France sous Decaen* (Paris 1901); Enrique Gandia, *Napoléon et l'indépéndance de l'Amérique latine* (Paris 1955); C. de Sassenay, *Napoleon I et la fondation de la République Argentine* (Paris 1892). See also two articles: Pardo de Leygonier, 'Napoléon et les libérateurs de l'Amérique latine', *Revue de l'Institut Napoléon* (1962) pp.29–33 and O. Baulny, 'La Naissance de l'Argentine el l'entreprise ibérique de Napoléon', *Revue de l'Institut Napoléon* (1970) pp.169–80.

CHAPTER TWENTY-SIX

Once again a mere twelve-month period produces a cascade of printed primary sources. Particularly important are three volumes of Talleyrand's letters: Gaston Palewski, ed., *Le Miroir de Talleyrand: Lettres inédites à la duchesse de Courlande pendant le Congrès de Vienne* (Paris 1976); *Talleyrand intime d'aprés sa correspondance avec la duchesse de Courlande: La Restauration en 1814* (Paris 1891); G. Pallin ed, *Correspondance inédite du Prince de Talleyrand et du Roi XVIII pendant le Congrès de Vienne* (Paris 1881). Other useful sources are M.H. Weil, ed., *Les Dessous du Congrès de Vienne d'après des documents originaux des Archives du Ministère impérial et royal de l'intérieur à Vienne*, 2 vols (Paris 1917); Abbé de Pradt, *Récit historique sur la restauration de la royauté en France, le 31 mars 1814* (Paris 1822) John Scott, *A Visit to Paris in 1814* (1816); C.K. Webster, ed, *British Diplomacy, 1813–1815: Select Documents dealing with the Reconstruction of Europe* (1921); Auguste de La Garde-Chambonas, *Souvenirs du Congrès de Vienne, 1814–1815* (Paris 1820); Dorothée de Courlande, *Souvenirs de la duchesse de Dino (Paris* 1908).

The Allies' choice of Elba as the locale for the Emperor's exile is dealt with in the following works: C. Buckland, *Metternich and the British Government* (1932); Harold Nicolson, *The Congress of Vienna* (1946); Dara Olivier, *Alexandre 1er: Prince des Illusions* (Paris 1973); Francis Ley, *Alexandre Ier et sa Sainte-Alliance, 1811–1825* (Paris 1975); C.K.

Webster, *The Foreign Policy of Castlereagh, 1812–1815* (1931); M. Chamberlain, *Lord Aberdeen: a Political Biography* (1983); Antoine d'Arjuzon, *Castlereagh* (Paris 1995); G. Bertier de Sauvigny, *Metternich* (Paris 1986); Wendy Hinde, *Castlereagh* (1981); Philip Ziegler, *The Duchess of Dino* (1962); F.D. Scott, *Bernadotte and the Fall of Napoléon* (Cambridge, Mass. 1935); L. Pingaud, *Bernadotte, Napoléon et les Bourbons* (Paris 1901); Gregor Dallas, *1815: The Roads to Waterloo* (1996); Evelyne Lever, *Louis XVIII* (Paris 1988); Philip Mansel, *The Court of France, 1789–1830* (Cambridge 1988). See also numerous articles on the subject, especially P. Schroeder, 'An unnatural "natural alliance": Castlereagh, Metternich and Aberdeen in 1813', *International History Review* 10 (1988) pp.522–40; F.D. Scott, 'Bernadotte and the Throne of France, 1814', *Journal of Modern History* 5 (1933) pp.465–78; Philip Mansel, 'Wellington and the French Restoration', *International History Review* 11 (1989) pp.76–83; Katherine MacDonagh, 'A Sympathetic Ear: Napoleon, Elba and the British', *History Today* (February 1994) pp.29–35.

The period at Fontainebleau comes alive in L. Madelin, ed., *Lettres inédites de Napoléon à Marie-Louise* (Paris 1960) and Palmastierna, ed., *Lettres de Marie-Louise à Napoléon (Paris* 1955), which can be supplemented by Baron C.F. Méneval, *Napoléon et Marie-Louise: souvenirs historiques (Paris* 1845), Frédéric Masson ed., *Private Diaries of Marie-Louise* (1922) and J.C. Hobhouse, *The Substance of some Letters written from Paris* (1817). On the alleged suicide bid see P. Hillemand, 'Napoléon a-t-il tenté de se suicider à Fontainebleau?' *Revue de l'Institut Napoléon* (1971), who traces the matter to an accidental dose of opium. On the possibility that there was an assassination bid, connected or unconnected to the 'suicide' attempt, see Frédéric Masson, *L'Affaire Maubreuil (Paris* 1907) and M. Gasson, *La tumulteuse existence de Maubreuil (Paris* 1954).

There is a wealth of material on the sojourn in Elba. Vital primary sources, apart from the memoirs of Caulaincourt, include Eugène d'Arnauld Vitrolles, *Mémoires de Vitrolles* (Paris 1951); André Pons de l'Hérault, *Souvenirs et anecdotes de l'Île d'Elbe* (1897) and Viscount Ebrington, *Memorandum of two conversations* (1823). In this bracket, too, should be classed Fernand Beaucour's monograph *Une visite à Napoléon à l'Île d'Elbe d'un membre du Parlement anglais* (Paris 1990). Secondary sources, where there is a clear correlation between degrees of excellence and those most recently published, include: Fernand Beaucour, *Napoléon a l'île d'Elbe* (Paris 1991); Louise Laflandre-Linden, *Napoléon et l'île d'Elbe* (Paris 1989) P. Bartel, *Napoléon à l'île d'Elbe* (Paris 1959); G. Godlewski, *Trois Cent Jours d'Exil* (Paris 1961); Neil Campbell, *Napoleon at Fontainebleau and Elba* (1869); P. Gruyer, *Napoléon, roi de l'île d'Elbe* (Paris 1904); R. Christophe, *Napoléon, Empereur de l'île d'Elbe* (Paris 1959); N. Young, *Napoleon in Exile: Elba* (1914); E. Foresi, *Napoléon I all'isola dell'Elba* (Florence 1884); M. Pellet, *Napoléon à l'île d'Elbe* (Paris 1888); L.G. Pelissier, *Le registre de l'île d'Elbe* (Paris 1897). There is a brilliant overview in Jean Tulard, 'L'île d'Elbe en l'an X', *Revue de l'Institut Napoléon* (1964) pp.64–68.

An extensive literature also covers the intrigues before Napoleon's breakout from Elba and the triumphant march to Paris at the beginning of the Hundred Days. Fundamental are Norman Mackenzie, *The Escape from Elba: the Fall and Flight of Napoleon, 1814–1815* (Oxford 1982) and Henry Houssaye, *1815: La Première Restauration, le Retour de l'île d'Elbe, les Cent Jours* (Paris 1920). See also F. Ponteil, *La Chute de Napoléon* (Paris 1943); Jean Thiry, *La Chute de Napoléon* (Paris 1938); J.H. Rose, *Napoleon's Last Voyages* (1906); C. Shorter, *Napoleon and his Fellow-travellers* (1908). For the politics and intrigues consult A. Espitalier, *Deux artisans du retour de l'île d'Elbe* (Paris 1934): A. Ernouf, *Maret, duc de Bassano* (Paris 1878); E. Bonnal, *Les Royalistes contre l'Armée (Paris* 1906). For the march to Paris, aside from L. Marchand, *Mémoires* (Paris 1955), there is Alexandre de Laborde, *Quarante-huite heures de garde au Château des Tuileries pendant les journées de 19 et 20 Mars 1815* (Paris 1816). There are very full accounts in: Paul Gaffarel, *Les Cent Jours à Marseille* (Paris 1906); L. Pingaud, *La Franche-Comté en* 1815 (Paris 1894); G. de Manteyer, *La Fin de l'Empire dans les Alpes* (Paris 1942); Jean Thiry, *Le Vol de l'Aigle* (Paris 1942); A. Chollier, *La Vraie Route Napoléon* (Paris 1946); S & A. Troussier, *La Chevauchée héroique du retour de l'île d'Elbe* (Paris 1965); C. Manceron, *Napoléon reprend Paris* (Paris 1965).

CHAPTER TWENTY-SEVEN

Apart from Houssaye's classic study cited in the notes to the last chapter, there are many good books on the Hundred Days: Alan Schom, *One Hundred Days: Napoleon's Road to Waterloo* (1993); Émile Le Gallo, *Les Cent Jours* (Paris 1923); G. de Bertier de Sauvigny, *La Restauration* (Paris 1955); C. Manceron, *Which Way to Turn: Napoleon's Last Choice* (1961); F. Sieburg, *Les Cent Jours* (Paris 1957). On Benjamin Constant and the Additional Act the following are indispensable: Constant's own *Journaux Intimes* (Paris 1952); his *Mémoires sur les Cent-Jours*, ed. Pozzo di Borgo (Paris 1961) and his *Œuvres*, ed. Alfred Roulin (Paris 1957); L. Radiguet,

L'Acte additionel (Paris 1911); Dennis Wood, *Benjamin Constant: A Biography* (1993); P. Bastid, *Benjamin Constant et sa doctrine* (Paris 1965).

Political aspects of Napoleon's return appear in M. Reinhard, *Le Grand Carnot* (Paris 1952); W. Sérieyx, *Drouot et Napoleon* (Paris 1931); H. Malo, *Le Bedau Montrond* (Paris 1926); R. Alexander, *Bonapartism and Revolutionary Tradition in France; the Fedérés of 1815* (1991); Frédéric Bluche, *Le Plebiscite des Cent Jours* (Geneva 1974); M. Bruguière, *La Première Restauration et son Budget* (Paris 1969); X. Gignoux, *La Vie du Baron Louis* (Paris 1928). Fouché, correctly identified by Houssaye as the key figure of 1815 in the imperial destiny is best approached by a quaternity of volumes: his own *Mémoires de Joseph Fouché, Duc d'Otrante*, ed. Michel Vovelle (Paris 1992); André Castelot, *Fouché* (Paris 1990); Louis Madelin, *Fouché, 1759–1820*, 2 vols (Paris 1910) and the classic account by Stefan Zweig, *Fouché* (Paris 1969). Useful articles for the politics of 1815 include: H. Kurtz, 'Napoleon in 1815: the second reign', *History Today*, October 1965 pp.673–87 and R. Alexander, 'The *fedérés* of Dijon in 1815', *Historical Journal* 30 (1987) pp.367–90.

There are many useful travellers' tales which set the scene in Paris: Lady Sidney Owenson Morgan, *La France* (1817); John Scott, *Paris Revisited in 1815* (1816); Samuel Romilly, *Life of Sir Samuel Romilly written by himself* (1842); John Hobhouse, *The Substance of Some Letters written by an Englishman Resident at Paris during the last reign of the Emperor Napoleon* (1816). For the general context in France and reactions in the regions consult the following: A. Jardin & A.J. Tudesq, *La France des notables, 1815–1848*, 2 vols (Paris 1973); Marc Blancpain, *La vie quotidienne dans la France du Nord sous les occupations (1814–1944)* (Paris 1983) Henry Contamine, *Metz et la Moselle de 1814 à 1870* (Paris 1932); J. Vidalenc, *Le Département de l'Eure sous la monarchie constitutionelle* (Paris 1952); P. Leulliot, *La Première Restauration et les cent jours en Alsace* (Paris 1958); G. Lavalley, *Le Duc d'Aumont et les Cent Jours en Normandie* (n.d.); R. Grand, *La Chouannerie de 1815* (Paris 1942); Bertrand Lasserre, *Le Général Lemarque et l'Insurréction royaliste en Vendée* (Paris 1906). An interesting sidelight is shed by E. Romberg and A. Malet, *Louis XVIII et les cent jours à Gard* (Paris 1902).

If, as is often claimed, far too much has been written about the Waterloo campaign, perhaps this is because of the embarrassment of riches when it comes to primary sources. Among the memoirs already cited one should point in particular to those by Lucien Bonaparte, Bourrienne, Fouché, Hortense, Lafayette, Chateaubriand, Molé, Réal, Savary, Talleyrand and Thibaudeau. Also essential are Emmanuel, Marquis de Grouchy, *Fragments Historiques* (Paris 1829) and *Mémoires*

(Paris 1873); Jean-Claude Beugnot, *Mémoires du comte Beugnot, 1779–1815*, ed. R. Lacour-Gayet (Paris 1959); François Guizot, *Mémoires pour servir à l'histoire de mon temps* Vol 1. (Paris 1858); Louis-Philippe d'Orléans, *Mon Journal*, 2 vols (Paris 1849); Cavalie Mercer, *Journal of the Waterloo Campaign, kept throughout the Campaign of* 1815, 2 vols (1870); Jules Michelet, *Ma Jeunesse* (Paris 1884); Eugène d'Arnauld, baron de Vitrolles, *Mémoires de Vitrolles*, ed. P. Farel, 2 vols (Paris 1951); but this by no means exhausts the huge memoir literature for 1815.

As might be expected, there is a massive literature on Ligny, Quatre Bras and Waterloo, beginning with Carl von Clausewitz, *La Campagne de 1815* (Paris 1900); Antoine Jomini, *Précis de la Campagne de 1815* (Paris 1939); Jean Charras, *Histoire de la Campagne de 1815* (Paris 1869) and L.D. Pontecoulant, *Napoléon à Waterloo* (Paris 1866). The classic study is Henry Houssaye's *1815: Waterloo* (Paris 1924). Thereafter, for each French study one can cite a British one. So A. Brett-James, *The Hundred Days; Napoleon's Last Campaign* from Eyewitness Accounts (1965); E. Lénient, *La Solution des Enigmes de Waterloo* (1915); A.F. Becke, *Napoleon and Waterloo* (1936); H. Lachouque, *Le Secret de Waterloo* (Paris 1952); J. Naylor, *Waterloo* (1960); Jean Thiry, *Waterloo* (Paris 1943); J. Weller, *Wellington at Waterloo* (1967); Hector Couvreur, *Le Drame belge de Waterloo* (Brussels 1959); A. Chalfont, ed. *Waterloo: Battle of the Three Armies* (1979); C. Piollet, *La Vérité sur le mot de Cambronne* (Paris 1921); Christopher Hibbert, *Waterloo: Napoleon's Last Campaign* (1967); Henry Houssaye, *La Garde meurt et ne se rend pas* (Paris 1907); David Howarth, *A Near-Run Thing; the Day of Waterloo* (1968). Three useful articles are J. Holland Rose, 'Wellington dans la campagne de Waterloo', *Revue des Études napoléoniennes*, 1915 pp.44–55; E. Kraehe, 'Wellington and the Reconstruction of the Allied Armies during the Hundred Days', *International History Review* 11 (1989) pp.84–97; C. Grouard, 'Les derniers historiens de 1815', *Revue des Études napoléoniennes* 1917 pp.163–98.

On the gloomy sequel to Waterloo and the Emperor's eventual surrender: Henry Houssaye, *1815: La Seconde Abdication, la Terreur Blanche* (Paris 1918); Jean Thiry, *La Seconde Abdication* (Paris 1945); J. Duhamel, *Les Cinquante Jours de Waterloo à Plymouth* (Paris 1963); G. de Bertier de Sauvigny, *La Restauration* (Paris 1955); G. Martineau, *Napoleon Surrenders* (1971). Two good articles are J. Gallaher, 'Marshal Davout and the Second Bourbon Restoration', *French Historical Studies* 6 (1970) pp.350–64 and G. Lewis, 'The White Terror of 1815 in the Department of the Gard: counter-revolution, continuity and the individual', *Past and Present* 58 pp.108–35.

CHAPTER TWENTY-EIGHT

The period on St Helena is particularly rich in eyewitness accounts. The following are fundamental: Marie-Joseph Emmanuel-Dieudonné de las Cases, *Mémorial de Saint-Hélène ou journal où se trouve consigné . . . tout ce qu'a dit et fait Napoléon . . . du 20 juin 1815 au 25 novembre 1816*, ed. M. Dunan, 2 vols (Paris 1822); Barry E. O'Meara, *Napoleon in Exile; or a Voice from St Helena* (1888); Francois Antommarchi, *Mémoires du docteur F. Antommarchi ou les derniers moments de Napoléon*, 2 vols (Paris 1825); Comte Charles-François-Tristan de Montholon, *Récits de la captivité de l'Empéreur Napoléon à Sainte-Hélène*, 2 vols (Paris 1847); Baron General Gaspar Gourgaud, *Sainte-Hélène, journal inédit de 1815 à 1818*, 2 vols (Paris 1889); Comte Louis-Joseph-Narcisse Marchand, *Mémoires de Marchand, premier valet de chambre et executeur testamentaire de l'empereur*, ed. J. Bourguignon, 2 vols (Paris 1955); Comte Général Henri-Gratien Bertrand, *Général Bertrand . . . Cahiers de Sainte-Hélène*, 3 vols (Paris 1959). See also the superb collectaneous volume: Jean Tulard, *Napoléon à Sainte-Hélène* (Paris 1981) and the bibliography by C. Albert-Samuel in *Revue de l'Institut Napoléon* (1971) pp.151–57.

For the voyage out on the *Northumberland*, add the following (in addition to Maitland and Keith's narratives cited in the last chapter): J.H. Rose, *Napoleon's Last Voyages* (1906); Gilbert Martineau, *Napoleon's Last Journey* (1976); Clement Shorter, *Napoleon and his Fellow-travellers* (1908); Félix Coquereau, *Souvenirs du voyage à Sainte Hélène* (Paris 1841); G. Bordonove, *Vers Sainte Hélène* (Paris 1977); Arnold Chaplin, *A St Helena Who's Who* (1919); G. Cockburn, *Napoleon's Last Voyage* (1888).

For the captivity on St Helena, the following primary sources (or collections thereof) should be added: Julian Park, trans. & ed, *Napoleon in Captivity: The Reports of Count Balmain, Russian Commissioner on the island of St Helena 1816–1820* (1928); Lady Pulteney Malcolm, *Diary of St Helena* (1899); J.N. Santini, *An Appeal to the British Nation* (1817); Elizabeth Balcombe Abell, *Recollections of the Emperor Napoleon* (1844); Montholon, *Lettres du comte et comtesse Montholon*, ed. P. Gonnard (Paris 1906); W. Henry, *Events of a Military Life* (1834); W. Warden, *Letters written on board the Northumberland and at St Helena* (1816); James Kemble, *St Helena during Napoleon's Exile* (1969); J. Stokoe, *With Napoleon at St Helena* (1902); Basil Jackson, *Reminiscences of a Staff Officer* (1877); E. Lutyens, *Letters of Captain Engelbert Lutyens* (1915); Henry Meynell, *Conversations with Napoleon at St Helena* (1911); Constance Russell, *Swallowfield and its Owners* (1901); Louis Étienne St-

Denis, *From the Tuileries to St Helena. Personal Recollections of Louis Étienne St-Denis* (1922); Firmin Didot, *La Captivité de Sainte-Hélène d'après les rapports du Marquis de Montchenu* (Paris 1894); E. St-Denis, *Souvenirs du Mamelouk Ali sur l'Empéreur Napoléon* (Paris 1926).

Among a vast secondary literature one might point especially to: G. Martineau, *Napoleon's St Helena* (1968); Julia Blackburn, *The Emperor's Last Island* (1991); Jean Thiry, *Sainte-Hélène* (Paris 1976); Earl Rosebery, *Napoleon, the Last Phase* (1900); R. Korngold, *The Last Years of Napoleon* (1960); Octave Aubry, *St Helena* (1937); W. Forsyth, *History of the Captivity of Napoleon at St Helena* (1853); P. Ganière, *Napoléon à St-Hélène* (Paris 1960); Frédéric Masson, *Autour de Sainte Hélène* (Paris 1935); Mabel Balcombe Brookes, *St Helena Story* (1960); Norwood Young, *Napoleon in Exile: St Helena*, 2 vols (1915); Léon Brice, *Les Espoirs de Napoléon à Sainte-Hélène* (Paris 1938); Ernest d'Hauterive, *Sainte-Hélène au temps de Napoléon et aujourd'hui* (Paris 1933); René Bouvier, *Sainte-Hélène avant Napoléon* (Paris 1938); Philip Gosse, *St Helena, 1502–1938* (Shropshire 1990); J. Mougins-Roquefort, *Napoléon prisonnier par les Anglais* (Paris 1978). For events in England and France with a direct bearing on the emperor and his imprisonment see H. Kurtz, *The Trial of Marshal Ney* (1957); J.P. Garnier, *Charles X* (Paris 1967); E. Tangye Lean, *The Napoleonists* (1970); M. Thornton, *England and the St Helena Decision* (1968); Roger Fulford, *Samuel Whitbread, 1764–1815: A Study in Opposition* (1967); J. Dechamps, 'Les défenseurs de Napoleon en Grande-Bretagne de 1815 à 1830', *Revue de l'Institut Napoléon* (1955) pp.129–40.

With Napoleon's death we are once again in controversial and hotly disputed territory. An important source, in addition to Antommarchi, etc. already cited, is Archibald Arnott, *An Account of the late illness, disease and post-mortem examination of Napoleon Bonaparte* (1822). The discredited theory of death by cancer is rehearsed in P. Hillemand, *Pathologie de Napoléon* (Paris 1970). It is significant that Antommarchi, previously dismissed as an incompetent, has been rehabilitated: J. Poulet, 'Le cas Antommarchi', *Revue de l'Institut Napoléon* (1971) pp.130–38. Fundamental to this discussion are Simon Leys, *The Death of Napoleon* (1991) and the works published by Ben Weider and Sten Forshufvud: *Assassination at St Helena* (1978); *Assassination at St Helena Revisited* (1995); (by Forshufud alone) *Who Killed Napoleon?* (1961); and by Weider with David Hapgood, *The Murder of Napoleon* (1983). Their identification of Montholon as the true killer is supported by René Maury, *L'Assassin de Napoléon* (Paris 1994). For the self-serving mendacity of Montholon's memoirs see Hélène Michaud, 'Que vaut le témoignage de Montholon à la lumière de fonds Masson?', *Revue de l'Institut Napoléon* (1971) pp.113–20.

Napoleon's will and death masks have attracted their share of attention. On the will: J. Savant, *Toute l'histoire de Napoléon* (Paris 1951); J. Lemaire, *Le Testament de Napoléon* (Paris 1975); F. Beaucour, *Le Codicille secret du Testament de Napoléon* (Paris 1976). On the death masks: E. de Veauce, *L'Affaire du Masque de Napoléon* (Paris 1957) and J. Jousset, 'L'Affaire du Masque de Napoléon', *Revue de l'Institut Napoléon* (1957) pp.100–06. On the deathbed itself there is G. Retif de la Bretonne, *La Vérité sur le Lit de Mort de Napoléon* (Paris 1960). On the tomb at Longwood and the return of Napoleon's body to Les Invalides in 1840 there is Albert Cahuet, *Après la mort de l'empéreur* (Paris 1913) and *Retours de Sainte-Hélène* (Paris 1943); J. Bourguignon, *Le Retour des Cendres* (Paris 1943); Arthur Bertrand, *Lettres sur l'expédition de Sainte-Hélène en 1840* (Paris 1841); George G. Bennett, *The St Helena Reminiscences*, ed. T. Hearl (Cheltenham 1989). There are even sceptics who doubt that the body in the Invalides really is Napoleon's: G. Retif de la Bretonne, *Anglais, rendez-nous Napoléon* (Paris 1969) and F. Cavanna, *Les Aventures de Napoléon* (Paris 1976).

INDEX